W9-ASV-992

To my parents, Wira and Mietek, my wife, Haya,
and my children, Lemor, Sivan and Aaron.

Avi Silberschatz

To my wife, Jeanne,
and my children, Jennifer and Kathryn.

Jim Peterson

Mark Dalton: Sponsoring Editor

Hugh Crawford: Manufacturing Supervisor
Karen Guardino: Production Manager
Thomas A. Philbrook and **Barbara Atkinson:** Cover Designers
Susan E. Vicenti: Art Editor
Natasha Wei: Production Editor

This book is in the Addison-Wesley series in Computer Science.

Michael A. Harrison: Consulting Editor

Library of Congress Cataloging in Publication Data

Peterson, James Lyle.
  Operating system concepts.

  Bibliography: p.
  Includes index.
  1. Operating systems (Computers)   I. Silberschatz,
Abraham.   II. Title.
QA76.6.P475   1985   001.64′2   84-21637
ISBN 0-201-06198-8

Scope® Registered trademark of Control Data Corporation

VMS™ Trademark of Digital Equipment Corporation

CP/M® Registered trademark of Digital Research Incorporated

UNIX™ Trademark of Bell Laboratories

Reproduced by Addison-Wesley from camera-ready copy prepared by the authors.

CDEFGHIJ-AL-89876

Operating System Concepts

Second Edition

James L. P

Abraham Silbe

University of Texas

▲▼ Addison-Wesley Publishing C

Reading, Massachusetts • Menlo Park, C
Don Mills, Ontario • Wokingham, England • An
Sydney • Singapore • Tokyo • Mexico City •
Santiago •

Preface

Operating systems are an essential part of a computer system. Similarly, a course on operating systems is an essential part of a computer science education. This book is intended as a text for an introductory course in operating systems at the junior, senior, or first-year graduate level. It provides a clear description of the *concepts* which underlie operating systems.

This book is not centered around any particular operating system or hardware. Instead, it discusses fundamental concepts which are applicable to a variety of systems. Our emphasis is on solving the problems encountered in designing an operating system, regardless of the underlying hardware on which the system will run.

Content of this Book

The overall content of the book is as follows:

1 Introduction
2 Operating System Services
3 File Systems
4 CPU Scheduling
5 Memory Management
6 Virtual Memory
7 Disk and Drum Scheduling
8 Deadlocks
9 Concurrent Processes
10 Concurrent Programming
11 Protection
12 Design Principles
13 Distributed Systems
14 The Unix Operating System
15 Historical Perspective

As prerequisites, we assume the reader is familiar with general assembly language programming and computer organization. We do not discuss in any detail the characteristics of I/O devices or how to write device drivers.

Chapters 1, 2, and 3 explain what operating systems *are* and what they *do*. These chapters explain how the concept of an operating system has developed, the common features of an operating system, what it does for the user, and what it does for the computer system operator. It is motivational, historical, and explanatory in nature. We try to avoid how things are done internally in these chapters. Therefore, these chapters are suitable for individuals or lower-level classes who want to learn what an operating system is, without getting into the details of the internal algorithms.

Chapters 4 to 8 deal with the classic internal algorithms and structures of operating systems: *cpu scheduling, memory management*, and *device management*. They provide a firm practical understanding of the algorithms used: their properties, advantages, and disadvantages. The algorithms are presented in a natural order, so that new, more complicated systems can be built upon the understanding of simpler systems.

Chapter 9 introduces the unifying concept of the computer system as a collection of cooperating sequential processes. Chapters 10, 11, 12, and 13 present advanced topics and current trends, including high-level languages for writing concurrent programs, protection systems, design principles, and distributed systems. These topics are still being researched and may well need later revision. However, we include them in the book for two reasons. First, although research is still ongoing and final solutions to these problems are still being sought, there is general agreement that these topics are important and students should be exposed to them. Second, existing systems use these solutions, and anyone working with operating systems over the next five years will need to be aware of the developments in these directions.

In response to many requests, however, we have included a new chapter to illustrate how the many described concepts can be put together in a real system. We have chosen the Unix operating system, specifically Berkeley's 4.2BSD, for this example system. This operating system was chosen in part because it was at one time almost small enough to understand and yet is not a "toy" operating system. Most of its internal algorithms were selected for *simplicity*, not speed or sophistication. Unix is readily available to computer science departments, so many students may have used Unix.

Each chapter ends with references to further reading. Chapter 15 is essentially a set of references to further reading for the entire book, describing briefly some of the most influential operating systems.

Organization

Operating systems first began to appear in the late 1950's, and for twenty years underwent major changes in concepts and technology. As a result, the first-generation operating system textbooks that appeared during this period (such as Brinch Hansen [1973a], Madnick and Donovan [1974], Shaw [1974], Tsichritzis and Bernstein [1974]) tried to explain a subject that changed even as they were being written.

Now, however, operating system theory and practice appears to have matured and stabilized. The fundamental operating system concepts are now well defined and well understood. While there will undoubtedly be new algorithms, the basic approach to cpu scheduling, memory management, the user interface, and so on, is not likely to change. Few really new operating systems are being written. Most large computers use operating systems that were designed in the 1960's. The newest operating systems are being developed for the multitude of microcomputer systems, but these are generally either CP/M, Unix, or imitations of these. It is now possible to write a book that presents well-understood, agreed-upon, classic operating system material.

This text is one of a second generation of operating system textbooks (such as Calingaert [1982]). Our text differs from other texts in the level of content and organization. The basic concepts have been carefully organized and presented; the material flows naturally from these basic principles to more sophisticated ones.

The only controversial aspect of this book is its organization, specifically the definition of the formal process model as late as Chapter 9. Almost every other text places this material at the beginning as Chapter 2. In our experience, this arrangement does not work. The process model is a powerful and convenient unifying concept. However, when operating systems are first introduced, the student does not know the basic principles. To benefit from the process model, the student needs to understand how cpu scheduling and memory management can present an image of separate virtual processors, each with its own separate virtual memory space. Then, and only then, will the student really be able to understand why the process model is useful. Once the student has the proper background to be able to appreciate the process model of operating systems, the standard material concerning processes, process coordination, synchronization, and communication can be presented.

Concurrency itself, in the form of overlapped I/O, spooling, multiprogramming, and time-sharing, is introduced as early as Chapter 1. However, we feel that the *formal* process model is best reserved until the basic concepts (cpu scheduling and memory management) are well understood.

The Second Edition

Many comments and suggestions were forwarded to us concerning our first edition. These, together with our own observations while teaching at the University of Texas and IBM, have prodded us to produce this second edition. Our basic procedure was to reorganize and rewrite the material in each chapter, to bring some of the older material up-to-date, to improve the exercises, and to add a new chapter on Unix.

Substantive revisions were made in the following chapters:

- **Chapter 1**. A new organization clearly separates the performance and protection aspects of operating systems.

- **Chapter 3**. Sections have been reorganized to present a more natural flow of information, discussing first files, and then directories.

- **Chapter 8**. Additional examples illustrate the behavior of the various algorithms. Section 8.6, on recovery, has been rewritten to obtain a better organization.

- **Chapter 9**. Section 9.5 has been rewritten to bring the material up-to-date. In particular, a new, more concise definition of the critical section problem has been included, Dekker's algorithm for the synchronization of two processes has been replaced with Peterson's algorithm, and a new synchronization algorithm using special hardware instructions (that is, test and set) has been included. The section of the RC4000 system has been replaced by a discussion of the more modern Accent system.

- **Chapter 13**. A new subsection on the Byzantine general problem has been added.

- **Chapter 14**. A problem common to students (and professors) using the first edition was that they felt overwhelmed by the variety of solutions to the many aspects of operating systems. It was difficult to see how a complete system would fit all the pieces together. To address this problem, we have added a chapter on a complete operating system. The initial problem was to create either a "paper" design (such as that used in Lister [1979]) or a real system. We decided to present a real system. The next problem was to choose a particular system. We chose Unix, specifically 4.2 BSD.

- **Chapter 15.** Since a new Chapter 14 was added, the old Chapter 14 (without the section on Unix) was renumbered Chapter 15.

Errata

We have attempted to clean up every error in this book, but as with operating systems, there will undoubtedly still be some obscure bugs. We would appreciate it if you, the reader, would notify us of any errors or omissions in the book. If you would like to suggest improvements or contribute exercises, we would be glad to hear from you. An errata sheet is available to instructors for the first edition, and we will update it with errors in this edition as they become known.

Acknowledgments

Eight years of CS 372 students at the University of Texas at Austin suffered through permutations of this material until we got it right. David Orshalick helped with the early table of contents. Dick Kieburtz helped with the contents of Section 11.9 on language-based protection. During the writing stage, we were invited to design and teach an operating system course for IBM, which helped clarify our organization.

As the text was written, Carol Engelhardt deciphered our handwriting and edited our text into Scribe format. Carol's efforts throughout this project were the only thing that got it done.

Jeff Ullman helped us to get draft copies on the Dover at Stanford. Arthur Keller helped get those drafts back to Texas. Susan Lilly was able to understand what we were trying to say in the drafts and edit them into readable text. Elaine Rich, Richard Cohen, and Brian Reid explained the subtleties of Scribe, helping us to define our documents and make them work. The manuscript was read in various forms by Michael Molloy, Gael Buckley, and the reviewers.

During the lengthy revision process for this Second Edition, the Information Technology Center of Carnegie-Mellon University provided a supportive work environment.

Chapter 14 is derived from a draft by John Quarterman, who received comments on earlier drafts from Samuel J. Leffler, Bill Shannon, William N. Joy, and John B. Chambers. John Quarterman endured months of our questions and endless reviews as we struggled to write and rewrite the chapter. The credit for this chapter should go to John Quarterman, while any errors in presentation or fact for Chapter 14, as with the rest of the book, are, of course, ours.

Finally, we would like to acknowledge the helpful reviewing of Larry Flanigan, University of Michigan; William Appelbe, University of California at San Diego; Christopher Haynes, Indiana University; and Raymond Hookway, Case Western Reserve University.

J.P.
A.S.

Contents

Chapter 4 CPU Scheduling

Chapter 5 Memory Management

Chapter 6 Virtual Memory

Chapter 7   Disk and Drum Scheduling

Chapter 8   Deadlocks

Chapter 9   Concurrent Processes

Chapter 10   Concurrent Programming

Chapter 11   Protection

Chapter 12   Design Principles

Chapter 13   Distributed Systems

Chapter 14   The Unix Operating System

Chapter 15   Historical Perspective

1

Introduction

An *operating system* is a program which acts as an interface between a user of a computer and the computer hardware. The purpose of an operating system is to provide an environment in which a user may execute programs. The primary goal of an operating system is thus to make the computer system *convenient* to use. A secondary goal is to use the computer hardware in an *efficient* manner.

To understand what operating systems are, it is necessary to understand how they have developed. In this chapter, we trace the development of operating systems from the first hands-on systems to current multiprogrammed and time-shared systems. As we move through the various stages, we see how the components of operating systems evolved as natural solutions to problems in early computer systems. Understanding the reasons behind the development of operating systems gives an appreciation for what an operating system does and how it does it.

1.1 What Is an Operating System?

An operating system is an important part of almost every computer system. A computer system can be roughly divided into 4 components (Figure 1.1):

- The **hardware** (cpu, memory, I/O devices).

- The **operating system**.

- The **applications programs** (compilers, database systems, video games, business programs).

- The **users** (people, machines or other computers).

The hardware provides the basic computing resources. The applications programs define the ways in which these resources are used to solve the

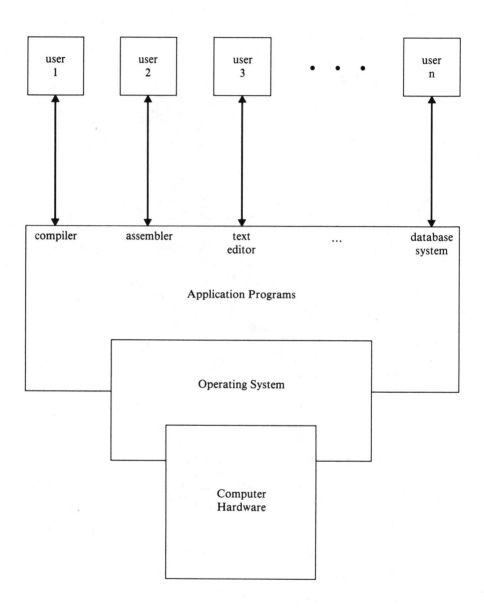

Figure 1.1   Abstract view of the components of a computer system

computing problems of the users. There may be many different users trying to solve different problems. Accordingly, there may be many different applications programs. The operating system controls and coordinates the use of the hardware among the various application programs for the various users.

An operating system is similar to a *government*. The basic resources of a computer system are provided by its hardware, software, and data. The operating system provides the means for the proper use of these resources in the operation of the computer system. Like a government, the operating system performs no useful function by itself. It simply provides an *environment* within which other programs can do useful work.

We can view an operating system as a *resource allocator*. A computer system has many resources (hardware and software) which may be required to solve a problem: cpu time, memory space, file storage space, input/output (I/O) devices, and so on. The operating system acts as the manager of these resources and allocates them to specific programs and users as necessary for their tasks. Since there may be many, possibly conflicting, requests for resources, the operating system must decide which requests are allocated resources to operate the computer system fairly and efficiently.

A slightly different view of an operating system focuses on the need to control the various I/O devices and user programs. An operating system is a *control program*. (At least three operating systems incorporate this view into their names. The primary operating system for most Burroughs computers is MCP, the Master Control Program. CP/67 is a Control Program for the IBM 360/67; CP/M, the popular microcomputer operating system, is a Control Program for Microcomputers.) A control program controls the execution of user programs to prevent errors and improper use of the computer. It is especially concerned with the operation and control of I/O devices.

In general, however, there is no completely adequate definition of an operating system. Operating systems exist because they are a reasonable way to solve the problem of creating a usable computing system. The fundamental goal of computer systems is to execute user programs and solve user problems. Towards this goal computer hardware is constructed. Since bare hardware alone is not very easy to use, applications programs are developed. These various programs require certain common operations, such as controlling the I/O devices. The common functions of controlling and allocating resources are then brought together into one piece of software: the operating system.

It is perhaps easier to define operating systems by what they *do*, rather than what they *are*. The primary goal of an operating system is *convenience for the user.* Operating systems exist because they are supposed to make it easier to compute with an operating system than without an operating system. This is particularly clear when you look at operating systems for small personal computers.

A secondary goal is *efficient* operation of the computer system. This goal is particularly important for large shared multi-user systems. These systems are typically very expensive, and so it is desirable to make them as efficient as possible. These two goals, convenience and efficiency, are sometimes contradictory. In the past, efficiency considerations were often more important than convenience. Thus much of operating system theory concentrates on optimal use of computing resources.

To see what operating systems are and what operating systems do, let us consider how they have developed over the last thirty years. By tracing that evolution we can identify the common elements of operating systems and see how and why they have developed as they have.

Operating systems and computer architecture have had a great deal of influence on each other. To facilitate the use of the hardware, operating systems were developed. As operating systems were designed and used, it became obvious that changes in the design of the hardware could simplify the operating system. In this short historical review, notice how the introduction of new hardware features is the natural solution to many operating system problems.

1.2 Early Systems

Initially, there was only computer hardware. Early computers were (physically) very large machines run from a console. The programmer would write a program and then operate the program directly from the operator's console. First, the program would be manually loaded into memory, either from the front panel switches, paper tape, or punched cards. Then the appropriate buttons would be pushed to load the starting address and to start the execution of the program. As the program ran, the programmer/operator could monitor its execution by the display lights on the console. If errors were discovered, the programmer could halt the program, examine the contents of memory and registers, and debug the program directly from the console. Output was printed, or punched onto paper tape or cards for later printing.

An important aspect of this environment was its *hands-on* interactive nature. The programmer was the operator. Most systems used a sign-up or *reservation scheme* for allocating machine time. If you wanted to use the computer, you went to the sign-up sheet, looked for the next convenient free time on the machine, and signed up for it.

There were, however, certain problems with this approach. Suppose you had signed up for an hour of computer time to run a program that you were developing. You might run into a particularly nasty bug and be unable to finish in an hour. If someone had reserved the following block of time, you would have to stop, collect what you could, and return at a later time to continue. On the other hand, if things went real well, you might finish in 35 minutes. Since you had thought you might need the machine longer, you had signed up for an hour, and so the machine would sit idle for 25 minutes.

As time went on, additional software and hardware were developed. Card readers, line printers, and magnetic tape became commonplace. Assemblers, loaders, and linkers were designed to ease the programming task. Libraries of common functions were created. Common functions could then be copied into a new program without having to be written again.

The routines which performed input and output were especially important. Each new I/O device had its own characteristics, requiring careful programming. A special subroutine was written for each I/O device. Such a subroutine is called a *device driver*. A device driver knows how the buffers, flags, registers, control bits, and status bits should be used for a particular device. Each different type of device has its own driver. A simple task, such as reading a character from a paper tape reader might involve complex sequences of device-specific operations. Rather than writing the necessary code every time, the device driver was simply used from the library.

Later, compilers for Fortran, Cobol, and other languages appeared, making the programming task much easier, but the operation of the computer more complex. To prepare a Fortran program for execution, for example, the programmer would first need to load the Fortran compiler into the computer. The compiler was normally kept on magnetic tape, so the proper tape would need to be mounted on a tape drive. The program would be read through the card reader and written onto another tape. The Fortran compiler produced assembly language output, which then needed to be assembled. This required mounting another tape with the assembler. The output of the assembler would need to be linked to its supporting library routines. Finally, the binary object form of the program would be ready to execute. It could be loaded into memory and debugged from the console, as before.

Notice that there could be a significant amount of *setup time* involved in the running of a job. Each job consisted of many separate steps: loading the Fortran compiler tape, running the compiler, unloading the compiler tape, loading the assembler tape, running the assembler, unloading the assembler tape, loading the object program, and running the object program. If an error occurred at any step, you might have to start over at the beginning. Each job step might involve the loading and unloading of magnetic tapes, paper tapes, and/or cards.

1.3 Simple Monitor

The job setup time was a real problem. During the time that tapes were being mounted or the programmer was operating the console, the cpu sat idle. Remember that in the early days there were very few computers and they were very expensive (millions of dollars). As an example, consider an IBM 7094 system costing $2,000,000 with an expected lifetime of 5 years. The capital costs are $45.66 per hour if it is run 24 hours per day, 365 days per year. In addition, there were the operational costs of power, cooling, paper, programmers, and so on. This was at a time when the minimum wage was $1.00 per hour.

Thus computer time was very valuable, and the owners of the computers wanted them to be used as much as possible. They needed high *utilization* to get as much as they could from their investments.

The solution was two-fold. First, professional computer operators were hired. The programmer no longer operated the machine. As soon as one job was finished, an operator could start the next; there was no idle time due to reserving computer time that turned out not to be needed. Since an operator had more experience with mounting tapes than a programmer, setup time was reduced. The user provided whatever cards or tapes were needed, as well as a short description of how the job was to be run. Of course the operators could not debug an incorrect program at the console, since they would not understand the program. Therefore, a dump of memory and registers was taken, and the programmer had to debug from the dump. This allowed the operators to continue immediately with the next job, but left the programmer with a much more difficult debugging problem.

The second major time savings involved reducing setup time. Jobs with similar needs were *batched* together and run through the computer as a group. For instance, suppose the operators received one Fortran job, one Cobol job and another Fortran job. If they ran them in that order, they would have to set up for Fortran (load the compiler tapes, and so on), then set up for Cobol, and then set up for Fortran again. If they ran the two Fortran programs as a batch, however, they could set up only once for Fortran, saving operator time.

These changes, making the operator distinct from the user and batching similar jobs, improved utilization quite a bit. Programmers would leave their programs with the operators. The operators would sort them into batches with similar requirements and as the computer became available, run each batch. The output from each job would be sent back to the appropriate programmer.

But there were still problems. For example, when a job stopped, the operators would have to notice that fact by observing the console, determine why the program stopped (normal or abnormal termination), take a dump if necessary, and then load the card reader or paper tape reader with the next job and restart the computer. During this transition from one job to the next, the cpu sat idle.

To overcome this idle time, *automatic job sequencing* was introduced, and with it, the first rudimentary operating systems were created. What was desired was a procedure for automatically transferring control from one job to the next. A small program, called a *resident monitor*, was created for this purpose (Figure 1.2). The resident monitor is always (resident) in memory.

Initially (when the computer was turned on) control of the computer resided with the resident monitor, which would transfer control to a

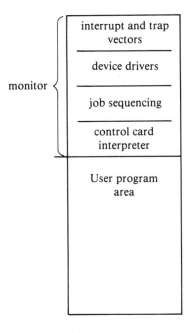

Figure 1.2   Memory layout for a resident monitor

program. When the program terminated, it would return control to the resident monitor, which would then go on to the next program. Thus the resident monitor would automatically sequence from one program to another and from one job to another.

But how would the resident monitor know which program to execute? Previously, the operator had been given a short description of what programs were to be run on what data. To provide that information directly to the monitor, *control cards* were introduced. The idea is quite simple. In addition to the program or data for a job, we include special cards (control cards) which are directives to the resident monitor indicating what program is to be run. For example, a normal user program might require one of three programs to run: the Fortran compiler (FTN), the assembler (ASM), or the user's program. We could use a separate control card for each of these:

> $FTN -- Execute the Fortran compiler.
> $ASM -- Execute the assembler.
> $RUN -- Execute the user program.

These cards tell the resident monitor which programs to run.

We can use two additional control cards to define the boundaries of each job:

> $JOB -- First card of a job.
> $END -- Last card of a job.

These two cards might be useful for accounting for the machine resources used by the programmer. Parameters can be used to define the job name, account number to be charged, and so on. Other control cards can be defined for other functions, such as asking the operator to load or unload a tape.

One problem with control cards is how to distinguish them from data or program cards. The usual solution is to identify them by a special character or pattern on the card. Several systems used the dollar sign character ($) in the first column to identify a control card. Others used a different code. IBM's Job Control Language (JCL) used slash marks (//) in the first two columns. Figure 1.3 shows a sample card deck setup for a simple batch system.

A resident monitor thus has several identifiable parts. One major part is the control card interpreter. The control card interpreter will at intervals need a loader to load systems programs and applications programs into memory. Thus a loader is a part of the resident monitor. Both the control card interpreter and the loader will need to perform

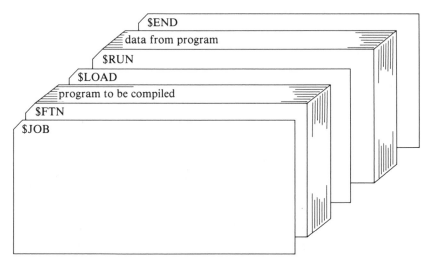

Figure 1.3   Card deck for a simple batch system

I/O, and so the resident monitor has a set of device drivers for the system's I/O devices. Often the system and application programs are linked to these same device drivers, providing continuity in their operation, as well as saving memory space and programming time.

These batch systems work fairly well. The resident monitor provides automatic job sequencing as indicated by the control cards. When a control card indicates that a program is to be run, the monitor loads it into memory and transfers control to it. When the program completes, it transfers control back to the monitor, which reads the next control card, loads the appropriate program, and so on. This is repeated until all control cards are interpreted for the job. Then the monitor automatically continues with the next job.

1.4 Performance

Computers, especially large mainframes, have traditionally been very expensive machines. Accordingly, the owners of these machines have wanted to get as much computation done as possible. The same is true even for today's cheaper microcomputers. Although microcomputers may not be very expensive, it is still desirable to get as much (useful) computing done as possible.

The switch to batch systems with automatic job sequencing was made to improve performance. The problem, quite simply, is that humans are extremely slow (relative to the computer, of course). Consequently, it is desirable to replace human operation by operating system software. Automatic job sequencing eliminates the need for human setup time and job sequencing.

Even with automatic job sequencing, however, the main cpu is often idle. The problem involves the speed of the mechanical I/O devices, which are intrinsically slower than electronic devices. Even a slow cpu works in the microsecond range, with millions of instructions executed per second. A fast card reader, on the other hand, might read 1000 cards per minute. Thus the difference in speed between the cpu and its I/O devices may be three orders of magnitude or more.

The (relative) slowness of the I/O devices can mean that the cpu is often waiting on I/O. As an example, an assembler or compiler may be able to process 300 or more cards per second. A fast card reader, on the other hand, may be able to read only 1200 cards per minute (or 2 cards per second). This means that assembling a 1200 card program would require only 4 seconds of cpu time, but 60 seconds to read. Thus the cpu is idle for 56 out of 60 seconds or 93.3 percent of the time. The resulting cpu utilization is only 6.7 percent. The process is similar for output operations. The problem is that while an I/O operation is occurring, the cpu is idle, waiting for the I/O to complete; while the cpu is executing, the I/O devices are idle.

1.4.1 Off-line Operation

Over time, of course, improvements in technology resulted in faster I/O devices. But cpu speeds increased even faster, so that the problem was not resolved; the cpu was still faster than the I/O devices.

One common solution was to replace the very slow card readers (input devices) and line printers (output devices) with magnetic tape units. The majority of computer systems in the late 1950's and early 1960's were batch systems reading from card readers and writing to line printers or card punches. Rather than have the cpu read directly from cards, however, the cards were first copied onto a magnetic tape. When the tape was sufficiently full, it was taken down and carried over to the computer. When a card was needed for input to a program, it was read from the tape. Similarly, output was written to tape and the contents of the tape would be printed later. The card readers and line printers were operated *off-line*, not by the main computer (Figure 1.4).

Two approaches to off-line processing were used. Special-purpose devices (card readers, line printers) were developed which output directly to or input directly from magnetic tape. These devices had additional hardware designed specifically for this task. The other approach was to dedicate a small computer (such as the IBM 1401) to the task of copying to and from tape. The small computer was a satellite of the main computer. *Satellite processing* was one of the first cases of multiple computer systems working together to improve performance.

The main advantage of off-line operation was that the main computer was no longer constrained by the speed of the card readers and line printers, but only by the speed of the much faster magnetic tape units. This technique of using magnetic tape for all I/O could be applied with any unit record equipment (card readers, card punches, plotters, paper tape, printers).

In addition, no changes need be made to the application programs to change from direct to off-line I/O operation. Consider a program which runs on a system with an attached card reader. When it wants a card, it calls the card reader device driver in the resident monitor. If we change to off-line operation of the card reader, only the device driver must be changed. When the program needs an input card, it calls the same system routine as before. However, now the code for that routine is not the card reader driver, but a call to the magnetic tape driver. The application program receives the same card image in either case.

This ability to run a program with different input/output devices is called *device independence.* Device independence is made possible by having the operating system determine which device a program actually uses when it requests I/O. Programs are written to use *logical* I/O devices. Control cards (or other commands) indicate how the logical devices should be mapped onto physical devices.

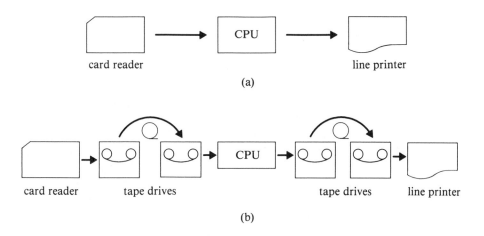

Figure 1.4   (a) On-line and (b) Off-line operation of I/O devices

The real gain in off-line operation comes from the possibility of using multiple reader-to-tape and tape-to-printer systems for one cpu. If the cpu can process input twice as fast as the reader can read cards, then two readers working simultaneously can produce enough tape to keep the cpu busy. On the other hand, there is now a longer delay in getting a particular job run. It must first be read onto tape. Then there is a delay until enough other jobs are read onto the tape to "fill" it. The tape must then be rewound, unloaded, hand-carried to the cpu, and mounted on a free tape drive. This is not unreasonable for batch systems, of course. Many similar jobs can be batched onto a tape before it is taken to the computer.

1.4.2 Buffering

Another solution to the slowness of I/O devices is *buffering*. Buffering attempts to keep both the cpu and the I/O device busy all the time. The idea is quite simple. After data has been read and the cpu is about to start operating on it, the input device is instructed to begin the next input immediately. The cpu and input device are then both busy. With luck, by the time that the cpu is ready for the next data item, the input device will have finished reading it. The cpu can then begin processing the newly read data, while the input device starts to read the following data.

Similar buffering can be done for output. In this case, the cpu creates data which is put into a buffer until an output device can accept it.

A *record* is a natural unit of data. It may be a physical record (such as a line image for a printer or a character from a keyboard or a block from a tape or disk), or it may be a logical record (such as an input line, an English word, or an array). Logical records are defined by the application problem; physical records are defined by the nature of the I/O device. Software blocking and unblocking can convert between the logical records of the application and the physical records of the device. Records are the units of data used for buffering.

In practice, buffering seldom keeps both the cpu and its I/O devices busy all the time. If the cpu is working on one record while an input device is working on another, either the cpu or the input device will finish first. If the cpu finishes first, it must wait; it cannot proceed until the next record is read and is in memory ready to be processed. Notice, however, that the cpu may not have to sit idle for long, and in the worst case, no longer than without buffering. If the input device finishes first, then either it must wait or it may proceed with reading the next record. The buffers that hold records that have been read but not yet processed (or processed but not yet output) are often made large enough to hold several records (for example a 255-character buffer, or a 10-card buffer). Thus an input device can read several records ahead of the cpu. If the input device is consistently faster than the cpu, however, the buffer will eventually become full and the input device must wait.

Buffering is a tricky business and can be difficult to code. One problem is to detect that an I/O device has finished an operation as soon as possible. The next I/O operation can only be started when the previous one has finished. *Interrupts* solve this problem. As soon as an I/O device is finished with an operation, it interrupts the cpu. When the cpu is interrupted, it stops what it is doing and immediately transfers to a fixed location. The instructions at this location are typically a service routine for the interrupt. The interrupt service routine checks to see if the buffer is not full (for an input device) or not empty (for an output device), then starts the next I/O request. The cpu can then resume the interrupted computation. In this way, I/O devices and the cpu can be operated at full speed.

Interrupts are an important part of a computer architecture. Each computer design has its own interrupt mechanism, but several functions are common. The interrupt must transfer control to the interrupt service routine. Generally, this is done by reserving a set of locations in low memory (the first 100 or so locations) to hold the addresses of the interrupt service routines for the various devices. This array, or *vector*, of addresses is then indexed by the device number to provide the address of the interrupt service routine for the interrupting device.

The interrupt architecture must also save the address of the interrupted instruction. Many old designs simply stored the interrupt address in a fixed location or in a location indexed by the device number. More recent architectures store the return address on the system stack. Other registers, such as accumulators or index registers, may need to be explicitly saved and restored by the programmer of the interrupt service routine. After the interrupt is serviced, a jump back to the interrupt address will resume the interrupted computation as if the interrupt had not occurred. Sophisticated interrupt architectures also deal with an interrupt arriving while another interrupt is being serviced, often by a priority scheme.

For example, consider a simple terminal output driver. When a line is to be displayed on the terminal, the first character is sent to the terminal. When that character is displayed, the terminal will interrupt the cpu. When the interrupt request from the terminal arrives, the cpu will be about to execute some instruction. (If the cpu is in the middle of executing an instruction, the interrupt is held pending until the instruction execution is complete.) The address of this interrupted instruction is saved, and control is transferred to the interrupt service routine for the output terminal.

The interrupt service routine saves the contents of any registers it will need to use. It checks for any error conditions which might have resulted from the last output operation. It then checks the buffer containing those characters which are yet to be displayed. If there are any characters in the buffer, one is removed from the buffer. Pointer and counter variables are adjusted appropriately. The character is output to the display and control bits are set to allow it to interrupt again when the character has been properly displayed. Then, the interrupt service routine restores the contents of any saved registers and transfers control back to the interrupted instruction.

If characters are being output to a 1200-baud terminal, the terminal can accept and display one character approximately every 8 milliseconds, or 8000 microseconds. A well-written interrupt service routine to output characters from a buffer to the display may require 20 microseconds per character, leaving 7980 microseconds out of every 8000 for cpu computation (and servicing other interrupts). A high-speed device, however, such as a tape, disk or communications network, may be able to transmit information at close to memory speeds; the cpu would need 20 microseconds to respond to each interrupt, with interrupts arriving every 4 microseconds (for example).

To solve this problem, direct-memory access (DMA) is used for high-speed I/O devices. After setting up buffers, pointers, and counters for the I/O device, the device transfers an entire block of data to or from memory directly, with no intervention by the cpu. Only one interrupt is generated per block, rather than the one interrupt per byte (or word) for low-speed devices.

The basic operation of the cpu is the same. When a DMA device interrupts the cpu, the interrupt service routine first checks for errors in the previous transfer. Then it finds a buffer (an empty buffer for input or a full buffer for output) from a queue of buffers for the next transfer. (A buffer is typically 128 to 4096 bytes, depending upon the device.) Device registers are set to the buffer address and size, and the I/O operation is started. The next interrupt from the device indicates that the entire block has been transferred (or an error has occurred).

Notice that buffering is directly related to interrupt processing. That fact, plus the difficulty of correctly programming the buffering routines (what if we are in the middle of removing a record from the buffer and updating the buffer pointers when an interrupt occurs?), means that buffering is generally an operating system function. The resident monitor or the device drivers include system I/O buffers for each I/O device. Subroutine calls to the device driver by applications programs

(I/O requests) normally cause only a transfer to or from a system buffer. The actual I/O operation has either already been done, or will be done later, as soon as the device is available.

How does buffering affect performance? Buffering mainly helps to smooth over variations in the time it takes to process a record. If the average speeds (in records per second) of the cpu and the I/O devices are the same, then buffering allows the cpu to get slightly ahead or behind the I/O devices, with both still processing everything at full speed.

However, if the cpu is, on the average, much faster than an input device, buffering is of little use. If the cpu is always faster, then it will always find an empty buffer and have to wait for the input device. For output, the cpu can proceed at full speed until, eventually, all system buffers are full. Then the cpu must wait for the output device. This situation occurs with *I/O-bound* jobs where the amount of I/O, relative to computation, is very great. Since the cpu is faster than the I/O device, the speed of execution is bounded by the speed of the I/O device, not by the speed of the cpu.

On the other hand, the amount of computation is so high for a *cpu-bound* job that the input buffers are always full and the output buffers always empty; the cpu cannot keep up with the I/O devices.

Consequently, buffering can be of some help, but it is seldom sufficient. Particularly in early computer systems, most jobs were I/O-bound. Buffering helped somewhat, but the I/O devices (such as card readers, line printers, and paper tape reader/punches) were simply too slow to keep up with the cpu.

1.4.3 Spooling

While off-line preparation of jobs continued for some time, it was quickly replaced in most systems. Disk systems became widely available and greatly improved on off-line operation. The problem with tape systems was that the card reader could not write onto one end of the tape while the cpu read from the other. The entire tape had to be written before it was rewound and read. Disk systems eliminated this problem. By moving the head from one area of the disk to another, a disk can rapidly switch from the area on the disk being used by the card reader to store new cards to the position needed by the cpu to read the "next" card.

In a disk system, cards are read directly from the card reader onto the disk. The location of card images is recorded in a table kept by the operating system. Each job is noted in the table as it is read in. When a job is executed, its requests for card reader input are satisfied by reading from the disk. Similarly, when the job requests the printer to output a line, that line is copied into a system buffer and written to disk. When the job is completed, the output is actually printed.

This form of processing is called *spooling* (Figure 1.5). The name is an acronym for Simultaneous Peripheral Operation On-Line. Spooling essentially uses the disk as a very large buffer, for reading as far ahead as possible on input devices and for storing output files until the output devices are able to accept them.

Buffering overlaps the I/O of a job with its own computation. The advantage of spooling over buffering is that spooling overlaps the I/O of one job with the computation of other jobs. Even in a simple system, the spooler may be reading the input of one job while printing the output of a different job. During this time still another job (or jobs) may be executed, reading their "cards" from disk and "printing" their output lines onto the disk. Buffering can only overlap the I/O of a job with its *own* computation and I/O; spooling can overlap the I/O and computation of many jobs.

Spooling is now a standard feature of most systems, but it was not an integral part of IBM's OS/360 operating system for the 360 family of computers when OS/360 was introduced in the early sixties. Instead, spooling was a special feature added by the Houston computation center of NASA. Hence it is known as HASP, the Houston Automatic Spooling Program.

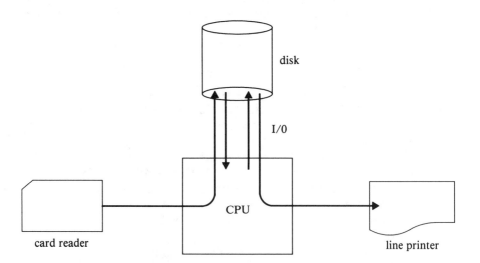

Figure 1.5   Spooling

An extreme form of spooling can be done with magnetic tape. It is possible to read the entire contents of a magnetic tape onto disk before using it. All operations then occur on the disk copy, at higher speeds, and with no wear to the tape. This scheme is known as *staging* a tape.

Spooling has a direct beneficial effect on performance. For the cost of some disk space and a few tables, the cpu can overlap the computation of one job with the I/O of other jobs. Thus spooling can keep both the cpu and the I/O devices working at much higher rates, particularly if there is a mix of cpu-bound and I/O-bound jobs to be run.

In addition, spooling provides a very important data structure: a *job pool*. Spooling will generally result in several jobs having been read and waiting on disk, ready to run. A pool of jobs on disk allows the operating system to select which job to run next, in order to increase cpu utilization. When jobs come in directly on cards or even on magnetic tape, it is not possible to skip around and run jobs in a different order. Jobs must be run sequentially, on a first-come-first-served basis. However, when several jobs are on a direct-access device, such as a disk, *job scheduling* becomes possible. We discuss job and cpu scheduling in greater detail in Chapter 4, but a few important aspects are covered here.

1.5 Multiprogramming

The most important aspect of job scheduling is the ability to *multiprogram*. Off-line operation, buffering, and spooling for overlapped I/O have their limitations. A single user cannot, in general, keep either the cpu or the I/O devices busy at all times. Multiprogramming is an attempt to increase cpu utilization by always having something for the cpu to execute.

The idea is as follows. The operating system picks one of the jobs in the job pool and begins to execute it. Eventually, the job may have to wait for something, such as a tape to be mounted, a command to be typed on a keyboard, or an I/O operation to complete. In a non-multiprogrammed system (uniprogramming) the cpu would sit idle. In a multiprogramming system, the operating system will simply switch to another job and execute it. When *that* job needs to wait, the cpu is switched to another job, and so on. Eventually the first job will have finished waiting and will get the cpu back. As long as there is always some job to execute, the cpu will never be idle.

This idea is quite common in other life situations. A lawyer does not have only one client at a time. Rather several clients may be in the process of being served at the same time. While one case is waiting to go to trial or for papers to be typed, the lawyer can work on another case. With enough clients, a lawyer need never be idle. (Idle lawyers tend to become politicians, so there is a certain social value in keeping them busy.)

Multiprogrammed operating systems are fairly sophisticated. In order to have several jobs ready to run, they must all be kept simultaneously in memory (Figure 1.6). Having several programs in memory at the same time requires some form of memory management, which is covered in Chapters 5 and 6. In addition, if several jobs are ready to run at the same time, some decision must be made to choose among them. This is *cpu scheduling*, which is discussed in Chapter 4. Also, multiprogrammed systems must provide device scheduling (Chapter 7), deadlock handling (Chapter 8), concurrency control (Chapter 9), and protection (Chapter 11). Thus multiprogramming is the central theme of modern operating systems, and the central theme of this book.

1.6 Time Sharing

When batch systems were first developed, they were defined by the "batching" together of similar jobs. Card and tape based systems allowed only sequential access to programs and data and so only one application system could be used at a time. As on-line disk storage became feasible, it was possible to provide immediate access to all of the

Figure 1.6   Memory layout for a multiprogramming system

application systems. Now batch systems are no longer defined by the batching together of similar jobs, but by other characteristics.

A batch operating system normally reads a stream of separate jobs, from a card reader, for example, each with its own control cards which predefine what the job does. When the job is complete, its output is usually printed (on a line printer, for example). The definitive feature of a batch system is the *lack* of interaction between the user and the job while it is executing. The job is prepared and submitted. At some later time (perhaps minutes, hours or days), the output appears. The delay between job submission and job completion (called *turnaround* time) may result from the amount of computing needed, or from delays before the operating system starts processing the job.

There are some difficulties with a batch system from the point of view of the programmer or user, however. Since users cannot interact with their jobs while they are executing, they must set up control cards to handle all possible outcomes. In a multi-step job, subsequent steps may depend upon the result of earlier ones. The running of a program, for example, may depend upon its successful compilation. It can be difficult to define completely what to do in all cases.

Another difficulty in a batch system is that programs must be debugged statically, from snapshot dumps. A programmer cannot modify a program as it executes to study its behavior. A long turnaround time inhibits experimentation with a program. (Conversely, this situation may instill a certain amount of discipline into the writing and testing of programs.)

An *interactive*, or *hands-on*, computer system provides on-line communication between the user and the system. The user gives instructions to the operating system or to a program directly, and receives an immediate response. Usually a keyboard is used to provide input, and a printer or display screen (such as a CRT) is used to provide output. When the operating system finishes the execution of one command, it seeks the next "control card" not from a card reader, but from the user's keyboard. The user gives a command, waits for the response, and decides on the next command, based upon the result of the previous one. The user can easily experiment and see immediate results. Most systems have an interactive text editor for entering programs and an interactive debugger to assist in debugging programs.

Batch systems are quite appropriate for executing large jobs which need little interaction. The user can submit them and return later for the results; it is not necessary to wait while the job is processed. Interactive jobs tend to be composed of many short actions where the results of the next command may be unpredictable. The user submits the command and then waits for the results. Accordingly, the *response* time should be quite short, on the order of seconds at the most. An interactive system is characterized by the desire for a short response time.

Early computers were interactive systems. That is, the entire system was at the immediate disposal of the programmer/operator. This allowed the programmer great flexibility and freedom in program testing and development. But, as we saw, this arrangement resulted in substantial idle time while the cpu waited for some action to be taken by the programmer/operator. Because of the high cost of these early computers, idle cpu time was undesirable. Batch operating systems developed in an attempt to avoid this problem. Batch systems improved system utilization for the owners of the computer systems.

Time sharing systems are the result of trying to provide interactive use of a computer system at a reasonable cost. A time-shared operating

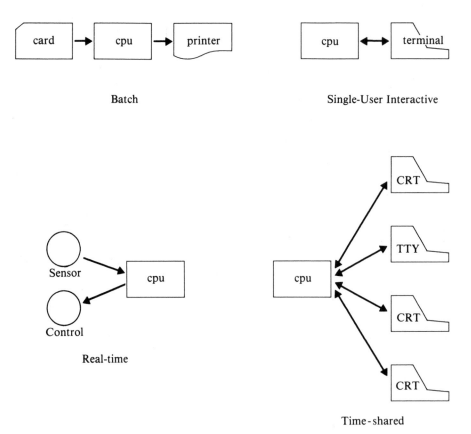

Figure 1.7   Types of operating systems

system uses cpu scheduling and multiprogramming to provide each user with a small portion of a time-shared computer. Each user has a separate program in memory. When a program executes, it typically executes for only a short time before it either finishes or needs to perform I/O. I/O may be interactive; that is, output is to a display for the user and input is from a user keyboard. Since interactive I/O is typically at people speeds, it may take a long time to complete. Input, for example, is bounded by typing speed; 5 characters per second is fairly fast for people, but very slow for computers. Rather than let the cpu sit idle when this happens, the operating system will rapidly switch the cpu to the program of some other user.

A time-shared operating system allows the many users to simultaneously *share* the computer. Since each action or command in a time-shared system tends to be short, only a little cpu time is needed for each user. As the system switches rapidly from one user to the next, users are given the impression that they each have their own computer, while actually one computer is shared among the many users.

The idea of time sharing was demonstrated as early as 1960, but since time-shared systems are more difficult and expensive to build, they did not become common until the early 1970's. As the popularity of time sharing has grown, there have been attempts to merge batch and time-shared systems into one system. Many computer systems which were designed as primarily batch systems have been modified to create a time-sharing subsystem. For example, IBM's OS/360, a batch system, was modified to support TSO, the Time-Sharing Option. At the same time, time-sharing systems have often added a batch subsystem. Today most systems provide both batch processing and time sharing, though their basic design and use tends to be one or the other.

1.7 Real-Time Systems

Still another form of operating system is the *real-time* system. A real-time system is often used as a control device in a dedicated application. Sensors bring data to the computer. The computer must analyze the data and possibly adjust controls to modify the sensor inputs. Systems which control scientific experiments, medical computer systems, industrial control systems, and some display systems are real-time systems. A real-time operating system has well-defined fixed time constraints. Processing *must* be done within the defined constraints or the system will fail. Contrast this requirement to a time-sharing system where it is desirable (but not mandatory) to respond quickly, or to a batch system where there may be no time constraints at all.

1.8 Protection

Early computer systems were single-user programmer-operated systems. When programmers operated the computer from the console, they had complete control over the system. As operating systems developed, however, this control was given to the operating system. Starting with the resident monitor, the operating system began performing many of the functions, especially I/O, for which the programmer had previously been responsible.

In addition, in order to improve system utilization, the operating system began to *share* system resources among several programs simultaneously. With spooling, one program might be executing while I/O was occurring for other jobs; the disk simultaneously held data for many jobs. Multiprogramming put several programs in memory at the same time.

This sharing created both improved utilization and increased problems. When the system was run without sharing, an error in a program could only cause problems for the one program that was running. With sharing, many jobs could be (adversely) affected by a bug in one program.

For example, consider the earliest resident monitor providing nothing more than automatic job sequencing (Section 1.3). Suppose a program gets stuck in a loop reading input cards. The program will read through all of its data and, unless something stops it, will continue reading the cards of the next job, and the next, and so on. This could prevent the correct operation of many jobs.

Even more subtle errors could occur in a multiprogramming system where one erroneous program might modify the program or data of another program or even the resident monitor itself.

Without protection against these sorts of errors, either the computer must be run one job at a time, or all output must be suspect. A properly designed operating system must ensure that an incorrect (or malicious) program cannot cause other programs to execute incorrectly.

Many programming errors are detected by the hardware. These errors are normally handled by the resident monitor. If a user program fails in some ways, such as an illegal instruction or a memory addressing fault, the hardware will trap to the resident monitor. (A *trap* is an internally generated interrupt, usually the result of a program error.) The trap, acting like an interrupt, will store the program counter of the offending instruction and transfer to a service routine in the resident monitor. Typically, the resident monitor automatically dumps memory and registers before going on to the next job.

This approach works fine as long as the error is detected by the hardware. We must be sure, however, that *all* errors are detected. We must protect the operating system and all other programs and their data from any malfunctioning program. Protection is needed for any shared resource. Thus at least three kinds of protection are needed: I/O protection, memory protection, and cpu protection.

1.8.1 I/O Protection

Consider a program which attempts to read input past the end of its own data. How can we stop this program? One approach is to use the common I/O subroutine which we mentioned before: the device driver (Section 1.2). The device driver for the card reader could be modified to detect an attempt to read a control card. Each card which is read would be examined to see if it was a control card (dollar sign in column one, for example). If not, the card and program control would be returned to the user program, as normal. However, if an attempt is made to read a control card, the card reader driver would transfer control directly to the resident monitor. The resident monitor would treat this situation as an error, dump memory, and go on to the next job.

This scheme works fine, except in the case where the user does not use the card reader driver. Use of these common I/O subroutines is voluntary, and there may be occasions when programmers may decide not to use them, but to write their own. For example, they may be really concerned with speed and feel they can program a better buffering scheme, or perhaps they just think it would be interesting to write their own device driver.

To provide proper service, however, we cannot let this happen. Unless we can prevent one user from reading the control cards of another user's job (whether accidentally or maliciously), we are not able to ensure that each job is correctly run. Notice that this problem did not arise when each job was run separately. We must prevent all users from reading control cards; only the monitor should be allowed to read control cards.

We want the computer to *allow* the operating system to read control cards, but *prevent* any user program from reading control cards. Thus we want the computer to behave differently for user programs and the operating system. We want two separate *modes* of operation: *user mode* and *monitor mode* (also called *supervisor mode* or *system mode*). A bit is added to the hardware of the computer to indicate the current mode: monitor (0) or user (1).

We then define all I/O instructions to be *privileged instructions*. The hardware allows privileged instructions to be executed only in monitor mode. If an attempt is made to execute a privileged instruction in user mode, the hardware does not execute it, but treats it as an illegal instruction and traps to the resident monitor. Whenever a trap or interrupt occurs, the hardware switches from user mode to monitor mode (that is, changes the state of the mode bit to be 0). Thus whenever the resident monitor gains control of the computer, it is in monitor mode. The monitor always switches to user mode (by setting the mode bit to 1) before passing control to a user program.

This *dual mode* operation allows us to be sure that only the device drivers (which are part of the resident monitor and hence are executed in monitor mode) can read cards. A user program, therefore, can never read a control card as data.

The operation of the computer is now quite simple. We start in monitor mode in the resident monitor. The resident monitor reads the first control card, and the desired program is loaded into memory. Then, changing from monitor mode to user mode (a privileged instruction), the monitor transfers control to the newly loaded program. When the program terminates, control is returned to the monitor which continues with the next control card. The user program cannot read a control card as data, because the user program is executed in user mode, and cannot directly execute any I/O instruction.

Since I/O instructions are privileged, they can only be executed by the operating system. Then how does the user program perform I/O? By making I/O instructions privileged, we have prevented user programs from doing any I/O, either valid or invalid. The solution to this problem is that since only the monitor can do I/O, the user must *ask* the monitor to do I/O on the user's behalf.

Most modern computers have a special instruction called a *monitor call* or *system call*. On the IBM 370, it is the SVC instruction; on the DEC-10, it is the UUO instruction; on the PDP-11, it is the TRAP instruction. Let us use the term *system call* for all of these. When a system call is executed, it is treated by the hardware as a software interrupt. Control passes through the interrupt vector to a service routine in the resident monitor. The monitor/user mode bit is set to monitor mode. The system call service routine is a part of the resident monitor. The monitor examines the interrupting instruction to determine that a system call has occurred. A parameter indicates exactly what the user program is requesting. Additional information needed for the request may be passed in registers or in memory (with pointers to the memory locations passed in registers). The monitor executes the request and returns control to the instruction following the system call.

Thus, to do I/O, a user program executes a system call to request that the (operating system) monitor perform I/O on its behalf (Figure

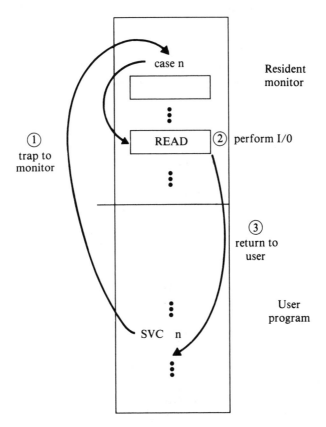

Figure 1.8   Use of a system call to perform I/O

1.8). The operating system monitor, executing in monitor mode, checks that the request is valid, and (if so) does the I/O requested. The monitor then returns to the user.

The dual mode approach allows the operating system to maintain complete control over the computer system at all times. User programs cannot directly do any I/O which might compromise the system's proper operation. They must request aid from the operating system monitor. The monitor always checks first to make sure that the request is reasonable and permissible for that user. If so, it executes the request on behalf of the user, and then returns control to the user. In addition, since the operating system is invoked for every I/O operation, it can perform spooling, buffering, and blocking to improve performance. It can also map logical devices to physical devices to provide device independence. Thus dual-mode I/O provides both I/O protection and allows improved performance.

1.8.2 Memory Protection

For I/O protection to be complete, we must be sure that a user program can never gain control of the computer in monitor mode. If the computer is executing in user mode, it will switch to monitor mode whenever an interrupt or trap occurs, jumping to the address determined from the interrupt vector. Suppose a user program, as part of its execution, stores a new address in the interrupt vector. This new address could overwrite the previous address of the interrupt service routine with an address in the user program. Then when a corresponding trap or interrupt occurs, the hardware would switch to monitor mode, and transfer control through the (modified) interrupt vector to the user program! The user program could gain control of the computer in monitor mode.

We must protect the interrupt vector from modification by a user program. In addition, we must also protect the interrupt service routines in the resident monitor from modification. Otherwise, a user program might overwrite instructions in the interrupt service routine with jumps to the user program, thus gaining control from the interrupt service routine which was executing in monitor mode. Even if the user did not gain unauthorized control of the computer, modifying the interrupt service routines would probably disrupt the proper operation of the computer system and its spooling and buffering.

We see then that we must provide memory protection at least for the interrupt vector and the interrupt service routines of the resident monitor. Similar reasoning shows that this protection must be provided by the hardware. It can be implemented in several ways, as we will see in Chapter 5.

In most cases, both the interrupt vector and the resident monitor occupy low memory, while user programs are loaded into high memory. Memory protection can then be a simple hardware *fence register* which separates memory into two parts: user and monitor (Figure 1.9). Monitor memory must not be accessed or modified in user mode. This protection is accomplished by comparing *every* address generated in user mode with the fence register. Any attempt by a program executing in user mode to access monitor memory results in a trap to the monitor, which treats the attempt as a fatal error. This prevents the user program from (accidentally or deliberately) modifying the code or data structures of the resident monitor.

The fence register can be loaded by the operating system by using a special privileged instruction. Since privileged instructions can only be executed in monitor mode, and only the operating system executes in monitor mode, only the operating system can load the fence register. This scheme allows the monitor to change the value of the fence register whenever the size of the monitor changes but prevents user programs from changing the contents of the fence register.

The operating system, executing in monitor mode, is generally given unrestricted access to both monitor and user memory. This provision allows the operating system to load user programs into user memory, dump them out in case of errors, access and modify parameters of system calls, and so on.

You might notice that although a simple fence register is enough to protect the interrupt vector and resident monitor from modification, it is not generally sufficient to protect user programs from each other. To illustrate this, consider the system of Figure 1.6. Suppose that program 3 is executing. We could move the fence register to point to the beginning

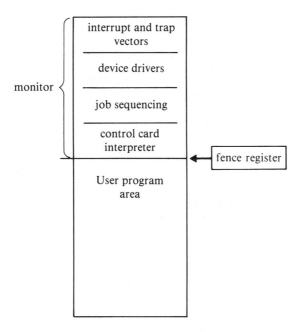

Figure 1.9   Hardware address protection for a resident monitor

of program 3 (see Figure 1.10). This will ensure that program 3 cannot access memory locations in the monitor, program 1, or program 2. It does not, however, protect other users (such as program 4) from unauthorized access by program 3.

What is needed is an ability to protect the memory space *before* and *after* an executing program. This protection can be provided by using *two* registers, as illustrated in Figure 1.11. These registers provide the upper and lower bounds on the addresses which can be legally generated by a user program. That is, the bounds registers contain the values of the smallest and largest physical addresses (for example, lower bound = 100040 and upper bound = 174640) that can be generated by an individual program. Other mechanisms for memory protection are discussed in Chapter 5.

Instructions to modify the contents of any memory management registers, such as fence or bounds registers, must of course be privileged instructions. Only the operating system should be able to modify these registers.

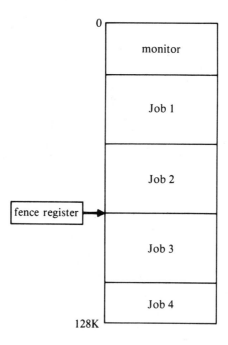

Figure 1.10   Attempting to execute a program by moving the fence

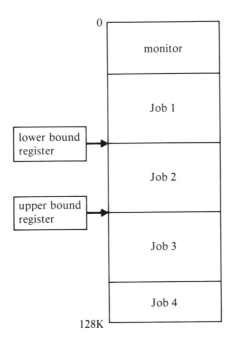

Figure 1.11   Two bounds registers define a logical address space

1.8.3 CPU Protection

One final change in the architecture of the computer system is the addition of a *timer*. A timer prevents a user program from getting stuck in an infinite loop, and never returning control to the monitor. A timer can be set to interrupt the computer after some period of time. The period may be fixed (for example, 1/60 second) or variable (for example, from 1 millisecond to a second in increments of a millisecond). A variable timer is generally implemented by a fixed rate clock and a counter. The operating system sets the counter. Every time the clock ticks, the counter is decremented. When the counter reaches zero, an interrupt occurs. A 10-bit counter with a 1 millisecond clock would allow interrupts at intervals from 1 millisecond to 1024 milliseconds, in steps of 1 millisecond.

Before turning over control to the user, the monitor makes sure that the timer is set to interrupt. If the timer interrupts, control transfers automatically to the monitor which may treat it as a fatal error or decide to give the program more time. Instructions which modify the operation of the timer are clearly privileged.

1.8.4 Resulting Architecture

The desire to reduce setup time and improve utilization of the computer system led to batching jobs together, buffering and spooling, and eventually to multiprogramming and time sharing. These approaches share the resources of the computer system among many different programs and jobs. Sharing led directly to modifications to the basic computer architecture, in order to allow the operating system monitor to maintain control over the computer system and especially input/output. Control must be maintained if we are to provide continuous, consistent, and correct operation.

To maintain control, a dual mode of execution (user mode and monitor mode) was introduced. This scheme supports the concept of privileged instructions, which can only be executed in monitor mode. I/O instructions and instructions to modify the memory management registers or the timer are privileged instructions.

As you can imagine, several other instructions are also classified as privileged. For instance, the HALT instruction is privileged; a user program should never be able to halt the computer. The instructions to turn the interrupt system on and off are also privileged, since proper operation of the timer and I/O depends upon the ability to respond to interrupts correctly. The instruction to change from user mode to monitor mode is privileged, and on many machines any change in the user/monitor mode bit is privileged.

Memory protection must be provided for the monitor, the interrupt vector, and user programs and data. The user program is confined by the operating system, preventing it from disrupting the proper operation of the computer (Figure 1.12).

It should be remembered that the primary purpose of buffering, spooling, multiprogramming, and time sharing is *performance*. We want to get maximum computational usage out of the computer system. The operating system, in addition to providing a convenient environment in which the user can write and run programs, must also take increasing responsibility for arranging the *efficient* use of the cpu and its I/O devices. This movement towards high cpu utilization (plus changing technology) caused profound changes in the environment which was created by the operating system for the programmer.

The changes in computer architecture which we have just discussed provide the mechanisms that are needed to ensure that an operating system functions *correctly*. A system designer can be assured that no

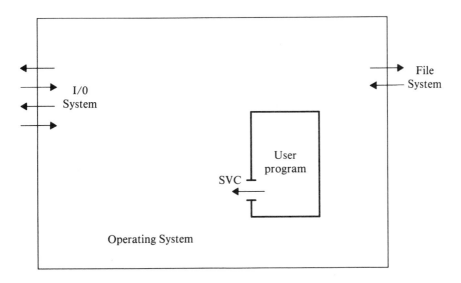

Figure 1.12   The operating system confines the user program

user program can disrupt the operation of the computer (unless there are bugs in the operating system, of course).

1.9 Different Classes of Computers

Most of our discussion up to now has referred to *mainframe* computer systems, the standard large computer systems found in computation centers and data processing centers. Most operating system theory and techniques were developed for mainframe computer systems. Mainframe operating systems have been developing over the last thirty years.

Minicomputers appeared in the mid-1960's, and are considerably smaller and less expensive than mainframe systems. *Microcomputers* appeared in the 1970's, and are even smaller and less expensive. Operating systems for these computers have benefited from the development of operating systems for mainframes in several ways. Minicomputers and microcomputers were immediately able to adopt the technology developed for larger operating systems. Thus they could avoid the mistakes made by the prototype operating systems for mainframes. Most minicomputer and microcomputer systems have avoided batch systems and gone directly to interactive and time-shared operating systems.

On the other hand, the hardware costs for minicomputers and microcomputers are sufficiently low that it may not be necessary to share the hardware among multiple users in order to maintain a high cpu utilization. Thus some of the design decisions which are made in operating systems for mainframes may not be appropriate for smaller systems.

In general, however, an examination of operating systems for mainframes, minicomputers, and microcomputers shows that features which were at one time available only on mainframes have been adopted by minicomputers. Those on minicomputers have been introduced on microcomputers. The same concepts and techniques are appropriate for all the various different classes of computers (Figure 1.13).

A good example of this movement can be seen by considering the Multics operating system. Multics was developed from 1965 to 1970 at MIT as a computing *utility*. It ran on a very large and complex mainframe computer (the GE 645). Many of the ideas which were developed for Multics were subsequently used at Bell Labs (one of the original partners in the development of Multics) in the design of Unix.

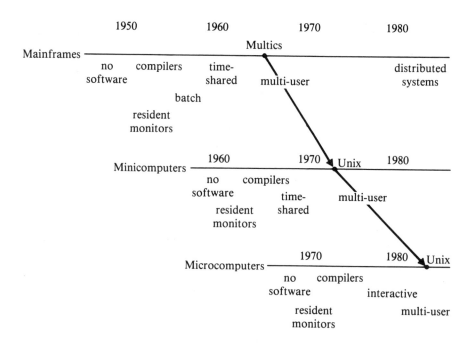

Figure 1.13   Migration of operating system concepts and features

Unix was designed around 1970 for a PDP-11 minicomputer. Around 1980, the features of Unix became the basis for Unix and Unix-like operating systems on microcomputer systems. Thus the features developed for a large mainframe system can be seen to have moved to minicomputers and microcomputers, over time.

Arguments have been raised that the development of cheap microprocessors and cheap memory will make operating systems (and courses which teach them) obsolete. We do not believe this to be true. Rather it is the case that the decrease in hardware costs allows relatively sophisticated operating system concepts (such as time sharing and virtual memory) to be implemented on an even greater number of systems. The movement from simple operating systems (such as CP/M) to multiprogramming systems (like MP/M or Unix) supports such a view.

Thus the decrease in the cost of computer hardware, such as microprocessors, will increase the need to understand the concepts of operating systems.

1.10 Multiprocessor Systems

There have been attempts to create *multiprocessor* computer systems. The standard system is *uniprocessor*, that is, it has one main cpu. A true multiprocessor system would have more than one cpu, sharing memory and peripherals. The obvious advantages would appear to be greater computing power and reliability. However, it is not yet known how to create a completely general multiprocessor operating system. More commonly one of the following two approaches is used.

The most common multiple processor systems assign to each processor a specific task. A master processor controls the system; the other processors either look to the master for instruction or have predefined tasks. This scheme defines a master/slave relationship. In particular, small processors, located at some distance from the main cpu, may be used to run card readers and line printers and transfer these jobs to and from the main computer. These locations are called Remote Job Entry (RJE) sites. Time-sharing systems are often composed of a large computer (like a DEC-20) which is the main computer and a smaller *front-end* computer (like a PDP-11) which is simply responsible for the terminal I/O.

The second fairly common multiple processor system is a computer *network*. In a network, multiple independent computer systems can communicate, sending files and information between them. However, each computer system has its own operating system and operates independently. Computer networks allow new possibilities in distributed processing, as discussed in Chapter 13.

1.11 Summary

Operating systems have developed over the past thirty years for two main purposes. First, they provide a convenient environment for the development and execution of programs. Second, operating systems attempt to schedule computational activities to ensure good performance of the computing system.

Initially, computers were used from the front console. Software such as assemblers, loaders, and compilers improved on the convenience of programming the system, but also required substantial setup time. To reduce the setup time, operators were hired and similar jobs were batched together.

Batch systems allowed automatic job sequencing by a resident monitor and improved the overall utilization of the computer greatly. The computer no longer had to wait for human operation. CPU utilization was still low, however, because of the slow speed of the I/O devices relative to the cpu. Off-line operation of slow devices was tried. Buffering was another approach to improving system performance by overlapping the input, output, and computation of a single job. Finally, spooling allowed the cpu to overlap the input of one job with the computation and output of other jobs.

Spooling also provides a pool of jobs which have been read and are waiting to be run. This job pool supports the concept of multiprogramming. With multiprogramming, several jobs are kept in memory at one time; the cpu is switched back and forth between them in order to increase cpu utilization and to decrease the total real time needed to execute a job.

Multiprogramming, which was developed to improve performance, also allows time sharing. Time-shared operating systems allow many users (from one to several hundred) to use a computer system interactively at the same time. Other operating system types include real-time systems and multiprocessor systems.

The operating system must ensure correct operation of the computer system. To prevent user programs from interfering with the proper operation of the system, the hardware was modified to create two modes: user mode and monitor mode. Various instructions (such as I/O instructions and halt instructions) are privileged, and can only be executed in monitor mode. The memory in which the monitor resides must also be protected from modification by the user. A timer prevents infinite loops. Once these changes (dual mode, privileged instructions, memory protection, timer interrupt) have been made to the basic computer architecture, it is possible to write a correct operating system.

Operating system techniques are migrating down from mainframes to minicomputer and microcomputer systems.

Exercises

1.1 What are the main purposes of an operating system?

1.2 List all the steps that are necessary in order to run a program on a completely dedicated machine.

1.3 Which of the following instructions are privileged?

P a. Set value of timer. *depends*

   b. Read the clock.

P c. Clear memory. *depends*

P d. Turn off interrupts.

P e. Switch from user to monitor mode.

1.4 Writing an operating system that can operate without interference from malicious or undebugged user programs requires some hardware assistance. Name three hardware aids to writing an operating system. *interrupts   dual mode buffers   registers*

1.5 The concept of multiprogramming was not useful (that is, could not be used to gain more performance from a computing system) until the direct access memory channel was developed. Explain why. *bec. cpu was still used to switch data I interrupts happened too often*

1.6 In a multiprogramming and time-sharing environment, several users share the system simultaneously. This results in a problem in security. *overwriting someone's space getting too much privilege beating the system*

   a. List several such problems.

   b. Can we ensure the same degree of security in a shared machine as we have in a dedicated machine? *no*

1.7 Show how a desire for control cards leads naturally to a separate user/monitor state.

1.8 How does the distinction between monitor mode and user mode function as a rudimentary form of protection system?

1.9 Some early computers protected the operating system by placing it in a memory partition that could not be modified by either the user job or the operating system itself. What difficulties may arise in such a scheme?

1.10 Many computer systems do not provide a user/monitor mode in hardware. Does this mean that it is not possible to construct an operating system for these computers? Give an argument both for and against this question.

1.11 Protecting the resident monitor is crucial to a correctly operating computer system. Providing this protection is the reason behind dual mode operation, memory protection, and the timer. To allow maximum flexibility, however, we would also like to place minimal constraints upon the user. The following is a list of operations which are normally protected. What is the *minimal* set of instructions which must be protected?

  a. Change to user mode.

  b. Change to monitor mode.

  c. Read from monitor memory.

  d. Write into monitor memory.

  e. Instruction fetch from monitor memory.

  f. Turn on timer interrupt.

  g. Turn off timer interrupt.

1.12 Define the essential differences between the following types of operating systems:

  a. Batch.

  b. Interactive.

  c. Time-sharing.

  d. Real-time.

1.13 What are the main difficulties in writing an operating system for a real-time environment?

1.14 What are the main advantages of multiprogramming? *time — efficiency of cpu use*

1.15 One of the drawbacks of early operating systems (for example, batch systems) was that users lost the ability to interact with their jobs. In what ways do modern operating systems overcome this problem?

1.16 Why is spooling necessary for batch multiprogramming? Is it needed for a time-shared system?

Bibliographic Notes

General overviews of operating system functions and concepts are presented by Warwick [1970], Hoare [1972a], Tsichritzis and Bernstein [1974, Chapter 1], Lister [1979, Chapter 2], and Habermann [1976, Section 1.2]. Discussions concerning the historical evolution of computer hardware and software systems are presented by Rosen [1969], Rosin [1969], Denning [1971], Sayers [1971, Chapters 7, 8, and 9], Shaw [1974, Section 1.3], and Weizer [1981].

An early batch processing system is described by Bratman and Boldt [1959]. An overview of a simple batch operating system is presented by Graham [1975, Chapter 2]. General discussions concerning batch systems are offered by Kurzban et al. [1975, Sections 1.2 and 1.3]. Job control languages are discussed by Brown [1970], Barron [1974], and Frank [1976].

Off-line systems (satellite processing) were used by the IBM Fortran Monitor system from the late 1950's into the middle of 1960. Spooling was pioneered on the Atlas computer system at Manchester University [Kilburn et al. 1961]. Spooling was also used on the Univac EXEC II system [Lynch 1967, 1972a].

Time-sharing systems were first proposed by Strachey [1959]. The advantages of an on-line man machine interaction were later discussed by Licklider and Clark [1962]. The earliest time-sharing systems were the CTSS system developed at MIT [Corbato et al. 1962] and the SDC Q-32 system built by the System Development Corporation [Schwartz et al. 1964, Schwartz and Weissman 1967]. Other early, but more sophisticated, systems include the Multics system developed at MIT [Corbato and Vyssotsky 1965], the XDS-940 system developed at the University of California at Berkeley [Lichtenberger and Pirtle 1965], and the IBM TSS/360 system [Lett and Konigsford 1968]. General discussions concerning time-sharing systems are offered by Watson [1970, Sections 1.1 to 1.4], and Graham [1975, Chapter 13].

Stone [1980] argued that the development of cheap microprocessors and cheap memory will make operating systems, and courses which teach them, obsolete. Denning [1980b, 1982a] replied that the basic old concepts of operating systems are simply being refined and put to good use on contemporary hardware.

General discussions concerning multiprocessing are given by Nutt [1977], Enslow [1977], Gula [1978], and Jones and Schwarz [1980]. Multiprocessor hardware is discussed by Satyanarayanan [1980a, 1980b]. An overview of computer networks is presented by Kimbleton and Schneider [1975], and Forsdick et al. [1978].

2

Operating System Services

An operating system provides the environment within which programs are executed. Since only the operating system can actually perform I/O, user programs must request all such operations from the operating system. In this chapter, we consider what services an operating system provides and how they are provided.

2.1 Types of Services

An operating system provides an environment for the execution of programs. The operating system provides certain services to programs and to the users of those programs. The specific services provided will, of course, differ from one operating system to another, but there are some common classes of services which can be identified. These operating system functions are provided for the convenience of the programmer, to make the programming task easier.

- **Program execution**. Users will want to execute programs. The system must be able to load a program into memory and run it. The program must be able to end its execution, either normally or abnormally.

- **Input/Output operations**. A running program may require input and output. This I/O may involve a file or an I/O device. For specific devices, special functions may be desired (such as, rewind a tape drive, blank the screen on a CRT, and so on). Since a user program cannot execute I/O operations directly, the operating system must provide some means to do so.

- **File system manipulation**. The file system is of particular interest. It should be obvious that programs want to read and write files. We also want to create and delete files by name. The file system is fully discussed in Chapter 3.

- **Error detection**. The operating system constantly needs to be aware of possible errors. Errors may occur in the cpu and memory hardware (such as a memory error or a power failure), in I/O devices (such as a parity error on tape, a card jam in the card reader, or the printer out of paper), or in the user program (such as an arithmetic overflow, an attempt to access illegal memory location, or using too much cpu time). For each type of error, the operating system should take the appropriate action to ensure correct and consistent computing.

In addition, another set of operating system functions exist not for the user but for the efficient operation of the system itself. Systems with multiple users can gain efficiency by sharing the computer resources among the users.

- **Resource allocation**. When there are multiple users or multiple jobs running at the same time, resources must be allocated to each of them. Many different types of resources are managed by the operating system. Some (such as cpu cycles, main memory, and file storage) may have special allocation code, while others (such as I/O devices) may have much more general request and release code.

- **Accounting**. We want to keep track of which users use how much and what kinds of computer resources. This record-keeping may be for the purpose of paying for the system and its operation, or simply for accumulating usage statistics. Usage statistics may be a valuable tool in trying to configure the system to improve computing services.

- **Protection**. The owners of information stored in a multi-user computer system may want to control its use. When several disjoint jobs are being executed simultaneously in order to increase utilization, it should not be possible for one job to interfere with the others. In addition, conflicting demands for various resources need to be reconciled fairly and scheduled reasonably.

2.2 The User View

Operating system services are provided in many different ways. Two basic methods of providing services are *system calls* and *systems programs*. Each method has its advantages.

2.2.1 System Calls

The more fundamental level of services is handled through the use of system calls. System calls provide the interface between a running program and the operating system. These calls are generally available as assembly language instructions, and are usually listed in the manuals used by assembly language programmers.

System calls can be roughly grouped into three major categories: *process or job control*, *device and file manipulation*, and *information maintenance*. In the following discussion, we briefly indicate the types of system calls that may be provided by an operating system. Unfortunately, our description may seem somewhat shallow, since at this point, most of these system calls support or are supported by, concepts and functions which are discussed in later chapters.

Process and Job Control

A running program needs to be able to halt its execution either normally (**end**) or abnormally (**abort**). If the program discovers an error in its input and wants to terminate abnormally, it may also want to define an error level. More severe errors can be indicated by a higher error level parameter. It is then possible to combine normal and abnormal termination by defining a normal termination as an abnormal termination at level 0.

A process or job executing one program may want to **load** and **execute** another program. This allows the control card interpreter to execute a program as directed by the control cards of the user job, for example. An interesting related question is where to return control when the loaded program terminates. This question is related to the problem of whether the existing program is lost, saved, or allowed to continue execution concurrently with the new program.

If control returns to the existing program when the new program terminates, we must save the memory image of the existing program and effectively have created a mechanism for one program to call another program. If both programs continue concurrently, we have created a new job or process to be multiprogrammed. Often there is a system call specifically for this purpose (**create process** or **submit job**).

If we create a new job or process, or perhaps even a set of jobs or processes, we should be able to control its execution. This control requires the ability to determine and reset the attributes of a job or process, including its priority, its maximum allowable execution time, and so on (**get process attributes** and **set process attributes**). We may also want to terminate a job or process that we created (**terminate process**) if we find that it is incorrect or no longer needed.

Having created new jobs or processes, we may need to wait for them to finish execution. We may want to wait for a certain amount of time (**wait time**), but more likely we want to wait for a specific event (**wait event**). The jobs or processes should then signal when that event has occurred (**signal event**). System calls of this type, dealing with the coordination of concurrent processes, are discussed in more detail in Chapter 9.

Another set of system calls are helpful in debugging a program. Many systems provide system calls to **dump** memory. This provision is useful for assembly language or machine language debugging, particularly in a batch system. A program **trace** lists each instruction as it is executed, and is provided by fewer systems.

A time profile of a program is provided by many systems. It indicates the amount of time that the program executes at a particular location or set of locations. A time profile requires either a tracing facility or regular timer interrupts. At every occurrence of the timer interrupt, the value of the program counter is recorded. With frequent enough timer interrupts, a statistical picture of the time spent on various parts of the program can be obtained.

File Manipulation

The file system will be discussed in more detail in Chapter 3. We can identify several common system calls dealing with files, however. Their exact meaning will become more clear when Chapter 3 is read.

We first need to be able to **create** and **delete** files. Such a system call requires the name of the file and perhaps some of its attributes. Once the file is created, we need to **open** it and use it. We may also **read**, **write**, and **reposition** (rewinding it or skipping to the end of the file, for example). Finally, we need to **close** the file, indicating that we are no longer using it.

We may need these same sets of operations for directories if we have a directory structure in the file system. In addition, for either files or directories, we need to be able to determine the values of various attributes, and perhaps reset them if necessary. File attributes include the file name, a file type, protection codes, accounting information, and so on. Two system calls, **get file attribute** and **set file attribute** are required for this function. Section 3.2.2 discusses commonly kept file attributes.

Device Management

Files can be thought of as abstract or virtual devices. Thus many of the system calls for files are also needed for devices. If there are multiple

- Process Control.

  ○ End, Abort

  ○ Load, Execute

  ○ Create Process, Terminate Process

  ○ Get Process Attributes, Set Process Attributes

  ○ Wait for Time

  ○ Wait Event, Signal Event

- File Manipulation.

  ○ Create File, Delete File

  ○ Open, Close

  ○ Read, Write, Reposition

  ○ Get File Attributes, Set File Attributes

- Device Manipulation.

  ○ Request Device, Release Device

  ○ Read, Write, Reposition

  ○ Get Device Attributes, Set Device Attributes

- Information Maintenance.

  ○ Get Time or Date, Set Time or Date

  ○ Get System Data, Set System Data

  ○ Get Process, File, or Device Attributes, Set Process, File, or Device Attributes

Figure 2.1   Types of system calls

users of the system, however, we must first **request** the device, to ensure that we have exclusive use of it. After we are finished with the device, we must **release** it. These functions are similar to the **open/close** system calls for files.

Once the device has been requested (and allocated to us), we can **read**, **write**, and (possibly) **reposition** the device, just as with files. In fact, the similarity between I/O devices and files is so great that many operating systems merge the two into a combined file/device structure. In this case, I/O devices are identified by special file names.

Information Maintenance

Many system calls exist simply for the purpose of transferring information between the user program and the operating system. For example, most systems have a system call to return the current **time** and **date**. Other system calls may return information about the system, such as the number of current users, the version number of the operating system, the amount of free memory or disk space, and so on.

In addition, the operating system keeps information about all of its jobs and processes, and there are system calls to access this information. Generally, there are also calls to reset it (**get process attributes** and **set process attributes**). In Section 4.2.1, we discuss what information is normally kept.

Figure 2.1 summarizes the types of system calls normally provided by an operating system.

2.2.2 System Call Implementation

System calls occur in different ways, depending upon the computer in use. On the IBM 360/370, for example, there is a special system call instruction which traps directly to the operating system. The lower eight bits of the system call specify a number that identifies the type of call being made.

CP/M runs on the Intel 8080, which does not have a special system call instruction. A call is made by placing the function number in register C and jumping directly to location 5 in memory.

Often more information is required than simply the identity of the desired system call. The exact type and amount of information varies according to the particular operating system and call. For example, to read a card image, we may need to specify the file or device to use and the address and length of the memory buffer into which it should be read. Of course, the device or file may be implicit in the call and, if the card images are always 80 characters, we may not need to specify the length.

   Two general methods are used to pass parameters to the operating
system. The simplest approach is to pass the parameters in *registers*.
However, in some cases there may be more parameters than registers.
In these cases the parameters are generally stored in a *block* or table in
memory and the address of the block is passed as a parameter in a
register (Figure 2.2). Some operating systems prefer this uniform
interface, even when there are enough registers for all of the parameters
for most cases.
   System calls are generally available only in assembly language.
Some systems may allow system calls to be made directly from a
higher-level language program, in which case the calls normally
resemble predefined function or subroutine calls. They may generate a
call to a special run-time routine that makes the system call, or the
system call may be generated directly in-line.
   Several languages, such as C [Kernighan and Ritchie 1978], Bliss
[Wulf et al. 1971], and PL/360 [Wirth 1968], have been defined to replace
assembly language for systems programming. These languages allow
system calls to be made directly. Some Pascal systems also provide an
ability to make system calls directly from a Pascal program to the
operating system. Most Fortran systems provide similar capabilities,
often by a set of library routines.

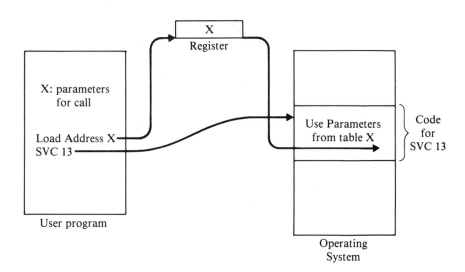

Figure 2.2   Passing parameters as a table

As an example of how system calls are used, consider writing a simple program to read data from one file and copy it to another file. The first thing the program will need is the names of the two files: the input file and the output file. These can be specified in two ways. One approach is for the program to ask the user for the names of the two files. In an interactive system, this will require a sequence of system calls to first write a prompting message on the terminal and then read from the terminal the characters which define the two files. Another approach, particularly used for batch systems, is to specify the names of the files with control cards. In this case, there must be a mechanism for passing these parameters from the control cards to the executing program.

Once the two file names are obtained, the program must open the input file and create the output file. Each of these operations requires another system call. There are also possible error conditions for each operation. When the program tries to open the input file, it may find that there is no file of that name or that the file is protected against access. In these cases, the program should print a message on the console (another sequence of system calls) and then terminate abnormally (another system call). If the input file exists, then we must create a new output file. We may find that there is already an output file with the same name. This situation may cause the program to abort (a system call), or we may delete the existing file (another system call) and create a new one (another system call). Another option, in an interactive system, is to ask the user (a sequence of system calls to output the prompting message and read the response from the terminal) whether to replace the existing file or abort.

Now that both files are set up, we enter a loop which reads from the input file (a system call) and writes to the output file (another system call). Each read and write must return status information regarding various possible error conditions. On input, the program may find that the end of the file has been reached, or that there was a hardware failure in the read (such as a parity error). The write operation may encounter various errors, depending upon the output device (no more disk space, physical end of tape, printer out of paper, and so on).

Finally, after the entire file is copied, the program may close both files (another system call), write a message to the console (more system calls) and finally terminate normally (the last system call). As we can see, programs may make heavy use of the operating system. All interactions between the program and its environment must occur as the result of requests from the program to the operating system.

Most users never see this level of detail, however. The run-time support system for most programming languages provides a much simpler interface. For example, a *write* statement in Pascal or Fortran most likely is compiled into a call to a run-time support routine that issues the necessary system calls, checks for errors, and finally returns to the user program. Thus most of the details of the operating system interface are hidden from the user programmer by the compiler and its run-time support package.

2.2.3 Systems Programs

Another aspect of a modern system is its collection of systems programs. While we could write a program to copy one file to another, as shown above, it is unlikely that we would want to. In addition to the actual operating system monitor code, most systems supply a large collection of systems programs to solve common problems and provide a more convenient environment for program development and execution.

Systems programs can be divided into several categories:

- **File manipulation**. These programs create, delete, copy, rename, print, dump, list, and generally manipulate files and directories.

- **Status information**. Some programs simply ask the operating system for the date, time, amount of available memory or disk space, number of users, or similar status information. That information is then formatted and printed to the terminal or other output device or file.

- **File modification**. Several text editors may be available to create and modify the content of files stored on disk or tape.

- **Programming language support**. Compilers, assemblers, and interpreters for common programming languages (such as Fortran, Cobol, Pascal, Basic, and so on) are often provided with the operating system. Recently many of these programs are being priced and provided separately.

- **Program loading and execution**. Once a program is assembled or compiled, it must be loaded into memory to be executed. The system may provide absolute loaders, relocatable loaders, linkage editors, and overlay loaders. Debugging systems for either higher-level languages or machine language are needed also.

- **Application programs**. In addition, most operating systems come with programs which are useful to solve some particularly common problems, such as compiler-compilers, text formatters, plotting packages, database systems, statistical analysis packages, and so on.

Perhaps the most important system program for an operating system is its *command interpreter*. The command interpreter is that program which is running when a job initially starts or a user first logs-in to a time-sharing system.

Many commands are given to the operating system by control cards. (Control cards are commands given in a batch environment; commands are control cards in an interactive environment.) When a new job is started in a batch system, or when a user logs-in to a time-shared system, a program which reads and interprets control cards is automatically executed. This program is variously called (1) the control card interpreter, (2) the command line interpreter, (3) the console command processor (in CP/M), (4) the shell (in Unix), and so on. Its function is quite simple: get the next command or control card and execute it.

Many of the commands given at this level manipulate files: create, delete, list, print, copy, execute, and so on. There are two general ways in which these commands are implemented. In one approach, the command interpreter itself contains the code to execute the command. For example, a command to delete a file may cause the command interpreter to jump to a section of its code that sets up the parameters and makes the appropriate system call. In this case, the number of commands that can be given determines the size of the command interpreter, since each command requires its own implementing code.

An alternative approach implements all commands by special systems programs. In this case, the command interpreter does not "understand" the command in any way; it merely uses the command to identify a file to be loaded into memory and executed. Thus a command:

delete G

would search for a file called *delete*, load it into memory, and pass it a parameter, G. The function associated with the **delete** command would be completely defined by the code in the file *delete*. In this way, new commands can be easily added to the system by creating new files of the proper name. The command interpreter program, which can now be quite small, need not be changed in order to add new commands.

There are problems with this approach to the design of a command interpreter. Notice first that since the code to execute a command is a separate system program, the operating system must provide a mechanism for passing parameters from the command interpreter to the system program. This task can often be quite clumsy, since the command interpreter and the system program may not both be in memory at the same time.

The other problem is that the interpretation of the parameters is totally left up to the programmer of the system program. This may mean that parameters are inconsistently provided across programs which appear similar to the user, but were written at different times by different programmers.

The view of the operating system seen by most users is thus defined by its systems programs, not by its actual system calls. Consequently, this view may be quite removed from the actual system. The problems of designing a useful and friendly user interface are many, but they are not direct functions of the operating system. In this book, we will concentrate upon the fundamental problems of providing adequate service to user programs. From the point of view of the operating system, we do not distinguish between user programs and systems programs.

2.3 The Operating System View

The view of an operating system seen by the user is defined mainly by the systems programs, particularly the command interpreter. The operating system programmer, on the other hand has a much different view. Where the user views those facilities provided by the operating system, the systems programmer sees only the physical resources and devices and must convert them into the logical facilities to be provided to the user. Let us consider how the operating system is structured.

Operating systems are *event-driven* programs. If there are no jobs to execute, no I/O devices to service, and no users to respond to, an operating system will sit quietly, waiting for something to happen. Events are almost always signaled by the occurrence of an interrupt or a trap. Thus an operating system is *interrupt-driven*.

The interrupt-driven nature of an operating system defines its general structure. When an interrupt (or trap) occurs, the hardware transfers control to the operating system. First, the operating system preserves the state of the cpu by storing registers and the program counter. Then, it determines which type of interrupt has occurred. This determination may require polling, or it may be a natural result of a vectored interrupt system. Several different types of interrupts may occur:

- A system call.

- An I/O device interrupt.

- A program error.

For each type of interrupt, separate segments of code in the operating system determine what action should be taken.

2.3.1 System Calls

System calls to the operating system are further classified according to the type of call. Each call has its own segment of code to implement the desired action. Generally we can consider:

- **Normal termination**. If a system call is made to terminate the currently running program normally, the operating system must transfer control to the command interpreter. The command interpreter then reads the next control card or command to determine the next job step.

- **Abnormal termination**. A program, detecting an error in its execution or data and deciding to terminate abnormally, may require a dump of memory and an error message. Next, the command interpreter is called. In an interactive system, the command interpreter simply continues with the next command; it is assumed that the user will issue an appropriate command to respond to the error. In a batch system, the command interpreter usually terminates the entire job and continues with the next job. Some systems allow control cards to indicate special recovery actions in case an error occurs.

- **Status requests**. One class of system calls simply ask the operating system for information. Such requests include asking for the date or time of day, the attributes of files or jobs, or the status of various resources (such as how much memory is available?). The requested information is computed, and control is returned to the running program.

- **Resource requests**. A program, as it is running, may need additional resources in order to proceed. Additional resources may be more memory, tape drives, access to files, and so on. If the resources are available, they can be granted and control returned to the user program; otherwise the program will have to wait until sufficient resources are available.

- **I/O requests**. The largest number of requests, however, will be for I/O. Most programs will read or write to devices or files often during their execution.

2.3.2 I/O Device Interrupts

A major class of events which an operating system must handle is the class of I/O interrupts. An I/O device will interrupt when it has finished an I/O request. This situation will occur, in general, as the result of a user system call requesting I/O. Once the I/O is started, two courses of action exist. In the simplest case, we start the requested I/O and wait until it is complete before returning control to the user program. The other possibility is to return control to the user program without waiting for the I/O to complete.

Waiting for I/O completion may be accomplished in one of two ways. Some computers, like the IBM 370 and PDP-11, have a special **wait** instruction that idles the cpu until the next interrupt. Machines which do not have such an instruction may have a wait loop:

Loop: **jmp** *Loop*

This very tight loop simply continues until an interrupt occurs, transferring control to another part of the operating system. The **wait** instruction is probably better, since a wait loop generates a series of instruction fetches, which may cause significant contention for memory access.

One advantage of always waiting for I/O completion is that at most one I/O request is outstanding at a time. Thus whenever an I/O interrupt occurs, the operating system knows exactly which device is interrupting. On the other hand, this approach severely limits the amount of simultaneous I/O which can be done.

An alternative is to start the I/O and immediately return control to the user program. A new system call is needed to allow the user to wait for I/O completion. Hence we still require the wait code needed before. We also need to be able to keep track of many I/O requests at the same time. For this purpose, the operating system uses a table containing an entry for each I/O device: the *device status table* (Figure 2.3). Each table entry indicates the type of device, its address, and its state (not functioning, idle, or busy). If the device is busy with a request, the type of request and other parameters will be stored in the table entry for that device. Since it is possible for a program to issue several requests to the same device, we may have a list or chain of waiting requests. Thus in addition to the I/O device table, an operating system may have a request list for each device.

An I/O device interrupts when it needs service. When an interrupt occurs, we first determine which I/O device caused the interrupt. We

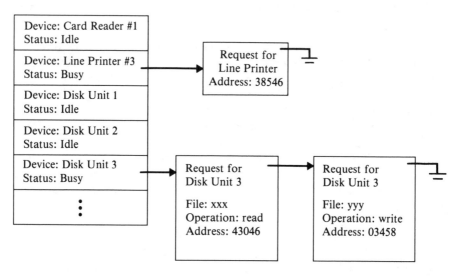

Figure 2.3   Device status table

then index into the I/O device table to determine the status of that device, and modify the table entry to reflect the occurrence of the interrupt. For most devices, an interrupt signals completion of an I/O request. If there are additional requests waiting for this device, we begin processing the next request.

Finally, control is returned from the I/O interrupt. If a program was waiting for this request to complete (as recorded in the device status table), we now return control to it. Otherwise, we return to whatever we were doing before the I/O interrupt: to the execution of the user program (the program started an I/O operation and that operation has now finished, but the program has not yet waited for the operation to complete) or to the wait loop (the program started two or more I/O operations and is waiting for a particular one to finish, but this interrupt was from one of the others).

Some input devices may vary from this scheme. Many interactive systems allow users to type ahead on their terminal. In this case, interrupts may occur signaling the arrival of characters from the terminal, while the device status block indicates that no program has requested input from this device. If type-ahead is to be allowed, then a buffer must be provided to store the type-ahead characters until some program wants them. In general, we may need a buffer for each input terminal.

A different situation exists when a timer interrupt occurs. A timer interrupt signals the passage of some period of time, allowing the operating system to compute the current time in reference to some initial time. If we have interrupts every 1 second, and we have had 1427 interrupts since we were told it was 1:00 PM, then we can compute that the current time is 1:23:47 PM. Most computers determine the current time in this manner.

Another use of the timer is to prevent a user program from running too long. A simple technique is to initialize a counter with the amount of time that a program is allowed to run. A program with a seven-minute time limit, for example, would have its counter initialized to 420. Every second, the timer interrupts and the counter is decremented by one. As long as the counter is positive, control is returned to the user program. When the counter becomes negative, we terminate the program for exceeding its time limit.

2.3.3 Program Errors

A third kind of interrupt involves program errors. Certain types of program errors (such as an illegal instruction, an attempt to execute a privileged instruction, or an illegal memory reference) cause hardware traps. The trap transfers control through the interrupt vector to the operating system just like an interrupt.

Whenever a program error occurs, the operating system must abnormally terminate the program. This situation is handled by the same code as a user-requested abnormal termination. An appropriate error message is given, and the memory of the program is dumped. In a batch system, the memory dump may be printed, allowing the user to try to find the cause of the error by examining the printed dump. In an interactive system, the memory dump may be written to a file. The user may then print it or examine it on-line, and perhaps correct and restart the program.

2.3.4 General Flow

Figure 2.4 illustrates this general flow of an operating system. Clearly, no real operating system will exactly match this structure. Most operating systems, however, will be similar. We can now identify certain common parts of an operating system.

An operating system will have device drivers, an interrupt handler, a set of system call routines, and a command or control card interpreter. Another major portion of an operating system is the file system, which we discuss in Chapter 3.

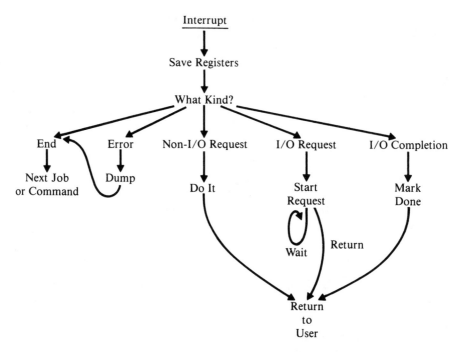

Figure 2.4   General flow of an operating system

These elements are sufficient to define an operating system. The CP/M operating system, which is extremely popular with microcomputer systems, has essentially this structure. It consists of device drivers (BIOS), a file system (BDOS), and a command interpreter (the console command processor) (Figure 2.5). Most operating systems provide additional functions, and hence are much more complex, as we shall see in the remainder of this book.

Notice however that a single-user, uniprogramming operating system is much less complex than a multi-user, multiprogrammed operating system. We are mainly concerned in this text with the problems and solutions which have been defined for multiprogrammed operating systems.

2.4 Summary

Operating systems provide a number of services. At the lowest level, system calls allow a running program to make requests from the operating system directly. At a higher level, the command interpreter provides a mechanism for a user to issue a request without needing to write a program. Commands may come from cards (in a batch system) or directly from a terminal (in an interactive or time-shared system). Systems programs provide another mechanism for satisfying user requests.

The types of requests vary according to the level of the request. The system call level must provide the basic functions, such as process control and file and device manipulation. Higher-level requests, satisfied by the command interpreter or systems programs, are translated into a sequence of system calls. System services can be

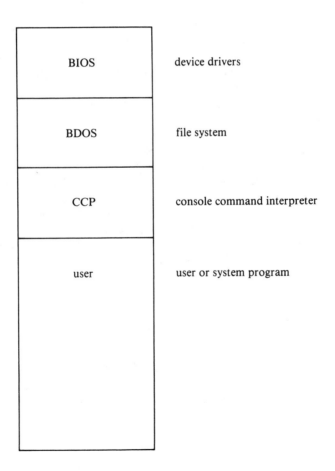

Figure 2.5   CP/M operating system structure

classified into several categories: program control, status requests, and I/O requests. Program errors can be considered implicit requests for service.

Once the system services are defined, the structure of the operating system can be developed. Various tables are needed to record the information which defines the state of the computer system and its jobs.

Operating systems are generally interrupt-driven. A different section of the operating system responds to each of the various interrupts, traps, and system calls.

Bibliographic Notes

Operating system services are covered by Shaw [1974, Section 1.4] and Kurzban et al. [1975, Chapter 3]. A good discussion on I/O device interrupts is presented by Lister [1979, Section 6.3].

To see actual operating system code, you might look at Madnick and Donovan [1974, Chapter 7] (a sample multiprogramming system for an IBM/360), Brinch Hansen [1977] (the Solo operating system for the PDP-11 written in Concurrent Pascal), Brinch Hansen [1983] (the Edison system for the IBM PC), or Lions [1977] (the source code of Unix version 6 in C for a PDP-11 plus a running commentary)

Unger [1975] is concerned with various aspects of command languages. Particularly interesting is the survey of Gram and Hertweck [1975]. Brown [1978] provides a somewhat more recent summary of developments with command languages.

Command languages can be seen as special-purpose programming languages. Brunt and Tuffs [1976] argue that a command language should provide a rich set of functions, while Frank [1976] argues for a more limited, simpler command language. An excellent case study is the Unix shell, as described by Bourne [1978].

3

File Systems

For most users, the file system is the most visible aspect of an operating system. Files store data and programs. The operating system implements the abstract concept of a file by managing mass storage devices, such as tapes and disks. In this chapter, we consider the various ways to map files onto devices. Also files are normally organized into directories to ease their use, so we look at a variety of directory structures. Finally, when multiple users have access to files, it may be desirable to control by whom and in what ways files may be accessed. This control is known as file protection.

3.1 File Concept

File management is one of the most visible services of an operating system. Computers can store information in several different physical forms; magnetic tape, disk, and drum are the most common forms. Each of these devices has its own characteristics and physical organization.

For convenient use of the computer system, the operating system provides a uniform logical view of information storage. The operating system abstracts from the physical properties of its storage devices to define a logical storage unit, the *file*. Files are mapped, by the operating system, onto physical devices.

What is a file? A file is a collection of related information defined by its creator. Commonly, files represent programs (both source and object forms) and data. Data files may be numeric, alphabetic or alphanumeric. Files may be free-form, such as text files, or may be rigidly formatted. In general, a file is a sequence of bits, bytes, lines or records whose meaning is defined by its creator and user. It is a very general concept.

A file is named, and is referred to by its name. It has certain other properties such as its type, the time of its creation, the name (or account number) of its creator, its length, and so on.

Think of a file as a magnetic tape. A tape is initially blank, but can have information written on it, which can then be stored and later read back into the computer. The same information may be read several times. Each tape is referred to by a tape name or number. The contents of a tape can be modified and additional information can be appended to the end. A tape can be rewound and rewritten with new information, erasing the old information.

3.1.1 File Types

The information in a file is defined by its creator. Many different types of information may be stored in a file: source programs, object programs, numeric data, text, payroll records, and so on. A file has a certain defined *structure* according to its use. A text file is a sequence of characters organized into lines (and possibly pages); a source file is a sequence of subroutines and functions, each of which is further organized as declarations followed by executable statements; an object file is a sequence of words organized into loader record blocks.

One major consideration is how much of this structure should be known and supported by the operating system. If an operating system knows the structure of a file, it can then operate on the file in reasonable ways. For example, a common mistake occurs when a user tries to print the binary object form of a program. This attempt normally produces garbage, but can be prevented *if* the operating system has been told that the file is a binary object program.

Another example comes from the TOPS-20 operating system. If the user tries to execute an object program whose source file has been modified (edited) since the object file was produced, the source file will be recompiled automatically. This function ensures that the user always runs an up-to-date object file, even if he forgets to recompile. Otherwise, the user could waste a significant amount of time executing the old object file. Notice that in order for this function to be possible, the operating system must be able to identify the source file from the object file, check the time that each file was last modified or created, and determine the language of the source program (in order to use the correct compiler).

There are disadvantages to having the operating system know the structure of a file. One problem is the resulting size of the operating system. If the operating system defines fourteen different file structures, it must then contain the code to support these file structures correctly. In addition, every file must be definable as one of the file types supported by the operating system. Severe problems may result from new applications that require information structured in ways not supported by the operating system.

For example, assume that a system supports two types of files: text files (composed of ASCII characters separated by a carriage return and line feed) and executable binary files. Now if we (as a user) want to define an encrypted file to protect our files from being read by unauthorized people, we may find neither file type to be appropriate. The encrypted file is not ASCII text lines but (apparently) random bits. But though it may appear to be a binary file, it is not executable. As a result we may have to circumvent or misuse the operating system's file types mechanism, or modify or abandon our encryption scheme.

The other extreme is to impose (and support) no file type in the operating system. This approach has been adopted in Unix, among others. Unix considers each file to be a sequence of 8-bit bytes; no interpretation of these bits is made by the operating system. This scheme provides maximum flexibility, but minimal support. Each application program must include its own code to interpret an input file into the appropriate structure.

3.1.2 Tape-Based Systems

Early file systems were tape-based. Each file was implemented by mapping it onto its own reel of tape. The advantage of this approach is its simplicity, but it suffers from a certain inefficiency, since physical tape reels are quite large (normally 2400 feet of tape). Studies have shown that most files are small. For example, Figure 3.1 shows the number of files of each size for a particular day on a PDP 11/70 with the Unix operating system. Since many files are quite small, they would only take up a small amount of tape. A tape can easily hold 5,000,000 bytes. Even a fairly large file of 100,000 bytes uses only 2 percent of the tape.

A separate but related problem occurs with some very large files, such as census data, which may require several tapes for storage. To handle this situation most systems provide for *multi-reel* or *multi-volume* tape files.

To solve the problem of using a large number of nearly empty tapes to store an equal number of small files, systems were created which store multiple files on one tape. This solution improves tape utilization considerably, since an average of 10 files per tape reduces the number of reels by a factor of 10.

Now, however, there is the problem of determining which files are on which tape. To solve this problem, a *directory* is added to the tape. In IBM systems, the tape reel is called a volume, and the directory is called the Volume Table of Contents (VTOC). The directory lists the name and location of each file on the tape. We may also keep additional

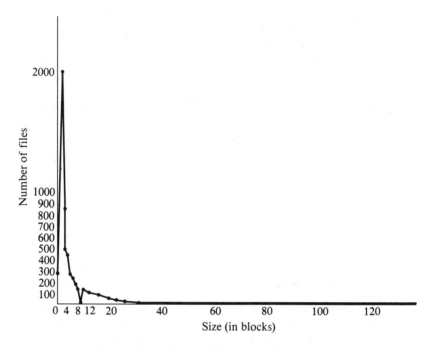

Figure 3.1   Sizes of files in a file system

information about a file in the directory, such as the size of the file, when it was created, and so on. Each tape, or device, will have its own device directory. The device directory is a convenient place to keep summary information about the files on that device.

Finding a file requires identifying the proper tape (often specified by the user), searching its directory, and then positioning the tape to the appropriate file. Reading the file proceeds as before, when we had one file per tape, with the exception that end-of-file is now different from end-of-tape. We must also distinguish between rewinding the file and rewinding the tape.

Other difficulties also exist. Consider a program which reads lines alternately from two files on the same tape. Either one file must first be copied to another tape, or the tape drive would spend significant amounts of time moving from one file on the tape to the other and back. Also, remember that the physical nature of tapes generally precludes rewriting in place. Thus if a file is to be modified, it requires copying the entire tape over. All files, even those which are not being modified, must be copied and rewritten. Typically, this is necessary even if a new file is being added to the end of the tape, since almost any change requires rewriting the directory. The directory is normally kept at the front of the tape to speed access. Thus if the directory is modified, the entire tape may need to be rewritten.

3.1.3 Disk-Based Systems

Many of the problems associated with storing multiple files on a tape are resolved when a disk-based or drum-based system is used. A disk is divided into tracks. The number of tracks varies from disk drive to disk drive. Each track is further divided into sectors. A sector is the smallest unit of information which can be read from or written to the disk. Depending upon the disk drive, sectors vary from 32 bytes to 4096 bytes; there are 4 to 32 sectors per track, and from 75 to 500 tracks per disk surface. Large disk systems may have several platters (see Figure 3.2). Each platter has two surfaces. To access a sector we must specify the surface, track, and sector. The read/write heads are moved to the correct track (seek time), electronically switched to the correct surface, and then we wait (latency time) for the requested sector to rotate below the heads. A cylinder is a set of tracks which are at the same track

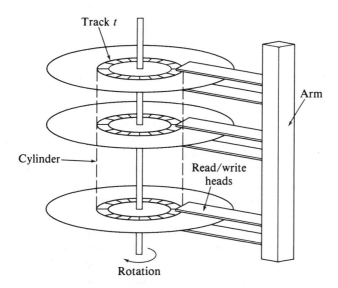

Figure 3.2   Moving head disk mechanism

position of the disk, but on different platter surfaces. No seek is necessary for accessing tracks in the same cylinder.

I/O transfers between memory and disk are performed in units of one or more sectors. Addressing a particular sector requires a track (or cylinder) number, a surface number, and a sector number. Thus the disk can be viewed as a three-dimensional array of sectors. Commonly, this is treated by the operating system as a one-dimensional array of *disk blocks*. Each block is a sector. Typically block addresses increase through all sectors on a track, then through all the tracks in a cylinder, and finally from cylinder 0 to the last cylinder on the disk. If s is the number of sectors per track and t is the number of tracks per cylinder, then clearly we can convert from a disk address of cylinder i, surface j, sector k to a one-dimensional block number b, by

$$b = k + s \times (j + i{\times}t)$$

Notice that with this mapping, accessing block $b+1$ when the last block accessed was b requires a seek only when b was the last block of one cylinder and $b+1$ is the first block of the next cylinder. Even in this case, the head is moved only one track.

A drum is effectively a one-cylinder disk. Since each track has its own read/write head, there is no seek time. The primary differences between disks and drums are performance, cost, and storage capacity, not their logical structure, so we do not distinguish between them in this book.

Disks and drums differ from tapes in two ways which are important now. First, they can be rewritten in place; it is possible to read a block from the disk, modify it and write it back into the same place. Second, we can directly access any given block of information on the disk. Switching from one file to another only requires moving the read/write heads and waiting for the drum to revolve. The combination of seek time and latency is generally less than 100 milliseconds; although disk access is not as fast as main memory, it is much faster than tape. These two differences make it much more convenient to store multiple files on a disk than on a tape.

As with a multi-file tape, a disk normally has a device directory indicating which files are on the disk. The directory lists the file by name, and includes such information as where the file is on the disk, its length, type, owner, time of creation, time of last use, and so on. Since blocks from disk can be rewritten in place, we can read, update and rewrite the directory whenever it needs to be changed, without having to copy the rest of the disk.

Each disk pack or floppy has its own device directory. The device directory is stored on the device, often at some fixed disk address, such as disk address 00001. (Address 00000 is generally a system boot loader.) This is particularly desirable for removable media devices, such as floppy disk drives or removable disk packs. If the media is dismounted, stored, and then remounted, perhaps on a different drive, we still want to be able to find the files on that device.

It is sometimes possible to use a large disk pack as a mountable volume, like a tape, but the size (and cost) of such a disk generally precludes this use except in very large systems or very small disks. Floppy disks are almost always removable, and are best treated as direct-access tapes.

3.1.4 Blocking

Disk systems typically have a well-defined block size determined by the size of a sector. All disk I/O is in units of one block (physical record), and all blocks are the same size. Tapes are somewhat more flexible and the physical block size can be defined by the software. A designation of 80 characters (one card image) per physical record is common, but this can introduce significant amounts of wasted space in interrecord gaps. A physical record of several thousand bytes makes better use of the tape.

In any case, with either tapes or disks, it is unlikely that the physical record size will exactly match the length of the desired logical record. Logical records may even vary in length. *Packing* a number of logical records into physical blocks is a common solution to this problem.

For example, the Unix operating system defines all files to be simply a stream of bytes. Each byte is individually addressable by its offset from the beginning (or end) of the file. In this case, the logical record is one byte. The file system automatically packs and unpacks bytes into physical disk blocks (say 512 bytes per block) as necessary.

Knowledge of the logical record size, physical block size and packing technique determine how many logical records are packed into each physical block. The packing can be done either by the user's application program or by the operating system.

In either case, the file may be considered to be a sequence of blocks. All of the basic I/O functions operate in terms of blocks. The conversion from logical records to physical blocks is a relatively simple software problem.

Notice that always allocating disk space in blocks means that, in general, some portion of the last block of each file may be wasted. If each block is 512 bytes, then a file of 1949 bytes would be allocated 4 blocks (2048 bytes); the last 99 bytes would be wasted. The wasted bytes allocated to keep everything in units of blocks (instead of bytes) is *internal fragmentation*. All file systems suffer from internal fragmentation. In general, larger block sizes cause more internal fragmentation.

3.1.5 Operations on Files

Files can be implemented on several different devices: tapes, disks, drums, and other, more unusual, storage devices. A file is a logical entity which represents a named piece of information. A file is *mapped* onto a physical device (Figure 3.3). There are many ways to map, or implement, files. To be able to compare the various implementations of files, we need to understand the definition of files independent of their implementation. A file is an *abstract data type*. To define a file properly, we need to consider the operations which can be performed on files.

A file is a means of storing information for later use. We want to (1) *create* a file and (2) *write* to the file. At some later time, we will want to (3) *rewind* the file, and (4) *read* from the file. Eventually we may no longer need it and may want to (5) *delete* the file. These five operations are certainly the minimal required file operations. More commonly, we will also want to *edit* the file and modify its contents. A common modification is *appending* new information to the end of an existing file. We may want to create a *copy* of a file, or copy it to an I/O device, such as a printer or a display. Since files are named objects, we may want to *rename* an existing file.

3.2 File Support

The file concept is implemented by the operating system. System calls are provided to create, write, read, rewind, and delete files.   To

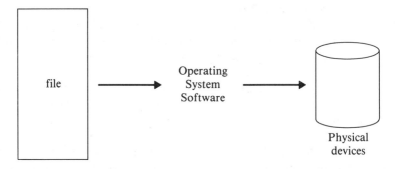

Figure 3.3   Mapping logical files onto a physical device

understand how file systems are supported, let us look at these five file operations in more detail. From this, we will see the importance of the device directory.

3.2.1 File Operations

For convenience, assume the file system is disk-based. Let us consider what the operating system must do for each of the five basic file operations. It should then be easy to see how similar operations, such as renaming a file, would be implemented.

- **Creating a file**. Two steps are necessary to create a file. First, space in the file system must be found for the file. Section 3.4 discusses how to allocate space for the file. Second, an entry for the new file must be made in the directory. The directory entry records the name of the file and its location in the file system.

- **Writing a file**. To write a file, a system call is made specifying both the name of the file and the information to be written to the file. Given the name of the file, the system searches the directory to find the location of the file. The directory entry will need to store a pointer to the current end of the file. Using this pointer, the address of the next block can be computed and the information can be written. The write pointer must be updated. In this way successive writes can be used to write a sequence of blocks to the file.

- **Reading a file**. To read from a file, a system call specifies the name of the file and where (in memory) the next block of the file should be put. Again, the directory is searched for the associated directory entry. And again, the directory will need a pointer to the next block to be read. Once that block is read, the pointer is updated.

  In general, a file is either being read or written, thus although it would be possible to have two pointers, a read pointer and a write pointer, most systems have only one, a *current file position*. Both the read and write operations use this same pointer, saving space in the directory entry, and reducing the system complexity.

- **Rewind a file**. Rewinding a file need not involve any actual I/O. Rather the directory is searched for the appropriate entry and the current file position is simply reset to the beginning of the file.

- **Delete a file**. To delete a file, we search the directory for the named file. Having found the associated directory entry, we release all file space (so it can be reused by other files) and invalidate the directory entry.

You may have noticed that all of the operations mentioned involve searching the directory for the entry associated with the named file. The directory entry contains all of the important information needed to operate on the file. To avoid this constant searching, many systems will *open* a file when it first becomes actively used. The operating system keeps a small table containing information about all open files. When a file operation is requested, only this small table is searched, not the entire directory. When the file is no longer actively used, it is *closed* and removed from the table of open files.

Some systems implicitly open a file when the first reference is made to it. The file is automatically closed when the job or program that opened the file terminates. Most systems, however, require that a file be opened explicitly by the programmer with a system call (open) before it can be used. The open operation takes a file name and searches the directory, copying the directory entry into the table of open files. Then the open system call will typically return a pointer to the entry in the table of open files. This pointer, not the actual file name, is used in all I/O operations, avoiding any further searching.

3.2.2 Device Directory

The particular information kept for each file in the directory varies from operating system to operating system. The following is a list of some of the information which may be kept in a directory entry. Not all systems keep all this information, of course.

- **File name**. The symbolic file name.

- **File type**. For those systems which support different types.

- **Location**. A pointer to the device and location on that device of the file.

- **Size**. The current size of the file (in bytes, words or blocks) and the maximum allowed size.

- **Current position**. A pointer to the current read or write position in the file.

- **Protection**. Access control information to control reading, writing, executing, and so on.

- **Usage count**. Indicating the number of processes which are currently using (have opened) this file.

- **Time, date, and process identification**. This information may be kept for (a) creation, (b) last modification, and (c) last use. These can be useful for protection and usage monitoring.

It may take from 16 to over 1000 bytes to record this information for each file. In a system with a large number of files, the size of the directory itself may be hundreds of thousands of bytes. Thus the device directory may need to be stored on the device and brought into memory piecemeal, as needed.

If we think of the directory as a symbol table which translates file names into their directory entries, it becomes apparent that the directory itself can be organized in many ways. We want to be able to insert entries, delete entries, search for a named entry and list all the entries in the directory. What data structure is used for the directory?

A linear list of directory entries requires a linear search to find a particular entry. This is simple to program but time-consuming in execution. To create a new file, we must first search the directory to be sure that no existing file has the same name. Then we can add a new entry at the end of the directory. To delete a file, we search the directory for the named file, then release the space allocated to it. To reuse the directory entry, we can do one of several things. We can mark it unused (a special name such as an all-blank name, or a used/unused bit in each entry), or attach it to a list of free directory entries. A third alternative is to copy the last entry in the directory in the freed location and decrease the length of the directory. A linked list can also be used to decrease the time to delete a file.

The real disadvantage of a linear list of directory entries is the linear search to find a file. A sorted list allows a binary search and decreases the average search time. However, the search algorithm is more complex to program. In addition, the list must be kept sorted. This requirement may complicate creating and deleting files, since we may have to move substantial amounts of directory information to maintain a sorted directory. (Notice, however, that if we want to be able to produce a list of all files in a directory sorted by file name, we do not have to sort separately before listing.) A linked binary tree might help here.

Another data structure which has been used for a file directory is a hash table. A hash table data structure can greatly improve the directory search time. Insertion and deletion are also fairly straightforward, although some provision must be made for *collisions* -- situations where two file names hash to the same location. The major difficulties with a hash table are the generally fixed size of the hash table and the dependence of the hash function on the size of the hash table.

For example, assume we establish a hash table of 64 entries. The hash function converts file names into integers from 0 to 63, probably by a final operation which uses the remainder of a division by 64. If we later try to create a 65th file, we must enlarge the directory hash table, say, to 100 entries. As a result, we need a new hash function, which must map file names to the range 0 to 99, and we must reorganize the existing directory entries to reflect their new hash function values.

3.3 Access Methods

Files store information. When it is used, this information must be accessed and read into computer memory. There are several ways that the information in the file can be accessed. Some systems provide only one access method for files, and so the concept is not important. On other systems, such as those of IBM, many different access methods are supported and choosing the right one for a particular application is a major design problem.

3.3.1 Sequential Access

The bulk of the operations on a file are reads and writes. A read reads the *next* portion of the file and automatically advances the file pointer. Similarly a write appends to the end of the file and advances to the end of the newly written material (the new end of file). Such a file can be rewound, and on some systems, a program may be able to skip forward or backward n records, for some integer n (perhaps only for $n = 1$). This scheme is known as *sequential access* to a file (Figure 3.4). Sequential access is based upon a tape model of a file.

3.3.2 Direct Access

An alternative access method is *direct access*, which is based upon a disk model of a file. For direct access, the file is viewed as a numbered

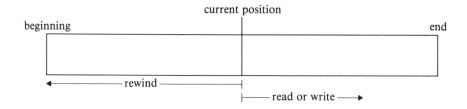

Figure 3.4   Sequential access file

sequence of blocks or records. A block is generally a fixed-length quantity, defined by the operating system as the minimal positioning unit (Figure 3.5). A block may be a byte, 512 words, 1024 bytes, or some other quantity, depending upon the system. Some systems allow the block size to be separately defined for each file.

A direct access file allows arbitrary blocks to be read or written. Thus we may read block 14, then read block 53, and then write block 7. There are no restrictions on the order of reading or writing for a direct access file.

Direct access files are of great use for immediate access to large amounts of information. They are often used in accessing large data bases. When a query concerning a particular subject arrives, we compute which block contains the answer and then read that block directly to provide the desired information.

For example, on an airline reservation system, we might store all of the information about a particular flight (for example, flight 713) in the block identified by the flight number. Thus the number of available seats for flight 713 is stored in block 713 of the reservation file. To store information about a larger set, such as people, we might compute a hash function on their name or search a small in-core index to determine a block to read and search.

The file operations must be modified to include the block number as a parameter. Thus we have *read n*, where *n* is the block number, rather than *read next* and *write n* rather than *write next*. An alternative approach is to retain *read next* and *write next*, as with sequential access, and to add an operation, *position file to n*, where *n* is the block number. Then to effect a *read n*, we would *position to n* and then *read next*.

The block number provided by the user to the operating system is normally a *relative block number*. A relative block number is an index relative to the beginning of the file. Thus the first relative block of the file is 0, the next is 1, and so on, even though the actual absolute disk address of the block may be 14703 for the first block, and 14704 for the second. The use of relative block numbers allows the operating system to decide where the file should be placed (the allocation problem as

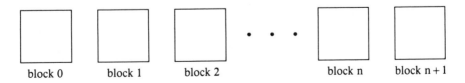

block 0   block 1   block 2   block n   block n + 1

Figure 3.5   Direct access file

discussed in Section 3.4, below), and helps prevent the user from accessing portions of the file system which may not be part of his file. Some systems start their relative block numbers at 0; others start at 1.

Not all operating systems support both sequential and direct access for files. Some systems allow only sequential file access; others allow only direct access. Some systems require that a file be defined as sequential or direct when it is created; such a file can only be accessed in a manner consistent with its declaration. Notice, however, that it is quite easy to simulate sequential access on a direct access file. If we simply keep a variable cp which defines our current position, then we can simulate sequential file operations as shown in Figure 3.6. On the other hand, it is extremely inefficient and clumsy to simulate a direct access file on a sequential file.

3.3.3 Other Access Methods

Other access methods can be built on top of a direct access method. These additional methods generally involve the construction of an *index* for the file. The index, like an index in the back of a book, contains pointers to the various blocks. To find an entry in the file, we first search the index and then use the pointer to directly access the file and find the desired entry.

For example, a retail price file might list the Universal Product Codes (UPC) for items with their associated prices. Each entry consists of a 10-digit UPC code and a 6-digit price, for a 16-byte entry. If our disk has 1024 bytes per block, we can store 64 entries per block. A file of 120,000 entries would occupy about 2,000 blocks (2 million bytes). By

Sequential Access	Implementation for Direct Access
rewind	$cp := 0;$
read next	*read cp;* $cp := cp+1;$
write next	*write cp;* $cp := cp+1;$

Figure 3.6 Simulating sequential access on a direct access file

keeping the file sorted by UPC code, we can define an index consisting of the first UPC code in each block. This index would have 2,000 entries of 10 digits each, or 20,000 bytes, and could be kept in memory. To find the price of a particular item we can (binary) search the index. From this search we would know exactly which block contains the desired entry and access that block. This structure allows us to search a large file with very little I/O.

With large files, the index file itself may become too large to be kept in memory. One solution is then to create an index for the index file. The primary index file would contain pointers to secondary index files which then point to the actual data items.

For example, IBM's ISAM (Indexed Sequential Access Method) uses a small master index which points to disk blocks of a secondary index (Figure 3.7). The secondary index blocks point to the actual file blocks. The file is kept sorted on a defined key. To find a particular item, a binary search is first made of the master index, which provides the block number of the secondary index. This block is read in, and again a binary search is used to find the block containing the desired record. Finally, this block is searched sequentially. In this way, any record can be located from its key by at most two direct access reads. For example, a search for *5-81*, might require reading block 7 of the secondary index and then block 494 of the main file.

3.4 Allocation Methods

From the user's point of view, a file is an abstract data type. It can be created, opened, written, rewound, read, closed, and deleted, without any real concern for its implementation. The implementation of a file is a problem for the operating system.

On a tape-based system, the implementation of files is fairly simple, due to the limitations of the physical devices. We can either map each file to a separate tape or several files onto the same tape. Only sequential access can be reasonably supported.

The direct access nature of disks allows us more flexibility in the implementation of files. In almost every case, many files will be stored on the same disk. The main problem is how to allocate space to these files so that disk space is effectively utilized and files can be quickly accessed. Three major methods of allocating disk space are in wide use: *contiguous*, *linked*, and *indexed*. Each method has its advantages and disadvantages. Accordingly, some systems (such as Data General's RDOS for its Nova line of computers) support all three. More commonly, a system will use one particular method for all files.

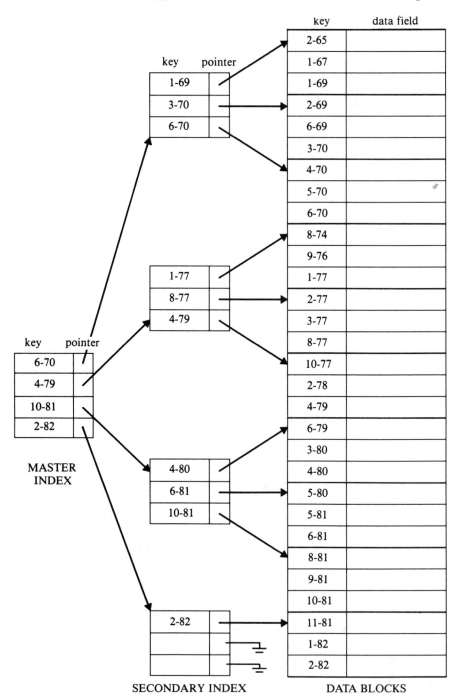

Figure 3.7   File structure for ISAM (Indexed Sequential Access Method)

3.4.1 Free Space Management

Files are created and deleted frequently during the operation of a computer system. Since there is only a limited amount of disk space, it is necessary to reuse the space from deleted files for new files. To keep track of free disk space, the file system maintains a *free space list*. The free space list records all disk blocks which are *free* (that is, not allocated to some file). To create a file, we search the free space list for the required amount of space and allocate it to the new file. This space is then removed from the free space list. When a file is deleted, its disk space is added to the free space list.

The free space list, despite its name, may not be implemented as a list. Frequently, it is implemented as a *bit map* or *bit vector*. Each block is represented by one bit. If the block is free, the bit is 0; if the block is allocated, the bit is 1. For example, consider a disk where blocks 2, 3, 4, 5, 8, 9, 10, 11, 12, 13, 17, 18, 25, 26, and 27 are free; the free space bit map would be

$$110000110000001110011111100011111 \ldots$$

Another approach is to link all the free disk blocks together, keeping a pointer to the first free block. This block contains a pointer to the next free disk block, and so on. In our example, we would keep a pointer to block 2, as the first free block. Block 2 would contain a pointer to block 3, which would point to block 4, which would point to block 5, which would point to block 8, and so on (Figure 3.8).

This scheme is not very efficient since to traverse the list, we must read each block, requiring substantial I/O time. A modification of this approach would store the addresses of n free blocks in the first free block. The first $n-1$ of these are actually free. The last one is the disk address of another block containing the addresses of another n free blocks. The importance of this implementation is that the addresses of a large number of free blocks can be found quickly.

Another approach is to take advantage of the fact that, generally, several contiguous blocks may be allocated or freed simultaneously, particularly when contiguous allocation (Section 3.4.2) is used. Thus rather than keeping a list of n free disk addresses, we can keep the address of the first free block and the number n of free contiguous blocks which follow it. Each entry in the free space list then consists of a disk address and a count. While each entry requires more space than a simple disk address, the overall list will be shorter, as long as the count is generally greater than one.

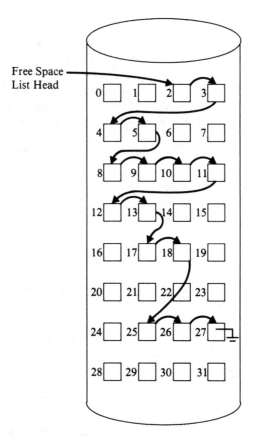

Figure 3.8   Linked free space list on disk

3.4.2 Contiguous Allocation

The *contiguous* allocation method requires each file to occupy a set of contiguous addresses on the disk. Disk addresses define a linear ordering on the disk. Notice that with this ordering, accessing block $b+1$ after block b normally requires no head movement. When head movement is needed (from the last sector of one cylinder to the first sector of the next cylinder), it is only one track.

Contiguous allocation of a file is defined by the disk address of the first block and its length. If the file is n blocks long, and starts at location b, then it occupies blocks b, $b+1$, $b+2$, ..., $b+n-1$. The directory entry for each file indicates the address of the starting block and the length of the area allocated for this file (Figure 3.9).

Accessing a file which has been contiguously allocated is fairly easy. For sequential access, the file system remembers the disk address of the last block and, when necessary, reads the next block. For direct access to block i of a file which starts at block b, we can immediately access block $b+i$. Thus both sequential and direct access can be supported by contiguous allocation.

The difficulty with contiguous allocation is finding space for a new file. Once the implementation of the free space list is defined, we can decide how to find space for a contiguously allocated file. If the file to be created is n blocks long, we must search the free space list for n free contiguous blocks. For a bit map we need to find n 0 bits in a row; for a list of addresses and counts, a count of at least n. This problem can then

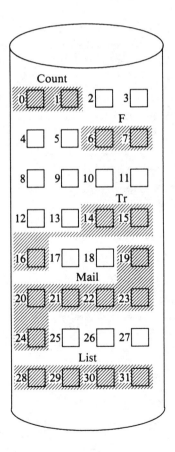

DIRECTORY

File	Start	Length
Count	0	2
Tr	14	3
Mail	19	6
List	28	4
F	6	2

Figure 3.9 Contiguous allocation

be seen to be a particular instance of the general *dynamic storage allocation* problem.

Dynamic Storage Allocation

Disk space can be viewed as a large array of disk blocks. At any given time, some of these blocks are allocated to files and others are free. Disk space can thus be seen as a collection of free and used segments; each segment is a contiguous set of disk blocks. An unallocated segment is called a *hole*. The dynamic storage allocation problem is how to satisfy a request of size *n* from a list of free holes. There are many solutions to this problem. The set of holes is searched to determine which hole is best to allocate. *First-fit*, *best-fit*, and *worst-fit* are the most common strategies used to select a free hole from the set of available holes.

- **First-fit**. Allocate the *first* hole that is big enough. Searching can start either at the beginning of the set of holes or where the previous first-fit search ended. We can stop searching as soon as we find a large enough free hole.

- **Best-fit**. Allocate the *smallest* hole that is big enough. We must search the entire list, unless the list is kept ordered by size. This strategy produces the smallest left-over hole.

- **Worst-fit**. Allocate the *largest* hole. Again, we must search the entire list, unless it is sorted by size. This strategy produces the largest left-over hole, which may be more useful than the smaller left-over hole from a best-fit approach.

Simulations have shown that both first-fit and best-fit are better than worst-fit in both time and storage utilization. Neither first-fit nor best-fit is clearly best in terms of storage utilization, but first-fit is generally faster.

These algorithms suffer from *external fragmentation*. As files are allocated and deleted, the free disk space is broken into little pieces. External fragmentation exists when enough total disk space exists to satisfy a request, but it is not contiguous; storage is fragmented into a large number of small holes. Depending upon the total amount of disk storage and the average file size, external fragmentation may be either a minor or a major problem.

Compaction

Some microcomputer systems use contiguous allocation on floppy disk systems. To prevent losing significant amounts of disk space to external fragmentation, the user must run a repacking routine which basically copies the entire file system onto another floppy disk or a tape. The original floppy is then completely freed, creating one large contiguous free hole. The files can then be copied back onto the floppy, by allocating contiguous space from this one large hole. This scheme effectively *compacts* all free space into one hole, solving the fragmentation problem. The cost of this compaction is time. Copying all the files from a disk to compact space may take hours and may be necessary on a weekly basis.

Problems with Contiguous Allocation

There are other problems with contiguous allocation. The major problem is determining how much space is needed for a file. When the file is created, the total amount of space it will need must be found and allocated: create a file of n blocks. How does the user (program or person) know the size of the file to be created? In some cases, this determination may be fairly simple (copying an existing file, for example), but in general the size of an output file may be quite hard to estimate.

If we allocate too little space to a file, we may find that it cannot be extended. Especially with a best-fit allocation strategy, the space on both sides of the file may be in use. We simply cannot make the file larger. Two possibilities then exist. First, the user program can be terminated, with an appropriate error message. The user must then allocate more space and run the program again. These repeated runs may be quite costly. To prevent them, the user will normally overestimate the amount of space needed, resulting in considerable wasted space.

The other possibility is to find a larger hole, copy the contents of the file to the new space and release the previous space. This action may be repeated as long as space exists, although it can also be quite time-consuming. Notice, however, that in this case the user need never be informed explicitly about what is happening; the system continues despite the problem, although more and more slowly.

Even if the total amount of space needed for a file is known in advance, it may be inefficient to pre-allocate it. A file which grows slowly over a long period of time (months or years) must be allocated enough space for its final size, even though much of that space may be unused for a long time.

3.4.3 Linked Allocation

The problems discussed above can be traced directly to the requirement that space be allocated contiguously. *Linked allocation* solves these problems. With linked allocation, each file is a linked list of disk blocks; the disk blocks may be scattered anywhere on the disk. The directory contains a pointer to the first (and last) blocks of the file. For example, a file of 5 blocks which starts at block 9, might continue at block 16, then block 1, block 10, and finally block 25 (Figure 3.10). Each block contains a pointer to the next block. These pointers are not made available to the user. Thus if each sector is 512 words, and a disk address (the pointer) requires two words, then the user sees blocks of 510 words.

Creating a file is easy; we simply create a new entry in the device directory. With linked allocation, each directory entry has a pointer to the first disk block of the file. This pointer is initialized to **nil** (the end-

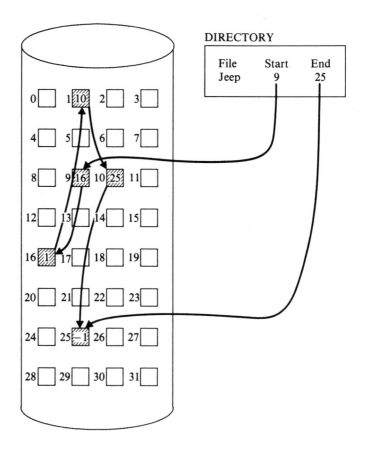

Figure 3.10   Linked allocation of disk space

of-list pointer value) to signify an empty file. A write to a file removes the first free block from the free space list and writes to it. This new block is then linked to the end of the file. To read a file, we simply read blocks by following the pointers from block to block.

There is no external fragmentation with linked allocation. Any free block on the free space list can be used to satisfy a request, since all blocks are linked together. Notice also that there is no need to declare the size of a file when it is created. A file can continue to grow as long as there are free blocks. Consequently, it is never necessary to compact disk space.

Linked allocation does have disadvantages, however. The major problem is that it can only be used effectively for sequential access files. To find the ith block of a file, we must start at the beginning of that file and follow the pointers until we get to the ith block. Each access to a pointer requires a disk read. Hence, we cannot support a direct access capability for linked allocation files.

Another disadvantage to linked allocation is the space required for the pointers. If a pointer requires two bytes out of a 256-byte block, then 2.3 percent of the disk is being used for pointers, not for information. Each file therefore requires slightly more space.

A more subjective problem is reliability. Since the files are linked together by pointers scattered all over the disk, consider what would happen if a pointer is lost or damaged. A bug in the operating system software or a disk hardware failure may result in picking up the wrong pointer. This error could result in linking into the free space list or into another file. One partial solution is to use doubly-linked lists or to store the file name and relative block number in each block; these schemes require even more overhead for each file.

3.4.4 Indexed Allocation

Linked allocation solves the external fragmentation and size declaration problems of contiguous allocation. However, linked allocation cannot support direct access, since the blocks are scattered all over the disk. More importantly, the pointers to the blocks are scattered all over the disk. Indexed allocation solves this problem by bringing all of the pointers together into one location: the *index block*.

Each file has its own index block, which is an array of disk block addresses. The ith entry in the index block points to the ith block of the file. The directory contains the address of the index block (Figure 3.11). To read the ith block, we use the pointer in the ith index block entry to find and read the desired block. When the file is created, all pointers in the index block are set to **nil**. When the ith block is first written, a block is removed from the free space list, and its address is put in the *i*th index block entry.

Indexed allocation supports direct access, without suffering from external fragmentation. Any free block anywhere on the disk may satisfy a request for more space.

Indexed allocation does suffer from wasted space. The pointer overhead of the index block is generally worse than the pointer overhead of linked allocation. Most files are small. Assume that we have a file of only one or two blocks. With linked allocation, we only lose the space of one pointer per block (one or two pointers). With indexed allocation, an entire index block must be allocated, even if only one or two pointers will be non-**nil**.

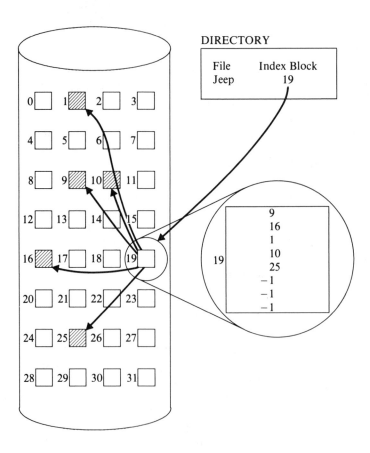

Figure 3.11   Indexed allocation of disk space

This point raises the question of how large the index block should be. Every file must have an index block, so we want the index block to be as small as possible. If the index block is too small, however, it will not be able to hold enough pointers for a large file. An index block is normally one disk block. Thus it can be read and written directly by itself. To allow for large files, several index files may be linked together. For example, an index block might contain a small header giving the name of the file, and a set of the first 100 disk block addresses. The next address (the last word in the index block) is **nil** (for a small file) or a pointer to another index file (for a large file). For a very large file, this second index file could point to a third, and so on.

Notice that this representation of the index block uses a linked allocation for the index blocks. A variant of this representation uses a separate index block to point to the index blocks which point to the file blocks themselves. To access a block, the operating system uses the first level index to find the second level index to find the desired data block. This approach could be continued to a third or fourth level, but two levels of indexes are generally sufficient. If we can get 256 pointers into an index block, then two levels of indexes allows 65,536 data blocks, which (at 1024 bytes each) allows a file of up to 67,108,864 bytes, a size which exceeds the physical capacity of many devices.

Another alternative is to keep the first, say 15, pointers of the index block in the device directory. If a file requires more than 15 blocks, a 16th pointer points to a list of index blocks. In this way, small files do not need a separate index block. The Unix operating system uses a scheme similar to this.

3.4.5 Performance

Storage efficiency is an important difference between the various allocation methods. They also differ in the time required to access a block on disk. This factor is particularly important for small, slow disk systems.

One difficulty in comparing the performance of the various systems is in determining how they will be used. For any type of access, contiguous allocation requires only one access to get a disk block. Since we can easily keep the initial address of the file in core, we can immediately calculate the disk address of the ith block (or the next block) and read it directly.

For linked allocation, we can also keep the address of the next block in memory and read it directly. This method is fine for sequential access, but for direct access, an access to the ith block might require i

disk reads. This problem indicates why linked allocation should not be used for an application requiring direct access.

As a result, some systems support direct access files by using contiguous allocation and sequential access by linked allocation. For these systems, the type of access to be made must be declared when the file is created. A file created for sequential access will be linked and cannot be used for direct access. A file created for direct access would be contiguous and could support both direct access and sequential access, but its maximum length must be declared when it is created. Notice that in this case the operating system must have appropriate data structures and algorithms to support *both* allocation methods. Files can be converted from one type to another by the creation of a new file of the desired type, into which the contents of the old file are copied. The old file may then be deleted, and the new file renamed.

Indexed allocation is more complex. If the index block is already in memory, then the access can be made directly. However, keeping the index block in memory requires considerable space. If this memory space is not available, then we may have to read first the index block and then the desired data block. For a two-level index, two index block reads might be necessary. For a very large file, accessing a block near the end of the file would require reading in all of the index blocks to follow the pointer chain before the data block could finally be read. Thus the performance of indexed allocation depends upon the index structure, the size of the file, and the position of the block desired.

Some systems combine contiguous allocation with indexed allocation by using contiguous allocation for small files (up to 3 or 4 blocks) and automatically switch to an indexed allocation if the file grows large. Since most files are small, and contiguous allocation is efficient for small files, average performance can be quite good.

3.5 Directory Systems

The previous discussion allows us to create files, read, write and reposition them, and, finally, to delete them. The files are represented by entries in a device directory or volume table of contents. The device directory records information, such as name, location, size, and type, for all files on that device.

A device directory may be sufficient for a single-user system with limited storage space. As the amount of storage and the number of users increase, however, it becomes increasingly difficult for the users to organize and keep track of all of the files. The solution to this problem is the imposition of a directory *structure* on the file system. A directory structure provides a mechanism for organizing the many files in the file system. It may span device boundaries and include several different disk units. In this way, the user need be concerned only with the logical directory and file structure, and can completely ignore the problems of physically allocating space for files.

In fact, many systems actually have two separate directory structures: the device directory and the file directories. The device directory is stored on each physical device and describes all files on that device. The device directory entry mainly concentrates on describing the physical properties of each file: where it is, how long it is, how it is allocated, and so on. The file directories are a logical organization of the files on all devices. The file directory entry concentrates on logical properties of each file: name, file type, owning user, accounting information, protection access codes, and so on. A file directory entry may simply point to the device directory entry to provide physical properties or may duplicate this information. Our main interest now is with the file directory structure; device directories should be well understood.

Many different file directory structures have been proposed and are in use. The directory is essentially a *symbol table*. The operating system takes the symbolic file name and finds the named file. We examine some directory structures here. When considering a particular directory structure, we need to keep in mind the operations which are to be performed on a directory.

- **Search**. We need to be able to search a directory structure to find the entry for a particular file. Since files have symbolic names and similar names may indicate a relationship between the files, we may want to be able to find all files which match a particular pattern.

- **Create file**. New files need to be created and added to the directory.

- **Delete file**. When a file is no longer needed, we want to remove it from the directory.

- **List directory**. We need to be able to list the files in a directory and the contents of the directory entry for each file in the list.

- **Backup**. For reliability, it is generally a good idea to save the contents and structure of the file system at regular intervals. This often consists of copying all files to magnetic tape. This provides a backup copy in case of system failure or if the file is simply no longer in use. In this case, the file can be copied to tape and the disk space of that file released for reuse by another file.

3.5.1 Single-Level Directory

The simplest directory structure is the single-level directory. The device directory is an example of a single-level directory. All files are contained in the same directory, which is very easy to support and understand (Figure 3.12).

A single-level directory has significant limitations, however, when the number of files increases or when there is more than one user. Since all files are in the same directory, they must have unique names. If we have two users who call their test data file TEST, then the unique name rule is violated. (For example, in one programming class, 23 students called the program for their second assignment PROG2; another 11 called it ASSGN2.) Although file names are generally selected to reflect the content of the file, they are often quite limited in length. (DEC's TOPS-10 allows only six-character file names; Unix allows fourteen characters.)

Even with a single user, as the number of files increases, it becomes difficult to remember the names of all the files in order to create only files with unique names. (It is not uncommon for a user to have hundreds of files on one computer system and an equal number of additional files on another system.)

3.5.2 Two-Level Directory

The major disadvantage to a single-level directory is the confusion of file names between different users. The standard solution is to create a

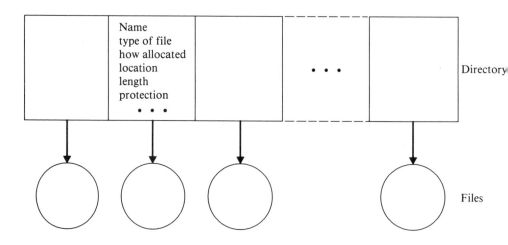

Figure 3.12   Single-level directory

separate directory for each user. Especially on a large system, this user directory is a *logical*, rather than physical, organization, since all of the files are still physically on the same device.

In the two-level directory structure, each user has his own User File Directory (UFD). Each user directory has a similar structure (linear, binary, or hashed) but lists only the files of a single user. When a user job starts or a user logs-in, the system's Master File Directory (MFD) is searched. The Master File Directory is indexed by user name or account number and each entry points to the user directory for that user (Figure 3.13).

When users refer to a particular file, only their own user file directory is searched. Thus different users may have files with the same name, as long as all the file names within each user file directory are unique.

To create a file for a user, the operating system searches only that user's directory to ascertain whether another file of that name already exists. To delete a file, the operating system confines its search to the local user file directory; thus it cannot accidentally delete another user's file with the same name.

The user directories themselves must be created and deleted as necessary. A special system program is run with the appropriate user

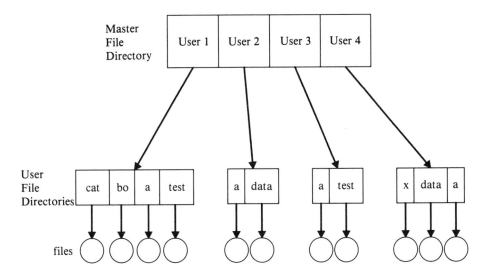

Figure 3.13   Two-level directory structure

name and account information. The program creates a new user file directory and adds an entry for it to the Master File Directory. The execution of this program might, of course, be restricted. The allocation of disk space for user directories can be handled using the techniques discussed in Section 3.4 for files themselves.

There are still problems with the two-level directory structure. This structure effectively isolates one user from another. This is an advantage when the users are completely independent, but a disadvantage when the users *want* to cooperate on some task and access files of other users. Some systems simply do not allow local user files to be accessed by other users.

If access is to be permitted, one user must have the ability to name a file in another user's directory. To name a particular file uniquely in a two-level directory, we must give both the user name and the file name. A two-level directory can be thought of as a tree of height 2. The root of the tree is the Master File Directory. Its direct descendants are the User File Directories. The descendants of the User File Directories are the files themselves. The files are the leaves of the tree. Specifying a user name and a file name defines a path in the tree from the root (the Master File Directory) to a leaf (the specified file). Thus a user name and a file name define a *path name*. Every file in the system has a unique path name. To uniquely name a file, a user must know the path name of the file desired.

For example, if user *A* wishes to access his own test file, he can simply refer to TEST. To access the test file of user *B*, however, he might have to refer to TEST[USERB] or /USERB/TEST. Every system has its own syntax for naming files in directories other than the user's own.

A special case of this situation occurs in regard to the system files. Those programs provided as a part of the system (loaders, assemblers, compilers, utility routines, libraries, and so on) are generally defined as files. When the appropriate commands are given to the operating system, these files are read by the loader and executed. Many command interpreters act by simply treating the command as the name of a file to load and execute. As the directory system is presently defined, this file name would be searched for in the current user file directory. One solution would be to copy the system files into each user file directory. However, copying all the system files would be enormously wasteful of space. (If the system files require 5 megabytes, then supporting twelve users would require sixty (5×12) megabytes just for copies of the system files.)

The standard solution is to complicate the search procedure slightly. A special user directory is defined to contain the system files (for example, user 0). Whenever a file name is given to be loaded, the operating system first searches the local user file directory. If the file is found, it is used. If it is not found, the system automatically searches the special user directory which contains the system files. The sequence of directories searched when a file is named is called the *search path*.

3.5.3 Tree-Structured Directories

Once a two-level directory is viewed as a two-level tree, the natural generalization is to extend the directory structure to an arbitrary tree (Figure 3.14). This allows users to create their own subdirectories and organize their files accordingly. The Unix file system, for instance, is structured as a tree. The tree has a root directory. Every file in the system has a unique path name. A path name is the path from the root, through all the subdirectories, to a specified file.

A directory (or subdirectory) contains a set of files and/or subdirectories. All directories have the same internal format. One bit in

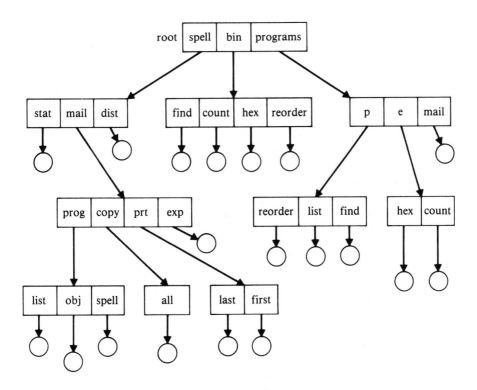

Figure 3.14   Tree-structured directory structure

each directory entry defines the entry as a file (0) or a subdirectory (1). Special system calls are used to create and delete directories.

In normal use, each user has a *current directory*. The current directory should contain most of the files that are of current interest to the user. When reference is made to a file, the current directory is searched. If a file is needed which is not in the current directory, then the user must either specify a path name or change the current directory. A system call will take a directory name as a parameter and use it to redefine the current directory. Thus users can change their current directory whenever desired. When a user job starts, or a user logs-in, the operating system searches the accounting file to find an entry for this user (for accounting purposes). Also stored in the accounting file is a pointer to (or the name of) the user's initial directory. A local variable for this user (or for this process) is defined, to specify the user's current directory.

Path names can be of two types: *complete* path names or *relative* path names. A complete path name begins at the root and follows a path down to the specified file, giving the directory names on the path. A relative path name defines a path from the current directory. For example, in the tree-structured file system of Figure 3.14, if the current directory is *root/spell/mail*, then the relative path name *prt/first* refers to the same file as the complete path name *root/spell/mail/prt/first*.

Allowing users to define their own subdirectories permits them to impose a structure upon their files. This structure might result in separate directories for files associated with different topics (for example, a subdirectory was created to hold the text of this book) or different forms of information (for example, the directory *programs* may contain source programs; the directory *bin* may store all the binaries).

An interesting policy decision in a tree-structured directory structure is how to handle the deletion of a directory. If a directory is empty, its entry in its containing directory can simply be deleted. However, suppose the directory to be deleted is not empty, but contains several files, or possibly subdirectories. One of two approaches can be taken. Some systems will not delete a directory unless it is empty. Thus to delete a directory, someone must first delete all the files in that directory. If there are any subdirectories, this procedure must be applied recursively to them, so that they can be deleted also. This approach may result in a substantial amount of work.

An alternative approach is just to assume that when a request is made to delete a directory that all of its files and subdirectories are also to be deleted. Note that either approach is fairly easy to implement; the choice of implementation is a policy decision. There are systems which have been implemented each way.

Files of other users can be easily accessed. For example, user B can access files of user A by specifying their path names. User B can specify either a complete or a relative path name. Alternatively, user B's current directory could be changed to be user A's directory and user B could access the files directly by their file names. Some systems also allow a user to define a own search path. In this case, user B could define a search path to be (1) his local directory, (2) the system file directory, and (3) user A's directory, in that order. As long as the name of a file of user A did not conflict with the name of a local file or system file, it could be referred to simply by its name.

3.5.4 Acyclic Graph Directories

Consider two programmers who are working on a joint project. The files associated with that project can be stored in a subdirectory, separating them from other projects and files of the two programmers. But since both programmers are equally responsible for the project, both want the subdirectory to be in their own directory. The common subdirectory should be *shared*. A shared directory or file will exist in the file system in two (or more) places at once. Notice that a shared file (or directory) is not the same as two copies of the file. With two copies, each programmer can view the copy rather than the original, but if one programmer changes the file, the changes will not appear in the other's copy. With a shared file, there is only *one* actual file and so any changes made by one person would be immediately visible to the other. This is particularly important for shared subdirectories; a new file created by one person will automatically appear in all of the shared subdirectories.

A tree structure prohibits the sharing of files or directories. An *acyclic graph* allows directories to have shared subdirectories and files (Figure 3.15). The *same* file or subdirectory may be in two different directories. An acyclic graph (that is, a graph with no cycles) is a natural generalization of the tree-structured directory scheme.

In a situation where several people are working as a team, all of the files to be shared may be put together into one directory. The user file directories of all the team members would each contain this directory of shared files as a subdirectory. Even when there is a single user, the desired file organization may require that some files be put into several different subdirectories. For example, a program written for a particular project should be in both the directory of all programs and in the directory for that project.

Shared files and subdirectories can be implemented in several ways. A common way is to create a new directory entry called a *link*. A link is effectively a pointer to another file or subdirectory. For example, a link

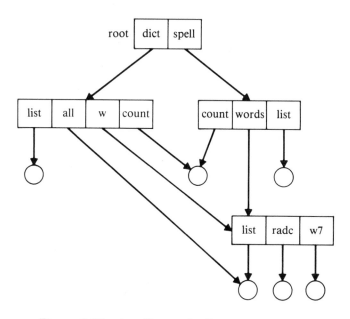

Figure 3.15   Acyclic graph directory structure

may be implemented as a complete path name (a *symbolic link*). When a reference to a file is made, we search the directory. The directory entry is marked as a link and the name of the real file (or directory) is given. The link is *resolved* by using the path name to locate the real file. Links are easily identified by their format in the directory entry, and are effectively named indirect pointers.

The other approach to implementing shared files is simply to duplicate all information about them in both sharing directories. Thus both entries are identical and equal. A link is clearly different from the original directory entry, thus the two are not equal. Duplicate directory entries, however, make the original and the copy indistinguishable. A major problem with duplicate directory entries is maintaining consistency if the file is modified.

An acyclic graph directory structure is more flexible than a simple tree structure, but it is also more complex. Several problems must be carefully considered. Notice that a file may now have multiple complete path names. Consequently, distinct file names may refer to the same file. This is similar to the aliasing problem for programming languages. If we are trying to traverse the entire file system (to find a file, accumulate statistics on all files, or copy all files to backup storage), this problem becomes significant, since we do not want to traverse shared structures more than once.

Another problem involves deletion. When can the space allocated to a shared file be deallocated and reused? One possibility is to remove the file whenever anyone deletes it, but this action may leave dangling pointers to the now non-existent file. Worse, if the remaining file pointers contain actual disk addresses, and the space is subsequently reused for other files, these dangling pointers may point into the middle of other files.

In a system where sharing is implemented by symbolic links, this situation is somewhat easier to handle. The deletion of a link need not affect the original file; only the link is removed. If the file entry itself is deleted, the space for the file is deallocated, leaving the links dangling. We can search for these links and remove them also, but unless a list of the associated links is kept with each file, this search can be quite expensive. Alternatively, we can leave the links until an attempt is made to use them. At that time, we can determine that the file of the name given by the link does not exist and fail to resolve the link name; the access is treated just like any other illegal file name. (In this case, the system designer should carefully consider what to do when a file is deleted and another file of the same name is created, before a symbolic link to the original file is used.)

Another approach to deletion is to preserve the file until all references to it are deleted. To implement this approach, we must have some mechanism for determining that the last reference to the file has been deleted. We could keep a list of all references to a file (directory entries or symbolic links). When a link or a copy of the directory entry is established, a new entry is added to the file reference list. When a link or directory entry is deleted, we remove its entry on the list. The file is deleted when its file reference list is empty.

The trouble with this approach is the variable and potentially large size of the file reference list. However, we really do not need to keep the entire list, only a count of the *number* of references. A new link or directory entry increments the reference count; deleting a link or entry decrements it. When the count is zero, the file can be deleted; there are no remaining references to it.

3.5.5 General Graph Directory

One serious problem with using an acyclic graph structure is ensuring that there are no cycles. If we start with a two-level directory and allow users to create subdirectories, a tree-structured directory results. It should be fairly easy to see that simply adding new files and subdirectories to an existing tree-structured directory preserves its tree-structured nature. However, when we add links to an existing tree-structured directory, the tree structure is destroyed, resulting in a simple graph structure (Figure 3.16).

The primary advantage of an acyclic graph is the relative simplicity of the algorithms to traverse it and to determine when there are no more references to a file. We want to avoid traversing shared sections of an acyclic graph twice, mainly for performance reasons. If we have just searched a major shared subdirectory for a particular file, without finding it, we want to avoid searching that subdirectory again; it would be a waste of time.

If cycles are allowed to exist in the directory, we likewise want to avoid searching any component twice, for reasons of correctness as well as performance. A poorly designed algorithm might result in an infinite loop continually searching through the cycle and never terminating.

A similar problem exists in trying to determine when a file can be deleted. As with acyclic graph directory structures, a zero in the reference count means that there are no more references to the file or directory, and it can be deleted. However, it is also possible, when cycles exist, that the reference count may be non-zero, even when it is

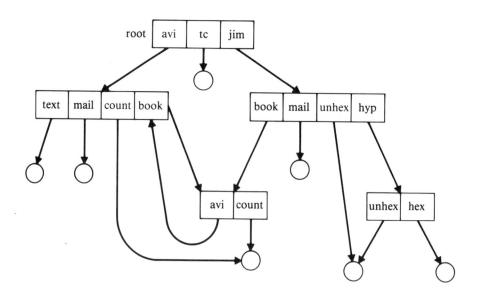

Figure 3.16   General graph directory

no longer possible to refer to a directory or file. This anomaly results from the possibility of self-referencing (a cycle) in the directory structure. In this case, it is generally necessary to use *garbage collection* to determine when the last reference has been deleted and the disk space can be reallocated. Garbage collection involves traversing the file system, marking everything which can be accessed. Then a second pass collects everything which is not marked onto a list of free space. (A similar marking procedure can be used to ensure that a traversal or search will cover everything in the file system once and only once.) Garbage collection for a disk-based file system, however, is extremely time-consuming and seldom attempted.

Garbage collection is only necessary because of possible cycles in the graph. Thus an acyclic graph structure is much easier to work with. The difficulty is to avoid cycles as new links are added to the structure. How do we know when a new link will complete a cycle? There are algorithms to detect cycles in graphs; however, they are computationally expensive, especially when the graph is on disk storage.

3.6 File Protection

When information is kept in a computer system, a major concern is its protection from both physical damage (*reliability*) and improper access (*protection*).

Reliability is generally provided by making duplicate copies of files. Many operating systems will automatically copy disk files to tape at regular intervals (once a day or week or month) to maintain a copy should a file system be accidentally destroyed. File systems can be damaged by hardware problems, such as errors in reading or writing, power surges or failures, head crashes, dirt, temperature, and vandalism. Bugs in the file system software can also cause file contents to be lost.

Protection can be provided in many ways. For a small single-user system, protection might be provided by physically removing the diskettes and locking them in a desk drawer or file cabinet. In a multi-user system, however, other mechanisms are needed.

The need for protecting files is a direct result of the ability to access files. On systems which do not permit access to the files of other users, protection is not needed. Thus one extreme would be to provide complete protection by prohibiting access. The other extreme is to provide free access with no protection. Both of these approaches are too extreme for general use. What is needed is *controlled access*.

Protection mechanisms provide controlled access by limiting the types of file access which can be made. Access is permitted or denied depending upon several factors, one of which is the type of access requested. Several different types of operations may be controlled:

- **Read**. Read from the file.

- **Write**. Write or rewrite the file.

- **Execute**. Load the file into memory and execute it.

- **Append**. Write new information at the end of the file.

- **Delete**. Delete the file and free its space for possible reuse.

Other operations, such as renaming the file or copying it or editing it, may also be controlled. For many systems, however, these higher-level functions (such as copying) may be implemented by a system program which makes lower-level system calls. Protection is provided only at the lower level. For instance, copying a file may be implemented simply by a sequence of read requests. In this case, a user with read access can also cause the file to be copied, printed, and so on.

The directory operations which must be protected are somewhat different. We want to control the creation and deletion of files in a directory. In addition, we probably want to control whether a user can determine the existence of a file in a directory. Sometimes, knowledge of the existence and name of a file may be significant in itself. Thus listing the contents of a directory must be a protected operation.

Many different protection mechanisms have been proposed. As always, each has its advantages and disadvantages and must be selected as appropriate for its intended application. A small computer system which is used by only a few members of a research group may not need the same types of protection as a large corporate computer which is used for research, finance, and personnel.

3.6.1 Naming

The protection schemes of several systems depend upon the inability of users to access a file which they cannot name. If users cannot name a file, then they cannot operate on it. This scheme assumes that there is no mechanism for obtaining the names of other user's files and that the names cannot be easily guessed. Since file names are generally picked to be mnemonic, they can often be easily guessed.

3.6.2 Passwords

Another approach is to associate a password with each file. Just as access to the computer system itself is often controlled by a password, access to each file can be controlled by a password. If the passwords are randomly chosen and changed often, this scheme may be quite effective in limiting access to a file to only those who know the password.

Commonly, however, only one password is associated with each file. Thus protection is on an all-or-nothing basis. To provide protection on a more detailed level, multiple passwords are needed.

3.6.3 Access Control

Another approach is to make access dependent on the identity of the user. Various users may need different types of access to a file or directory. An *access list* can be associated with each file and directory, specifying the user name and the types of access allowed for each user. When a user requests a particular file, the operating system checks its access list. If that user is listed for the requested access, the access is allowed. Otherwise, a protection violation occurs and the user job is terminated.

A condensed version of this approach to file protection is used in many systems. The main problem with access lists can be their length. If we want to allow everyone to read a file, we must list all users with read access. To condense the length of the access list, many systems recognize three classifications of users: *owner, group,* and *everyone else.* Each file has an owner -- the user who created the file. In addition, the owner may belong to a group of users who are sharing the file and need similar access. For example, the members of a programming team, or the members of a class or a department may define a group. Finally, there is everyone else.

With this classification, only three fields are needed to define protection. Each field is often a collection of bits which either allow or prevent the access associated with that bit. For example, the Unix system defines three fields of three bits each: **rwx**, where **r** controls read access, **w** controls write access, and **x** controls execution. A separate field is kept for the file owner, for the owner's group and for all other users. In this scheme, nine bits per file are needed to record protection information.

Protection can be associated either with the file itself or with the path used to specify the file. The more common scheme provides protection on the path. Thus if a path name refers to a file in a directory, the user must be allowed access to both the directory and the file. In systems where files may have numerous path names (such as acyclic or general graphs), a given user may then have different access rights to a file depending upon the path name used.

3.7 Implementation Issues

A file system consists of two quite different design problems. The first problem is defining how the file system should look to the user. This involves the definition of a file and its attributes, operations allowed on a file, and the directory structure. Next, algorithms and data structures must be created to map the logical file system onto the physical devices which exist for use with the file system.

The file system itself is generally composed of many different levels, as shown in Figure 3.17. This is an example of a layered design. Each level in the design uses the features of lower levels to create new features for use by higher levels.

The lowest level, I/O Control, consists of device drivers and interrupt handlers to actually transfer information between memory and the disk system. The Basic File System uses this to read and write particular blocks to and from the disk. Each disk block is identified by its numeric disk address (for example, drive 1, cylinder 73, surface 2, sector 10).

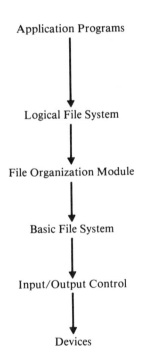

Figure 3.17   Layered file system

The File Organization Module knows about both files and disk blocks. By knowing the type of file allocation used and the location of the file, the File Organization Module can generate the addresses of the blocks for the Basic File System to read. Finally, the Logical File System uses the directory structure to provide the File Organization Module with the values it needs from a symbolic file name.

To create a new file, an application program calls the Logical File System. The Logical File System knows the format of the directory structures. To create a new file, we read the appropriate directory into memory, update it with the new entry and write it back to the disk. The directories can be treated exactly like files -- files with a type field indicating that they are directories. Thus the Logical File System can call the File Organization Module to map the directory I/O into disk block numbers which are passed on to the Basic File System and I/O Control System.

Once the directory has been updated, the Logical File System can use it to perform I/O. When a file is opened, the directory structure is searched for the desired file entry. It would be possible to search the directory structure for every I/O operation, but that would be inefficient. To speed the search, a table of opened files is generally kept in memory by the operating system. The first reference to a file (normally an open) causes the directory structure to be searched and the directory entry for this file to be copied into the table of opened files. The index into this table is returned to the user program and all further references are made through the index (a file descriptor) rather than with a symbolic name. All changes to the directory entry are made to the copy in the table of opened files. When the file is closed, the updated entry is copied back to the disk-based directory structure.

While this approach is much faster than constant references to the disk copy of the directory entry, it can cause problems. If the operating system fails, the table of opened files is generally lost and with it any changes in the directories of opened files. This can leave the file system in an inconsistent state where the actual state of some files is not as they are described in the directory structure.

Another aspect of file use which must be carefully defined is access control (protection). Every access to a file or directory must be checked for correctness. Systems have been designed which check file protection only when the file is opened. Separate system calls are used for **open for read** and **open for write**. Although the operating system can certainly check protection at this point, it must continue to check that a file which is **open for read** is never written to. Thus *every* access must be checked for validity.

3.8 Summary

A file is an abstract data type defined and implemented by the operating system. A file is a sequence of logical records. A logical record may be a byte, a line (fixed or variable length), or a more complex data item. The operating system may specifically support various record types or may leave that to the application program.

The major problem for the operating system is to map the logical file concept onto physical storage devices such as magnetic tape or disk. Since the physical record size of the device may not be the same as the logical record size, it may be necessary to block logical records into physical records. Again, this task may be supported by the operating system or left for the application program.

Tape-based file systems are quite constrained; most file systems are disk based. Tapes are commonly used for data transport between machines, or for backup or archival storage.

On a disk system, files may be either sequential access or direct access. Files can be allocated space on the disk in three ways: contiguous, linked, or indexed. Contiguous allocation can suffer from external fragmentation. Direct access files cannot be supported with linked allocation. Indexed allocation may require substantial overhead for its index block.

Each device in a file system keeps a volume table of contents or device directory listing the location of the files on the device. In addition, it is useful to create directories to allow files to be organized. A single-level directory causes naming problems, since each file must have a unique name. A two-level directory solves this problem by creating a separate directory for each user. Users have their own directory containing their own files.

The natural generalization of a two-level directory is a tree-structured directory. A tree-structured directory allows users to create subdirectories to organize their files. Acyclic graph directory structures allow subdirectories and files to be shared, but complicate searching and deletion. A general graph structure allows complete flexibility in the sharing of files and directories, but sometimes requires garbage collection to recover unused disk space.

Since files are the main information storage mechanism in most computer systems, file protection is needed. Access to files can be controlled separately for each type of access: read, write, execute, append, list directory, and so on. File protection can be provided by passwords, access lists, or special *ad hoc* techniques.

File systems are often implemented in a layered or modular structure. The lower levels deal with the physical properties of storage devices. Upper levels deal with symbolic file names and logical properties of files. Intermediate levels map the logical file concepts into physical device properties.

Exercises

3.1 Consider a file system where a file can be deleted and its disk space reclaimed while links to it still exist. What problems may occur if a new file is created in the same storage area? How can this be avoided?

3.2 Some systems automatically delete all user files when a user logs off or a job terminates, unless the user explicitly requests that they be kept, while others keep all files unless the user explicitly deletes them. Discuss the relative merits of each approach.

3.3 Operating system designers should limit the *size* of their modules because of the adverse effect on such things as number of errors, resulting expense, unreliability, and system complexity. It may be argued, therefore, that in a file system, such functions as the provision of different file structures and access methods are best accomplished by library routines rather than by the system itself. What more *basic* functions would you have the file system itself provide? Justify your answer.

3.4 Give an example of an application in which data in a file should be accessed:

a. Sequentially.

b. Randomly.

3.5 In many systems a subdirectory can be read and written by an authorized user just as ordinary files.

a. What protection problems can arise?

b. Suggest a scheme for dealing with these protection problems.

3.6 Suggest a scheme for implementing the current directory scheme efficiently.

3.7 Could you simulate a multi-level directory structure with a single-level directory structure in which arbitrary long names can be used? If your answer is yes, explain how and contrast these two schemes. How would your answer change if file names were limited to 7 characters?

3.8 Consider a file currently consisting of 100 blocks. How many disk I/O operations are involved with contiguous, linked, and indexed allocation strategies, if one block:

		C	l	C
a.	is added at the beginning?	100	2	1
b.	is added in the middle?	50	2	1
c.	is added at the end?	1	2	1
d.	is removed from the beginning?	1	2	1
e.	is removed from the middle?	50	2	1
f.	is removed from the end?	1	2	1

3.9 Some systems provide file sharing by maintaining a single copy of a file, while others maintain several copies, one for each of the users sharing the file. Discuss the relative merits of each approach. *changes not in both / one could change w/o telling other*

3.10 Some systems automatically open a file when it is referenced for the first time, and close the file when the job terminates. Discuss the advantages and disadvantages of this scheme as compared to the more traditional one where the user has to explicitly open and close the file. *saves memory / always know where stf is / won't close file so easily*

3.11 It has been suggested that instead of having an access list associated with each file (which users can access the file and how), one should have a user control list associated with each user (which files a user can access and how). Discuss the relative merits of these two schemes.

3.12 Consider a system where free space is kept in a free space list.

a. Suppose that the pointer to the free list is lost. Can the system reconstruct the free list? *not if d's singly linked*

b. Suggest a scheme to ensure that the pointer is never lost as a result of memory failure.

store d in hw register / doubly linked list / print out at begin of session

3.13 Explain the purpose of the *open* and *close* operations.

3.14 Consider a system that supports the allocation strategies contiguous, linked, and indexed. What criteria should be used in deciding which strategy should be utilized for a particular file?

3.15 Why must the bit map for file allocation be kept on mass storage rather than main memory?

3.16 Consider a system consisting of 5000 users. Suppose that you want to allow 4990 of these users to be able to access one file.

   a. How would you specify this?

   b. Could you suggest another protection scheme that can be used more effectively for this purpose?

3.17 We have a file system on a disk with 512-word blocks. Assume that each file has a directory entry giving the file name, first block (or first index block), length of file, and last block position. The directory entry is in memory. For indexed allocation, the directory entry points to first index block, which in turn points to 511 file blocks and one pointer to next index block. For each of the three allocation strategies: contiguous, linked and indexed,

   a. Explain how the logical to physical address mapping is accomplished in this system.

   b. If we are currently at logical block 10 (the last block accessed was block 10) and want to access logical block 4, how many physical blocks must be read from the disk?

3.18 One problem with contiguous allocation is that the user must preallocate enough space for each file. If the file grows to be larger than the space allocated for it, special actions must be taken. One solution to this is to define a file structure consisting of an initial contiguous area (of a specified size). If this is filled, the operating system automatically defines an overflow area which is linked to the initial contiguous area. If the overflow area is filled, another overflow area is allocated. Compare this implementation of a file with the standard contiguous and linked implementations.

Bibliographic Notes

A multi-level directory structure was first implemented on the Multics system [Daley and Neumann 1965]. Other systems using a multi-level directory structure include Atlas [Wilkes 1975], TENEX [Bobrow et al. 1972], and Unix [Ritchie and Thompson 1974]. Watson [1970], Organick [1972] and Katzan [1973] discussed the implementation of directory structures.

File organization techniques were discussed by Knuth [1973] and Lefkovitz [1969]. Chapin [1969] gave a comparison of various file organization techniques. The various ways a file may be organized were presented by Dodd [1969] in a very nice tutorial paper.

Dynamic storage allocation is discussed by Knuth [1973, Section 2.5] who found through simulation results that first-fit is generally superior to best-fit. Additional discussions are offered by Shore [1975] and Bays [1977].

Hierarchies of I/O function were discussed by Madnick and Alsop [1969], Shaw [1974, Section 9.6], Tsichritzis and Bernstein [1974, Section 6.1], Dependahl and Presser [1976] and Calingaert [1982, Section 6.3].

File system integrity was discussed by Wilkes [1975] and Fraser [1969, 1972] for the Cambridge Multiple-Access system and by Organick [1972] for the Multics system.

Basic textbook discussions are offered by Shaw [1974, Chapter 9], Tsichritzis and Bernstein [1974, Chapter 6], Lister [1979, Chapter 6], Habermann [1976, Chapter 9], and Calingaert [1982, Chapter 9].

4

CPU Scheduling

CPU scheduling is the basis of multiprogrammed operating systems. By switching the cpu between processes, the operating system can make the computer more productive. In this chapter we introduce the basic scheduling concepts and present several different cpu scheduling algorithms. We also consider the problem of selecting an algorithm for a particular system.

4.1 Review of Multiprogramming Concepts

The most important concept in modern operating systems is undoubtedly *multiprogramming*. By having a number of programs in memory at the same time, the cpu may be shared among them. This scheme improves the overall efficiency of the computer system by getting more work done in less time.

The idea of multiprogramming is relatively simple. A job is executed until it must wait, typically for the completion of some I/O request. In a simple computer system, the cpu would then just sit idle. All of this waiting time is wasted; no useful work is accomplished. With multiprogramming, we try to use this time productively. Several jobs are kept in memory at one time. When one job has to wait, the operating system takes the cpu away from that job and gives it to another job. This pattern continues. Every time one job has to wait, another job may take over the use of the cpu.

The benefits of multiprogramming are increased cpu utilization and higher total job *throughput*. Throughput is the amount of work accomplished in a given time interval (for example, 17 jobs per hour). As an extreme example, assume we have two jobs, A and B, to be executed (Figure 4.1). Each job executes for one second, then waits for one second. This pattern is repeated 60 times. If we run first job A and then job B, one after the other, it will take four minutes to run the two jobs (Figure 4.2). Job A takes two minutes to run, then job B takes two minutes to run. We actually compute for only two minutes of this time,

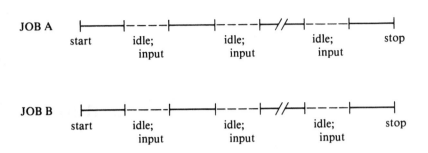

Figure 4.1   Two jobs, A and B, for execution

however; the other two minutes are idle time. Our cpu utilization is only 50 percent.

If we multiprogram job A and job B, we can greatly improve the system performance (Figure 4.3). We start with job A, which executes for one second. Then, while job A waits for one second, we execute job B. When job B waits, job A is ready to run. Now the elapsed time to execute both jobs is only two minutes, and there is no idle cpu time. Thus we have improved cpu utilization from 50 percent to 100 percent, increasing throughput at the same time. Notice that job A finishes no earlier, but job B is now finished in half the time.

This example is an extreme case, and is highly unlikely to occur in practice. It does, however, illustrate the concept of multiprogramming. In the next section, we examine cpu scheduling in much greater detail.

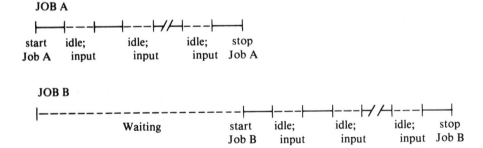

Figure 4.2   Job execution without multiprogramming

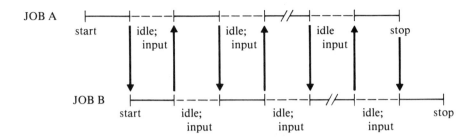

Figure 4.3   Job execution with multiprogramming

4.2 Scheduling Concepts

Scheduling is a fundamental operating system function, since almost all computer resources are scheduled before use. The cpu is, of course, one of the primary computer resources. Thus its scheduling is central to operating system design.

4.2.1 Basic Components

The cpu executes a large number of jobs or tasks. While its main concern is the execution of user jobs and programs, the cpu is also needed for other system activities. Every action of the computer system is initiated by the cpu. The cpu must respond to error traps, program requests, and I/O interrupts. Interrupts may be individual characters at a time-sharing terminal keyboard, or the result of a channel program transferring large blocks between memory and mass storage devices.

A persistent problem with operating systems is what to call all the cpu activities. A batch system executes *jobs*, while a time-shared system has *user programs*. Even on a single-user system, a user may be able to run several programs at one time: one interactive and several batch programs. Even if the user can only execute one program at a time, the operating system may need to support its own internal programmed activities, such as spooling.

In many respects, all of these activities are similar, so we call all of them *processes*. A process is a program in execution. Typically, a batch job is a process. A time-shared user program is a process. A system task, such as spooling, is also a process. In various operating systems, processes may be called jobs, users, programs, tasks, or activities. For now, a process may be considered as a job or a time-shared program, but the concept is actually more general. For example, as we will see in Chapter 9, it is possible to provide system calls that allow processes to create subprocesses to execute simultaneously.

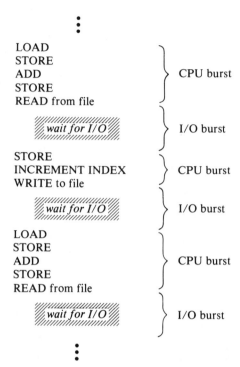

Figure 4.4   Execution is an alternating sequence of cpu and I/O bursts

The terms *job* and *process* are used almost interchangeably in this text. While we personally prefer the term *process*, much of the operating system theory and terminology was developed during a time when the major activity of operating systems was job processing. It would be misleading to avoid the use of commonly-accepted terms that include the word *job* (like job scheduling) simply because the term *process* has superseded it.

CPU-I/O Burst Cycle

The success of cpu scheduling depends upon the following observed property of processes: process execution is a *cycle* of cpu execution and I/O wait. Processes alternate back and forth between these two states. Process execution begins with a *cpu burst*. It is followed by an *I/O burst*, which is followed by another cpu burst, then another I/O burst, and so on. Eventually, the last cpu burst will end with a system request to terminate execution, rather than another I/O burst (Figure 4.4).

The durations of these cpu bursts have been measured. Although they vary greatly from process to process and computer to computer, they tend to have a frequency curve similar to that in Figure 4.5. The curve is generally characterized as exponential or hyper-exponential. There are a very large number of very short cpu bursts and a small number of very long ones. An I/O-bound program would typically have many very short cpu bursts. A cpu-bound program might have a few very long cpu bursts. This distribution can be quite important in selecting an appropriate cpu scheduling algorithm.

Process State

A process is a program in execution. As the program executes, the process changes *state*. The state of a process is defined by its current activity. Process execution is an alternating sequence of cpu and I/O bursts, beginning and ending with a cpu burst. Thus each process may be in one of the following states: *new, active, waiting,* or *halted*. These states are illustrated in Figure 4.6.

In fact, these states can be further refined. Since the cpu may be shared among several processes, an active process may either be waiting for the cpu or executing on it. A process which is waiting for the cpu is

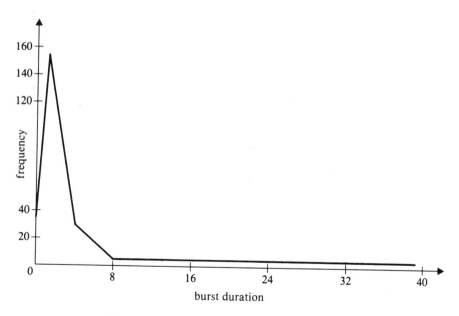

Figure 4.5   Histogram of cpu burst times

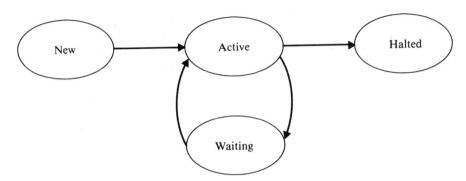

Figure 4.6   Process state diagram

ready. A process which has been allocated the cpu is *running*. A more detailed state diagram is illustrated in Figure 4.7.

Process Control Block

Each process is represented in the operating system by its own *process control block* (also called a task control block or a job control block) (Figure 4.8). A process control block (PCB) is a data block or record containing many pieces of the information associated with a specific process, including:

- The **process state** may be new, ready, running, waiting, or halted.

- The **program counter** indicates the address of the next instruction to be executed for this process.

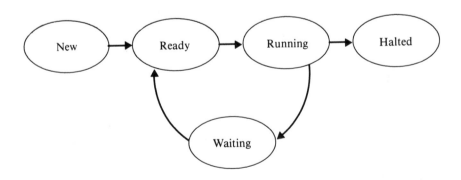

Figure 4.7   Refined process state diagram

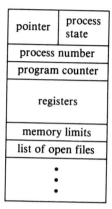

Figure 4.8   Process control block

- The **cpu registers** vary in number and type, depending upon the computer architecture. They include accumulators, index registers, and general purpose registers, plus any condition code information. Along with the program counter, this state information must be saved when an interrupt occurs, to allow the process to be continued correctly afterwards (Figure 4.9).

- Any **memory management information**, including base and bounds registers or page tables (Chapter 5).

- Any **accounting information**, including the amount of cpu and real time used, time limits, account numbers, job or process numbers, and so on.

- **I/O status information**, including outstanding I/O requests, I/O devices (like tape drives) allocated to this process, a list of open files, and so on.

- **CPU scheduling information**, including a process priority, pointers to scheduling queues, and any other scheduling parameters.

The PCB simply serves as the repository for any information that may vary from process to process.

PCBs must be stored in monitor memory. This memory may be managed in several ways. By far the easiest approach is to predeclare the maximum number of processes and preallocate statically enough room for all PCBs. More generally, the number of PCBs will change over time. Thus a dynamic memory management policy might be better. The

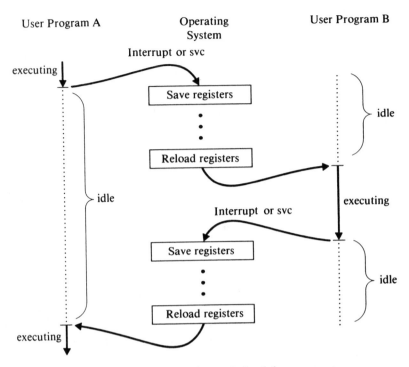

Figure 4.9   The cpu can be switched from user to user

system designer must weigh the extra flexibility and possibly higher memory utilization against the more complex algorithms and the potential for error or the overallocation of memory.

4.2.2 Scheduling Queues

The objective of multiprogramming is to have a process running at all times, in order to maximize cpu utilization. For a uniprocessor system, there will never be more than one running process. If there are more processes, the rest will have to wait until the cpu is free and can be rescheduled. The processes which are ready and waiting to execute are kept on a list called the *ready queue*. This list is generally a linked list. A ready queue header will contain pointers to the first and last PCBs in the list. Each PCB has a pointer field which points to the next process in the ready queue.

We should note that the ready queue is not necessarily a first-in-first-out (FIFO) queue, as used in data structure texts. As we will see when we consider the various scheduling algorithms, a ready queue

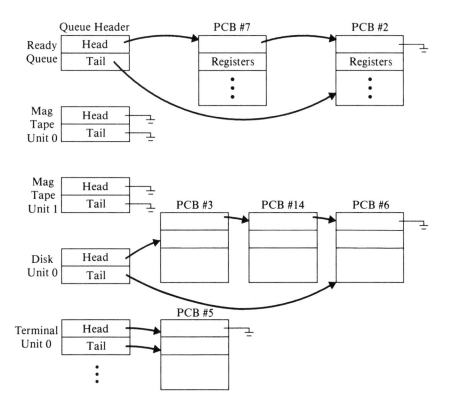

Figure 4.10　The ready queue and various I/O device queues

may be implemented as a FIFO queue, a priority queue, a tree, a stack, or simply an unordered linked list. Conceptually, however, all of the processes in the ready queue are lined up waiting for a chance to run on the cpu.

There are also other queues in the system (Figure 4.10). When a process is allocated the cpu, it executes for a while and eventually either quits or waits for an I/O request. The I/O request may be to a dedicated terminal or to a shared device, such as a disk. Since there are many processes in the system, the disk may be busy with the I/O request of some other process. Thus the process may have to wait for the disk. The list of processes waiting for a particular I/O device is called a *device queue*. Each device has its own device queue. If the device is a dedicated device, like a time-sharing terminal, the device queue will never have more than one process in it. If the device is sharable, several processes may be in the device queue.

A common representation for a discussion of cpu scheduling is a *queueing diagram* such as Figure 4.11. Each rectangular box represents a queue. Two types of queues are present: the ready queue and a set of device queues. The circles represent the resources which serve the queues, and the arrows indicate the flow of processes in the system.

A process enters the system from the outside world and is put in the ready queue. It waits in the ready queue until it is selected for the cpu. After running on the cpu, it waits for an I/O operation by moving to an I/O queue. Eventually, it is served by the I/O device and returns to the ready queue. A process continues this cpu-I/O cycle until it finishes; then it exits from the system.

Since our main concern at this time is cpu scheduling, we will abstract the details of the multiple I/O device subsystem, replacing it with one I/O waiting queue and I/O server (Figure 4.12). I/O scheduling is discussed more in Chapters 7 and 8.

4.2.3 Schedulers

An operating system has many schedulers. There are two main cpu schedulers: the long-term scheduler and the short-term scheduler.

The *long-term scheduler* (or job scheduler) determines which jobs are admitted to the system for processing. In a batch system, there are often more jobs submitted than can be executed immediately. These jobs are spooled to a mass storage device (typically a disk), where they are kept for later execution. The long-term scheduler selects jobs from this job

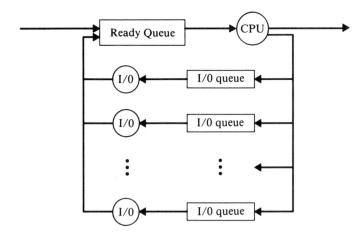

Figure 4.11   Queueing diagram representation of cpu scheduling

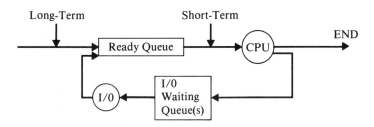

Figure 4.12   Simplified queueing diagram

pool and loads them into memory for execution. The *short-term scheduler* (or cpu scheduler) selects from among the jobs in memory which are ready to execute and allocates the cpu to one of them.

The primary distinction between these two schedulers is the frequency of their execution. The short-term scheduler must select a new process for the cpu quite often. A process may execute only a few milliseconds before waiting for an I/O request. Often the short-term scheduler executes at least once every 10 milliseconds. Because of the short duration between executions, the short-term scheduler must be very fast. If it takes 1 millisecond to decide to execute a process for 10 milliseconds, then $1/(10+1) \approx 9$ percent of the cpu is being used (wasted) simply for scheduling the work.

The long-term scheduler, on the other hand, executes much less frequently. It may be minutes between the arrival of new jobs in the system. The long-term scheduler controls the *degree of multiprogramming* (the number of processes in memory). If the degree of multiprogramming is stable, then the average arrival rate of jobs entering the system must be equal to the average departure rate of jobs leaving the system. Thus the long-term scheduler may need to be invoked only when a job leaves the system. Because of the longer interval between executions, the long-term scheduler can afford to take more time to decide which job should be selected for execution.

It may also be more important that the long-term scheduler make a careful selection. In general, most jobs can be described as either I/O-bound or cpu-bound jobs. It is important that the long-term scheduler select a good *job mix* of I/O-bound and cpu-bound jobs. If all jobs are I/O-bound, the ready queue will almost always be empty and the short-term scheduler will have little to do. If all jobs are cpu-bound, the I/O waiting queue will almost always be empty and again the system will be unbalanced. The system with the best performance will have a combination of cpu-bound and I/O-bound jobs.

On some systems, the long-term scheduler may be absent or minimal. For example, time-sharing systems often have no long-term scheduler, but simply put every new process in memory for the short-term scheduler. The stability of these systems depends either upon a physical limitation (such as a limited number of available terminals) or the self-adjusting nature of human users. If the performance gets too bad, some users will simply quit and go do something else.

Some systems, especially those with virtual memory or time sharing, may introduce an additional, intermediate level of scheduling. This *medium-term scheduler* is diagrammed in Figure 4.13. The key idea behind a medium-term scheduler is that it can sometimes be advantageous to remove processes from memory (and from active contention for the cpu) and thus reduce the degree of multiprogramming. At some later time, the process can be reintroduced into memory and continued where it left off. This scheme is often called *swapping*. The process is swapped out and swapped in later by the medium-term scheduler. Swapping may be necessary to improve the job mix, or because a change in memory requirements has overcommitted available memory, requiring memory to be freed up. Swapping is discussed in more detail in Chapter 5.

Another component involved in the cpu scheduler function is the *dispatcher*. The dispatcher is the module that actually gives control of the cpu to the process selected by the short-term scheduler. This function involves loading the registers of the process, switching to user mode, and jumping to the proper location in the user program to restart it. Obviously, the dispatcher should be as fast as possible.

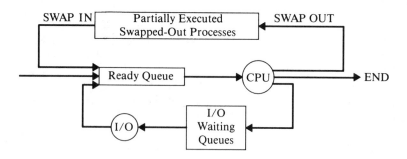

Figure 4.13   Adding medium-term scheduling to the queueing diagram

4.3 Scheduling Algorithms

CPU scheduling deals with the problem of deciding which of the processes in the ready queue is to be allocated the cpu. There are many different cpu scheduling algorithms. In this section we will describe several of these algorithms.

4.3.1 Performance Criteria

Different algorithms have different properties and may favor one class of processes over another. In choosing which algorithm to use in a particular situation, the properties of the various algorithms must be considered.

Many criteria have been suggested for comparing cpu scheduling algorithms. Which characteristics are used for comparison can make a substantial difference in the determination of the best algorithm. Criteria which are used include:

- **CPU utilization**. When the cpu is very expensive, we want to keep it as busy as possible. CPU utilization may range from 0 percent to 100 percent. In a real system, it should range from 40 percent (for a lightly loaded system) to 90 percent (for a heavily used system).

- **Throughput**. If the cpu is busy, then work is being done. One measure of work is the number of jobs which are completed per time unit, called throughput. For long jobs this rate may be one job per hour; for short transactions, throughput might be ten jobs per second.

- **Turnaround time**. From the point of view of a particular job, the important criterion is how long it takes to execute that job. The interval from the time of submission to the time of completion is the turnaround time. Turnaround time is the sum of the periods spent waiting to get into memory, waiting in the ready queue, executing on the cpu, and doing I/O.

- **Waiting time**. The cpu scheduling algorithm does not really affect the amount of time that a job executes or does I/O. The algorithm only affects the amount of time that a job spends waiting in the ready queue. Thus rather than looking at turnaround time, we might simply consider the waiting time for each job.

- **Response time**. In an interactive system, turnaround time may not be the best criterion. Often a process can produce some output fairly early and can continue computing new results while previous results are being output to the user. Thus another measure is the time from the submission of a request until the first response is produced. This measure, called *response time*, is the amount of time it takes to start responding, but not the time that it takes to output that response. The turnaround time is generally limited by the speed of the output device.

Once we have selected a criterion for comparison, we generally want to optimize it. It is desirable to maximize cpu utilization and throughput, and to minimize turnaround time, waiting time and response time. In most cases, it is the average measure that is optimized. However, it may sometimes be desirable to optimize the minimum or maximum values, rather than the average. For example, to guarantee that all users get good service, we may want to minimize the maximum response time.

It has also been suggested that for interactive systems (such as time-sharing systems), it is more important to minimize the *variance* in the response time than to minimize the average response time. A system with reasonable and *predictable* response time may be considered better than a system which is faster on the average, but highly variable. There has been very little work done on cpu scheduling algorithms to minimize variance.

As we discuss various cpu scheduling algorithms, we want to illustrate their operation. An accurate illustration should involve many jobs, each being a sequence of several hundred cpu and I/O bursts. For simplicity of illustration, we consider only one cpu burst per job, in our examples. One measure of comparison is the average turnaround time: how long does it take to schedule and execute these jobs? More elaborate evaluation mechanisms are discussed in Section 4.4.

4.3.2 First-Come-First-Served

By far the simplest cpu scheduling algorithm is *First-Come-First-Served* (FCFS). That is, the process which requests the cpu first is allocated the cpu first. The implementation of FCFS is easily managed with a FIFO queue. When a process enters the ready queue, its process control block is linked onto the tail of the queue. When the cpu is free, it is allocated to the process at the head of the ready queue. The running process is then removed from the ready queue. The code for FCFS scheduling is simple to write and understand.

The performance of FCFS, however, is often quite poor. Consider the following three jobs. For each job, assume that we know the length of the next cpu burst. We can compute the average turnaround time to service these three cpu bursts.

Job	Burst Time
1	24
2	3
3	3

If the jobs arrive in the order 1, 2, 3, and are served in FCFS order, we get the result shown in the following *Gantt chart*.

The turnaround time for job 1 is 24; for job 2, 27; and for job 3, 30. Thus the average turnaround time is (24+27+30)/3 = 27. If the jobs arrive in the order 2, 3, 1, however, the following Gantt chart shows the results.

The average turnaround time is now (30+3+6)/3 = 13 -- a substantial reduction. Thus the average turnaround time for FCFS is generally not minimal, and may vary substantially.

In addition, consider the performance of FCFS in a dynamic situation. Assume we have one cpu-bound job and many I/O-bound jobs. As the jobs flow around the system, the following scenario may result. The cpu-bound job will get the cpu and hold it. During this time all the other jobs will finish their I/O and move into the ready queue, waiting for the cpu. While they wait in the ready queue, the I/O devices are idle. Eventually, the cpu-bound job finishes its cpu burst and moves to an I/O device. All the I/O-bound jobs, which have very short cpu bursts, execute quickly and move back to the I/O queues. At this point the cpu sits idle. The cpu-bound job will then move back to the ready queue and be allocated the cpu. Again, all the I/O processes end up waiting in the ready queue until the cpu-bound job is done. There is a *convoy effect* as all the other processes wait for the one big process to get off the cpu. This effect results in lower cpu and device utilization than might be possible if the shorter jobs were allowed to go first.

4.3.3 Shortest-Job-First

A different approach to cpu scheduling is the *Shortest-Job-First* (SJF) algorithm. Shortest-Job-First associates with each job the length of its next cpu burst. When the cpu is available, it is assigned to that job with the smallest next cpu burst. If two jobs have the same next cpu burst, FCFS is used.

As an example, consider the following set of jobs.

Job	Burst Time
1	6
2	3
3	8
4	7

Using Shortest-Job-First scheduling, we would schedule these jobs according to the following Gantt chart.

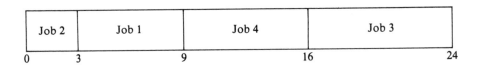

Job 2	Job 1	Job 4	Job 3
0 3	9	16	24

The average turnaround time is 13.

Shortest-Job-First is provably *optimal*, in that it gives the minimum average waiting time for a given set of jobs. The proof shows that moving a short job before a long one decreases the waiting time of the short job more than it increases the waiting time of the long job (Figure 4.14). Consequently, the *average* waiting time decreases.

The real difficulty with Shortest-Job-First is knowing the length of the next cpu request. For job (long-term) scheduling in a batch system, we can use the job time limit. Thus users are motivated to estimate the job time limit accurately, since a lower value may mean faster turnaround. (Too low a value will cause a "time limit exceeded" error and require resubmission.) Shortest-Job-First is frequently used in job scheduling.

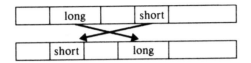

Figure 4.14   Proving that SJF is optimal

Although Shortest-Job-First is optimal, it cannot be implemented at the (short-term) cpu scheduling level. There is no way to know the length of the next cpu burst. One approach is to try to approximate Shortest-Job-First scheduling. We may not *know* the length of the next cpu burst, but we may be able to *predict* its value. We would expect that the next cpu burst will be similar in length to the previous ones. Thus by computing an approximation of the length of the next cpu burst, we can pick the job with the shortest predicted cpu burst.

The next cpu burst is generally predicted as an *exponential average* of the measured lengths of previous cpu bursts. Let t_n be the length of the nth cpu burst, and let τ_{n+1} be our predicted value for the next cpu burst. Then, for α, $0 \le \alpha \le 1$, define:

$$\tau_{n+1} = \alpha t_n + (1-\alpha)\tau_n.$$

This formula defines an *exponential average*. The value of t_n contains our most recent information; τ_n stores the past history. The parameter α controls the relative weight of recent and past history in our prediction. If $\alpha = 0$, then $\tau_{n+1} = \tau_n$, and recent history has no effect (current conditions are assumed to be transient); if $\alpha = 1$, then $\tau_{n+1} = t_n$ and only the most recent cpu burst matters (history is assumed to be old and irrelevant). More commonly, $\alpha = 1/2$, so that recent history and past history are equally weighted. Figure 4.15 shows an exponential average with $\alpha = 1/2$. The initial τ_0 can be defined as a constant or an overall system average.

To understand the behavior of the exponential average, we can expand the formula for τ_{n+1} by substituting for τ_n, to find:

$$\tau_{n+1} = \alpha t_n + (1-\alpha)\alpha t_{n-1} + \dots + (1-\alpha)^j \alpha t_{n-j} + \dots$$

Since both α and $(1-\alpha)$ are less than 1, each successive term has less weight than its predecessor.

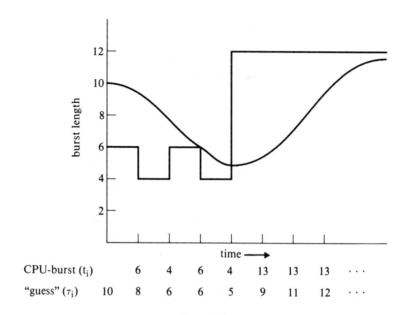

CPU-burst (t_i)		6	4	6	4	13	13	13	$\cdots$
"guess" (τ_i)	10	8	6	6	5	9	11	12	$\cdots$

Figure 4.15   Predicting the next cpu burst using an exponential average

4.3.4 Priority

Shortest-Job-First is a special case of the general *priority* scheduling algorithm. A priority is associated with each job, and the cpu is allocated to the job with the highest priority. Equal priority jobs are scheduled FCFS.

A Shortest-Job-First algorithm is simply a priority algorithm where the priority (p) is the inverse of the (predicted) next cpu burst (τ), $p = 1/\tau$. The larger the cpu burst, the lower the priority, and vice versa.

It should be noted that we discuss scheduling in terms of *high* priority and *low* priority. Priorities are generally some fixed range of numbers, such as 0 to 7 or 0 to 4095. However, there is no general agreement on whether 0 is the highest or lowest priority. Some systems use low numbers to represent low priority; others have low numbers for high priority. This difference can lead to some confusion.

Priorities can be defined either internally or externally. Internally defined priorities use some measurable quantity or quantities to compute the priority of a process. For example, time limits, memory requirements, the number of open files, and the ratio of average I/O burst to average cpu burst have been used in computing priorities. External priorities are set by criteria which are external to the operating system, such as the type and amount of funds being paid for computer use, the department sponsoring the work, and other external, often political, factors.

A major problem with priority scheduling algorithms is *indefinite blocking* or *starvation*. A process which is ready to run but lacking the cpu can be considered blocked, waiting for the cpu. A priority scheduling algorithm can leave some low-priority processes waiting indefinitely for the cpu. In a heavily loaded computer system, a steady stream of higher-priority processes can prevent a low-priority process from ever getting the cpu. Generally, one of two things will happen. Either the job will eventually be run (at 2 AM Sunday morning when the system is finally lightly loaded) or the computer system will crash and lose all unfinished low-priority jobs. (Rumor has it that when they closed down the 7094 at MIT in 1973, they found a low-priority job that had been submitted in 1967 and had not yet been run.)

Another solution to the problem of indefinite blockage of low-priority jobs is *aging*. Aging is a technique of gradually increasing the priority of jobs that wait in the system for a long time. For example, if priorities range from 0 (low) to 127 (high), we could increment a waiting job's priority by 1 every fifteen minutes. Eventually, even a job with an initial priority of 0 would have the highest priority in the system and would be executed. In fact, it would take no more than 32 hours for a priority 0 job to age to a priority 127 job.

4.3.5 Preemptive Algorithms

FCFS, Shortest-Job-First, and priority algorithms, as described so far, are *non-preemptive* scheduling algorithms. Once the cpu has been allocated to a process, it can keep the cpu until it wants to release it, either by terminating or by requesting I/O. FCFS is intrinsically non-preemptive, but the other two can be modified to be *preemptive* algorithms.

Shortest-Job-First may be either preemptive or non-preemptive. The question arises when a new job arrives at the ready queue while a previous job is executing. The new job may have a shorter next cpu burst than what is left of the currently executing job. A preemptive Shortest-Job-First algorithm will preempt the currently executing job, while a non-preemptive Shortest-Job-First algorithm will allow the currently running job to finish its cpu burst. Preemptive Shortest-Job-First is sometimes called *Shortest-Remaining-Time-First*.

Priority scheduling can also be either preemptive or non-preemptive. When a job arrives at the ready queue (as a result of finishing its previous I/O request, for example), its priority is compared with the priority of the currently running process. A preemptive priority scheduling algorithm will preempt the cpu if the priority of the newly arrived process is higher than the priority of the currently running process. A non-preemptive priority scheduling algorithm will simply put the new process at the head of the ready queue.

Non-preemptive cpu scheduling algorithms (especially FCFS scheduling) are particularly troublesome for time-sharing systems. In a time-sharing system, it is very important that each user get a share of the cpu at regular intervals. It would be disastrous to allow one process to be allowed to keep the cpu for an extended period of time.

As an example, consider the following 4 jobs.

Job	Arrival Time	Burst Time
1	0	8
2	1	4
3	2	9
4	3	5

If the jobs arrive at the ready queue at the times shown and need the indicated times, then the following Gantt chart illustrates the resulting preemptive Shortest-Job-First schedule.

Job 1 is started at time 0, since it is the only job in the queue. Job 2 arrives at time 1. The remaining time for job 1 (7 time units) is larger than the time required by job 2 (4 time units), so job 1 is preempted, and job 2 is scheduled. The average turnaround time for this example is $((17-0) + (5-1) + (26-2) + (10-3))/4 = 52/4 = 13$ time units. A non-preemptive Shortest-Job-First scheduling would result in an average turnaround time of 14.25.

4.3.6 Round-Robin

The *round-robin* (RR) scheduling algorithm is designed especially for time-sharing systems. A small unit of time, called a *time quantum* or time slice, is defined. A time quantum is generally from 10 to 100 milliseconds. The ready queue is treated as a circular queue. The cpu scheduler goes around the ready queue, allocating the cpu to each process for a time interval up to a quantum in length.

To implement round-robin scheduling, the ready queue is kept as a FIFO queue of processes. New processes are added to the tail of the ready queue. The cpu scheduler picks the first job from the ready queue, sets a timer to interrupt after one time quantum, and dispatches the process. One of two things will then happen. The process may have a cpu burst less than the time quantum. In this case, the process itself releases the cpu voluntarily, by issuing an I/O request or terminating. We then proceed to the next job in the ready queue.

Otherwise, if the cpu burst of the currently running process is larger than the time quantum, the timer will go off and cause an interrupt to the operating system. The registers for the interrupted process are saved in its process control block, and the process is put at the *tail* of the ready queue. The cpu scheduler then selects the next job in the ready queue and gives it the next time quantum.

For example, consider the following set of jobs, which were previously used to illustrate FCFS scheduling.

Job	Burst Time
1	24
2	3
3	3

If we use a time quantum of 4, the resulting round-robin schedule is:

Job 1	Job 2	Job 3	Job 1	Job 1	Job 1	Job 1	Job 1
4	7	10	14	18	22	26	30

Job 1 gets the first 4 time units. Since it requires another 20, it is preempted after the first time quantum, and the cpu is given to the next job in the queue, job 2. Since job 2 does not need 4 units, it quits before its time quantum expires. The cpu is then given to the next process, job 3. Once each job has received one time quantum, the cpu is returned to job 1 for an additional time quantum. The average turnaround time is $47/3 \approx 16$.

In the round-robin scheduling algorithm, no process is allocated the cpu for more than one time quantum in a row. If its cpu burst exceeds a time quantum, it is *preempted* and put back in the ready queue. Round-robin is a preemptive scheduling algorithm.

If there are n processes in the ready queue and the time quantum is q, then each process gets $1/n$ of the cpu time in chunks of at most q time units at a time. Each process must wait no longer than $(n-1) \times q$ time units until its next time quantum. For example, if there are five processes, with a time quantum of 20 milliseconds, then each process would get up to 20 milliseconds every 100 milliseconds.

The performance of round-robin depends heavily on the time quantum. At one extreme, if the time quantum is very large (infinite), round-robin is the same as FCFS. If the time quantum is very small (say 1 microsecond), round-robin is called *processor sharing* and appears (in theory) as if each of n processes has its own processor running at $1/n$ the speed of the real processor. This approach is used in hardware in the CDC 6600 to implement ten peripheral processors with only one set of hardware and ten sets of registers [Thornton 1970]. The hardware executes one instruction for one set of registers, then goes on to the next. This cycle continues, resulting in ten slow processors rather than one fast one. (Actually, since the processor is much faster than memory and each instruction references memory, the processors are not much slower than a single processor would be.)

In software, however, we have other problems. Specifically, at the end of each time quantum, we get an interrupt from the timer. Processing the interrupt to switch the cpu to another process requires saving all the registers for the old process and loading the registers for the new process. This task is known as a *context switch*. Context switch time is pure overhead. It varies from machine to machine, depending upon memory speed, the number of registers, and the existence of special instructions (such as a single instruction to load or store all registers). Typically, it takes from 10 to 100 microseconds.

To illustrate the effect of context switch time on the performance of round-robin scheduling, let's assume that we have only one job of 10 time units. If the quantum is 12 time units, the job finishes in less than one time quantum, with no overhead. If the quantum is 6 time units, however, the job requires two quanta, resulting in a context switch. If the time quantum is 1 time unit, then 9 context switches will occur, slowing the execution of the job accordingly (Figure 4.16).

Thus we want the time quantum to be large with respect to the context switch time. If the context switch time is approximately 10 percent of the time quantum, then about 10 percent of the cpu time will be spent in context switch time.

Turnaround time also depends on the time quantum (Figure 4.17). It can be improved if most jobs finish their next cpu burst in a single

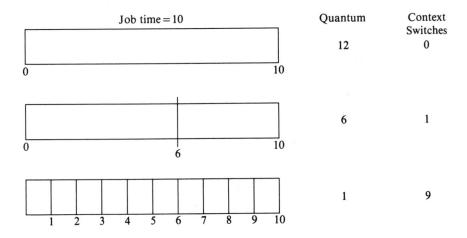

Figure 4.16   A smaller time quantum increases context switches

time quantum. For example, given three jobs of 10 time units each and a quantum of 1 time unit, the average turnaround time is 29. If the time quantum is 10, however, the average turnaround time drops to 20. If context switch time is added in, things are even worse for a smaller time quantum, since more context switches will be required.

On the other hand, if the time quantum is too large, round-robin degenerates to FCFS. A suggested rule-of-thumb is that 80 percent of the cpu bursts should be shorter than the time quantum.

4.3.7 Multi-Level Queues

Another class of scheduling algorithms has been created for situations in which jobs are easily classified into different groups. For example, a common division is made between *foreground* (interactive) jobs and *background* (batch) jobs. These two types of jobs have quite different response time requirements, and so might have different scheduling algorithms. In addition, foreground jobs may have priority (externally defined) over background jobs.

A *multi-queue scheduling algorithm* partitions the ready queue into separate queues (Figure 4.18). Jobs are permanently assigned to one queue, generally based upon some property of the job, such as memory size or job type. Each queue has its own scheduling algorithm. For example, separate queues might be used for foreground and background jobs. The foreground queue might be scheduled by a round-robin algorithm, while the background queue is scheduled FCFS.

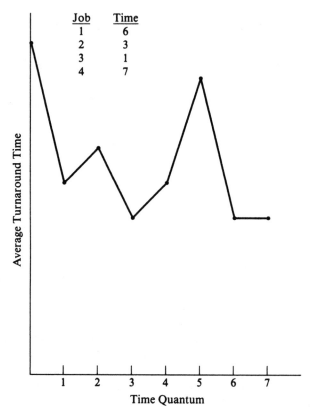

Figure 4.17   The average turnaround time varies with the time quantum

In addition, there must be scheduling between the queues. This is commonly a fixed-priority preemptive scheduling. For example, the foreground queue may have absolute priority over the background queue.

As an example of a multi-queue scheduling algorithm, one OS/MFT system had five queues:

- System Jobs.
- Interactive Programs.
- Interactive Editing.
- Batch Jobs.
- Student Jobs.

highest priority

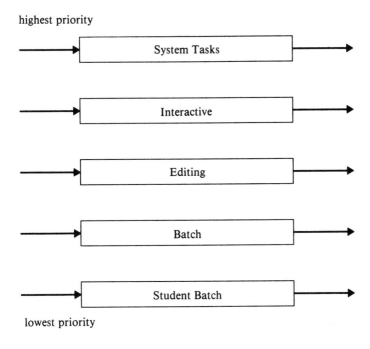

lowest priority

Figure 4.18   Multi-queue scheduling

Each queue had absolute priority over lower priority queues. No job in the batch queue, for example, could run unless the queues for system jobs, interactive jobs, and interactive editing jobs were all empty. If an interactive editing job entered the ready queue while a batch job was running, the batch job would be preempted.

Another possibility is to time slice between the queues. Each queue gets a certain portion of the cpu time, which it can then schedule among the various processes in its queue. For instance, in the foreground/background queue example, the foreground queue can be given 80 percent of the cpu time to round-robin among its processes, while the background queue receives 20 percent of the cpu to give to its processes in a FCFS manner.

4.3.8 Multi-Level Feedback Queues

Normally, in a multi-queue scheduling algorithm, jobs are permanently assigned to a queue upon entry to the system. Jobs do not move between queues. If there are separate queues for foreground and background jobs, for example, jobs would not move from one queue to the other, since jobs do not change their foreground or background nature.

Multi-level feedback queues, however, allow a job to move between queues. The idea is to separate out jobs with different cpu-burst characteristics. If a job uses too much cpu time, it will be moved to a lower priority queue. This scheme leaves I/O-bound and interactive jobs in the higher priority queues. Similarly, a job which waits too long in a lower-priority queue may be moved to a higher-priority queue.

For example, consider a multi-level feedback queue scheduler with three queues, numbered from 0 to 2 (Figure 4.19). The scheduler first executes all jobs in queue 0. Only when queue 0 is empty will it execute jobs in queue 1. Similarly, jobs in queue 2 will only be executed if queues 0 and 1 are empty. A job which arrives for queue 1 will preempt a job in queue 2. A job in queue 1 will in turn be preempted by a job arriving for queue 0.

A job entering the ready queue is put in queue 0. A job in queue 0 is given a time quantum of 8 milliseconds. If it does not finish within this time, it is moved to the tail of queue 1. If queue 0 is empty, the job at the head of queue 1 is given a quantum of 16 milliseconds. If it does not complete, it is preempted and put into queue 2. Jobs in queue 2 are run FCFS only when queues 0 and 1 are empty.

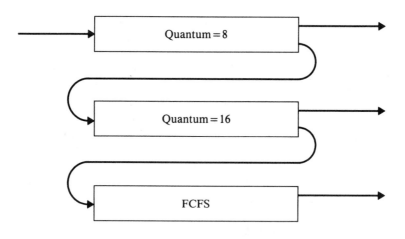

Figure 4.19   Multi-level feedback queues

This scheduling algorithm gives highest priority to any job with a cpu burst of 8 milliseconds or less. Such a job will quickly get the cpu, finish its cpu burst, and go off to its next I/O burst. Jobs which need more than 8, but less than 24, milliseconds are also served quickly, although with lower priority than shorter jobs. Long jobs automatically sink to queue 2 and are served FCFS with any cpu cycles left over from queues 0 and 1.

In general, a multi-queue feedback scheduler is defined by the following parameters:

- The number of queues.

- The scheduling algorithm for each queue.

- A method of determining when to upgrade a job to a higher priority queue.

- A method of determining when to demote a job to a lower priority queue.

- A method of determining which queue a job will enter when it needs service.

The definition of a multi-queue feedback scheduler makes it the most general cpu scheduling algorithm. It can be configured to match a specific system under design. Unfortunately, it also requires some means of selecting values for all of the parameters to define the best scheduler. Although a multi-level feedback queue is the most general scheme, it is also the most complex.

4.4 Algorithm Evaluation

How do we select a cpu scheduling algorithm for a particular system? As we have seen in Section 4.3, there are many scheduling algorithms, each with its own parameters. As a result, selecting an algorithm can be quite difficult.

The first problem is defining the criteria to be used in selecting an algorithm. As we saw in Section 4.3.1, criteria are often defined in terms of cpu utilization, response time, or throughput. To select an algorithm, we must first define the relative importance of these measures. Our criteria may include several measures, such as,

- Maximize cpu utilization under the constraint that the maximum response time is 1 second.

- Maximize throughput such that turnaround time is (on average) linearly proportional to total execution time.

Once the selection criteria have been defined, we want to evaluate the various algorithms under consideration. There are a number of different evaluation methods, which we describe in the following sections.

4.4.1 Analytic Evaluation

One major class of evaluation methods is called *analytic evaluation*. Analytic evaluation uses the algorithm and the system workload to produce a formula or number which evaluates the performance of the algorithm for that workload.

Deterministic Modeling

One type of analytic evaluation is *deterministic modeling*. This method takes a particular predetermined workload and defines the performance of each algorithm for that workload.

For example, assume we have the workload shown below. All five jobs arrive at time 0, in the order given.

Job	Burst Time
1	10
2	29
3	3
4	7
5	12

Considering FCFS, Shortest-Job-First, and round-robin (quantum = 10) scheduling algorithms for this set of jobs, which algorithm would give the minimum average waiting time?

For FCFS, we would execute the jobs as

1	2	3	4	5

```
    10                          39  42      49      61
```

Job	Waiting Time
1	0
2	10
3	39
4	42
5	49
	140

The average waiting time is then 140/5 = 28.

With Shortest-Job-First (non-preemptive), we execute the jobs as,

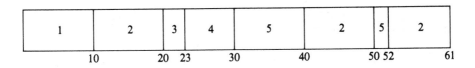

Job	Waiting Time
1	10
2	32
3	0
4	3
5	20
	65

The average waiting time is 65/5 = 13.

With round-robin (quantum = 10), we start job 2, but preempt it after 10 time units, putting it in the back of the queue.

1	2	3	4	5	2	5	2

10   20 23   30   40   50 52   61

Job	Waiting Time
1	0
2	32
3	20
4	23
5	40
	115

The average waiting time is then 115/5 = 23.

We see that *in this case* Shortest-Job-First has less than half the average waiting time of FCFS; round-robin has an intermediate value.

Deterministic modeling is simple and fast. It gives exact numbers allowing the algorithms to be compared. However, it requires exact numbers for input and its answers apply only to those cases. The main use of deterministic scheduling is in describing scheduling algorithms and providing examples. In cases where we may be running the same programs over and over again and can measure their processing requirements exactly, we may be able to use deterministic scheduling to select a scheduling algorithm. Over a set of examples, deterministic modeling may indicate trends which can then be analyzed and proven separately. For example, it can be shown for the environment described (all jobs and their times available at time zero), Shortest-Job-First will always have the minimum waiting time.

In general, however, deterministic modeling is too specific to be very useful in most cases. It requires too much exact knowledge and provides results of limited usefulness.

Queueing Models

The jobs which are run on many systems vary from day to day, and so there is no static set of jobs (and times) to use for deterministic modeling. What can be determined, however, is the distribution of cpu and I/O bursts. These distributions may be measured and then approximated or simply estimated. The result is a mathematical formula describing the probability of a particular cpu burst. Commonly this distribution is exponential and is described by its mean. Similarly, the distribution of times when jobs arrive in the system (the arrival time distribution) must be given. From these two distributions, it is possible to compute the average throughput, utilization, waiting time, and so on for most algorithms.

The computer system is described as a network of servers. Each server has a queue of waiting jobs. The cpu is a server with its ready queue, as is the I/O system with its device queues. Knowing arrival rates and service rates, we can compute utilization, average queue length, average wait time, and so on. This area of study is called *queueing network analysis*.

For example, let n be the average queue length (excluding the job being serviced), let W be the average waiting time in the queue, and let λ be the average arrival rate for new jobs in the queue (such as 3 jobs per second). Then we would expect that during the time, W, that a job waits, $\lambda \times W$ new jobs will arrive in the queue. If the system is in a steady state, then the number of jobs leaving the queue must equal the number of jobs which arrive. Thus,

$$n = \lambda \times W.$$

This equation is known as *Little's formula*. Little's formula is particularly useful because it is true for any scheduling algorithm and arrival distribution.

We can use Little's formula to compute one of the three variables, if we know the other two. For example, if we know that 7 jobs arrive every second (on average), and that there are normally 14 jobs in the queue, then we can compute the average waiting time per job as 2 seconds.

Queueing analysis can be quite useful in comparing scheduling algorithms, but it also has its limitations. At the moment, the class of algorithms and distributions which can be handled are fairly limited. The mathematics of complicated algorithms or distributions can be difficult to work with. Thus arrival and service distributions are often defined in unrealistic, but mathematically-tractable ways. It is also generally necessary to make a number of independent assumptions, which may not be accurate. Thus to be able to compute the answer, queueing models are often only an approximation of the real system. As a result, the accuracy of the answer may be questionable.

4.4.2 Simulations

To get a more accurate evaluation of scheduling algorithms, *simulations* are often used. Simulations involve programming a model of the computer system. Software data structures represent the major components of the system. The simulator has a variable representing a clock, and as its value is increased, the simulator modifies the system state to reflect the activities of the devices, the jobs, and the scheduler. As the simulation executes, statistics are gathered and printed to indicate algorithm performance.

The data to drive the simulation can be generated in several ways. The most common method uses a random number generator, which is programmed to generate jobs, cpu burst times, arrivals, departures, and so on, according to probability distributions. The distributions may be defined mathematically (uniform, exponential, Poisson) or may be defined empirically. To define a distribution empirically, measurements of the actual system under study are taken. The results can then be used to define the actual distribution of events in the real system. This distribution can then be used to drive the simulation.

However, a distribution-driven simulation may be inaccurate, due to relationships between successive events in the real system. The frequency distribution only indicates how many of each event occur, but does not indicate anything about the order of their occurrence. To correct this problem, *trace tapes* can be used. A trace tape is created by monitoring the real system, recording the sequence of actual events (Figure 4.20). This sequence is then used to drive the simulation. Trace tapes are an excellent way to compare two algorithms on exactly the

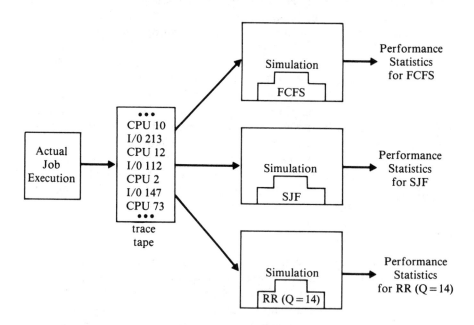

Figure 4.20   Evaluation of cpu schedulers by simulation

same set of real inputs. This method can produce very accurate results for its inputs.

Simulations can be very expensive, however, often requiring hours of computer time. A more detailed simulation provides more accurate results, but also requires more computer time. In addition, trace tapes can require large amounts of storage space. The design, coding, and debugging of the simulator can be a major task.

4.4.3 Implementation

Even a simulation is of limited accuracy. The only completely accurate way of evaluating a scheduling algorithm is to code it up and put it in the operating system to see how it works. This approach puts the actual algorithm in the real system for evaluation under real operating conditions.

The major difficulty is the cost of this approach. The expense is not only in coding the algorithm and modifying the operating system to support it as well as its required data structures, but also in the reaction of the users to a constantly changing operating system. Most users are not interested in building a better operating system; they merely want to get their jobs executed and to use their results. A constantly changing operating system does not help the users get their work done.

The other difficulty with any algorithm evaluation is that the environment in which the algorithm is used will change. The environment will change not only in the usual way, as new programs are written and the types of problems change, but also as a result of the performance of the scheduler. If short jobs are given priority, then a user may break a larger job into a set of smaller jobs. If interactive jobs are given priority over non-interactive jobs, then users may switch to interactive use.

For example, one system tried to automatically classify interactive and non-interactive processes by looking at the amount of terminal I/O. If a process did not input or output to the terminal in a 1 second interval, it was classified as non-interactive and moved to a lower priority queue. As a result, one programmer modified his programs to write an arbitrary character to the terminal at regular intervals of less than 1 second. The system gave his programs a high priority, even though the terminal output was completely meaningless.

4.5 Multiple Processor Scheduling

Our major discussion of cpu scheduling has focused on the problems of scheduling the cpu in a system with a single processor. If multiple cpus are available, the scheduling problem is correspondingly more complex. Many possibilities have been tried, and as with single processor cpu scheduling, there is no one best solution.

One major factor is the types of processors involved. The processors may be identical (a *homogeneous* system) or different (a *heterogeneous* system). If the processors are different, the options are relatively limited. Each processor has its own queue and its own scheduling algorithm. Jobs are intrinsically typed by their structure; they must be run on a particular processor. A program written in PDP-11 assembly language cannot be run on an IBM Series/1; it must be run on a PDP-11. Hence the processes are self-segregating, and each processor can schedule itself.

If several identical processors are available, then *load sharing* can occur. It would be possible to provide a separate queue for each processor. However, in this case, then one processor could be idle, with an empty queue, while another processor is very busy. To prevent this situation, a common ready queue is used. All jobs go into one queue and are scheduled onto any available processor.

In such a scheme one of two scheduling approaches may be used. One approach is for each processor to be self-scheduling. Each processor examines the common ready queue and selects a process to execute. As we will see in Chapter 9, if we have multiple processors trying to access and update a common data structure, each processor must be programmed very carefully. We must insure that two processors do not choose the same process, and that processes are not lost from the queue. The other approach avoids this problem by appointing one processor as scheduler for the other processors, and a master/slave structure exists.

4.6 Summary

CPU scheduling is the process of selecting and allocating the cpu to a waiting process. Each process is represented by a process control block. The process control blocks can be linked together to form queues of processes. There are two major classes of queues in an operating system: I/O request queues and the ready queue. The ready queue contains all of the processes which are ready to execute and are waiting for the cpu.

Job scheduling is the selection of jobs to be allowed to contend for the cpu. Normally, job scheduling is heavily influenced by resource allocation considerations, especially memory management. CPU scheduling is the selection of one process from the ready queue. The cpu is allocated to the selected process by the dispatcher.

First-Come-First-Served scheduling is the simplest scheduling algorithm, but it can cause short jobs to wait for very long jobs. Shortest-Job-First scheduling is provably optimal, providing the shortest average waiting time. Shortest-Job-First is difficult to implement because it is difficult to predict the length of the next cpu burst. Shortest-Job-First is a special case of the general priority scheduling algorithm, which simply allocates the cpu to the highest priority process. Both priority and Shortest-Job-First scheduling may suffer from starvation. Aging is a technique to prevent starvation.

Round-robin scheduling is more appropriate for a time-shared system. Round-robin is a preemptive algorithm; FCFS is non-preemptive. Shortest-Job-First and priority algorithms may be either preemptive or non-preemptive. Round-robin allocates the cpu to the first process in the ready queue for q time units, where q is the time quantum. After q time units, the cpu is preempted and the process is put at the tail of the ready queue. The major problem is the selection of the time quantum. If the quantum is too large, round-robin degenerates to FCFS scheduling; if the quantum is too small, scheduling overhead in the form of context switch time becomes excessive.

Multiple queue algorithms allow different algorithms to be used for various classes of jobs. The most common is a foreground interactive queue, scheduled round-robin, and a background batch queue, scheduled FCFS. Feedback queues allow jobs to move from one queue to another.

The wide variety of scheduling algorithms demands an ability to select between them. Analytic methods use mathematical analysis to determine the performance of an algorithm. Simulation methods determine performance by imitating the scheduling algorithm on a "representative" sample of processes and computing the resulting performance.

Exercises

4.1 Describe the differences between short-term, medium-term, and long-term scheduling.

4.2 What advantage is there in having different quantum sizes on different levels of a multi-level queueing system?

4.3 Explain the operation of multi-level scheduling.

4.4 What are some scheduling decisions which must be taken *above* the level of cpu scheduling?

4.5 Which of the following are reasonable long-term scheduling algorithms and which are reasonable short-term scheduling algorithms?

    a. First-Come-First-Served.

    b. Round-robin.

    c. Shortest-Job-First.

    d. Highest-Priority-First.

    e. Longest-Job-First.

    f. Last-Come-First-Served.

4.6 Assume you have the following jobs to execute with one processor:

Job	Burst Time	Priority
1	10	3
2	1	1
3	2	3
4	1	4
5	5	2

The jobs are assumed to have arrived in the order 1, 2, 3, 4, 5.

    a. Give a Gantt chart illustrating the execution of these jobs using First-Come-First-Served, Round-robin (quantum = 1), Shortest-Job-First, and a non-preemptive priority scheduling algorithm.

    b. What is the turnaround time of each job for each of the above scheduling algorithms?

    c. What is the waiting time of each job for each of the above scheduling algorithms?

    d. What is the schedule with the minimal average waiting time (over all jobs)?

4.7 Define the difference between preemptive and non-preemptive scheduling. State why strict non-preemptive scheduling is unlikely to be used in a computer center.

4.8 Suppose the following jobs arrive for processing at the times indicated. Each job will run the listed amount of time. What is the average turnaround time for these jobs? Use non-preemptive scheduling and base all decisions on the information you have at the time the decision must be made.

Job	Arrival Time	Burst Time
1	0.0	8
2	0.4	4
3	1.0	1

a. FCFS.

b. Shortest-Job-First.

c. Shortest-Job-First is supposed to improve performance, but notice that we choose to run job 1 at time 0 because we did not know that two shorter jobs would arrive shortly. Compute average turnaround time if the cpu is left idle for the first 1 unit and then Shortest-Job-First scheduling is used. Remember that job 1 and job 2 are waiting during this idle time so their waiting time may increase. This algorithm could be known as Future Knowledge Scheduling.

4.9 Consider a round-robin scheduling algorithm where the entries in the ready queue are pointers to the process control blocks.

a. What would be the effect of putting two pointers to the same process in the ready queue?   *would get 2x the cpu time*

b. What would be the advantages and disadvantages of this scheme?   *not fair. —defeats purpose*
   get the job done faster

c. How would you modify the basic round-robin algorithm to achieve the same effect without the duplicate pointers?
   priority, double the quantum time

4.10 Give an equation to relate the following three times for a job.
   Q length
   $$n = \lambda W$$

a. Turnaround time.

b. CPU busy time.

c. Waiting time.

$$T = W + C$$

4.11 Many cpu scheduling algorithms are parameterized. For example, the round-robin algorithm requires a parameter to indicate the time slice. Multi-level feedback queues require parameters to define the number of queues, the scheduling algorithms for each queue, and the criteria used to move jobs between queues, and so on.

This means that these algorithms are really sets of algorithms (for example, the set of round-robin algorithms for all time slices, and so on). It may be that one set of algorithms includes another (for example, FCFS is round-robin with an infinite time quantum). What (if any) relation holds between the following pairs of sets of algorithms?

a. Priority, Shortest-Job-First.

b. Multi-level feedback queues, FCFS.

c. Priority, FCFS.

d. Round-robin, Shortest-Job-First.

4.12 Kleinrock has described a preemptive priority scheduling algorithm based on dynamically changing priorities. Larger priority numbers imply higher priority. When a job is waiting for the cpu (in the ready queue, but not running), its priority changes at a rate α; when it is running its priority changes at a rate β. All processes are given a priority of 0 when they enter the ready queue. The parameters α and β can be set to give many different scheduling algorithms.

a. What is the algorithm which results from $\beta > \alpha > 0$?

b. What is the algorithm which results from $\alpha < \beta < 0$?

4.13 A cpu scheduling algorithm determines an order for the execution of its scheduled jobs. Given n jobs to be scheduled on one processor, how many possible different schedules are there? Give a formula in terms of n.

4.14 Suppose a scheduling algorithm (at the level of short-term cpu scheduling) favors those programs which have used little processor time in the recent past. Why will this algorithm favor I/O-bound programs and yet not permanently starve cpu-bound programs?

4.15 Explain the differences in the degree to which the following scheduling algorithms discriminate in favor of short jobs.

  a. First-Come-First-Served.

  b. Round-robin.

  c. Multi-level feedback queues.

4.16 Differentiate between a multi-level feedback scheduling algorithm and a multi-queue (foreground/background) cpu scheduling algorithm which uses round-robin for the foreground and a preemptive priority algorithm for the background.

Bibliographic Notes

General discussions concerning scheduling have been written by Lampson [1968], Coffman and Kleinrock [1968a], Bull and Packham [1971, Chapter 2], Colin [1971, Chapter 15], Hoare and Perrott [1972], Lister [1979, Section 8.4], and Bunt [1976]. More formal treatments of scheduling theory are contained in Conway et al. [1967], Coffman and Denning [1973] and Kleinrock [1975].

Job scheduling has been discussed by Abell et al. [1970], Browne et al. [1972], and Coffman and Kleinrock [1968a]. Sayers [1971], Hoare and Perrott [1972] and Lorin [1972] also presented general discussions on job scheduling.

Process scheduling has been discussed by Oppenheimer and Weizer [1968], Lampson [1968], Coffman and Kleinrock [1968a], Kleinrock [1970], Baskett [1971], Brinch Hansen [1971], Varney [1971] and Buzen [1971, 1973].

Priority cpu scheduling has been discussed by Lampson [1968], Coffman and Kleinrock [1968a] and Kleinrock [1970]. Multi-level feedback queues were originally implemented on the CTSS system in 1962 [Corbato et al. 1962]. This queueing system was analyzed by Schrage [1967]; variations on multi-level feedback queues were studied by Coffman and Kleinrock [1968b]. Additional studies were presented by Coffman and Denning [1973] and Svobodova [1976]. Multi-level queues were implemented in the TOPS-10 operating system for the DEC-10.

Dispatching has been discussed by Shaw [1974, Section 7.5] and Tsichritzis and Bernstein [1974, Section 3.3]. Implementation issues concerning a dispatcher were discussed by Brinch Hansen [1973a, Section 4.2]. General implementation issues are discussed by Tsichritzis and Bernstein [1974, Section 3.4], Habermann [1976, Section 6.5] and Calingaert [1982, Section 3.6].

Lynch [1972c] gave a discussion of the practical aspects and goals of performance evaluation. A survey on performance evaluation was written by Lucas [1971]. Discussions concerning queueing system models have been given by McKinney [1969], Coffman and Denning [1973, Chapter 3], Brinch Hansen [1973a, Chapter 6], Muntz [1975] and Habermann [1976, Chapter 6].

5

Memory Management

In Chapter 4, we showed how the cpu can be shared by a set of processes. As a result of cpu scheduling, we can improve both the utilization of the cpu and the speed of the computer's response to its users. To realize this increase in performance, however, we must keep several processes in memory; we must *share* memory.

In this chapter, we discuss various ways to manage memory. The memory management algorithms vary from a primitive bare-machine approach to paging and segmentation strategies. Each approach has its own advantages and disadvantages.

5.1 Preliminaries

Memory is central to the operation of a modern computer system. As shown in Figure 5.1, both the cpu and I/O system interact with memory. Memory is a large array of words or bytes, each with its own address. Interaction is achieved through a sequence of reads or writes to specific memory addresses. The cpu fetches from and stores in memory.

In most cases, a user program goes through several steps before being executed (Figure 5.2). Addresses may be represented in different ways during these steps. Addresses in the source program are generally

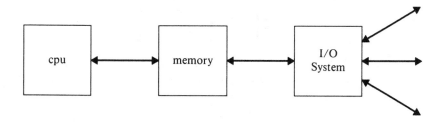

Figure 5.1 Central nature of memory in a computer system

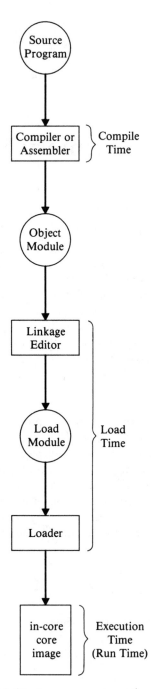

Figure 5.2   Multi-step processing of a user program

symbolic (such as *x*). A compiler will typically *bind* these symbolic addresses to relocatable addresses (such as 14 bytes from the beginning of this module). The linkage editor or loader will in turn bind these relocatable addresses to absolute addresses (such as 74014). Each binding is a mapping from one address space to another.

A program must eventually be mapped to absolute addresses and loaded into memory to be executed. As the program executes, it accesses program instructions and data from memory by generating these absolute addresses. Eventually, the program terminates, its memory space is declared available, and the next program may be loaded and executed.

A typical instruction execution cycle, for example, will first fetch an instruction from memory. The instruction will be decoded and may cause operands to be fetched from memory. After executing the instruction on the operands, results may be stored back in memory. Notice that the memory unit sees only a stream of memory addresses; it does not know how they are generated (the program counter, indexing, indirection, literal addresses, and so on) or what they are for (instructions or data). Accordingly we can ignore *how* a memory address is generated by a program; the program can use any programming technique it wants to generate its addresses. We are interested only in the sequence of memory addresses generated by the running program.

In this chapter, we consider many different memory management schemes. These schemes reflect various approaches to memory management, and the effectiveness of the different algorithms depends on the particular situation. Selection of a memory management scheme for a specific system depends upon many factors, but especially upon the *hardware* design of the system. Each algorithm requires its own hardware support. We begin with the least complex hardware and work slowly up to more complex and sophisticated schemes.

5.2 Bare Machine

By far the simplest memory management scheme is *none*. The user is provided with the bare machine and has complete control over the entire memory space (Figure 5.3).

This approach has some definite advantages. It provides maximum flexibility to the user: the user can control the use of memory in whatever manner desired. It has maximum simplicity and minimum cost. There is no need for special hardware for this approach to memory management. Nor is there a need for operating system software.

This system has its limitations also: it provides no services. The user has complete control over the computer, but the operating system

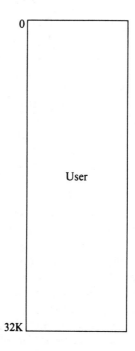

Figure 5.3   Bare machine

has no control over interrupts, no resident monitor to process system calls or errors, and no space to provide control card sequencing or job sequencing. Hence the bare-machine approach has its limitations. It is generally used only on dedicated systems where the users require flexibility and simplicity and are willing to program their own support routines.

5.3 Resident Monitor

The next simplest scheme is to divide memory into two sections, one for the user and one for the resident monitor of the operating system (Figure 5.4). It is possible to place the resident monitor in either low memory or high memory. The major factor affecting this decision is generally the location of the interrupt vector. Since the interrupt vector is often in low memory, it is more common to place the resident monitor in low memory. Thus we will only discuss the situation where

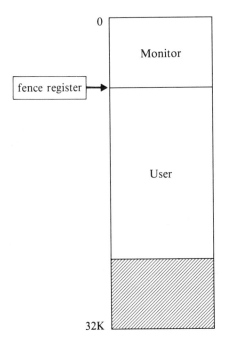

Figure 5.4   Resident monitor

the monitor is in low memory; the development of the other situation is similar.

This approach was used in the Fortran Monitoring System for the 7094, one of the first "operating systems". It is the primary approach for many current microcomputer systems, such as CP/M.

5.3.1 Protection Hardware

If the monitor is residing in low memory and a user program is executing in high memory, we need to protect the monitor code and data from changes (accidental or malicious) by the user program. This protection must be provided by the hardware and can be implemented in several ways. The general approach is shown in Figure 5.5. Every address (instruction or data) generated by the user program is compared with a *fence* address. If the generated address is greater than or equal to the fence, then it is a legitimate reference to user memory and is sent to the memory unit as usual. If the generated address is less than the fence, however, the address is an illegal reference to monitor memory. The reference is intercepted and a trap to the operating system is generated (addressing error). The operating system will then take the appropriate action (generally terminating the program with an appropriate error message and memory dump).

Notice that *every* reference to memory by the user program must be checked. In general, this checking will slow every memory access by the time of comparison; thus a memory reference may take 995 nanoseconds instead of 980 nanoseconds. Careful circuit design can often overlap this comparison with other activities to reduce the effective access time.

The operating system, executing in monitor mode, is generally given unrestricted access to both monitor and user memory. This provision allows the operating system to load user programs into user memory, dump them out in case of errors, access and modify parameters of system calls, and so on.

A major difference in computer systems is the way in which the fence address is specified. One approach is to build it into the hardware as a fixed constant. For example, on the HP 2116B computer, the basic binary loader was stored in locations 77700 to 77777 (high memory of a 32K word machine). During user program execution, it was not possible

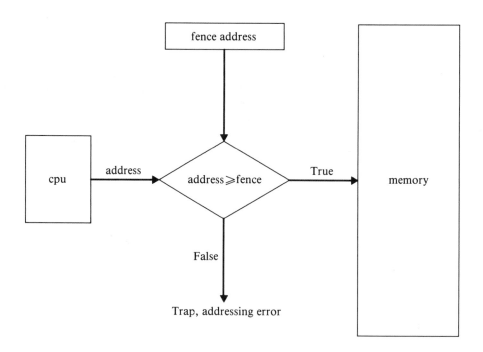

Figure 5.5   Hardware address protection for a resident monitor

to access any location above location 77700; the fence value was built into the hardware.

The difficulty with a fixed, hardware-supplied fence address is the selection of a correct address. If the address is too small, the monitor is not completely protected; if the address is too large, memory that is not needed by the monitor is protected, and hence unavailable to the user. Aggravating the problem is the fact that the monitor, like all software, will change over time, growing bigger or smaller. Hence the "correct" fence value today may not be correct tomorrow.

To solve this problem, a *fence register* is commonly used. The fence register contains the address of the fence and is used to check the correctness of all user memory references. It can be loaded by the operating system by using a special privileged instruction. The fence register can only be loaded by a program executing in monitor mode. This scheme allows the monitor to change the value of the fence register whenever the size of the monitor changes.

5.3.2 Relocation

Another problem to consider is the loading of user programs. Although the address space of the computer starts at 00000, the first address of the user program is not 00000, but the first address beyond the fence. This arrangement may affect the addresses that the user program uses. Classically, the binding of instructions and data to memory addresses can be done at either at compile time or load time. If the fence address is known at compile time, absolute code can be generated. This code will start at the fence and extend up from there. If the fence address subsequently changes, however, it will be necessary to recompile this code. As an alternative, the compiler may generate relocatable code. In this case, binding is delayed until load time. If the fence address changes, the user code need only be reloaded in order to incorporate this changed value.

In both cases, however, the fence must be *static* during the execution of the program. Clearly, if the user addresses are bound to physical addresses by use of the fence, then these addresses will be invalid if the fence changes. Thus the fence can only be moved when no user program is executing. There are cases, however, when it is desirable to change the size of the monitor (and hence the fence location) during program execution. For example, the monitor contains code and buffer space for device drivers. If a device driver (or other operating system service) is not commonly used, it is undesirable to keep that code and data in memory, since we might be able to use that space for other purposes. Such code is sometimes called *transient* monitor code; it comes

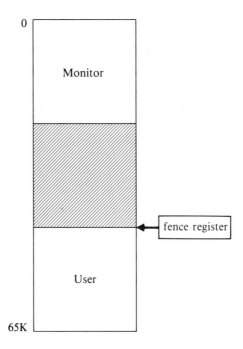

Figure 5.6   Loading the user into high memory

and goes as needed. Thus using this code changes the size of the monitor during program execution.

There are two ways to modify the basic scheme that we have presented to allow the monitor size to change dynamically. An early PDP-11 operating system used the approach shown in Figure 5.6. The user was loaded into high memory down towards the fence, rather than from the fence towards high memory. The advantage here is that all unused space is in the middle and either the user or the monitor can expand into this unused memory, as necessary.

A more general approach, used on the CDC 6600 computers, is to delay address binding until *execution* time. This dynamic relocation scheme requires slightly different hardware support, as illustrated in Figure 5.7. The fence register is now called a *relocation* or *base* register. The value in the base register is *added* to every address generated by a user process at the time it is sent to memory. For example, if the fence is at 1400, then an attempt by the user to address location 0 is dynamically relocated to location 1400; an access to location 346 is relocated to location 1746.

Notice that the user never sees the *real* physical addresses. The user can create a pointer to location 346, store it in memory, manipulate it, compare it to other addresses -- all as the number 346. Only when it is used as a memory address (in an indirect load or store perhaps) is it relocated relative to the base register. The user program deals with *logical* addresses. The memory mapping hardware converts logical addresses into physical addresses.

For this hardware, a change in the fence only requires changing the base register and *moving* all user memory to the correct locations relative to the new fence value. This scheme may require a significant amount of memory to be copied, but it allows the fence to be changed at any time.

Notice also that we now have two different types of addresses: logical addresses (in the range 0 to *max*) and physical addresses (in the range $R+0$ to $R+max$ for a fence value R). The user generates only logical addresses and thinks that the program runs in locations 0 to *max*.

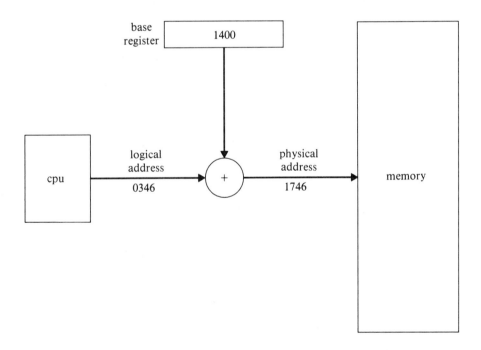

Figure 5.7   Dynamic relocation using a relocation register

The operating system knows better and can access physical memory directly in monitor mode. All information passed from the user program to the operating system (such as buffer addresses in system calls) must be explicitly relocated by operating system software before it is used. This necessity is especially true for addresses given to the I/O devices. The user supplies logical addresses; these logical addresses must be mapped to physical addresses before they are used.

The concept of a *logical address space* which is mapped to a separate *physical address space* is central to proper memory management.

5.4 Swapping

The resident monitor memory management scheme may seem of little use since it appears to be inherently single-user. However, it was the basic scheme used in two early time-sharing systems: the CTSS and the Q-32 system. These systems used a resident monitor with the remainder of memory available to the currently executing user. When they switched to the next user, the current contents of user memory were

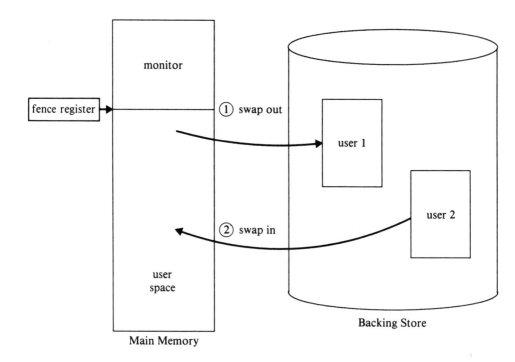

Figure 5.8   Swapping two users using a drum as a backing store

written out to a backing store (a disk or drum), and the memory of the next user was read in. This scheme is called *swapping* (Figure 5.8).

5.4.1 Backing Store

Swapping requires a *backing store*. The backing store is commonly a fast drum or disk. It must be large enough to accommodate copies of all memory images for all users, and must provide direct access to these memory images. The ready queue consists of all processes whose memory images are on the backing store and which are ready to run. A separate system variable indicates which process is currently in memory. Whenever the cpu scheduler decides to execute a process, it calls the dispatcher. The dispatcher checks to see whether that process is in memory; if not, it swaps out the process currently in memory and swaps in the desired process. It then reloads registers as normal and transfers control to the selected process.

5.4.2 Swap Time

It should be clear that the context switch time in such a swapping system is fairly high. To get an idea of the context switch time, assume that the user program is 20K words and the backing store is a fixed head drum with an average latency of 8 milliseconds and a transfer rate of 250,000 words per second. Then a transfer of the 20K-word program to or from memory takes:

$$8 \text{ msec} + (20K \text{ words} / 250,000 \text{ words/sec}) = 8 \text{ msec} + (2/25) \text{ sec}$$
$$= 8 \text{ msec} + (2000/25) \text{ msec}$$
$$= 88 \text{ msec}$$

Since we must both swap out and swap in, the total swap time is then about 176 milliseconds.

In the Q-32 time-sharing system, a drum with an average latency of 10 milliseconds and a transfer rate of 363,000 words per second was used, resulting in an expected swap time of 130 milliseconds for 20K words.

For efficient cpu utilization, we want our execution time for each process to be long relative to the swap time. Thus in a round-robin cpu scheduling algorithm, for example, the time quantum should be substantially larger than 0.176 seconds.

Notice that the major part of the swap time is transfer time. The total transfer time is directly proportional to the *amount* of memory swapped. If we have a 32K computer system with a resident monitor of 12K, the maximum user program is 20K. However, many user programs may be much smaller than this size, say 4K. A 4K program could be swapped out in only 24 milliseconds, compared to the 88 milliseconds for swapping 20K. Therefore, it would be useful to know exactly how much memory a user program *is* using, not simply how much it *might be* using. Then we would only need to swap what is actually used, reducing swap time. For this scheme to be effective, the user must keep the monitor informed of any changes in memory requirements. Thus a program with dynamic memory requirements will need to issue system calls (Request Memory/Release Memory) to inform the monitor of its changing memory needs.

The effectiveness of swapping can also be improved by increasing the backing store performance. Consider, for example, IBM's Large Core Storage (LCS) and CDC's Extended Core Storage (ECS). LCS has an access time of 8 microseconds and a 400,000 word per second transfer rate. LCS takes only 100 milliseconds to swap 20K out and in. ECS has an access time of 3 microseconds and a transfer rate of 10,000,000 words per second. Total swap time for 20K words is thus only 4 milliseconds. New mass core, mass semiconductor, and bubble memories allow similarly speedy swaps from main memory to backing store.

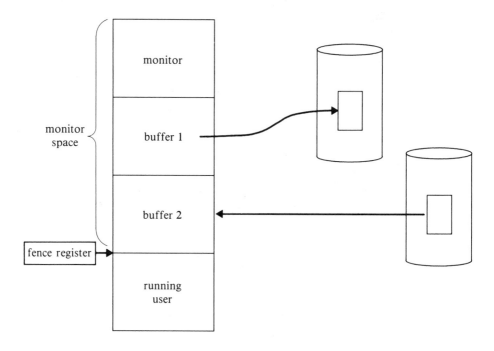

Figure 5.9   Overlapped swapping

5.4.3 Overlapped Swapping

The effect of swapping on the context switch time can be further
reduced by overlapping the swapping and program execution. Consider
the scheme shown in Figure 5.9. The objective is to overlap the
swapping of one process with the execution of another. Thus the cpu
will not sit idle while swapping is going on. While one user program is
executing, the previous user program is being swapped out from buffer
1, and the next user program to be executed is being swapped into
buffer 2.

Notice, however, that after the current user program releases the
cpu, we must move the next user program from buffer 2 to the user
region, before it can be executed. The program currently in the user
region must also be moved into one of the buffers for swapping. If this
was not done, we could only execute the program in buffer 2 by moving
the fence, as shown in Figure 5.10. The previous user program (in the
user region) is then exposed to improper modification by the program in
buffer 2. Thus we must do a memory-to-memory swap.

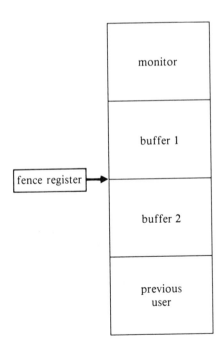

Figure 5.10   Attempting to execute a program by moving the fence

This approach is also somewhat limited if truly high-speed swapping devices are used. ECS, for example, has a transfer rate equal to the speed of main memory. When ECS is transferring, there are no remaining memory cycles for the cpu to use. Thus cpu operation is completely halted whenever ECS is used, and cpu/swap overlap is not possible.

There are other constraints on swapping also. If we want to swap a process, we must be sure that it is completely idle. Of particular concern is any pending I/O. If a process waits for an I/O operation, we may want to swap that process to free up its memory. However, if the I/O is asynchronously accessing the user memory for I/O buffers, then the process cannot be swapped. Assume that the I/O operation was queued, because the device was busy. If we swap out process 1 and swap in process 2, the I/O operation may then attempt to use memory which now belongs to process 2. The two main solutions to this problem are either (1) never swap a process with pending I/O, or (2) execute I/O operations only into operating system buffers. Transfers between operating system and user memory occur only when the process is swapped in.

5.5 Multiple Partitions

The memory configuration resulting from overlapped swapping is effectively the same as the memory configuration for multiprogramming: more than one program is in memory at the same time. For multiprogramming, the cpu is switched rapidly back and forth between these programs. The memory management problem is to allocate memory to the many programs which may be in the job pool to be executed.

Memory is divided into a number of *regions* or *partitions*. Each region may have one program to be executed. Thus the degree of multiprogramming is bounded by the number of regions. When a region is free, a program is selected from the job queue and loaded into the free region. When it terminates, the region becomes available for another program.

Two major memory management schemes are possible. Each approach divides memory into a number of *regions* or *partitions*. The major distinction between the two approaches is whether the regions are static or dynamic. These schemes are *multiple contiguous fixed partition allocation* and *multiple contiguous variable partition allocation*. The two most widely known examples of these algorithms are the MFT (multiprogramming with a fixed number of tasks) and MVT (multiprogramming with a variable number of tasks) versions of IBM's OS/360 operating system. For brevity we use these acronyms to denote these two main classes of algorithms.

5.5.1 Protection Hardware

As we saw in Section 1.8.2, and again in Figure 5.10, however, we must first provide a way to protect the code and data in one region from programs in other regions. What is needed is an ability to protect the memory space *before* and *after* an executing program. This protection can be provided by using *two* registers, as illustrated in Figure 5.11.

These two registers provide the upper and lower bounds on the addresses which can be legally generated by a user program. They can be defined in either of two ways:

- **Bounds registers**. The values of the smallest and largest physical addresses (for example, lower bound = 100040 and upper bound =

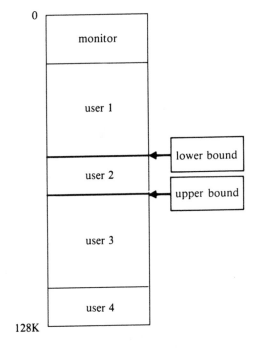

Figure 5.11   Two bounds registers define a logical address space

174640). Legal user addresses range from the lower bound to the upper bound.

- **Base and limit registers**. The value of the smallest physical address and the range of logical addresses (for example, *base* = 100040 and *limit* = 74600). Legal user addresses range from 0 to the *limit* and are dynamically relocated to physical addresses ranging from *base* to *base* + *limit*.

As shown in Figure 5.12, the hardware for using these two registers differs slightly. Bounds registers require static relocation, at assembly or load time. Each logical address must be greater than or equal to the lower bound and less than the upper bound. With base and limit registers, each logical address must be less than the limit register, and is then *dynamically* relocated by adding the value in the base register. This relocated address is sent to memory. The CDC 6600 computer and its descendants use base and limit registers.

5.5.2 Fixed Regions (MFT)

In MFT, the region sizes are fixed, and do not change as the system runs. For example, a memory of 32K words might be divided into regions of the following sizes:

Resident Monitor	10K
Very small jobs	4K
Average jobs	6K
Large jobs	12K

MFT Job Scheduling

As jobs enter the system, they are put into a job queue. The job scheduler takes into account the memory requirements of each job and the available regions in determining which jobs are allocated memory. When a job is allocated space, it is loaded into a region (relocating it if necessary). It can then compete for the cpu. When a job terminates, it releases its memory region, which the job scheduler may then fill with another job from the job queue.

A number of variations are possible in the allocation of memory to jobs. One strategy is to classify all jobs on entry to the system, according to their memory requirements. This classification can be done by requiring the user to specify the maximum amount of memory required. Alternatively, the system can attempt to determine memory

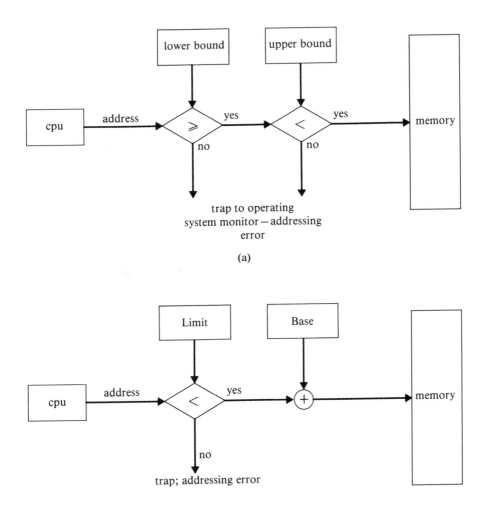

Figure 5.12　(a) Bounds registers and (b) Base/Limit registers

requirements automatically. For example, a prepass of the control cards may be used to determine the maximum memory requirement. Each memory region has its own job queue (Figure 5.13). The job classification is used to select the appropriate queue for the job.

For example, if we have three user memory regions, of sizes 2K, 6K, and 12K, we need three queues: Q2, Q6, and Q12. An incoming job requiring 5K of memory would be appended to Q6; a new job needing

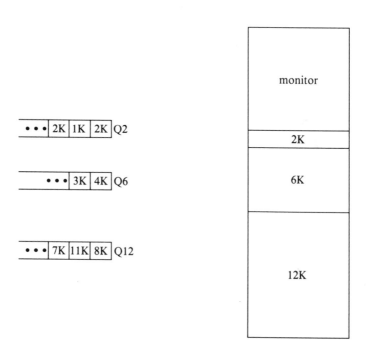

Figure 5.13   MFT with separate queues for each region

10K would be put in Q12; a job of 2K would go in Q2. Each queue is scheduled separately. Since each queue has its own memory region, there is no competition between queues for memory.

Another approach is to throw all jobs into one queue (Figure 5.14). The job scheduler selects the next job to be run and waits until a memory region of that size is available. Suppose that we had a FCFS job scheduler, the job queue of Figure 5.14, and regions of 2K, 6K, and 12K. We would first assign job 1 to the 6K region and job 2 to the 2K region. Since our next job requires 3K, we need the 6K region. Since the 6K region is being used by job 1, we must wait until job 1 terminates; then job 3 will be allocated the 6K region. Job 4 must wait until job 3 is scheduled (since our job scheduler is FCFS) even though the region for job 4 is free.

An immediately obvious variant of this scheme tries to keep memory regions from sitting idle. Thus when a region becomes available, we _skip_ down the job queue looking for the first job which can fit into that region. We schedule this job, even if higher-priority (but larger) jobs are waiting before it in the job queue. These higher-priority jobs cannot use the available region, since they are too large. Thus we are not preventing them from advancing by starting a smaller (but lower-priority) job.

Another variant considers the following question: Why are we keeping job 3 waiting when there is an idle region which is large enough to run job 3? We can obviously schedule job 3 in the 12K region. While it is true that job 3 could run in the 6K region, this region happens to be occupied. Should we schedule job 3 in the 12K region (wasting space) or should it wait while the lower-priority job 4 (which can *only* run in the 12K region) is scheduled? If we decide to run job 4, making job 3 wait, what do we do when job 4 terminates? Do we let the 12K region sit idle (reserved for any large job which may arrive) or do we use it for some job which could run in a smaller region?

These decisions reflect the choice between a *best-fit-only* or a *best-available-fit* job memory allocation policy.

Still another variation on MFT is created by adding swapping. If we have several jobs that each fit in a given region, we can swap them in and out of that region. For example, assume that we have 4 regions, each with a round-robin cpu scheduling algorithm. When a quantum

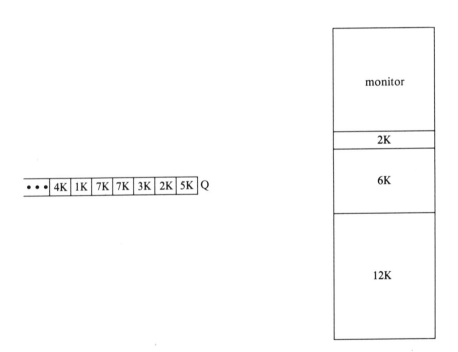

Figure 5.14   MFT with a unified queue

expires, the memory manager would start to swap out the job which just finished, and swap in another job for this region. In the meantime, the cpu scheduler would allocate a time slice to some job in another region. When each job finishes its quantum, it is swapped with another job for that region. Hopefully, the memory manager can swap jobs fast enough that there are always jobs in memory, ready to execute, when the cpu scheduler wants to reschedule the cpu.

A variant of this swapping policy is used for priority-based scheduling algorithms. If a higher-priority job arrives and wants service, the memory manager can swap out the lower-priority job in order to load and execute the higher-priority job. When the higher-priority job finishes, the lower-priority job can be swapped back in and continued. This variant of swapping is sometimes called *roll-out/roll-in*.

Normally a job which is swapped out in MFT will be swapped back in to the same region. This restriction is dictated both by the region allocation policy and by the method of relocation. If relocation is done at assembly or load time (static relocation), then the job cannot be moved to a different region. With dynamic relocation, such as with base/limit registers, it is possible to swap a job into a different region.

We saw in Chapter 2 that a running program may be able to issue requests for more memory (*Getmain/Freemain* on the IBM systems, for example). This provision allows a program to determine its memory requirements dynamically, based upon its input data, rather than statically. However, this ability can cause problems for an MFT memory management policy. Assume that we have a job of 4K placed in a region of 6K. The job can request and release memory freely, as long as it does not request more than 6K (the region size) at one time. Notice that these requests have no real influence on the amount of memory allocated to the job. The job always has 6K of memory, even if it only uses 4K.

What can the system do if the job requests still more memory? There are three main possibilities:

- We can *terminate* the job. If we require the user to state the maximum amount of memory that the job will need, and we use this value to select a region, then a request for memory space in excess of this region is a run-time error.

- We can simply *return* control to the user program, with a status indicator that no more memory exists. The user program can then either quit or modify its operation to work in the space available. Many algorithms exhibit a space-time tradeoff: more space allows the program to run faster, but it can run (more slowly) in less memory space.

- We can (1) *swap* out the job, (2) wait for a larger region to be available, (3) swap into the larger region (relocating the job as necessary), and (4) continue execution. This solution is only possible when the hardware supports dynamic relocation, and can be quite expensive, but it provides the maximum flexibility for programs to modify their memory requirements as necessary.

Remember also that if the operating system is kept informed by the application program of the actual amount of memory that it needs, swapping time can be reduced. If a program is allocated a region of 12K, but is only using 8K, then only 8K needs to be swapped.

Region Size Selection

Another design problem with MFT involves the determination of the sizes of the regions. If we have 32K total memory and a 10K resident monitor, we are left with 22K to partition among the users. We must decide how many regions of what size to create. The initial decision is generally based on an educated guess of the memory requirements of the input programs. For a batch system running small I/O utilities (from 1K to 3K), an 8K Fortran compiler, and a 4K assembler, we might create a 10K region to allow compilation and other large programs and two 4K regions for I/O and assembly programs. Since this partition leaves 4K unallocated, we might increase the 10K region to 14K, or one 4K region to 8K, or both 4K regions to 6K.

Once the system is operational, we can collect information about the number and sizes of the jobs which are actually run. These statistics may indicate that a different set of regions would be better.

The major problem with MFT is finding a good fit between the region sizes and the actual memory requirements of jobs. The overall performance of the computer system is generally proportional to the multiprogramming level; the multiprogramming level is directly affected by how well we manage memory. If half of memory is not being used, then we could run twice as many jobs by finding a way to use that space.

Memory Fragmentation

A job which needs m words of memory may be run in a region of n words, where $n \geq m$. The difference between these two numbers $(n - m)$ is *internal fragmentation*, memory which is internal to a region, but is not being used. *External fragmentation* occurs when a region is unused and available, but too small for any waiting job. Both types of fragmentation are sources of memory waste in MFT.

For example, suppose that we break a 22K user space into a 10K region and three 4K regions. If our job queue contains jobs requiring 7K, 3K, 6K, and 6K, we can allocate the 7K job to the 10K region (producing 3K of internal fragmentation) and the 3K job to one of the 4K regions (producing 1K of internal fragmentation). Since the two remaining jobs are too large for the two available regions, we are left with two unusable regions of 4K each, a total of 8K of external fragmentation. Our total fragmentation, both internal and external, is 12K, more than half our memory.

If we divide memory into regions of 10K, 8K, and 4K, we could run the 7K job in the 8K region and the 3K job in the 4K region, producing 2K of internal fragmentation. Depending upon our job scheduler we would make both 6K jobs wait (producing 10K of external fragmentation) or run one of them in the 10K region. If we run one job, we will produce an additional 4K of internal fragmentation, but will eliminate the external fragmentation. If our regions just matched the job sizes, we would be able to run all 4 jobs with neither internal nor external fragmentation.

5.5.3 Variable Partitions (MVT)

The main problem with MFT is determining the best region sizes to minimize internal and external fragmentation. Unfortunately, with a dynamic set of jobs to run, there is probably no *one* right partition of memory. For example, suppose that 120K of memory is available for user programs and that all user jobs are 20K, *except* one big job of 80K, which runs once a day. We must allocate an 80K region to allow this program to run, but since all other jobs are 20K, we are faced with 60K (half of the user memory space) of internal fragmentation, except when that one big job is run once a day.

The solution to this problem is to allow the region sizes to vary *dynamically*. This approach is called multiple contiguous *variable* partition allocation. We use MVT to denote this class of memory management algorithms, after OS/360 MVT (multiprogramming with a variable number of tasks).

MVT memory management is fairly simple: The operating system keeps a table indicating which parts of memory are available and which are occupied. Initially, all memory is available for user programs, and is considered as one large block of available memory, a *hole*. When a job arrives and needs memory, we search for a hole large enough for this job. If we find one, we allocate only as much as is needed, keeping the rest available to satisfy future requests.

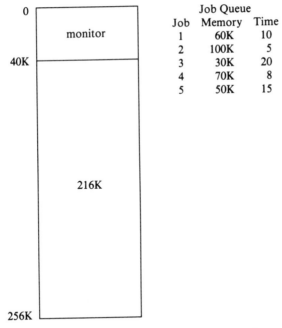

Figure 5.15   MVT scheduling example

For example, assume that we have 256K memory available and a
resident monitor of 40K. This situation leaves 216K for user programs,
as shown in Figure 5.15. Given the job queue in the figure, and FCFS
job scheduling, we can immediately allocate memory to jobs 1, 2, and 3,
creating the memory map of Figure 5.16(a). We have 26K of external
fragmentation. Using a round-robin cpu scheduling algorithm with a
quantum of 1 time unit, job 2 will terminate at time 14, releasing its
memory allocation. This situation is illustrated in Figure 5.16(b). We
then return to our job queue and schedule the next job, job 4, to
produce the memory map of Figure 5.16(c). Job 1 will terminate at time
28 to produce Figure 5.16(d), and job 5 is then scheduled, producing
Figure 5.16(e).

This example illustrates several points about MVT. In general, there
is at any time a *set* of holes, of various sizes, scattered throughout
memory. When a job arrives and needs memory, we search this set for a
hole that is large enough for this job. If the hole is too large, it is split
into two: one part is allocated to the arriving job; the other is returned
to the set of holes. When a job terminates, it releases its block of

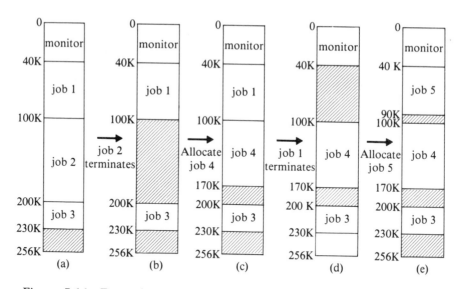

Figure 5.16   Example memory allocation and job scheduling for MVT

memory, which is then placed back in the set of holes. If the new hole is adjacent to other holes, we would merge these adjacent holes to form one larger hole. At this point we may need to check whether there are jobs waiting for memory and whether this newly freed and recombined memory could satisfy the demands of any of these waiting jobs.

This scheme is a particular application of the general *dynamic storage allocation* problem, discussed in Section 3.4.2. The most common algorithms for allocating memory are *first-fit* and *best-fit*.

Once a block of memory has been allocated to a job, its program can be loaded into that space and executed. The minimal hardware support needed is the same as with MFT: two registers containing the upper and lower bounds of the region of memory allocated to this job. When the cpu scheduler selects this process, the dispatcher loads these bounds registers with the correct values. Since every address generated by the cpu is checked against these registers, we can protect other users' programs and data from being modified by this running process.

Notice that *software* determines the difference between MFT and MVT; the *hardware* is identical.

Another problem that arises with MVT is illustrated by Figure 5.17. Consider the hole of 18,464 bytes. If the next job requests 18,462 bytes, what do we do? If we allocate exactly the requested block, we are left with a hole of 2 bytes. The overhead to keep track of this hole will be substantially larger than the hole itself. The general approach is to allocate very small holes as part of the larger request. Thus the allocated memory may be slightly larger than the requested memory, reintroducing one small amount of internal fragmentation. For example, the CDC 6600 allocates memory only in 64-word quantities, the IBM 360 allocates in 2-Kbyte quantities, and the PDP-11 uses an 8-word minimum block.

MVT Job Scheduling

As with MFT, MVT interacts strongly with job scheduling. At any given time, we have a list of available block sizes and a queue of jobs requesting memory. The job scheduler can order the job queue according to a scheduling algorithm. Memory is allocated to jobs until, finally, the memory requirements of the next job cannot be satisfied; no available block of memory (hole) is large enough. The job scheduler can then wait until a large enough block is available, or it can skip down the job queue to see if the smaller memory requirements of some lower-

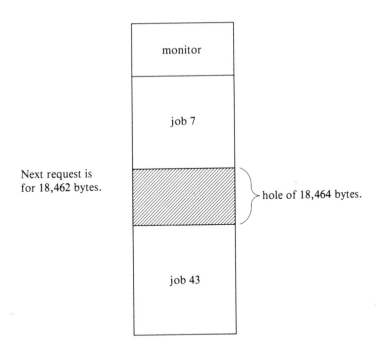

Figure 5.17   Allocation is in some multiple of bytes

priority job can be met. This decision produces a choice between cpu scheduling with or without skip.

Memory utilization is generally better for MVT than for MFT. There is little or no internal fragmentation in MVT, since the regions are created to be the size requested by the job. However, we can have external fragmentation. Looking back at Figure 5.16, we can see two such situations. In Figure 5.16(a), there is a total external fragmentation of 26K, a space that is too small to satisfy any job request. In Figure 5.16(c), however, we have a total external fragmentation of 56K (= 30K + 26K). This space would be large enough to run job 5 (which needs 50K) *except* this free memory is not contiguous. The free memory space is fragmented into two pieces, neither one of which is large enough, by itself, to satisfy the memory request of job 5.

This fragmentation problem can be quite severe. In the worst case, we could have a block of free (wasted) memory between every two jobs. If all of this memory were in one big free block, we might be able to run several more jobs. The selection of first-fit or best-fit can affect the amount of fragmentation. (First-fit is better for some systems and best-fit for others.) Another factor is which end of a free block is allocated (which is the leftover piece, the one on the top or the bottom?). No matter what algorithms are used, however, external fragmentation will be a problem.

Compaction

One solution to this problem is *compaction*. The goal is to shuffle the memory contents to place all free memory together in one large block. For example, the memory map of Figure 5.16(e) can be compacted, as shown in Figure 5.18. The three holes of sizes 10K, 30K, and 26K can be compacted into one hole of 66K.

Compaction is not always possible. Notice that in Figure 5.18, we moved jobs 4 and 3. For these programs to be able to work in their new locations, all internal addresses must be relocated. If relocation is static and done at assembly or load time, compaction cannot be done; compaction is possible *only* if relocation is dynamic, at execution time, using base and limit registers.

If addresses are dynamically relocated (as on the CDC 6600), relocation requires only moving the program and data, and then changing the base register to reflect the new base address.

When compaction is possible, we must determine its cost. The simplest compaction algorithm is to simply move all jobs towards one end of memory; all holes move in the other direction, producing one large hole of available memory. This scheme can be quite expensive.

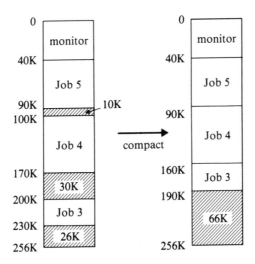

Figure 5.18   Compaction

Consider the memory allocation shown in Figure 5.19. If we use this simple algorithm, we must move jobs 3 and 4, for a total of 600K moved. In this situation, we could simply move job 4 above job 3, moving only 400K, or move job 3 down below job 4, moving only 200K. Note that in this last instance, our one large hole of available memory is not at the end of memory, but in the middle. Also notice that if the queue contained only one job that wanted 450K, we could satisfy that *particular* request by moving job 2 somewhere else (like below job 4). Although this solution does not create a single large hole, it does create a hole big enough to satisfy the immediate request. Selecting an optimal compaction strategy is quite difficult.

The SCOPE operating system for the CDC 6600 used an MVT memory management policy with compaction. Up to eight jobs were allowed in main memory at one time. When a job terminated, memory was compacted to keep all free space in one hole at the bottom of memory.

As with other systems, swapping can be combined with MVT. A job can be rolled out of main memory to a backing store and rolled in again later. When the job is rolled out, its memory is released and perhaps reused for another job. When the job is to be rolled back in, several problems may arise. If static relocation is used, the job must be rolled in to the exact same memory locations that it previously occupied. This restriction may require that other jobs be rolled out to free that memory.

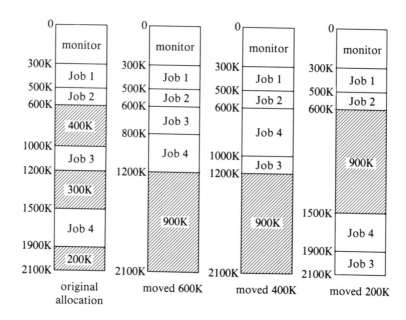

Figure 5.19   Comparison of some different ways to compact memory

If dynamic relocation (such as base/limit registers) is used, then a job can be rolled in to a different location. In this case, we find a free block, compacting if necessary, and roll in the job.

One approach to compaction is to roll out those jobs to be moved, and roll them in to different memory locations. If swapping or roll-in/roll-out is already a part of the system, the additional code for compaction may be minimal.

We can also reduce the average amount of external fragmentation by reducing the average size of a job. Another approach, used on several machines, is to break the memory that a job needs into two parts; each part is smaller than the whole.

The PDP-10 has two pairs of base/limit registers. Memory is split in half by use of the high order address bit. Low memory is relocated/limited by base/limit register pair 0; high memory is relocated/limited by base/limit register pair 1. By convention, compilers and assemblers put read-only values (such as constants and instructions) in high memory and variables in low memory. Protection bits are associated with each register pair and can enforce the read-only nature of high memory. This arrangement allows programs (stored in high memory as read-only) to be shared among many user programs, each with its own separate low-memory segment.

The Univac 1108 has a similar arrangement, which is based on a different type of separation scheme. The cpu knows whether it wants an instruction (instruction fetch) or data (data fetch or store). Therefore, the Univac 1108 has two base/limit register pairs: one for instructions and one for data. The instruction base/limit-register pair is automatically read-only, so programs can be shared between different users.

In both cases, by separating the instructions and data, and relocating each separately, we can share programs among different users. Thus we make better use of memory, by reducing both fragmentation and multiple copies of the same code, particularly commonly used code such as compilers, editors, and so on.

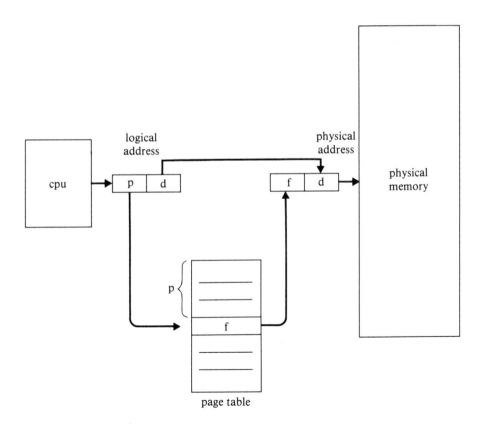

Figure 5.20   Paging hardware

5.6 Paging

MVT suffers from external fragmentation. Generally, this situation occurs when available memory is not contiguous, but fragmented into many scattered blocks. Since the memory allocated to a particular job must be contiguous, this scattered, noncontiguous memory cannot be used. This problem has two general solutions. *Compaction* changes the allocation of memory to make free space contiguous, and hence useful. *Paging* permits a program's memory to be noncontiguous, thus allowing a program to be allocated physical memory wherever it is available.

5.6.1 Hardware

The hardware support for paging is illustrated in Figure 5.20. Every address generated by the cpu is divided into two parts: a *page number* (*p*) and a *page offset* (*d*). The page number is used as an index into a *page table*. The page table contains the base address of each page in physical memory. This base address is combined with the page offset to define the physical memory address that is sent to the memory unit.

The paging model of memory is shown in Figure 5.21. Physical memory is broken into fixed-size blocks called *frames*. Logical memory is

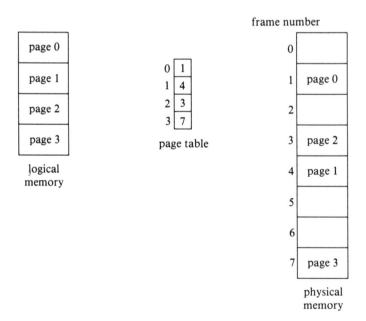

Figure 5.21   Paging model of logical and physical memory

also broken into blocks of the same size called *pages*. When a program is to be executed, its pages are loaded into any available frames, and the page table is defined to translate from user pages to memory frames.

The page size (and frame size) is defined by the hardware. The size of a page is typically a power of two. For example, the IBM 370 uses 2048 or 4096 bytes per page, the XDS-940 used 2048 words per page, the Nova 3/D uses 1024 words per page and the DEC-10 uses 512 words per page. The Atlas machine and the Sigma 7 also used 512-word pages (Figure 5.22). In general, if the page size is P then a logical address, U, produces a page number, p, and offset, d, by

$$p = U \text{ div } P$$
$$d = U \text{ mod } P$$

where *div* is integer division and *mod* is the integer remainder. The selection of a power of two as a page size makes the translation of a logical address into a page number and page offset particularly easy. If a page is 2^n addressing units (bytes or words) long, then the low-order n bits of a logical address designate the page offset and the remaining, high-order, bits designate the page number. Thus if the page size is a power of two, we can avoid the division.

For a concrete example, consider the memory of Figure 5.23. Using a page size of 4 words and a physical memory of 32 words (8 pages), we show an example of how the user's view of memory can be mapped into physical memory. Logical address 0 is page 0, offset 0. Indexing into the page table, we find that page 0 is in frame 5. Thus logical address 0 maps to physical address 20 (= 5×4 + 0). Logical address 3

Machine	Address	Page Bits	Offset
Atlas	20	11	9
DEC-10	18	9	9
Sigma 7	17	8	9
Nova 3/D	15	5	10
XDS-940	14	3	11
IBM 370	24	13 or 12	11 or 12

Figure 5.22 Number of address bits for various computers with paging

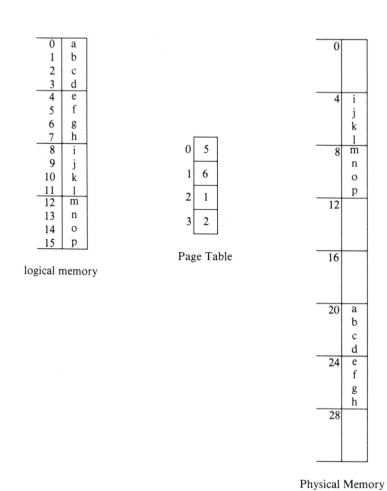

Figure 5.23   Paging example for a 32-word memory with 4-word pages

(page 0, offset 3) maps to physical address 23 (= 5×4 + 3). Logical
address 4 is page 1, offset 0; according to the page table, page 1 is
mapped to frame 6. Thus logical address 4 maps to physical address
(6×4 + 0 =) 24. Logical address 13 maps to physical address 9.

It is important to notice that paging itself is a form of dynamic
relocation. *Every* logical address is mapped by the paging hardware to
some physical address.

5.6.2 Job Scheduling

As before, the memory management scheme influences the job scheduler. When a job arrives to be executed, the job scheduler examines its size. The size of the job is expressed in pages. The job scheduler then looks at available memory, which is kept as a list of unallocated page frames. Each user page needs one frame. Thus if the job requires n pages, there must be n frames available in memory. If there are n frames available, the job scheduler allocates them to this job. The first page of the job is loaded into one of the allocated frames, and the frame number is put in the page table for this job. The next page is loaded into another frame, and its frame number is put into the page table, and so on (Figure 5.24).

Using a paging scheme, we have no external fragmentation: *any* free frame can be allocated to a job that needs it. However, we may have some internal fragmentation. Notice that frames are allocated as units. If the memory requirements of a program do not happen to fall on page boundaries, the *last* frame allocated may not be completely full. For example, if pages are 512 words, a program of 8629 words would need 16 pages plus 437 words. It would be allocated 17 frames, resulting in an internal fragmentation of $512 - 437 = 75$ words. In the worst case, a program would need n pages plus 1 word. It would be allocated $n+1$ frames, resulting in an internal fragmentation of almost an entire frame. If job size is independent of page size, we would expect internal fragmentation of half a page per job. This consideration suggests that small page sizes are desirable.

Each job has its own page table, which is stored with the other register values (like the program counter) in the job control block. When the dispatcher is told to start a job, it must reload the user registers and define the correct hardware page table values from the stored user page table.

5.6.3 Implementation of the Page Table

The hardware implementation of the page table is of interest. In the simplest case, the page table is implemented as a set of dedicated *registers*. The cpu dispatcher reloads these registers just as it reloads the other program registers. Instructions to load or modify the page table registers are, of course, privileged, so that only the operating system can change the memory map. This approach was used on the XDS-940, which had 8 pages of 2048 words each and 8 page table registers. The Nova 3/D has 32 pages of 1024 words each with 32 page table registers. The Sigma 7 had an 8-bit page number, requiring 256 registers for its

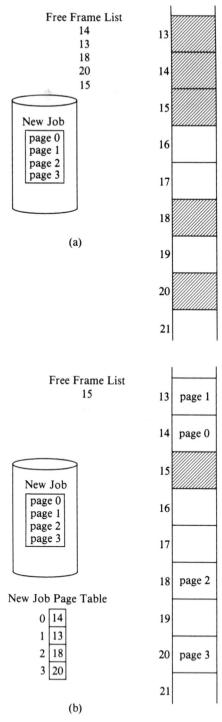

Figure 5.24 Allocation of free frames (a) Before and (b) After

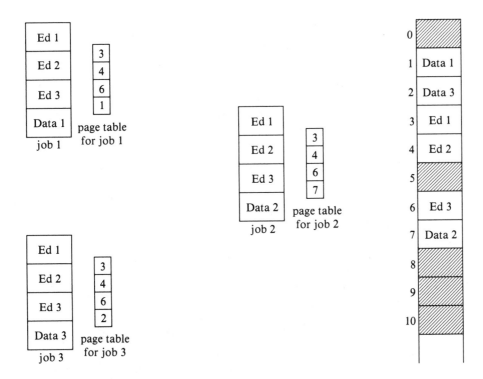

Figure 5.25   Sharing code in a paging environment

for its execution. The data for two different processes will of course vary for each process.

Only one copy of the editor needs to be kept in physical memory. Each user's page table maps onto the same physical copy of the editor, but data pages are mapped onto different frames. Thus to support 40 users, we need only one copy of the editor (30K), plus 40 copies of the 5K of data space per user. The total space required is now 230K, instead of 1400K, a significant savings.

Other heavily used programs can also be shared: compilers, assemblers, data-base systems, and so on. To be sharable, the code must be *reentrant* (non-self-modifying). This term means that there should never be any attempt to store in the code; it is read-only or fetch-only. Obviously, it is crucial for shared pages to be unchanging. If one user were to change a location, it would change for all users. The read-only nature of shared code should not be left to the correctness of the code; the operating system should enforce this property.

5.6.5 Protection

Memory protection in a paged environment is accomplished by protection bits associated with each page. Normally these bits are kept in the page table. One bit can define a page to be read/write or read-only. Every reference to memory goes through the page table to find the correct frame number. At the same time the physical address is being computed, the protection bits can be checked to verify that no writes are being made to a read-only page. An attempt to write to a read-only page causes a hardware trap to the operating system (memory protection violation).

This approach to protection can be easily expanded in order to provide a finer level of protection. We can provide hardware to provide read-only, read-write, or execute-only protection. Or, by providing separate protection bits for each kind of access, any combination of these accesses can be allowed, while illegal attempts are trapped to the operating system.

One more bit is generally attached to each entry in the page table: a valid/invalid bit. The underlying machine architecture defines some maximum address range which can be generated. For example, a 16-bit address allows addresses in the range 0 to 65,535; a 24-bit address allows addresses from 0 to 16,777,215. However, each particular job is generally constrained to a smaller address space, depending upon the program. With the bounds registers hardware, we can trap incorrect program-generated addresses.

Illegal addresses are trapped by using the valid/invalid bit. The operating system sets this bit for each page to allow or disallow accesses to that page. For example, in a system with a 14-bit address space (0 to 16,383), we may have a program which should use only addresses 0 to 10,468. Given a page size of 2K, we get the situation shown in Figure 5.26. Addresses in pages 0, 1, 2, 3, 4, and 5 are mapped normally through the page table. Any attempt to generate an address in pages 6 or 7, however, finds that the valid/invalid bit is set to invalid, and the computer will trap to the operating system (invalid page reference).

Notice that since the program extends only to address 10,468, any reference beyond that address is illegal. However, references to page 5 are classified as valid, so accesses to addresses up to 12,287 are valid. Only addresses from 12,288 to 16,383 are invalid. This problem is a result of the 2K page size and reflects the internal fragmentation of paging.

The XDS-940 attached a bit to each page to control Read-Only (RO) or Read-Write (RW) access. A frame number of 0 was interpreted as an invalid page table entry. The designers reasoned that the operating

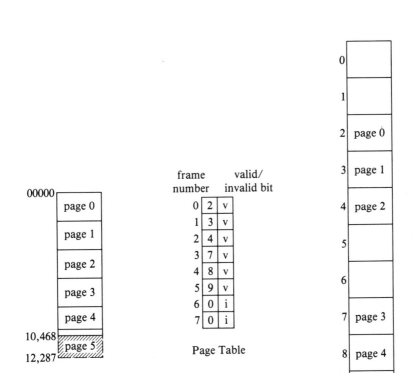

Figure 5.26   Valid (v) or invalid (i) bit in a page table

system would occupy frame 0 of memory and therefore no user page table should ever map into frame 0.

5.6.6 Two Views of Memory

A very important aspect of paging is the clear separation between the user's view of memory and the actual physical memory. The user program believes that memory is one contiguous space, containing only this one program. In fact, the user program is scattered throughout physical memory, which also holds other programs. The difference between the user's view of memory and the actual physical memory is reconciled by the *address translation*, or *mapping*, hardware. The mapping hardware translates logical addresses into physical addresses. This mapping is hidden from the user and controlled by the operating system.

One result of the separation of logical and physical addresses is that they may in fact not be the same. On the XDS-940, for example, a logical address is 14 bits; a physical address is 16 bits. A 3-bit page number indexes into the page table to select a 5-bit frame number. Thus there can be up to four times as much physical memory as any one user can address. Multiprogramming is easy; at least four users can reside in memory simultaneously.

This technique was especially adopted by minicomputer manufacturers. Many minicomputers were designed in the 1960's, when memory was expensive and programs had to be small. Thus most addresses were limited to 15 or 16 bits. With the availability of cheaper semiconductor memory, it became feasible to add more physical memory to these minicomputers. But increasing the address size, in order to allow the larger 17-bit or 18-bit addresses needed for the increased physical memory, meant either redesigning the instruction set or extending the word size to accommodate the extra bits. Either solution would involve a major change, invalidating all existing programs and documentation. The solution which most manufacturers adopted was memory mapping. Logical addresses (15 or 16 bits) are mapped onto larger (17-bit or 18-bit) physical addresses. By multiprogramming the system, all of the memory can be used. Individual users, however, cannot use more memory than before, since the logical address space has not been increased.

For example, the Nova 3/D maps a 5-bit page number into a 7-bit frame number. The HP 2100 does the same. The DEC-10 maps a 9-bit page number into a 13-bit frame number, changing an 18-bit logical address into a 22-bit physical address.

The operating system controls this mapping and can turn it on for the user and off for the operating system. Since the operating system is managing physical memory, it must be aware of the nature of physical memory: which frames are allocated, which frames are available, how many total frames there are, and so on. This information is generally kept in a data structure called a *frame table*. The frame table has one entry for each physical page frame, indicating whether it is free or allocated and, if allocated, to which page of which process.

In addition, the operating system must be aware that user processes operate in user space, and all logical addresses must be mapped to produce physical addresses. If a user makes a system call (to do I/O, for example) and provides an address as a parameter (a buffer, for instance), that address must be mapped to produce the correct physical address. The operating system maintains a copy of the page table for each user, just as it maintains a copy of the program counter and register contents. This copy is used to translate logical addresses to physical addresses whenever the operating system must manually map a logical address to a physical address. It is also used by the dispatcher to define the hardware page table when a process is to be allocated the cpu.

5.7 Segmentation

An important aspect of memory management that became unavoidable with paging is the separation of the user's view of memory and the actual physical memory. The user's view of memory is not the same as the actual physical memory. The user's view is mapped onto physical memory. The mapping allows the difference between logical memory and physical memory.

5.7.1 User's View of Memory

What is the real user's view of memory? Does the user think of memory as a linear array of words, some of which contain instructions while others contain data, or is there some other preferred memory view? There is general agreement that the user or programmer of a system does not think of memory as a linear array of words. Rather, the user prefers to view memory as a collection of variable-sized segments, with no necessary ordering among segments (Figure 5.27).

Consider how you think of a program when you are writing it. You think of it as a main program with a set of subroutines, procedures, functions, or modules. There may also be various data structures: tables, arrays, stacks, variables, and so on. Each of these modules or data elements is referred to by name. You talk about "the symbol table," "function Sqrt," "the main program," without caring what addresses in memory these elements occupy. You are not concerned with whether the symbol table is stored before or after the Sqrt function. Each of these segments is of variable length; the length is intrinsically defined by the purpose of the segment in the program. Elements within a segment are identified by their offset from the beginning of the segment: the first statement of the program, the 17th entry in the symbol table, the fifth instruction of the Sqrt function, and so on.

Segmentation is a memory management scheme which supports this user's view of memory. A logical address space is a collection of segments. Each segment has a name and a length. Addresses specify

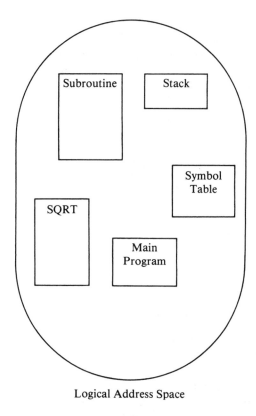

Logical Address Space

Figure 5.27   User's view of a program

both the segment name and the offset within the segment. The user therefore specifies each address by two quantities: a segment name and an offset. (Contrast this scheme with paging, where the user specified only a single address, which was partitioned by the hardware into a page number and an offset, all invisible to the programmer.)

For simplicity of implementation, segments are numbered and referred to by a segment number rather than a segment name. Normally, the user program is assembled (or compiled), and the assembler (or compiler) automatically constructs segments reflecting the input program. A Pascal compiler might create separate segments for (1) the global variables, (2) the procedure call stack, to store parameters and return addresses, (3) the code portion of each procedure or function, and (4) the local variables of each procedure and function. A Fortran compiler might create a separate segment for each common block.

Arrays might be assigned separate segments. The loader would take all of these segments and assign them segment numbers.

5.7.2 Hardware

Although the user can now refer to objects in the program by a two-dimensional address, the actual physical memory is still, of course, a one-dimensional sequence of words. Thus we must define an implementation to map two-dimensional user-defined addresses into one-dimensional physical addresses. This mapping is effected by a *segment table*.

The use of a segment table is illustrated in Figure 5.28. A logical address consists of two parts: a segment number, s, and an offset into that segment, d. The segment number is used as an index into the segment table. Each entry of the segment table has a segment *base* and a segment *limit*. The offset d of the logical address must be between 0 and the segment limit. If it is not, we trap to the operating system (logical addressing attempt beyond end of segment). If this offset is legal, it is added to the segment base to produce the address in physical memory of the desired word. The segment table is thus essentially an array of base/limit register pairs.

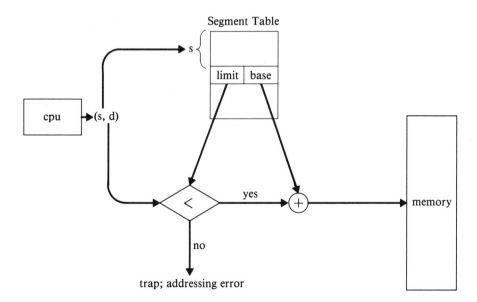

Figure 5.28   Segmentation hardware

As an example, consider the situation shown in Figure 5.29. We
have five segments numbered from 0 through 4. The segments are
actually stored in physical memory as shown. The segment table has a
separate entry for each segment, giving the beginning address of the
segment in physical memory (the base) and the length of that segment
(the limit). For example, segment 2 is 400 words long, beginning at
location 4300. Thus a reference to word 53 of segment 2 is mapped onto
location 4300 + 53 = 4353. A reference to segment 3, word 852 is
mapped to 3200 (the base of segment 3) + 852 = 4052. A reference to
word 1222 of segment 0 would result in a trap to the operating system,
since this segment is only 1000 words long.

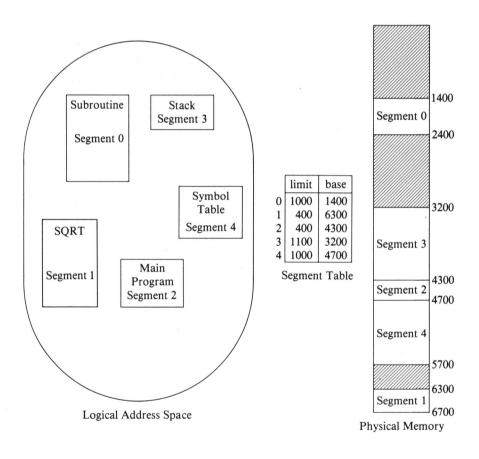

Figure 5.29   Example segmentation

Figure 5.30   Segmentation addressing for the PDP-11/45

5.7.3 Implementation of Segment Tables

Like the page table, the segment table can be put either in fast registers or in memory. A segment table kept in registers can be very quickly referenced; the addition to the base and comparison with the limit can be done simultaneously to save time. The PDP-11/45 uses this approach; it has eight segment registers. A 16-bit address is formed from a 3-bit segment number and a 13-bit segment offset. This arrangement allows up to eight segments; each segment can be up to 8K bytes (Figure 5.30). Each segment table entry has a base address, length, and a set of access control bits specifying no access, read-only access, or read/write access to the segment.

The Burroughs B5500 allowed 32 segments of up to 1024 words each. These specifications defined a 5-bit segment number and a 10-bit offset. However, experience with this system showed that there were too few segments and that the segment size limit was too small (arrays over 1K had to be broken into several segments). Thus the GE 645 used for Multics allows up to 256K segments of up to 64K words.

With this many segments, it is not feasible to keep the segment table in registers, so it must be kept in memory. A *Segment Table Base Register* (STBR) points to the segment table. Also, since the number of segments used by a program may vary widely, a *Segment Table Length Register* (STLR) is used. For a logical address (s,d), we first check that the segment number s is legal ($s <$ STLR). Then we add the segment number to the STBR resulting in the address (STBR + s) in memory of the segment table entry. This entry is read from memory and we proceed as before: check the offset against the segment length and compute the physical address of the desired word as the sum of the segment base and offset.

As with paging, this mapping requires two memory references per logical address, effectively slowing the computer system by a factor of two, unless something is done. The normal solution is to use a set of associative registers to hold the most recently used segment table entries. A relatively small set of associative registers (8 or 16) can generally reduce the delay of memory accesses to no more than 10 percent or 15 percent slower than unmapped memory accesses.

5.7.4 Protection and Sharing

A particular advantage of segmentation is the association of protection with the segments. Since the segments represent a semantically defined portion of the program, it is likely that all entries in the segment are used the same way. Hence we have some segments which are instructions, while other segments are data. In a modern architecture, instructions are non-self-modifying, so instruction segments can be defined as read-only or execute-only. The memory-mapping hardware will check the protection bits associated with each segment-table entry to prevent illegal accesses to memory, such as attempts to write into a read-only segment or to use an execute-only segment as data. By placing an array in its own segment, the memory-management hardware will automatically check that array indexes are legal and do not stray outside the array boundaries. Thus many common program errors will be detected by the hardware before they can cause serious damage.

Another advantage of segmentation involves the *sharing* of code or data. Each job has a segment table associated with its process control block, which the dispatcher uses to define the hardware segment table when this job is given the cpu. Segments are shared when entries in the segment tables of two different jobs point to the same physical locations. (Figure 5.31).

The sharing occurs at the segment level. Thus any information can be shared by defining it to be a segment. Several segments can be shared, so a program composed of several segments can be shared.

For example, consider the use of a text editor in a time-sharing system. A complete editor might be quite large, composed of many segments. These segments can be shared among all users, limiting the physical memory needed to support editing tasks. Rather than *n* copies of the editor, we need only one copy. For each user, we still need separate, unique segments to store local variables. These segments, of course, would not be shared.

It is also possible to share only parts of programs. For example, common subroutine packages can be shared among many users by defining them as sharable, read-only segments. Two Fortran programs, for instance, may use the same *Sqrt* subroutine, but only one physical copy of the *Sqrt* routine would be needed.

Although this sharing appears quite simple, there are some subtle considerations. Code segments typically contain references to themselves. For example, a conditional jump normally has a transfer

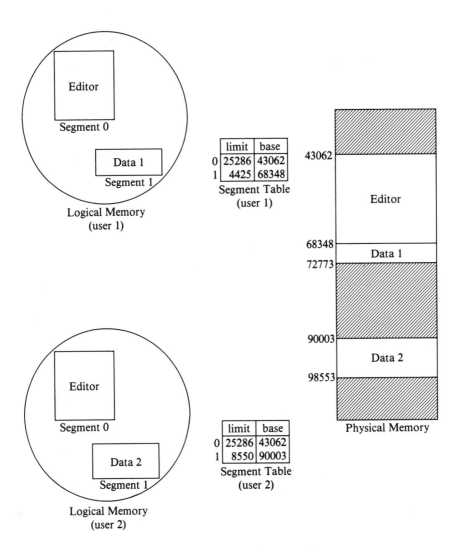

Figure 5.31   Sharing segments in a segmented memory system

address. The transfer address is a segment number and offset. The segment number of the transfer address will be the segment number of the code segment. If we try to share this segment, all sharing processes must define the shared code segment to have the same segment number.

For instance, if we want to share the *Sqrt* routine, and one process wants to make it segment 4 and another wants to make it segment 17, how should the *Sqrt* routine refer to itself? Since there is only one physical copy of *Sqrt*, it must refer to itself in the same way for both users: it must have a unique segment number. As the number of users sharing the segment increases, so does the difficulty of finding an acceptable segment number.

Read-only data segments (without pointers) may be shared as different segment numbers, as may code segments which do not refer to themselves directly but only indirectly. For example, conditional branches which specify the branch address as an offset from the current program counter or relative to a register containing the current segment number would allow code to avoid direct reference to the current segment number.

The GE 645 computer used for Multics had four registers containing the segment numbers of the current segment, the stack segment, the linkage segment, and a data segment. Programs seldom refer directly to a segment number, but always indirectly through these four segment registers. This allows code to be freely shared.

5.7.5 Fragmentation

The job scheduler must find and allocate memory for all the segments of a user program. This situation is similar to paging *except* that the segments are of *variable* length; pages are all the same size. Thus, as with MVT, memory allocation is a dynamic storage allocation problem, probably solved by using a best-fit or first-fit algorithm.

Segmentation may then cause external fragmentation, when all blocks of free memory are too small to accommodate a segment. In this case, the job may simply have to wait until more memory (or at least larger holes) become available, or compaction may be used to create larger holes. Since segmentation is by its nature a dynamic relocation algorithm, we can compact memory whenever we want. If the cpu scheduler must wait for one job, due to a memory allocation problem, it may (or may not) skip through the cpu queue looking for a smaller, lower-priority job to run.

How bad is external fragmentation for a segmentation scheme? Would job scheduling with skip or compaction help? The answers to these questions depend mainly on the average segment size. At one extreme, we could define each job to be one segment; this scheme is MVT. At the other extreme, every word could be put in its own segment and relocated separately. This arrangement eliminates external fragmentation altogether. If the average segment size is small, external fragmentation will also be small. (By analogy, consider putting suitcases in the trunk of a car; they never quite seem to fit. However, if you open the suitcases and put the individual items in the trunk, everything fits.) Since the individual segments are smaller than the overall job, they are more likely to fit in the available memory blocks.

5.8 Combined Systems

Both paging and segmentation have their advantages and disadvantages. It is also possible to combine these two schemes to improve on each. These combinations are best illustrated by two specific systems: the IBM 360/67 (and later IBM 370) and the GE 645 for Multics.

5.8.1 Segmented Paging

The IBM 360/67 was an early paged system. The basic 24-bit byte address was divided into a 12-bit page number and a 12-bit offset. (Programmers familiar with the instruction format for the IBM 360/370 will recognize why a 12-bit page offset was used.) Each page table entry was 2 bytes (a half word) containing a 12-bit frame number and a valid/invalid bit. The problem was that a 12-bit page number allowed 4096 pages, requiring 8K bytes for each page table. In addition, it was desired to expand the logical address to 32 bits with a 20-bit page number. This would have required a page table of 1,048,576 entries, or 2,097,152 bytes.

Particularly with the larger address space, most of the page table would be empty, since most programs would use only a fraction of the total possible address space. Therefore, the *page table* was segmented. The upper 4 bits of a page number are considered a segment number, which is used to select one of sixteen segment table entries. Each segment can be up to 268,435,456 bytes in length, although its length must be a multiple of 4096 bytes. The segment table entry points to the base of a page table for this segment, and also indicates the length of the page table (Figure 5.32). In this way, large sections of the page table which were zero could be collapsed by setting the address of the page table to zero.

Naturally, this scheme now requires, in the worst case, *three* memory accesses per desired memory reference. A set of eight associative registers reduces the overhead to only 150 nanoseconds slower than an unmapped reference (750 nanoseconds) when a hit occurs.

The important concept here is that the user still sees a linear paged address space. One result of this arrangement is that it is possible to

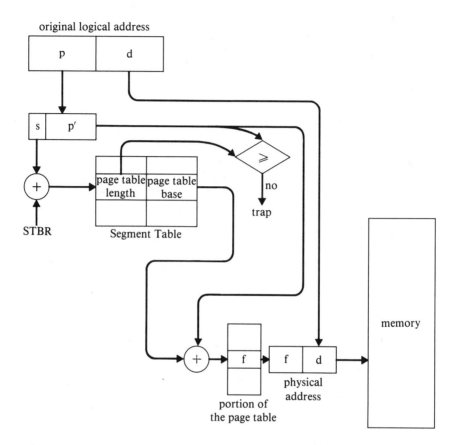

original logical address

Figure 5.32   Segmented paging on the IBM 360/67

increment an index and produce first the last location of segment i and then the first location of segment $i+1$; memory is still basically linear.

5.8.2 Paged Segmentation

The Multics system faced a different problem. Logical addresses were formed from an 18-bit segment number and a 16-bit offset. Although this scheme creates a 34-bit address space, the table overhead is quite tolerable since the variable number of segments naturally implies a Segment Table Length Register. We need only as many segment table entries as we have segments; there need be no empty segment table entries.

However, with segments of 64K words, the average segment size could be quite large and external fragmentation could be a problem. Even if external fragmentation is not a problem, the search time to allocate a segment, using first-fit or best-fit, could be long. Thus we may waste memory due to external fragmentation, or waste time due to lengthy searches, or both.

The solution adopted was to *page* the *segments*. Paging eliminates external fragmentation and makes the allocation problem trivial: any empty frame can be used for a desired page. The result is shown in Figure 5.33. Notice that the difference between this solution and pure segmentation is that the segment table entry does not contain the base

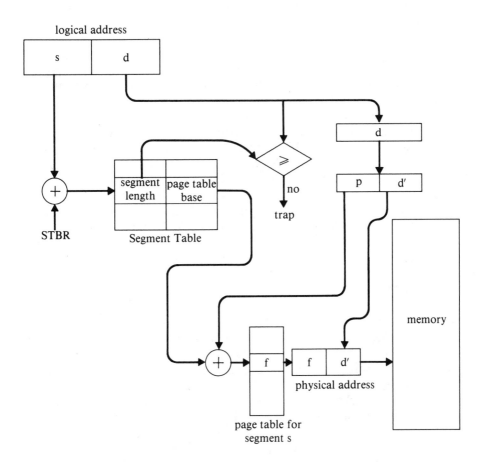

Figure 5.33   Paged segmentation on the GE 645 (Multics)

address of the segment, but the base address of a *page table* for this segment. The segment offset is then broken into a 6-bit page number and a 10-bit page offset. The page number indexes into the page table to give the frame number. Finally, the frame number is combined with the page offset to form a physical address.

We must now have a separate page table for each segment. However, since each segment is limited in length by its segment table entry, the page table need not be full sized. It requires only as many entries as are actually needed. In addition, the last page of each segment will generally not be completely full. Thus we will have, on the average, half a page of *internal* fragmentation per segment. Consequently, although we have eliminated external fragmentation, we have introduced internal fragmentation and increased table space overhead.

Other systems also use paged segmentation. The Prime 500 system uses a 12-bit segment number and a word offset split into a 6-bit page number and a 10-bit offset. The RCA Spectra 70/46 had a 5-bit segment number, and an 18-bit offset, composed of a 6-bit page number and 12-bit byte displacement.

To tell the truth, even the paged segmentation view of Multics just presented is simplistic. Since the segment number is an 18-bit quantity, we could have up to 262,144 segments, requiring a very large segment table. To ease this problem, Multics pages the segment table. Thus in general, an address in Multics uses the segment number to define a page index into a page table for the segment table. From this entry, it locates the part of the segment table with the entry for this segment. The segment table entry points to a page table for this segment, which specifies the frame containing the desired word.

5.9 Summary

Memory management algorithms for multiprogrammed operating systems range from the simple resident monitor approach to paged segmentation. The greatest determinant of the policy used in a particular system is the hardware provided. Every memory address generated by the cpu must be checked for legality and possibly mapped to a physical address. The checking cannot be implemented (efficiently) in software. Hence we are constrained by the hardware available.

The memory-management algorithms discussed (bare machine, resident monitor, MFT, MVT, paging, segmentation, and combinations of paging and segmentation) differ in many aspects. The following list indicates some important considerations in comparing different memory management strategies.

- **Hardware support**. A simple fence register or a pair of bounds registers are sufficient for a resident monitor, MFT, or MVT, while paging and segmentation need mapping tables to define the address map.

- **Performance**. As the algorithm becomes more complex, the time required to map a logical address to a physical address increases. For the simple systems, we need only compare or add to the logical address, operations that are quite fast. Paging and segmentation can be as fast if the table is implemented in fast registers. If the table is in memory, however, user memory accesses can be substantially degraded. A set of associative registers can reduce the performance degradation to an acceptable level.

- **Fragmentation**. A multiprogrammed system will generally perform better with a higher level of multiprogramming. For a given set of jobs, the multiprogramming level can only be increased by packing more jobs into memory. To accomplish this task, we must reduce memory waste or fragmentation. Systems with fixed-size allocation units, such as MFT or paging, suffer internal fragmentation; systems with variable-sized allocation units, such as MVT and segmentation, suffer external fragmentation.

- **Relocation**. One solution to the external fragmentation problem is compaction. Compaction involves shifting a program in memory without the program noticing the change. This consideration requires that logical addresses be relocated dynamically, at execution time. If addresses are relocated only at load time, we cannot compact storage.

- **Swapping**. Any algorithm can have swapping added to it. At intervals determined by the operating system, usually dictated by cpu-scheduling policies, jobs are copied from main memory to a backing store and later copied back to main memory. This scheme allows more jobs to be run than can be fit into memory at one time.

- **Sharing**. Another means of increasing the multiprogramming level is to share code and data among different users. Sharing generally requires that either paging or segmentation be used, to provide small packets of information (pages or segments) which can be shared. Sharing is a means of running many users with a limited amount of memory, but shared programs and data must be carefully designed.

- **Protection**. If paging or segmentation is provided, different sections of a user program can be declared execute-only, read-only, or read-write. This restriction is necessary with shared code or data, and is generally useful in any case to provide simple runtime checks for common programming errors.

Exercises

5.1 Explain the following allocation algorithms:

    a. First-fit.

    b. Best-fit.

    c. Worst-fit.

5.2 When a job is rolled out, it loses its ability to use the cpu (at least for a while). Name another situation where a job loses its ability to use the cpu, but where the job does not get rolled out.

5.3 Consider a logical address space of 8 pages of 1024 words mapped onto a physical memory of 32 frames.

    a. How many bits are there in the logical address?

    b. How many bits are there in the physical address?

5.4 Consider a paged system with page size of 100 words. For the following assembly language program (starting at location 0) generate the sequence of memory addresses accessed. (Include both data and instruction accesses.)

    0. Load from 263.

    1. Store into 264.

    2. Store into 265.

    3. Read from I/O device.

    4. Branch to location 4 if I/O device busy.

    5. Store into 901.

    6. Load from 902.

    7. Halt.

5.5 Explain the difference between logical and physical addresses.

5.6 Consider a paging system with the page table stored in memory.

a. If a memory reference takes 1.2 microseconds, how long does a paged memory reference take?

b. If we add 8 associative registers, and 75 percent of all page table references are found in the associative registers, what is the effective memory reference time? (Assume that finding a page table entry in the associative registers takes zero time, if it is there.)

5.7 Why could OS/MVT on the IBM 360 not do compaction? How was this problem solved on the CDC 6600 to allow compaction?

5.8 Explain the difference between internal and external fragmentation.

5.9 Describe the hardware which is required to support paging with an acceptable amount of overhead.

5.10 On the IBM/360, pages are 4096 bytes long. Since addresses are 24 bits long, this means that there can be 4096 pages in logical memory, which requires a page table of 4096 entries. Since each page table entry takes 2 bytes, this requires two pages of memory just to hold the page table. Assuming that processes access memory from 0 to m and do not access memory from $m+1$ to 16,777,215 ($2^{24} - 1$), give a modification to the normal paging hardware which would decrease the average size of the page tables.

What if programs tend to access a set of sequential blocks of memory (from a to b, and from c to d, and from e to f, and so on) but not access the areas between the blocks (from b to c, d to e, f to g, and so on)? This might result from programs which allocate their arrays or matrices to the maximum amounts (several thousand locations) but only use the first few in each (on average). Define a new paging table structure and associated address translation scheme for keeping the size of the page tables small for this situation.

5.11 Most machines do not have either paging or segmentation hardware. If a problem requires a very large address space, can either of these schemes be implemented in software? Sketch how. Which would be easier, paging or segmentation?

5.12 Assume we have a paged memory system with associative registers to hold the most active page table entries. If the page table is normally held in memory, and memory access time is 1 microsecond, what is the effective access time if 85 percent of all memory references find their entries in the associative registers? What is the effective access time if the hit ratio to the associative registers is only 50 percent?

5.13 What is the effect of allowing two entries in a page table to point to the same page frame in memory? Could this be used to decrease the amount of time needed to copy a large amount of memory from one place to another? What would be the effect on the one page of storing in the other?

5.14 Consider the segment table,

Segment	Base	Length
0	219	600
1	2300	14
2	90	100
3	1327	580
4	1952	96

What are the physical addresses for the following logical addresses?

a. 0,430

b. 1,10

c. 1,11

d. 2,500

e. 3,400

f. 4,112

5.15 Why are segmentation and paging sometimes combined into one scheme?

5.16 Explain why it is easier to share a reentrant module using segmentation rather than pure paging.

5.17 Describe a mechanism by which one segment could belong to the address space of two different processes.

5.18 Consider a time-shared swapping system with one swapping drum and three fixed regions in memory. Average latency time for the drum is 4 milliseconds; transfer time for one region is 6 milliseconds. The idea is to be swapping in and out of one region while executing the processes in the other two. A job is swapped out to the drum only when it waits for input from its user; it is swapped in when there is a free region and an input line from its user.

  a. If this is the best of all possible worlds, we would hope to achieve 100 percent utilization of cpu and disk (both busy all the time). For utilization to be 100 percent, how long does a job execute while processing an input line, before waiting for the next line?

  b. If users submit one line every second to be processed, what is the maximum number of users which can be serviced?

5.19 In the IBM/360, memory protection is by the use of *keys*. A key is a 4 bit quantity. Each 2048 byte block of memory has a key (the storage key) associated with it. The cpu also has a key associated with it (the protection key). A store operation is allowed only if both keys are equal, or either is zero. Which of the following memory management schemes could be successfully used with this hardware?

  a. Bare Machine.

  b. Resident Monitor.

  c. Multiprogramming with a fixed number of processes.

  d. Multiprogramming with a variable number of processes.

  e. Paging.

  f. Segmentation.

5.20 Consider a machine with a relocation register and a limit register (like the CDC 6600). We would like to write an operating system which provides many users with a time-shared BASIC interpreter and editor. No user programs will be compiled; BASIC programs will only be interpreted. No other languages will be provided. Users will be able only to input from and output to their terminals, and to disk files. We have 100K memory, and the BASIC interpreter code takes about 15K. We also have 4 moving head disks.

The BASIC program being interpreted will be stored in memory as compressed text and may declare vector and matrix data structures, so the amount of memory for each user is 15K plus program text storage plus data storage. Discuss how the system should allocate memory.

5.21 The ability to share segments between processes without requiring the same segment number is possible in a dynamically linked segmentation system.

a. Define a system which allows static linking and sharing of segments without needing the same segment numbers.

b. Give a paging scheme which allows pages to be shared without needing the same page numbers (for demand paging).

Bibliographic Notes

External and internal fragmentation are discussed by Randell [1969].

The fixed partition allocation scheme is used in the IBM OS/360 MFT (Multiprogramming with a Fixed number of Tasks). The variable partition allocation scheme is used in the IBM OS/360 MVT (Multiprogramming with a Variable number of Tasks). Discussions of both types of systems are presented by Knight [1968], Madnick and Donovan [1974, Section 3.3] and Hoare and McKeag [1972].

The concept of paging can be credited to the designers of the Atlas system [Kilburn et al. 1961, 1962]. An early paging system is the XDS-940, which is described by Lichtenberger and Pirtle [1965] and Lampson et al. [1966].

The concept of segmentation was first discussed by Dennis [1965]. Systems which employ contiguous allocation per segment include the Burroughs B5700, B6500, and B7600 computer systems, in which address mapping is done in hardware [Organick 1973] and the PDP-11/45 computer system.

Systems which employ paging with segmentation include the GE 645 on which Multics was originally implemented [Organick 1972], the IBM 360/67 system [Comfort 1965], and the RCA Spectra 70/46 [Oppenheimer and Weizer 1968].

Boynton

Exercises

ch 5   4, 5, 11, 13, 14, 16

6   2, 9, 13, 18, 24, 25, 29

8   2, 4, 8, 9, 13, 15, 16

9   1, 2, 6, 10, 11, 13, (21, 25)

6

Virtual Memory

In the last chapter we discussed various memory management strategies that have been used in computer systems. All of these strategies have the same goal: to keep many processes in memory simultaneously to allow multiprogramming. However, they all require the entire process to be in memory before the process can execute.

Virtual memory is a technique which allows the execution of processes that may not be completely in memory. The main visible advantage of this scheme is that user programs can be larger than physical memory. Virtual memory is not easy to implement, however, and may substantially decrease performance, if it is used carelessly. In this chapter, we discuss virtual memory in the form of demand paging and examine its complexity and cost.

6.1 Overlays

The memory management algorithms of Chapter 5 are necessary because of one basic requirement: the entire logical address space of a process must be in physical memory before the process can execute. This restriction seems both necessary and reasonable, but it is also unfortunate, since it limits the size of a program to the size of physical memory.

In fact, an examination of real programs shows that in many cases, the entire program is not needed. For instance:

- Programs often have code to handle unusual error conditions. Since these errors seldom, if ever, occur in practice, this code is almost never executed.

- Arrays, lists, and tables are often allocated more memory than they actually need. An array may be declared 100 by 100, even though it is seldom larger than 10 by 10. An assembler symbol table may have room for 3000 symbols, although the average program has less than 200 symbols.

- Certain options and features of a program may be rarely used, such as a text editor command to convert all characters in a range of lines to upper case.

Even in those cases where the entire program is needed, it may not all be needed at the same time.

The ability to execute a program which is only partially in memory would have many benefits:

- A program would no longer be constrained by the amount of physical memory that is available. Users would be able to write programs for a very large *virtual* address space, simplifying the programming task.

- Since each user could take less physical memory, more users can be run at the same time, with a corresponding increase in cpu utilization and throughput, but no increase in response time or turnaround time.

- Less I/O would be needed to load or swap each user into memory, so each user would run faster.

Thus running a program which is not entirely in memory would benefit both the system and the user.

A technique called *overlays* is sometimes used to allow a program to be larger than the amount of memory allocated to it. The idea of overlays is to keep in memory only those instructions and data that are needed at any given time. When other instructions are needed, they are loaded into space that was previously occupied by instructions that are no longer needed.

As an example, consider a two-pass assembler. During pass 1, it constructs a symbol table, and then generates machine language code during pass 2. We may be able to partition such an assembler into pass 1 code, pass 2 code, the symbol table, and common support routines used by both pass 1 and pass 2. Assume the sizes of these components are:

Pass 1	8K
Pass 2	10K
Symbol Table	14K
Common Routines	5K

To load everything at once requires 37K of memory. If only 32K is available, we cannot run our program. However, notice that pass 1 and pass 2 do not need to be in memory at the same time. We thus define two overlays: (*A*) the symbol table, common routines, and pass 1, and (*B*) the symbol table, common routines, and pass 2.

We add an overlay driver (2K) and start with overlay *A* in memory. When we finish pass 1, we jump to the overlay driver, which reads overlay *B* into memory, overwriting overlay *A*, and then transfers control to pass 2. Overlay *A* needs only 29K, while overlay *B* needs 31K (Figure 6.1). We can now run our assembler in the 32K of memory available. However, it will run somewhat more slowly, due to the extra I/O to read the code for overlay *B* over the code for overlay *A*.

The code for overlay *A* and the code for overlay *B* are kept on disk or tape as absolute memory images, and read by the overlay driver as needed. Special relocation and linking algorithms are needed to construct the overlays.

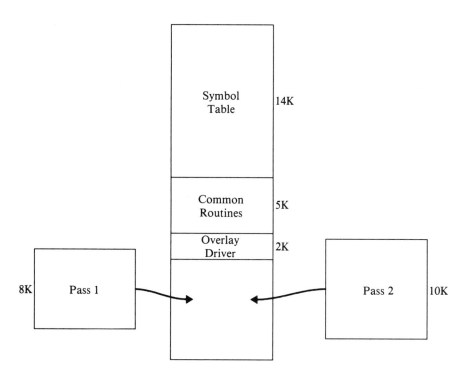

Figure 6.1   Overlays for a two-pass assembler

A related topic is *dynamic loading*. With dynamic loading, a routine is not loaded until it is called. All routines are kept on disk in a relocatable load format. The main program is loaded into memory and executed. When a routine wants to call another routine, the calling routine first checks to see whether the other routine has been loaded. If not, the relocatable linking loader is called to load the desired routine into memory and update the tables to reflect this change. Then control is passed to the newly loaded routine. The advantage of dynamic loading is that an unused routine is never loaded. This scheme is particularly useful when large amounts of code are needed to handle infrequently occurring cases, such as various error routines. In this case, although the total program size may be large, that portion which is actually used (and hence actually loaded) may be much smaller.

Neither overlays nor dynamic loading need special support from the operating system. Both can be implemented completely by the user with simple file structures, reading from the files into memory and then jumping to that memory and executing the newly read instructions. The operating system only notices more I/O than usual.

The user programmer, on the other hand, must properly design and program the overlay structure. This task can be a major undertaking, requiring complete knowledge of the structure of the program, its code, and its data structures. Since the program is, by definition, very large (small programs do not need to be overlaid), sufficient understanding of the program may be very difficult. Automatic techniques to run large programs in limited amounts of physical memory would be preferable.

6.2 Demand Paging

Virtual memory describes a set of techniques that allow us to execute a program which is not entirely in memory. *Demand paging* is the most common virtual memory system.

Demand paging is similar to a paging system with swapping (Figure 6.2). Programs reside on a swapping device, the *backing store*. When we want to execute a program, we swap it into memory. Rather than swapping the entire program into memory, however, we use a "lazy" swapper. The lazy swapper never swaps a page into memory unless it is needed. There are many advantages to using a lazy swapper. It decreases the swap time and the amount of physical memory needed, allowing an increased degree of multiprogramming.

But what happens when the program tries to use a page that was not brought into memory? The hardware will attempt to translate the user address into a physical address by using the page table. What is

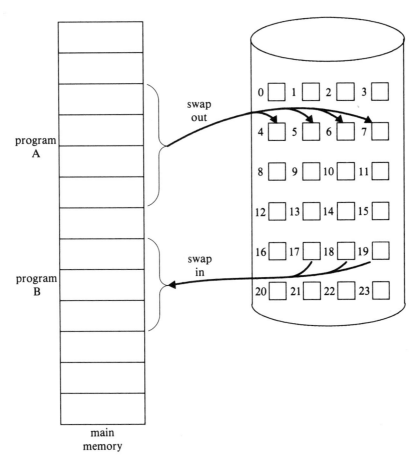

Figure 6.2   Swapping a paged memory to contiguous disk space

the entry in the page table for a page which has not been brought into memory? There is no associated page frame; the access must be invalid. We can prevent the attempted access by setting the valid/invalid bit in the page table to invalid for pages that have not been brought into memory (Figure 6.3).

Notice that this invalidation will have no effect if the program never attempts to access that page. Hence, if we guess right and swap in all and only those pages which are actually needed, the program will run exactly as if we had brought in all pages.

If we guess wrong, however, and the program tries to access a page which was not brought into memory, then a *page fault* will occur. The

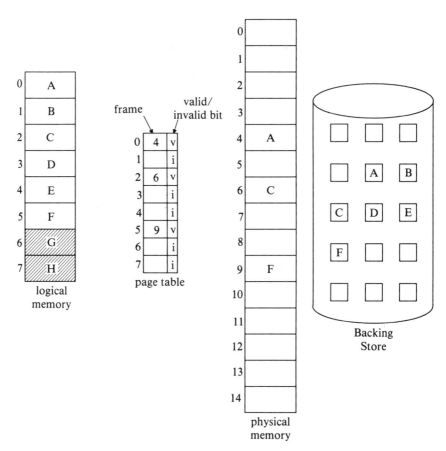

Figure 6.3   Page table when some pages are not in main memory

paging hardware, in translating the address through the page table will notice that the invalid bit is set, causing a trap to the operating system (invalid address error). Normally, an invalid address error is the result of an attempt to use an illegal memory address (such as an incorrect array subscript). In such a case, the program should be terminated. In this case, however, the trap is the result of the operating system's failure to bring a valid part of the program into memory, in an attempt to minimize swapping overhead and memory requirements. We must therefore correct this oversight. The procedure is quite simple (Figure 6.4):

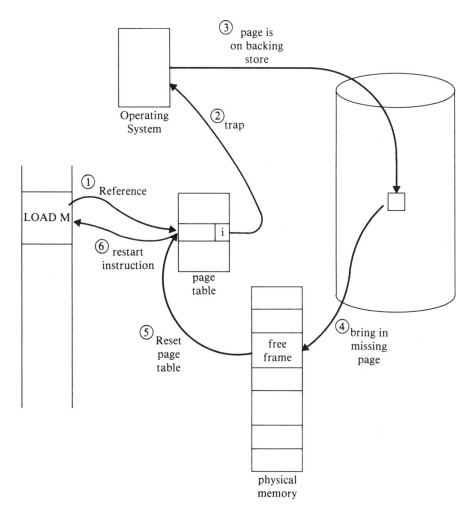

Figure 6.4   Steps in handling a page fault

1. First we check an internal table kept with the process control block
   for this process, to determine if the reference was a valid or invalid
   memory access. If it was invalid, we terminate the program.

2. If it was a valid reference, but we have not yet brought in that page,
   we must now bring it in.

3. Find a free frame (by taking one from the free frame list, for example).

4. Schedule a disk operation to read the desired page into the newly allocated frame.

5. When the disk read is complete, modify the internal table kept with the process and the page table to indicate that the page is now in memory.

6. Restart the instruction that was interrupted by the illegal address trap. The process can now access the page as if it had always been in memory.

It is important to realize that, by saving the state (registers, condition code, program counter) of the interrupted process when the illegal address trap (page fault) occurs, we can restart the process in *exactly* the same place and state, except that the desired page is now in memory and accessible. In this way we are able to execute a program, even though portions of it are not (yet) in memory. When the process tries to access locations which are not in memory, the hardware traps to the operating system (page fault). The operating system reads the desired page into memory and restarts the process as if the page had always been in memory.

In the extreme case, we could start executing a process with *no* pages in memory. The process would immediately fault for the page with the first instruction. After this page was brought into memory, the process would continue to execute, faulting as necessary until every page that it needed was actually in memory. At that point, it could execute with no more faults. This is *pure demand paging*: never bring a page into memory until it is required.

The hardware to support demand paging is the same as the hardware for paging and swapping:

- A **page table** with the ability to mark an entry invalid through a valid/invalid bit or special value of protection bits.

- A **backing store** to hold those pages not in memory. The backing store is usually a high-speed disk or drum or bulk core storage, such as IBM's ECS.

In addition to this hardware support, considerable software is needed, as we shall see.

Some additional architectural constraints must be imposed. A crucial issue is the need to be able to restart any instruction after a page fault.

In most cases this requirement is easily met. A page fault could occur at any memory reference. If the page fault occurs on the instruction fetch, we can restart by fetching the instruction again. If we page fault while fetching an operand, we must refetch the instruction, decode it again, and then fetch the operand.

As a worst case, consider a 3-address instruction such as *ADD A* to *B* placing the result in *C*. The steps to execute this instruction would be:

1. Fetch and decode the instruction (*ADD*).

2. Fetch *A*.

3. Fetch *B*.

4. Add.

5. Store the sum in *C*.

If we faulted when we tried to store in *C* (because *C* is in a page not currently in memory), we would have to go get the desired page, bring it in, correct the page table, and restart the instruction. The restart would require fetching the instruction again, decoding it again, fetching the two operands again, and then adding again. However, there is really not much repeated work (less than 1 complete instruction), and it is only necessary when a page fault occurs.

The major difficulty occurs when one instruction may modify several different locations. For example, consider the IBM 370 MVC (move character) instruction which can move up to 256 bytes from one location to another (possibly overlapping) location. If either block (source or destination) straddles a page boundary, a page fault might occur after the move is partially done. In addition, if the source and destination blocks overlap, the source block may have been modified, in which case we cannot simply restart the instruction.

This problem is solved in two different ways, depending upon the model. In one solution, the microcode computes and attempts to access both ends of both blocks. If a page fault is going to occur, it will happen at this step, before anything is modified. The move can then take place, knowing that no page fault can occur since all of the relevant pages are in memory. The other solution uses temporary registers to hold the values of overwritten locations. If there is a page fault, all of the old values are written back into memory before the trap occurs. This action restores memory to its state before the instruction was started, so that the instruction can be repeated.

A similar architectural problem occurs in the PDP-11, which uses special addressing modes including auto-decrement and auto-increment modes. These addressing modes use a register as a pointer and automatically decrement or increment the register as indicated. Auto-decrement automatically decrements the register *before* using its contents as the operand address; auto-increment automatically increments the register *after* using its contents as the operand address. Thus the instruction

$$MOV \ (R2)+,-(R3)$$

copies the contents of the location pointed to by register 2 into the location pointed to by register 3. Register 2 is incremented (by two for a word, since the PDP-11 is a byte-addressable computer) after it is used as a pointer; register 3 is decremented (by two) before it is used as a pointer. Now consider what will happen if we get a fault when trying to store into the location pointed to by register 3. To restart the instruction we must reset the two registers to the values they had before we started the execution of the instruction. In the PDP-11/45 and 11/70, a special register (SR1: Status Register 1) was created to record the register number and amount modified for any register which is changed during the execution of an instruction. This register allows the operating system to "undo" the effects of a partially executed instruction which causes a page fault.

These are by no means the only architectural problems resulting from adding paging to an existing architecture to allow demand paging, but they illustrate some of the difficulties. Paging is added between the cpu and the memory in a computer system. It should be entirely transparent to the user program. Thus it is often assumed that paging could be added to any system. While this assumption is true for paging for relocation, where a page fault represents a fatal error, it is not correct when a page fault means only that an additional page must be brought into memory and the program restarted.

6.3 Performance of Demand Paging

Demand paging can have a significant effect on the performance of a computer system. To see why, let us compute the *effective access time* for a demand paged memory. The memory access time, *ma*, for most computer systems now ranges from 500 nanoseconds to 2 microseconds. As long as we have no page faults, the effective access time is equal to the memory access time. If, however, a page fault occurs, we must first read the relevant page from backing store, and then access the desired word.

Let p be the probability of a page fault ($0 \leqslant p \leqslant 1$). We would expect p to be very close to zero; that is, there will be only a few page faults. The *effective* access time is then

effective access time = $(1-p) \times ma + p \times$ "page fault time"

To compute the effective access time, we must know how much time is needed to service a page fault. A page fault causes the following sequence to occur.

1. Trap to the operating system.

2. Save the user registers and program state.

3. Determine that the interrupt was a page fault.

4. Check that the page reference was legal and determine the location of the page on the backing store.

5. Issue a read from the backing store to a free frame:

   a. Wait in a queue for this device until the read request is serviced.

   b. Wait for the device seek and/or latency time.

   c. Begin the transfer of the page to a free frame.

6. While we wait, we can allocate the cpu to some other user (cpu scheduling).

7. Interrupt from the backing store (I/O completed).

8. Save the registers and program state for the other user.

9. Determine that the interrupt was from the backing store.

10. Correct the page table and other tables to show that the desired page is now in memory.

11. Wait for the cpu to be allocated to this process again.

12. Restore the user registers, program state, and new page table, then resume the interrupted instruction.

Not all of these steps may be necessary in every case. For example, we are assuming that, in step 5, the cpu is allocated to another process while the I/O occurs. This arrangement allows multiprogramming to maintain cpu utilization, but requires additional time to resume the page fault service routine when the I/O transfer is complete.

In any case, we are faced with three major components of the page fault service time:

- Service the page fault interrupt.

- Swap in the page.

- Restart the process.

The first and third tasks may be reduced, with careful coding, to several hundred instructions. These tasks may take from 100 to 1000 microseconds. The page-swap time, on the other hand, will probably be close to 9 milliseconds (msec). For example, a drum typically has an 8 msec latency and a 1 msec transfer time. If a moving-head disk is used as a paging device (a practice which is becoming more common), then we must include seek time, as well as latency and transfer time. A moving-head device could raise the total swap time to over 30 msec. Remember also that we are looking only at the device service time. If a queue of processes is waiting for the device (other processes which have caused page faults), we have to add device queueing time as we wait for the paging device to be free to service our request, increasing the time to swap even more.

If we take an average page fault service time of 10 msec and a memory access time of 1 microsecond (μsec), then

$$
\begin{aligned}
\text{effective access time} &= (1-p) \times (1\ \mu\text{sec}) + p \times (10\ \text{msec}) \\
&= (1-p) + 10000 \times p\ \mu\text{sec} \\
&= 1 + 9999 \times p\ \mu\text{sec}.
\end{aligned}
$$

We see then that the effective access time is directly proportional to the page fault rate. If one access out of a thousand causes a page fault, the effective access time is 11 microseconds. The computer would be slowed down by a factor of 11 because of demand paging. If we want less than 10 percent degradation, we need

$$
\begin{aligned}
1.10 &> 1 + 9999 \times p \\
.10 &> 9999 \times p \\
p &< .00001
\end{aligned}
$$

That is, to keep the slowdown due to paging to a reasonable level, less than 1 memory access out of 100,000 can be allowed to page fault.

It is very important to keep the page fault rate low in a demand paging system. Otherwise, the effective access time increases, slowing program execution dramatically.

6.4 Page Replacement

In our presentation so far, the page fault rate is not really a problem, since each page is faulted for at most once, when it is first referenced. This representation is not strictly true. Consider that if a program of ten pages actually uses only half of them, then demand paging saves the I/O necessary to load the five pages which are never used. We could also increase our degree of multiprogramming by running twice as many programs. Thus if we had forty frames, we could run eight programs, rather than the four which could run if each required ten frames (five of which were never used).

If we increase our degree of multiprogramming, we are *overallocating* memory. If we run six programs, each of which is ten pages in size, but actually uses only five pages, we have higher cpu utilization and throughput, with ten frames to spare. It is possible, however, that each of these programs, for a particular data set, may suddenly try to use all ten of its pages, resulting in a need for sixty frames, when only forty are available. While this situation may be unlikely, it becomes much more likely as we increase the multiprogramming level, so that the average memory usage is close to the available physical memory. (In our example, why stop at a multiprogramming level of six, when we can move to a level of seven or eight?)

Overallocation will show up in the following way. While executing a user program, a page fault occurs. The hardware traps to the operating system, which checks its internal tables to see that this is a page fault and not an illegal memory access. The operating system determines where the desired page is on the backing store, but then finds there are *no* free frames on the free frame list; all of memory is in use (Figure 6.5).

The operating system has several options at this point. It could terminate the user program. However, demand paging is something that *the operating system* is doing to improve the computer system's utilization and throughput. Users should not be aware that their programs are running on a paged system. Paging should be logically transparent to the user. So this option is not the best choice.

We could swap out a program, freeing all its frames, and reducing the level of multiprogramming. This is a good idea at times, and we consider it further in Section 6.8.1, but for now there is a more intriguing possibility: *page replacement*.

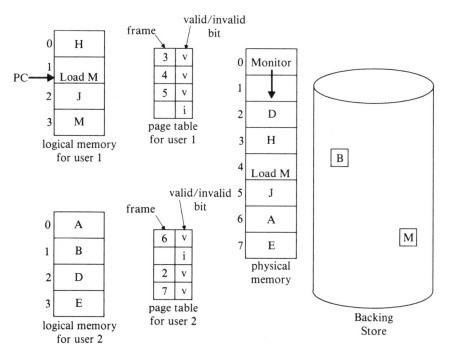

Figure 6.5   Need for page replacement

Page replacement takes the following approach. If no frame is free, find one which is not currently being used and free it. We can free a frame by writing its contents to the backing store, and changing the page table (and all other tables) to indicate that the page is no longer in memory (Figure 6.6). The freed frame can now be used to hold the page for which the program faulted. The page fault service routine is now modified to include page replacement:

1. Find the location of the desired page on the backing store.

2. Find a free frame.

   a. If there is a free frame, use it.

   b. Otherwise, use a page-replacement algorithm to select a *victim* frame.

   c. Write the victim page to the backing store; change the page and frame tables accordingly.

3. Read the desired page into the (newly) free frame; change the page and frame tables.

4. Restart the user process.

Notice that, if no frames are free, *two* page transfers (one out and one in) are required. This situation effectively doubles the page fault service time and will increase the effective access time accordingly.

This overhead can be reduced by the use of a *dirty bit*. Each page or frame may have a dirty bit associated with it in the hardware. The dirty bit for a page is set by the hardware whenever any word or byte in the page is written into, indicating when the page has been modified. When we select a page for replacement, we examine its dirty bit (each page has its own dirty bit). If the bit is set, we know that the page has been modified since it was read in from the backing store. In this case, we

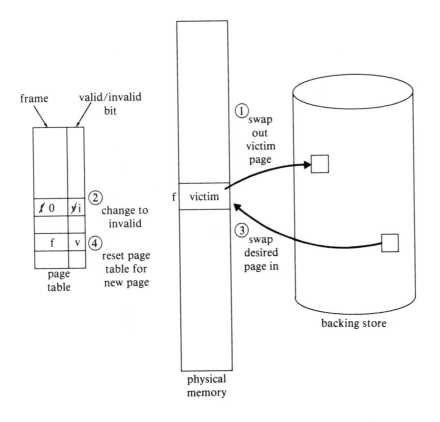

Figure 6.6 Page replacement

must write that page to the backing store. If the dirty bit is not set, however, the page has *not* been modified since it was read into memory. Therefore, if the copy of the page on the backing store has not been overwritten (by some other page, for example), we can avoid writing the memory page to the backing store; it is already there. This scheme can significantly reduce the time to service a page fault, since it reduces I/O time by half *if* the page is not dirty.

6.5 Virtual Memory Concepts

Page replacement is basic to demand paging. It completes the separation between logical memory and physical memory. With non-demand paging, user addresses were mapped into physical addresses, allowing the two sets of addresses to be quite different. With demand paging, the size of the logical address space is no longer constrained by physical memory. If we have a user program of 20 pages, we can execute it in 10 frames simply by using demand paging, and using a replacement algorithm to find a free frame whenever necessary. If a page is to be replaced, its contents are copied to the backing store. A later reference to that page will cause a page fault. At that time, the page will be brought back into memory, perhaps replacing some other page in the process.

Virtual memory is the separation of user logical memory from physical memory and is commonly implemented by demand paging. In this way a very large virtual memory can be provided for programmers on a smaller physical memory (Figure 6.7). Virtual memory makes the task of programming much easier, since the programmer need no longer worry about the amount of physical memory available, but can concentrate on the problem to be programmed. One result of virtual memory has been the virtual disappearance of overlays.

Virtual memory can also be implemented in a segmentation system. Several systems, such as Multics, provide a paged segmentation scheme, where segments are broken into pages. In this way, the user view is segmentation, but the operating system can implement this view with demand paging. *Demand segmentation* can also be used to provide virtual memory; Burroughs computer systems have used demand segmentation. However, segment replacement algorithms are more complex than page replacement algorithms because of the variable-sized nature of segments.

Two major problems must be solved to implement demand paging: the *frame allocation algorithm* and the *page replacement algorithm*. If we have multiple processes in memory, we must decide how many frames to

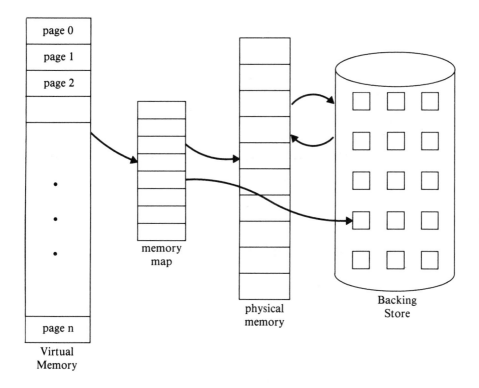

Figure 6.7   Virtual memory can be much larger than physical memory

allocate to each process. Further, when page replacement is required, we must select which frames are to be replaced.

6.6 Page Replacement Algorithms

There are a large number of different page replacement algorithms. Probably every operating system has its own unique replacement scheme. How do we select a particular replacement algorithm? In general, we want the one with the lowest *page fault rate*.

An algorithm is evaluated by running it on a particular string of memory references and computing the number of page faults. The string of memory references is called a *reference string*. Reference strings can be generated artificially (by a random number generator, for example) or by tracing a given system and recording the address of each memory reference. The latter choice produces a very large amount of data (on the order of a million addresses per second). To reduce the amount of data, we note two things.

First, for a given page size (and the page size is generally fixed by the hardware or system), we need only consider the page number, not the entire address. Second, if we have a reference to a page p, then any *immediately* following references to page p will never cause a page fault. Page p will be in memory after the first reference; the immediately following references will not fault.

For example, if we trace a particular program, we might record the following address sequence:

0100, 0432, 0101, 0612, 0102, 0103, 0104, 0101, 0611, 0102, 0103,
0104, 0101, 0610, 0102, 0103, 0104, 0101, 0609, 0102, 0105

which, at 100 words per page, is reduced to the following reference string

1, 4, 1, 6, 1, 6, 1, 6, 1, 6, 1.

To determine the number of page faults for a particular reference string and page replacement algorithm, we also need to know the number of page frames available. Obviously, as the number of frames available increases, the number of page faults will decrease. For the reference string considered above, for example, if we had three or more frames, we would have only three faults, one fault for the first reference to each page. On the other hand, with only one frame available, we would have a replacement with every reference, resulting in 11 faults. In general, we expect a curve such as Figure 6.8. As the number of frames increases, the number of page faults drops to some minimal level.

To illustrate the following page replacement algorithms, let us use the following reference string,

7, 0, 1, 2, 0, 3, 0, 4, 2, 3, 0, 3, 2, 1, 2, 0, 1, 7, 0, 1

for a memory with three frames.

6.6.1 FIFO

The simplest page replacement algorithm is *First-In-First-Out* (FIFO). A FIFO replacement algorithm associates with each page the time when it was brought into memory. When a page must be replaced, the oldest

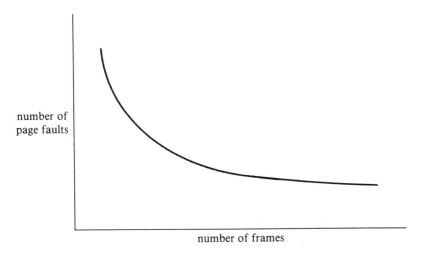

Figure 6.8   Graph of page faults versus the number of frames

page is chosen. Notice that it is not strictly necessary to keep the time when a page is brought in. We can create a FIFO queue to hold all pages in memory. We replace the page at the head of the queue. When a page is brought into memory, we insert it at the tail of the queue.

For our example reference string, our three frames are initially empty. The first three references (7, 0, 1) cause page faults, and are brought into these empty frames. The next reference (2) replaces page 7 since page 7 was brought in first. Since 0 is the next reference and 0 is already in memory, we have no fault for this reference. The first reference to 3 results in page 0 being replaced, since it was the first of the three pages in memory (0, 1, and 2) to be brought in. This replacement means that the next reference, to 0, will fault. Page 1 is then replaced by page 0. This process continues as shown in Figure 6.9. Every time a fault occurs, we show which pages are in our three frames. There are 15 faults altogether.

The FIFO page replacement algorithm is easy to understand and program. However, its performance is not always good. The page replaced may be an initialization module which was used a long time ago and is no longer needed. On the other hand, it could contain a heavily used variable which was initialized very early and is in constant use.

Notice that, even if we select for replacement a page that is in active use, everything still works correctly. After we page out an active page to bring in a new one, we almost immediately fault for the active page.

reference string

7 0 1 2 0 3 0 4 2 3 0 3 2 1 2 0 1 7 0 1

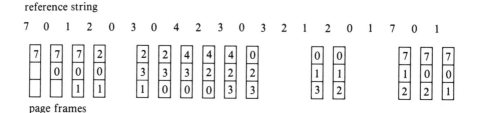

page frames

Figure 6.9   FIFO page replacement

Some other page will need to be replaced in order to bring the active page back into memory. Thus a bad replacement choice increases the page fault rate and slows program execution, but does not cause incorrect execution.

To illustrate the problems which are possible with a FIFO page replacement algorithm, consider the reference string

$$1, 2, 3, 4, 1, 2, 5, 1, 2, 3, 4, 5.$$

Figure 6.10 shows the curve of page faults versus the number of available frames. We notice that the number of faults for four frames (10) is *greater* than the number of faults for three frames (9)! This result is most unexpected and is known as *Belady's anomaly*. Belady's anomaly reflects the fact that for some page replacement algorithms, the page fault rate may *increase* as the number of allocated frames increases. One would expect that giving more memory to a program would improve its performance. In some early research it was noticed that this assumption was not always true. Belady's anomaly was discovered as a result.

6.6.2 Optimal Replacement

One result of the discovery of Belady's anomaly was the search for an *optimal* page replacement algorithm. An optimal page replacement algorithm has the lowest page fault rate of all algorithms. An optimal algorithm would never suffer from Belady's anomaly. An optimal page replacement algorithm exists, and has been called OPT or MIN. It states simply

> Replace that page which will not be used
> for the longest period of time.

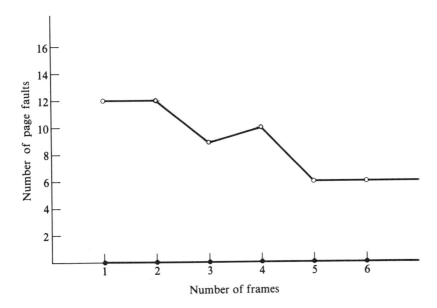

Figure 6.10   Page fault curve for FIFO replacement on a reference string

Using this page replacement algorithm guarantees the lowest possible page fault rate for a fixed number of frames.

For example, on our sample reference string, the optimal page replacement algorithm would yield nine page faults, as shown in Figure 6.11. The first three references cause faults which fill the three empty frames. The reference to page 2 replaces page 7, because 7 will not be used until reference 18, while page 0 will be used at 5, and page 1 at 14. The reference to page 3 replaces page 1, since page 1 will be the last of the three pages in memory to be referenced again. With only nine page faults, optimal replacement is much better than FIFO, which had fifteen faults. (If we ignore the first three, which all algorithms must suffer, then optimal is twice as good as FIFO). In fact, no replacement algorithm can process this reference string in three frames with less than nine faults.

Unfortunately, the optimal page replacement algorithm is difficult to implement, since it requires future knowledge of the reference string. (We encountered a similar situation with the Shortest-Job-First cpu scheduling algorithm in Section 4.3.3.) As a result, the optimal algorithm is used mainly for comparison studies. It may be quite useful to know

reference string

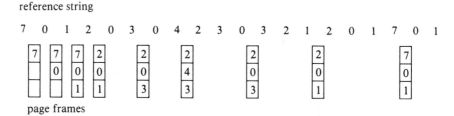

page frames

Figure 6.11   Optimal page replacement

that although a new algorithm is not optimal, it is within 12.3 percent of optimal at worst and 4.7 percent on average.

6.6.3 Least Recently Used

If the optimal algorithm is not feasible, perhaps an approximation to the optimal algorithm is possible. The key distinction between FIFO and OPT (other than looking backwards or forwards in time) is that FIFO uses the time when a page was brought into memory; OPT uses the time when a page is to be *used*. If we use the recent past as an approximation of the near future, then we would replace that page which *has not been used* for the longest period of time (Figure 6.12). This is the *Least Recently Used* (LRU) algorithm.

LRU replacement associates with each page the time of its last use. When a page must be replaced, LRU chooses that page which has not been used for the longest period of time. This is the optimal page replacement algorithm looking backwards in time, rather than forwards. (In fact, a common technique used to generate the number of faults for OPT for a particular reference string is to reverse the entire string and use LRU on this time-reversed reference string.)

The result of applying LRU to our example reference string is shown in Figure 6.12. LRU produces twelve faults. Notice that the first five faults are the same as the optimal replacement. When the reference to page 4 occurs, however, LRU sees that of the three frames in memory, page 2 was used least recently. The most recently used page is page 0, and just before that page 3 was used. Thus LRU replaces page 2, not knowing that it is about to be used. When it then faults for page 2, LRU replaces page 3 since of the three pages in memory {0, 3, 4}, page 3 is the least recently used. Despite these problems, LRU with twelve faults is still much better than FIFO with fifteen.

LRU is often used as a page replacement algorithm and is considered to be quite good. The major problem is *how* to implement

reference string

7   0   1   2   0   3   0   4   2   3   0   3   2   1   2   0   1   7   0   1

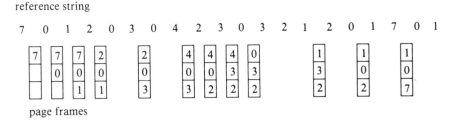

page frames

Figure 6.12   Least recently used page replacement

LRU. An LRU page replacement algorithm may require substantial hardware assistance. The problem is to determine an order for the frames defined by the time of last use. Two implementations are feasible.

- **Counters**. In the simplest case, we associate with each page table entry a time-of-use register and add to the cpu a logical clock or counter. The clock is incremented for every memory reference. Whenever a reference to a page is made, the contents of the clock register are copied to the time-of-use register in the page table for that page. In this way, we always have the "time" of the last reference to each page. We replace the page with the smallest time value. This scheme requires a search of the page table to find the least recently used page. The times must also be maintained when page tables are changed (due to cpu scheduling). Overflow of the clock must be considered.

- **Stack**. Another approach to implementing LRU is to keep a *stack* of page numbers. Whenever a page is referenced, it is removed from the stack and put on the top. In this way, the top of the stack is always the most recently used page and the bottom is the least recently used page (Figure 6.13). Since entries must be removed from the middle of the stack, it is best implemented by a doubly-linked list, with a head and tail pointer. Removing a page and putting it on the top of the stack then requires changing six pointers at worst. Each update is a little more expensive, but there is no search for a replacement; the tail pointer points to the bottom of the stack which is the least recently used page. This approach is particularly appropriate for software or microcode implementations of LRU.

Neither optimal replacement nor LRU replacement suffers from Belady's anomaly. There is a class of page replacement algorithms, called *stack algorithms*, that can never exhibit Belady's anomaly. A stack algorithm is an algorithm for which it can be shown that the set of pages in memory for n frames is always a *subset* of the set of pages which would be in memory with $n+1$ frames. For LRU, the set of pages in memory would be the n most recently referenced pages. If the number of frames is increased, these n pages will still be the most recently referenced and so will still be in memory.

Note that neither implementation of LRU would be conceivable without hardware assistance. The updating of the clock registers or stack must be done for *every* memory reference. If we were to use an interrupt for every reference, to allow software to update such data structures, it would slow every memory reference by a factor of at least 10, hence slowing every user program by a factor of 10. Few systems could tolerate that level of overhead for memory management.

6.6.4 LRU Approximation

Few systems provide sufficient hardware support for true LRU page replacement. Some systems provide no hardware support and other page replacement algorithms (such as FIFO) must be used. Many systems provide some help, however, in the form of a *reference bit*. The reference bit for a page is set, by the hardware, whenever that page is

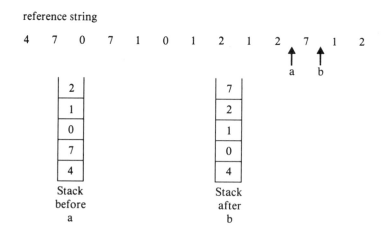

Figure 6.13   Use of a stack to record the most recent page references

referenced (either a read or a write to any word or byte in the page). Reference bits are associated with each entry in the page table, or as a separate register with one bit per frame. Special instructions are provided for reading and clearing these bits.

Initially, all bits are cleared (to 0) by the operating system. As a user program executes, the bit associated with each page referenced is set (to 1) by the hardware. After some time, we can determine which pages have been used and which have not been used by examining the reference bits. We do not know the *order* of use, but we know which were used and which were not used. This partial ordering information leads to many page replacement algorithms which try to approximate LRU replacement.

Additional Reference Bits

Additional ordering information can be gained by recording the reference bits at regular intervals. We can keep an 8-bit byte for each page in a table in memory. At regular intervals (say every 100 msec), a timer interrupt transfers control to the operating system. The operating system shifts the reference bit for each page into the high-order bit of its 8-bit byte, shifting the other bits right one bit, discarding the low-order bit. These 8-bit shift registers contain the history of page use for the last eight time periods. If the shift register contains 00000000, then the page has not been used for eight time periods; a page that is used at least once each period would have a shift register value of 11111111.

A page with a history register value of 11000100 has been used more recently than one with 01110111. If we interpret these 8-bit bytes as unsigned integers, the page with the lowest number is the least recently used, and it can be replaced. Notice that the numbers are not guaranteed to be unique, however. We can either replace (swap out) all pages with the smallest value or use a FIFO selection among them.

The number of bits of history can be varied, of course, and would be selected to make the updating as fast as possible. In the extreme case, it can be reduced to zero bits of history, leaving only the reference bit itself. This algorithm is called the *Second Chance* page replacement algorithm.

Second Chance Replacement

The basic algorithm of Second Chance replacement is a FIFO replacement algorithm. When a page has been selected, however, we inspect its reference bit. If it is 0, we proceed to replace this page. If the reference bit is 1, however, we give that page a second chance and move on to select the next FIFO page. When a page gets a second

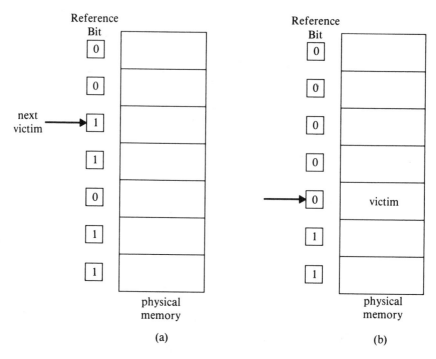

Figure 6.14   Second chance page replacement

chance, its reference bit is cleared and its arrival time is reset to the current time. Thus a page which is given a second chance will not be replaced until all other pages are replaced (or given second chances). In addition, if a page is used often enough to keep its reference bit set, it will never be replaced.

One way to view the second chance algorithm is as a circular queue. A pointer indicates which page is to be replaced next. When a frame is needed, the pointer advances until it finds a page with a zero reference bit. As it advances, it clears the reference bits (Figure 6.14). In the worst case, when all bits are set, the pointer cycles through the whole queue, giving each page a second chance. It clears all the reference bits before selecting the next page for replacement. Second chance degenerates to FIFO if all bits are set.

Least Frequently Used

Least Frequently Used (LFU) keeps a counter of the number of references which have been made to each page. The page with the smallest count is replaced. The motivation for this selection is that an actively used page should have a large reference count. This algorithm suffers from the situation in which a page is used very heavily during the initial phase of a program, but then is never again used. Since it was heavily used, it has a large count and remains in memory even though it is no longer needed. One solution is to shift the counts right one bit at regular intervals, forming an exponentially decaying average usage count.

Most Frequently Used

Another page replacement algorithm is *Most Frequently Used* (MFU) replacement, which argues that the page with the smallest count was probably just brought in and has yet to be used. As you might expect, neither MFU nor LFU are very common. The implementation of these algorithms is fairly expensive.

Page Classes

There are many other algorithms used for page replacement. For example, if we consider both the reference bit and the dirty bit (Section 6.4) as an ordered pair we have the following four classes:

0. (0,0) neither used nor dirty.

1. (0,1) not used (recently) but dirty.

2. (1,0) used but clean.

3. (1,1) used and dirty.

When page replacement is necessary, each page is in one of these four classes. We replace any page in the lowest non-empty class. If there are multiple pages in the lowest class, we can use FIFO or choose randomly among them.

6.6.5 Ad Hoc Algorithms

Other procedures are often used in addition to a specific page replacement algorithm. For example, systems commonly keep a *pool* of free frames. When a page fault occurs, a victim frame is chosen as before. However, the desired page is read into a free frame from the pool before the victim is written out. This procedure allows the program to restart as soon as possible, without waiting for the victim page to be written out. When the victim is later written out, its frame is added to the free frame pool.

An expansion of this idea maintains a list of dirty pages. Whenever the paging device is idle, a dirty page is selected and written to the backing store. Its dirty bit is then reset. This scheme increases the probability that a page will be clean when it is selected for replacement, and will not need to be written out.

Another modification is to keep a pool of free frames but to remember which page was in each frame. Since the frame contents are not modified by writing the frame to the backing store, the old page can be reused directly from the free frame pool if it is needed before that frame is reused. No I/O is needed in this case. When a page fault occurs, we first check if the desired page is in the free frame pool. If not, we must select a free frame and read into it.

This technique is used in the VAX/VMS system, along with a FIFO replacement algorithm. When the FIFO replacement algorithm mistakenly replaces a page which is still in active use, it is quickly retrieved from the free-frame buffer and no I/O is necessary. The free-frame buffer provides protection against the relatively poor, but simple, FIFO replacement algorithm.

6.7 Allocation Algorithms

Once we have selected a replacement algorithm, we have considerable flexibility in memory management. User virtual memory can be much larger than physical memory. Demand paging and page replacement allow us to execute large programs even with a small physical memory.

The simplest case of virtual memory is the single-user system. Consider a single-user microcomputer system with 128K bytes of memory composed of 1K pages. The operating system may take 35K bytes, leaving 93 frames for the user program. Under pure demand paging, all 93 frames would initially be put on the free frame list. When a user program started execution, it would generate a sequence of page faults. The first 93 page faults would all get free frames from the free frame list. When the free frame list was exhausted, a page replacement algorithm would be used to select one of the 93 in-core pages to be replaced with the 94th, and so on. When the program terminated, the 93 frames would once again be placed on the free frame list.

There are many variations on this simple strategy. We can require that the operating system allocate all of its buffer and table space from the free frame list. When this space is not in use by the operating system, it can be used to support user paging. We could try to keep three free frames reserved on the free frame list at all times. Thus when a page fault occurs, there is a free frame available to page into. While the page swap is taking place a replacement can be selected, which is then written to the backing store as the user program continues to execute.

Other variants are also possible, but the basic strategy is clear: the user program is allocated any free frame.

A different problem arises when demand paging is combined with multiprogramming. Multiprogramming puts two (or more) programs in memory at the same time. How do we allocate the fixed amount of free memory among the various processes? If we have 93 free frames and 2 processes, how many frames does each process get?

6.7.1 Minimum Number of Frames

There are, of course, constraints on our allocation. We cannot allocate more than the total number of available frames (unless there is page sharing). There is also a minimum number of frames which can be allocated. Obviously, as the number of frames allocated to each process decreases, the page fault rate (and effective access time) increase, slowing process execution.

Besides the undesirable performance properties of allocating only a few frames, there is a minimum number of frames which must be allocated. This minimum number is defined by the instruction set architecture. Remember that when a page fault occurs before an executing instruction is complete, the instruction must be restarted. Consequently, we must have enough frames to hold all the different pages that any single instruction can reference.

For example, consider the PDP-8. All of its memory reference instructions have only one memory address. Thus we need at least one frame for the instruction and one frame for the memory reference. In addition, the address specified in the instruction may be an indirect reference. So, a load instruction on page 16 can refer to an address on page 0, which is an indirect reference to page 23. Therefore, paging on the PDP-8 requires at least three frames per process. Think about what might happen if a process had only two frames.

The minimal number of frames is defined by the computer architecture. While the PDP-8 requires three frames, the PDP-11 requires at least six. The move instruction for some addressing modes is more than one word and thus the instruction itself may straddle two pages. In addition, each of its two operands may be indirect references, for a total of six frames. The worst case for the IBM 370 is probably the Move Character instruction. Since the instruction is storage-to-storage, it takes 6 bytes and can straddle two pages. The block of characters to move and the area to be moved to can each also straddle two pages. This situation would require 6 frames. (Actually, the worst case is if the Move

Character instruction is the operand of an Execute instruction which straddles a page boundary; in this case, we need 8 frames.)

The Data General Nova 3 architecture allowed multiple levels of indirection: each 16-bit word could contain a 15-bit address plus a 1-bit indirect indicator. Theoretically, a simple load instruction could reference an indirect address that could reference an indirect address (on another page) that could also reference an indirect address (on yet another page), and so on, until every page in virtual memory had been touched. Thus in the worst case, the entire virtual memory must be in physical memory. Noting that no real program ever made much use of this "feature", however, the engineers modified the architecture when paging was added to limit an instruction to at most 16 levels of indirection. When the first indirection occurs, a counter is set to 16 and decremented for each successive indirection for this instruction. If the counter is decremented to zero, a trap occurs (excessive indirection). This limitation reduces the maximum number of memory references per instruction to 17, requiring the same number of frames.

The minimum number of frames per process is defined by the architecture, while the maximum number is defined by the amount of available physical memory. In between, we are still left with significant choice in frame allocation.

6.7.2 Global versus Local Allocation

It is not necessary for us to decide explicitly how many frames to allocate to each process. With multiple processes competing for frames, we can classify page replacement algorithms into two broad categories: *global replacement* and *local replacement*. Global replacement allows a process to select a replacement frame from the set of all frames, even if that frame is currently allocated to some other process; one process can take a frame from another. Local replacement requires that each process select only from its own set of allocated frames.

With a local replacement strategy, the number of frames allocated to a process does not change. With global replacement, a process may happen to select only frames allocated to other processes, thus increasing the number of frames allocated to it (assuming that other processes do not choose *its* frames for replacement).

One problem of a global replacement algorithm is that a program cannot control its own page fault rate. The set of pages in memory for a process depends not only upon the paging behavior of that process, but also on the paging behavior of other processes. Therefore, the same program may perform quite differently (taking 0.5 seconds for one execution and 10.3 seconds for the next execution) due to totally external circumstances. This is not the case with a local replacement algorithm. Under local replacement, the set of pages in memory for a process is affected only by the paging behavior of that process.

6.7.3 Allocation Algorithms

The easiest way to split m frames among n processes is to give everyone an equal share, m/n frames. For instance, if there are 93 frames and 5 processes, each process would get 18 frames. The leftover 3 frames could be used as a free frame buffer pool. This is called *equal allocation*.

An alternative is to recognize that various processes will need differing amounts of memory. If a small student program of 10K and an interactive data base of 127K are the only two processes running in a system with 62 free frames, it does not make much sense to give each process 31 frames. The student program does not need more than 10 frames so the other 21 are strictly wasted.

To solve this problem, we can use *proportional allocation*. We allocate available memory to each process according to its size. Let the size of the virtual memory for process p_i be s_i and define

$$S = \Sigma \, s_i$$

Then if the total number of available frames is m, we allocate a_i frames to process p_i, where a_i is approximately

$$a_i = s_i/S \times m$$

Of course, we must adjust the a_i's to be integers, greater than the minimum number of frames required by the instruction set, with a sum not exceeding m.

For proportional allocation, we would split 62 frames between two processes, one of 10 pages and one of 127 pages, by allocating 4 frames and 57 frames, respectively, since,

$$10/137 \times 62 \approx 4$$
$$127/137 \times 62 \approx 57$$

In this way, both processes share the available frames according to their "needs", rather than equally.

In both of these cases, equal and proportional allocation, of course, the allocation to each process may vary according to the multiprogramming level. If the multiprogramming level is increased, each process will lose a couple of frames to provide the memory needed for the new process. On the other hand, if the multiprogramming level decreases, the frames which had been allocated to the departed process can now be spread over the remaining processes.

Notice that with either equal or proportional allocation, a high-priority process is treated the same as a low-priority process. By its definition, however, we may want to give the high-priority process more memory to speed its execution, to the detriment of low-priority processes.

One approach is to use a proportional allocation scheme, where the ratio of frames depends not upon the relative sizes of programs, but upon their priorities, or on a combination of size and priority.

Another approach is to allow high-priority processes to select frames from low-priority processes for replacement. A process can select a replacement from among its own frames or the frames of any lower priority process. This approach allows a high-priority process to increase its frame allocation at the expense of the low-priority process.

6.8 Thrashing

If the number of frames allocated to a low-priority process falls below the minimum number required by the computer architecture, we must suspend its execution. We should then page out its remaining pages, freeing all of its allocated frames. This provision introduces a swap-in/swap-out level of intermediate cpu scheduling.

In fact, look at any process which does not have "enough" frames. Although it is technically possible to reduce the number of allocated frames to the minimum, there is some (larger) number of pages that are in active use. If the process does not have this number of frames, it will very quickly page fault. At this point, it must replace some page. However, since all of its pages are in active use, it must replace a page which will be needed again right away. Consequently, it very quickly faults again, and again, and again. The program continues to fault, replacing pages for which it will then fault and bring back in right away.

This very high paging activity is called *thrashing*. A process is thrashing if it is spending more time paging than executing. Thrashing can cause severe performance problems. Consider the following scenario, which is based upon the actual behavior of early paging systems.

The operating system monitors cpu utilization. If cpu utilization is too low, the degree of multiprogramming is increased by introducing a new process to the system. A global page replacement algorithm is used. Now suppose a process enters a new phase in its execution and needs more frames. It starts faulting and taking pages away from other processes. These processes need those pages, however, and so they also fault, taking pages from other processes. These faulting processes must use the paging device to swap pages in and out. As they queue up for the paging device, the ready queue empties. As processes wait for the paging device, cpu utilization decreases.

The cpu scheduler sees the decreasing cpu utilization, and increases the degree of multiprogramming as a result. The new process tries to get started by taking pages from running processes, causing more page faults, and a longer queue for the paging device. As a result, cpu utilization drops even further, and the cpu scheduler tries to increase the degree of multiprogramming even more. Thrashing has occurred and system throughput plunges. The page fault rate increases tremendously. As a result, the effective memory access time increases. No work is getting done because the processes are spending all their time paging.

This phenomenon is illustrated in Figure 6.15. CPU utilization is plotted against the degree of multiprogramming. As the degree of multiprogramming increases, cpu utilization also increases, although more slowly, until a maximum is reached. If the degree of multiprogramming is increased even further, thrashing sets in and cpu utilization drops sharply. At this point, to increase cpu utilization and stop thrashing, we must *decrease* the degree of multiprogramming.

The effects of thrashing can be limited by using a local or priority replacement algorithm. With local replacement, if one process starts thrashing, it cannot steal frames from another process and cause it to thrash also. However, if processes are thrashing, they will be in the

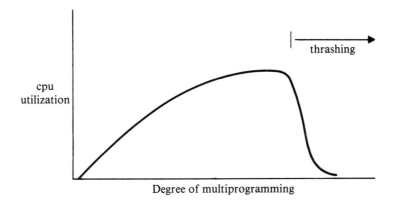

Figure 6.15   Thrashing

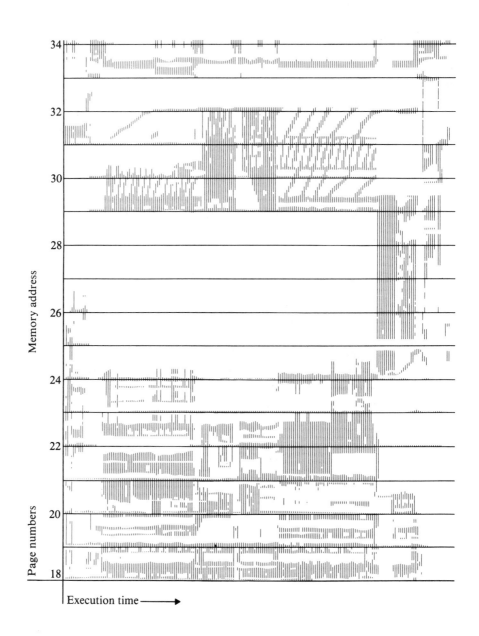

Figure 6.16   Locality in a memory reference pattern

Redrawn from [Hatfield and Gerald 1971] by permission.

queue for the paging device most of the time. The average service time for a page fault will increase, due to the longer average queue for the paging device. Thus the effective access time will increase even for a process which is not thrashing.

6.8.1 Locality

To prevent thrashing, we must provide a process with as many frames as it needs. But how do we know how many frames it "needs"? There are several techniques. The working set strategy (discussed in Section 6.8.2) starts by looking at what a program is actually using. This approach defines the *locality model* of program execution.

The locality model states that as a program executes, it moves from locality to locality. A locality is a set of pages which are actively used together (Figure 6.16). A program is generally composed of several different localities, which may overlap.

For example, when a subroutine is called, it defines a new locality. In this locality, memory references are made to the instructions of the subroutine, its local variables, and a subset of the global variables. When the subroutine is exited, the process leaves this locality, since the local variables and instructions of the subroutine are no longer in active use. We may return to this locality later. Thus we see that localities are defined by the program structure and its data structures. The locality model states that all programs will exhibit this basic memory reference structure.

Suppose we allocate enough frames to a process to accommodate its current locality. It will fault for the pages in its locality until all of these pages are in memory and then it will not fault again until it changes localities. If we allocate fewer frames than the size of the current locality, the process will thrash, since it cannot keep in memory all of the pages that it is actively using.

6.8.2 Working Set Model

The *working set model* is based on the assumption of locality. This model uses a parameter, Δ, to define the *working set window*. The idea is to examine the most recent Δ page references. The set of pages in the most recent Δ page references is the *working set* (Figure 6.17). If a page is in active use, it will be in the working set. If it is no longer being used, it will drop from the working set Δ time units after its last reference. Thus the working set is an approximation of the program's locality.

For example, given the sequence of memory references shown in Figure 6.17, if $\Delta = 10$ memory references, then the working set at time t_1 is $\{1, 2, 5, 6, 7\}$. By time t_2, the working set has changed to $\{3, 4\}$.

page reference trace

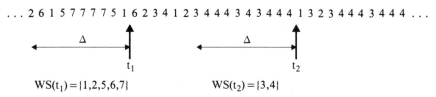

Figure 6.17   Working set model

The accuracy of the working set depends upon the selection of Δ. If Δ is too small, it will not encompass the entire working set; if Δ is too large, it may overlap several localities. In the extreme, if Δ is infinite, the working set is the entire program. Madnick and Donovan [1974] suggest that Δ should be about 10,000 references.

The most important property of the working set is its size. If we compute the working set size, WSS_i, for each process in the system, we can then consider

$$D = \Sigma \; WSS_i$$

where D is the total demand for frames. Each process is actively using the pages in its working set. Thus process i needs WSS_i frames. If the total demand is greater than the total number of available frames, thrashing will occur, since some processes will not have enough frames.

The use of the working set model is then quite simple. The operating system monitors the working set of each process and allocates to it enough frames to provide it with its working set size. If there are enough extra frames, another process can be initiated. If the sum of the working set sizes increases, exceeding the total number of available frames, the operating system selects a process to suspend. Its pages are written out and its frames are reallocated to other processes. The suspended process can be restarted later.

This working set strategy prevents thrashing while keeping the degree of multiprogramming as high as possible. Thus it tries to optimize cpu utilization.

The difficulty with the working set model is keeping track of the working set. The working set window is a moving window. At each memory reference, a new reference appears at one end and the oldest reference drops off the other end. A page is in the working set if it is referenced anywhere in the working set window. We can approximate the working set model with a fixed interval timer interrupt and a reference bit.

For example, assume Δ is 10,000 references and we can cause a timer interrupt every 5,000 references. When we get a timer interrupt, we copy and clear the reference bit values for each page. Thus if a page fault occurs, we can examine the current reference bit and the two in-memory bits to determine if a page was used within the last 10,000 to 15,000 references. If it was used, at least one of these bits will be on. If it has not been used, these bits will be off. Those pages with at least one bit on will be considered to be in the working set. Note that this arrangement is not entirely accurate, since we cannot tell where within an interval of 5,000 a reference occurred. We can reduce the uncertainty by increasing the number of our history bits and the number of interrupts (for example, 10 bits and interrupts every 1,000 references). However, the cost to service these more frequent interrupts will be correspondingly higher.

6.8.3 Page Fault Frequency

The Working Set Model is quite successful and knowledge of the working set can be useful for prepaging (Section 6.9.1), but it seems a rather clumsy way to control thrashing. The *Page Fault Frequency* (PFF) strategy takes a more direct approach.

The specific problem is to prevent thrashing. Thrashing is a high page fault rate. Thus we want to control the page fault rate. When it is too high, we know that the process needs more frames. Similarly, if the

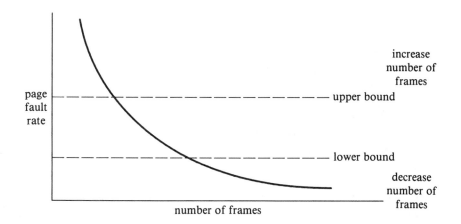

Figure 6.18   Page fault frequency

page fault rate is too low, then the process may have too many frames. We can establish upper and lower bounds on the desired page fault rate (Figure 6.18). If the actual page fault exceeds the upper limit, we allocate that process another frame; if the page fault rate falls below the lower limit, we remove a frame from that process. Thus we can directly measure and control the page fault rate to prevent thrashing.

As with the working set strategy, we may have to suspend a process. If the page fault rate increases and no free frames are available, we must select some process and suspend it. The freed frames are then distributed to processes with high page fault rates.

6.9 Other Considerations

The selection of a replacement algorithm and allocation policy are the major decisions to make for a paging system, but there are many other considerations.

6.9.1 Prepaging

An obvious property of a pure demand paging system is the large number of page faults that occur when a program is started. This situation is a result of trying to get the initial locality into memory. The same thing may happen at other times. For instance, when a swapped-out process is restarted, all of its pages are on the backing store and each must be brought in by its own page fault. *Prepaging* is an attempt to prevent this high level of initial paging. The strategy is to bring into memory at one time all of the pages which will be needed.

In a system using the working set model, for example, we keep with each process a list of the pages in its working set. If we must suspend a process (due to an I/O wait or a lack of free frames), we remember the working set for that process. When the process is to be resumed (I/O completion or enough free frames), we automatically bring its entire working set back into memory before restarting the process.

Prepaging may be an advantage in some cases. The question is simply whether the cost of prepaging is less than the cost of servicing the corresponding page faults. It may well be the case that many of the pages brought back into memory by prepaging are not used. Assume that s pages are prepaged and a fraction α of these s pages are actually used ($0 \leq \alpha \leq 1$). The question is whether the cost of the αs saved page faults is more or less than the cost of prepaging $(1-\alpha)s$ unnecessary pages. If α is close to zero, prepaging loses; if α is close to one, prepaging wins.

6.9.2 I/O Interlock

When demand paging is used, it is sometimes necessary to allow some of its pages to be *locked* in memory. One such situation occurs when I/O is done to or from user (virtual) memory. I/O is often implemented by a separate I/O processor. For example, a magnetic tape controller is generally given the number of words (or bytes) to transfer and a memory address for the buffer (Figure 6.19). When the transfer is complete, the cpu is interrupted.

We must be sure the following sequence of events does not occur: A process issues an I/O request, and is put in a queue for that I/O device.

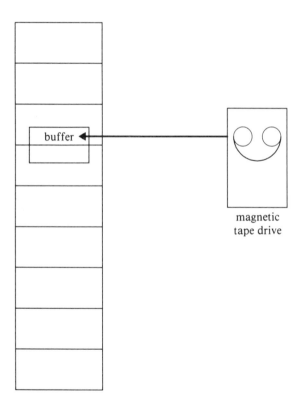

magnetic
tape drive

Figure 6.19   Frames which are being used for I/O must be kept in memory

Meanwhile, the cpu is given to other processes. These processes cause page faults, and, using a global replacement algorithm, one of them replaces the page containing the memory buffer for the waiting process. The pages are swapped out. Some time later, when the I/O request advances to the head of the device queue, the I/O occurs to the specified address. However, this frame is now being used for a different page belonging to another process.

There are two common solutions to this problem. One solution is never to execute I/O to user memory. Instead, data is always copied between system memory and user memory. I/O only takes place between system memory and the I/O device. To write a block on tape, the block is first copied to system memory and then written to tape.

This extra copying may result in unacceptably high overhead. Another solution is to allow pages to be *locked* into memory. A lock bit is associated with every frame. If the frame is locked, it cannot be selected for replacement. Under this approach, to write a block on tape, the pages containing the block are locked into memory. The system can then continue as usual. Locked pages cannot be replaced. When the I/O is complete, the pages are unlocked.

Another use for a lock bit involves normal page replacement. Consider the following sequence of events: A low-priority process faults. Selecting a replacement frame, the paging system swaps the necessary page into memory. Ready to continue, the low-priority process enters the ready queue and waits for the cpu. Since it is a low-priority process, it may not be selected by the cpu scheduler for awhile. While the low-priority process waits, a high-priority process faults. Looking for a replacement, the paging system sees a page which is in memory but has not been referenced or modified: the page the low-priority process just brought in. It looks like a perfect replacement; it is clean and will not need to be written out, and it apparently has not been used for a long time.

Deciding whether the high-priority process should be able to replace the low-priority process is a policy decision. After all, we are simply delaying the low-priority process for the benefit of the high-priority process. On the other hand, we are wasting the effort spent to bring in the page of the low-priority process. If we decide to prevent replacing a newly swapped-in page until it can be used at least once, then we can use the lock bit to enforce this policy. When a page is selected for replacement, its lock bit is turned on and remains on until the faulting process is again dispatched.

Using a lock bit can be dangerous, however, if it gets turned on and never turned off. Should this situation occur (due to a bug in the operating system, for example), the locked frame becomes unusable.

6.9.3 Page Size

The designers of an operating system for an existing machine seldom have a choice concerning the page size. However, when new machines are being designed, a decision regarding the best page size must be made. As you might expect, there is no single best page size. Rather there are a set of factors which support various sizes. Page sizes are invariably powers of two, generally ranging from 256 (2^8) to 4096 (2^{12}) bytes or words.

How do we select a page size? One concern is the size of the page table. For a given virtual memory space, decreasing the page size increases the number of pages, and hence the size of the page table. For a virtual memory of 4 megawords (2^{22}), there would be 16,384 pages of 256 words but only 1024 pages of 4096 words. Since each active process must have its own copy of the page table, we see that a large page size is desirable.

On the other hand, memory is better utilized with smaller pages. If a program is allocated memory starting at location 00000, continuing until it has as much as it needs, it is unlikely that the program will end exactly on a page boundary. Thus a part of the last page must be allocated (since pages are the units of allocation) but is unused (internal fragmentation). Assuming independence of program size and page size, we would expect that, on the average, half of the last page of each program is wasted. This loss would be only 128 words for a page of 256 words, but 2048 words for a page of 4096 words. To minimize internal fragmentation, we need a small page size.

Another problem is the time required to read or write a page. I/O time is composed of (for a fixed head device) latency and transfer time. Transfer time is proportional to the amount transferred (that is, the page size), a fact which would seem to argue for a small page size. Remember, however, that latency time normally dwarfs transfer time. At a transfer rate of 256,000 words per sec, it takes only 2 msec to transfer 512 words. Latency, on the other hand, is perhaps 8 msec. Of the total I/O time (10 msec), therefore, 20 percent is attributable to the actual transfer. Decreasing the page size to 128 words only reduces total I/O time from 10 to 9 msec. Doubling the page size increases I/O time to only 12 msec. It takes 12 msec to read a single page of 1024 words, but 36 msec to read the same amount as four pages of 256 words each. Thus a desire to minimize I/O time argues for a larger page size.

But, with a smaller page size, total I/O should be reduced, since locality will be improved. A smaller page size allows each page to better match program locality. For example, consider a program of 20K words, of which only half (10K) are actually used in an execution. If we have only one large page, we must bring in the entire page, a total of 20K words transferred and allocated. If we had pages of only one word, then we could bring in only the 10,000 words that are actually used, resulting in only 10,000 words being transferred and allocated. With a smaller page size, we have better resolution, allowing us to isolate only the memory which is actually needed. With a larger page size we must allocate and transfer not only what is needed but also anything else which happens to be in the page, whether it is needed or not. Thus a smaller page size should result in less I/O and less total allocated memory.

On the other hand, did you notice that with a page size of 1 word, we would have a page fault for *each* word? A program of 20K, using only half of that memory, would generate only 1 page fault with a page size of 20K, but 10,000 page faults for a page size of 1 word. Each page fault generates the large amount of overhead needed for saving registers, replacing a page, queueing for the paging device, and updating tables. To minimize the number of page faults, we need to have a large page size.

There are other factors to consider (such as the relationship between page size and sector size on the paging device), but the problem has no best answer. Some factors (internal fragmentation, locality) argue for a small page size while others (table size, I/O time) argue for a large page size. To illustrate the problem, two systems allow two different page sizes. The Multics hardware (GE 645) allows pages of either 64 words or 1024 words. The IBM/370 allows pages of either 2K or 4K bytes. The difficulty of picking a page size is illustrated by the fact that MVS on the IBM/370 selected 4K pages, while VS/1 selected 2K pages.

6.9.4 Program Structure

Demand paging is designed to be transparent to the user program. In many cases, the user is completely unaware of the paged nature of memory. In other cases, however, system performance can be improved by an awareness of the underlying demand paging.

For example, assume pages are 128 words in size. Consider a Pascal program with a 128 by 128 array to initialize to zero. The following code is typical.

var A: **array** [1..128] **of array** [1..128] **of** *integer*;

for j := 1 **to** 128
   do for i := 1 **to** 128
      do $A[i][j]$:= 0;

This code looks innocent enough, but notice that the array is stored row major. That is, the array is stored $A[1][1]$, $A[1][2]$, ..., $A[1][128]$, $A[2][1]$, $A[2][2]$, ..., $A[128][128]$. For pages of 128 words, each row takes one page. Thus the code above zeroes one word in each page, then another word in each page, and so on, resulting in $128 \times 128 = 16,384$ page faults. Changing the code to

> **var** A: **array** [1..128] **of array** [1..128] **of** *integer*;

> **for** $i :=$ 1 **to** 128
>   **do for** $j :=$ 1 **to** 128
>   **do** $A[i][j] :=$ 0;

on the other hand, zeroes all the words on one page before starting the next page, reducing the number of page faults to 128.

Careful selection of data structures and programming structures can increase locality and hence lower the page fault rate and the number of pages in the working set. A stack has good locality since access is always made to the top. A hash table, on the other hand, is designed to scatter references, producing bad locality.

At a later stage, the compiler and loader can have a significant effect on paging. Separating code and data and generating reentrant code means that code pages can be read-only and hence will never be dirty. Clean pages do not have to be paged out to be replaced. The loader can avoid placing routines across page boundaries, keeping each routine completely in one page. Routines which call each other many times can be packed into the same page. This is a variant of the bin packing problem of operations research: try to pack the variable-sized load segments into the fixed-size pages so that interpage references are minimized. Such an approach is particularly useful for large page sizes.

6.9.5 Storage Hierarchy

It should also be pointed out that our discussion has concentrated on only one level of what is a storage hierarchy in most systems. Many computers now contain a high-speed cache for main memory. When a memory access is made, the contents of the accessed location, plus its neighbors, are copied to the cache. If another reference is made to these locations they can be fetched directly from the cache without having to go to the slower-speed main memory. For a reasonably sized cache, a hit ratio of 80 percent is common.

As a historical aside, the first paging computer was the Atlas computer. Main memory was a 96K drum. Drum memories were fairly common in the late 1950's, being used also on the IBM 650. The Atlas had a small amount (16K words) of a new, faster memory called a magnetic core memory. It was still experimental and was very expensive. The core memory was used as a cache for the slower drum memory. Paging techniques were developed to implement the cache management.

Extending this view, internal programmable registers, such as index registers and accumulators, are a high-speed cache for main memory. The programmer (or compiler) implements the register (page) allocation and replacement algorithms to decide what information to keep in primary memory (registers) and what to keep in backing memory (main memory). The optimal page replacement algorithm can often be used here, since the programmer or compiler can look ahead to see what will be needed in the future.

Looking in the other direction, the file system can be viewed as a backing store for the paging device. Files are transferred from the file system to the paging device when they are referenced (demand transfer). The file system itself may have several levels of storage. The faster (but more limited) disk storage can be backed up by larger (but slower) tape storage. Transfers between these two storage levels are generally explicitly requested, but many systems now automatically archive a file which has not been used for a long time (a month) and will then automatically fetch it back to disk when it is next referenced.

Stepping back, we can see a wide variety of storage in a computer system, which can be organized in a hierarchy (Figure 6.20). The higher levels are expensive, but very fast. As we move down the hierarchy, the cost per bit decreases, while the access time increases and the amount of storage at each level increases. The movement of information between levels may be either explicit or implicit. Paging algorithms are suitable for many of these transfers.

This view of storage was carried to its natural conclusion in the Multics system. Multics provides a very large segmented address space. The segments are named, and all files are segments. Thus explicit I/O commands are not needed. A file can be accessed by specifying the file name as a segment name and loading or storing directly into the segment. The reference will cause a segment fault (and then a page fault) to transfer the desired information from the file system to memory.

6.10 Summary

It is desirable to be able to execute a process whose logical address space is larger than the available physical address space. The programmer can

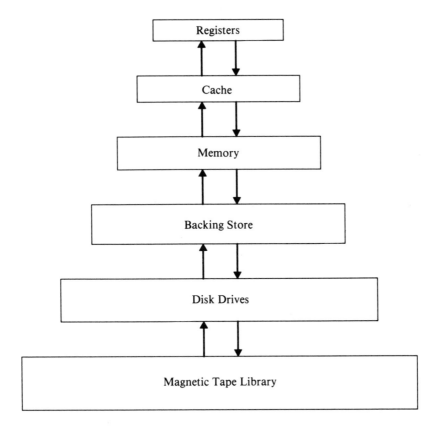

Figure 6.20   Memory hierarchies

make such a process executable by restructuring it using overlays, but this is generally a difficult programming task. Virtual memory is a technique to allow a large logical address space to be mapped onto a smaller physical memory. Virtual memory allows very large programs to be run, and also allows the degree of multiprogramming to be raised, increasing cpu utilization.

Pure demand paging never brings in a page until it is actually referenced. The first reference causes a page fault to the operating system resident monitor. The operating system consults an internal table to determine where the page is located on the backing store. It then finds a free frame and reads the page in from the backing store. The page table is updated to reflect this change and the instruction that caused the page fault is restarted. This approach allows a program to run even though its entire memory image is not in main memory at once. As long as the page fault rate is reasonably low, performance is acceptable.

Demand paging can be used to reduce the number of frames allocated to a process. This arrangement can raise the degree of multiprogramming (allowing more processes to be available for execution at one time) and, hopefully, the cpu utilization of the system. It also allows programs to be run even though their memory requirements exceed the total available physical memory. Such programs run in virtual memory.

If total memory requirements exceed the physical memory, then it may be necessary to replace pages from memory, in order to free frames for new pages. Various page replacement algorithms are used. FIFO is easy to program, but suffers from Belady's anomaly. Optimal page replacement requires future knowledge. Least Recently Used (LRU) is an approximation of optimal, but even it may be difficult to implement. Most page replacement algorithms, such as second chance, are approximations of LRU.

In addition to a page replacement algorithm, a frame allocation policy is needed. Allocation can be fixed, suggesting local page replacement, or dynamic, suggesting global replacement. The working set model assumes that programs execute in localities. The working set is the set of pages in the current locality. Accordingly, each process should be allocated enough frames for its current working set.

If a process does not have enough memory for its working set, it will thrash. Providing enough frames to each process to avoid thrashing may require process swapping and scheduling.

In addition to the major problems of page replacement and frame allocation, the proper design of a paging system requires consideration of page size, I/O, locking, prepaging, program structure, and other topics. Virtual memory can be thought of as one level of a hierarchy of storage levels in a computer system. Each level has its own access time, size, and cost parameters.

Exercises

6.1 What relationship exists between the choice of a system file structure and the system's virtual memory?

6.2 When do page faults occur? Describe the actions taken by the operating system when a page fault occurs.

6.3 Would a drum or a disk be better for a paging device?

6.4 Assume you have a page reference string for a process with m frames (initially all empty). The page reference string has length p with n distinct page numbers occurring in it. For any page replacement algorithms,

   a. What is a lower bound on the number of page faults?

   b. What is an upper bound on the number of page faults?

6.5 Just as paging can be demand paging, so segmentation can be demand segmentation. We need a segment replacement algorithm (similar to a page replacement algorithm). Describe a reasonable segment replacement algorithm. What problems are there with segment replacement that do not occur with page replacement?

6.6 Which of the following programming techniques and structures are "good" for a demand paged environment and which are "not good"?

   a. Stack.

   b. Hashed Symbol Table.

   c. Sequential Search.

   d. Binary Search.

   e. Pure Code.

   f. Vector Operations.

   g. Indirection.

6.7 Consider the following page replacement algorithms:

   a. LRU.

   b. FIFO.

   c. Optimal.

   d. Second Chance.

Rank these algorithms from bad to perfect according to their page fault rate. Separate those algorithms which suffer from Belady's anomaly from those which do not.

6.8 A certain computer provides its users with a virtual memory space of 2^{24} words. The computer has 2^{18} words of physical memory. The virtual memory is implemented by paging, and the page size is 256 words. A user program generates the virtual address 11123456 (octal). Explain how the system establishes the corresponding physical location. Distinguish between software and hardware operations.

6.9 Consider the following sequence of memory references from a 460-word program:

10, 11, 104, 170, 73, 309, 185, 245, 246, 434, 458, 364

- Give the reference string assuming a page size of 100 words.
- Find the page fault rate for this reference string, assuming 200 words of primary memory available to the program and a FIFO replacement algorithm.
- What would the page fault rate be if we used an LRU replacement algorithm?
- What is the page fault rate for the optimal replacement algorithm?

6.10 Suppose your replacement policy (in a paged system) consists of regularly examining each page and discarding it if it has not been used since the last examination. What would you gain and what would you lose by using this policy rather than (say) LRU or second chance?

6.11 Consider a paging system with a paging drum of 4 million words of memory with an average access and transfer time of 5 milliseconds, and a paged core memory of 262,144 words with a 2 microsecond access time. If we want our paging system to look to the user like a memory of 4 million words with a 4 microsecond (average) access time, what percentage of accesses must occur without a page fault?

6.12 When virtual memory is implemented in a computing system, there are certain costs associated with the technique, and certain benefits. List the costs and the benefits. Is it possible for the costs to exceed the benefits? What measures can be taken to ensure that this does not happen?

6.13 Consider a demand paging system. Measured utilizations are,

CPU utilization	20%
Paging drum	99.7%
Other I/O devices	5%

Which (if any) of the following will (probably) improve cpu utilization? Why?

a. Get a faster cpu.

b. Get a bigger paging drum.

c. Increase the degree of multiprogramming.

d. Decrease the degree of multiprogramming.

e. Get faster other I/O devices.

6.14 An operating system supports a paged virtual memory, using a central processor with a cycle time of 1 microsecond. Pages have 1000 words, and the paging device is a drum which rotates at 3000 revolutions per minute, and transfers 1,000,000 words per second. The following statistical measurements were obtained from the system:

- 0.1 percent of all instructions executed accessed a page other than the current page.

- Of the instructions which accessed another page, 80 percent accessed a page already in memory.

- When a new page was required, the replaced page was dirty 50 percent of the time.

Calculate the effective instruction time (the average time required to execute an instruction) on this system, assuming that the system is running one program only, and that the processor is idle during drum transfers.

6.15 Suppose we want to use a paging algorithm which requires a reference bit (like second chance or working set), but the hardware does not provide one. Can you sketch how we could simulate a reference bit even if one is not provided by the hardware, or is this not possible? If it is possible, what would be the cost?

6.16 We have devised a new page replacement algorithm which is rather complex, but it is thought that it may be optimal. In some contorted test cases, Belady's anomaly occurs. Is the new algorithm optimal?

6.17 Consider the two-dimensional array A:

var A: **array** $[1..100]$ **of array** $[1..100]$ **of** *integer*;

where $A[1][1]$ is at location 200, in a paged memory system with pages of size 200. A small program is in page 0 (locations 0-199) for manipulating the matrix, thus every instruction fetch will be from page 0.

For three page frames, how many page faults are generated by the following array initialization loops, using LRU replacement, and assuming page frame 1 has the program in it, and the other two are initially empty.

>   a. **for** $j := 1$ **to** 100 **do**
>   **for** $i := 1$ **to** 100 **do**
> $A[i][j] := 0$;

>   b. **for** $i := 1$ **to** 100 **do**
>   **for** $j := 1$ **to** 100 **do**
> $A[i][j] := 0$;

6.18 Consider the following page reference string:

1, 2, 3, 4, 2, 1, 5, 6, 2, 1, 2, 3, 7, 6, 3, 2, 1, 2, 3, 6

How many page faults would occur for the following replacement algorithms, assuming 1, 2, 3, 4, 5, 6, or 7 frames? Remember all frames are initially empty, so your first unique pages will all cost one fault each.

- LRU.
- FIFO.
- Optimal.

6.19 Segmentation is very similar to paging but with variable-sized "pages". Define two segment replacement algorithms based on FIFO and LRU page replacement schemes. Remember that since segments are not the same size, the segment which is chosen to be replaced may not be big enough to leave enough consecutive locations for the needed segment. Consider strategies for systems where segments cannot be relocated and systems where they can.

6.20 Consider a demand paging system with a paging drum with an average access and transfer time of 5 milliseconds. Addresses are translated through a page table in main memory, with an access time of 1 microsecond per memory access. Thus each memory reference through the page table takes two accesses. To improve this time, an associative memory has been added which reduces access time to one memory reference, if the page table entry is in the associative memory.

Assuming that 80 percent of the accesses are in the associative memory, and that of the remaining, 10 percent (or 2 percent of the total) cause page faults, what is the effective memory access time?

6.21 Consider a system with 1 microsecond core memory and a drum secondary storage system with average latency time of 5 microseconds and transfer rate of a million words per second.

    a. For a page size p and page fault rate x $(0 \leq x \leq 1)$ what is the effective access time?

    b. Assume that the page fault rate varies inversely exponentially with page size, $x = e^{-p/500}$. Thus, the larger the page size, the smaller the page fault rate. What page size gives the minimal effective access time?

6.22 Suppose we have a demand paged memory. The page table is held in registers. It takes 8 milliseconds to service a page fault if an empty page is available or the replaced page is not dirty, and 20 milliseconds if the replaced page is dirty. Memory access time is 1 microsecond.

Assume that the page to be replaced is dirty 70 percent of the time, what is the maximum acceptable page fault rate for an effective access time of no more than 2 microseconds?

6.23 A page replacement algorithm should minimize the number of page faults. This minimization can be done by distributing heavily used pages evenly over all of memory rather than having them compete for a small number of page frames. We can associate with each page frame a counter of the number of pages which are associated with that frame. Then to replace a page we search for the page frame with the smallest counter.

   a. Define a page replacement algorithm using this basic idea. Specifically address the problems of:

   1. The initial value of the counters.

   2. When counters are increased.

   3. When counters are decreased.

   4. How the page to be replaced is selected.

   b. How many page faults occur for your algorithm for the following reference string, for 4 page frames?

   1, 2, 3, 4, 5, 3, 4, 1, 6, 7, 8, 7, 8, 9, 7, 8, 9, 5, 4, 5, 4, 2

   c. What is the minimal number of page faults for an optimal page replacement strategy for the reference string in (b) with 4 page frames?

6.24 Is it necessary to always put a page of a process back in the same place on the drum (or disk) each time it is written out? If it is not, explain the circumstances under which it is unnecessary.

6.25 What is the cause of thrashing? How does the system detect thrashing, and once detected what can the system do to eliminate it?

6.26 As a normal consumer, you have begun to acquire lots of stuff. Having a small house, you store some of it in the attic, but now you are considering renting a storage locker. This would give three places to keep things: the house (active use), the attic (easily accessed storage), and the storage locker (hard-to-access storage). Suggest a scheme to decide what should be kept in the attic and what should be in the storage locker.

6.27 We have an operating system for a machine which uses base and limit registers, but we have modified the machine to provide a page table. Can the page tables be set up to simulate base and limit registers? How or why not?

6.28 IBM has a Large Core Storage (LCS) which is a large, relatively inexpensive, relatively slow memory. Unlike CDC's ECS, programs can be executed directly out of LCS. Direct access of a single word takes about 4 microseconds as opposed to 1 microsecond for primary core memory. Assume that memory could be paged into pages of size 256 words. Although random access to LCS gives a 4 microsecond access time, a page of consecutive memory can be transferred to main memory in only 259 microseconds (4 for the first and then one microsecond for each additional location). Two memory management schemes are under consideration: (i) paging into primary memory from LCS, or (ii) executing directly from LCS. Calculate the effective memory access time for both schemes for the following types of programs. For what page fault rates should which scheme be used?

  a. A program with good locality and a page fault rate of one percent.

  b. A program with bad locality and a page fault rate of 37 percent.

6.29 Consider a demand paged computer system using a paging drum, global LRU replacement, and an allocation policy which shares frames equally among processes (that is, if there are m frames and n processes, and each gets m/n frames). The degree of multiprogramming is currently fixed at four. The system was recently measured to determine utilization of cpu and the paging drum. The results are one of the following.

  a. CPU utilization 13 percent; Drum utilization 97 percent.

  b. CPU utilization 87 percent; Drum utilization 3 percent.

  c. CPU utilization 13 percent; Drum utilization 3 percent.

For each case, what is happening and can the degree of multiprogramming be increased to increase the cpu utilization? Is the paging helping?

6.30 Consider a machine with the following paging hardware: There
are 32 page frames for pages of 512 words. Page tables have 32
entries and are kept in memory, starting at addresses which are
multiples of 32 (so that the low order 5 bits are zero). Two
special registers UPT and SPT point to the User Page Table and
the Supervisor Page Table, respectively. In user mode, the UPT
is used for address translation until a page fault or other
interrupt occurs, then the program counter is stored in the
address contained in the IA (Interrupt Address) register and
execution continues at IA+1 in supervisor mode using the page
tables pointed at by SPT. If an interrupt occurs in supervisor
mode, the same procedure is followed. Each page table entry
uses the sign bit as the valid/invalid bit (0 = in memory, 1 = not
in memory) and the low order 15 bits (16-bit words) specify the
starting address of the page. The low order 9 bits must be zero
(all pages start at multiples of the page size, 512). Every memory
access is translated by one of the tables, UPT or SPT, depending
upon the mode of the cpu, user or supervisor.

a. What happens if the page for the address in IA is not in?

b. How can the operating system address memory absolutely
(that is, without page table translation)?

Bibliographic Notes

Demand paging was first used in the Atlas system, implemented on the
Manchester University MUSE computer around 1960 [Kilburn et al.
1961, 1962]. Another early demand paging system was Multics,
implemented on the GE 645 system [Daley and Dennis 1968; Bensoussan
et al. 1972; Organick 1972]. Other early demand paging systems include
the THE operating system [Bron 1972] (where the paging was
implemented in software) and the TENEX operating system [Bobrow et
al. 1972].

Belady et al. [1969] was the first to observe that the FIFO
replacement strategy may have the anomaly that bears his name.
Mattson et al. [1970] demonstrated that stack algorithms are not subject
to Belady's anomaly.

The optimal replacement algorithm is due to Belady [1966]. It was
proven to be optimal by Mattson et al. [1970]. Belady's optimal
algorithm is for a fixed allocation; Prieve and Fabry [1976] have an

optimal algorithm if the allocation can vary. Gustavson [1968], Denning [1970], Colin [1971], and Aho et al. [1971] discussed various page replacement algorithms. Belady [1966], Mattson et al. [1970], Coffman and Varian [1968], and Belady and Kuehner [1969] compared page replacement algorithms. Comeau [1967], Brawn and Gustavson [1968], McKellar and Coffman [1969], Sayre [1969], and Winograd et al. [1971] were particularly concerned with performance issues.

Thrashing was discussed by Denning [1968] and Alderson et al. [1972]. The working set model is due to Denning [1968]. Denning [1970, 1980a], Doherty [1970], Denning and Schwartz [1972], and Coffman and Ryan [1972] continued work on the working set model. The page fault rate monitoring scheme is due to Wulf [1969] who successfully applied this technique to the Burroughs B5500 computer system. Operdeck and Chu [1974] also discuss the page fault frequency algorithm.

Belady [1966], Fine et al. [1966], Coffman and Varian [1968], Freibergs [1968], Brawn and Gustavson [1968], Hatfield [1972], and Baer and Sager [1972] conducted experiments to study the dynamic behavior of programs under paging. Denning [1968], Oppenheimer and Weizer [1968], DeMeis and Weizer [1969], and Alderson et al. [1972] considered various load control strategies to prevent thrashing.

Wolman [1965], Randell [1969], Arden and Boettner [1969], Batson et al. [1970], Denning [1970], and Hatfield and Gerald [1971] discussed page and segment sizes.

Vareha et al. [1969], Kuck and Lawrie [1970], and Mattson et al. [1970] discussed multi-level main storage. Such schemes were implemented in several large machines including the IBM 370/168 and IBM 370/195 [Liptay 1968].

Randell and Kuehner [1968], Denning [1970], Doran [1976] and Hoare and McKeag [1972] presented survey papers on paging. Basic textbook discussions are offered by Watson [1970, Sections 2.4 and 2.5], Madnick and Donovan [1974, Chapter 3], Tsichritzis and Bernstein [1974, Chapter 5], Shaw [1974, Chapter 5], Lister [1975, Chapter 5], Habermann [1976, Chapters 7 and 8], and Calingaert [1982, Chapter 2].

Disk and Drum Scheduling

In the last few chapters, we have seen how both the central processor and the memory of a computer system can be allocated to users. The dynamic scheduling of these resources allows the computer system to operate more efficiently. In this chapter, we consider another crucial scheduler, the disk scheduler, and some of the different algorithms used for accessing the disk.

Most of the processing of modern computer systems centers on the disk system. Disks provide the primary on-line storage of information, both programs and data. Most programs, like compilers, assemblers, sort routines, editors, formatters, and so on, are stored on a disk until loaded into memory, and then use the disk as both the source and destination of their processing. Hence the proper management of disk storage is of central importance to a computer system.

There are few alternatives. Magnetic tape systems are generally too slow. In addition, they are limited to sequential access. Thus tapes are more suited for storing infrequently used files, where speed is not a primary concern.

7.1 Physical Characteristics

Physically, disks are relatively simple (Figure 7.1). Each disk has a flat circular shape, like a phonograph record. Its two surfaces are covered with a magnetic material, similar to magnetic tape. Information is recorded on the surfaces.

When the disk is in use, a drive motor spins it at high speed (for example, 3600 revolutions per minute). There is a read/write head positioned just above the surface of the disk. The disk surface is logically divided into *tracks*. Information is stored by recording it magnetically on the track under the read/write head. There may be hundreds of tracks on a disk surface.

A *fixed-head disk* has a separate head for each track. This arrangement allows the computer to switch from track to track quickly,

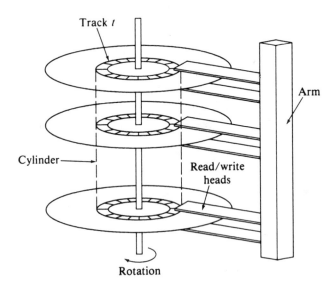

Figure 7.1   Moving-head disk mechanism

but it requires a large number of heads, making the device very expensive. More commonly, there is only one head, which moves in and out to access different tracks. This *moving-head disk* requires hardware to move the head, but only a single head is needed, resulting in a much cheaper system.

A fixed-head disk is logically the same as a drum. A drum is shaped as a cylinder, rather than a platter, and recording is done on its side, rather than its ends. Although it would be possible to create a moving-head drum, all drums are in fact fixed-head. Drums tend to have higher transfer rates than disks, but have smaller storage capacity. Drums are generally quite expensive, but their uses may be appropriate in situations that demand high performance.

Drums were commonly used as the backing store for early paging systems. The backing store was then called the swapping drum or *paging drum*. Many systems now use a high-speed disk or, more recently, a large semiconductor or core memory device that acts like a drum, but has even higher access and transfer speeds.

Disks were originally designed for file storage, so the primary design criteria were cost, size, and speed. To provide additional storage capacity, several approaches were taken. The primary gain has been made by improving the recording density, allowing more bits to be put on a surface. The density is reflected by the number of tracks per inch, and hence the total number of tracks on a surface. In addition, with separate heads on each side of the platter, disk capacity can be doubled at minimal cost. This approach can be extended by stacking several disks, each with two recording surfaces, on one spindle. Since they all rotate together, only one drive motor is needed, although each surface still needs its own read/write head.

Finally, the disk can be *removable*, allowing different disks to be mounted as needed. Removable disk packs may consist of one or several platters. Generally, they are held in hard plastic cases to prevent damage while not in the disk drive.

Such large disks are rigid aluminum platters covered with magnetic recording material. The read/write heads are kept as close as possible to the disk surface. Often the head floats or flies only microns from the disk surface, supported by a cushion of air. Because the head floats so close to the surface, platters must be carefully machined to be very flat.

Head crashes can be a problem. If the head contacts the disk surface (due to a power failure, for example), the head will scrape the recording media off the disk, destroying the data which had been there.

Floppy disks take a different approach. The disks are coated with a hard surface, so the read/write head can sit directly on the disk surface without destroying the data. Thus the disk itself is much cheaper to produce and use. The coating (and the read/write head) will wear after enough use, however, and need to be replaced over time.

Floppies are usually much smaller than hard disks, from 100K to 500K bytes per disk. They come in many variations (single-sided, double-sided, single-density and double-density) and sizes (8 inch, 5-1/4 inch, and so on). Hard disks vary from 5 megabytes to over 300 megabytes per drive. Hard disks are also faster and more expensive.

The hardware for a disk system can be divided into two parts. The *disk drive* is the mechanical part, including the device motor, the read/write heads, and associated logic. The other part, called the *disk controller*, determines the logical interaction with the computer. The controller takes instructions from the cpu and orders the disk drive to carry out the instruction. This division allows many disk drives to be attached to the same disk controller. If an initial system has one disk controller and one disk drive, the disk storage of the system can be doubled for less than twice the cost simply by attaching a second drive to the existing controller.

Information on the disk is referenced by a multi-part address, which includes the drive number, the surface, and the track. All of the tracks on one drive that can be accessed without moving the heads (basically the tracks on the different surfaces) are called a *cylinder*.

Within a track, information is written in blocks. The blocks may be a fixed size, specified by the hardware. These are called *sectors*. Each sector can be separately read or written. Alternatively, the information on a track may be composed of variable length blocks, separated by record gaps. This scheme is more flexible, but more difficult to work with. Many systems, even with hardware-variable disk blocks, will pick a block size and fix it in software. In either case, information is read and written in blocks. Blocking and unblocking of records in software can easily hide the fixed or variable nature of the physical block size.

Disk speed is composed of three parts. To access a block on the disk, the system must first move the head to the appropriate track or cylinder. This head movement is called a *seek*, and the time to complete it is *seek time*. Once the head is at the right track, it must wait until the desired block rotates under the read/write head. This delay is *latency* time. Finally, the actual transfer of data between the disk and main memory can take place. This last part is *transfer* time. The total time to service a disk request is the sum of the seek time, latency time, and transfer time.

Since most jobs depend heavily upon the disk for loading and input and output files, it is important that disk service be as fast as possible. The operating system can improve on the average disk service time by scheduling the requests for disk access.

As we discussed in Chapter 2, every I/O device, including each disk drive, has a queue of pending requests. Whenever a process needs I/O to or from the disk, it issues a system call to the operating system. The request specifies several pieces of necessary information:

- Is this an input or output operation?

- The disk address (drive, cylinder, surface, block).

- The memory address.

- The amount of information to be transferred (a byte or word count).

If the desired disk drive and controller is available, the request can be serviced immediately. However, while the drive or controller is serving one request, any additional requests, normally from other processes, will need to be queued.

For a multiprogramming system with many processes, the disk queue may often be non-empty. Thus, when a request is complete, we must pick a new request from the queue and service it. A disk service requires that the head be moved to the desired track, then a wait for latency, and finally the transfer of data.

7.2 First-Come-First-Served Scheduling

The simplest form of disk scheduling is, of course, *First-Come-First-Served* (FCFS). This algorithm is easy to program and intrinsically fair. However, it may not provide the best (average) service. Consider, for example, an ordered disk queue with requests involving tracks,

98, 183, 37, 122, 14, 124, 65, and 67,

listed first (98) to last (67). If the read/write head is initially at track 53, it will first move from 53 to 98, then to 183, 37, 122, 14, 124, 65, and finally to 67, for a total head movement of 640 tracks. This schedule is diagrammed in Figure 7.2.

The problem with this schedule is illustrated by the wild swing from 122 to 14 and then back to 124. If the requests for tracks 37 and 14 could be serviced together, before or after the requests at 122 and 124, the total head movement could be substantially decreased and the average time to service each request would decrease, improving disk throughput.

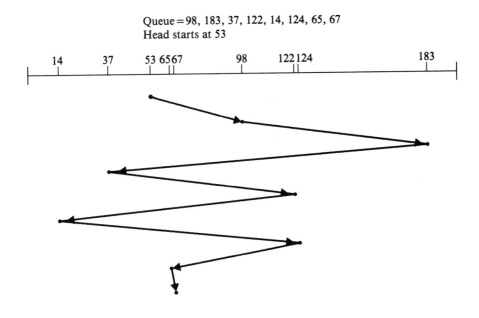

Figure 7.2   First-Come-First-Served disk scheduling

7.3 Shortest-Seek-Time-First

It seems reasonable to service all requests close to the current head position together, before moving the head far away to service another request. This assumption is the basis for the *Shortest-Seek-Time-First* (SSTF) disk scheduling algorithm. SSTF selects the request with minimum seek time from the current head position. Since seek time is generally proportional to the track difference between the requests, this approach is implemented by moving the head to the closest track in the request queue.

For our example request queue, the closest request to the initial head position (53) is at track 65. Once we are at track 65, the next closest request is at track 67. At this point, the distance to track 37 is 30, while the distance to 98 is 31. Therefore the request at track 37 is closer and is served next. Continuing, we service the request at track 14, then 98, 122, 124, and finally at 183 (Figure 7.3). This scheduling method results in a total head movement of only 236 tracks, a little more than a third of the distance needed for FCFS. This algorithm would result in a substantial improvement in average disk service.

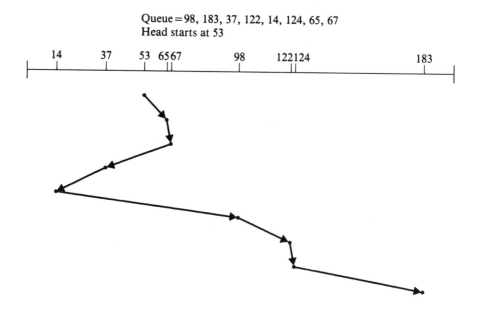

Figure 7.3   Shortest-Seek-Time-First disk scheduling

SSTF is essentially a form of SJF scheduling, and like SJF, it may cause *starvation* of some requests. Remember that, in a real system, requests may arrive at any time. Assume that we have two requests in the queue, for 14 and 186. If a request near 14 arrives while we are servicing that request, it will be serviced next, making the request at 186 wait. While this request is being serviced, another request close to 14 could arrive. In theory, a continual stream of requests near each other could arrive, causing the request for track 186 to wait indefinitely.

The SSTF algorithm, while a substantial improvement over FCFS, is not optimal. For example, if we move the head from 53 to 37, even though it is not closest, and then to 14 before turning around to service 65, 67, 98, 122, 124, and 183, we can reduce the total head movement to 208 tracks.

7.4 SCAN

Recognition of the dynamic nature of the request queue leads to the SCAN algorithm. The read/write head starts at one end of the disk, and moves toward the other end, servicing requests as it reaches each track, until it gets to the other end of the disk. At the other end, the direction of head movement is reversed and servicing continues. The head continuously scans the disk from end to end.

Before applying SCAN to our example,

98, 183, 37, 122, 14, 124, 65, and 67,

we need to know the direction of head movement, in addition to its last position. If the head was moving toward 0, the head movement would service 37 and 14 as it moved to 0. At track 0, the head would reverse and move to the other end of the disk, servicing the requests at 65, 67, 98, 122, 124, and 183 as it moves (Figure 7.4). If a request arrives in the queue just in front of the head, it will be serviced almost immediately, while a request arriving just behind the head will have to wait until the head moves to the end of the disk, reverses direction, and returns, before being serviced.

The SCAN algorithm is sometimes called the "elevator" algorithm, since it is similar to the behavior of elevators as they service requests to move from floor to floor in a building. Another analogy is to shoveling snow from a sidewalk while it is snowing. Starting from one end, we remove snow as we move toward the other end. As we move, new snow falls behind us. At the far end, we reverse direction and remove the newly fallen snow behind us.

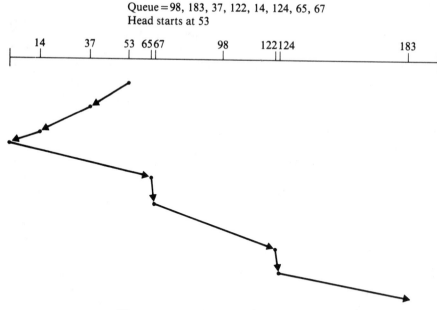

Queue = 98, 183, 37, 122, 14, 124, 65, 67
Head starts at 53

Figure 7.4   SCAN disk scheduling

Assuming a uniform distribution of requests for tracks, consider the density of requests when the head reaches one end and reverses direction. At this point, there are relatively few requests immediately behind the head, since these tracks have recently been serviced. The heaviest density of requests is at the other end of the disk. These requests have also waited the longest.

C-SCAN (Circular-SCAN) is a variant of SCAN designed to provide a more uniform wait time. As with SCAN, C-SCAN moves the head from one end of the disk to the other, servicing requests as it goes. When it reaches the other end, however, it immediately returns to the beginning of the disk, without servicing any requests on the return trip. C-SCAN essentially treats the disk as if it were circular, with the last track adjacent to the first one (Figure 7.5).

Notice that our descriptions of both SCAN and C-SCAN always move the head from one end of the disk to the other. In practice, neither algorithm is implemented in this way. More commonly, the head is only moved as far as the last request in each direction. As soon as there are no requests in the current direction, the head movement is reversed. These versions of SCAN and C-SCAN are called LOOK and C-LOOK. ("Look" for a request before moving in that direction.)

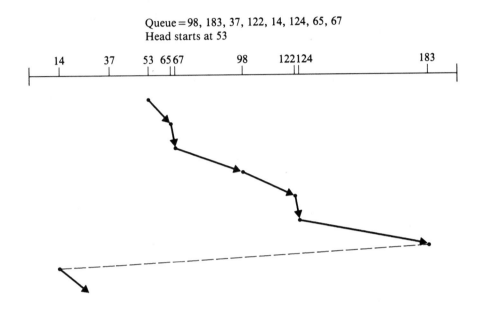

Queue = 98, 183, 37, 122, 14, 124, 65, 67
Head starts at 53

Figure 7.5   C-LOOK disk scheduling

7.5 Selecting a Disk Scheduling Algorithm

With so many disk scheduling algorithms, how do we choose a particular algorithm? SSTF is quite common and has a natural appeal. SCAN and C-SCAN are more appropriate for systems with a heavy load on the disk. It is possible to define an optimal algorithm, but the computation needed for an optimal schedule may not justify the savings over SSTF or SCAN. Teorey and Pinkerton [1972] compared the various algorithms using simulations and recommended using either SCAN or C-SCAN, depending upon the load.

With any scheduling algorithm, however, performance depends heavily on the number and types of requests. In particular, if the queue seldom has more than one outstanding request, then all scheduling algorithms are effectively equivalent. Some studies have suggested [Lynch 1972b] that the queue normally will have only one request. In this case, FCFS is also a reasonable algorithm.

Notice also that the requests for disk service can be greatly influenced by the file allocation method. A program reading a contiguously allocated file will generate a number of requests which are close together on the disk, resulting in limited head movement. A linked or indexed file, on the other hand, may include blocks which are widely scattered on the disk, resulting in better disk space utilization at the expense of head movement.

The location of directories and index blocks is also important. Since every file must be opened to be used, and opening a file requires a search of the directory structure, the directories will be frequently accessed. Placing the directories in the *middle* of the disk, rather than at either end, can significantly reduce disk head movement.

As a result of these considerations, it should be clear that the disk scheduling algorithm, like all others, should be written as a separate module of the operating system, allowing it to be removed and replaced with a different algorithm if necessary. Initially, either FCFS or SSTF would be reasonable choices.

7.6 Sector Queueing

The disk-scheduling algorithms we have just discussed (FCFS, SSTF, SCAN, and C-SCAN) are all aimed at minimizing disk head movement, in order to minimize total service time and wait time. Fixed-head devices, such as drums, do not have this problem, however, since there is no head movement and no significant time to select a track. Thus different algorithms are used for these devices.

Sector queueing is an algorithm for scheduling fixed-head devices. It is based on the division of each track into a fixed number of blocks, called sectors. The disk address in each request specifies the track and sector. Since seek time is zero for fixed-head devices, the main service time is latency time. For FCFS scheduling, assuming that requests are uniformly distributed over all sectors, the expected latency is one-half of a revolution.

Consider, however, the following example. Assume the head is currently over sector 2 and the first request in the queue is for sector 12. To service this request we must wait until sector 12 revolves under the read/write heads. If there is a request in the queue for sector 5, it could be serviced before the request for sector 12, without causing the request for sector 12 to be delayed. Thus we can greatly improve our throughput by servicing a request for each sector as it passes under the head, even if the request is not at the head of the waiting queue.

Sector queueing defines a separate queue for each sector of the drum. When a request arrives for sector i, it is placed in the queue for sector i (Figure 7.6). As sector i rotates beneath the read/write heads, the first request in its queue is serviced.

Sector queueing is primarily used with fixed-head devices. However, it can also be used with moving-head devices, if there is more than one request for service within a particular track or cylinder. Once the head is moved to a particular cylinder, all requests for this cylinder can be serviced without further head movement. Hence sector queueing can be used to order multiple requests within the same cylinder. As with other scheduling algorithms, of course, sector queueing will only have an effect if the operating system must choose from a set of more than one request.

Figure 7.6   Sector queueing

7.7 Summary

Disk systems are the major I/O device on most computers. Requests for disk I/O are generated both by the file system and by virtual memory systems. Each request specifies the address on the disk to be referenced. This address includes a track or cylinder number. Moving-head disk scheduling algorithms try to minimize total head movement. FCFS, SSTF, SCAN, and C-SCAN are various disk scheduling algorithms. Sector queueing is a scheduling algorithm for fixed-head devices, such as drums.

Exercises

7.1 Suppose the head of a moving-head disk with 200 tracks, numbered 0 to 199, is currently serving a request at track 143 and has just finished a request at track 125. If the queue of requests is kept in the FIFO order:

86, 147, 91, 177, 94, 150, 102, 175, 130

what is the total head movement to satisfy these requests for the following disk scheduling algorithms?

   a. FCFS.

   b. SSTF.

   c. SCAN.

   d. LOOK.

   e. C-SCAN.

7.2 Fragmentation on a storage device could be eliminated by recompacting the information. Typical disk and drum devices do not have relocation or base registers (such as are used when memory is to be compacted), so how can we relocate files? Why are recompacting and relocation of files often avoided?

7.3 Why would a drum be used in preference to a disk for a paging device?

7.4 When the average queue length is small, all the disk scheduling algorithms reduce to FCFS scheduling. Explain why.

7.5 What is the major conceptual difference between disk scheduling and "elevator scheduling"? (Hint: Are we trying to minimize elevator movement?)

7.6 All the disk scheduling disciplines except FCFS are not truly fair (starvation may occur).

   a. Explain why.

   b. Come up with a scheme to ensure fairness.

   c. Why is fairness an important goal in a time-sharing system?

7.7 Compare the throughput of C-SCAN and SCAN, assuming a uniform distribution of requests.

7.8 SSTF tends to favor mid-range cylinders over the innermost and outermost cylinders. Explain why.

7.9 Requests are not usually uniformly distributed. For example, the cylinders on which the file directory structures reside are more frequently accessed than most files. Suppose that you know that 50 percent of the requests are for a small fixed number of cylinders.

   a. What scheduling algorithm would you use?

   b. Can you suggest a new scheduling algorithm for this case?

7.10 Why is latency optimization not usually employed in disk scheduling? How would the standard algorithms (FCFS, SSTF, SCAN, and C-SCAN) be modified to include latency optimization?

7.11 Is disk scheduling other than FCFS useful in a single-user environment?

7.12 With the decline in semiconductor memory prices, several companies have begun to make semiconductor "disks". These devices use memory chips rather than disks for storage. As a result, these disks have no moving parts, and hence are both faster and more reliable than normal mechanical disks. These new devices are designed to be *plug-compatible* with existing disks, so programming and addressing is identical to normal disks. However, they are much faster. How would this affect the selection of a disk scheduling algorithm?

7.13 While job hunting, a student hears an employer mention that their system uses sector queueing to minimize head movement on their moving-head disks. What do you think of this statement?

Bibliographic Notes

Denning [1967] described the FCFS, SSTF, and SCAN disk scheduling algorithms. A complete survey of all the various disk scheduling algorithms was presented by Teorey [1972] and Teorey and Pinkerton [1972].

Wilhelm [1976] and Hofri [1980] compared the FCFS and the SSTF seek scheduling algorithms. Frank [1969], Gotlieb [1973], Fuller [1974], and Perros [1980] computed various performance aspects of disk scheduling algorithms.

Lynch [1972b] and Wilhelm [1976] discussed the consequences of having nonuniform request distributions.

Denning [1967] presented various drum scheduling algorithms, including FCFS and SATF (Shortest-Access-Time-First). Analyses of a paging drum can be found in the articles by Weingarten [1966], Coffman [1969], and Fuller [1972]. Abate and Dubner [1969], Stone [1973], and Fuller [1974] discussed rotational optimization for fixed-head devices such as drums.

8

Deadlocks

In a multiprogramming environment, several processes may compete for a finite number of resources. A process requests resources, and if the resources are not available at that time, the process enters a wait state. It may happen that waiting processes will never again change state, because the resources they have requested are held by other waiting processes. For example, this situation occurs in a system with four tape drives and two processes. If each process holds two tape drives but needs three, then each will wait for the other to release its tape drives. This situation is called a *deadlock*. To prevent a deadlock, or recover from one if it occurs, the system may take some relatively extreme action, such as preemption of resources from one or more of the deadlocked processes. In this chapter we describe some of the various methods which operating systems may use to handle the deadlock problem.

8.1 The Deadlock Problem

The problem of deadlocks is not unique to the operating system environment. Generalizing our interpretation of resources and processes, we can see that the deadlock problem may be a part of our daily environment. For example, consider the problem of crossing a river that has a number of stepping stones (Figure 8.1). At most one foot can be on each stepping stone at a time. To cross the river, a person must use each of the stepping stones. We can view each person crossing the river as a process and each stepping stone as a resource. A deadlock occurs when two people start crossing the river from opposite sides and meet in the middle (Figure 8.2).

Stepping on a stone can be viewed as acquiring the resource, while removing the foot corresponds to releasing the resource. A deadlock occurs when two people try to step on the same stone. The deadlock can be resolved if either person retreats to the side of the river from which they started. In operating system terms, this retreat is called a *rollback*. Observe that if several people are crossing the river from the

Figure 8.1   River crossing

same side, more than one person may be required to retreat in order to resolve the deadlock. If a person starts to cross the river without finding out whether someone else is trying to cross from the other side, then a deadlock is always possible.

The only way to ensure that a deadlock will not occur is to require each person crossing the river to follow an agreed-upon protocol. One such protocol would require each person who wants to cross the river to find out whether someone else is crossing from the other side. If the answer is no, they may proceed. Otherwise, they must wait until the other person has finished crossing. Several remarks should be made concerning this protocol.

- We must have a mechanism to determine whether someone is crossing the river. If it is always possible to examine the state of all the stepping stones, this condition is sufficient. If not (for example, the river may be too wide or fog may obscure the view), another mechanism is required.

- Suppose two people want to cross the river from opposite sides at the same time. Our protocol does not specify what should be done

Figure 8.2   Deadlock situation in river crossing

in this case. If they both start crossing the river, a deadlock will occur. If each waits for the other to start, another form of deadlock will occur. One remedy to this difficulty is to assign one bank of the river (say, east) higher priority. That is, the person on the east side will always cross first, while the person on the west will have to wait.

- If this protocol is observed, one or more processes may have to wait indefinitely to cross the river. This situation is referred to as *starvation*. It may occur in the river-crossing example if a continuous stream of people are crossing the river from the high-priority side. In order to guard against starvation, the previous protocol must be extended. For example, we may define an algorithm that alternates the direction of crossing from time to time. The design of such an algorithm is left to the reader as an exercise.

8.1.1 System Model

A system consists of a finite number of resources to be distributed among a number of competing processes. The resources are partitioned into several types, each of which consists of some number of identical instances. CPU cycles, memory space, files, and I/O devices (such as printers, tape drives, and card readers) are examples of resource types. If a system has two cpus, then the resource type *cpu* has two instances. Similarly, the resource type *printer* may have five instances.

If a process requests an instance of a resource type, the allocation of *any* instance of the type will satisfy the request. If this is not the case, then the instances are not identical, and the resource type classes have not been properly defined. For example, a system may have two printers. These two printers may be defined to be in the same resource class if no one cares which printer prints their output. However, if one printer is on the ninth floor and the other is in the basement, then people on the ninth floor may not see both printers as equivalent, and separate resource classes may need to be defined for each printer.

A process must request a resource before using it and release the resource after using it. A process may request as many resources as it requires to carry out its designated task. Obviously, the number of resources requested may not exceed the total number of resources available in the system. In other words, a process cannot request three printers if the system only has two.

Under the normal mode of operation, a process may utilize a resource only in the following sequence:

1. **Request**. If the request cannot be immediately granted (for example, the resource is being used by another process), then the requesting process must wait until it can acquire the resource.

2. **Use**. The process can operate on the resource (for example, if the resource is a line printer, the process can print on the printer).

3. **Release**. The process releases the resource.

The request and release of resources are system calls, as explained in Section 2.2.1. Examples are the Request/Release Device, Open/Close File, and Allocate/Free memory system calls. The use of resources can also only be made through system calls (for example, to read or write a file or I/O device). Therefore, for each use, the operating system checks to make sure that the using process has requested and been allocated the resource. A system table records whether each resource is free or allocated, and if allocated, to which process. If a process requests a resource that is currently allocated to another process, it can be added to a queue of processes waiting for this resource.

8.1.2 Deadlock Definition

A set of processes is in a deadlock state when every process in the set is waiting for an event that can only be caused by another process in the set. The events with which we are mainly concerned here are resource acquisition and release. However, other types of events may result in deadlocks, as shown in Chapters 9 and 13.

To illustrate a deadlock state, consider a system with three tape drives. Suppose that there are three processes, each holding one of these tape drives. If each process now requests another tape drive, the three processes will be in a deadlock state. Each is waiting for the event "tape drive is released", which can only be caused by one of the other waiting processes. This example illustrates a deadlock involving processes competing for the same resource type.

Deadlocks may also involve different resource types. For example, consider a system with one printer and one card reader. Suppose that process P is holding the card reader and process Q is holding the printer. If P now requests the printer and Q requests the card reader, a deadlock occurs.

8.2 Deadlock Characterization

It should be obvious that deadlocks are undesirable. In a deadlock, processes never finish executing and system resources are tied up, preventing other jobs from ever starting. Before we discuss the various methods for dealing with the deadlock problem, it would be helpful to describe some features that characterize deadlocks.

8.2.1 Necessary Conditions

A deadlock situation can arise if and only if the following four conditions hold simultaneously in a system.

- **Mutual exclusion.** At least one resource is held in a non-sharable mode; that is, only one process at a time can use the resource. If another process requests that resource, the requesting process must be delayed until the resource has been released.

- **Hold and wait.** There must exist a process that is holding at least one resource and is waiting to acquire additional resources that are currently being held by other processes.

- **No preemption**. Resources cannot be preempted; that is, a resource can only be released voluntarily by the process holding it, after the process has completed its task.

- **Circular wait**. There must exist a set $\{p_0, p_1, \ldots, p_n\}$ of waiting processes such that p_0 is waiting for a resource which is held by p_1, p_1 is waiting for a resource which is held by p_2, $\ldots$, p_{n-1} is waiting for a resource which is held by p_n, and p_n is waiting for a resource which is held by p_0.

We emphasize that all four conditions must hold for a deadlock to occur. The circular-wait condition implies the hold-and-wait condition, so the four conditions are not completely independent. However, we will see (in Section 8.3) that it is quite useful to consider each condition separately.

We can see these four conditions in our river-crossing example. A deadlock occurs if and only if two people from opposite sides of the river meet in the middle. The mutual-exclusion condition obviously holds, since at most one person can be stepping on a stone at one time. The hold-and-wait condition is satisfied, since each person is stepping on one stone and waiting to step on the next one. The no-preemption condition holds, since a stepping stone cannot be forcibly removed from the person stepping on it. Finally, the circular-wait condition holds, since the person coming from the east is waiting on the person coming from the west, while the person coming from the west is, in turn, waiting on the person coming from the east. Neither of the two can proceed, and each is waiting for the other to remove their foot from one of the stepping stones.

8.2.2 Resource Allocation Graph

Deadlocks can be described more precisely in terms of a directed graph called a *system resource allocation graph*. This graph consists of a pair $G = (V,E)$, where V is a set of vertices and E is a set of edges. The set of vertices is partitioned into two types $P = \{p_1, p_2, \ldots, p_n\}$, the set consisting of all the processes in the system, and $R = \{r_1, r_2, \ldots, r_m\}$, the set consisting of all resource types in the system.

Each element in the set E of edges is an ordered pair (p_i, r_j) or (r_j, p_i), where p_i is a process ($p_i \in P$) and r_j is a resource type ($r_j \in R$). If $(p_i, r_j) \in E$, then there is a directed edge from process p_i to resource type r_j, implying that process p_i requested an instance of resource type r_j and is currently waiting for that resource. If $(r_j, p_i) \in E$, then there is a directed edge from resource type r_j to process p_i, implying that an instance of resource type r_j has been allocated to process p_i. An edge (p_i, r_j) is called a *request edge*, while an edge (r_j, p_i) is called an *assignment edge*.

Pictorially, we represent each process p_i as a circle and each resource type r_j as a square. Since resource type r_j may have more than one instance, we represent each such instance as a dot within the square. Note that a request edge only points to the square r_j, while an assignment edge must also designate one of the dots in the square.

When process p_i requests an instance of resource type r_j, a request edge is inserted in the resource allocation graph. When this request can be fulfilled, the request edge is *instantaneously* transformed to an assignment edge. When the process later releases the resource, the assignment edge is deleted.

The resource allocation graph in Figure 8.3 depicts the following situation.

- The sets P, R, and E:

$$P = \{p_1, p_2, p_3\}$$
$$R = \{r_1, r_2, r_3, r_4\}$$
$$E = \{(p_1, r_1), (p_2, r_3), (r_1, p_2), (r_2, p_2), (r_2, p_1), (r_3, p_3)\}$$

- Resource instances:

   ○ One instance of resource type r_1.

   ○ Two instances of resource type r_2.

   ○ One instance of resource type r_3.

   ○ Three instances of resource type r_4.

- Process states:

   ○ Process p_1 is holding an instance of resource type r_2 and is waiting for an instance of resource type r_1.

   ○ Process p_2 is holding an instance of r_1 and r_2 and is waiting for an instance of resource type r_3.

   ○ Process p_3 is holding an instance of r_3.

Given the definition of a resource allocation graph, it can be easily shown that if the graph contains no cycles, then no process in the system is deadlocked. If, on the other hand, the graph contains a cycle, then a deadlock may exist.

If each resource type has exactly one instance, then a cycle implies that a deadlock has occurred. If the cycle involves only a set of resource types, each of which have only a single instance, then a deadlock has occurred. Each process involved in the cycle is deadlocked. In this case, a cycle in the graph is both a necessary and sufficient condition for the existence of deadlock.

If each resource type has several instances, then a cycle does not necessarily imply that a deadlock occurred. In this case, a cycle in the graph is a necessary but not a sufficient condition for the existence of deadlock.

To illustrate this concept, let us return to the resource allocation graph depicted in Figure 8.3. Suppose that process p_3 requests an instance of resource type r_2. Since no resource instance is available, a request edge (p_3, r_2) is added to the graph (Figure 8.4). At this point two minimal cycles exist in the system:

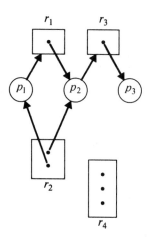

Figure 8.3   Resource allocation graph

$$p_1 \rightarrow r_1 \rightarrow p_2 \rightarrow r_3 \rightarrow p_3 \rightarrow r_2 \rightarrow p_1$$

$$p_2 \rightarrow r_3 \rightarrow p_3 \rightarrow r_2 \rightarrow p_2$$

Processes p_1, p_2, and p_3 are deadlocked. Process p_2 is waiting for the resource r_3, which is held by process p_3. Process p_3, on the other hand, is waiting for either process p_1 or p_2 to release resource r_2. Meanwhile, process p_2 is waiting on process p_3. In addition, process p_1 is waiting for process p_2 to release resource r_1.

Now consider Figure 8.5. In this example, we also have a cycle:

$$p_1 \rightarrow r_1 \rightarrow p_3 \rightarrow r_2 \rightarrow p_1$$

However, there is no deadlock. Observe that process p_4 may release its instance of resource type r_2. That resource can then be allocated to p_3, breaking the cycle.

To summarize, if a resource allocation graph does not have a cycle then the system is *not* in a deadlock state. On the other hand, if there is a cycle, then the system may or may not be in a deadlock state. This observation is important in dealing with the deadlock problem.

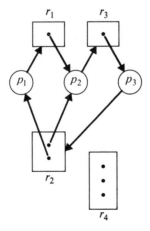

Figure 8.4   Resource allocation graph with a deadlock

8.2.3 Methods for Handling Deadlocks

Principally, there are two methods for dealing with the deadlock problem. We can use some protocol to ensure that the system will *never* enter a deadlock state. Alternatively, we can allow the system to enter a deadlock state and then recover. As we show in Section 8.6, recovery from a deadlock may be quite difficult and expensive. Therefore, we first consider methods of ensuring that deadlocks never occur. There are two common methods: deadlock prevention and deadlock avoidance.

8.3 Deadlock Prevention

As we noted in Section 8.2.1, for a deadlock to occur, each of the four necessary conditions must hold. By ensuring that at least one of these conditions cannot hold, we can *prevent* the occurrence of a deadlock. Let us elaborate on this approach by examining each of the four necessary conditions separately.

8.3.1 Mutual Exclusion

The mutual-exclusion condition must hold for non-sharable types of resources. For example, a printer cannot be simultaneously shared by

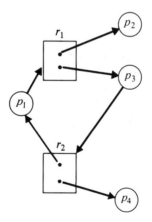

Figure 8.5   Resource allocation graph with a cycle but no deadlock

several processes. Sharable resources, on the other hand, do not require mutually exclusive access, and thus cannot be involved in a deadlock. Read-only files are a good example of a sharable resource. If several processes attempt to open a read-only file at the same time, they can be granted simultaneous access to the file. A process never needs to wait for a sharable resource. In general, however, it is not possible to prevent deadlocks by denying the mutual-exclusion condition. Some resources are intrinsically non-sharable.

8.3.2 Hold and Wait

In order to ensure that the hold-and-wait condition never holds in the system, we must guarantee that whenever a process requests a resource it does not hold any other resources. One protocol that can be used requires each process to request and be allocated all of its resources before it begins execution. This provision can be implemented by requiring that system calls requesting resources for a process precede all other system calls.

An alternative protocol allows a process to request resources only when it has none. A process may request some resources and use them. Before it can request any additional resources, however, it must release all the resources that it is currently allocated.

To illustrate the difference between these two protocols, consider a process which copies from a card reader to a disk file, sorts the disk file, and then prints the results to a line printer and copies them to a magnetic tape. If all resources must be requested at the beginning of the process, then the process must initially request the card reader, disk file, line printer, and tape drive. It will hold the magnetic tape drive for its entire execution, even though it needs it only at the end.

The second method allows the process to request initially only the card reader and disk file. It copies from the card reader to the disk, then releases both the card reader and the disk file. The process must then re-request the disk file and the line printer. After copying the disk file to the line printer, it releases both, and then requests the disk file and tape drive. It copies the disk file to tape, then releases these two resources and terminates.

There are two main disadvantages to these protocols. First, *resource utilization* may be very low, since many of the resources may be allocated but unused for a long period of time. In the example given, for instance, we can release the card reader and disk file and then re-request the disk file and printer only if we can be sure that our data will remain on the disk file. If this cannot be ensured, then we must request all resources at the beginning for both protocols.

Second, *starvation* is possible. A process that needs several popular resources may have to wait indefinitely while at least one of the resources that it needs is always allocated to some other process.

8.3.3 No Preemption

The third necessary condition is that there be no preemption of resources that have already been allocated. In order to ensure that this condition does not hold, the following protocol may be used. If a process that is holding some resources requests another resource that cannot be immediately allocated to it (that is, the process must wait), then all resources currently being held are preempted. That is, these resources are implicitly released. The preempted resources are added to the list of resources for which the process is waiting. The process will only be restarted when it can regain its old resources, as well as the new ones that it is requesting.

Alternatively, if a process requests some resources, we first check if they are available. If so, we allocate them. If they are not available, we check whether they are allocated to some other process that is waiting for additional resources. If so, we preempt the desired resources from the waiting process and allocate them to the requesting process. If the resources are not available or held by a waiting process, the requesting process must wait. While it is waiting, some of its resources may be preempted, but only if another process requests them. A process can only be restarted when it is allocated the new resources it is requesting and recovers any resources that were preempted while it was waiting.

This protocol is often applied to resources whose state can be easily saved and restored later, such as cpu registers and memory space. It cannot generally be applied to such resources as printers, card readers, or tape drives. However, in the THE system (Bron [1972]), the line printer could be preempted. It was assumed that if the printer was preempted, and output from two jobs was therefore intermixed, then the operator would sort out the printed pages.

8.3.4 Circular Wait

In order to ensure that the circular wait condition never holds, we may impose a total ordering of all resource types. That is, we assign to each resource type a unique integer number, which allows us to compare two resources and determine whether one precedes another in our ordering.

More formally, let $R = \{r_1, r_2, ..., r_m\}$ be the set of resource types. We can define a one-to-one function $F: R \rightarrow N$, where N is the set of natural numbers. For example, if the set of resource types R includes disk drives, tape drives, card readers, and printers, then the function F might be defined as follows:

$$F(\text{card reader}) = 1$$
$$F(\text{disk drive}) = 5$$
$$F(\text{tape drive}) = 7$$
$$F(\text{printer}) = 12$$

We can now consider the following protocol to prevent deadlocks: each process can only request resources in an increasing order of enumeration. That is, a process can initially request any number of instances of a resource type, say r_i. After that, the process can request instances of resource type r_j if and only if $F(r_j) > F(r_i)$. If several instances of the same resource type are needed, a *single* request for all of these must be issued. For example, using the function defined above, a process that wants to use the card reader and printer at the same time must request first the card reader and then the printer.

Alternatively, we can simply require that whenever a process requests an instance of resource type r_j, it has released any resources r_i such that $F(r_i) \geq F(r_j)$.

If these protocols are used, the circular wait condition cannot hold. We can demonstrate this fact by assuming that a circular wait exists (proof by contradiction). Let the set of processes in the circular wait be $\{p_0, p_1, \ldots, p_n\}$, where p_i is waiting for a resource r_i, which is held by process p_{i+1}. (Modulo arithmetic is used on the indexes, so that p_n is waiting for a resource r_n held by p_0.) Then since process p_{i+1} is holding resource r_i while requesting resource r_{i+1}, we must have $F(r_i) < F(r_{i+1})$, for all i. But this means that $F(r_0) < F(r_1) < \ldots < F(r_n) < F(r_0)$. By transitivity, $F(r_0) < F(r_0)$, which is impossible. Therefore, there can be no circular wait.

It should be noted that the function F should be defined according to the normal order of usage of the resources in a system. For example, since the card reader is usually needed before the printer, it would be reasonable to define $F(\text{card reader}) < F(\text{printer})$.

8.4 Deadlock Avoidance

Deadlock prevention algorithms, as discussed in Section 8.3 above, prevent deadlocks by restraining how requests can be made. The restraints ensure that at least one of the necessary conditions for deadlock cannot occur, and hence, that deadlocks cannot hold. A side effect of preventing deadlocks by this method, however, is possibly low device utilization and reduced system throughput.

An alternative method for avoiding deadlocks is to require additional information about how resources are to be requested. For example, in a system with one card reader and one line printer, we might be told that process P will request first the card reader, and later the line printer, before releasing both resources. Process Q, on the other hand, will request first the line printer, and then the card reader. With this knowledge of the complete sequence of requests and releases for each process, we can decide for each request whether or not the process should wait. Each request requires that the system consider the resources currently available, the resources currently allocated to each process, and the future requests and releases of each process, to decide if the current request can be satisfied or must wait to avoid a possible future deadlock.

There are various algorithms which differ in the amount and type of information required. The simplest and most useful model requires that each process declare the *maximum number* of resources of each type that it may need. Given *a priori* information, for each process, about the maximum number of resources of each type that may be requested, it is possible to construct an algorithm that ensures that the system will never enter a deadlock state. This algorithm defines the deadlock *avoidance* approach. A deadlock avoidance algorithm dynamically examines the resource allocation state to ensure that there can never be a circular-wait condition. The resource allocation *state* is defined by the number of available and allocated resources, and the maximum demands of the processes. A state is *safe* if the system can allocate resources to each process (up to its maximum) in some order and still avoid a deadlock.

More formally, a system is in a safe state only if there exists a *safe sequence*. A sequence of processes $<p_1, p_2, ..., p_n>$ is a safe sequence for the current allocation state if for each p_i, the resources which p_i can still request can be satisfied by the currently available resources plus the resources held by all the p_j, with $j < i$. In this situation, if the resource need of process p_i is not immediately available, then p_i could wait until all p_j have finished. When they have finished, p_i can obtain all of its needed resources, complete its designated task, return its allocated resources, and terminate. When p_i terminates, p_{i+1} can obtain its needed resources, and so on. If no such sequence exists, then the system state is said to be *unsafe*.

A safe state is not a deadlock state. Conversely, a deadlock state is an unsafe state. Not all unsafe states are deadlocks, however (Figure 8.6). An unsafe state *may* lead to a deadlock. As long as the state is safe, the operating system can avoid unsafe (and deadlock) states. In an unsafe state, the operating system cannot prevent processes from requesting resources in such a way that a deadlock occurs: the behavior of the processes controls unsafe states.

To illustrate, consider a system with twelve magnetic tape drives and three processes: p_0, p_1, and p_2. Process p_0 requires ten tape drives, process p_1 may need as many as four, and process p_2 may need up to nine tape drives. Suppose that at time T_0, process p_0 is holding five tape drives, process p_1 is holding two, and process p_2 is holding two. (Thus there are three free tape drives.)

	Maximum Needs	Current Needs
p_0	10	5
p_1	4	2
p_2	9	2

At time T_0, the system is in a safe state. The sequence $<p_1, p_0, p_2>$ satisfies the safety condition, since process p_1 can immediately be allocated all of its tape drives and then return them (the system will then have five available tape drives), process p_0 can get all of its tape drives and return them (the system will then have ten available tape drives), and finally process p_2 could get all of its tape drives and return them. (The system will then have all twelve tape drives available.)

Note that it is possible to go from a safe state to an unsafe state. Suppose that at time T_1, process p_2 requests and is allocated one more tape drive. The system is no longer in a safe state. At this point, only process p_1 can be allocated all of its tape drives. When it returns them,

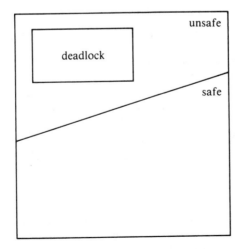

Figure 8.6 Safe, unsafe, and deadlock state spaces

the system will have only four available tape drives. Since process p_0 is allocated five tape drives, but has a maximum of ten, it may then request five more. Since they are unavailable, process p_0 must wait. Similarly, process p_2 may request an additional six tape drives and have to wait, resulting in a deadlock.

Our mistake is in granting the request from process p_2 for one more tape drive. If we had made p_2 wait until either of the other processes had finished and released its resources, then we could have avoided the deadlock situation.

Given the concept of a safe state, we can define avoidance algorithms which ensure that the system will never deadlock. The idea is simply to ensure that the system will always remain in a safe state. Initially the system is in a safe state. Whenever a process requests a resource that is currently available, the system must decide if the resource can be immediately allocated or if the process must wait. The request is granted only if it leaves the system in a safe state.

Note that in this scheme if a process requests a resource which is currently available, it may still have to wait. Thus resource utilization may be lower than without a deadlock avoidance algorithm.

8.4.1 Several Instances of a Resource Type

The avoidance algorithm described below is commonly known as *the banker's algorithm*. The name was chosen since this algorithm could be used in a banking system to ensure that the bank never allocates its available cash in such a way that it can no longer satisfy the needs of all its customers.

When a new process enters the system, it must declare the maximum number of instances of each resource type that it may need. This number may not exceed the total number of resources in the system. When a user requests a set of resources, it must be determined whether the allocation of these resources will leave the system in a safe state. If so, the resources are allocated; otherwise, the process must wait until some other process releases enough resources.

Several data structures must be maintained to implement the banker's algorithm. These data structures encode the state of the resource allocation system. Let n be the number of processes in the system and m be the number of resource types. We need the following data structures:

- *Available.* A vector of length m indicating the number of available resources of each type. If *Available*[j] $= k$, there are k instances of resource type r_j available.

- *Max.* An $n \times m$ matrix defining the maximum demand of each process. If $Max(i,j) = k$, then process p_i may request at most k instances of resource type r_j.

- *Allocation.* An $n \times m$ matrix defining the number of resources of each type currently allocated to each process. If $Allocation[i,j] = k$, then process p_i is currently allocated k instances of resource type r_j.

- *Need.* An $n \times m$ matrix indicating the remaining resource need of each process. If $Need(i,j) = k$, then process p_i may need k more instances of resource type r_j, in order to complete its task. Note that $Need(i,j) = Max(i,j) - Allocation(i,j)$.

These data structures vary both in size and value as time progresses.

To simplify the presentation of the algorithm, let us establish some notation. Let X and Y be vectors of length n. We say that $X \leq Y$ if and only if $X[i] \leq Y[i]$ for all $i = 1, 2, ..., n$. For example, if $X = (1,7,3,2)$ and $Y = (0,3,2,1)$, then $Y \leq X$. $Y < X$ if $Y \leq X$ and $Y \neq X$.

We can treat each row in the matrices *Allocation* and *Need* as vectors and refer to them as *Allocation$_i$* and *Need$_i$*, respectively. *Allocation$_i$* specifies the resources currently allocated to process p_i, while *Need$_i$* specifies the additional resources the process p_i may still request in order to complete its task.

Banker's Algorithm

Let *Request$_i$* be the request vector for process p_i. If *Request$_i$[j]* $= k$, then process p_i wants k instances of resource type r_j. When a request for resources is made by process p_i, the following actions are taken:

1. If *Request$_i$* $\leq$ *Need$_i$* then proceed to step 2. Otherwise we have an error, since the process has exceeded its maximum claim.

2. If *Request$_i$* $\leq$ *Available* then proceed to step 3. Otherwise the resources are not available, and p_i must wait.

3. The system pretends to have allocated the requested resources to process p_i by modifying the state as follows.

$$Available := Available - Request_i;$$
$$Allocation_i := Allocation_i + Request_i;$$
$$Need_i := Need_i - Request_i;$$

If the resulting resource allocation state is safe, the transaction is completed and process p_i is allocated its resources. However, if the new state is unsafe, then p_i must wait for $Request_i$ and the old resource allocation state is restored.

Safety Algorithm

The algorithm for finding out whether a system is in a safe state or not can be described as follows:

1. Let *Work* and *Finish* be vectors of length m and n, respectively. Initialize *Work* := *Available* and *Finish*[i] := *false* for i= 1, 2, ..., n.

2. Find an i such that:

   a. *Finish*[i] = *false*, and

   b. $Need_i \leq Work$.

   If no such i exists, go to step 4.

3. *Work* := *Work* + *Allocation*$_i$
   Finish[i] := *true*
   go to step 2.

4. If *Finish*[i] = *true* for all i, then the system is in a safe state.

An Example

Consider a system with five processes $\{p_0, p_1, ..., p_4\}$ and three resource types $\{A, B, C\}$. Resource type A has 10 instances, resource type B has 5 instances, and resource type C has 7 instances. Suppose that at time T_0 the following snapshot of the system has been taken.

	Allocation	Max	Available
	A B C	A B C	A B C
p_0	0 1 0	7 5 3	3 3 2
p_1	2 0 0	3 2 2	
p_2	3 0 2	9 0 2	
p_3	2 1 1	2 2 2	
p_4	0 0 2	4 3 3	

The content of the matrix *Need* is defined to be *Max* − *Allocation* and is:

Need

A B C

	A B C
p_0	7 4 3
p_1	1 2 2
p_2	6 0 0
p_3	0 1 1
p_4	4 3 1

We claim that the system is currently in a safe state. Indeed, the sequence $<p_1, p_3, p_5, p_2, p_0>$ satisfies the safety criteria.

Suppose now that process p_1 requests one additional instance of resource type A and two instances of resource type C, so $Request_1 = (1,0,2)$. In order to decide whether this request can be immediately granted, we first check that $Request_1 \leq Available$ (that is, $(1,0,1) \leq (3,2,2)$) which is true. We then pretend that this request has been fulfilled and arrive at the following new state:

	Allocation	*Need*	*Available*
	A B C	A B C	A B C
p_0	0 1 0	7 4 3	2 3 0
p_1	3 0 2	0 2 0	
p_2	3 0 2	6 0 0	
p_3	2 1 1	0 1 1	
p_4	0 0 2	4 3 1	

We must determine whether this new system state is safe. To do so we execute our safety algorithm and find out that the sequence $<p_1, p_3, p_4, p_0, p_2>$ satisfies our safety requirement. Hence we can immediately grant the request of process p_1.

You should be able to see, however, that in this state, a request for $(3,3,0)$ by p_4 cannot be granted since the resources are not available. A request for $(0,2,0)$ by p_0 cannot be granted even though the resources are available, since the resulting state is unsafe.

8.4.2 Single Instance of Each Resource Type

Although the banker's algorithm is quite general and will work for any resource allocation system, it may require $m \times n^2$ operations. If we have a resource allocation system with only one instance of each resource type, a more efficient algorithm can be defined.

This algorithm uses a variant of the resource allocation graph defined in Section 8.2.2. In addition to the request and assignment edges, we introduce a new type of edge called a *claim edge*. A claim edge (p_i, r_j) indicates that process p_i may request resource r_j sometime in the future. This edge resembles a request edge in direction, but is represented by a dashed line. When process p_i requests resource r_j the claim edge (p_i, r_j) is converted to a request edge. Similarly, when a resource r_j is released by p_i, the assignment edge (r_j, p_i) is reconverted to a claim edge (p_i, r_j). We note that the resources must be claimed *a priori* in the system. That is, before process p_i starts executing all of its claim edges must already appear in the resource allocation graph. This condition can be relaxed by allowing a claim edge (p_i, r_j) to be added to the graph only if all the edges associated with process p_i are claim edges.

Suppose that process p_i requests resource r_j. The request can be granted only if converting the request edge (p_i, r_j) to an assignment edge (r_j, p_i) does not result in the formation of a cycle in the resource allocation graph. Note that the check for safety is done by using a cycle detection algorithm. An algorithm for detecting a cycle in this graph requires an order of n^2 operation, where n is the number of processes in the system.

If no cycle exists, then the allocation of the resource will leave the system in a safe state. If a cycle is found, then the allocation will put the system in an unsafe state. Therefore, process p_i will have to wait for its requests to be satisfied.

To illustrate this algorithm, consider the resource allocation graph of Figure 8.7. Suppose that p_2 requests r_2. Although r_2 is currently free, we

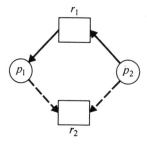

Figure 8.7 Resource allocation graph for deadlock avoidance

cannot allocate it to p_2 since this action will create a cycle in the graph (Figure 8.8). A cycle indicates that the system is in an unsafe state. If p_1 then requests r_2, a deadlock will occur.

8.5 Deadlock Detection

If a system does not employ some protocol that ensures that no deadlock will ever occur, then a detection and recovery scheme must be implemented. An algorithm that examines the state of the system is invoked periodically to determine whether a deadlock has occurred. If so, the system must attempt to recover from the deadlock. In order to do so the system must:

a. Maintain information about the current allocation of resources to processes, as well as any outstanding resource allocation requests.

b. Provide an algorithm that utilizes this information to determine whether the system has entered a deadlock state.

In the following sections, we will elaborate on issues (a) and (b) as they pertain to systems with several instances of each resource type, as well as systems with only a single instance of each resource type. At this point, however, let us note that a detection and recovery scheme requires overhead that includes not only the run-time costs of maintaining the necessary information and executing the detection algorithm, but also the potential losses inherent in recovering from a deadlock.

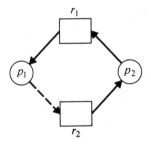

Figure 8.8   An unsafe state in a resource allocation graph

8.5.1 Several Instances of a Resource Type

The detection algorithm employs several time-varying data structures that are very similar to those used in the banker's algorithm (Section 8.4.1).

- *Available.* A vector of length m indicating the number of available resources of each type.

- *Allocation.* An $n \times m$ matrix defining the number of resources of each type currently allocated to each process.

- *Request.* An $n \times m$ matrix indicating the current request of each process. If $Request(i,j) = k$, then process p_i is requesting k more instances of resource type r_j.

The less-than relation ($<$) between two vectors is defined as in Section 8.4. To simplify notation, we will again treat the rows in the matrices *Allocation* and *Request* as vectors and refer to them as $Allocation_i$ and $Request_i$, respectively. The detection algorithm described below is due to Shoshani and Coffman [1970]. The algorithm simply investigates every possible allocation sequence for the processes that remain to be completed. Compare this algorithm with the banker's algorithm of Section 8.4.1.

1. Let *Work* and *Finish* be vectors of length m and n, respectively. Initialize *Work* := *Available*. For $i = 1, 2, \ldots, n$, if $Allocation_i \neq 0$ then *Finish*[i] := *false*; otherwise, *Finish*[i] := *true*.

2. Find an index i such that:

    a. *Finish*[i] = *false*, and

    b. $Request_i \leq Work$.

    If no such i exists go to step 4.

3. *Work* := *Work* + $Allocation_i$
   Finish[i] := *true*
   go to step 2.

4. If *Finish*[i] = false, for some i, $1 \leq i \leq n$, then the system is in a deadlock state. Moreover, if *Finish*[i] = *false* then process p_i is deadlocked.

You may wonder why we reclaim the resources of process p_i as soon as we determine that $Request_i \leq Work$. We know that p_i is currently *not* involved in a deadlock. Thus we take an optimistic attitude, and assume that p_i will require no more resources to complete its task; it will thus return all its resources to the system. If this is not the case, a deadlock may occur later which will be detected the next time the deadlock detection algorithm is invoked.

An Example — WRONG

Consider a system with five processes $\{p_0, p_1, ..., p_4\}$ and three resource types $\{A, B, C\}$. Resource type A has 7 instances, resource type B has 2 instances, and resource type C has 6 instances. Suppose that at time T_0 we have the following resource allocation state:

	Allocation	Request	Available
	A B C	A B C	A B C
p_0	0 1 0	0 0 0	0 0 1
p_1	2 0 0	2 0 2	
p_2	3 0 2	0 0 0	
p_3	2 1 1	1 0 0	
p_4	0 0 2	0 0 2	

We claim that the system is not in a deadlocked state. Indeed, if we execute our algorithm, we will find that the sequence $<p_0, p_2, p_3, p_1, p_4>$ will result in $Finish[i]$ = true for all i.

Suppose now that process p_2 makes one additional request for an instance of type C. The $Request$ matrix is modified as follows.

	Request
	A B C
p_0	0 0 0
p_1	2 0 2
p_2	0 0 1
p_3	1 0 0
p_4	0 0 2

We claim that the system is now deadlocked. Although we can reclaim the resources held by process p_0, the number of available resources is not sufficient to fulfill the requests of the other processes. Thus a deadlock exists, consisting of processes p_1, p_2, p_3 and p_4.

8.5.2 Single Instance of Each Resource Type

As with the avoidance algorithm, the deadlock detection algorithm is of order $m \times n^2$. If all resources have only a single instance, we can define a faster algorithm. Again, we will use a variant of the resource allocation graph, called a *wait-for* graph. This graph is obtained from the resource allocation graph by removing the nodes of type resource and collapsing the appropriate edges.

More precisely, an edge from p_i to p_j in a wait-for graph implies that process p_i is waiting for process p_j to release a resource that it needs. An edge (p_i, p_j) exists in a wait-for graph if and only if the corresponding resource allocation graph contains two edges (p_i, r_q) and (r_q, p_j) for some resource r_q. For example, in Figure 8.9, we present a resource allocation graph and its corresponding wait-for graph.

As before, a deadlock exists in the system if and only if the wait-for graph contains a cycle. In order to detect deadlocks, the system needs to *maintain* the wait-for graph and periodically *invoke an algorithm* that searches for a cycle in the graph.

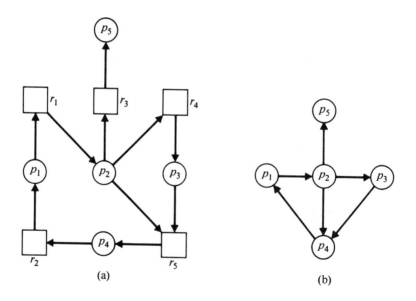

Figure 8.9   Resource allocation graph (a) and its wait-for graph (b)

An algorithm to detect a cycle in a graph requires an order of n^2 operations, where n is the number of vertices in the graph. While this cost is less than that of the general deadlock algorithm, there is considerable overhead in detecting such cycles.

8.5.3 Detection Algorithm Usage

When should we invoke the detection algorithm? The answer depends on two factors:

- How *often* do we believe a deadlock occurs?

- How *many* processes will be affected by deadlock, when it happens?

If deadlocks occur frequently, then the detection algorithm should be invoked more frequently. Resources allocated to deadlocked processes will be idle until the deadlock can be broken. In addition, the number of processes involved in the deadlock cycle may grow.

Deadlocks can only come into being when some process makes a request which cannot be immediately granted. It is possible that this request is the request which completes a chain of waiting processes. In the extreme, we could invoke the deadlock detection algorithm every time a request for allocation cannot be immediately granted. In this case we can identify not only the set of processes which are deadlocked, but the specific process which "caused" the deadlock. (In reality, each of the deadlocked processes is a link in the cycle in the resource graph, and so all of them, jointly, caused the deadlock.) If there are many different resource types, one request may cause many cycles in the resource graph, each cycle completed by the most recent request, and "caused" by the one identifiable process.

Of course, invoking the deadlock detection algorithm for every request would be a considerable overhead in computation time. A less expensive alternative would be to simply invoke it at less frequent intervals, for example once an hour, or whenever cpu utilization drops below 40 per cent. (A deadlock eventually cripples system throughput and will cause cpu utilization to drop.) If the detection algorithm is invoked at arbitrary points in time, there may be many cycles in the resource graph. We would generally not be able to tell which of the many deadlocked processes "caused" the deadlock.

8.6 Recovery from Deadlock

When a detection algorithm determines that a deadlock exists, the system must *recover* from the deadlock. There are two options for breaking a deadlock. One solution would be to simply kill one or more processes in order to break the circular wait. The second option is to preempt some resources from one or more of the deadlocked processes.

8.6.1 Process Termination

In order to eliminate the deadlock by killing a process, two methods can be utilized. In both methods the system reclaims all resources allocated to the terminated processes.

- **Kill all deadlocked processes.** This clearly will break the deadlock cycle, but at a great expense, since these processes may have computed for a long period of time, and the results of these partial computations must be discarded, and probably recomputed later.

- **Kill one process at a time until the deadlock cycle is eliminated.** This method requires considerable overhead, since after each process is killed, a deadlock detection algorithm must be invoked to determine whether any processes are still deadlocked.

Notice that killing a process may not be easy. If the process was in the midst of updating a file, aborting it in the middle will leave that file in an incorrect state. Similarly, if the process was in the midst of printing data on the line printer, the system must reset the state of the printer to a correct state before proceeding with the printing of the next job.

If the partial termination method is used, then given a set of deadlocked processes, we must determine which process (or processes) should be terminated to try to break the deadlock. This is a policy decision, similar to CPU scheduling problems. The question is basically an economical one; we should abort those processes that will incur the minimum cost. Unfortunately, the term "minimum cost" is not a precise one. Many factors may determine which process is chosen, including:

1. The priority of the process.

2. How long the process has computed, and how much longer the process will compute before completing its designated task.

3. How many and what type of resources the process has used (for example, are the resources simple to preempt?).

4. How many more resources the process needs in order to complete.

5. How many processes will be involved in the rollback.

8.6.2 Resource Preemption

To eliminate deadlocks using resource preemption, we successively preempt some resources from processes and give these resources to other processes until the deadlock cycle is broken.

If preemption is required in order to deal with deadlocks, then three issues need to be addressed.

- **Selecting a victim.** Which resources and which processes are to be preempted? As in process abortion, we must determine the order of preemption in order to minimize cost.

  Returning to our river-crossing example, suppose there are 1000 stepping stones. Consider a deadlock situation involving two people, P and Q.

  > Suppose that P has a higher priority than Q (for example, P may be a policeman). Then Q will have to back up, no matter what their situation may be.

  > Suppose that P needs only 2 more stepping stones to cross the river (that is, P has already used 998 stepping stones). In this case, it would be more reasonable to require Q to back up.

  > Suppose that P and Q deadlock in the middle of the river. No one is behind Q, but there are ten people behind P. In this case, it would be more reasonable to require Q to back up. Otherwise, eleven people will have to back up.

- **Rollback.** If we preempt a resource from a process, what should be done with that process? Clearly, it cannot continue with its normal execution; it is missing some needed resource. We must roll the process back to some safe state, and restart it from that state. But what constitutes a safe state and how easy is it to determine?

  The simplest solution is a total rollback: abort the process and then restart it. However, it is more effective to roll back the process only as far as necessary to break the deadlock. This method, however, requires the system to keep more information about the state of all the running processes.

  Let us return to the river-crossing example. Total rollback is analogous to returning the person to the place where their journey started. For example, a New Yorker who is trying to cross a river in California must return to New York.

  Clearly, this solution is not cost effective. It is more natural to break the deadlock cycle by retreating to one of the banks of the river. An even more effective method is to place several additional stepping stones in the river, so that one of the people involved in the deadlock may step aside to break the deadlock (Figure 8.10). In a computer system, a checkpoint can be taken. A checkpoint is a recording of the state of the process to allow rollback.

● **Starvation**. How do we ensure that starvation will not occur? That is, how can we guarantee that resources will not always be preempted from the same process?

In a system where victim selection is based primarily on cost factors, it may happen that the same process is always picked as a victim. As a result, this process never completes its designated task. This situation is called *starvation*, and needs to be dealt with in any practical system. Clearly, we must ensure that a process can be picked as a victim only a (small) finite number of times. The most common solution is to include the number of rollbacks in the cost factor.

8.7 Combined Approach to Deadlock Handling

It has been argued that none of the basic approaches for handling deadlocks (that is, prevention, avoidance, and detection) alone is appropriate for the entire spectrum of resource allocation problems encountered in operating systems. Howard [1973] has suggested that these basic approaches can be combined, allowing the use of the optimal approach for each class of resources in the system. The proposed method is based on the notion that resources can be partitioned into classes that are hierarchically ordered. A resource-ordering technique (Section 8.3.4) is applied to the classes. Within each class the most appropriate technique for handling deadlocks can be used.

It is easy to show that a system that employs this strategy will not be subjected to deadlocks. Indeed, a deadlock cannot involve more than one class, since the resource-ordering technique is used. Within each class, one of the basic approaches is used. Consequently, the system is not subject to deadlocks.

To illustrate this technique, consider a system that consists of the four classes of resources described below:

● **Internal resources**. Resources used by the system, such as a process control block.

● **Central memory**. Memory used by a user job.

Figure 8.10   Adding stones to allow limited rollback

- **Job resources**. Assignable devices (such as a tape drive) and files.

- **Swappable space**. Space for each user job on the backing store.

An ideal mixed deadlock solution for this system orders the classes as shown, and uses the following approaches to each class:

- **Internal resources**. Prevention through resource ordering can be used, since run-time choices between pending requests are unnecessary.

- **Central memory**. Prevention through preemption can be used, since a job can always be swapped out, and the central memory can be preempted.

- **Job resources**. Avoidance can be used, since the information needed about resource requirements can be obtained from the job control cards.

- **Swappable space**. Preallocation may be used, since the maximum storage requirements are usually known.

This example shows how various basic approaches can be mixed within the framework of resource ordering, in order to obtain an effective solution to the deadlock problem.

8.8 Summary

A deadlock state occurs when two or more processes are waiting indefinitely for an event that can only be caused by one of the waiting processes. Principally, there are two methods for dealing with deadlocks:

- Use some protocol to ensure that the system will never enter a deadlock state.

- Allow the system to enter deadlock state and then recover.

A deadlock situation may occur if and only if four necessary conditions simultaneously hold in the system: mutual exclusion, hold and wait, no preemption, and circular wait. To prevent deadlocks, we ensure that at least one of the necessary conditions never holds. There are three basic methods for deadlock prevention.

- **Hold and wait**. Before proceeding with its execution, each process must acquire all the resources it needs.

- **No preemption**. If a process is holding some resources and it requests another resource and this resource cannot be immediately allocated to that process (that is, the process must wait), then the process must release all the resources it is currently holding.

- **Circular wait**. Impose a linear ordering on all resource types. Each process can request resources only in an increasing order.

Another method for avoiding deadlocks which is less stringent than the above prevention algorithm is to have some *a priori* information on how each process will be utilizing the resources. The banker's algorithm needs to know the maximum number of each resource class that may be requested by each process. Using this information, a deadlock avoidance algorithm can be defined.

If a system does not employ some protocol to ensure that deadlocks will never occur, then a detection and recovery scheme must be employed. A deadlock detection algorithm must be invoked to determine whether a deadlock has occurred. If a deadlock is detected, the system must recover by either aborting some of the deadlocked processes or by preempting resources from some of the deadlocked processes.

In a system that selects victims for rollback primarily on cost factors, starvation may occur. As a result the selected process never completes its designated task.

Finally, it has been argued that none of these basic approaches alone is appropriate for the entire spectrum of resource allocation problems in operating systems. The basic approaches can be combined, allowing the selection of the optimal one for each class of resources in a system.

Exercises

8.1 List several examples of deadlocks which are not related to a computer system environment.

8.2 Are all of the necessary conditions introduced in Section 8.2.1 independent, or does one (or more) have to hold for another to hold. If so, can you give a "minimal" set of necessary conditions.

8.3 Design an algorithm for crossing the river such that starvation and deadlock are not possible.

8.4 Is it possible to have a deadlock involving only one single process?

8.5 Hardware is not unbreakable. How does the failure of a device affect each of the three methods for handling deadlocks (prevention, avoidance, and detection)? What steps can be taken (if any are necessary) to try to improve things after a device goes down?

8.6 It has been stated that proper spooling would eliminate deadlocks. Certainly, it eliminates card readers, plotters, line printers, and so on from contention. It is even possible to spool tapes (called *staging* them). This would leave us with the resources of cpu time, memory, and disk space. Is it possible to have a deadlock involving these resources? If so, how? What deadlock scheme would seem best to eliminate these deadlocks (if any are possible) or what condition is violated (if they are not possible)?

8.7 Prove that the safety algorithm of Section 8.4 requires an order of $m \times n^2$ operations.

8.8 Consider the traffic deadlock depicted in Figure 8.11.

 a. Show that the four necessary conditions for deadlock indeed hold in this example.

 b. Come up with a simple rule that will avoid deadlocks.

8.9 What is the main difference between deadlock and starvation?

8.10 [Holt 1971] Consider a system consisting of 4 resources of the same type, being shared by 3 processes, each of which needs at most 2 resources. Show that the system is deadlock free.

8.11 [Holt 1971] Consider a system consisting of m resources of the same type, being shared by n processes. Show that the system is deadlock free if:

 a. $Need_i > 0$ for $i = 1, 2, ..., m$.

 b. The sum of all maximum needs is less than $m+n$.

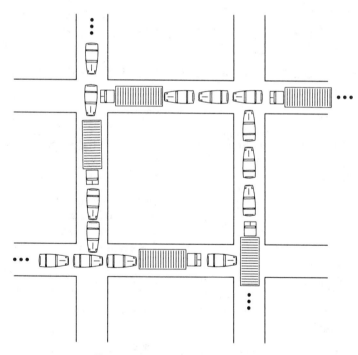

Figure 8.11   Traffic deadlock

8.12 Suppose that a system is in an unsafe state. Show that it is possible for the processes to complete their execution without entering a deadlock state.

8.13 In a real computer system, neither the resources available nor the demands of processes for resources is consistent over long periods of time (months). Resources break or are replaced, new processes come and go, new resources are bought and added to the system. If deadlock is controlled by the banker's algorithm, which of the following changes can be safely made (without introducing the possibility of deadlock) and under what circumstances?

    a. Increase *Available* (new resources added).

    b. Decrease *Available* (resource permanently removed from system). *make sure Max ≤ Avail !!*

    c. Increase *Max* (for one process, it may want more).

    d. Decrease *Max* (a process decides it will not need that much).

    e. Increase the number of processes. *make sure safe state exist*

    f. Decrease the number of processes.

8.14 Consider a system which runs 5000 jobs per month with no deadlock prevention or avoidance scheme. Deadlocks occur about twice a month and require the operator to terminate and rerun about 10 jobs per deadlock. Each job is worth about $2 (in cpu time) and the jobs terminated tend to be about half done when they are killed.

    A systems programmer has estimated that a deadlock avoidance algorithm (like the banker's algorithm) would be installed in the system with an increase in the average execution time per job of about 10 percent. Since the machine currently has 30 percent idle time, all 5000 jobs per month could still be run, although turnaround time would increase by about 20 percent on average.

    a. What are the arguments for installing the deadlock avoidance algorithm?

    b. What are the arguments against installing the deadlock avoidance algorithm?

8.15 Consider the following resource allocation policy. Requests and releases for resources are allowed at any time. If a request for resources cannot be satisfied because the resources are not available, then we check any processes which are blocked, waiting for resources. If they have the desired resources, then they are taken away from the waiting process and given to the requesting process. The vector of resources for which the waiting process is waiting is increased to include the resources which were taken away.

For example, consider a system with three resource types and the vector *Available* initialized to (4,2,2). If process A asks for (2,2,1), it gets them. If B asks for (1,0,1), it gets them. Then if A asks for (0,0,1) it is blocked (resource not available). If C now asks for (2,0,0), it gets the available one (1,0,0) and one which was allocated to A (since A is blocked.) A's *Allocation* vector goes down to (1,2,1) and its *Need* vector goes up to (1,0,1).

a. Can deadlock occur? If so, give an example. If not, which necessary condition can not occur?

b. Can indefinite blocking occur?

8.16 Consider the following snapshot of a system.

		Allocation	Need	Available
	P_0	0 0 1 2	0 0 1 2	1 5 2 0
	P_1	1 0 0 0	1 7 5 0	
	P_2	1 3 5 4	2 3 5 6	
	P_3	0 6 3 2	0 6 5 2	
	P_4	0 0 1 4	0 6 5 6	

Answer the following questions using the banker's algorithm:

a. What is the content of the array *Need*?

b. Is the system in a safe state?

c. If a request from process p_1 arrives for (0,4,2,0), can the request be immediately granted?

8.17 What are the difficulties that may arise when a process is rolled back as the result of a deadlock?

8.18 Can a system detect that some of its processes are starving? If the answer is yes, explain how. If the answer is no, explain how the system may deal with the starvation problem.

8.19 The banker's algorithm for a single resource type can be simply obtained from the general banker's algorithm by reducing the dimensionality of the various arrays by one. Show through an example that the multiple resource type banker scheme cannot be implemented by individually applying the single resource type scheme to each resource type.

8.20 Suppose that you have coded the deadlock avoidance safety algorithm and now wish to implement the deadlock detection algorithm. Can this be done by simply using the safety algorithm code and redefining $Max_i = Waiting_i + Allocation_i$, where $Waiting_i$ is a vector specifying the resources process i is waiting for, and $Allocation_i$ is as defined in Section 8.4?

8.21 Show how the four prevention algorithms can be applied to our river crossing problem.

Bibliographic Notes

Dijkstra [1965a] was one of the first and most influential contributors in the deadlock area. Holt [1971b, 1972] was the first to formalize the notion of deadlocks in terms of a graph theoretical model similar to the one presented in this chapter.

The various prevention algorithms were suggested by Havender [1968] who has devised the resource ordering scheme for the IBM OS/360 system.

The banker's algorithm for avoiding deadlocks was developed for a single resource type by Dijkstra [1965a], and was extended to multiple resource types by Habermann [1969]. General discussions concerning deadlock avoidance by stating claims have been written by Habermann [1969], Holt [1971a, 1972], and Parnas and Habermann [1972].

A parallel deadlock avoidance scheme was presented by Fontao [1971]. A practical approach to managing resources and avoiding deadlocks was discussed by Frailey [1973]. A deadlock avoidance scheme in which the system resources are partitioned into subsystems, each of which can be scheduled independently was presented by Lomet [1980].

The issue of computational intractability of some deadlock avoidance algorithms has been studied by Devillers [1977], Gold [1978], and

Minoura [1982]. The issue of testing for deadlock-freedom in a computer system was discussed by Kameda [1980].

Survey papers have been written by Coffman et al. [1971] and Isloor et al. [1980]. A formal treatment of deadlocks was presented by Shaw [1974, Chapter 8] and Coffman and Denning [1973, Section 2.3].

Concurrent Processes

Until now we have only considered the issue of concurrency as it relates to hardware components or user processes. In this chapter we examine the general issue of concurrency as it relates to arbitrary algorithms. In particular, we exploit concurrency both within a single process and concurrency across processes.

9.1 Precedence Graphs

Consider the following program segment, Program 1, which performs some simple arithmetic operations.

$$a := x + y;$$
$$b := z + 1;$$
$$c := a - b;$$
$$w := c + 1;$$

Suppose we want to execute some of these statements concurrently. We may have multiple functional units (such as adders) in our processor, or multiple cpus. The "addition" and "subtraction" might be operations on matrices or vectors, or on very large sets (union and intersection), or on files (concatenation and difference). With multiple cpus we may be able to execute some statements concurrently with others, reducing our total execution time.

Clearly, the statement $c := a - b$ cannot be executed before both a and b have been assigned values. Similarly, $w := c + 1$ cannot be executed before the new value of c has been computed. On the other hand, the statements $a := x + y$ and $b := z + 1$ could be executed concurrently since neither depends upon the other.

The point of this example is that, within a single program, there are *precedence constraints* among the various statements. In the following sections, we formalize these ideas.

9.1.1 Definition

A *precedence graph* is a directed acyclic graph whose nodes correspond to individual statements. An edge from node S_i to node S_j means that statement S_j can be executed only after statement S_i has completed execution.

For example, in the precedence graph depicted in Figure 9.1, the following precedence relations exist:

- S_2 and S_3 can be executed after S_1 completes.
- S_4 can be executed after S_2 completes.
- S_5 and S_6 can be executed after S_4 completes.
- S_7 can execute only after S_5, S_6, and S_3 complete.

Note that S_3 can be executed concurrently with S_2, S_4, S_5, and S_6.

The precedence graph must be acyclic. The graph in Figure 9.2 has the following precedence constraints: S_3 can be executed only after S_2 has completed and S_2 can be executed only after S_3 has completed. Obviously, these constraints cannot both be satisfied at the same time.

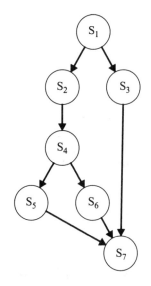

Figure 9.1 Precedence graph

9.1.2 Concurrency Conditions

When can two statements in a program be executed concurrently and still produce the same results? That is, should there be an edge from S_1 to S_2 in the precedence graph corresponding to this program? Before we answer this question, let us first define some notation.

- $R(S_i) = \{a_1, a_2, ..., a_m\}$, the *read set* for S_i, is the set of all variables whose values are referenced in statement S_i during its execution.

- $W(S_i) = \{b_1, b_2, ..., b_n\}$, the *write set* for S_i, is the set of all variables whose values are changed (written) by the execution of statement S_i.

To illustrate this notation, consider the statement $c := a - b$. The values of the variables a and b are used to compute the new value of c. Hence a and b are in the read set. The (old) value of c is not used in the statement, but a new value is defined as a result of the execution of the statement. Hence c is in the write set, but not the read set.

$$R(c := a - b) = \{a,b\}$$
$$W(c := a - b) = \{c\}$$

For the statement, $w := c + 1$ the read and write sets are:

$$R(w := c + 1) = \{c\}$$
$$W(w := c + 1) = \{w\}$$

The intersection of $R(S_i)$ and $W(S_i)$ need not be null. For example, in the statement $x := x + 2$, $R(x := x + 2) = W(x := x + 2) = \{x\}$.

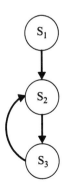

Figure 9.2   Precedence graph with cycles

As another example, consider the statement $read(a)$. Notice that a is being read into, thus its value is changing. The read and write sets are:

$$R(read(a)) = \{\,\}$$
$$W(read(a)) = \{a\}$$

The following three conditions must be satisfied for two successive statements S_1 and S_2 to be executed concurrently and still produce the same result. These conditions were first stated by Bernstein [1966] and are commonly known as *Bernstein's conditions*.

1. $R(S_1) \cap W(S_2) = \{\,\}$.
2. $W(S_1) \cap R(S_2) = \{\,\}$.
3. $W(S_1) \cap W(S_2) = \{\,\}$.

As an illustration, consider S_1: $a := x + y$ and S_2: $b := z + 1$. These two statements can be executed concurrently because

$$R(S_1) = \{x,y\}$$
$$R(S_2) = \{z\}$$
$$W(S_1) = \{a\}$$
$$W(S_2) = \{b\}$$

However, S_2 cannot be executed concurrently with S_3: $c := a - b$, since

$$W(S_2) \cap R(S_3) = \{b\}.$$

9.2 Specification

The precedence graph is a useful device for defining the precedence constraints of the parts of a computation. However, a precedence graph would be difficult to use in a programming language, since it is a two-dimensional object. Other means must be provided to allow the programmer to specify the precedence relations among the various statements in a program.

9.2.1 The Fork and Join Constructs

The **fork** and **join** instructions were introduced by Conway [1963] and Dennis and Van Horn [1966]. They were one of the first language notations for specifying concurrency.

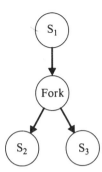

Figure 9.3   Precedence graph for the **fork** construct

The **fork** L instruction produces two concurrent executions in a program. One execution starts at the statement labeled L, while the other is the continuation of the execution at the statement following the **fork** instruction.

To illustrate this concept, consider the following program segment:

$$S_1;$$
$$\textbf{fork } L;$$
$$S_2;$$
$$\cdot$$
$$\cdot$$
$$\cdot$$
$$L:\ S_3;$$

Part of the precedence graph corresponding to this program is presented in Figure 9.3. When the **fork** L statement is executed, a new computation is started at S_3. This new computation executes concurrently with the old computation, which continues at S_2.

Note that the execution of a **fork** statement splits one single computation into two independent computations; hence the name **fork**.

The **join** instruction provides the means to recombine two concurrent computations into one. Each of the two computations must request to be joined with the other. Since computations may execute at different speeds, one may execute the **join** before the other. In this case, the computation which executes the join first is terminated, while the second computation is allowed to continue. If there were three computations to be joined, the first two to execute the join are terminated, while the third is allowed to continue.

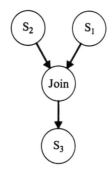

Figure 9.4   Precedence graph for the **join** construct

We need to know the number of computations which are to be joined, so that we can terminate all but the last one. The **join** instruction has a parameter to specify the number of computations to join. Thus the execution of the **join** instruction with a parameter *count* has the following effect:

$$count := count - 1;$$
$$\textbf{if } count \neq 0 \textbf{ then } quit;$$

where *count* is a non-negative integer variable, and *quit* is an instruction which results in the termination of the execution. For 2 computations, the variable *count* would be initialized to 2.

The **join** instruction must be executed atomically; that is, the concurrent execution of two **join** statements is equivalent to the serial execution of these two statements, in some undefined order. The importance of this statement will be demonstrated in Section 9.5.

To illustrate this concept, consider the following program segment:

$$count := 2;$$
$$\textbf{fork } L1;$$

$$.$$
$$.$$
$$.$$

$$S_1;$$
$$\textbf{go to } L2;$$
$$L1: \; S_2;$$
$$L2: \; \textbf{join } count;$$

Part of the precedence graph corresponding to this program is presented in Figure 9.4.

Note that the execution of the **join** statement merges several concurrent executions; hence the name **join**.

Let us further illustrate these concepts through additional examples. Consider again Program 1. To allow the concurrent execution of the first two statements, this program could be rewritten using **fork** and **join** instructions:

```
         count := 2;
         fork L1;
         a := x + y;
         go to L2;
L1:      b := z + 1;
L2:      join count;
         c := a − b;
         w := c + 1;
```

Now return to the precedence graph of Figure 9.1. The corresponding program using the **fork** and **join** instructions is:

```
         S_1;
         count := 3;
         fork L1;
         S_2;
         S_4;
         fork L2;
         S_5;
         go to L3;
L2:      S_6;
         go to L3;
L1:      S_3;
L3:      join count;
         S_7;
```

Note that in Figure 9.1 there exists only one **join** node S_7, which has an in-degree of 3. Hence, only one **join** statement is needed. The counter for this **join** is initialized to 3.

As a final example, consider a program that copies from a sequential file f to another file g. By using double-buffering with r and s, this program can read from f concurrently with writing g.

```
var  f, g: file of T;
     r, s: T;
     count: integer;
     begin
         reset(f);
         read(f,r);
         while not eof(f)
             do begin
                     count := 2;
                     s := r;
                     fork L1;
                     write(g,s);
                     go to L2;
               L1: read(f,r);
               L2: join count;
                   end;
         write(g,r);
     end.
```

The **fork** and **join** instructions are a powerful means of writing concurrent programs. Unfortunately, programs that use these statements have an awkward control structure. The **fork** instruction is similar to the **go-to** statement in its effect on the point of execution. Much has been said about the undesirable effects of the **go-to** statement. Rather than repeating these, we refer the interested reader to Dijkstra's [1968a] letter.

9.2.2 The Concurrent Statement

A higher-level language construct for specifying concurrency is the **parbegin/parend** statement of Dijkstra [1965a], which has the following form:

$$\textbf{parbegin}\ S_1;\ S_2;\ ...;\ S_n\ \textbf{parend};$$

Each S_i is a single statement. All statements enclosed between **parbegin** and **parend** can be executed concurrently. Thus the precedence graph which corresponds to the statement above is depicted in Figure 9.5, where S_0 and S_{n+1} are the statements appearing just before and after the **parbegin/parend** statement, respectively. Note that statement S_{n+1} can be executed only after *all* S_i, $i = 1, 2, ..., n$, have completed.

Let us illustrate these concepts through additional examples. Consider again Program 1. To allow the concurrent execution of the first

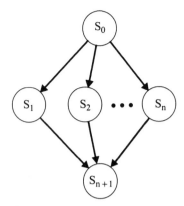

Figure 9.5   Precedence graph for the concurrent statement

two   statements,   this   program   could   be   rewritten   using   the
parbegin/parend construct:

> **parbegin**
> $a := x + y;$
> $b := z + 1;$
> **parend;**
> $c := a - b;$
> $w := c + 1;$

We can write the following program to correspond to the precedence
graph in Figure 9.1:

> $S_1;$
> **parbegin**
> $S_3;$
> **begin**
> $S_2;$
> $S_4;$
>   **parbegin**
> $S_5;$
> $S_6;$
>   **parend;**
> **end;**
> **parend;**
> $S_7;$

Finally, let us rewrite the program that copies a file *f* to another file *g*, using the concurrent statement.

> **var** *f, g*: **file of** *T*;
>   *r, s*: *T*;
> **begin**
>   *reset(f)*;
>   *read(f,r)*;
>   **while not** *eof(f)*
>   **do begin**
>   *s := r*;
>   **parbegin**
>   *write(g,s)*;
>   *read(f,r)*;
>   **parend**;
>   **end**;
>   *write(g,r)*;
> **end**.

The concurrent statement is easily added to a modern block-structured higher-level language and exhibits many of the advantages of other structured control statements.

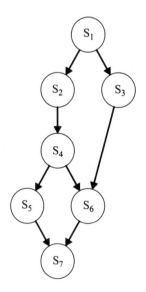

Figure 9.6   Precedence graph with no corresponding concurrent statement

9.2.3 Comparison

Is the concurrent statement powerful enough to model all possible precedence graphs? Unfortunately, the answer is no! To illustrate this point, suppose that we change the graph in Figure 9.1, adding an edge from node S_3 to S_6 (Figure 9.6). Note that the edge from S_3 to S_7 was removed since the addition of an edge from S_3 to S_6 made it redundant. We claim, without proof, that this new graph does not have a corresponding program that uses only the concurrent statement. Try to construct an equivalent program using **parbegin** and **parend**.

In terms of modeling precedence graphs, the **fork/join** construct is more powerful than the concurrent statement. The precedence graph of Figure 9.6, which has no corresponding program using the concurrent statement, has the following program using the **fork/join** construct.

$$
\begin{aligned}
&S_1; \\
&count1 := 2; \\
&\textbf{fork } L1; \\
&S_2; \\
&S_4; \\
&count2 := 2; \\
&\textbf{fork } L2; \\
&S_5; \\
&\textbf{go to } L3; \\
L1:\ &S_3; \\
L2:\ &\textbf{join } count1; \\
&S_6; \\
L3:\ &\textbf{join } count2; \\
&S_7;
\end{aligned}
$$

Although the concurrent statement alone is not enough to implement all precedence graphs, other mechanisms (such as the semaphores of Section 9.6) can be added to the concurrent statement to match the power of precedence graphs. In addition, we would not expect *all* possible precedence graphs to need implementing, but only those corresponding to real-world problems. It is not clear that the concurrent statement is insufficient for all real-world problems.

9.3 Review of Process Concept

In the previous section, we introduced precedence graphs and showed how concurrency can be represented within a single program. In this section we formalize the notion of concurrent execution by reintroducing the sequential process concept. The notion of a process was discussed in more detail in Chapter 4.

Informally, a *sequential process* is a program in execution. We emphasize that a program by itself is not a process; a program is a *passive* entity, while a process is an *active* entity. The execution of a process must progress in a sequential fashion (hence the name *sequential* process). That is, at any point in time at most one instruction is executed on behalf of the process. Thus although two processes may be associated with the same program, they are nevertheless considered two separate execution sequences. The relation between the process concept and the precedence graph concept will be explored shortly.

9.3.1 State of a Process

A sequential process may be in one of the following four states:

- **Running**. Instructions are being executed.

- **Blocked**. The process is waiting for some event to occur (such as an I/O completion).

- **Ready**. The process is waiting to be assigned to a processor.

- **Deadlocked**. The process is waiting for some event that will never occur.

The state diagram corresponding to these four states is presented in Figure 9.7. It is essentially the same as the state diagram in Figure 4.7, with the addition of the deadlocked state.

9.3.2 Relation to Precedence Graphs

We have seen that concurrent computation within a single program can be modeled by a precedence graph. We have also presented two different specification notations (**fork/join** and **parbegin/parend**) to describe a concurrent computation. Since we are interested in describing such a computation as a set of sequential processes, we must now relate these two concepts: processes and precedence graphs.

It is convenient to view each node in a precedence graph as a sequential process. In such an environment, processes appear and disappear dynamically during the lifetime of a single program execution. This scheme, however, may result in significant overhead, in terms of the number of processes that need to be created and destroyed. The overhead could be minimized if we collapse those activities that can be carried out sequentially into a single process. This change, however, needs to be made cautiously, so that we do not reduce the amount of concurrency allowed in a computation. For example, in the precedence graph of Figure 9.1, statements S_2 and S_4 could be collapsed into a single process.

Let us now formally describe the effect of Dijkstra's concurrent statements and the **fork/join** instructions, as they relate to sequential processes. To simplify our discussion, we consider only the **fork/join** constructs. We can always simulate the concurrent statement using the **fork/join** constructs as follows. Let

$$\textbf{parbegin } S_1; S_2; ...; S_n \textbf{ parend};$$

be a general statement. It can be simulated by:

```
          count := n;
          fork L2;
          fork L3;

              .
              .
              .
          fork Ln;
          S1;
          go to Lj;
     L2:  S2;
          go to Lj;
     L3:  S3;
          go to Lj;

              .
              .
              .
     Ln:  Sn;
     Lj:  join count;
```

When process P_i executes the statement **fork** L, a new process P_j is created. P_i and P_j share the same program, as well as any global variables. (It should be clear that in such an environment programs should be written as reentrant code). The main difference between P_i and P_j is that the instruction counter of P_j is set to L and its internal hardware registers are initialized appropriately.

When the **join** *count* instruction is encountered, the value of *count* is decremented by one. If the result is equal to zero, the process continues with its execution. Otherwise, the process terminates.

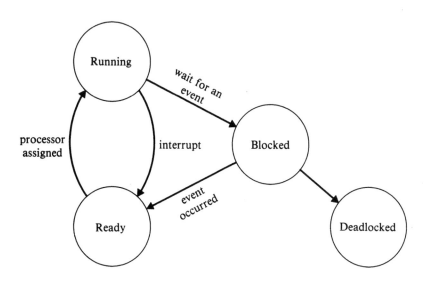

Figure 9.7   State diagram of a process

9.4 Hierarchy of Processes

In this section we shift our attention to the issues of how the various processes are related, and what kind of operations may be invoked on a process. It is convenient to define a new graphical representation of a computation, which we call a process graph.

A *process graph* is a directed rooted tree, whose nodes correspond to processes. An edge from node P_i to node P_j means that P_i created P_j. In this case we shall say that P_i is the parent of P_j, or that P_j is the child of P_i. The graph must be a rooted tree, since each process can have at most one parent, but as many children as it creates (Figure 9.8).

Note the difference between a process graph (which depicts a process creation relation) and a precedence graph (which depicts a precedence relation). In a process graph, an edge from P_i to P_j does not imply that P_j can only execute after P_i, only that P_i created P_j; P_i and P_j may execute concurrently.

9.4.1 Operations on a Process

Given the concept of a process graph, we can now discuss how parent/child relations are formed and the main differences that exist between a parent and a child process.

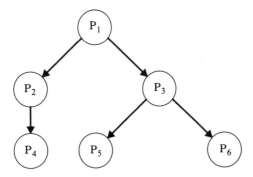

Figure 9.8   Process graph

Process Creation

When one process creates a new process (or processes), by some create operation (such as a **fork**), several possible implementations exist:

1. **Execution**. Concurrent versus sequential.

   a. The parent continues to execute concurrently with its children.

   b. The parent waits until all of its children have terminated.

2. **Sharing**. All versus partial.

   a. The parent and children share all variables in common.

   b. The children share only a subset of their parent's variables.

Let us now briefly elaborate on each of these possibilities.

Option 1a has been adopted in the **fork/join** constructs. When process P_i executes **fork** L, a new process P_j is created, where P_i is the parent of P_j. Both processes continue to execute concurrently.

Option 1b has been adopted in the concurrent statements. When process P_i executes the statement

$$\textbf{parbegin } S_1; S_2; ...; S_n \textbf{ parend};$$

n new processes are created, all executing concurrently. Process P_i, however, is delayed until all of these processes terminate. Then process

P_i continues with its execution at the statement following the concurrent statement.

Option 2a has been adopted in both the **fork/join** constructs and the concurrent statement. In both schemes, the parent and children share all variables in common.

Option 2b has been adopted in the Unix operating system. When process P_i creates a new process P_j, this new process has an independent memory image of P_i, including access permission to all opened files of P_i. The variables accessible to P_j, however, cannot be accessed by P_i since P_i and P_j have independent memory images. Thus, in Unix, P_i and P_j can only communicate by the use of shared files.

In general, a process will need certain resources (cpu time, memory, files, I/O devices) to accomplish its task. When a process creates a subprocess, the subprocess may be able to obtain its resources directly from the operating system or it may be constrained to a subset of the resources of the parent process. The parent may have to partition its resources among its children or it may be able to share some resources (such as memory or files) among several of its children. Restricting a child process to a subset of the parent's resources prevents a process from overloading the system by spawning too many subprocesses.

Process Termination

A process terminates when it finishes executing its last statement. However, there are additional circumstances when termination occurs. A process can cause the termination of another process by issuing the command:

$$\textbf{kill } id;$$

where *id* is the name of the process to be terminated. The **kill** operation can usually only be invoked by the parent of the process to be terminated. Note that a parent needs to know the identities of its children. Thus when one process creates a new process, the identity of the newly created process is passed to the parent. For example,

$$id := \textbf{fork } L$$

creates a new process (executing at L) whose identity is stored in the variable *id*.

A parent may terminate the execution of one of its children for a variety of reasons, such as:

a. The child has exceeded its usage of some of the resources it has been allocated.

b. The task assigned to the child is no longer required.

In order to determine (a), a mechanism must be available to allow the parent to inspect the state of its children.

Many systems do not allow a child to exist if its parent has terminated. In such systems, if process P_j terminates (either normally or abnormally), then all of its children must also be terminated. This phenomenon is referred to as *cascading termination* and is normally initiated by the operating system.

9.4.2 Static and Dynamic Processes

A process that does not terminate while the operating system is functioning is called *static*; a process that may terminate is called *dynamic*. If a system consists of only a bounded number of static processes, then its corresponding process graph is also static; that is, it never changes. Obviously, we must be careful when we define our terms, since initially the graph has no nodes. Rather than worrying about this technicality, let us agree that by *static process graph* we mean one that reaches a static state after some initial "short" period of time.

What are the main advantages and disadvantages of each of these schemes? The difference between the two schemes is similar in many respects to differences between block-structured languages, (such as Algol, PL/1, or Pascal) and languages with static memory allocation (such as Fortran). In the former, blocks/processes appear and disappear dynamically, while in the latter, blocks/processes are fixed at declaration time. The dynamic scheme is more flexible than the static scheme, but it requires more overhead, since process creation and deletion can be quite expensive.

9.5 The Critical Section Problem

In the last section, we developed a model of a system consisting of a number of cooperating sequential processes, all running asynchronously and sharing some data in common. Let us illustrate this model with a simple example that is representative of operating systems.

Producer/consumer processes are quite common in operating systems. A *producer* process produces information that is consumed by a *consumer* process. For example, a line printer driver produces characters which are consumed by the line printer. A compiler may produce assembly code, which is consumed by an assembler. The assembler, in turn, may produce load modules, which are consumed by the loader.

To allow producer and consumer processes to run concurrently, we must create a pool of buffers that can be filled by the producer and emptied by the consumer. A producer can produce into one buffer while the consumer is consuming from another buffer. The producer and consumer must be synchronized, so that the consumer does not try to consume items which have not yet been produced. In this situation, the consumer must wait until an item is produced.

The *unbounded-buffer* producer/consumer problem places no limit on the number of buffers. The consumer may have to wait for new items, but the producer can always produce new items; there are always empty buffers. The *bounded-buffer* producer/consumer problem assumes that there is a fixed number, n, of buffers. In this case, the consumer must wait if all the buffers are empty and the producer must wait if all the buffers are full.

In the following solution to the bounded buffer problem, the shared pool of buffers is implemented as a circular array with two logical pointers: *in* and *out*. The variable *in* points to the next free buffer, while *out* points to the first full buffer. The pool is empty when *in* = *out*; the pool is full when *in*+1 **mod** n = *out*.

The *skip* is a do-nothing instruction. Thus, **while** *condition* **do** *skip* simply tests the condition repetitively until it becomes false.

```
type item = ... ;
    var buffer: array [0..n−1] of item;
        in, out: 0..n−1;
        nextp, nextc: item;
        in := 0;
        out := 0;
        parbegin

            producer: begin
                repeat
                    ...
                    produce an item in nextp
                    ...
                    while in+1 mod n = out do skip;
                    buffer[in] := nextp;
                    in := in+1 mod n;
                until false;
            end;
```

consumer: **begin**
　　　　　　　repeat
　　　　　　　　　while *in* = *out* **do** *skip*;
　　　　　　　　　nextc := *buffer*[*out*];
　　　　　　　　　out := *out*+1 **mod** *n*;
　　　　　　　　　　　…
　　　　　　　　　consume the item in *nextc*
　　　　　　　　　　　…
　　　　　　　　until *false*;
　　　　　end;
　　parend;

This algorithm allows at most $n-1$ buffers to be full at the same time. Suppose that we wanted to modify the algorithm to remedy this deficiency. One possibility is to add an integer variable *counter*, initialized to 0. *Counter* is incremented every time a new full buffer is added to the pool and decremented whenever we remove one of the full buffers from the pool. The code for the producer process can be modified as follows:

repeat
　　　…
　　produce an item in *nextp*
　　　…
　　while *counter* = *n* **do** *skip*;
　　buffer[*in*] := *nextp*;
　　in := *in*+1 **mod** *n*;
　　counter := *counter* + 1;
until *false*;

The code for the consumer process can be modified as follows:

repeat
　　while *counter* = 0 **do** *skip*;
　　nextc := *buffer*[*out*];
　　out := *out*+1 **mod** *n*;
　　counter := *counter* − 1;
　　　…
　　consume the item in *nextc*
　　　…
until *false*;

Although both the producer and consumer routines are correct separately, they may not function correctly when executed concurrently. To illustrate this, suppose that the value of variable *counter* is currently 5 and that the producer and consumer processes execute the statements "*counter* := *counter* + 1" and "*counter* := *counter* − 1" concurrently. Following the execution of these two statements the value of the variable *counter* may be 4, 5 or 6! The only correct result is *counter* = 5, which is generated correctly if the producer and consumer execute separately.

We can show that *counter* may be incorrect, as follows. Note that the statement "*counter* := *counter* + 1" is implemented in machine language as:

$$register_1 := counter;$$
$$register_1 := register_1 + 1;$$
$$counter := register_1$$

where $register_1$ is a local cpu register. Similarly, the statement "*counter* := *counter* − 1" is implemented as follows:

$$register_2 := counter$$
$$register_2 := register_2 - 1;$$
$$counter := register_2$$

where again $register_2$ is a local cpu register. Even though $register_1$ and $register_2$ may be the same physical registers (an accumulator, say), remember that the contents of this register will be saved and restored by the cpu scheduling routines: the interrupt handler and the dispatcher (Section 4.2.3).

The concurrent execution of the statements "*counter* := *counter* + 1" and "*counter* := *counter* − 1" is equivalent to a sequential execution where the lower level statements presented above are interleaved in some arbitrary order (but the order within each high level statement is preserved). One such interleaving is:

T_0:	producer	execute	$register_1 := counter$	$\{register_1 = 5\}$
T_1:	producer	execute	$register_1 := register_1 + 1$	$\{register_1 = 6\}$
T_2:	consumer	execute	$register_2 := counter$	$\{register_2 = 5\}$
T_3:	consumer	execute	$register_2 := register_2 - 1$	$\{register_2 = 4\}$
T_4:	producer	execute	$counter := register_1$	$\{counter = 6\}$
T_5:	consumer	execute	$counter := register_2$	$\{counter = 4\}$

Notice that we have arrived at the incorrect state "*counter* = 4," recording that there are four full buffers when in fact there are five full buffers. If we reverse the order of the statements at T_4 and T_5 we would arrive at the incorrect state "*counter* = 6."

We may arrive at this incorrect state because we allowed both processes to manipulate the variable *counter* concurrently. (Note that executing these two statements concurrently violates Bernstein's conditions.) In order to remedy this difficulty, we need to ensure that only one process at a time may be manipulating the variable *counter*. This observation leads us to the *critical section problem*.

9.5.1 Problem Definition

Consider a system consisting of n cooperating processes $\{P_1, P_2, ..., P_n\}$. Each process has a segment of code, called a *critical section*, in which the process may be reading common variables, updating a table, writing a file, and so on. The important feature of the system is that when one process is executing in its critical section, no other process is to be allowed to execute in its critical section. Thus the execution of critical sections by the processes is *mutually exclusive* in time. The critical section problem is to design a protocol which the processes may use to cooperate. Each process must request permission to enter its critical section. The section of code implementing this request is the *entry* section. The critical section may be followed by an *exit* section. The remaining code is the *remainder* section.

A solution to the mutual exclusion problem must satisfy the following three requirements:

a. **Mutual Exclusion**. If process P_i is executing in its critical section then no other process can be executing in its critical section.

b. **Progress**. If no process is executing in its critical section and there exists some process that wishes to enter its critical section, then only those processes that are not executing in their remainder section can participate in the decision as to who will enter the critical section next, and this selection cannot be postponed indefinitely.

c. **Bounded Waiting**. There must exist a bound on the number of times that other processes are allowed to enter their critical sections after a process has made a request to enter its critical section and before that request is granted.

It is assumed that each process is executing at a non-zero speed. However, no assumption can be made concerning the *relative* speed of the n processes.

In Sections 9.5.2 and 9.5.3 we work up to solutions to the critical section problem which satisfy the three requirements stated above, and which do not rely on any assumptions concerning the hardware instructions or the number of processors the hardware supports. It is, however, assumed that the basic machine language instructions (the primitive instructions such as load, store, and test) are executed atomically. That is, if two such instructions are executed simultaneously, the result is equivalent to their sequential execution in some unknown order. Thus, if a load and a store are executed simultaneously, the load will either get the old value or the new value, but not some combination of the two.

In Section 9.5.4 we present some simple hardware instructions that are available on many systems, and show how they can be effectively utilized in solving the critical section problem.

9.5.2 Two-Process Software Solutions

In this section we trace the initial attempts made in trying to develop algorithms for ensuring mutual exclusion. We restrict our attention to algorithms that are applicable to only two processes at a time. In Section 9.5.3 we deal with the more general problem of n processes. The processes are numbered P_0 and P_1 and the general structure of the problem is:

> **begin**
>   common variable declarations;
>   **parbegin**
> P_0;
> P_1;
>   **parend**;
> **end**.

For brevity, when presenting the algorithm, we define only the common variables and describe process P_i. For convenience, we use P_j to denote the other process; that is, $j = 1 - i$.

The general structure of process P_i is presented below. The *entry section* and *exit section* are enclosed in boxes to highlight the important segments of code.

repeat

> entry section;

critical section

> exit section;

remainder section

until *false*;

Algorithm 1

Our first approach is to let the processes share a common integer variable *turn* initialized to 0 (or 1). If *turn* = i, then process P_i is allowed to execute in its critical section.

repeat

> **while** *turn* ≠ i **do** *skip*;

critical section

> *turn* := j;

remainder section

until *false*;

This solution ensures that only one process at a time can be in its critical section. However, it does not satisfy the progress requirement, since it requires strict alternation of processes in the execution of the critical section. For example, if *turn* = 0 and P_1 wants to enter its critical section, it cannot do so, even though P_0 may be in its remainder section.

Algorithm 2

The problem with Algorithm 1 is that it fails to remember the state of each process, but remembers only which process is allowed to enter its critical section. To remedy this problem, we can replace the variable *turn* with the following array.

var *flag*: **array** [0..1] **of** *boolean*;

The elements of the array are initialized to *false*. If *flag[i]* is *true*, then process P_i is executing in its critical section.

The general structure of process P_i would be:

repeat

> **while** *flag[j]* **do** *skip*;
> *flag[i]* := *true*;

critical section

> *flag[i]* := *false*;

remainder section

until *false*;

Here we first check if the other process is in its critical section (*flag[j]* = *true*) and if so, we wait. Then we set our *flag[i]* to be *true* and enter our critical section. When we leave our critical section, we reset our *flag* to be *false*, allowing the other process into its critical section if it was waiting.

This algorithm does not ensure that only one process at a time will be executing in its critical section. For example, consider the following execution sequence:

T_0: P_0 enters the **while** statement and finds *flag[1]* = *false*.

T_1: P_1 enters the **while** statement and finds *flag[0]* = *false*.

T_2: P_1 sets *flag[1]* = *true* and enters the critical section.

T_3: P_0 sets $flag[0]$ = $true$ and enters the critical section.

We now have arrived at a state where P_0 and P_1 are both in their critical sections, violating the mutual-exclusion requirement.

This algorithm is crucially dependent on the exact timing of the two processes. The sequence above could have been derived in an environment where there are several processors executing concurrently, or where an interrupt (such as a timer interrupt) has occurred immediately after step T_0 was executed (and another interrupt after T_2), and the cpu is switched from one process to another.

Algorithm 3

The problem with Algorithm 2 is that process P_i made a decision concerning the state of P_j before P_j had the opportunity to change the state of the variable $flag[j]$. We can try to correct this problem. As in Algorithm 2, we still maintain the array $flag$. This time, however, the setting of $flag[i]$ = $true$ indicates only that P_i *wants* to enter the critical section.

repeat

> $flag[i] := true;$
> **while** $flag[j]$ **do** *skip*;

critical section

> $flag[i] := false;$

remainder section

until *false*;

So, in this algorithm, we first set our $flag[i]$ to be $true$, signaling that we want to enter our critical section. Then we check that the other process does not also want to enter its critical section. We wait if so. Then we enter our critical section. When we exit the critical section, we set our $flag$ to be $false$, allowing the other process (if it is waiting) to enter its critical section.

In this solution, unlike Algorithm 2, the mutual-exclusion requirement is satisfied. Unfortunately, the progress requirement is not met. To illustrate this problem, consider the following execution sequence.

$$T_0: \quad P_0 \text{ sets } flag[0] = true.$$
$$T_1: \quad P_1 \text{ sets } flag[1] = true.$$

Now P_0 and P_1 are looping forever in their respective **while** statements.

Algorithm 4

By now the reader is probably convinced that there is no simple solution to the critical section problem. It appears that every time we fix one bug in a solution, another bug appears. However, we now (finally) present a correct solution, due to Peterson [1981]. This solution is basically a combination of Algorithm 3 and a slight modification of Algorithm 1.

The processes share two variables in common:

var *flag*: **array** [0..1] **of** *boolean*;
turn: 0..1;

Initially *flag*[0] = *flag*[1] = *false* and the value of *turn* is immaterial (but either 0 or 1). The structure of process P_i is:

repeat

```
flag[i] := true;
turn := j;
while (flag[j] and turn=j) do skip;
```

critical section

```
flag[i] := false;
```

remainder section

until *false*;

To enter our critical section, we first set our *flag[i]* to be *true*, and assert that it is the other process' turn to enter if it wants to (*turn* = *j*). If both processes try to enter at the same time, *turn* will be set to both *i* and *j* at roughly the same time. Only one of these assignments will last; the other will occur, but be immediately overwritten. The eventual value of *turn* decides which of the two processes is allowed to enter its critical section first.

We now prove that Peterson's solution is correct. To do so we need to show that (a) mutual exclusion is preserved, (b) the progress requirement is satisfied, and (c) the bounded-waiting requirement is met.

To prove property (a) we note that each P_i enters its critical section only if either *flag[j]* = *false* or *turn* = *i*. Also note that if both processes could be executing in their critical sections at the same time then *flag[0]* = *flag[1]* = *true*. These two observations imply that P_0 and P_1 could not have successfully executed their *while* statement at about the same time, since the value of *turn* can be either 0 or 1, but not both. Hence, one of the processes, say P_j, must have successfully executed the *while* statement, while P_i had to at least execute one additional statement "*turn* = *j*". However, since at that point in time *flag[j]* = *true*, and *turn* = *i*, and this condition will persist as long as P_j is in its critical section, the result follows: mutual exclusion is preserved.

To prove properties (b) and (c), we note that a process P_i can be prevented from entering the critical section only if it is stuck in the *while* loop with the condition *flag[j]* = *true* and *turn* = *j*; this is the only loop. If P_j is not interested in entering the critical section, then *flag[j]* = *false* and P_i can enter its critical section. If P_j has set *flag[j]* = *true* and is also executing in its *while* statement, then either *turn* = *i* or *turn* = *j*. If *turn* = *i*, then P_i will enter the critical section. If *turn* = *j*, then P_j will enter the critical section. However, once P_j exits its critical section, it will reset *flag[j]* to *false* allowing P_i to enter its critical section. If P_j should reset *flag[j]* to *true*, it must also set *turn* = *i*. Thus, since P_i does not change the value of the variable *turn* while executing the *while* statement, P_i will enter the critical section (progress) after at most one entry by P_j (bounded-waiting).

9.5.3 N-Process Software Solutions

We have seen that Peterson's solution solves the critical section problem for two processes. Now let us develop an algorithm for solving the critical section problem for *n* processes. Algorithm 5 is due to Eisenberg and McGuire [1972] while Algorithm 6 is due to Lamport [1974].

Algorithm 5

The common data structures are:

$$\textbf{var } \textit{flag}: \textbf{array } [0..n-1] \textbf{ of } (\textit{idle, want-in, in-cs});$$
$$\textit{turn}: 0..n-1;$$

All the elements of *flag* are initially *idle*, the initial value of *turn* is immaterial (between 0 and $n-1$).

The structure of process P_i is:

var j: $0..n$;
repeat

```
repeat
    flag[i] := want-in;
    j := turn;
    while j ≠ i
        do if flag[j] ≠ idle
            then j := turn
            else j := j+1 mod n;
    flag[i] := in-cs;
    j := 0;
    while (j < n) and (j = i or flag[j] ≠ in-cs) do j := j+1;
    until (j ≥ n) and (turn = i or flag[turn] = idle);
turn := i;
```

critical section

```
j := turn+1 mod n;
while (flag[j] = idle) do j := j+1 mod n;
turn := j;
flag[i] := idle;
```

remainder section

until *false*;

To prove that Eisenberg and McGuire's algorithm is correct, we need to show that (a) mutual exclusion is preserved, (b) the progress requirement is satisfied, and (c) the bounded-waiting requirement is met.

To prove property (a) we note that each P_i enters its critical section only if $flag[j] \neq in\text{-}cs$ for all $j \neq i$. Since only P_i can set $flag[i] = in\text{-}cs$, and since P_i inspects $flag[j]$ only while $flag[i] = in\text{-}cs$, the result follows.

To prove property (b) we observe that the value of *turn* can be modified only when a process enters its critical section and when it leaves its critical section. Thus if no process is in its critical section or leaving it, the value of *turn* remains constant. The first contending process in the cyclic ordering $(i, i+1, ..., n-1, 0, ..., i-1)$ will enter the critical section.

To prove property (c) we observe that when a process leaves the critical section, it must designate as its unique successor the first contending process in the cyclic ordering, ensuring that any process wanting to enter its critical section will do so within $n-1$ turns.

Algorithm 6

A different approach was provided by Lamport [1974], who presented an algorithm called the *bakery algorithm*. This algorithm was developed for a distributed environment. We are only concerned with those aspects of the algorithm that pertain to a centralized environment.

The bakery algorithm is based upon a scheduling algorithm commonly used in bakeries, ice cream stores, meat markets, and similar situations. Upon entering the store, each customer receives a number. The customer with the lowest number is served next. Unfortunately, the bakery algorithm cannot guarantee that two processes do not receive the same number. In the case of a tie, the process with the lowest name is served first. That is, if P_i and P_j receive the same number and if $i < j$, then P_i is served first. Since process names are unique and totally ordered, our algorithm is completely deterministic.

The common data structures are:

$$\text{var } choosing: \textbf{array } [0..n-1] \textbf{ of } boolean;$$
$$number: \textbf{array } [0..n-1] \textbf{ of } integer;$$

Initially these data structures are initialized to *false* and 0, respectively. For convenience, we define the following notation:

- $(a,b) < (c,d)$ if $a < c$ or if $a = c$ and $b < d$.

- $max(a_0, ..., a_{n-1})$ is a number, k, such that $k \geq a_i$ for $i = 0, ..., n-1$.

The structure of process P_i is:

repeat

```
choosing[i] := true;
number[i] := max(number[0], number[1], ..., number[n-1]) + 1;
choosing[i] := false;
for j := 0 to n-1
    do begin
            while choosing[j] do skip;
            while number[j] ≠ 0
                and (number[j],j) < (number[i],i) do skip;
    end;
```

critical section

```
number[i] := 0;
```

remainder section

until *false;*

In order to prove that the bakery algorithm is correct, we need to first show that if P_i is in its critical section and P_k $(k \neq i)$ has already chosen its *number[k]* $\neq 0$, then $(number[i],i) < (number[k],k)$. The proof of this is left as an exercise to the reader.

Given the above, it is now simple to show that mutual exclusion is observed. Indeed, consider P_i in its critical section and P_k trying to enter the critical section. When P_k executes the second **while** statement for $j = i$ it finds that:

- *number[k]* $\neq 0$, and
- $(number[i],i) < (number[k],k)$.

Thus it continues looping in the **while** statement until P_i leaves its critical section.

To show that the progress and bounded-waiting requirements are preserved and that the algorithm ensures fairness, it is sufficient to observe that the processes enter their critical section on a first-come-first-served basis.

9.5.4 Hardware Solutions

Many machines provide special hardware instructions that allow one to either test and modify the content of a word, or to swap the contents of two words, in one memory cycle. These special instructions can be used to solve the critical section problem. Rather than discussing one specific instruction for one specific machine, let us abstract the main concepts behind these types of instructions by defining the *Test-and-Set* instruction as follows:

```
function Test-and-Set (var target: boolean): boolean;
    begin
        Test-and-Set := target;
        target := true;
    end;
```

and the *Swap* instruction as follows:

```
procedure Swap (var a, b: boolean);
    var temp: boolean;
    begin
        temp := a;
        a := b;
        b := temp;
    end;
```

The important characteristic is that these instructions are executed atomically; that is, in one memory cycle. Thus if two *Test-and-Set* (or *Swap*) instructions are executed simultaneously (each on a different cpu), they will be executed sequentially in some arbitrary order.

If the machine supports the *Test-and-Set* instruction, then mutual exclusion can be implemented by declaring a boolean variable *lock*, initialized to *false*.

repeat

> **while** *Test-and-Set*(*lock*) **do** *skip*;

critical section

> *lock* := *false*;

remainder section

until *false*;

If the machine supports the *Swap* instruction, then mutual exclusion can be provided in a similar manner. A global boolean variable *lock* is initialized to *false*. Each process also has a local boolean variable *key*.

repeat

> *key* := *true*;
> **repeat**
>   *Swap*(*lock*,*key*);
> **until** *key* = *false*;

critical section

> *lock* := *false*;

remainder section

until *false*;

The algorithms presented above do not satisfy the bounded-waiting requirement. To do so additional variables must be used. Below, we present an algorithm, due to Burns [1978], that uses the *Test-and-Set* instruction, and which satisfies all the required critical section requirements.

The common data structures are:

> **var** *waiting*: **array** [0..*n*−1] **of** *boolean*
> *lock*: **boolean**

These data structures are initialized to *false*.
The structure of process P_i is:

> **var** *j*: 0..*n*−1;
> *key*: *boolean*;
> **repeat**

```
waiting[i] := true;
key := true;
while waiting[i] and key do key := Test-and-Set(lock);
waiting[i] := false;
```

critical section

```
j := i+1 mod n;
while (j ≠ i) and (not waiting[j]) do j := j+1 mod n;
if j = i then lock := false
        else waiting[j] := false;
```

remainder section

> **until** *false*;

To prove that the mutual-exclusion requirement is met, we note that process P_i can enter its critical section only if either *waiting*[*i*] = *false* or *key* = *false*. *Key* can become *false* only by executing the *Test-and-Set*. The first process to execute the *Test-and-Set* will find *key* = *false*; all others must wait. *Waiting*[*i*] can become false only if another process leaves its critical section; only one *waiting*[*i*] is set *true*, maintaining the mutual-exclusion requirement.

To prove the progress requirement, we note that the arguments presented above for mutual exclusion also apply here, since a process exiting the critical section either sets *lock* to *false*, or *waiting*[*j*] = *false*. Both allow a trying process to enter its critical section.

To prove bounded-waiting, we note that when a process leaves its critical section, it scans the array *waiting* in the cyclic ordering ($i+1$, $i+2$, ..., $n-1$, 0, ..., $i-1$). It designates the first process in this ordering which is in its entry section (*waiting*[j] = *true*) as the next one to enter its critical section. Any process waiting to enter its critical section will thus do so within $n-1$ turns.

9.6 Semaphores

The solutions to the mutual exclusion problem presented in the last section are not easy to generalize to more complex problems. To overcome this difficulty, a new synchronization tool, called a *semaphore*, was introduced by Dijkstra [1965a]. A semaphore S is an integer variable that, apart from initialization, can be accessed only through two standard *atomic* operations: P and V. The classical definitions of P and V are:

$$P(S): \textbf{while } S \leq 0 \textbf{ do } skip;$$
$$S := S - 1;$$

$$V(S): S := S + 1;$$

Modifications to the integer value of the semaphore in the P and V operations are executed indivisibly. That is, when one process modifies the semaphore value, no other process can simultaneously modify that same semaphore value. In addition, in the case of the $P(S)$, the testing of the integer value of S ($S \leq 0$), and its possible modification ($S := S - 1$) must also be executed without interruption. We see how these operations can be implemented in Section 9.6.2, but first let us see how semaphores can be used.

9.6.1 Usage

Semaphores can be used in dealing with the n-process critical section problem. The n processes share a common semaphore, *mutex*, initialized to 1. Each process P_i is organized as follows:

repeat

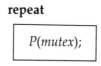

critical section

$$\boxed{V(mutex);}$$

remainder section

until *false;*

Semaphores can also be used in solving various synchronization problems. For example, consider two concurrently running processes: P_1 with a statement S_1, and P_2 with a statement S_2. Suppose that we require that S_2 be executed only after S_1 has completed. This scheme can be readily implemented by letting P_1 and P_2 share a common semaphore *synch*, initialized to 0, and by inserting the statements:

$$S_1;$$
$$V(synch);$$

in process P_1, and the statements

$$P(synch);$$
$$S_2;$$

in process P_2. Since *synch* is initialized to 0, P_2 will execute S_2 only after P_1 has invoked $V(synch)$, which is after S_1.

Let us present a more complicated example. Consider the precedence graph of Figure 9.6 and the corresponding program below:

```
var a, b, c, d, e, f, g: semaphores;
(* initial value of all semaphores is 0 *)
    begin
        parbegin
            begin S₁; V(a); V(b); end;
            begin P(a); S₂; S₄; V(c); V(d); end;
            begin P(b); S₃; V(e); end;
            begin P(c); S₅; V(f); end;
            begin P(d); P(e); S₆; V(g); end;
            begin P(f); P(g); S₇; end;
        parend;
    end;
```

Recall that we argued that the graph of Figure 9.6 does not have a corresponding program that employs the concurrent statement. This program, however, demonstrates that, with the addition of semaphores, the concurrent statement is as powerful as the **fork/join** construct.

9.6.2 Implementation

The main disadvantage of the mutual exclusion solutions of Section 9.5, and the semaphore definition given above is that they all require *busy-waiting*. While a process is in its critical section, any other process that tries to enter its critical section must continuously loop in the entry code. This is clearly a problem in a real multiprogramming system where a single cpu is shared among many processes. Busy-waiting wastes cpu cycles that some other process might be able to use productively.

To overcome the need for busy-waiting, we can modify the definition of the P and V semaphore operations. When a process executes the P operation and finds that the semaphore value is not positive, it must wait. However, rather than busy-waiting, the process can *block* itself. The block operation places a process into a waiting state. It then transfers control to the cpu scheduler, which selects another process to execute from the ready queue.

A process which is blocked, waiting on a semaphore S, should be restarted by the execution of a V operation by some other process. The process is restarted by a *wakeup* operation, which changes the state of the process from blocked to ready and puts it into the ready queue. (The cpu may or may not be switched from the running process to the newly ready process, depending upon the cpu scheduling algorithm.)

To implement semaphores under this definition, we define a semaphore as a record.

> **type** *semaphore* = **record**
>   *value: integer;*
>   *L:* **list of** *process;*
>   **end;**

Each semaphore has an integer value and a list of processes. When a process must wait on a semaphore, it is added to the list of processes. A V operation removes one process from the list of waiting processes and awakens it.

The semaphore operations can now be defined as:

$P(S)$:   *S.value* := *S.value* − 1;
        if *S.value* < 0
          then begin
                  add this process to *S.L*;
                  block;
          end;

$V(S)$:   *S.value* := *S.value* + 1;
        if *S.value* ≤ 0
          then begin
                  remove a process *P* from *S.L*;
                  wakeup(P);
          end;

The *block* operation suspends the process that invokes it. The *wakeup(P)* operation resumes the execution of a blocked process *P*. These two operations are provided by the operating system as basic system calls.

Note that while the classical definition of semaphores with busy waiting is such that the semaphore value is never negative, this implementation may have negative semaphore values. If the semaphore value is negative, its magnitude is the number of processes waiting on that semaphore. This fact is a result of switching the order of the decrement and the test in the implementation of the *P* operation.

The list of processes can be easily implemented by a link field in each process control block (PCB). Each semaphore contains an integer value and a pointer to a list of PCBs. The simplest way to add and remove processes from the list would be last-in-first-out (a stack), but this scheme could cause starvation. Consequently, the list is more commonly implemented as a queue, and the semaphore contains both head and tail pointers to the queue. In general, however, the list may use *any* queueing strategy (FIFO, LIFO, priority, or some other strategy). Correct usage of semaphores does not depend upon a particular queueing strategy for the semaphore lists.

The critical aspect of semaphores is that they are executed atomically. We must guarantee that no two processes can execute *P* and *V* operations on the same semaphore at the same time. This situation is a critical section problem, and can be solved in either of two ways.

In a uniprocessor environment (that is, where only one cpu exists), we can simply inhibit interrupts during the time the *P* and *V* operations are executing. This scheme works in a uniprocessor environment because once interrupts are inhibited, instructions from different processes cannot be interleaved.

In a multiprocessor environment, inhibiting interrupts does not work. Instructions from different processes (running on different processors) may be interleaved in some arbitrary way. If the hardware does not provide any special instructions, one can employ any of the correct software solutions for the critical section problem (Algorithms 4, 5, or 6 above), where the critical sections consist of the P and V procedures.

It is important to admit that we have not completely eliminated busy-waiting with this definition of the P and V operations. Rather we have removed busy-waiting from the entry to the critical sections of application programs. Furthermore, we have limited it to only the critical sections of the P and V operations, which are quite short. (If properly coded, they should be no more than about ten instructions.) Thus the critical section is almost always empty and virtually no busy-waiting ever occurs. When busy-waiting does occur, it is for a very short period of time. An entirely different situation exists with application programs whose critical sections may be quite long (hours) or may be almost always occupied. In this case, busy-waiting would be very inefficient.

9.7 Classical Process Coordination Problems

In this section we present a number of different synchronization problems that are important mainly because they are examples for a large class of concurrency control problems. These problems are used in testing nearly every newly proposed synchronization scheme. Semaphores are used for synchronization in our solutions.

9.7.1 The Bounded-Buffer Problem

The bounded-buffer problem was introduced in Section 9.5, and is commonly used to illustrate the power of synchronization primitives. We present here a general structure of this scheme, without committing ourselves to any particular implementation. We assume that the pool consists of n buffers, each capable of holding one item. The *mutex* semaphore provides mutual exclusion for accesses to the buffer pool. The *empty* and *full* semaphores count the number of empty and full buffers, respectively.

```
type item = ... ;
    var buffer = ... ;
    full, empty, mutex: semaphore;
    nextp, nextc: item;
    begin
        full := 0;
        empty := n;
        mutex := 1;
        parbegin
            producer: repeat
                            ...
                        produce an item in nextp
                            ...
                        P(empty);
                        P(mutex);
                            ...
                        add nextp to buffer
                            ...
                        V(mutex);
                        V(full);
                    until false;

            consumer: repeat
                        P(full);
                        P(mutex);
                            ...
                        remove an item from buffer to nextc
                            ...
                        V(mutex);
                        V(empty);
                            ...
                        consume the item in nextc
                            ...
                    until false;

        parend;
    end.
```

Note the symmetry between the producer and the consumer. We can interpret this code as the producer producing full buffers for the consumer, or as the consumer producing empty buffers for the producer. A more detailed example is presented in Chapter 10.

9.7.2 The Readers/Writers Problem

A data object (such as a file or record) is to be shared among several concurrent processes. Some of these processes may want only to read the content of the shared object, while others may want to update (that is, read and write) the shared object. We distinguish between these two types of processes by referring to those processes which are only interested in reading as *readers* and to the rest as *writers*. Obviously, if two readers access the shared data object simultaneously, no adverse effects will result. However, if a writer and some other process (either a reader or a writer) access the shared object simultaneously, chaos may ensue. Such concurrent access would violate Bernstein's conditions.

In order to ensure that these difficulties do not arise, we require that the writers have exclusive access to the shared object. This synchronization problem is referred to as the readers/writers problem. It was originally stated and solved by Courtois et al. [1971]; since then it has been used to test nearly every new synchronization primitive. The readers/writers problem has several variations, all involving priorities. The simplest one, referred to as the *first* readers/writers problem, requires that no reader will be kept waiting unless a writer has already obtained permission to use the shared object. In other words, no reader should wait for other readers to finish simply because a writer is waiting. The *second* readers/writers problem requires that once a writer is ready, it performs its write as soon as possible. In other words, if a writer is waiting to access the object, no new readers may start reading.

We note that a solution to either problem may result in *starvation*. In the first case, writers may starve; in the second case, readers may starve. For this reason other variants of the problem have been proposed. In this section we present a solution to the first readers/writers problem. In Chapter 10 we present a solution that avoids starvation to a variant of the second readers/writers problem.

In this solution to the first readers/writers problem, the reader processes share the following data structures.

$$\textbf{var} \;\; \textit{mutex, wrt: semaphore;}$$
$$\textit{readcount : integer;}$$

The semaphores *mutex* and *wrt* are initialized to 1, while *readcount* is initialized to 0. The semaphore *wrt* is common to both the reader and writer processes. The *mutex* semaphore is used to ensure mutual exclusion when the variable *readcount* is updated. *Readcount* keeps track of how many processes are currently reading the object. The semaphore *wrt* functions as a mutual exclusion semaphore for the writers. It also is used by the first/last reader that enters/exits the critical section. It is not used by readers who enter or exit while other readers are in their critical section.

The general structure of a reader process is:

$$P(mutex);$$
$$readcount := readcount + 1;$$
$$\textbf{if } readcount = 1 \textbf{ then } P(wrt);$$
$$V(mutex);$$

$$\cdots$$

reading is performed

$$\cdots$$

$$P(mutex);$$
$$readcount := readcount - 1;$$
$$\textbf{if } readcount = 0 \textbf{ then } V(wrt);$$
$$V(mutex);$$

while the general structure of a writer process is:

$$P(wrt);$$

$$\cdots$$

writing is performed

$$\cdots$$

$$V(wrt);$$

Note that if a writer is in the critical section and n readers are waiting, then one reader is queued on wrt, while $n-1$ readers are queued on $mutex$. Also observe that when a writer executes $V(wrt)$, we may resume the execution of either the waiting readers or a single waiting writer. The selection is up to the scheduler.

9.7.3 The Dining Philosophers Problem

The dining philosophers problem was originally stated and solved by Dijkstra [1965a]. Since then, it has been considered a classic synchronization problem, not because of its practical importance, but because it is an example for a large class of concurrency control problems.

The problem can be stated as follows. Five philosophers spend their lives thinking and eating. The philosophers share a common circular table surrounded by five chairs, each belonging to one philosopher. In the center of the table there is a bowl of rice, and the table is laid with five chopsticks (Figure 9.9). When a philosopher thinks, he does not interact with his colleagues. From time to time, a philosopher gets hungry and tries to pick up the two chopsticks that are closest to him (the chopsticks that are between him and his left and right neighbors). A philosopher may only pick up one chopstick at a time. Obviously, he cannot pick up a chopstick that is already in the hand of a neighbor. When a hungry philosopher has both his chopsticks at the same time, he eats without releasing his chopsticks. When he is finished eating, he puts down both of his chopsticks and starts thinking again.

One simple solution is to represent each chopstick by a semaphore. A philosopher tries to grab the chopstick by executing a *P* operation on that semaphore; the chopstick is released by executing a *V* on the semaphore. Thus the shared data is:

var chopstick: array [0..4] of semaphore;

where all the elements of *chopstick* are initialized to 1. The structure of philosopher *i* can now be described as follows:

repeat

$$P(chopstick[i]);$$
$$P(chopstick[i+1 \textbf{ mod } 5]);$$

$$\cdots$$

eat

$$\cdots$$

$$V(chopstick[i]);$$
$$V(chopstick[i+1 \textbf{ mod } 5]);$$

$$\cdots$$

think

$$\cdots$$

until false;

Although this solution guarantees that no two neighbors are eating simultaneously, it nevertheless must be rejected because of the possibility of creating a deadlock. Suppose that all five philosophers become hungry simultaneously, and each grabs his left chopstick. All the elements of *chopstick* now equal zero. When each philosopher tries to grab his right chopstick, he will be delayed forever.

Several possible remedies to the deadlock problem are listed below. Rather than presenting an algorithm for each of these solutions, we leave part of them as an exercise to the reader, and present one solution in Chapter 10.

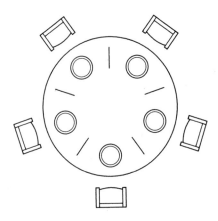

Figure 9.9   Dining philosophers

- Allow at most four philosophers to be sitting simultaneously at the table.

- Allow a philosopher to pick up his chopsticks only if both of them are available (note that this should be done in a critical section).

- Use an asymmetric solution. That is, an odd philosopher picks up first his left chopstick and then his right chopstick, while an even philosopher picks up his right chopstick and then his left chopstick.

Finally, any satisfactory solution to the dining philosophers problem must guard against the possibility that one of the philosophers will starve to death. A deadlock-free solution does not necessarily eliminate the possibility of starvation.

9.8 Interprocess Communication

Many of the problems which we have described, and more, are presented as synchronization problems. But, in a larger sense, they are simple examples of the larger problem of allowing *communication* between processes which wish to cooperate. In this section we are concerned with the general problem of interprocess communication. Principally, there exist two complementary communication schemes: shared memory and message systems.

Shared-memory systems require communicating processes to share some variables. The processes are expected to exchange information through the use of these shared variables. For example, the bounded-buffer scheme discussed in Section 9.5 could be used for this purpose. In a shared-memory scheme the responsibility for providing communication rests with the application programmers; the operating system only needs to provide the shared memory. The *message-system* scheme allows the processes to exchange messages. In this scheme, the responsibility for providing communication rests with the operating system itself.

Obviously, these two schemes are not mutually exclusive, and could be used simultaneously within a single operating system. In this section, we focus primarily on message systems, since the shared-memory scheme is basically application oriented. Also, we consider only systems with processes whose logical address spaces are disjoint.

The function of a message system is to allow processes to communicate with each other without the need to resort to shared variables. An interprocess communication facility basically provides two operations: **send**(*message*) and **receive**(*message*).

If processes P and Q want to communicate they must send and receive messages from each other. In order to do so, a *communication link* must exist between them. This link can be implemented in a variety of ways. We are not concerned here with the physical implementation of a link (such as shared memory or a hardware bus), but more in the issues of its logical implementation, such as its logical properties. Some basic implementation questions are:

- How are links established?

- Can a link be associated with more than two processes?

- How many links can there be between every pair of processes?

- What is the capacity of a link? That is, does the link have some buffer space? If so, how much?

- What is the size of messages? Can the link accommodate variable-size or fixed-size messages?

- Is a link unidirectional or bidirectional? That is, if a link exists between P and Q, can messages flow in one direction (such as only from P to Q) or in both directions?

The definition of unidirectional must be more carefully stated, since a link may be associated with more than two processes. Thus we say that a link is unidirectional only if each process connected to the link can either send or receive, but not both, and each link has at least one receiver process connected to it.

In addition, there are several methods for logically implementing a link and the **send/receive** operations:

- Direct or indirect communication.

- Send to a process or to a mailbox.

- Symmetric or asymmetric communication.

- Automatic or explicit buffering.

- Send by copy or send by reference.

- Fixed-size or variable-size messages.

In the following, we elaborate on these types of message systems.

9.8.1 Naming

In this section we consider the first three issues concerning the logical implementation of a link. Primarily, communication between two processes can be either direct or indirect.

Direct Communication

In the direct communication discipline, each process that wants to send or receive a message must explicitly name the recipient or sender of the communication. In this scheme, the **send** and **receive** primitives are defined as follows:

> **send**(P, *message*). Send a *message* to process P.

> **receive**(Q, *message*). Receive a *message* from process Q.

A communication link in this scheme has the following properties:

- A link is established automatically between every pair of processes that want to communicate. The processes need only know each other's identity to communicate.

- A link is associated with exactly two processes.

- Between each pair of communicating processes, there exists exactly one link.

- The link is bidirectional.

For example, the producer/consumer problem can be coded in this scheme in the following way:

```
type item = ... ;
    var nextp, nextc: item;
    parbegin
        producer: repeat
                    ...
                    produce an item in nextp
                    ...
                    send(consumer,nextp);
                  until false;

        consumer: repeat
                    receive(producer,nextc);
                    ...
                    consume the item in nextc
                    ...
                    until false;
    parend;
```

If this example is considered as a bounded-buffer scheme, then the size of the buffer equals the capacity of the communication link. This is discussed in more detail in Section 9.8.2.

This scheme exhibits a symmetry in addressing; that is, both the sender and the receiver have to name one another in order to communicate. A variant of this scheme employs asymmetry in addressing. Only the sender names the recipient; the recipient is not required to name the sender. In this scheme, the **send** and **receive** primitives are defined as follows:

- **send**(P, message). Send a message to process P.

- **receive**(id, message). Receive a message from any process; id is set to the name of the process with whom communication has taken place.

The disadvantage in both of these schemes (symmetric and asymmetric) is the limited modularity of the resulting process definitions. Changing the name of a process may necessitate the examination of all other process definitions. All references to the old name must be found, in order to modify them to the new name. This situation is not desirable from the viewpoint of separate compilation.

Indirect Communication

With indirect communication, the messages are sent to and received from mailboxes (also referred to as *ports*). A mailbox can be abstractly viewed as an object into which messages may be placed by processes and from which messages may be removed. Each mailbox has a unique identification that distinguishes it. In this scheme, a process may communicate with some other process by a number of different mailboxes. Two processes may communicate only if they have a shared mailbox. The **send** and **receive** primitives are defined as follows:

- **send**(A, *message*). Send a *message* to mailbox A.

- **receive**(A, *message*). Receive a *message* from mailbox A.

In this scheme, a communication link has the following properties:

- A link is established between a pair of processes only if they have a shared mailbox.

- A link may be associated with more than two processes.

- Between each pair of communicating processes there may be a number of different links, each corresponding to one mailbox.

- The link may be either unidirectional or bidirectional.

Now suppose that processes P_1, P_2, and P_3 all share mailbox A. Process P_1 sends a message to A, while P_2 and P_3 each execute a **receive** from A. Who will receive the message sent by P_1? This question can be resolved in a variety of ways:

- Allow a link to be associated with at most two processes.

- Allow at most one process at a time to execute a **receive** operation.

- Allow the system to select who will receive the message arbitrarily (that is, either P_2 or P_3, but not both, will receive the message). The system may identify the receiver to the sender.

Ownership of Mailboxes

A mailbox may be owned either by a process or by the system. If the mailbox is owned by a process (that is, the mailbox is attached to or defined as part of the process), then we distinguish between the owner (who can only receive messages through this mailbox) and the user of the mailbox (who can only send messages to the mailbox). Since each mailbox has a unique owner, there can be no confusion about who should receive a message sent to this mailbox. When a process that owns a mailbox terminates, the mailbox disappears. Any process that subsequently sends a message to this mailbox must be notified that the mailbox no longer exists (a form of exception handling).

There are a number of ways to designate the owner and users of a particular mailbox. One possibility is to allow a process to declare variables of type *mailbox*. The process that declares a mailbox is its owner. Any other process that knows the name of this mailbox can use it. It is also possible to declare a shared mailbox and then externally declare the identity of the owner.

On the other hand, a mailbox that is owned by the operating system, has an existence of its own. It is independent and not "attached" to any particular process. The operating system provides a mechanism that allows a process to:

- Create a new mailbox.

- Send and receive messages through the mailbox.

- Destroy a mailbox.

The process that creates a new mailbox is its owner by default. Initially, the owner is the only process that can receive messages through this mailbox. However, the ownership and receive privilege may be passed to other processes through appropriate system calls. Of course, this provision could result in multiple receivers for each mailbox. Processes may also share a mailbox through the process-creation facility. For example, if process P created mailbox A, and then created a new process Q, P and Q may share mailbox A. Since all processes with access rights to a mailbox may ultimately terminate, after some time a mailbox may no longer be accessible by any process. In this case, the operating system should reclaim whatever space was used for the mailbox. This task may require some form of garbage collection.

9.8.2 Buffering

In this section we consider two more issues concerning the logical implementation of a link: capacity and message properties.

Capacity

A link has some capacity that determines the number of messages that can temporarily reside in it. This property can be viewed as a queue of messages attached to the link. Basically, there are three ways such a queue can be implemented:

- **Zero capacity**. The queue has maximum length 0; thus the link cannot have any messages waiting in it. In this case, the sender must wait until the recipient receives the message. The two processes must be synchronized for a message transfer to take place. This synchronization is called a *rendezvous*.

- **Bounded capacity**. The queue has finite length n; thus at most n messages can reside in it. If the queue is not full when a new message is sent, it is placed in the queue (either by copying the message or by keeping a pointer to the message), and the sender can continue execution without waiting. The link has a finite capacity, however. If the link is full, the sender must be delayed until space is available in the queue.

- **Unbounded capacity**. The queue has potentially infinite length; thus any number of messages can wait in it. The sender is never delayed.

The zero capacity case is sometimes referred to as a message system with no buffering; the other cases provide automatic buffering.

We note that, in the non-zero capacity cases, a process does not know whether a message has arrived at its destination after the **send** operation is completed. If this information is crucial for the computation, the sender must explicitly communicate with the receiver to find out if it received the message. For example, suppose process P sends a message to process Q and can only continue with its execution after the message is received. Process P executes the sequence:

send(Q ,*message*);
receive(Q, *message*);

and process Q executes:

receive(P, *message*);
send(P, "acknowledgement");

Messages

Messages sent by a process can be of three varieties:

- Fixed-sized.
- Variable-sized.
- Typed messages.

If only fixed-sized messages can be sent, the physical implementation is straightforward. This restriction, however, makes the task of programming more difficult. On the other hand, variable-sized messages require a more complex physical implementation, but the programming becomes simpler.

The last case, associating a type with each mailbox, is basically applicable only to indirect communication. The messages that can be sent to and received from a mailbox are restricted to the designated type. This is particularly appropriate for mailboxes declared in a strongly-typed program language. For example, a mailbox to hold n *items* for the producer/consumer problem might be declared as:

$$m: \textbf{mailbox}[n] \textbf{ of } item;$$

Special Cases

There are two special cases that do not directly fit into any of the categories we have discussed.

- The process sending a message is never delayed. However, if the receiver has not received the message before the sending process sends another message, the first message is lost. This scheme is based on the physical implementation of "send a reference" rather than "send a copy". The advantage of this scheme is that large messages need not be copied more than once. The main disadvantage is that the programming task becomes more difficult. Processes need to synchronize explicitly, to ensure that messages are not lost, and that the sender and receiver do not manipulate the message buffer simultaneously.

- The process sending a message is delayed until it receives a reply. This scheme was adopted in the Thoth operating system (Cheriton et al. [1979]). In this system, messages are of fixed size (eight words). A process P that sends a message is blocked until the receiving process has received the message and sent back an eight-word reply by the **reply**(P, *message*) primitive. The reply message overwrites the original message buffer. The only difference between the **send** and **reply** primitives is that a **send** causes the sending process to be blocked, while the **reply** allows both the sending process and the receiving process to continue immediately with their executions.

9.8.3 Exception Conditions

A message system is particularly useful in a distributed environment, where processes may reside at different sites (machines). In such an environment the probability that an error will occur during communication (and processing) is much larger than in a single-machine environment. In a single-machine environment, messages are usually implemented in shared memory. If a failure occurs, the entire system fails. In a distributed environment, however, messages are usually handled by communication lines, and the failure of one site does not necessarily result in the failure of the entire system.

When a failure occurs in either a centralized or distributed system, some error recovery (exception condition handling) must take place. Let us briefly discuss some of the exception conditions that a system must handle in the context of a message scheme.

Process Terminates

Either a sender or receiver may terminate before a message is processed. This situation will leave messages that will never be received or processes waiting for messages that will never be sent. We consider two cases here.

1. A receiver process P may wait for a message from a process Q that has terminated. If no action is taken, P will be blocked forever. (Notice that this condition is not deadlock in the classical definition, since there is no circular wait.) In this case, the system may either terminate P or notify it that Q has terminated.

2. Process P may send a message to a process Q that has terminated. In the automatic-buffering scheme, no harm is done; P simply

continues with its execution. If P needs to know that its message has been processed by Q, it must explicitly program for an acknowledgment. In the no-buffering case, P will be blocked forever. As in case (1), the system may either terminate P or notify it that Q has terminated.

Lost messages

A message from process P to process Q may become lost somewhere in the communications network, due to a hardware or communication line failure. There are three basic methods for dealing with this event.

1. The operating system is responsible for detecting this event and for resending the message.

2. The sending process is responsible for detecting this event and for retransmitting the message, if it so wants.

3. The operating system is responsible for detecting this event; it then notifies the sending process that the message has been lost. The sending process can proceed as it wants.

It is not always necessary to detect lost messages. The user must specify (that is, either notify the system, or program this requirement itself) that such a detection should take place.

How do we detect that a message is lost? The most common detection method is to use *time-outs*. When a message is sent out, a reply message, acknowledging reception of the message, is always sent back. The operating system or a process may then specify a time interval during which it expects the acknowledgment message to arrive. If this time period elapses before the acknowledgment arrives, the operating system (or process) may assume that the message is lost. It is possible, however, that a message did not get lost, but simply took a little longer than expected to travel through the network. In this case, we may have multiple copies of the same message flowing through the network. A mechanism must exist to distinguish between these various types of messages. This problem is discussed in more detail in Chapter 13.

Scrambled messages

The message may be delivered to its destination, but be scrambled on the way (because of noise in the communications channel, for example). This case is similar to the case of a lost message. Either the operating system will retransmit the original message, or it will notify the process of this event. Checksums (such as parity or CRC) are commonly used to detect this type of error.

9.8.4 An Example: Accent

As an example of a message-based operating system, consider the Accent operating system, developed at Carnegie-Mellon University [Rashid and Robertson 1981] for the Perq computer. The Accent operating system kernel supports the creation and destruction of multiple processes. Each process has its own paged virtual memory with a 32-bit address space. No process shares memory with another process, as all communication is by *messages*. Messages are sent to and received from *mailboxes* (which Accent calls ports).

Even system calls are made by messages. When each process is created, two special mailboxes, the Kernel mailbox and the Data mailbox, are also created. A system call is made by sending a message to the Kernel mailbox; any return values are sent by the operating system as a message to the Data mailbox and can then be received by the process. Only the message communication operations (send/receive) are primitive.

The *AllocatePort* system call creates a new mailbox and allocates space for its queue of messages. The maximum size of the message queue must be specified when the mailbox is created. The process which creates the mailbox is its owner. The owner also is given receive access to the mailbox. Only one process at a time can either own or receive from a mailbox, but these rights can be sent to other processes if desired.

The mailbox has an initially empty queue of messages. As messages are sent to the mailbox, the message is copied into the mailbox. Messages are queued by priority. Two classes of messages are commonly used: *normal* and *emergency*. Emergency messages have high priority; normal messages have low priority. Messages of the same priority are queued First-In-First-Out, but high priority messages are queued before low priority messages.

The messages themselves consist of a fixed-length header, followed by a variable-length data portion. The header includes the length of the entire message, its class (normal or emergency) and two mailbox names. When a message is sent, one mailbox name is the mailbox to which the message is being sent. Commonly, the sending process expects a reply; the other mailbox name is passed on to the receiving process, which may use it as a "return address" to send messages back.

The variable part of the message is a list of typed data items. Each entry in the list has a type, size, and value. The type of the objects in the message is important since operating system defined objects, such as the ownership or receive access rights, process states, and memory segments, may be sent in messages.

The send and receive operations themselves are quite flexible. When a message is sent to a mailbox, the mailbox may be full. If the mailbox is not full, the message is copied to the mailbox and the sending process continues. If the mailbox is full, the process has four options:

1. Wait indefinitely until there is room in the mailbox.

2. Wait at most n milliseconds.

3. Do not wait at all, but return immediately.

4. One message can be given to the operating system to keep even though the mailbox to which it is being sent is full. When the operating system can actually put the message in the mailbox, a message is sent back to the sender; only one such message to a full mailbox can be pending at any time for a given sending process.

The last option is meant for server processes, such as a line printer driver. After finishing a request, they may need to send a one-time reply to the process which had requested service, but must continue with other service requests, even if the reply mailbox for a client is full.

The receive operation must specify from which mailbox or mailboxes to receive a message. A process can only receive from a mailbox for which it has receive access. In addition, mailboxes may be *locked*. Messages cannot be received from a locked mailbox. A *MessagesWaiting* system call returns a list of the mailboxes with waiting messages. The receive operation attempts to receive from (1) any unlocked mailbox for which the process has receive access, or (2) a specific (named) mailbox. If no message is waiting to be received, the receiving process may wait, wait at most n milliseconds, or not wait.

The Accent system was especially designed for distributed systems, which we discuss in Chapter 13, but Accent is also suitable for single processor systems. The major problem with message systems has generally been performance. A particular problem is caused by copying the message first from the sender to the mailbox, and then from the mailer to the receiver. The Accent message system attempts to avoid double copy operations by manipulation of the page table whenever possible. For example, if a 512-byte (one page) message is sent and received from message buffers which are aligned on page boundaries, no data copying is necessary; the page table entry for the sending process is simply copied to the page table of the receiving process.

9.9 Summary

In this chapter we have examined the general issue of concurrency as it relates to arbitrary algorithms. Within a single program, there are precedence constraints among the various statements. A precedence graph may be used to express these constraints formally. Bernstein's conditions can be used to determine how a precedence graph can be constructed for an arbitrary program.

A programmer can specify the precedence relations among the various statements in a program, using the concept of a sequential process. In particular, two language constructs for this purpose have been suggested: the **fork** and **join** constructs and the **concurrent** statement (**parbegin/parend**).

The notion of concurrent execution can be formalized by using the precedence graph and sequential process concepts.

Given a collection of cooperating sequential processes that share some data, mutual exclusion must be provided. A number of different algorithms exist for solving the critical section problem, with the assumption that only storage interlock is available.

The main disadvantage of these solutions is that they all require *busy-waiting*. Semaphores overcome this difficulty. Semaphores can be used to solve various synchronization problems and they can be implemented efficiently.

A number of different synchronization problems (such as the bounded-buffer problem, the readers/writers problem, and the dining philosophers problem) are important mainly because they are examples for a large class of concurrency control problems. These problems are used to test nearly every newly proposed synchronization scheme.

Interprocess communication is best provided by a message system. Message systems can be defined in many different ways.

Exercises

9.1 Transform the precedence graph of Figure 9.10 to a program using:

    a. The concurrent statement.

    b. The **fork** and **join** constructs.

9.2 Why is it necessary for the **join** instruction to be executed as an indivisible operation?

9.3 Write a program to implement a double buffering scheme with no copying using the **parbegin/parend** construct.

9.4 The producer consumer algorithm presented in Section 9.5 allows only $n-1$ buffers to be full at any point in time. Modify the algorithm to allow all the buffers to be fully utilized. Do not use semaphores in your solution.

9.5 Explain the necessity for mutual exclusion. What is the minimum level of mutual exclusion that is *necessary* for the implementation of useful mutual exclusion in operating systems? What other forms are useful?

9.6 Consider the precedence graph of Figure 9.10. Suppose that we add the edge (S_2, S_4) to the graph.

    a. Can this new precedence graph be expressed using only the concurrent statement? If so, show how; if not, explain why.

    b. How can this precedence graph be expressed if semaphores can also be used?

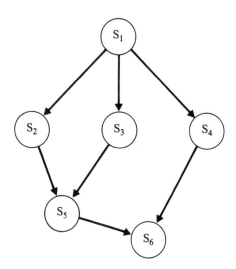

Figure 9.10   Precedence graph

9.7 Prove that in the bakery algorithm, the following property holds: if P_i is in its critical section and P_k ($k \neq i$) has already chosen its *number*[k] $\neq$ 0, then (*number*[i],i) < (*number*[k],k).

9.8 Consider the river crossing example from Chapter 8. Write an algorithm for a person crossing from bank A or from bank B. The algorithm should ensure that several persons from the same bank can cross simultaneously and that no deadlocks will occur. Show how the algorithm can be extended to also avoid starvation.

9.9 The following algorithm, due to Dekker, is the first known correct software solution to the critical section problem for two processes. The two processes, P_0 and P_1, share the following variables:

> **var** *flag*: **array** [0..1] **of** *boolean*; (* initially false *)
> *turn*: 0..1;

The program below is for process P_i (i = 0 or 1) with process P_j (j = 1 or 0) being the other one.

```
repeat
    flag[i] := true;
    while flag[j]
        do if turn = j
            then begin
                    flag[i] := false;
                    while turn = j do skip;
                    flag[i] := true;
                end;
        ...
    critical section
        ...
    turn := j;
    flag[i] := false;
        ...
    remainder section
        ...
until false;
```

Prove that the algorithm satisfies all three requirements for the critical section problem.

9.10 Show that if the P and V operations are not executed atomically, then mutual exclusion may be violated.

9.11 A *binary* semaphore is a semaphore whose integer value can range only between 0 and 1. Show how a general semaphore can be implemented using binary semaphores.

9.12 Semaphore waiting lists are often implemented as queues served in FIFO order. Could they be implemented as stacks? What problems might this cause?

9.13 Consider a set of sequential processes that cannot share any variables except semaphores. Can these processes communicate with each other? (Hint: it will suffice to consider the transmission of a single bit.)

9.14 Two synchronization primitives, *ENQ* and *DEQ* are defined as follows. r is a resource object, p is a process, *queue(r)* is a FIFO queue of processes waiting to acquire resource r, and *inuse(r)* is a boolean variable.

$$
\begin{aligned}
ENQ(r)\text{:} \quad &\textbf{if } inuse(r) \\
&\quad \textbf{then begin} \\
&\qquad\qquad \text{insert } p \text{ in } queue(r)\text{;} \\
&\qquad\qquad \text{block } p\text{;} \\
&\qquad\quad \textbf{end} \\
&\quad \textbf{else } inuse(r) := true\text{;} \\
DEQ(r)\text{:} \quad &p := \text{head of } queue(r)\text{;} \\
&\quad \textbf{if } p \neq nil \\
&\qquad \textbf{then } \text{activate } p\text{;} \\
&\qquad \textbf{else } inuse(r) := false\text{;}
\end{aligned}
$$

Construct an implementation of *ENQ/DEQ* using semaphores. Be sure that the ordering implicit in the reactivation of the process is implemented properly. Use any additional data structures and variables you need.

9.15 What is the meaning of the term *busy-waiting*? What other kinds of waiting are there? Can busy-waiting be avoided altogether?

9.16 Write an algorithm for implementing semaphores using:

   a. The Swap instruction.

   b. The Test-and-Set instruction.

9.17 A multiple semaphore allows the P and V primitives to operate on several semaphores simultaneously. It is useful for acquiring and releasing several resources in one atomic operation. Thus the P primitive (for two semaphores) can be defined as follows:

$$P(S,R): \quad \textbf{while } (S \leq 0 \textbf{ or } R \leq 0) \textbf{ do } skip;$$
$$S := S - 1;$$
$$R := R - 1;$$

Show how a multiple semaphore can be implemented using regular semaphores.

9.18 The following "solution" to the critical section problem was presented by Hyman [1966]. Determine its correctness. If it is incorrect, show an example which violates one of the three requirements for the critical section problem.

The two processes P_0 and P_1 share the following variables:

var *flag*: **array** [0..1] **of** *boolean*; (* initially false *)
    turn: 0..1;

The program below is for process P_i ($i = 0$ or 1) with process P_j ($j = 1$ or 0) being the other one.

```
repeat
    flag[i] := true;
    while turn ≠ i
        do begin
                while flag[j] do skip
                turn := i;
        end
            ...
        critical section
            ...
    flag[i] := false
            ...
        remainder section
            ...
until false;
```

9.19 Is busy-waiting a property of the P/V solution to process synchronization and mutual exclusion?

9.20 Consider a system which supports an interprocess communication scheme but does not provide semaphores. Indicate what declarations and code would be needed to program an interaction which wants to use P and V operations on semaphores rather than **send/receive**. You must show how to represent the P/V operations and semaphores using the **send/receive** operations and messages.

9.21 [Dijkstra 1965a] *The Sleepy Barber Problem.* A barbershop consists of a waiting room with n chairs, and the barber room containing the barber chair. If there are no customers to be served the barber goes to sleep. If a customer enters the barbershop and all chairs are occupied, then the customer leaves the shop. If the barber is busy, then the customer sits in one of the available free chairs. If the barber is asleep, the customer wakes the barber up. Write a program to coordinate the barber and the customers.

9.22 [Patil 1971] *The Cigarette Smokers Problem.* Consider a system with three *smoker* processes and one *agent* process. Each smoker continuously makes a cigarette and smokes it. But to make a cigarette, three ingredients are needed: tobacco, paper, and matches. One of the processes has paper, another tobacco and the third has matches. The agent has an infinite supply of all three. The agent places two of the ingredients on the table. The smoker who has the remaining ingredient can then make and smoke a cigarette, signaling the agent upon completion. The agent then puts out another two of the three ingredients and the cycle repeats. Write a program to synchronize the agent and the smokers.

9.23 Consider a system of processes which communicate only through *pipes*; that is, unidirectional message queues using a system-wide shared buffer pool. Each pipe has exactly one producer and exactly one consumer process.

    a. Under what circumstances will a process be forced to wait in this system?

    b. Outline an appropriate deadlock detection mechanism for this system.

    c. Having detected a deadlock and chosen a "victim" process to be terminated, what must you do to the message queues?

    d. State and justify a rule for selecting the victim.

9.24 Consider the interprocess communication scheme using mailboxes.

    a. Suppose a process P wants to wait for a message from mailbox A and from mailbox B (one from each). What sequence of **send** and **receives** should it do?

    b. What sequence of **send** and **receive** should be done if P wants to wait for a message from either mailbox A or mailbox B (or both).

    c. A **receive** operation makes a process wait until the mailbox is non-empty. Can you devise a scheme which allows a process to wait until a mailbox is empty?

9.25 Provide a deadlock-free solution to the dining philosophers problem. Does your solution ensure freedom from starvation? If yes, explain why; if not, modify your algorithm to provide a starvation-free solution.

Bibliographic Notes

The concepts of concurrent statements, critical sections, and semaphores were all introduced in the classic paper by Dijkstra [1965a]. This paper also presented the mutual exclusion algorithms 1 to 4 for two processes, concluding with Dekker's algorithm (see Exercise 9.9), the first correct software solution to the two-process mutual exclusion problem. It is due to the Dutch mathematician T. Dekker. Simpler solutions to the two-process mutual exclusion problem have since been presented by Doran and Thomas [1980] and Peterson [1981].

The first solution to the mutual exclusion problem for n processes was presented by Dijkstra [1965b]. A simpler solution has been given by Peterson [1981]. Neither of these solutions, however, have an upper bound on the amount of time a process must wait before it is allowed to enter the critical section. Knuth [1966] presented the first algorithm with a bound. His bound was 2^n turns. A refinement of Knuth's algorithm by DeBruijn [1967] reduced the waiting time to n^2 turns, while Eisenberg and McGuire [1972] succeeded in reducing the time to the lower bound of $n-1$ turns. The bakery algorithm of Lamport [1974] also requires $n-1$ turns, but it is easier to program and understand.

Complexity results concerning the number of shared variables needed to implement the various n-process mutual exclusion algorithms are presented by Burns [1978], Burns and Lynch [1980], and Burns et al. [1982].

Discussions concerning the various aspects of semaphores are offered by Dijkstra [1965a, 1968b, 1971] and Habermann [1972]. The names of the *P* and *V* operations come from the Dutch *proberen* (to test) and *verhogen* (to increment). Many authors (such as Brinch Hansen [1973a]) prefer to use *wait* (for *P*) and *signal* (for *V*).

Patil [1971] examined the question of whether semaphores can solve all possible synchronization problems. Parnas [1975a] discussed some of the flaws with Patil's arguments. Kosaraju [1973] and Agerwala and Flynn [1973] followed up on Patil's work to produce a problem which cannot be solved by *P* and *V* operations. Similar observations were also discovered by Keller [1972]. Lipton [1974] has discussed the limitation of various synchronization primitives such as PV multiple [Patil 1971], PV general [Cerf 1972] and PV chunk [Vantilborgh and Van Lamsweerde 1972]. Additional results concerning these issues are described by Henderson and Zalcstein [1980].

The classic process coordination problems we have described are paradigms for a large class of concurrency control problems. The bounded-buffer problem and the dining philosophers problem were suggested by Dijkstra [1965a, 1971]. The readers/writers problems were suggested by Courtois et al. [1971].

Discussions concerning the process concept and its implementation are given by Horning and Randell [1973], Brinch Hansen [1970] (the RC 4000 system), Dijkstra [1968b] (the THE system), and Liskov [1972a] (the Venus system).

The subject of interprocess communication is discussed by Morenoff and McLean [1967], Brinch Hansen [1970] (the RC 4000 system), and Cheriton et al. [1979] (the Thoth real time operating system). Brinch Hansen [1970] was the first to suggest the use of messages for synchronization.

Tutorial and survey articles include Presser [1975] and Atwood [1976]. Textbook discussions are offered by Brinch Hansen [1973a, Chapter 3], Shaw [1974, Chapter 3], Tsichritzis and Bernstein [1974, Chapter 2] and Habermann [1976, Chapters 3 and 4].

Concurrent Programming

Operating systems are now almost always written in a system implementation language or a higher-level language. This feature improves their implementation, maintenance, and portability. In this chapter, we will trace the evolution of higher-level language constructs for concurrent programming.

10.1 Motivation

An operating system consists of a large number of programs that run asynchronously and cooperate in fulfilling the operating system's task. Traditionally, these programs were written in assembly language for the following three reasons:

- Higher-level languages did not provide mechanisms for writing machine-dependent code (such as device drivers).

- Higher-level languages did not provide the appropriate tools for writing concurrent programs.

- Higher-level languages for concurrent programs were not efficient.

Recently, however, we have witnessed the definition of new languages that support concurrency and are relatively efficient. Moreover, many of the arguments against the use of higher-level languages have been based on an assumption that the language in question is to be used in programming the central functions of an operating system: the physical storage management, process management, and protection kernel, for instance. However, most of the code of an operating system is not concerned with providing this level of operating system function. Therefore, with the appropriate higher-level language, this code need not be written in assembly language.

There are advantages to using a higher-level programming language, instead of assembly language. Higher-level language programs are simpler and easier to test and verify, to modify, and to transfer from one machine to another. Consequently, the programmer spends less time developing and testing programs.

The main disadvantage of a higher-level language is the problem of inefficient code generation. This problem can be resolved by the use of various compiler optimization techniques. We now have optimizing compilers that generate code that is at least as good as hand-written assembly language programs. The amount of optimization that can be achieved by a compiler obviously depends heavily on the higher-level language. It is the responsibility of the language designer to make sure that the language constructs proposed can be efficiently implemented.

In this chapter we are mainly concerned with higher-level languages that are to be used in writing concurrent programs. Such languages must provide facilities for modularization and synchronization.

10.2 Modularization

Modularization is the term used to describe the partitioning of a single large program into a set of smaller modules. In this section we will survey the types of modules that we would expect to see in an operating system written in some higher-level language.

10.2.1 Processes

As we saw in Chapters 4 and 9, the process is a fundamental building block in the design of an operating system. An operating system is composed of a number of asynchronous processes that must communicate and synchronize their actions.

In the most lenient case, processes can share all variables. In this case, to guard against time-dependent errors, programmers must build their own synchronization schemes. The compiler cannot aid the programmer in this task. In the most restrictive case, processes do not share any variables. Communication and synchronization can be accomplished only by a message-passing facility which we discussed in Chapter 9, or by parameter passing between separate procedures, which we will discuss in this chapter. The compiler can ensure at compile time that no sharing occurs, hence there will be no time-dependent errors caused by sharing variables.

A process thus consists of some local data, and a sequential program that can operate on the data (Figure 10.1). The local data can only be accessed by the sequential program encapsulated within the same process. That is, one process cannot directly access the local data of another process. If processes can share global data, this data must be either defined in a common area, or encapsulated in a procedure or abstract data type as described in the next section.

10.2.2 Procedures

Another unit of modularization is the procedure (subroutine) or function that we expect to find in any higher-level language. If a procedure can include its own persistent variables (variables that do not disappear between procedure calls), then some global data can be encapsulated within a procedure. Thus a process cannot access this data directly; it must invoke the procedure for this purpose.

This encapsulation shields the users of the procedure from its implementation details, allowing them to concentrate on how to use the procedure rather than on how the procedure is actually implemented.

10.2.3 Abstract Data Types

A procedure provides us with a limited mechanism for information hiding. To hide the method of defining data completely, we must resort to a more complicated set of mechanisms. We need a facility that allows

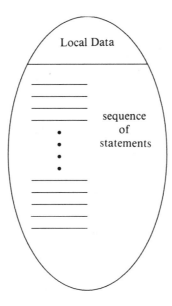

Figure 10.1   Schematic view of a process

a programmer to create a class of abstract objects that were not explicitly anticipated in the design of the programming language. This kind of mechanism is becoming available in a number of programming languages. It is commonly referred to as an *abstract data type*. An abstract data type is characterized by a set of programmer-defined operators. The representation of an abstract data type consists of declarations of variables whose values define the state of an instance of the type, as well as the bodies of procedures or functions that implement operations on the type (Figure 10.2).

The classic example of an abstract data type is a stack. Most languages do not provide stacks as built-in data types, in the same way that they provide integers, arrays, and other basic types. Thus a stack is a programmer-defined data type, not a language-defined data type. A stack has a small set of well defined operations (push, pop, empty, top, and so on). A stack should only be accessed by these operations; elements of the stack should never be directly accessed.

We refer to a program module that gives the representation of an abstract type as a *class*. This term was introduced in *Simula 67* [Dahl et al. 1968] and is used in the language *Concurrent Pascal* [Brinch Hansen 1975]. The syntax of a class is:

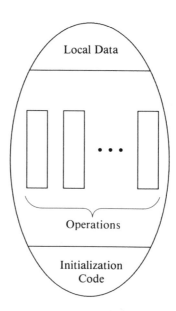

Figure 10.2   Schematic view of an abstract data type

```
type class-name = class
      variable declarations

      procedure P1 ( ... );
           begin ... end;

      procedure P2 ( ... );
           begin ... end;
                   .

                   .

                   .

      procedure Pn ( ... );
           begin ... end;

      begin
           initialization code
      end.
```

Quite obviously, the representation of an abstract data type should not be used directly by program components other than its operators; otherwise, the consistency of the abstraction could be compromised. This restriction is the basic requirement imposed on a language that supports programmer-defined abstractions. Thus a procedure defined within a class can only access the variables declared locally within the class and the formal parameters. Similarly, the local variables of a class can only be accessed by the local procedures.

The mechanism with which a language implementation provides static enforcement of protection for types defined by modules is based on a reformulation of the traditional scope rules of block-structured languages. A module *exports* the names (and types) of its operators, but does not export the representation of the type it defines. A user of an abstract data type can only invoke the operations that are exported. If a new type is exported, users may define instances of that type. Users may not, however, manipulate the elements directly. Direct access to the representation of the type can only be done within the class in which the new type is defined.

A class need not export all of its procedures. To distinguish between procedures that are exported and those that are not, we use the notation:

procedure entry P (...);

Only entry procedures can be invoked from outside the class.

Let us illustrate these concepts with a simple, but typical, example. Suppose that we want to define a class for distributing fixed-size storage (such as pages in memory or blocks on a disk). The information about the free storage is kept in a bit vector (Section 3.4), which is encapsulated within the *frames* class described below.

```
type frames = class
    var free: array [1..n] of boolean;

    procedure entry acquire (var index: integer);
        begin
            for index := 1 to n
                do if free[index]
                        then begin
                                free[index] := false;
                                exit;
                            end;
                index := -1;
        end

    procedure entry release (index: integer);
        begin
            free[index] := true;
        end;

    begin
        for index := 1 to n
            do free[index] := true;
    end.
```

An instance of the *frames* class (for example, for memory management) can be obtained by declaring:

```
var memory: frames;
```

A process needing to acquire a free page will execute:

```
memory.acquire (in);
```

If a free page is not available, the variable *in* will be set to −1. At this point, the process must either wait or request page swapping. The process may return the allocated page by executing:

memory.release (in);

After this procedure has been executed, the returned page may be reallocated to another process.

The advantage of the *class* definition of *frames* is that we can easily change the implementation of *frames* without changing its use. For instance, it would be easy to replace the bit vector implementation of the *frames* class with a linked list implementation. Only the class declaration need be changed.

10.3 Synchronization

In the *frames* example, several processes may invoke the procedures *acquire* and *release* simultaneously. This situation may result in inconsistent data (for example, two processes may find the same free frame). To guard against this possibility, the language must also provide appropriate synchronization tools.

A language must provide the means to guard against time-dependent errors. Such errors can occur if several concurrent processes communicate with each other by the use of either common variables or explicit messages. Obviously, we could disallow such communication entirely, thus eliminating time-dependent errors. This restriction, however, will drastically reduce the amount of concurrency allowed in an operating system. Clearly, this solution is not viable. Therefore, we will have to compromise. Instead of completely eliminating time-dependent errors, we will provide language constructs that will reduce them considerably.

10.3.1 Critical Regions

Semaphores can be effectively used in solving the critical section problem, as well as arbitrary synchronization schemes. Let us review this solution to the critical section problem. All processes share a semaphore variable *mutex*, which is initialized to 1. Each process must execute *P(mutex)* before entering the critical section, and *V(mutex)* afterwards. If this sequence is not observed, two processes may be in their critical sections simultaneously, resulting in time-dependent errors.

Let us examine the various difficulties that may result. Note that these difficulties will arise even if a *single* process is not well behaved. This situation may be the result of an honest programming error or an uncooperative programmer.

- Suppose that a process interchanges the operations on the semaphore *mutex*. That is, it executes

$$V(mutex);$$
$$\ldots$$
$$\text{critical section}$$
$$\ldots$$
$$P(mutex);$$

In this situation, several processes may be executing in their critical section simultaneously, violating the mutual exclusion requirement. This time-dependent error may be discovered only if several processes are simultaneously active in their critical sections. Note that this situation may not always be reproducible.

- Suppose that a process exchanges *V(mutex)* with *P(mutex)*. That is, it executes

$$P(mutex);$$
$$\ldots$$
$$\text{critical section}$$
$$\ldots$$
$$P(mutex);$$

In this case, a deadlock will occur.

- Suppose that a process omits the *P(mutex)* or the *V(mutex)* or both. In this case, either mutual exclusion is violated or a deadlock will occur.

The example above illustrates that time-dependent errors can be easily generated when semaphores are used to solve the critical section problem. To overcome this deficiency, Brinch Hansen [1972b] and Hoare [1972b] introduced a new language construct, the *critical region*. A variable v of type T, which is to be shared among many processes, can be declared:

var v: **shared** T;

The variable v can be accessed only inside a *region* statement of the following form:

region v **do** S;

This construct means that while statement *S* is being executed, no other process can access the variable *v*. Thus, if the two statements,

region *v* **do** *S1*;

region *v* **do** *S2*;

are executed concurrently in distinct sequential processes, the result will be equivalent to the sequential execution "*S1* followed by *S2*," or "*S2* followed by *S1*."

To illustrate this construct, consider the *frames* class defined in Section 10.2.3. Since mutual exclusion is required when accessing the array *free*, we need to declare it as a shared array.

var *free*: **shared array** [1..*n*] **of** *boolean*;

The *acquire* procedure must be rewritten as follows:

```
procedure entry acquire (var index: integer);
    begin
        region free
            do for index := 1 to n
                do if free[index]
                    then begin
                            free[index] := false;
                            exit;
                        end;
            index := −1;
    end;
```

It turns out that the *release* procedure and initialization part of the class *frames* need not be rewritten. We leave the proof of this statement to the reader.

The critical-region construct guards against some simple errors associated with the semaphore solution to the critical section problem which may be made by a programmer. Note that it does not necessarily eliminate time-dependent errors, but rather reduces the number of them. If errors occur in the logic of the program, reproducing a particular sequence of events may not be simple.

Let us illustrate now how a compiler could implement the critical region construct. For each declaration

var *v*: **shared** *T*;

the compiler generates a semaphore *v-mutex* initialized to 1. For each statement,

$$\textbf{region } v \textbf{ do } S;$$

the compiler generates the following code:

$$P(v\text{-}mutex);$$
$$S;$$
$$V(v\text{-}mutex);$$

Clearly, mutual exclusion is preserved as required by the semantics of the critical region statement.

Critical regions may also be nested. In this case, however, deadlocks may result. The following program illustrates this situation.

$$\textbf{var } x,y\text{: } \textbf{shared } T;$$
$$\textbf{parbegin}$$
$$Q\text{: } \textbf{region } x \textbf{ do region } y \textbf{ do } S1;$$
$$R\text{: } \textbf{region } y \textbf{ do region } x \textbf{ do } S2;$$
$$\textbf{parend};$$

If P and Q enter the regions x and y, respectively, at about the same time, a deadlock will occur. Consider the following execution sequence, using semaphores to implement the critical region construct.

T_0: Q executes $P(x\text{-}mutex)$.
T_1: R executes $P(y\text{-}mutex)$.
T_2: R executes $P(x\text{-}mutex)$, R waits since $x\text{-}mutex = 0$.
T_3: Q executes $P(y\text{-}mutex)$, Q waits since $y\text{-}mutex = 0$.

We now have a deadlock situation involving Q and R. The deadlock occurs because region x is nested in region y and vice versa. In order to prevent such a situation, a resource ordering may be imposed (Section 8.3.4). If no such ordering can be constructed, deadlocks may occur. The compiler can detect the possibility of such deadlocks and issue error messages notifying the programmer of the situation. The compiler would use the nesting of two regions to define a binary relation as follows. If we have two regions x and y such that **region** y is nested in **region** x, then we define $y < x$. If this binary relation is a partial ordering, then no deadlock can occur.

10.3.2 Conditional Critical Regions

The critical region construct can be effectively used to solve the critical-section problem. It cannot, however, be used to solve some general synchronization problems. For this reason the *conditional critical region* was introduced by Hoare [1972b]. The major difference between the critical region and the conditional critical region constructs is in the region statement, which now has the form:

region *v* **when** *B* **do** *S*;

where *B* is a boolean expression. As before, regions referring to the same shared variable exclude each other in time. Now, however, when a process enters the critical section region, the boolean expression *B* is evaluated. If the expression is true, statement *S* is executed. If it is false, the process relinquishes the mutual exclusion and is delayed until *B* becomes true and no other process is in the region associated with *v*.

Let us illustrate these concepts by coding the bounded-buffer problem. The buffer space and its pointers are encapsulated in:

var *buffer*: **shared record**
                    pool: **array** $[0..n-1]$ **of** *item*;
                    count,in,out: *integer*;
          end;

The producer process inserts a new item *nextp* in buffer by executing

```
region buffer when count < n
    do begin
        pool[in] := nextp;
        in := in+1 mod n;
        count := count + 1;
    end;
```

The consumer process removes an item from the shared buffer and puts it in *nextc* by executing

```
region buffer when count > 0
    do begin
        nextc := pool[out];
        out := out+1 mod n;
        count := count - 1;
    end;
```

Let us illustrate how the conditional critical region could be implemented by a compiler. With each shared variable x, the following variables are associated:

$$\textbf{var}\ x\text{-}mutex,\ x\text{-}wait\text{: } semaphore;$$
$$x\text{-}count,\ x\text{-}temp\text{: } integer;$$

Mutual exclusive access to the critical section is provided by $x\text{-}mutex$. If a process cannot enter the critical section because the boolean condition B is false, it waits on the $x\text{-}wait$ semaphore. We keep track of the number of processes waiting on $x\text{-}wait$ with $x\text{-}count$. When a process leaves the critical section, it may have changed the value of some boolean condition B that prevented another process from entering the critical section. Accordingly, we must trace through the queue of processes waiting on $x\text{-}wait$ allowing each process to test its boolean condition. We use $x\text{-}temp$ to determine when we have allowed each process to test its condition. Accordingly, $x\text{-}mutex$ is initialized to 1, while $x\text{-}wait$, $x\text{-}count$, and $x\text{-}temp$ are initialized to 0. A statement

$$\textbf{region}\ x\ \textbf{when}\ B\ \textbf{do}\ S;$$

can be implemented as follows:

```
P(x-mutex);
if not B
   then begin
           x-count := x-count + 1;
           V(x-mutex);
           P(x-wait);
           while not B
              do begin
                     x-temp := x-temp + 1;
                     if x-temp < x-count
                        then V(x-wait)
                        else V(x-mutex);
                     P(x-wait);
                 end;
           x-count := x-count - 1;
       end;
S;
```

$$\textbf{if } \textit{x-count} > 0$$
$$\qquad \textbf{then begin}$$
$$\qquad\qquad \textit{x-temp} := 0;$$
$$\qquad\qquad V(\textit{x-wait});$$
$$\qquad \textbf{end};$$
$$\textbf{else } V(\textit{x-mutex});$$

This implementation assumes a FIFO ordering in the queueing of processes for a semaphore.

Note that this implementation requires the reevaluation of the expression B for any waiting processes every time a process leaves the critical region. If several processes are delayed, waiting for their respective boolean expressions to become true, this reevaluation overhead may result in inefficient code. There are various optimization methods that can be used to reduce this overhead. The interested reader is referred to Brinch Hansen [1972b] and Schmid [1976] for a discussion of this subject.

Hoare's construct allows processes to be delayed only at the beginning of a critical region. There are, however, circumstances where synchronization conditions must be placed anywhere within the critical region. This observation led Brinch Hansen [1972b] to the following region construct:

$$\textbf{region } v$$
$$\qquad \textbf{do begin}$$
$$\qquad\qquad \textit{S1};$$
$$\qquad\qquad \textbf{await}(B);$$
$$\qquad\qquad \textit{S2};$$
$$\qquad \textbf{end};$$

When a process enters the region it executes statement $S1$ ($S1$ may be null). It then evaluates B. If B is true, $S2$ is executed. If B is false, the process relinquishes mutual exclusion and is delayed until B becomes true and no other process is in the region associated with v.

We illustrate this new construct by coding a variant of the second readers/writers problem. The second readers/writers problem requires that once a writer is ready, it may write as soon as possible. Thus a reader can enter its critical section only if there are no writers either waiting or in its critical section.

The conditional critical region construct is combined with our previously described class construct.

```
type reader-writer = class
    var v: shared record
                    nreaders, nwriters: integer;
                    busy: boolean;
                end;


    procedure entry open-read;
        region v
            do begin
                    await(nwriters = 0);
                    nreaders := nreaders + 1;
                end;

    procedure entry close-read;
        region v
            do begin
                    nreaders := nreaders − 1;
                end;

    procedure entry open-write;
        region v
            do begin
                    nwriters := nwriters + 1;
                    await((not busy) and (nreaders = 0));
                    busy := true;
                end;

    procedure entry close-write;
        region v
            do begin
                    nwriters := nwriters − 1;
                    busy := false;
                end;


    begin
        busy := false;
        nreaders := 0;
        nwriters := 0;
    end.
```

A reader process must invoke a read operation on the file instance and operations upon an instance *rw* of the *reader-writer* class only in the following sequence:

rw.open-read;

...

read file

...

rw.close-read;

Similarly, a writer process must invoke operations in the sequence:

rw.open-write;

...

write file

...

rw.close-write;

However, the class concept alone cannot guarantee that such sequences will be observed. In particular,

- A process might operate on the file without first gaining access permission to it (by a direct call to read or to write the file);

- A process might never release the file once it has been granted access to it;

- A process might attempt to release a file that it never requested;

- A process might request the same file twice (without first releasing it); and so on.

Note that we have now encountered difficulties that are similar in nature to those that motivated us to develop the critical region construct in the first place. Previously, we had to worry about the correct use of semaphores. Now we have to worry about the correct use of higher-level programmer-defined operations, with which the compiler can no longer assist us.

One way to ensure that the readers and writers indeed observe the appropriate sequences is to incorporate the shared file itself within the *reader-writer* class. In addition, we will define the following two new external procedures within the *reader-writer* class:

procedure entry *read* (...);
   begin
      open-read;
      ...
      read file
      ...
      close-read;
   end;

procedure entry *write* (...);
   begin
      open-write;
      ...
      write file
      ...
      close-write;
   end;

Now the procedures *open-read, close-read, open-write,* and *close-write* are local to the class (that is, they are not entry procedures) and cannot be invoked from outside.

This solution ensures that the user processes access the file correctly. However, it is not very satisfactory. We have assumed that the programmer who has coded the *reader-writer* class knows precisely how the user processes want to access the file. This is not a reasonable assumption, since the reading and writing may be application oriented. For example, one user may want to issue five consecutive *reads*, while another user may want a *read* followed by a *write* to update the file.

In general, it is not acceptable to encapsulate the resource itself within the module that schedules the resource. The programmer of this module cannot and should not be required to anticipate all the possible uses of the resource.

10.3.3 Monitors

In the preceding sections, we have described the critical-region mechanisms for process synchronization. We have also combined this mechanism with the class concept to achieve a greater degree of protection. One unattractive feature of this combination was that every procedure had to provide its own synchronization explicitly. A desire to provide the appropriate synchronization automatically led Brinch Hansen [1973a] and Hoare [1974] to the development of a new language construct, a *monitor*.

A monitor is a mechanism that allows the safe and effective sharing of abstract data types among several processes. The syntax of a monitor is identical to that of a class, except that the keyword *class* is replaced by the keyword *monitor*. The main semantic difference is that the monitor ensures mutual exclusion; that is, only one process at a time can be active within the monitor. This property is guaranteed by the monitor itself. Consequently, the programmer need not explicitly code this synchronization constraint (Figure 10.3).

The monitor, as defined so far, is similar in many respects to the critical region. As we have seen, the critical region is not sufficiently powerful for modeling some synchronization schemes, and has thus been extended to the conditional critical region. Similarly, we need additional mechanisms with monitors for synchronization. These mechanisms are provided by the *condition* construct. Programmers who need to write their own tailor-made synchronization scheme can define one or more variables of type **condition**:

var *x,y: condition;*

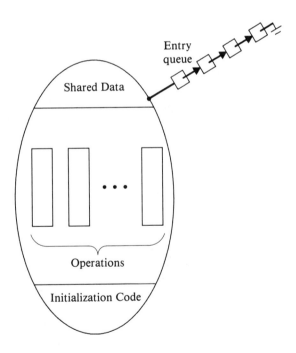

Figure 10.3   Schematic view of a monitor

The only operations that can be invoked on a condition variable are *wait* and *signal*. Thus a condition variable can be viewed as an abstract data type that provides those two operations (Figure 10.4). The operation

$$x.wait;$$

means that the process invoking this operation is suspended until another process invokes

$$x.signal;$$

The *x.signal* operation resumes exactly one suspended process. If no process is suspended, then the *signal* operation has no effect; that is, the state of *x* is as if the operation was never executed. Contrast this with the *V* operation, which always affects the state of the semaphore.

Now suppose that when the *x.signal* operation is invoked by a process *P*, there is a suspended process *Q* associated with condition *x*. Clearly, if the suspended process *Q* is allowed to resume its execution,

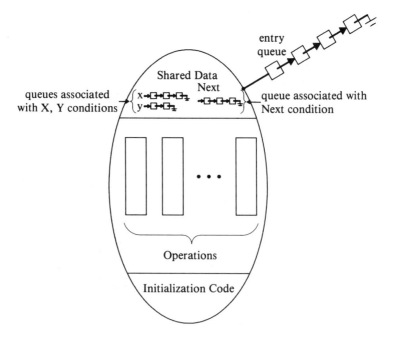

Figure 10.4   Monitor with condition variables

the signaling process P must wait. Otherwise, both P and Q will be active simultaneously within the monitor. Note, however, that both processes can conceptually continue with their execution. Two possibilities exist:

a. P waits until Q either leaves the monitor, or waits for another condition.

b. Q waits until P either leaves the monitor, or waits for another condition.

There are reasonable arguments in favor of adopting either (a) or (b). Since P was already executing in the monitor, choice (b) seems more reasonable. However, if we allow process P to continue, the "logical" condition for which Q was waiting may no longer hold by the time Q is resumed.

Hoare has adopted choice (a), mainly because the above argument in favor of it translates directly to simpler and more elegant proof rules [Hoare 1974]. Brinch Hansen [1975], on the other hand, elected a compromise. When process P executes the *signal* operation, it immediately leaves the monitor. Hence Q is immediately resumed. This scheme is less powerful than Hoare's scheme, since a process cannot signal more than once during a single procedure call. Let us illustrate these concepts by writing a monitor that simulates a binary semaphore.

```
type semaphore = monitor
        var busy: boolean;
            nonbusy: condition;

        procedure entry P;
            begin
                if busy then nonbusy.wait;
                busy := true;
            end;

        procedure entry V;
            begin
                busy := false;
                nonbusy.signal;
            end;

        begin
            busy := false;
        end.
```

The boolean variable *busy* indicates the state of the semaphore. When the first *P* operation is executed, the state of the semaphore is set to busy; if any additional *P* operations are attempted, these processes must wait until a *V* operation occurs. Notice that the *V* operation always sets *busy* to false. If there is a waiting process, it immediately resets *busy* to true. If no process is waiting, *busy* remains false.

Let us now consider a more complicated example, the dining philosophers problem. We present a deadlock-free solution by allowing a philosopher to pick up his chopsticks only if both of them are available. In order to code this solution, we need to distinguish between three states that a philosopher may be in. For this purpose, we introduce the following data structure:

var *state*: **array** [0..4] **of** (*thinking, hungry, eating*);

Philosopher *i* can set *state*[*i*] = *eating* only if its neighbors are not eating (that is, *state*[*i*−1 **mod** 5] ≠ *eating* **and** *state*[*i*+1 **mod** 5] ≠ *eating*).

We also need to declare

var *self*: **array** [0..4] **of** *condition*;

where philosopher *i* can delay himself when he is hungry, but unable to obtain the needed chopsticks.

We are now in a position to describe our solution. The distribution of the chopsticks is controlled by the monitor:

```
type dining-philosophers = monitor
    var state : array [0..4] of (thinking, hungry, eating);
    var self : array [0..4] of condition;

    procedure entry pickup (i: 0..4);
        begin
            state[i] := hungry;
            test (i);
            if state[i] ≠ eating then self[i].wait;
        end;

    procedure entry putdown (i: 0..4);
        begin
            state[i] := thinking;
            test (i−1 mod 5);
            test (i+1 mod 5);
        end;
```

```
procedure test (k: 0..4);
    begin
        if state[k−1 mod 5] ≠ eating
        and state[k] = hungry
        and state[k+1 mod 5] ≠ eating
        then begin
                state[k] := eating;
                self[k].signal;
            end;
    end;

begin
    for i := 0 to 4
        do state[i] := thinking;
end.
```

Philosopher *i* must invoke the operations *pickup* and *putdown* on an instance *dp* of the *dining-philosophers* monitor in the following sequence:

$$dp.pickup(i);$$
$$\ldots$$
$$eat$$
$$\ldots$$
$$dp.putdown(i);$$

It is easy to show that this solution ensures that no two neighbors are eating simultaneously, and that no deadlocks will occur. We note, however, that it is possible for a philosopher to starve to death. We will not present a solution to this problem, but rather leave it as an exercise for the reader.

We will now consider a possible implementation of the monitor mechanism. For each monitor, a semaphore *mutex* (initialized to 1) is provided. *P(mutex)* must be executed before entering the monitor, while *V(mutex)* must be executed after leaving the monitor.

Since a signaling process must wait until the resumed process either leaves or waits, an additional semaphore, *next*, is introduced, initialized to 0, on which the signaling processes may suspend themselves. An integer variable *next-count* will also be provided to count the number of processes suspended on *next*. Thus each external procedure *F* will be replaced by

$$P(mutex);$$
$$\ldots$$
$$\text{body of } F;$$
$$\ldots$$
if *next-count* > 0
   then $V(next)$
   else $V(mutex);$

Mutual exclusion within a monitor is ensured.

We can now describe how condition variables are implemented. For each condition x we introduce a semaphore x-sem and an integer variable x-count, both initialized to 0. The operation $x.wait$ can now be implemented as

$$x\text{-}count := x\text{-}count + 1;$$
if *next-count* > 0
   then $V(next)$
   else $V(mutex);$
$$P(x\text{-}sem);$$
$$x\text{-}count := x\text{-}count - 1;$$

The operation $x.signal$ can be implemented as

if x-count > 0
   then begin
        $next\text{-}count := next\text{-}count + 1;$
        $V(x\text{-}sem);$
        $P(next);$
        $next\text{-}count := next\text{-}count - 1;$
   end;

This implementation is applicable to the definition of monitors of both Hoare and Brinch Hansen. In some cases, however, the generality of the implementation is unnecessary and a significant improvement in efficiency is possible. We leave this problem as an exercise for the reader.

Note that if a monitor $M1$ calls another monitor $M2$, the mutual exclusion in $M1$ is not released while execution proceeds in $M2$. This fact has two consequences:

● Any process calling $M1$ will be blocked outside $M1$ on *mutex* during this time period.

- If the process enters a condition queue in *M2*, a deadlock may occur.

This problem is called the *nested monitor calls problem*.

We turn now to the subject of process resumption order. That is, if several processes are suspended on condition *x*, and an *x.signal* operation is executed, which process is resumed next? One simple scheme is to use a first-come-first-served scheme. Thus the process waiting longest is resumed first. There are, however, many circumstances when such a simple scheduling scheme is not adequate. For this reason, Hoare [1974] introduced the *conditional wait* construct. It has the form

$$x.wait(c);$$

where *c* is an integer expression that is evaluated when the wait operation is executed. The value of *c*, which is called a priority number, is then stored with the name of the process that is suspended. When *x.signal* is executed, the process with the smallest associated priority number is resumed next.

Let us illustrate this new mechanism by developing a scheduling algorithm that allocates a resource in a Shortest-Job-First order. We assume that when each process requests an allocation, it specifies the maximum time it plans to use the resource.

```
type SJN = monitor
    var busy: boolean;
        x: condition;

    procedure entry acquire (time: integer);
        begin
            if busy then x.wait(time);
            busy := true;
        end;

    procedure entry release;
        begin
            busy := false;
            x.signal;
        end;

    begin
        busy := false;
    end.
```

A more complicated example, in which we code the C-SCAN disk head scheduling algorithm for a disk with n cylinders (as described in Section 7.4), is shown below.

```
type diskhead = monitor
    var busy: boolean;
        up: condition;
        headpos, count: integer;

    procedure entry acquire (dest: integer);
        begin
            if busy
                then if headpos ≤ dest
                        then up.wait(dest + count)
                        else up.wait(dest + count+n);
            busy := true;
            if dest < headpos
                then count := count + n;
            headpos := dest;
        end;

    procedure entry release;
        begin
            busy := false;
            up.signal;
        end;

    begin
        headpos := 0;
        count := 0;
    end.
```

The variable *count* serves to block the requests into two groups: those below the disk head, and those above the disk head. If the disk head is at 50, and we have a request at 75 and one at 25, the request at 25 is treated as a request at 25+n. Since $75 < n$, $75 < 25+n$, and the request at 75 is scheduled first. An overflow may eventually occur on the variable *count*. This problem can be remedied by inserting additional code to reset *count* to zero if the queue is empty.

A process that needs to access the disk must observe the following sequence:

$$da.acquire(i);$$
$$\cdots$$
$$\text{access cylinder } i;$$
$$\cdots$$
$$da.release;$$

where *da* is an instance of type *diskhead*. As in the readers/writers problem (Section 10.3.2), failure to observe this sequence may result in time-dependent errors. In addition, if a process acquires cylinder *i* and then uses cylinder $j \neq i$, the whole scheduling scheme is defeated. In contrast to the scheme of Section 10.3.2, where we could include the reading and writing operations in the monitor, we cannot include disk access operations within the scheduling monitor, *diskhead*. If we did, scheduling would operate according to the monitor scheduling algorithm, rather than the one we have coded. (This is another instance of the nested monitor calls problem.)

In order to ensure that the processes observe the appropriate sequences, we must inspect all the programs which make use of the *diskhead* monitor and its managed disk. There are two conditions that must be checked to establish the correctness of this system. First, user processes must always make their calls upon the monitor in a correct sequence. Second, we must be sure that an uncooperative process does not simply ignore the mutual-exclusion gateway provided by the monitor, and try to access the shared resource directly, without using the access protocols. Only if these two conditions can be ensured can we guarantee that no time-dependent errors will occur, and that the scheduling algorithm is not defeated.

While this inspection may be possible for a small static system, it is not reasonable for a large system or a dynamic system. This *access control problem* can only be solved by additional mechanisms that will be elaborated on in Chapter 11.

10.4 Concurrent Languages

In this section we will briefly survey some of the most widely referenced languages that have incorporated mechanisms for process communication and synchronization. These languages vary in the way that communication primitives are supported. Concurrent Pascal uses parameter passing, CSP uses message passing, and Ada uses a combination of both methods.

10.4.1 Concurrent Pascal

Concurrent Pascal is a programming language designed for the structured programming of computer operating systems. Developed by Brinch Hansen [1975], the language is based upon the sequential language Pascal [Wirth 1971]. One of the most noteworthy aspects of Concurrent Pascal is that it supports modularity in the construction of programs. A system programmed in this language is constructed from three kinds of modules: *processes, classes,* and *monitors.*

Processes are sequential and do not share any variables. Classes are abstract data types; each class can be accessed by one and only one process. Communication between processes must be accomplished through monitors. Concurrent Pascal monitors are similar to the description in Section 10.3.3, with the following two differences:

- Condition variables (called *queues* in Concurrent Pascal) can have only a single entry. If two processes try to enter a blocked state on the condition variable, an error occurs.

- When a process invokes the *signal* operation on a queue, it resumes a blocked process (if there is one) and *immediately* leaves the monitor.

These differences result in the generation of more efficient code by the compiler. However, they restrict the type of programs we may write. For example, it is not possible to signal twice within one monitor procedure.

Concurrent Pascal goes significantly beyond merely providing a mechanism by which a data segment may be safely shared; it will only allow processes to share access to a data segment if that segment has been declared within a monitor. The semantics of the language do not allow a programmer to declare a shared instance of a data type in any other way.

To a large extent, Concurrent Pascal supports the design of reliable programs by restricting the complexity of resource management strategies. The language does not allow recursive procedures nor the definition of recursive data types. Therefore, all main storage can be statically allocated at compilation. All program components (instances of processes, classes, and monitors) are created by declaration and are permanent. Finally, condition variables (queues) can have only a single entry.

The utility of such a restrictive mechanism embedded within a higher-level language remains to be proven by its adoption in practice.

However, there are at least two very compelling arguments for its use:

- A programmer who implements a system with Concurrent Pascal need not worry about intermittent errors that are sometimes caused by faulty synchronization protection of shared variables.

- The simplicity and standardization of a mechanism for sharing data among concurrently executing processes is likely to result in the production of an efficient system implementation. Inefficiency in systems is often traceable to a lack of conceptual unity and clarity in the underlying design.

A Concurrent Pascal compiler is available for the PDP-11 family of computers, and several (small) operating systems have been written in that language.

10.4.2 CSP

Communicating Sequential Processes (CSP) is a language framework for concurrent programming which is suitable for a microcomputer network environment with distributed storage [Hoare 1978]. The following concepts are central to the language.

- A CSP program consists of a fixed number of sequential processes that are mutually disjoint in address spaces.

- Communication and synchronization are accomplished through the input and output constructs.

- The sequential control structures are based on Dijkstra's guarded commands [Dijkstra 1975].

Communication in CSP occurs when one process names a second as the destination for output and the second process names the first as the source for input (you may view the output operation as a **send** and the input operation as a **receive**). The output values are copied from the first process to the second (the message is sent and received). Messages are typed. The types of the output message and the input message must match for communication to take place. Transfer of information occurs only when both the source and destination processes have invoked the output and input commands, respectively. Therefore, either the source or the destination process may be suspended until the other process is ready with the corresponding output or input. (This is a zero capacity communication scheme, as described in Section 9.8.2.) The I/O facility serves both as a communication mechanism and a synchronization tool.

The syntactic notation of CSP programs is extremely concise and therefore somewhat unconventional. While we could change the notation to make it more conventional, we have chosen to present the actual syntax used by Hoare. You should concentrate on the concepts involved rather than the notation.

To illustrate these concepts, consider two processes, *producer* and *consumer*, that want to exchange messages. The output command in *producer* has the form:

> *consumer* ! *m*   (meaning: **send** *m* to the *consumer*).

The input command in *consumer* has the form:

> *producer* ? *n*   (meaning: **receive** *n* from the *producer*).

Communication between these two processes occur when both processes invoke the above defined I/O commands. The effect is equivalent to the assignment:

$$n := m;$$

In the example above, if the type associated with variable *m* does not match the type of *n*, then the communication cannot take place, and both processes will wait (forever). In addition, if one of the communicating processes terminates, the subsequent invocation of a message operation by the other process will result in its abnormal termination.

In CSP, sequential control is accomplished through the use of Dijkstra's guarded commands notation. A guarded command has the form:

$$<guard> \rightarrow <command\text{-}list>$$

A guard consists of a list of declarations, boolean expressions, and an input command (each of these is optional). A guard fails if any of its boolean expressions have the value *false*, or if the process named in its input command has terminated. If a guard fails, then the process in which this statement is defined aborts. If it does not fail, then the *command-list* is executed. This action takes place only after the input command (if present) has been completed.

Guarded commands may be combined into an alternative command that has the form:

$$[G_1 \rightarrow C_1 \ [] \ G_2 \rightarrow C_2 \ [] \ ... \ [] \ G_n \rightarrow C_n]$$

An alternative command specifies execution of one of its constituent guarded commands. Consequently, if all guards fail, the alternative command fails and the process aborts. If more than one guarded command can be executed successfully, an *arbitrary* one is selected for execution.

Alternative commands can be executed as many times as possible by the use of the repetitive command that has the form:

$$*[G_1 \rightarrow C_1 \ [] \ G_2 \rightarrow C_2 \ [] \ ... \ [] \ G_n \rightarrow C_n]$$

The alternative command is executed repeatedly as long as it does not fail. When all of its guards fail, the alternative command fails, and the repetitive command terminates. Control is transferred to the following statement.

This scheme can be illustrated best through an example. Suppose that we want to write a CSP program to implement the producer/consumer problem, with a bounded-buffer consisting of ten elements. The ten buffers are to be encapsulated in a CSP process *bounded-buffer* defined below.

```
buffer: (0..9) item;
in,out: integer;
in := 0;
out := 0;
*[in < out+10; producer ? buffer(in mod 10)
        → in := in+1;
 [] out < in; consumer ? more()
        → consumer ! buffer(out mod 10);
            out := out+1
 ]
```

The producer process outputs an item p to the *bounded-buffer* process by executing:

$$bounded\text{-}buffer \ ! \ p;$$

The consumer process inputs an item q from the *bounded-buffer* process by executing:

$$bounded\text{-}buffer \ ! \ more();$$
$$bounded\text{-}buffer \ ? \ q;$$

The asymmetry between the way the *producer* and *consumer* processes invoke *bounded-buffer* is due to the requirement that only input commands may appear in guards.

10.4.3 Ada

Ada is a higher-level programming language, sponsored by the United States Department of Defense, designed under the leadership of Jean Ichbiah [Ada 1980]. The language can be used for conventional programming, as well as for special technical requirements, such as driving or monitoring various devices in real time. In this section, we are only concerned with those language constructs that are intended to provide a facility for writing concurrent programs. Central to this facility is the concept of the *task*, which is a program module that is executed asynchronously (a task can be viewed as a sequential process, as defined in Chapter 9). Tasks may communicate and synchronize their actions through the following:

- The **accept statement** is a combination of procedure calls and message transfer.

- The **select statement** is a non-deterministic control structure based on Dijkstra's guarded command construct.

We now briefly elaborate on these two language constructs.

Central to the communication facility is the **accept** statement, which has the following form. (Square brackets [ ] denote an optional part, while braces { } denote a repetition of zero or more times.)

> **accept** *<entry-name>* [*<formal parameter list>*]
> [**do** *<statements>* **end**;]

The statements of an **accept** statement can be executed only if another task invokes the entry-name. Invoking an entry-name is syntactically the same as a procedure call. At this point, parameters are also passed. After the **end** statement has been reached, parameters may be passed back, and both tasks are free to continue. Either the calling task or the called task may be suspended until the other task is ready with its corresponding communication. Thus the facility serves both as a communication mechanism and a synchronization tool.

Choices among several entry calls is accomplished by the **select** statement, which is based on Dijkstra's guarded command concept. For brevity, we describe a restricted form of the **select** statement, with no *delay* and *terminate* statements. The **select** statement has the form:

```
select
    [when <boolean-expression> ⇒ ]
        <accept-statement>
        [<statements>]
    {or [when <boolean-expressions> ⇒ ]
        <accept-statement>}
        [<statements>]
    [else <statements>]
end select;
```

Execution of a **select** statement proceeds as follows:

1. All the boolean expressions appearing in the **select** statement are evaluated. Each **accept** statement whose corresponding boolean expression is evaluated to be true is tagged as *open*. An **accept** statement that is not preceded by a **when** clause is always tagged as open.

2. An open **accept** statement may be selected for execution only if another task has invoked an entry corresponding to that **accept** statement. If several open statements may be selected, an arbitrary one will be chosen for execution. If none can be selected and there is an **else** part, the **else** part is executed. If there is no **else** part, then the task waits until an open statement can be selected.

3. If no **accept** statement is open and there is an **else** part, the **else** part is executed. Otherwise an exception condition is raised.

The **accept** statement provides a task with a mechanism to wait for a predetermined event in another task. On the other hand, the **select** statement provides a task with a mechanism to wait for a set of events whose order cannot be predicted in advance.

These concepts can be illustrated with the bounded-buffer producer/consumer problem:

```
task body bounded-buffer is
    buffer: array [0..9] of item;
    in,out: integer;
    count: integer;
    in := 0;
    out := 0;
    count := 0;
```

```
begin
  loop
    select
       when count < 10 ⇒
       accept insert (it: item)
            do buffer[in mod 10] := it end;
       in := in + 1;
       count := count + 1;
    or when count > 0 ⇒
       accept remove (it: out item)
            do it := buffer[out mod 10] end;
       out := out + 1;
       count := count − 1;
    end select;
  end;
end.
```

The producer task puts an item p into the bounded-buffer by executing:

$$bounded\text{-}buffer.insert\ (p);$$

The consumer task gets an item q from the bounded-buffer task BB by executing:

$$bounded\text{-}buffer.remove\ (q);$$

In contrast to CSP, we have complete symmetry between the producer and consumer tasks.

10.5 Summary

The advantage of higher-level programming languages over assembly languages is that they provide the means for the writing of programs that are simpler and easier to test and verify, modify, and transfer from one machine to another. Less time has to be spent by programmers on developing and testing their programs.

Higher-level languages that can be used in writing concurrent programs must provide a facility for:

- **Modularization.** Three types of modules are most common in an operating system written in a higher-level language.

- ○ **Processes** are the active sequential modules that run asynchronously.

- ○ **Procedures** are the elementary program structure for information hiding.

- ○ **Abstract data types** provide the mechanism for encapsulating data and procedures.

- **Synchronization.** A language must provide the means to guard against time-dependent errors. Several language constructs have been proposed to deal with these problems:

  - ○ **Critical regions** can be used to implement mutual exclusion in a safe and efficient manner.

  - ○ **Conditional critical regions** are similar to critical regions but can be used in solving arbitrary synchronization problems.

  - ○ **Monitors** provide the synchronization mechanism for sharing abstract data types.

The three most widely referenced languages that have incorporated mechanisms for process communication and synchronization are: Concurrent Pascal, CSP, and Ada. These languages vary in the ways that they support the communication primitives. Concurrent Pascal uses parameter passing, CSP uses message passing, and Ada uses a combination of both.

Exercises

10.1 Transform P and V operations on a semaphore S into equivalent critical regions without busy-waiting.

10.2 Demonstrate that monitors, conditional critical regions, and semaphores are all equivalent in the type of synchronization problems that can be implemented with them.

10.3 Extend the frames class of Section 10.2.3, to allow a process to acquire m consecutive blocks.

10.4 Write a bounded-buffer monitor in which the buffers (portions) are embedded within the monitor itself.

10.5 The strict mutual exclusion within a monitor makes the bounded-buffer monitor of Exercise 10.4 mainly suitable for small portions.

    a. Explain why.

    b. Design a new scheme which is suitable for larger portions.

10.6 Write a monitor for disk scheduling using the SCAN disk scheduling algorithm.

10.7 In the C-SCAN algorithm described in Section 10.3.3, the integer count may overflow since it is always incremented but never decremented.

    a. Modify the program to ensure that no overflow will occur.

    b. Suppose that we allow the overflow to occur. What will be the consequences, and could these be tolerated?

10.8 Suppose that the *signal* statement can only appear as the last statement in a monitor procedure. How can the implementation suggested in Section 10.3.3 be simplified?

10.9 Write a monitor for solving the dining philosopher problem. Make sure that your solution is deadlock free.

10.10 Write a monitor for solving the sleepy barber problem (Exercise 9.21).

10.11 Write a monitor for solving the cigarette smokers problem (Exercise 9.22).

10.12 A spooling system consists of an input process *I*, a user process *U*, and an output process *O*, which exchanges data through two bounded-buffer monitors *In* and *Out* (Figure 10.5). Write a program to implement such a scheme, assuming that the *read* and *write* operations allow you to read from the card reader and write onto the printer.

10.13 Consider the river crossing example from Chapter 8. Write a monitor for coordinating the crossing from the two opposite banks. Make sure that your solution ensures that several persons from the same bank can cross simultaneously and that no deadlocks will occur.

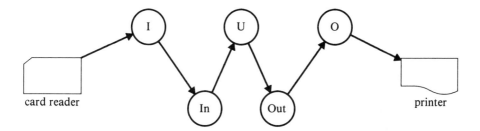

Figure 10.5   Spooling system

10.14 Show how the algorithm of Exercise 10.13 can be extended to also avoid starvation.

10.15 A file is to be shared among a number of different processes, each having a unique number. The file can be accessed simultaneously by several processes subject to the following constraint: the sum of all unique numbers associated with all the processes currently accessing the file must be less than n. Write a monitor to coordinate the access to the file.

10.16 Suppose that we replace the *wait/signal* construct of monitors with a single construct **await**(B), where B is a general boolean expression which causes the process executing it to wait until B becomes true.

   a. Write a monitor using this scheme to implement the readers/writers problem.

   b. This construct cannot be efficiently implemented in general; explain why.

   c. What restrictions need to be put on the await statement so that it can be efficiently implemented. (Hint: restrict the generality of B; see Kessels [1977].)

10.17 Although a monitor ensures mutual exclusion, the procedures must be reentrant. Explain why.

10.18 Consider a system consisting of processes $P_1, P_2, ..., P_n$, each having a unique priority number. Write a monitor that allocates three identical line printers to these processes, using the priority numbers for deciding on the order of allocation.

10.19 Write a monitor that implements an *alarm clock* which enables a calling program to delay itself for a specified number of time units (*ticks*). You may assume the existence of a real hardware clock, which invokes a procedure *tick* in your monitor at regular intervals.

Bibliographic Notes

The critical region concept is due to Hoare [1972b] and Brinch Hansen [1972b]. The conditional critical region was proposed by Hoare [1972b] and generalized by Brinch Hansen [1972b]. A comparison of the semaphore, critical region, and conditional region concepts is given by Brinch Hansen [1972a]. General discussions have been written by Brinch Hansen [1973a, 1973b]. The issue of efficient implementation of conditional critical region has been considered by Schmid [1976].

The monitor concept was developed by Brinch Hansen [1973a]; it was based on the secretary concept of Dijkstra [1971]. A complete description of the monitor was given by Hoare [1974]. A discussion concerning the various ways signaling can be implemented was offered by Howard [1976b]. An extension to the monitor to allow automatic signaling was proposed by Kessels [1977]. Implementation issues were discussed by Lister and Maynard [1976] and Schmid [1976].

Another synchronization concept, the coroutine, was invented by Conway [1963] and illustrated by Knuth [1973]. This construct is mainly suited to a strictly interleaved execution of processes on a single processor and is the basic concept of pipes in the Unix operating system.

Abstract data types have evolved from the work of Parnas [1971] on information hiding, and the class concept of Simula 67 [Dahl et al. 1968]. Discussions concerning various aspects of language notations have been presented by Liskov and Zilles [1974, 1975].

Various higher-level languages for writing concurrent programs in a centralized environment have recently emerged. Concurrent Pascal was developed by Brinch Hansen [1975] as an extension to sequential Pascal. The language was successfully used in the writing of three different types of operating systems [Brinch Hansen 1977]. Wirth [1977] developed another concurrent language called Modula, which also extends sequential Pascal. The language also incorporates machine-dependent features so that device drivers can be programmed using the language. Other languages include CSP/k [Holt et al. 1978], which is based upon PL/1, Pascal-Plus [Welsh and Bustard 1979], and Mesa [Lampson and Redell 1980], which employs the monitor concept.

Various higher-level languages for writing distributed programs have also been proposed. Communicating Sequential Processes [Hoare 1978], Distributed Processes [Brinch Hansen 1978], Ada [Ada 1980], Plits [Feldman 1979], MOD* [Cook 1980], and Synchronizing Resources [Andrews 1981] are among the most often mentioned languages. These languages vary in the type of synchronization and communication facilities they provide.

An important research topic concerning concurrent languages is correctness proofs. Owicki and Gries [1976a, 1976b] and Lamport [1977] were the first to develop such proof systems. Howard [1976a] presented proof rules for Hoare-like monitors. Owicki [1978] presented a method of verifying parallel programs containing shared classes rather than monitors. Other work in this area includes Apt et al. [1980], Levin and Gries [1981], Hoare [1981], and Misra and Chandy [1981].

11

Protection

The various processes in an operating system must be protected from each other's activities. For that purpose, various mechanisms have been introduced, which can be used to ensure that the files, memory segments, cpu, and other resources can be operated on only by those processes that have gained proper authorization from the operating system.

For example, the access control facility in a file system allows users to dictate how and by whom their files can be accessed. Memory addressing hardware ensures that a process can only execute within its own address space. The timer ensures that no process can gain control of the cpu without relinquishing it. Finally, users are not allowed to do their own I/O, to protect the integrity of the various peripheral devices.

In this chapter, we will examine the problem of protection in greater detail, and develop a unifying model for implementing protection.

11.1 Goals of Protection

As computer systems have become more sophisticated and pervasive in their applications, the need to protect their integrity has also grown. Protection was originally conceived as an adjunct to multiprogramming operating systems, so that untrustworthy users might safely share a common logical name space, such as a directory of files, or a common physical name space, such as memory. Modern protection concepts have evolved to increase the reliability of any complex system that makes use of shared resources.

Protection refers to a mechanism for controlling the access of programs, processes, or users to the resources defined by a computer system. This mechanism must provide a means for specification of the controls to be imposed, together with some means of enforcement. We distinguish between protection and *security*, which is a measure of confidence that the integrity of a system and its data will be preserved.

Security is a much broader topic than protection, and we address it only briefly in this text (Section 11.11).

There are several motivations for protection. Most obvious is the need to prevent mischievous, intentional violation of an access restriction by a system user. Of more general importance, however, is the need to ensure that each program component active in a system uses system resources only in ways consistent with the stated policies for the uses of these resources. This is an absolute requirement for a reliable system.

Protection can improve reliability by detecting latent errors at the interfaces between component subsystems. Early detection of interface errors can often prevent contamination of a healthy subsystem by a subsystem that is malfunctioning. An unprotected resource cannot defend against use (or misuse) by an unauthorized or incompetent user. A protection-oriented system provides means to distinguish between authorized and unauthorized usage.

11.2 Mechanisms and Policies

A computer system in the most general sense may be viewed as a collection of processes and resources. To ensure the orderly and efficient operation of a system, the processes are subjected to *policies* that govern the use of resources. The role of protection in a computer system is to provide a mechanism for the enforcement of the policies governing resource use. These policies may be established in a variety of ways. Some are fixed in the design of the system, while others are formulated by the management of a system. Still others are defined by the individual users to protect their own files and programs. A protection system must have the flexibility to enforce a variety of policies that can be declared to it.

Policies for resource use may vary, depending on the application, and they may be subject to change over time. For these reasons, protection can no longer be considered solely as a matter of concern to the designer of an operating system. It should also be available as a tool for the applications programmer, so that resources created and supported by an applications subsystem can be guarded against misuse. In this chapter we describe the protection mechanisms the operating system should provide, so that application designers can use them in designing their own protection software.

One very important principle is the separation of *policy* from *mechanism*. Mechanisms determine how to do something. Policies decide *what* will be done, but not how it will be done. The separation of policy and mechanism is very important for flexibility. Policies are likely to change from place to place or time to time. In the worst case, every change in policy would require a change in the underlying mechanism. General mechanisms would be more desirable, since a change in a policy would then require only the modification of some system parameters or tables.

11.3 Domain of Protection

A computer system is a collection of processes and *objects*. By objects we mean both hardware objects (such as the cpu, memory segments, printers, card readers, and tape drivers), and software objects (such as files, programs, and semaphores). Each object has a unique name that differentiates it from all other objects in the system, and it can be accessed only through well-defined and meaningful operations. Objects are essentially *abstract data types*.

The operations that are possible may depend on the object. For example, a cpu can only be executed on. Memory segments can be read and written, while a card reader can only be read. Tape drivers can be read, written, and rewound. Data files can be created, opened, read, written, closed, and deleted, while program files can be read, written, and executed.

Obviously, a process should be allowed to access only those resources it has been authorized to access. Furthermore, at any time it should be able to access only those resources that it currently requires to complete its task. This requirement, commonly referred to as the *need-to-know* principle, is useful in limiting the amount of damage a faulty process can cause in the system. For example, when process p invokes procedure A, the procedure should only be allowed to access its own variables and the formal parameters passed to it; it should not be able to access all the variables of process p. Similarly, consider the case where process p invokes a compiler to compile a particular file. The compiler should not be able to access any arbitrary files, but only a well-defined subset of files (such as the source file, listing file, and so on) related to the file to be compiled. Conversely, the compiler may have private files used for accounting or optimization purposes, which process p should not be able to access.

To facilitate this scheme, we introduce the concept of a *protection domain*. A process operates within a protection domain, which specifies the resources that the process may access. Each domain defines a set of objects and the types of operations that may be invoked on each object. The ability to execute an operation on an object is an *access right*. A domain is a collection of access rights, each of which is an ordered pair *<object-name, rights-set>*. For example, if domain D has the access right

<file F, {read,write}>, then a process executing in domain D can both read and write file F; it cannot, however, perform any other operation on that object.

Domains need not be disjoint; they may share access rights. For example, in Figure 11.1, we have three domains: D_1, D_2, and D_3. The access right $<O_4$, {print}> is shared by both D_2 and D_3, implying that a process executing in either one of these two domains can print object O_4. Note that a process must be executing in domain D_1 to read and write object O_1. On the other hand, only processes in domain D_3 may execute object O_1.

Consider the standard dual mode (monitor/user mode) model of operating system execution. When a process executes in the monitor mode, it can execute privileged instructions and thus gain complete control of the computer system. On the other hand, if the process executes in user mode, it can only invoke non-privileged instructions. Consequently, it can only execute within its pre-defined memory space. These two modes protect the operating system (executing in monitor domain) from the user processes (executing in user domain). In a multiprogrammed operating system, two protection domains are insufficient, since users also want to be protected from each other. Therefore a more elaborate scheme is needed.

11.4 Access Matrix

Our model of protection can be abstractly viewed as a matrix, called an *access matrix*. The rows of the access matrix represent domains, and the columns represent objects. Each entry in the matrix consists of a set of access rights. Since objects are explicitly defined by the column, we can omit the object name from the access right. The entry **access**(i,j) defines the set of operations that a process, executing in domain D_i, can invoke on object O_j.

To illustrate these concepts, consider the access matrix shown in Figure 11.2. There are four domains and five objects: three files (F_1, F_2,

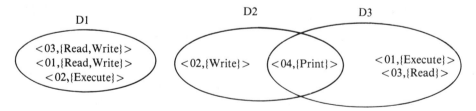

Figure 11.1   System with three protection domains

Object ⟍ Domain	F1	F2	F3	Card Reader	Printer
D1	Read		Read		
D2				Read	Print
D3		Read	Execute		
D4	Read Write		Read Write		

Figure 11.2   Access matrix

F_3), one card reader, and one printer. When a process executes in domain D_1, it can read files F_1 and F_3. A process executing in domain D_4 has the same privileges as in domain D_1. In addition, it can write onto files F_1 and F_3. Note that the card reader and printer can only be accessed by a process executing in domain D_2.

11.5 Implementation of Access Matrix

How can the access matrix be effectively implemented? In general, the matrix will be sparse; that is, most of the entries will be empty. Although there are data structure techniques available for representing sparse matrices, they are not particularly useful for this application, because of the way in which the protection facility is used.

11.5.1 Global Table

The simplest implementation of the access matrix is a global table consisting of a set of ordered triples <domain, object, rights-set>. Whenever an operation M is executed on an object O_j within domain D_i, the global table is searched for a triple $<D_i, O_j, R_k>$ where $M \in R_k$. If this triple is found, the operation is allowed to continue; otherwise, an exception (error) condition is raised. This implementation suffers from several drawbacks. The table is usually quite large and thus cannot be kept in main memory, implying additional I/O is needed. Virtual memory techniques are often used for managing this table. In addition, it is difficult to take advantage of special groupings of objects or domains. For example, if a particular object can be read by everyone, it must have a separate entry in every domain.

11.5.2 Access Lists

Each column in the access matrix can be implemented as an access list for one object, as described in Section 3.6.3. Obviously, the empty entries can be discarded. The resulting list for each object consists of ordered pairs <domain, rights-set>, which define all domains with a non-empty set of access rights for that object.

This approach can be simply extended to define a list plus a *default* set of access rights. When an operation M on an object O_j is attempted in domain D_i, we search the access list for object O_j, looking for an entry $<D_j, R_k>$ with $M \ \varepsilon \ R_k$. If the entry is found, we allow the operation; if not, we check the default set. If M is in the default set, we also allow the access. Otherwise, access is denied and an exception condition occurs. Note that for efficiency we may check the default set first and then search the access list.

11.5.3 Capability Lists

Rather than associating the columns of the access matrix with the objects as access lists, we can associate each row with its domain. A *capability list* for a domain is a list of objects and the operations allowed on those objects. An object is often represented by its physical name or address, called a *capability*. To execute operation M on object O_j, the process executes the operation M, specifying the capability (pointer) for object O_j as a parameter. Simple *possession* of the capability means that access is allowed.

The capability list is associated with a domain, but is never directly accessible to a process executing in that domain. Rather, the capability list is itself a protected object, maintained by the operating system and accessed by the user only indirectly. Capability-based protection relies on the fact that the capabilities are never allowed to migrate into any address space directly accessible by a user process (where they could be modified). If all capabilities are secure, the object they protect is also secure against unauthorized access.

Capabilities were originally proposed as a kind of secure pointer, to meet the need for resource protection that was foreseen as multiprogrammed computer systems came of age. The idea of an inherently protected pointer (from the point of view of a user of a system) provides a foundation for protection that can be extended up to the applications level.

In order to provide inherent protection, capabilities have to be distinguished from other kinds of objects and interpreted by an abstract machine on which higher-level programs run. Capabilities are usually distinguished from other data in one of two ways:

- Each object has a *tag* to denote its type as either a capability or as accessible data. The tags themselves must not be directly accessible by an applications program. Hardware or firmware support may be used to enforce this restriction. Although only one bit is necessary to distinguish between capabilities and other objects, more bits are often used. This extension allows all objects to be tagged with their types by the hardware. Thus the hardware can distinguish integers, floating point numbers, pointers, booleans, characters, instructions, capabilities, and uninitialized values by their tags.

- Alternatively, the address space associated with a program can be split into two parts. One part is accessible to the program and contains its normal data and instructions. The other part, containing the capability list, is accessible only by the operating system. A segmented memory space (Section 5.7) is useful to support this approach.

Several capability-based protection systems have been developed and are briefly described in Section 11.8.

11.5.4 A Lock/Key Mechanism

The lock/key scheme is a compromise between access lists and capability lists. Each object has a list of unique bit patterns, called *locks*. Similarly, each domain has a list of unique bit patterns, called *keys*. A process executing in a domain can access an object, only if that domain has a key which matches one of the locks of the object.

As with capability lists, the list of keys for a domain must be managed by the operating system on behalf of the domain. Users are not allowed to examine or modify the list of keys (or locks) directly.

11.5.5 Comparison

Access lists correspond directly to the needs of the users. When a users create objects, they can specify which domains can access the objects, as well as the operations allowed. However, since access rights information for a particular domain is not localized, it is difficult to determine the set of access rights for each domain. In addition, every access to the object must be checked, requiring a search of the access list. In a large system with long access lists, this search can be quite time-consuming.

Capability lists do not correspond directly to the needs of the users; they are useful, however, for localizing information for a particular process. We do not need to search a list to verify that access is allowed. The process attempting access must present a capability for that access.

Then the protection system need only verify that the capability is valid. Revocation of capabilities, however, may be quite inefficient (Section 11.7).

The lock/key mechanism is a compromise between these two schemes. The mechanism can be both effective and flexible, depending on the length of the keys. The keys can be passed freely from domain to domain. In addition, access privileges may be effectively revoked by simply changing some of the keys associated with the object (Section 11.7).

Most systems use a combination of access lists and capabilities. When a process first tries to access an object, the access list is searched. If access is denied, an exception condition occurs. Otherwise, a capability is created and attached to the process. Additional references use the capability to demonstrate swiftly that access is allowed. After the last access, the capability is destroyed. This strategy is used in the Multics system and in the CAL system, where both access lists and capability lists are employed.

As an example, consider a file system. Each file has an associated access list. When a process opens a file, the directory structure is searched to find the file, access permission is checked, and buffers are allocated. All of this information is recorded in a new entry in a file table associated with the process. The operation returns an index into this table for the newly opened file. All operations on the file are made by specifying the index into the file table. The entry in the file table then points to the file and its buffers. When the file is closed, the file table entry is deleted. Since the file table is maintained by the operating system, it cannot be corrupted by the user. Thus the only files which the user can access are those which have been opened. Since access is checked when the file is opened, protection is ensured.

Note that the right to access *must* still be checked on each access, and the file table entry has a capability only for the allowed operations. If a file is opened for reading, then a capability for read access is placed in the file table entry. If an attempt is made to write, this protection violation is determined by comparing the requested operation with the capability in the file table entry.

11.5.6 Policies

The access matrix scheme provides us with the mechanism for specifying a variety of policies. The mechanism consists of implementing the access matrix and ensuring that the semantic properties we have outlined in Section 11.4 indeed hold. More specifically, we must ensure that a process executing in domain D_i can access only those objects specified in row i, and then only as allowed by the access matrix entries.

Policy decisions concerning protection can be implemented by the access matrix. The policy decisions involve which rights should be included in the (i,j)th entry. We must also decide the domain in which each process executes. This last policy is usually decided by the operating system.

The users normally decide the contents of the access matrix entries. When a user creates a new object O_j, the column O_j is added to the access matrix with the appropriate initialization entries, as dictated by the creator. The user may decide to enter some rights in some entries in column j and other rights in other entries, as needed.

11.6 Dynamic Protection Structures

The association between a process and a domain may be either static (if the set of resources available to a process is fixed throughout its lifetime) or dynamic. As might be expected, the problems inherent in establishing dynamic protection domains require more careful solution than the simpler problems of the static case.

If the association between processes and domains is fixed, and we want to adhere to the need-to-know principle, then a mechanism must be available to change the content of a domain. A process may execute in two different phases. For example, it may need read access in one phase and write access in another. If the access matrix is static, we must define the domain to include both read and write access. However, this arrangement provides more rights than are needed in each of the two phases, since we have read access in the phase where we only need write access, and vice versa. Thus the need-to-know principle is violated. We must allow the contents of the access matrix to be modified, so that it always reflects the minimum necessary access rights for the process and its domain.

If the association is dynamic, a mechanism is available to allow a process to switch from one domain to another. We may also want to allow the content of a domain to be changed. If we cannot change the content of a domain, we can provide the same effect by creating a new domain with the change contents, and switching to that new domain when we want to change domain contents.

Clearly, both the static and dynamic schemes require strict control. Otherwise, protection policies could be violated. Fortunately, we already have a mechanism for defining and implementing that control: the access matrix. When we switch a process from one domain to another, we are executing an operation (switch) on an object (the domain). We can control domain switching by including domains among the objects of the access matrix. Similarly, when we change the content of the access matrix, we are performing an operation on an object: the access matrix. Again, we can control these changes by including the access matrix itself as an object. Actually, since each entry in the access matrix may be individually modified, we must consider each entry in the access matrix as an object to be protected.

Now, we need only consider the operations that are possible on these new objects (domains and the access matrix) and how we want processes to be able to execute these operations.

Processes should be able to switch from one domain to another. Domain switching from domain D_i to domain D_j is allowed to occur if and only if the access right *switch* ε **access**(i,j). Thus in Figure 11.3, a process executing in domain D_2 can switch to domain D_3 or to domain D_4. A process in domain D_4 can switch to D_1, and in domain D_1 a process can switch to domain D_2.

Allowing controlled change to the content of the access matrix entries requires three additional operations: **copy, owner,** and **control**.

The ability to copy an access right from one domain (row) of the access matrix to another is denoted by appending an asterisk (*) to the access right. The *copy* right only allows the copying of the access right within the column (that is, for the object) for which the right is defined. For example, in Figure 11.4a, a process executing in domain D_2 can copy the read operation into any entry associated with file F_2. Hence, the access matrix of Figure 11.4a can be modified to the access matrix shown in Figure 11.4b.

Object Domain	F1	F2	F3	Card Reader	Printer	D1	D2	D3	D4
D1	Read		Read				Switch		
D2				Read	Print			Switch	Switch
D3		Read	Execute						
D4	Read Write		Read Write			Switch			

Figure 11.3   Access matrix of Figure 11.2 with domains as objects

Domain \ Object	F1	F2	F3
D1	Execute		Write*
D2	Execute	Read*	Execute
D3	Execute		

(a)

Domain \ Object	F1	F2	F3
D1	Execute		Write*
D2	Execute	Read*	Execute
D3	Execute	Read	

(b)

Figure 11.4 Access matrix with copy rights

There are two variants to this scheme:

a. When a right is copied from **access**(i,j) to **access**(k,j), it is removed from **access**(i,j). This is a *transfer* of a right rather than a copy.

b. Propagation of the *copy* right may be limited. That is, when the right R^* is copied from **access**(i,j) to **access**(k,j), only the right R (not R^*) is created. A process executing in domain D_k cannot further copy the right R.

A system may select only one of these three *copy* rights, or it may provide all three by identifying them as separate rights: *copy*, *transfer*, and *limited-copy*.

The *copy* right allows a process to copy some rights from an entry in one column to another entry in the same column. We also need a mechanism to allow adding new rights and removing some rights. The *owner* right controls these operations. If **access**(i,j) includes the *owner* right, then a process executing in domain D_i, can add and remove any right in any entry in column j. For example, in Figure 11.5a, domain D_1 is the owner of F_1 and thus can add and delete any valid right in column F_1. Similarly, domain D_2 is the owner of F_2 and F_3, and thus can add and remove any valid right within these two columns. Thus the access matrix of Figure 11.5a can be modified to the access matrix shown in Figure 11.5b.

The *copy* and *owner* rights allow a process to change the entries in a column. A mechanism is also needed to change entries in a row. The *control* right is only applicable to domain objects. If **access**(i,j) includes the *control* right, then a process executing in domain D_i can remove any access right from row j. For example, suppose that in Figure 11.3 we include the *control* right in **access**(D_2,D_4). Then a process executing in domain D_2 could modify domain D_4, as shown in Figure 11.6.

These operations on the domains and the access matrix are not in themselves particularly important. What is more important is that they

Domain \ Object	F1	F2	F3
D1	Owner Execute		Write
D2		Read* Owner	Read* Owner Write*
D3	Execute		

(a)

Domain \ Object	F1	F2	F3
D1	Owner Execute		
D2		Owner Read* Write*	Read* Owner Write*
D3		Write	Write

(b)

Figure 11.5   Access matrix with owner rights

Object Domain	F1	F2	F3	Card Reader	Printer	D1	D2	D3	D4
D1	Read		Read				Switch		
D2				Read	Print			Switch	Switch Control
D3		Read	Execute						
D4	Write		Write			Switch			

Figure 11.6   Modified access matrix of Figure 11.3

illustrate the ability of the access matrix model to allow the implementation and control of dynamic protection requirements. New objects and new domains can be created dynamically and included in the access matrix model. However, we have only shown that the basic mechanism is here; the policy decisions concerning which domains are to have access to which objects in which ways must be made by the system designers and users. The access matrix is a general mechanism which does not require any particular protection policy.

The dynamic protection model provides a mechanism to solve the access control problem of Section 10.3.3. We saw that monitors were insufficient to allow users to create their own resources and control their use. If the resources were embedded in a monitor, their use would be controlled by the built-in monitor-scheduling policy; the users could not enforce their own scheduling policy. In addition, the fact that only one process can execute in a monitor at a time prevents simultaneous access to the resources, which is needed for the readers in the readers/writers problem.

To solve these problems, the resources must be external to the monitor. Now, however, we have no control over the use of the resources. To provide this control, a monitor, called a *manager*, is created for each resource. This manager schedules and controls access to the resources. To use a resource, a process first calls the manager, which returns to the user process a capability for the resource. The process must present the capability when it accesses the resource. When the process finishes, it returns the capability to the manager, which may then allocate it to other waiting processes, according to its own scheduling algorithm. Thus capabilities provide a solution to the access control problem of Section 10.3.3. A malfunctioning user process can only cause limited mischief that will affect other processes; it may acquire a capability to the shared resource and refuse to release it. This circumstance can be remedied, at the cost of some additional execution overhead, by providing for preemptive revocation of capabilities.

11.7 Revocation

In a dynamic protection system, it may sometimes be necessary to revoke access rights to objects that are shared by a number of different users. A number of different questions about revocation may arise:

- **Immediate/delayed**. Does revocation occur immediately or is it delayed? If revocation is delayed, can we find out when it will take place?

- **Selective/general**. When an access right to an object is revoked, does it affect *all* the users who have an access right to that object, or can we specify a select group of users whose access rights should be revoked?

- **Partial/total**. Can a subset of the rights associated with an object be revoked or must we revoke all access rights for this object?

- **Temporary/permanent**. Can access be revoked permanently (that is, the revoked access right will never again be available) or can access be revoked and later be obtained again?

   With an access list scheme, revocation is quite easy. The access list is searched for the access right(s) to be revoked and they are deleted from the list. Revocation is immediate, and can be general or selective, total or partial, and permanent or temporary.

   Capabilities, however, present a much more difficult revocation problem. Since the capabilities are distributed throughout the system, we must find them before we can revoke them. There are a number of different schemes for implementing revocation for capabilities, including:

- **Reacquisition**. Periodically, capabilities are deleted from each domain. If a process wants to use a capability, it may find that capability has been deleted. The process may then try to reacquire the capability. If access has been revoked, the process will not be able to reacquire the capability.

- **Back-pointers**. A list of pointers is maintained with each object, pointing to all capabilities associated with that object. When revocation is required, we can follow these pointers, changing the capabilities as necessary. This scheme has been adopted in the Multics system. It is quite general, although it is a very costly implementation.

- **Indirection**. The capabilities do not point to the objects directly, but instead point indirectly [Redell 1974]. Each capability points to a unique entry in a global table, which in turn points to the object. Revocation is implemented by searching the global table for the desired entry and deleting it. When an access is attempted, the capability is found to point to an illegal table entry. Table entries can be reused for other capabilities without difficulty, since both the capability and the table entry contain the unique name of the object. The object for a capability and its table entry must match. This scheme was adopted in the CAL system. It does not, however, allow selective revocation.

- **Keys**. A key is a unique bit pattern that can be associated with each capability. This key is defined when the capability is created, and it can neither be modified nor inspected by the process owning that capability. A *master key* associated with each object can be defined or replaced with the **set-key** operation. When a capability is created, the current value of the master key is associated with the capability. When the capability is exercised, its key is compared to the master key. If the keys match, the operation is allowed to continue; otherwise, an exception condition is raised. Revocation replaces the master key with a new value by the **set-key** operation, invalidating all previous capabilities for this object.

  Note that this scheme does not allow selective revocation, since only one master key is associated with each object. If we associate a list of keys with each object, then selective revocation can be implemented. Finally, we can group all keys into one global table of keys. A capability is valid only if its key matches some key in the global table. Revocation is implemented by removing the matching key from the table. With this scheme, a key can be associated with several objects, and several keys can be associated with each object, providing maximum flexibility.

  In key-based schemes, the operations of defining keys, inserting them into lists, or deleting them from lists, should not be available to all users. In particular, it would be reasonable to allow only the owner of an object to set the keys for its objects. This choice, however, is a policy decision that the protection system can implement, but should not define.

11.8 Existing Systems

So far we have avoided pinpointing exactly what a domain is. A domain is an abstract concept which can be realized in a variety of ways:

- A domain may be defined for each **user**. The set of objects which can be accessed depend on the identity of the user. Domain switching occurs when the user is changed, generally when a user logs-out and another user logs-in.

- Each **process** may be a domain. In this case, each row in the access matrix describes which objects can be accessed by that process, as well as which operations are allowed. Domain switching corresponds to one process sending a message to another process, and then waiting for a response.

- Each **procedure** may be a domain. Each row in the access matrix then describes which objects can be accessed by that procedure. In this situation, procedure calls cause domain switching.

In this section we briefly survey some of the most widely known protection systems. These systems vary in their complexity and in the type of policies that can be implemented on them.

11.8.1 Unix

In the Unix system, the protection scheme is basically centered around the file system. Three protection fields are associated with each file, corresponding to owner, group, and universal classification. Each field consists of three bits, r, w, and x. The r bit controls read access, w controls write access, and x controls execute access. A domain in Unix is associated with the user.

Domain switching corresponds to changing the user identification temporarily. This change is accomplished through the file system as follows. An owner identification and a domain bit are associated with each file. When a user (with *user-id* = A) starts executing a file owned by B, whose associated domain bit is *on*, the *user-id* is set to B. When the computation exits the file, the *user-id* is reset to A.

11.8.2 Multics

In the Multics system, the protection scheme is centered around the file system and a *ring* structure. The protection facility associated with the file system was described in Section 3.6.3. Briefly, an access list, as well as owner and universal access fields, is associated with each file.

The protection domains in Multics are hierarchically organized into a ring structure. Each ring corresponds to a single domain (Figure 11.7). The rings are numbered from 0 to 7. Let D_i and D_j be any two domain rings. If $j < i$, then D_i is a subset of D_j. That is, a process executing in domain D_j has more privileges than a process executing in domain D_i. A process executing in domain D_0 has the most privileges. If there are only two rings, this scheme is equivalent to the monitor/user mode of execution, where monitor mode corresponds to D_0 and user mode corresponds to D_1.

Multics has a segmented address space; each segment is a file. Each segment is associated with one of the rings. A segment description includes an entry that identifies the ring number. In addition, it includes three access bits to control reading, writing, and execution. The association between segments and rings is a policy decision which we are not concerned with in this book. With each process, a *current-ring-number* counter is associated, identifying the ring in which the process is currently executing. When a process is executing in ring i, it cannot access a segment associated with ring j, $j < i$. It can, however, access a

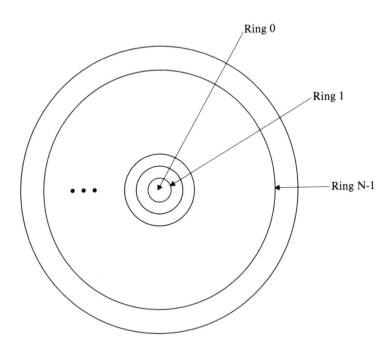

Figure 11.7   Multics ring structure

segment associated with ring k, $k \geq i$. The type of access, however, is restricted, according to the access bits associated with that segment.

Domain switching in Multics occurs when a process crosses from one ring to another by calling a procedure in a different ring. Obviously, this switch must be done in a controlled manner; otherwise, a process can start executing in ring 0, and no protection will be provided. To allow controlled domain switching, the ring field of the segment descriptor is modified to include:

- **Access bracket**. A pair of integers, $b1$ and $b2$, such that $b1 \leq b2$.

- **Limit**. An integer $b3$, such that $b3 > b2$.

- **List of gates**. The entry points (gates) at which the segments may be called.

If a process executing in ring i calls a procedure (segment) with access bracket $(b1,b2)$, then the call is allowed if $b1 \leq i \leq b2$, and the current ring number of the process remains i. Otherwise, a trap to the operating system occurs, and the situation is handled as follows:

- If $i < b1$, then the call is allowed to occur, since we have a transfer to a ring (domain) with fewer privileges. However, if parameters are passed which refer to segments in a lower ring (that is, segments which are not accessible to the called procedure), then these segments must be copied into an area that can be accessed by the called procedure.

- If $i > b2$, then the call is allowed to occur only if the limit ($b3$) is less than or equal to i, and the call has been directed to one of the designated entry points in the list-of-gates. This scheme allows processes with limited access rights to call procedures in lower rings with more access rights, but only in a carefully controlled manner.

The main disadvantage of the ring (hierarchical) structure is that it does not allow us to enforce the need-to-know principle. In particular, if an object must be accessible in domain D_j but not accessible in domain D_i, then we must have $j < i$. But this means that every segment accessible in D_i is also accessible in D_j.

11.8.3 Hydra

Hydra is a capability-based protection system that provides considerable flexibility. The system provides a fixed set of possible access rights, known to the system and interpreted by it. These rights include such basic forms of access as the right to read, to write, or to execute a memory segment. In addition, however, the system provides the means for a user (of the protection system) to declare additional rights. The interpretation of user-defined rights is performed solely by the user's program, but the system provides access protection for the use of these rights, as well as for the use of system-defined rights. The facilities provided by this system are quite interesting, and constitute a significant development in protection technology.

Operations upon objects are defined procedurally. The procedures that implement such operations are themselves a form of object, and are accessed indirectly by capabilities. The names of user-defined procedures must be identified to the protection system if it is to deal with objects of the user-defined type. When the definition of an object is made known to Hydra, the names of operations on the type become *auxiliary rights*. Auxiliary rights can be described in a capability for an instance of the type. In order for a process to perform an operation upon a typed object, the capability it holds for that object must contain the name of the operation being invoked among its auxiliary rights. This restriction enables discrimination of access rights to be made on an instance-by-instance, and process-by-process basis.

Another interesting concept in Hydra is called rights *amplification* [Cohen and Jefferson 1975]. This scheme allows certification of a procedure as "trustworthy" to act upon a formal parameter of a specified type, on behalf of any process that holds a right to execute the procedure. The rights held by a trustworthy procedure are independent of, and may exceed, the rights held by the calling process. However, it is not necessary to regard such a procedure as universally trustworthy (it is not allowed to act on other types, for instance), nor to extend trustworthiness to any other procedures or program segments that might be executed by a process.

Amplification is useful in allowing implementation procedures access to the representation variables of an abstract data type. If a process holds a capability to a typed object A, for instance, this capability may include an auxiliary right to invoke some operation P, but would not include any of the so-called kernel rights, such as read, write, or execute, on the segment that represents A. Such a capability gives a process a means of indirect access (through the operation P) to the representation of A, but only for specific purposes.

On the other hand, when a process invokes the operation P on an object A, the capability for access to A may be amplified as control passes to the code body of P. This may be necessary, in order to allow P the right to access the storage segment representing A, to implement the operation that P defines on the abstract data type. The code body of P may be allowed to read or to write to the segment of A directly, even though the calling process cannot. Upon return from P, the capability for A is restored to its original, unamplified state. This is a typical case in which the rights held by a process for access to a protected segment must change dynamically, depending on the task to be performed. The dynamic adjustment of rights is performed to guarantee consistency of a programmer-defined abstraction. Amplification of rights can be explicitly stated in the declaration of an abstract type to the Hydra system.

A Hydra subsystem is built on top of its protection kernel and may require protection of its own components. A subsystem interacts with the kernel through calls upon a set of kernel-defined primitives that define access rights to resources defined by the subsystem. Policies for use of these resources by user processes can be defined by the subsystem designer, but are enforceable by use of the standard access protection afforded by the capability system.

A programmer can make direct use of the protection system, after becoming acquainted with its features in the appropriate reference manual [Newcomer et al. 1976]. Hydra provides a large library of system-defined procedures that can be called by user programs. A user of the Hydra system would explicitly incorporate calls upon these system procedures into the code of their programs, or would use a program translator that had been interfaced to Hydra.

11.8.4 Cambridge CAP System

Quite a different approach to capability-based protection has been taken in the design of the Cambridge CAP system [Needham and Walker 1977]. Its capability system is apparently simpler and superficially less powerful than that of Hydra. However, closer examination shows that it too can be used to provide secure protection of user-defined objects. In CAP, there are two kinds of capabilities. The ordinary kind is called a *data capability*. It can be used to provide access to objects, but the only rights provided are the standard read, write, or execute of the individual storage segments associated with the object. Data capabilities are interpreted by microcode in the CAP machine.

A so-called *software capability* is protected by, but not interpreted by, the CAP microcode. It is interpreted by a *protected* (that is, a privileged) procedure, which may be written by an applications programmer as part of a subsystem. A particular kind of rights amplification is associated with a protected procedure. When executing the code body of such a procedure, a process temporarily acquires the rights to read or write the contents of a software capability itself. This specific kind of rights amplification corresponds to an implementation of the **seal** and **unseal** primitives on capabilities that were proposed by Morris [1973]. Of course, this privilege is still subject to type-verification to ensure that only software capabilities for a specified abstract type are allowed to be passed to any such procedure. Universal trust is not placed in any code other than the CAP machine's microcode.

The interpretation of a software capability is completely up to the subsystem, through the protected procedures it contains. This scheme allows a variety of protection policies to be implemented. Although programmers can define their own protected procedures (any of which might be incorrect), the security of the overall system cannot be compromised. The basic protection system will not allow an unverified, user-defined, protected procedure access to any storage segments (or capabilities) that do not belong to the protection environment in which it resides. The worst consequence of an insecure protected procedure is a protection breakdown of the subsystem for which it has responsibility.

The designers of the CAP system have noted that the use of software capabilities has allowed them to realize considerable economies in formulating and implementing protection policies commensurate with the requirements of abstract resources. However, subsystem designers who want to make use of this facility cannot simply study a reference manual, as is the case with Hydra. Instead, they must learn the principles and techniques of protection, since the system provides them with no library of procedures to be used.

11.9 Language-Based Protection

To the degree that protection is provided in existing computer systems, it has usually been achieved through the device of an operating system kernel, which acts as a security agent to inspect and validate each attempt to access a protected resource. Since comprehensive access validation is potentially a source of considerable overhead, either it must be given hardware support to reduce the cost of each validation, or one must accept that the system designer may be inclined to compromise the goals of protection. It is difficult to satisfy all of these goals if the flexibility to implement various protection policies is restricted by the support mechanisms provided or if protection environments are made larger than necessary in order to secure greater operational efficiency.

As operating systems have become more complex, and particularly as they have attempted to provide higher-level user interfaces, the goals of protection have become much more refined. In this refinement, we find that the designers of protection systems have drawn heavily on ideas that originated in programming languages and especially on the concept of abstract data types (Chapter 10). Protection systems are now concerned not only with the identity of a resource to which access is attempted but also with the functional nature of that access. In the newest protection systems, concern for the function to be invoked extends beyond a set of system-defined functions, such as standard file access methods, to include functions that may be user-defined as well.

Policies for resource use may also vary, depending on the application, and they may be subject to change over time. For these reasons, protection can no longer be considered solely as a matter of concern to the designer of an operating system. It should also be available as a tool for use by the applications designer, so that resources of an applications subsystem can be guarded against tampering or the influence of an error.

At this point, programming languages enter the picture. Specifying the desired control of access to a shared resource in a system is a declarative statement about the resource. This kind of statement can be integrated into a language by an extension of its typing facility. When protection is declared along with data typing, the designer of each subsystem can specify its requirements for protection, as well as its need for use of other resources in a system. Such a specification should be given directly as a program is composed, and in the language in which the program itself is stated. There are several significant advantages to this approach:

1. Protection needs are simply declared, rather than programmed as a sequence of calls on procedures of an operating system.

2. Protection requirements may be stated independently of the facilities provided by a particular operating system.

3. The means for enforcement need not be provided by the designer of a subsystem.

4. A declarative notation is natural because access privileges are closely related to the linguistic concept of data type.

How can a protection mechanism be implemented by the translator of a programming language? The conventional responsibility of a language implementation is the translation of algorithm statements in the programming language into a sequence of machine code that will carry out the algorithm on a target machine. If protection domains can also be specified, then an implementation must ensure that any translation it provides cannot enable a process to gain access to resources outside of its prescribed domain, regardless of the correctness of the algorithm statement given by the programmer. There is a significant difference between providing an implementation of program statements and of protection specifications. Statements are procedural and can be translated directly on a line-by-line basis into a sequence of machine code. Protection specifications, however, are non-procedural. They must be interpreted by an agent provided by an implementation.

Perhaps the greatest obstacle to embedding protection specifications in a programming language has been the lack of standard, or even roughly equivalent, means of protection enforcement mechanisms across a variety of computer systems. Although most commercially available computers provide sufficient hardware and operating system support to perform a straightforward translation of programs written in any of the statement-oriented programming languages, such as Fortran, Cobol, Algol, PL/1, or Pascal, relatively few systems provide support for the protection of individual storage segments within the workspace of a user.

There are a variety of techniques that can be provided by a programming language implementation to enforce protection, but any of these must depend for security upon some degree of support from an underlying machine and its operating system. For example, suppose a language were used to generate code to run on the Cambridge CAP system. On this system, every storage reference made on the underlying hardware occurs indirectly through a capability. This restriction prevents any process from accessing a resource outside of its protection environment at any time. However, a program may impose arbitrary restrictions on how a resource may be used during execution of a particular code segment by any process. Such restrictions can most readily be implemented by using the software capabilities provided by CAP. A language implementation might provide standard, protected procedures to interpret software capabilities that would realize the protection policies that could be specified in the language. This scheme puts policy specification at the disposal of the programmers, while freeing them from the details of implementing its enforcement.

Even if a system does not provide a protection kernel as powerful as those of Hydra, CAP, or Multics, there are still mechanisms available for implementing protection specifications given in a programming language. The principal distinction will be that the *security* of this protection will not be as great as that supported by a protection kernel, because the mechanism must rely on more assumptions about the operational state of the system. A compiler can separate references for which it can certify that no protection violation could occur from those for which a violation might be possible and treat them differently. The security provided by this form of protection rests on the assumption that the code generated by the compiler will not be modified prior to or during its execution.

What, then, are the relative merits of enforcement based solely on a kernel, as opposed to enforcement provided largely by a compiler?

- **Security**. Enforcement by a kernel provides a greater degree of security of the protection system itself, than does the generation of protection-checking code by a compiler. In a compiler-supported scheme, security rests on correctness of the translator, on some underlying mechanism of storage management that protects the segments from which compiled code is executed, and ultimately, on the security of files from which a program is loaded. Some of these same considerations also apply to a software-supported protection kernel, but to a lesser degree, since the kernel may reside in fixed physical storage segments and may be loaded only from a designated file. With a tagged capability system, in which all address computation is performed either by hardware or by a fixed microprogram, even greater security is possible. Hardware-supported protection is also relatively immune to protection violations that might occur as a result of either hardware or system software malfunction.

- **Flexibility**. There are limits to the flexibility of a protection kernel in implementing a user-defined policy, although it may supply adequate facilities for the system to provide enforcement for its own policies. With a programming language, protection policy can be declared and enforcement provided as needed by an implementation. If a language does not provide sufficient flexibility, it can be extended or replaced, with less perturbation of a system in service than would be caused by the modification of an operating system kernel.

- **Efficiency**. The best efficiency is obtained when enforcement of protection is directly supported by hardware (or microcode). Insofar as software support is required, language-based enforcement has the advantage that static access enforcement can be verified off-line at compile time. Also, since the enforcement mechanism can be tailored by an intelligent compiler to meet the specified need, the fixed overhead of kernel calls can often be avoided.

In summary, the specification of protection in a programming language allows the high-level description of policies for the allocation and use of resources. A language implementation can provide software for protection enforcement when automatic hardware-supported checking is unavailable. In addition, it can interpret protection specifications to generate calls on whatever protection system is provided by the hardware and the operating system.

Morris [1973] proposed a kind of "software capability" that could be used as an object of computation. Inherent in his concept was the idea that certain program components might have the privilege of creating or of examining these software capabilities. A capability-creating program would be able to execute a primitive operation that would seal a data structure, rendering its contents inaccessible to any program components that did not hold either the seal or unseal privileges. They might copy it, or pass its address to other program components, but could not gain access to its contents. The motivation for introducing such software capabilities is to bring a protection mechanism into the programming language. The only problem with the concept as proposed is that the use of the **seal** and **unseal** operations takes a procedural approach to specifying protection. A non-procedural or declarative notation seems a preferable way to make protection available to the applications programmer.

What is needed is a safe, dynamic access control mechanism for distributing capabilities to system resources among user processes. If it is to contribute to the overall reliability of a system, the access control mechanism should be safe to use. If it is to be useful in practice, it should also be reasonably efficient. This requirement has led to the development of a number of new language constructs that provide a mechanism for the safe and efficient distribution of capabilities among customer processes ([Silberschatz et al. 1977], [Kieburtz and Silberschatz 1978], and [McGraw and Andrews 1979]). These mechanisms ensure that a user process will use the managed resource only if it was granted a capability. However, they do not ensure that the user process will use the shared resources correctly. A mechanism is needed to allow the programmer to declare:

- Restrictions on the specific operations that a particular process may invoke on an allocated resource (for example, a reader of a file should only be allowed to read the file, while a writer should be able both to read and to write). It should not be necessary to grant the same set of rights to every user process, and it should be impossible for a process to enlarge its set of access rights, except with the authorization of the access control mechanism.

- Restrictions on the order in which a particular process may invoke
  the various operations of a resource (for example, a file must be
  opened before it can be read). It should be possible to give two
  processes different restrictions on the order in which they can
  invoke the operations of the allocated resource.

A specification notation called *access right expressions* for allowing
such restrictions to be declared was recently proposed by Kieburtz and
Silberschatz [1983]. Access right expressions ensure that a process can
only use specified operations and that the process invokes the
operations only in a sequence anticipated by the designer of the
resource. The notation is based on regular expressions, which provide a
familiar framework and seem to have sufficient expressive power to
describe most of the sequencing constraints of practical interest.

The incorporation of protection concepts into programming
languages, as a practical tool for system design, is at present only in its
infancy. It is likely that protection will become a matter of greater
concern to the designers of new systems with distributed architectures
and increasingly stringent requirements on data security. As this comes
to pass, the importance of suitable language notations in which to
express protection requirements will be more widely recognized.

11.10 Protection Problems

The mechanisms we have outlined so far provide an operating system
with powerful tools for the construction of arbitrary protection policies.
The problem of protecting information in an operating system has
received significant attention in recent years. Several important problems
have been defined, not all of which have easy (or possible) solutions.

- **Modification**. When a user passes an object as an argument to a
  procedure, it may be necessary to ensure that the procedure cannot
  modify the object. This restriction can be readily implemented by
  passing an access right that does not have the modification (write)
  right. However, if amplification may occur (such as in Hydra), the
  right to modify may be reinstated. Thus the user protection
  requirement can be circumvented.

  In general, of course, a user may trust that a procedure indeed
  performs its task correctly. This assumption, however, is not true,
  because of hardware or software errors. Hydra solves this problem
  by restricting amplifications.

- **Limiting propagation of access rights**. When the owner of an object wants to allow some users to share access to its object, it may also want to ensure that those users cannot in turn propagate the access rights to other unauthorized users. This can be accomplished by associating the *copy* and *owner* rights only with the owner of the object. Note that this restriction does not completely solve the problem, since user A (who has access permission) may allow user B (who does not have access permission) to log in as user A and access the object.

- **Revocation**. A user or a system may want to revoke a previously granted access right to an object for a number of different reasons. We discussed how revocation can be accomplished in Section 11.7.

- **Trojan horse**. Many systems have mechanisms for allowing programs written by users to be used by other users. If these programs are executed in a domain which provides the access rights of the executing user, they may misuse these rights. Inside a text editor program, for example, there may be code to search the file to be edited for certain keywords. If any are found, the entire file may be copied to a special area accessible to the creator of the text editor. A code segment which misuses its environment is called a Trojan horse.

- **Mutual suspicion**. Consider the case where a program is provided that can be invoked as a service by a number of different users. This service program may be a subroutine to sort an array, a compiler, an auditor, or a game. When users invoke this service program, they take the risk that the program may malfunction and either damage their data or retain some access right to their files to be used (without authority) later. Similarly, the service program may have some private files (for accounting purposes, for example) that should not be accessed directly by the calling user program. This problem is called the *mutually suspicious subsystem problem*. The procedure call mechanism of Hydra was designed as a direct solution to this problem.

- **Confinement**. The *copy* and *owner* rights provide us with a mechanism to limit the propagation of access rights. They do not, however, provide us with the appropriate tools for preventing the propagation of information (that is, disclosure of information). The problem of guaranteeing that no information initially held in an object can migrate outside of its execution environment is called the *confinement problem* [Lampson 1973]. This problem is in general unsolvable.

11.11 Security

Protection, as we have discussed it, is strictly an *internal* problem: How do we provide controlled access to programs and data stored in a computer system? Security, on the other hand, requires not only an adequate protection system, but consideration of the *external* environment within which the system operates. Internal protection is not useful if the operator's console is exposed to unauthorized personnel, or if files (that is, tapes and disks) can simply be removed from the computer system and taken to a system with no protection. These security problems are essentially management, not operating system, problems.

The major security problem for operating systems is the *authentication* problem. The protection system depends on an ability to properly identify the programs and processes that are executing. This ability, in turn, eventually rests on our power to correctly identify each user of the system. Users normally identify themselves. How do we determine if a user's identity is authentic?

The most common approach to authenticating a user identity is the use of user *passwords*. When users identify themselves, they are asked for a password. If the user-supplied password matches the password stored in the system, it is assumed that the user is legitimate.

Passwords are often used to protect objects in the computer system, in the absence of more complete protection schemes. They can be considered a special case of either keys or capabilities. Associated with each resource (such as a file) is a password. Whenever a request is made to use the resource, the password must be given. If the password is correct, access is granted. Different passwords may be associated with different access rights. For example, different passwords may be used for reading, appending, and updating a file.

Passwords have problems, but are extremely common, because they are easy to understand and use. The problems with passwords are related to the difficulty of keeping a password secret. Passwords can be compromised by being guessed or accidentally exposed. Exposure is particularly a problem if the password is written down where it can be read or lost. Short passwords do not leave enough choices to prevent a password from being guessed by repeated trials. For example, a four-digit password provides only 10,000 variations. On the average, only 5,000 would need to be tried before the correct one would be guessed. If a program could be written that would try a password every millisecond, it would then take only about 5 seconds to guess a password. Longer passwords are less susceptible to enumeration.

Passwords can be either system generated or user selected. However, system-generated passwords may be difficult to remember, and thus may be commonly written down. User-selected passwords, however, are often easy to guess (the user's name or initials, for example). Some sites have administrators who occasionally check programmer passwords and notify the programmers if the password is too short or easy to guess.

Several variants on the simple password scheme can be used. For example, the password can be changed frequently. In the extreme, the password is changed for each session. A new password is selected (either by the system or by the user) at the end of *each* session, and that password must be used for the next session. Note that even if a password is misused, it can only be used once, and its use prevents the legitimate user from using it. Consequently, the legitimate user discovers the security violation at the next session, by the use of a now invalid password. Steps can then be taken to correct the situation.

Another approach is to have a set of paired passwords. When a session begins, the system randomly selects and presents one part of a password pair; the user must supply the other part. This approach can be generalized to the use of an algorithm as a password. The algorithm might be an integer function, for example. The system selects a random integer and presents it to the user. The user applies the function and replies with the result of the function. The system also applies the function. If the two results match, access is allowed.

One problem with all of these approaches is the difficulty of keeping the password (or list of password pairs or algorithms) secret. The Unix system uses a variant of the algorithmic password to avoid the necessity of keeping its password list secret [Morris and Thompson 1979]. Each user has a password. The system contains a function that is very difficult (hopefully impossible) to invert, but simple to compute. That is, given a value x, it is very easy to compute the function value $f(x)$. Given a function value $f(x)$, however, it is impossible to compute x. This function is used to encode all passwords. Only the encoded passwords are stored. When a user presents a password, it is encoded and compared against the stored encoded password. Even if the stored encoded password is seen, it cannot be decoded to determine the password. Thus the password file need not be kept secret.

Two management techniques can be used to improve the security of a system. One is *threat monitoring*. The system can check for suspicious patterns of activity in an attempt to detect a security violation. A common example of this scheme is a time-sharing system which counts the number of incorrect passwords given when a user is trying to log in.

More than a few incorrect attempts may signal an attempt to guess a password. Another common technique is an *audit log*. An audit log simply records the time, user and type of all accesses to an object. After security has been violated, the audit log can be used to determine how and when the problem occurred and perhaps the amount of damage done. This information can be useful, both for recovery from the violation and, possibly, in the development of better security measures to prevent future problems.

11.12 Summary

Computer systems contain many objects. These objects need to be protected from misuse. Objects may be hardware (such as memory, cpu time, or I/O devices) or software (such as files, programs, and abstract data types). An access right is permission to perform an operation on an object. A domain is a set of access rights. Processes execute in domains and may use any of the access rights in the domain to access and manipulate objects.

The access matrix is a general model of protection. The access matrix provides a mechanism for protection without imposing a particular protection policy on the system or its users. The separation of policy and mechanism is an important design property.

The access matrix is sparse. It is normally implemented either as access lists associated with each object, or as capability lists associated with each domain. Dynamic protection can be included in the access matrix model by considering domains and the access matrix itself as objects.

Real systems are much more limited, and tend to provide protection only for files. Unix is representative, providing read, write, and execution protection separately for the owner, group, and general public for each file. Multics uses a ring structure in addition to file access. Hydra and the Cambridge CAP system are capability systems which extend protection to user-defined software objects.

Protection is an internal problem. Security must consider both the computer system and the environment (people, buildings, businesses, valuable objects, and threats) within which the system is used. Passwords are commonly used to solve the authentication problem.

Exercises

11.1 What are the main differences between capability lists and access lists?

11.2 A Burroughs B7000/B6000 MCP file can be tagged as sensitive-data. When such a file is deleted, its storage area is overwritten by some random bits. For what purpose would such a scheme be useful?

11.3 In a ring protection system, where level 0 has the greatest access to objects and level n (greater than zero) has fewer access rights, if the access rights of a program at a particular level in the ring structure are considered as a set of capabilities, what is the relationship between the capabilities of a domain at level j and a domain at level i to an object (for $j > i$)?

11.4 Consider a system in which "computer games" can be played by students only between 10 PM and 6 AM, by faculty members between 5 PM and 8 AM, and by the computer center staff at all times. Suggest a scheme for efficiently implementing this policy.

11.5 The RC 4000 system (and others) have defined a tree of processes (called a process tree) such that all of the descendants of a process are given resources (objects) and access rights by their ancestors only. Thus a descendant can never have the ability to do anything that its ancestors cannot do. The root of the tree is the operating system which has the ability to do anything. Assume the set of access rights was represented by an access matrix, A. $A(x,y)$ defines the access rights of process x to object y. If x is a descendant of z, what is the relationship between $A(x,y)$ and $A(z,y)$ for an arbitrary object y?

11.6 A password may become known to other users in a variety of ways. Is there a simple method for detecting that such an event has occurred?

11.7 The list of all passwords is kept within the operating system. Thus if a user manages to read this list, password protection is no longer provided. Suggest a scheme that will avoid this problem. (Hint: use different internal and external representations.)

11.8 What hardware features are needed for efficient capability manipulation? Can these be used for memory protection?

11.9 Consider an environment where a number is associated with each process and object in the system. Suppose that we allow a process with number n to access an object with number m only if $n > m$. What type of protection structure do we have?

11.10 What protection problems may arise if a shared stack is used for parameter passing?

11.11 Suppose a process is given the privilege of accessing an object only n times. Suggest a scheme for implementing this policy.

11.12 If all the access rights to an object are deleted, the object can no longer be accessed. At this point in time the object should also be deleted, and the space it occupies returned to the system. Suggest an efficient implementation of this scheme.

11.13 What is the need-to-know principle? Why is it important for a protection system to adhere to this principle?

11.14 Why is it difficult to protect a system in which users are allowed to do their own I/O?

11.15 Capability lists are usually kept within the address space of the user. How does the system ensure that the user cannot modify the contents of the list?

Bibliographic Notes

The access matrix model of protection between domains and objects developed from the work of Lampson [1969, 1971] and Graham and Denning [1972]. Popek [1974], Saltzer and Schroeder [1975], and Jones [1978] provide excellent surveys on the subject of protection. Harrison et al. [1976] used a formal version of this model to enable them to mathematically prove properties of a protection system.

The concept of a capability has evolved from Iliffe's and Jodeit's *codewords* which were implemented in the Rice University computer [Iliffe 1962]. The term capability was introduced by Dennis and Van Horn [1966]. The capability concept was further developed by Lampson [1969, 1971] and Jones [1973].

Capability-based protection systems include the Chicago Magic Number Computer [Fabry 1971], the BCC 5000 of the Berkeley Computer Corporation [Lampson 1969], the SUE system for the IBM 360 at the University of Toronto [Sevick 1972], the CAL system [Lampson and Sturgis 1976], the Plessey System 250 [Cosserat 1974, England 1974], Hydra [Wulf et al. 1974, Cohen and Jefferson 1975, Levin et al. 1975, Wulf et al. 1981], the CAP system [Needham and Walker 1974, 1977], UCLA Secure Unix [Popek et al. 1979], and iMAX for the Intel iAPX 432 [Kahn et al. 1981]. A general discussion concerning capability machines has been written by Lampson and Sturgis [1976].

The use of capabilities for addressing has been discussed by Evans and Leclerc [1967], Williams [1972], England [1974], Fabry [1974], and Saltzer and Schroeder [1975]. Capability-based addressing systems include the Plessey System 250 [England 1974] and CAP system [Needham and Walker 1977]. Descriptors, which are similar to capabilities, are used for addressing in Multics [Organick 1972] and the large Burroughs systems [Organick 1973].

Discussions concerning the Multics ring protection system have been written by Graham [1968], Organick [1972], Schroeder and Saltzer [1972], and Saltzer [1974].

Revocation has been discussed by Redell [1974], Redell and Fabry [1974], Neumann et al. [1975], Cohen and Jefferson [1975], and Ekanadham and Bernstein [1979].

The confinement problem was first discussed by Lampson [1973]. Additional discussion has been offered by Lipner [1975]. The Trojan horse problem was discussed by Anderson [1972], Branstad [1973], and Linde [1975].

Popek [1974], Saltzer and Schroeder [1975], and Rushby [1981] have discussed the principle of the least common mechanism.

The use of higher-level languages for specifying access control was first suggested by Morris [1973]. Silberschatz et al. [1977], Kieburtz and Silberschatz [1978], and Andrews and McGraw [1979] have proposed various language constructs for dealing with general dynamic resource management schemes. Jones and Liskov [1976, 1978] considered the problem of how a static access control scheme can be incorporated in a programming language that supports abstract data types, and how compile-time checking can be effectively used to check access control.

The issue of security was discussed by Comber [1969], Weissman [1969], Conway et al. [1972], Popek [1974], Saltzer [1974], Saltzer and Schroeder [1975], Hoffman [1977], Hsiao et al. [1979], and Denning [1982b].

Survey papers have been written by Popek [1974], Denning [1976], and Linden [1976]. Textbook discussions are offered by Watson [1970, Section 5.4], Tsichritzis and Bernstein [1974, Chapter7], Lister [1975, Chapter 9], Wilkes [1975, Chapter 6], Habermann [1976, Sections 9.4 and 9.5], and Levy [1984].

12

Design Principles

Most of this book has dealt with algorithms and data structures for solving specific problems that arise in operating systems. How do all of these parts fit together in an operating system? In this chapter, we will discuss the problems of designing and implementing an operating system. There are, of course, no complete solutions to the design problems, but there are approaches which have been successfully tried.

12.1 Goals

The first problem in designing an operating system is to define the goals and specifications of the system. At the highest level, the design of the system will be significantly affected by the choice of hardware and type of system: batch, time-shared, single-user, multi-user, distributed, real-time, or general purpose.

Beyond this highest design level, on the other hand, the requirements may be much harder to specify. The requirements can basically be divided into two groups: *user* goals and *system* goals.

12.1.1 User Goals

Users desire certain obvious properties in a system. The system should be convenient to use, easy to learn, easy to use, reliable, safe, and fast. Of course, these specifications are not very useful in the system design, since there is no general agreement on how to achieve these goals.

12.1.2 System Goals

A similar set of requirements can be defined by those people who must design, create, maintain, and operate the system. The operating system should be easy to design, implement, and maintain; it should be flexible, reliable, error-free, and efficient. Again, these requirements are vague and have no general solution.

There is no unique solution to defining the requirements for an operating system. The wide range of systems shows that different requirements can result in quite a variety of solutions for different environments. For example, the requirements for CP/M, a single-user system for microcomputers, must have been quite different from those for MVS, the large multi-user, multi-access operating system for IBM mainframes.

The specification and design of an operating system is a highly creative task. No mere textbook can solve that problem. There are, however, some general principles which have been suggested. *Software engineering* is the general field for these principles, but some ideas from this field are especially applicable to operating systems.

12.2 Mechanisms and Policies

One very important principle is the separation of *policy* from *mechanism*. Most of the discussion of this book has centered on mechanisms. Mechanisms determine how to do something. In contrast, policies decide *what* will be done.

For example, a priority cpu scheduling algorithm specifies how the cpu can be switched from process to process. The definition of priorities for the processes is a policy decision. The discussion in Chapter 11 showed several mechanisms for controlling access to resources. Protection mechanisms only provide the means to control access; policy decisions must decide how they are to be used.

The separation of policy and mechanism is very important for flexibility. Policies are likely to change from place to place or time to time. In the worst case, each change in policy would require a change in the underlying mechanism. A general mechanism would be more desirable. A change in policy would then only require redefining certain parameters of the system.

Policy decisions are important for all resource allocation and scheduling problems. Whenever it is necessary to decide whether or not to allocate a resource, a policy decision is being made.

12.3 Layered Approach

A system as large and complex as a modern operating system can only be created by partitioning it into smaller pieces. Each of these smaller pieces should be a well-defined portion of the system with carefully defined inputs, outputs, and function. The modularization can be done in many ways, but the most appealing is the layered approach.

The layered approach consists of breaking the operating system into a number of layers, each built on top of lower layers. The bottom layer is the hardware; the highest is the user interface. Dijkstra [1968b] used the layer approach to design the THE operating system. (The initials stand for his Dutch university: Technische Hogeschool, Eindhoven.) The THE system was defined in 6 layers, as shown in Figure 12.1.

The bottom layer was the hardware. The next layer implemented cpu scheduling as a priority system. The priority of each process was an exponential average of cpu time over real time. This approach gave I/O-bound jobs a higher priority, so they received faster service.

The next layer implemented memory management. The memory-management scheme was paging (512-word pages), using a drum for a backing store. The paging was implemented in software because there was no hardware memory mapping to support it. Pages were therefore extremely visible to the programmer. Before a page was accessed, the operating system was called to bring it into memory. A Least-Recently-Used (LRU) replacement policy was implemented. Global replacement was used, although pages could be temporarily locked into memory. Memory management was above cpu scheduling, since it was necessary to swap pages in and out of memory. During the I/O time required for these transfers, the cpu could be rescheduled.

Level 3 contained the device driver for the operator's console. By placing it, as well as the I/O buffering at Level 4, above memory management, the device buffers could be placed in virtual memory. The

Level 5: User Programs

Level 4: Buffering for input and output devices

Level 3: Operator Console Device Driver

Level 2: Memory Management (Software Paging)

Level 1: CPU Scheduling (priority) P and V operations

Level 0: Hardware

Figure 12.1   THE layer structure

I/O buffering was also above the operator's console, so that I/O error conditions could be output to the operator's console.

The main advantage of the layered approach is *modularity*. The layers are selected in such a way that a layer uses functions and services only of lower-level layers. This approach can make the debugging and verification of the system much easier. The first level can be debugged without any concern for the rest of the system, since, by definition, it uses only the basic hardware (which is assumed correct) to implement its functions. Once the first level is debugged, its correct functioning can be assumed while working on the second level, and so on. If an error is found during the debugging of a particular level, we know that the error must be on that level, since the levels below it are already debugged. Thus the design and implementation of the system is simplified by breaking it into layers.

This approach can be used in many ways. For example, the Venus system [Liskov 1972a], was also designed using a layered approach. The lower levels (0 to 4), dealing with cpu scheduling and memory management, were then put into microcode. This decision provided the advantages of additional speed of execution and a clearly defined interface between the microcoded levels and the higher levels (Figure 12.2).

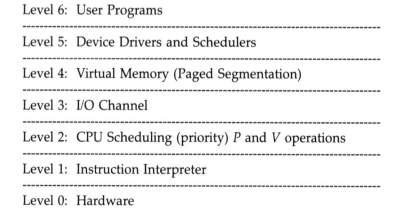

Figure 12.2   Venus layer structure

CP/M also uses a layered design (Figure 12.3). Since CP/M is a single-user system, it is mainly concerned with device drivers and the file system. The first software layer includes the device drivers. The next layer builds a logical file system on the physical device drivers. Finally the user interface, the command interpreter, is built on the logical file system.

The major difficulty with the layered approach involves defining the levels. Since a layer can only use layers at a lower level, careful planning is necessary. For example, the device driver for the backing store must be at a lower level than the virtual memory routines, since virtual memory requires the ability to use the backing store.

Other requirements may not be so obvious. The backing store driver would normally be above the cpu scheduler, since the driver may need to wait for I/O and the cpu can be rescheduled during this time. However, on a large system, the cpu scheduler may have more process control blocks (PCBs) than can fit in memory. Therefore, PCBs may need to be paged in and out of memory, requiring the backing store driver routine to be below the cpu scheduler.

Saxena and Bredt [1975] designed a system to support a very large number of processes. Their system had four levels relating to cpu and memory management. The lowest level was provided by physical memory. The next level used physical memory to represent the state of a fixed number of processes. This scheme allowed the next level to consist of those system processes necessary to implement virtual memory. This virtual memory was then used to store the large number of PCBs that are needed for an arbitrary number of processes. A general cpu scheduler was then implemented in virtual memory.

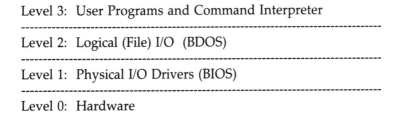

Level 3: User Programs and Command Interpreter

Level 2: Logical (File) I/O (BDOS)

Level 1: Physical I/O Drivers (BIOS)

Level 0: Hardware

Figure 12.3   CP/M layer structure

The requirement that only lower level layers be used by a layer can be a very severe constraint on the system design. It was an important design problem with the SUE system [Sevick 1972], for example. On the other hand, removing this constraint introduces the possibility of infinite recursion and infinite loops. Without the constraint, higher levels may call lower levels which call the higher level back, which calls the lower level again, and so on.

12.4 Virtual Machines

A particularly interesting application of the layered approach to design is the virtual machine concept. The VM operating system for IBM systems is the best example of the virtual machine concept.

By using cpu scheduling and virtual memory techniques, an operating system can create the illusion of multiple processes each executing on its own processor with its own (virtual) memory. Of course, normally, the process has additional features, such as system calls and a file system, which are not provided by the bare hardware. The virtual machine approach, on the other hand, does not provide any additional function, but provides an interface which is *identical* to the underlying bare hardware. Each process is provided with a (virtual) copy of the underlying computer.

The resources of the physical computer are shared to create the virtual machines. CPU scheduling can be used to share the cpu and make it appear that users have their own processor. Demand paging can provide each (virtual) processor with its own (virtual) memory. In fact, the virtual memory for a virtual machine can be larger or smaller than the physical memory of the physical machine. Spooling and a file system can provide virtual card readers and virtual line printers. A normal user time-sharing terminal provides the function of the virtual machine operator's console.

The only real difficulty involves disk systems. Suppose the physical machine has three disk drivers but wants to support seven virtual machines. Clearly, it cannot allocate a disk drive to each virtual machine. Remember that the virtual machine software itself will need substantial disk space to provide virtual memory and spooling. The solution is to provide virtual disks which are identical in all respects except size. These are termed *minidisks* for IBM's VM operating system. Each minidisk is implemented by allocating as many tracks as it needs on the physical disks. Obviously, the sum of the sizes of all minidisks must be less than the actual amount of physical disk space available.

Users thus are given their own virtual machine. They can then run, on their virtual machine, any software desired. For the IBM VM system, a user normally runs CMS, a single-user interactive operating system. The user, therefore, sees a single-user system running on a virtual machine. The virtual machine software is concerned with multiprogramming multiple virtual machines onto a physical machine, but need not consider any user support software. This arrangement may provide a very useful partitioning of the problem of designing a multiuser interactive system into two smaller pieces.

While the virtual machine concept is quite useful and gaining in popularity, it is quite difficult to implement. The difficulty is in providing an *exact* duplicate of the underlying machine. Remember, for example, that the underlying machine has two modes: user mode and monitor mode. The virtual machine software can run in monitor mode, since it is the operating system. The virtual machine itself, can only execute in user mode. Just as the physical machine has two modes, however, so must the virtual machine. Consequently, we must have a virtual user mode and a virtual monitor mode, both of which run in a physical user mode. Those actions which cause a transfer from user mode to monitor mode on a real machine (such as a system call or an attempt to execute a privileged instruction) must also cause a transfer from virtual user mode to virtual monitor mode on a virtual machine.

This transfer can generally be done fairly easily. When a system call, for example, is made by a program running on a virtual machine in virtual user mode, it will cause a transfer to the virtual machine monitor in the real machine. The virtual user mode is also a physical user mode. When the virtual machine monitor gains control, it can then change the register contents and program counter for the virtual machine to simulate the effect of the system call. It can then restart the virtual machine, noting that it is now in virtual monitor mode. If the virtual machine then tries, for example, to read from its virtual card reader, it will execute a privileged I/O instruction. Since the virtual machine is running in physical user mode, this instruction will trap to the virtual machine monitor. The virtual machine monitor must then simulate the effect of the I/O instruction. First it finds the spooled file that implements the virtual card reader. Then it translates the read of the virtual card reader into a read on the spooled disk file and transfers the next virtual "card image" into the virtual memory of the virtual machine. Finally, it can restart the virtual machine. The state of the virtual machine has been modified exactly as if the I/O instruction had been executed with a real card reader for a real machine executing in a real monitor mode.

The major difference is, of course, time. While the real I/O might have taken 100 milliseconds, the virtual I/O might take less time (since it is spooled) or more (since it is interpreted). In addition, the cpu is being multiprogrammed among many virtual machines, further slowing down the virtual machines in unpredictable ways. In the extreme case, it may be necessary to simulate all instructions to provide a true virtual machine. VM works for IBM machines because normal instructions for the virtual machines can execute directly on the hardware. Only the privileged instructions (needed mainly for I/O) must be simulated and hence execute more slowly.

The virtual machine concept has several advantages. Notice that there is complete protection. Each machine is completely isolated from all other virtual machines, so there is no problem with protection. On the other hand, there is no sharing. To provide sharing, two approaches have been implemented. First, it is possible to share a minidisk. This scheme is modeled after a physical shared disk, but implemented by software. With this technique, files can be shared. Second, it is possible to define a network of virtual machines, each of which can send information over the virtual communications network. Again, the network is modeled after physical communication networks, but implemented in software.

Such a virtual machine system is a perfect vehicle for operating systems research and development. Normally, changing an operating system is a difficult process. Since operating systems are large and complex programs, it is difficult to be sure that a change in one point does not cause obscure bugs in some other part. This situation can be particularly dangerous because of the power of the operating system. Since the operating system executes in monitor mode, a wrong change in a pointer could cause an error that would destroy the entire file system. Thus it is necessary to test all changes to the operating system carefully.

But the operating system runs on and controls the entire machine. Therefore, the current system must be stopped and taken out of use, while changes are made and tested. This is commonly called system development time. Since it makes the system unavailable to users, system development time is often scheduled late at night or on weekends.

A virtual machine system can eliminate much of this problem. System programmers are given their own virtual machine and system development is done on the virtual machine, instead of on a physical machine. Normal system operation seldom need be disrupted for system development.

12.5 Multiprocessors

Most of this book has been concerned with single-processor systems, since most systems appear to be single-processor systems. However, there is an increasing trend towards multiprocessor systems, for several reasons. One advantage is throughput. By increasing the number of processors, we would hope to get more work done in a shorter period of time. The speedup ratio with n processors is not n, however, but less than n. When multiple processors cooperate on a task, there is a certain amount of overhead in keeping everything working correctly. This overhead, plus contention for shared resources, lowers the expected gain from additional processors.

Another reason for multiprocessor systems is reliability. If functions can be properly distributed among several processors, then the failure of one processor will not halt the system, but only slow it down. If we have ten processors and one fails, then each of the remaining nine processors must pick up a share of the work of the failed processor. Thus the entire system runs only 10 percent slower, rather than failing altogether. This ability to continue despite hardware failures is called *graceful degradation*. Systems which are designed for graceful degradation are also called *fail-soft*.

Continued operation in the presence of failures requires a mechanism to allow the failure to be detected, diagnosed, and corrected. The Tandem system uses both hardware and software duplication to ensure continued operation despite faults. The system consists of two identical processors, each with its own local memory. The processors are connected by a bus. One processor is the primary and the other is the backup. Two copies are kept of each process; one on the primary machine and the other on the backup. At fixed checkpoints in the execution of the system, all process state information (including a copy of the memory image) is copied from the primary machine to the backup. When a failure is detected, the backup copy is activated and restarted from the most recent checkpoint.

Designing a multiprocessor system is more difficult than designing a single-processor system. The earliest multiprocessor systems used a master/slave mode of operation. One processor, designated the master, would schedule and allocate work to the slave processors. This scheme results in a specialization of function, and is quite common.

For example, one of the most time-consuming activities in a large time-sharing system is simply processing the input and output of characters between the terminals and the computer. If the main cpu must be interrupted for every character for every terminal, it may spend all of its time simply processing characters. To avoid this situation, most systems have a separate front-end processor which handles all the terminal I/O. For example, a large IBM system might use an IBM Series/1 minicomputer as a front-end. The front-end acts as a buffer between the terminals and the main cpu, allowing the main cpu to handle lines and blocks of characters instead of individual characters.

As microprocessors become less expensive and more powerful, additional operating system functions may be off-loaded to slave processors. For example, it would be fairly easy to add a microprocessor with its own memory to manage a disk system. The microprocessor could receive a sequence of requests from the main cpu and implement its own disk queue and scheduling algorithm. This arrangement would relieve the main cpu of the overhead of disk scheduling.

The master/slave design structure has its limitations, however. Although it may increase system efficiency, it decreases system reliability by increasing specialization. An alternative approach is to use several separate identical processors. Each processor runs its own separate copy of the operating system. This scheme increases the overall system availability. However, efficiency may suffer. Since each system is completely separate, one system may sit idle for lack of work, while another is overloaded.

To avoid these inefficiencies, the processors can share certain data structures, such as the job table, resource allocation state, and file system. A multiprocessor system of this form will allow jobs and resources to be shared dynamically between the various processors and can lower the variance between the systems. However, such a system must be very carefully written, because of the shared data structures. As we saw in Chapter 9, a data structure that is shared among concurrently executing processes must be carefully programmed to avoid time-dependent errors. The design and construction of multiprocessor operating systems is still very much an art.

12.6 Implementation

Once an operating system is designed, it must be implemented. Traditionally, operating systems have been written in assembly language. However, that is generally no longer true. Operating systems can now be written in higher-level languages (as described in Chapter 10).

The first system that was not written in assembly language was probably the Master Control Program (MCP) for Burroughs computers. MCP was written in a variant of Algol. Multics, developed at MIT, was written mainly in PL/1. The Unix operating system was mainly written in C. Only some 900 lines of code was in assembly language, most of

which was the dispatcher and device drivers. The Primos operating
system for Prime computers is written in a dialect of Fortran. The Solo
operating system is written in Concurrent Pascal.

The advantages of using a higher-level language, or at least a
systems implementation language, for implementing operating systems
is the same as for application programs: the code can be written faster, it
is more compact, and it is easier to understand and debug. The major
claimed disadvantage is speed and storage requirements. While it is
true that no compiler can produce consistently better code than an
expert assembly language programmer, it is probable that a compiler can
produce code at least as good as that written by the average assembly
language programmer. In addition, replacing the compiler with a better
compiler will uniformly improve the generated code for the entire
operating system by simple recompilation.

As with other systems, major performance improvements are more
likely to be the result of better data structures and algorithms than the
result of cleaner coding. In addition, though operating systems are very
large systems, only a small amount of the code is critical to high
performance; the page fault handler, the cpu scheduler and the
dispatcher are probably the most critical routines. After the system is
written and working correctly, bottleneck routines can be identified and
replaced.

To identify bottlenecks, it is necessary to be able to monitor the
system performance. Code must be added to compute and display
measures of system behavior. In a number of systems, this task is done
by producing trace tapes of system behavior. All interesting events are
logged with their time and important parameters and written to a file or
tape. Later, an analysis program can process the log file to determine
system performance and identify bottlenecks and inefficiencies. These
same trace tapes could also be run as input for a simulation of a
suggested improved system. Trace tapes may also be useful in finding
errors in operating system behavior.

An alternative possibility is to compute and display performance
measures in real time. This approach may allow the system operators to
become more familiar with system behavior and modify its operation in
real time.

12.7 System Generation

It is possible to design, code, and implement an operating system
specifically for one machine at one site. More commonly, however,
operating systems are designed to run on any of a class of machines at a
variety of sites with a variety of peripheral configurations. The system

must then be configured or generated for each specific computer site. This process is known as *system generation* (SYSGEN).

The operating system is normally distributed on tape or disk. To generate a system, a special program is used. The system generation program reads from a file or asks the operator for information concerning the specific *configuration* of the hardware system:

- What cpu is to be used? What options (extended instruction sets, floating point arithmetic, and so on) are installed? For multiple cpu systems each cpu must be described.

- How much memory is available? Some systems will determine this value themselves by referencing memory location after memory location until an "illegal address" fault is generated. This procedure defines the last legal address and hence the amount of available memory.

- What devices are available? The system will need to know how to address each device (its device number), where the device interrupts, its type and model, and any special characteristics.

- What operating system options are desired or what parameter values are to be used? These might include how many buffers of which sizes should be used, what cpu-scheduling algorithm is desired, the maximum number of processes to be supported, the round-robin time quantum, and so on.

Once this information is defined, it can be used in several ways. At one extreme, it may be used to modify a copy of the source of the operating system. The operating system would then be completely compiled. Data declarations, initializations, and constants, along with conditional compilation, would produce an output object version of the operating system that is tailored to exactly the system described.

At a slightly less tailored level, the system description could cause the creation of some tables and the selection of modules from a precompiled library. These modules would be linked together to form the generated operating system. Selection would allow the library to contain the device drivers for all supported I/O devices, but only those actually needed would be linked into the operating system. Since none of the system would be recompiled, system generation would be faster, but may result in a system with more generality than is actually needed.

At the other extreme, it would be possible to construct a system which was completely table driven. All of the code would always be a part of the system and selection would occur at execution time, not compile or link time. System generation involves simply creating the appropriate tables to describe the system.

The major differences among these approaches are the size and generality of the generated system and the ease of modification as the hardware configuration changes. Consider the cost of modifying the system to support a newly acquired graphics terminal or another disk drive. Balanced against that cost, of course, is the frequency (or infrequency) of such changes.

12.8 Summary

The design of a new operating system is a major task. It is very important that the goals of the system be well-defined before the design begins. The type of system desired is the foundation for choices between various algorithms and strategies that will be necessary.

Since an operating system is quite large, modularity is very important. The design of a system as a sequence of layers is considered an important design technique. The virtual machine is a particular layered design that can separate the problems of designing a user interface from the problems of providing a multiprogrammed system.

Operating systems are now almost always written in a systems implementation language or a higher-level language. This feature improves their implementation, maintenance, and portability. To create an operating system for a particular machine configuration, system generation is needed.

Exercises

12.1 Describe the following operating system components

   a. Memory management.

   b. CPU scheduling.

   c. File system directory.

   d. Deadlock considerations.

   for a basic dedicated interactive (such as APL or BASIC) time-shared system that has only one set of bounds (1 upper/1 lower bound) registers.

12.2 What design changes would occur in the system of Exercise 12.1 if you are given 2 bounds registers?

12.3 Someone once defined an operating system as "...that large store overhead provided, by a thoughtful manufacturer, to use large amounts of processor time in order to delay normal work turnaround!" For each of the following modules, describe what it is that justifies the *overhead* of having a file system: an I/O system, a job control system, console control, store management, and processor scheduling.

12.4 If operating systems have always been, in reality, the *control mechanisms* of our computer systems, what are some of the specific *control problems* (that is, supervisory and control functions) involved in operating systems viewed as processor schedulers and memory managers?

12.5 For the following parts of a layered operating system, what is the order of the layers?

a. Paged memory management.

b. CPU scheduling.

c. I/O scheduling and handling.

d. Pascal compiler.

e. Control card interpreter.

Assume the lowest level is the hardware and the highest level is the user.

12.6 Suppose you need to design a time-shared operating system to provide BASIC and APL for engineering students. The system will have 32 hardwired CRT terminals, a line printer and two big moving-head disks. The hardware supports user/supervisor modes, protected I/O instructions, and paging memory management hardware. Describe briefly how you would approach the following problems:

a. CPU scheduling.

b. Memory management.

c. Disk scheduling.

d. File system.

e. User identification and access control protection.

f. Deadlock.

12.7 Compare and contrast the various operating system organization for multiprocessor systems.

12.8 Why is it necessary to have multiple processors in a fail-soft system?

12.9 Is it simpler to provide a copy of the host machine, rather than an arbitrary machine, in a virtual machine environment?

Bibliographic Notes

Design issues have been considered by Watson [1970, Sections 1.3 and 1.4] and Tsichritzis and Bernstein [1974, Chapter 8]. Fundamental ideas on the design methodology for large systems like operating systems have been presented by Liskov [1972b] and Parnas [1972a, 1972b, 1972c].

The layered approach to operating systems design has been advocated by Dijkstra [1968b]. A good general discussion of the overall philosophy was presented by Saxena and Bredt [1975], Habermann et al. [1976], and Denning [1976]. The bottom-up method of design has been used by Dijkstra [1968b] (the THE system), Sevick [1972] (the SUE system), Liskov [1972a] (the Venus system), and Neumann et al. [1975] (the SRI provably secure operating system). Parnas and Darringer [1967], Zurcher and Randell [1968], and Graham et al. [1971] have considered the top-down approach to design.

Brinch Hansen [1970] was an early proponent of the construction of an operating system as a kernel (or nucleus) upon which can be built more complete systems. A computer architecture for supporting level structured operating systems was described by Bernstein and Siegel [1975].

The first operating system to provide a virtual machine was CP/67 on an IBM 360/67 [Meyer and Seawright 1970]. CP/67 provided each user with a virtual 360 Model 65 including I/O devices. The commercially available IBM VM/370 operating system is derived from CP/67 [Seawright and MacKinnon 1979]. Hall et al. [1980] promoted the use of virtual machines for increasing operating system portability. Jones [1978] suggested the use of virtual machines to enforce the isolation of processes for protection purposes.

The issue of reliability has been discussed by Parnas [1975b], Randell [1975], and Wulf [1975]. Survey papers were written by Denning [1976], Linden [1976], and Randell et al. [1978]. The Tandem approach to fail-soft design has been described by Levy [1978], Katzman [1978], and Bartlett [1978].

The issue of operating system portability has been discussed by Cox [1975], Miller [1978] (a portable Unix operating system), and Cheriton et al. [1979] (the Thoth portable operating system).

Corbato [1969], Lang [1970], Wulf et al. [1971], and Sammet [1971] have discussed higher-level system implementation languages. A variant of Algol was used in writing the Burroughs MCP operating system. PL/1 was used in writing the Multics system [Corbato 1969]. A variant of Fortran was used in writing the Primos operating system. The TI 990 operating system was written in a Pascal-like language with features for controlling concurrency. Higher-level languages that have been designed specifically for system implementation include PL/360 [Wirth 1968] for the IBM system/360 family of computers, SAL [Lang 1969] for the Atlas II computer, BCPL [Richards 1969] for the KDF9 computer, Bliss [Wulf et al. 1971] for the PDP-10 computer, and C [Kernighan and Ritchie 1978] for the Unix operating system.

13

Distributed Systems

A recent trend in computer systems is to distribute computation among several physical processors. There are basically two schemes for building such systems. In a **tightly coupled** system, the processors share memory and a clock. In these *multiprocessor* systems, communication usually takes place through the shared memory (Chapter 9).

In a **loosely coupled** system, the processors do not share memory or a clock. Instead, each processor has its own local memory. The processors communicate with each other through various communication lines, such as high-speed buses or telephone lines. These systems are usually referred to as *distributed* systems.

In this chapter we consider distributed systems. We contrast the main differences in operating system design between these types of systems and the centralized systems with which we were previously concerned.

13.1 Motivation

The processors in a distributed system may vary in size and function. They may include small microprocessors, work stations, minicomputers, and large general-purpose computer systems. These processors are referred to by a number of different names such as *sites*, *nodes*, *computers*, and so on, depending on the context in which they are mentioned. We mainly use the term *site*, in order to emphasize the physical distribution of these systems.

There are four major reasons for building distributed systems: *resource sharing*, *computation speed-up*, *reliability*, and *communication*. In this section, we briefly elaborate on each of them.

13.1.1 Resource Sharing

If a number of different sites (with different capabilities) are connected to each other, then a user at one site may be able to use the resources available at another. For example, a user at site *A* may be using a laser printer available only at site *B*. Meanwhile, a user at *B* may access a file that resides at *A*. In general, resource sharing in a distributed system provides mechanisms for sharing files at remote sites, processing information in a distributed database, printing files at remote sites, using remote specialized hardware devices (such as a high-speed array processor), and other operations.

13.1.2 Computation Speed-up

If a particular computation can be partitioned into a number of subcomputations that can run concurrently, then the availability of a distributed system may allow us to distribute the computation among the various sites, to run it concurrently. In addition, if a particular site is currently overloaded with jobs, some of them may be moved to other, lightly loaded, sites. This movement of jobs is called *load sharing*.

13.1.3 Reliability

If one site fails in a distributed system, the remaining sites can potentially continue operating. If the system is composed of a number of large autonomous installations (that is, general-purpose computers), the failure of one of them should not affect the rest. If, on the other hand, the system is composed of a number of small machines, each of which is responsible for some crucial system function (such as terminal character I/O or the file system), then a single failure may effectively halt the operation of the whole system. In general, if enough redundancy exists in the system (in both hardware and data), the system can continue with its operation, even if some of its sites have failed.

The failure of a site must be detected by the system, and appropriate action may be needed to recover from the failure. The system must no longer use the services of that site. In addition, if the function of the failed site can be taken over by another site, the system must ensure that the transfer of function occurs correctly. Finally, when the failed site recovers or is repaired, mechanisms must be available to integrate it back into the system smoothly.

13.1.4 Communication

When a number of sites are connected to each other by a communication network, the users at different sites have the opportunity to exchange information. Many systems have modeled this communication system on the post office. In a distributed system we refer to such activity as *electronic mail*.

Each user in the network is given a *mailbox*, a unique name within each site. A user can send mail to another user at the same site or at a different site. *Mail* is text that is not interpreted by the operating system. The user must provide an address to which the mail can be sent. An address is a mailbox name plus the name of a site. (The site name can be omitted in intra-site communication.) When the operating system transmits mail to its destination, it also appends the address (mailbox name) of the sender. This return address can be used if mail cannot be delivered, or if the receiver wants to reply to the sender.

Mail that has not yet been delivered is kept in a queue associated with the mailbox. Once a mail message has been read, the user has several options, including **saving** it for later use, **deleting** it, **forwarding** it to another mailbox (this choice requires the generation of a new address), or sending a **reply** message to the original sender. An application program generally provides the interface between the user and the mail subsystem. Users can read new mail and browse through old mail at their convenience.

The similarity between an electronic mail system, which is an application visible to the users, and a message system (as discussed in Section 9.8), which is intended for communication between processes, should be apparent. An operating system which was designed as a collection of processes that communicate through a message system (like the Accent system), can be easily extended to a distributed system.

13.2 Topology

The sites in the system can be physically connected in a variety of ways. Each configuration has some advantages and disadvantages. We briefly describe some of the most common configurations implemented to date, and compare them with respect to the following criteria:

- **Basic cost**. How expensive is it to link the various sites in the system?

- **Communication cost**. How long does it take to send a message from site A to site B?

- **Reliability**. If a link or a site in the system fails, can the remaining sites still communicate with each other?

The various topologies are depicted as graphs whose nodes correspond to sites. An edge from node A to node B corresponds to a direct connection between the two sites.

13.2.1 Fully Connected

In a fully connected network, each site is directly linked with all other sites in the system (Figure 13.1). The basic cost of this configuration is very high, since a direct communication line must be available between every two sites. The basic cost grows as the square of the number of sites. In this environment, however, messages between the sites can be sent very fast; a message only needs to use one link to travel between any two sites. In addition, such systems are very reliable, since many links must fail to partition the system. A system is *partitioned* if it has been split into two (or more) subsystems whose sites can no longer communicate with sites in other subsystems.

13.2.2 Partially Connected

In a partially connected network, direct links exist between some, but not all, pairs of sites (Figure 13.2). Hence, the basic cost of this configuration is lower than that of the fully connected network. However, a message from one site to another may have to be sent through several intermediate sites, resulting in slower communication. For example, in the system depicted in Figure 13.2, a message from site *A* to site *D* must be sent through sites *B* and *C*.

In addition, a partially connected system is not as reliable as a fully connected network. The failure of one link may partition the network. For the example in Figure 13.2, if the link from *B* to *C* fails, then the network is partitioned into two subsystems. One subsystem includes sites *A*, *B*, and *E*; the second subsystem includes sites *C* and *D*. The sites in one partition cannot communicate with the sites in the other. To minimize this possibility, each site is usually linked to at least two other sites. For example, if we add a link from *A* to *D*, the failure of a single link cannot result in the partition of the network.

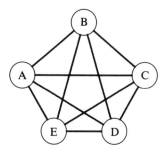

Figure 13.1   Fully connected network

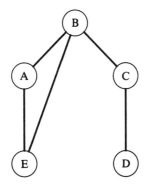

Figure 13.2   Partially connected network

13.2.3 Hierarchy

In a hierarchical network, the sites are organized as a tree (Figure 13.3). This is a common organization for corporate computer networks. Individual offices are linked to the local main office. Main offices are linked to regional offices; regional offices are linked to corporate headquarters.

Each site (except the root) has a unique parent, and some number of children. The basic cost of this configuration is generally less than the partially connected scheme. In this environment, a parent and child communicate directly. Siblings may communicate with each other only through their common parent. A message from one sibling to another must be sent up to the parent, and then down to the sibling. Similarly,

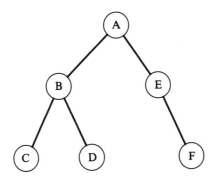

Figure 13.3   Tree structured network

cousins can communicate with each other only through their common grandparent.

If a parent site fails, then its children can no longer communicate with each other or with other processes. In general, the failure of any node (except a leaf) may partition the network into several disjoint subtrees.

13.2.4 Star

In a star network, one of the sites in the system is connected to all other sites (Figure 13.4). None of the other sites is connected to each other. The basic cost of this system is linear in the number of sites. The communication cost is also low, since a message from process A to B requires at most two transfers (from A to the central site and then from the central site to B). This speed may be somewhat misleading, however, since the central site may become a bottleneck. Consequently, even though the number of message transfers needed is low, the time required to send these messages may be high. In many star systems, therefore, the central site is completely dedicated to the message-switching task.

If the central site fails, the network is completely partitioned.

13.2.5 Ring

In a ring network, each site is physically connected to exactly two other sites (Figure 13.5a). The ring can be either unidirectional or bidirectional. In a unidirectional architecture, a site can transmit information to only

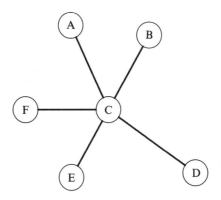

Figure 13.4   Star network

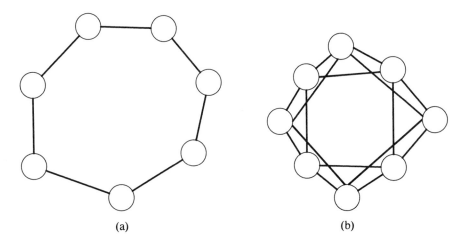

(a)   (b)

Figure 13.5   Ring networks (a) Single links and (b) Double links

one of its neighbors. All sites must send information in the same
direction. In a bidirectional architecture, a site can transmit information
to both of its neighbors. The basic cost of a ring is again linear in the
number of sites. However, the communication cost can be quite high. A
message from one site to another travels around the ring until it reaches
its destination. In a unidirectional ring, this could require $n-1$ messages.
In a bidirectional ring, at most $n/2$ messages are needed.

In a bidirectional ring, two links must fail to partition the network.
In a unidirectional ring, a single site failure (or link failure) would
partition the network. One remedy is to extend the architecture by
providing double links, as depicted in Figure 13.5b.

13.2.6 Multi-Access Bus

In a multi-access bus network, there is a single shared link (the bus). All
of the sites in the system are directly connected to that link, which may
be organized as a straight line (Figure 13.6a) or as a ring (Figure 13.6b).
The sites can communicate with each other directly through this link.
The basic cost of the network is linear in the number of sites. The
communication cost is quite low, unless the link becomes a bottleneck.
Notice that this network topology is similar to the star network with a
dedicated central site. The failure of one site does not affect
communication between the rest of the sites. However, if the link fails,
the network is completely partitioned.

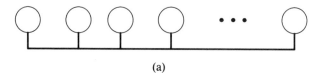

(a)

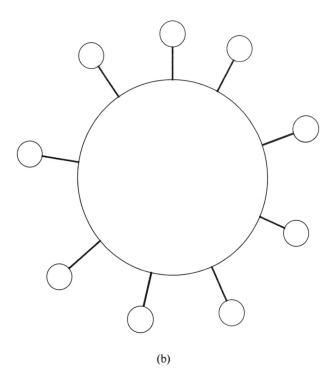

(b)

Figure 13.6   Bus network (a) Linear bus and (b) Ring bus

13.3 Communication

The designer of a communication network must address five basic issues:

- **Routing strategies**. How are the messages sent through the network?

- **Connection strategies**. How do two processes send a sequence of messages?

- **Contention**. Since the network is a shared resource, how do we resolve conflicting demands for its use?

- **Security**. How do we keep the content of messages private?

- **Design strategies**. What is the overall design for communication between applications?

In the following sections we elaborate on each of these.

13.3.1 Routing Strategies

When a process at site A wants to communicate with a process at site B, how is the message sent? If there is only one physical path from A to B (such as in a star or hierarchical network), the message must be sent through that path. However, if there are multiple physical paths from A to B, then several routing options exist. Each site has a *routing table*, indicating the alternative paths that can be used to send a message to other sites. The table may include information about the speed and cost of the various communication paths, and it may be updated as necessary.

- **Fixed routing**. A path from A to B is specified in advance and does not change unless a hardware failure disables this path. Usually, the shortest path is chosen, to minimize communication costs.

- **Virtual circuit**. A path from A to B is fixed for the duration of one session. Different sessions involving messages from A to B may have different paths.

- **Dynamic routing**. The path used to send a message from site A to site B is chosen only when a message is sent. Since the decision is made dynamically, separate messages may be assigned different paths. Site A will make a decision to send the message to site C; C, in turn, will decide to send it to site D, and so on. Eventually, a site will deliver the message to B. Usually a site sends a message to another site on that link which is the least used at that particular time.

There are some tradeoffs between these three schemes. Fixed routing cannot adapt to load changes. In other words, if a path has been established between A and B, the messages must be sent along this path, even if the path is heavily used while another possible path is lightly used. This problem is partially remedied by using virtual circuits and can be completely avoided by using dynamic routing. Fixed routing and virtual circuits ensure that messages from *A* to *B* will be delivered in the order in which they were sent. In dynamic routing, messages may arrive out of order. This problem can be remedied by appending a sequence number to each message.

13.3.2 Connection Strategies

There are a number of different ways to connect pairs of processes that want to communicate over the network. The three most common schemes are *circuit switching*, *message switching*, and *packet switching*.

- **Circuit switching**. If two processes want to communicate, a permanent physical link is established between them. This link is allocated for the duration of the communication, and no other process can use that link during this time period (even if the two processes are not actively communicating for a while). This scheme is similar to the telephone system. Once a communication line has been opened between two parties (that is, party *A* calls party *B*), no one else can use this circuit, until the communication is explicitly terminated (for example, when one of the parties hangs up).

- **Message switching**. If two processes want to communicate, a *temporary* link is established for the duration of one message transfer. Physical links are dynamically allocated among users as needed and only allocated for short periods of time. Each message is a block of data, together with some system information (such as the source, the destination, and error-correction codes) that allow the communication network to deliver the message to its destination correctly. This scheme is similar to the post office mailing system. Each letter is considered a message that contains both the destination address and source (return) address. Note that many messages (from different users) can be shipped over the same link.

- **Packet switching**. Messages are generally of variable length. To simplify the system design, communication is commonly implemented with fixed-length messages called *packets*. One logical message may have to be divided into a number of packets. Each packet may be sent to its destination separately, and each one may take a different path through the network. The packets must be reassembled into messages as they arrive.

There are obviously tradeoffs between these schemes. Circuit switching requires setup time but less overhead for shipping each message. Message and packet switching, on the other hand, require less setup time but more overhead per message. Also, in packet switching, each message must be divided into packets and later reassembled.

13.3.3 Contention

Since a link may connect multiple sites, it is possible that several sites may want to transmit information over a link simultaneously. This difficulty occurs mainly in a ring or multi-access bus network. In this case, the transmitted information may become scrambled and must be discarded. The sites must be notified about the problem, so that they can retransmit the needed information. If no special provisions are made, this situation may be repeated, resulting in degraded performance. Several techniques have been developed to avoid repeated collisions, including *collision detection*, *token passing*, and *message slots*.

- **Collision detection.** Before transmitting a message over a link, a site must listen to determine whether another message is currently being transmitted over that link. If the link is free, the site can start transmitting. Otherwise, it must wait (listening) until the link is free. If two or more sites begin transmitting at exactly the same time (each thinking that no one else is using the link), then they must stop transmitting. Each site tries again after some random time interval. Note that when site *A* starts transmitting over a link, it must continuously listen to detect collisions with messages from other sites. The main problem with this approach is that when the system is very busy, many collisions may occur, and thus performance is degraded. This approach has been successfully used in the Ethernet system [Metcalfe and Boggs 1976].

- **Token passing.** A unique message type, known as a *token*, continuously circulates in the system (usually a ring structure). A site wanting to transmit information must wait until the token arrives. It removes the token from the ring and begins to transmit its messages. When the site completes its round of message passing, it retransmits the token. This action, in turn, will allow another site to get hold of the token and start its message transmission. If the token gets lost, then the system must detect the loss and generate a new token. The token is usually generated by declaring an *election*, whose purpose is to elect a unique site. The elected site then starts the token going again. Later, in Section 13.12, we present one election algorithm. A token-passing scheme has been adopted by Primenet [Nelson and Gordon 1978].

- **Message slots**. A number of fixed-length message slots continuously circulate in the system (usually a ring structure). Each slot can hold a fixed-size message along with some control information (such as the source, the destination, and whether the slot is empty or full). A message must wait until an empty slot arrives. It then inserts its message into the slot, setting the appropriate control information. The slot with its message then continues in the network. When it arrives at a particular site, the control information must be inspected to determine whether the slot contains a message for this site. If not, it recirculates the slot and message. Otherwise, it removes the message, resetting the control information to indicate that the slot is empty. The site can then either use the slot to send its own message or release the slot. Since a slot can only contain fixed-size messages, a logical message may have to be broken down into a number of smaller packets, each of which is sent in a separate slot. This scheme has been adopted in the Cambridge Digital Communication Ring [Wilkes and Wheeler 1979].

13.3.4 Security

As computer networks gain popularity, more and more sensitive (classified) information is being transmitted over channels where eavesdropping and message interception are possible. For example, bank accounts, medical records, and criminal records are now routinely transferred between various sites, generally in separate, special-purpose networks. To keep such sensitive information secure, mechanisms must be available to allow a user to protect data transferred over the network.

Encryption is one common method of protecting information transmitted over unreliable links. The information (data) is *encrypted* (encoded) before it is transmitted. On arrival at its destination the data is *decrypted* (decoded). Even if the encrypted information is accessed by an unauthorized person, it will be useless unless it can be decoded. The main issue is the development of encryption schemes that are impossible (or very difficult) to break.

There are a variety of methods to accomplish this task. The most common ones provide a general encryption algorithm E, a general decryption algorithm D, and a secret key (or keys) to be supplied for each application. Let E_k and D_k denote the encryption and decryption algorithms, respectively, for a particular application with a key k. Then the encryption algorithm must satisfy the following properties for any message m:

a. $D_k(E_k(m)) = m$.

b. Both E_k and D_k can be computed efficiently.

c. The security of the system should depend only on the secrecy of the key and not on the secrecy of the algorithms E and D.

One such scheme, called the Data Encryption Standard, was recently adopted by the National Bureau of Standards. This scheme suffers from the *key distribution* problem: before communication can take place, the secret keys must be securely sent to both the sender and receiver. This task cannot be effectively done in a communication network environment. A solution to this problem is to use a *public key encryption* scheme [Diffie and Hellman 1976]. Each user has both a public and a private key, and two users can communicate knowing only each other's public key.

An algorithm based on this concept was recently proposed by Rivest, Shamir, and Adleman [1978]. This algorithm is believed to be almost unbreakable. The public encryption key is a pair (e,n); the private key is a pair (d,n), where e, d, and n are positive integers. Each message is represented as an integer between 0 and $n-1$. (A long message is broken into a series of smaller messages, each of which can be represented as such an integer.) The functions E and D are defined as

$$E(m) = m^e \bmod n = C.$$

$$D(C) = C^d \bmod n.$$

The main problem is choosing the encryption and decryption keys. The integer n is computed as the product of two large (100 digits or more) randomly chosen prime numbers p and q with

$$n = p \times q.$$

The integer d is chosen to be a large, randomly chosen integer relatively prime to $(p-1)\times(q-1)$. That is, d satisfies

$$\text{greatest common divisor}[d,(p-1)\times(q-1)] = 1$$

Finally, the integer e is computed from p, q, and d to be the *multiplicative inverse* of d modulo $(p-1)\times(q-1)$. That is, e satisfies

$$e \times d \bmod (p-1)\times(q-1) = 1.$$

It should be pointed out that although n is publicly known, p and q are not. This condition is due to the well-known fact that it is very difficult to factor n. Consequently, the integers d and e cannot be easily guessed.

Let us illustrate this scheme with an example. Let $p = 5$ and $q = 7$. Then $n = 35$ and $(p-1)\times(q-1) = 24$. Since 11 is relatively prime to 24, we can choose $d = 11$, and since 11×11 **mod** $24 = 121$ **mod** $24 = 1$, $e = 11$. Suppose now that $m = 3$. Then

$$C = m^e \text{ mod } n = 3^{11} \text{ mod } 35 = 12$$

and

$$C^d \text{ mod } n = 12^{11} \text{ mod } 35 = 3 = m$$

Thus, if we encode m using e, we can decode m using d.

13.3.5 Design Issues

When designing a communication network, we must deal with the inherent complexity of coordinating asynchronous operations communicating in a potentially slow and error-prone environment. The design problem (and related implementation) could be simplified by partitioning the problem into multiple layers. Following the International Standards Organization (ISO), we may refer to the layers with the following descriptions:

1. The **physical** layer is responsible for handling both the mechanical and electrical details of the physical transmission of a bit stream.

2. The **data link** layer is responsible for handling the packets, including any error detection and recovery that occurred in the physical layer.

3. The **network** layer is responsible for providing connections and routing packets in the communication network, including handling the address of outgoing packets, decoding the address of incoming packets, and maintaining routing information for proper response to changing loads.

4. The **transport** layer is responsible for low-level access to the network and the transfer of messages between the users, including partitioning messages into packets, maintaining packet order, flow control, and physical address generation.

5. The **session** layer is responsible for implementing the process-to-process protocols.

6. The **presentation** layer is responsible for resolving the differences in formats among the various sites in the network, including character conversions, and half duplex/full duplex (echoing).

7. The **application** layer is responsible for interacting directly with the users. This layer deals with electronic mail, as well as schemas for distributed data bases.

13.4 System Type

There are basically two types of distributed systems: *computer networks* and *local area networks*. The main difference between the two is the way in which they are geographically distributed. Computer networks are composed of a number of autonomous processors that are distributed over a large geographical area (such as the United States), while local area networks are composed of processors that are distributed over small geographical areas, such as a single building or a number of adjacent buildings. These differences imply major variations in the speed and reliability of the communications network, and are reflected in the operating system design.

13.4.1 Computer Networks

Computer networks emerged in the late 1960s, mainly as an academic research project to provide efficient communication between sites, allowing hardware and software to be conveniently and economically shared by a wide community of users. The first network to be designed and developed was the Arpanet [McQuillan and Walden 1977]. Work on the Arpanet began in 1968. It has grown from a four-site experimental network to a nationwide communication system comprising approximately one hundred computer systems. Recently, a number of commercial networks have also appeared on the market. The Telenet system is available within the continental United States, while the Datapac system is available in Canada. These networks provide their customers with the ability to access a wide range of various hardware and software computing resources.

Since the sites in a computer network are physically distributed over a large geographical area, the communication links are by default relatively slow and unreliable. Typical links are telephone lines, microwave links, and satellite channels. These communication links are

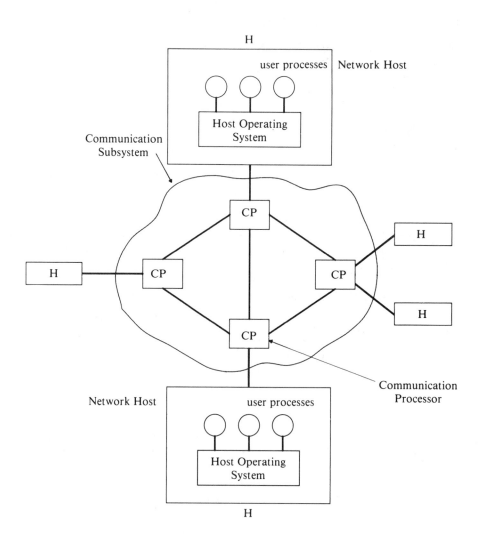

Figure 13.7   Communication processors in a computer network

controlled by special *communication processors* (Figure 13.7), which are responsible for defining the interface through which the sites communicate over the network, as well as transferring information between the various sites.

As a specific example, let us consider the Arpanet. The system provides an ability for geographically separated sites, called *hosts*, to communicate with each other. The host computers typically differ from one another in type, speed, word length, operating system, and so on. Each host computer is connected to the network through a local small computer called an *Interface Message Processor* (IMP). The complete network is formed by interconnecting the IMPs, all of which are virtually identical, through wideband (50 kilobits per second) communications lines supplied by the telephone company. Each IMP is programmed to store and forward packets to the neighboring IMPs in the network. When a host passes a message to its local IMP, the first 32 bits of the message include the network address of a destination host. The message is passed from IMP to IMP through the network until it finally arrives at the destination IMP. The destination IMP passes the message along to the destination host.

13.4.2 Local Area Networks

Local area networks (LANs) emerged in the early 1970s, as a substitute for large mainframe computer systems. It had become apparent that for many enterprises it is more economical to have a number of small computers, each with its own self-contained applications, rather than a single large system. Since each small computer is likely to need a full complement of peripheral devices (such as disks and printers), and since some form of data sharing is likely to occur in a single enterprise, it was a natural step to connect these small systems into a network.

Local area networks are usually designed to cover a very small geographical area (such as a single building, or a number of adjacent buildings) and are generally used in an office type environment. Since all the sites in such systems are close to each other, the communication links have a higher speed and lower error rate than their counterparts in computer networks. The most common links are twisted pair, baseband coaxial cable, broadband coaxial cable, and fiber optics. The most common configurations are star, ring, and multi-access bus networks.

A typical LAN may consist of a number of different minicomputers, various shared peripheral devices (such as laser printers or magnetic tape units), work stations, and one or more gateways (specialized processors) that provide access to other networks (Figure 13.8). An Ethernet scheme is commonly used to construct LANs. The

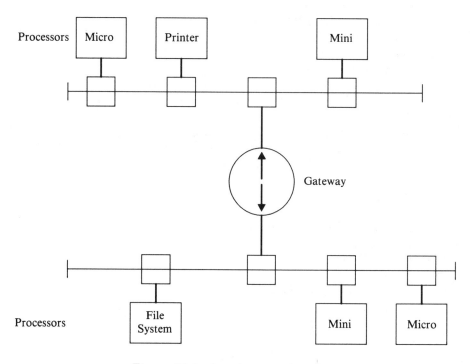

Figure 13.8   Local area network

communication medium is a multi-access coaxial cable with the collision detection scheme described in Section 13.3.3. Messages between the various nodes in the network are sent in packets. Since there is no central controller, new sites can be easily added to the network.

13.5 File Systems

There are two major issues that dominate the design criteria in a distributed file system:

- **Transparency**. Does a user access all of the files in a system in the same manner, regardless of where they reside?

- **Locality**. Where do files reside in the system?

In the following sections, we discuss these issues as they relate to the three most common ways file systems are organized in a distributed environment.

13.5.1 Arpanet FTP

Each site maintains its own local file system. If a user at site A wants to access a file at site B, the file must be explicitly copied from one site to another.

The Arpanet provides a mechanism for such a transfer with the File Transfer Protocol (FTP) program. Suppose that a user wants to copy a remote file F_1 from site B to a local file F_2, and copy local file F_3 to a remote file F_4 at site B. The user must first invoke the FTP program. The program then asks the user for the following information:

a. The name of the site with which the file transfer is to take place (that is, site B).

b. Access information (user name and password), to verify that the user has the appropriate access privileges at site B.

Once this checking has been done, the user can copy remote file F_1 from B by executing:

$$\textbf{get } F_1 \textbf{ to } F_2.$$

Local file F_4 is copied to F_3 by executing:

$$\textbf{send } F_3 \textbf{ to } F_4.$$

In this scheme, the file location is not transparent to the user. Users must know exactly where each file is. Moreover, there is no real file sharing, since a user can only copy a file from one site to another. Thus several copies of the same file may exist, resulting in a waste of space. In addition, if these copies are modified, we may find that the various copies are inconsistent.

13.5.2 Centralized Approach

Each site maintains its own local file system. A file can be accessed only by the users residing on that site. All shared files reside at a single centralized site (called a *file server*). If a user opens a non-local file, the *open* request is channeled to the file server.

In this scheme, the location of a file is transparent to users, who access remote files in the same way as local files. The operating system automatically converts accesses to shared (non-local) files into messages to the file server. The main problem with this scheme is that the file server may become a bottleneck. Every access to a remote file may require a considerable amount of message transfer overhead.

13.5.3 Distributed Approach

Each site maintains its own local file system. In contrast to the centralized approach, a local file can be accessed by a user residing on any site in the system. There are two complementary schemes for handling this approach. The simplest scheme requires the user to know the location of every file to be accessed. The file location is not transparent to users, who must include the file location in every access call. It is not convenient to move files around the system with this scheme since all users must be informed of the new location of the file.

The alternative scheme makes the file location transparent to the user. The user does not need to know where the file resides; remote files are accessed in the same manner as local files. In this scheme it is convenient to move files around the system. The operating system must maintain tables and use algorithms which allow it to find a file anywhere in the network.

13.6 Mode of Computation

A distributed system provides a user with access to the various resources that the system provides. By resources we mean both hardware (such as printers) and software (such as files and programs). In this section, we briefly discuss the various ways access to shared resources is accomplished.

13.6.1 Data Migration

When a user on site A wants to access data (such as a file) that resides at site B, there are two basic methods for the system to transfer the data. One approach is to transfer the entire file to site A. From that point on, all access to the file is local. When the user no longer needs access to the file, a copy of it (if it has been modified) is sent back to site B. Of course, even if only a modest change has been made to a large file, the entire amount of data must be transferred.

The other approach is to transfer to site A only those portions of the file that are actually *necessary* for the immediate task. If another portion is required later, another transfer will take place. When the user no longer wants to access the file, any part of it that has been modified must be sent back to site B. (Note the similarity to demand paging.)

Clearly, if only a small part of a large file is being accessed, the latter approach is preferable. If significant portions of the file are being accessed, it would be more efficient to copy the entire file.

It should be pointed out that it is not sufficient to merely transfer data from one site to another. The system must also perform various data translations if the two sites involved are not directly compatible (for instance, if they use different character code representations or represent integers with a different number of bits).

13.6.2 Computation Migration

In some circumstances, it may be more efficient to transfer the computation, rather than the data, across the system. For example, consider a job that needs to access a number of large files that reside at different sites, to obtain a summary of those files. It would be more efficient to access the files at the sites where they reside and then to return the desired results to the site that initiated the computation.

Such a computation can be carried out in a number of different ways. Suppose that process p wants to access a file at site A. Access to the file is carried out at site A, and could be initiated by a *remote procedure call*. Process p invokes a predefined procedure at site A. The procedure executes appropriately and then returns the needed parameters to p.

Alternatively, process p can send a *message* to site A. The operating system at site A creates a new process q whose function is to carry out the designated task. When process q completes its execution, it sends the needed result back to p by the message system. Note that in this scheme process p may execute concurrently with process q and in fact may have several processes running concurrently on several sites.

Both schemes could be used to access several files residing at various sites. One remote procedure call may result in the invocation of another remote procedure call, or even in the transfer of messages to another site. Similarly, process q could, during the course of its execution, send a message to another site, which in turn creates another process. This process may either send a message back to q or repeat the cycle above.

13.6.3 Job Migration

When a job arrives in the system at a particular site, it may be advantageous to perform the entire job, or parts of it, at different sites. This scheme may be used for several reasons:

- **Load balancing**. The jobs (or subjobs) may be distributed across the network to even the workload.

- **Computation speed-up**. If a single job can be divided into a number of subjobs that may run concurrently on different sites, then the total job turnaround time can be reduced.

- **Hardware preference**. The job may have characteristics that make it more suitable for execution on some specialized processor (such as matrix inversion on an array processor, rather than a microprocessor).

- **Software preference**. The job may require software that is only available at a particular site, and either the software cannot be moved, or it is cheaper to move the job.

There are basically two complementary techniques used to move jobs in a network. The system can attempt to hide the fact that the job has migrated from the user. This scheme has the advantage that programmers do not need to code their programs explicitly to accomplish the migration. This method is usually employed for achieving load balancing and computation speed-up.

The other approach is to allow (or require) the user to specify explicitly how the job should migrate. This method is usually employed when the job must be moved to satisfy some hardware or software preference.

13.7 Event Ordering

In a centralized or tightly coupled system, it is always possible to determine the order in which two events have occurred, since there is a single common memory and clock. In many applications, it is of utmost importance to be able to determine order. For example, in a resource allocation scheme, we specify that a resource can be used only *after* the resource has been granted. In a distributed system, however, there is no common memory and no common clock. Therefore, it is sometimes impossible to say which of two events occurred first. The *happened-before* relation is only a partial ordering of the events in distributed systems. Since the ability to define a total ordering is crucial in many applications, we present below a distributed algorithm, due to Lamport [1978a], for extending the *happened-before* relation to a consistent total ordering of all the events in the system.

13.7.1 The Happened-Before Relation

Since processes are sequential, all events executed in a single process are totally ordered. Also, by the law of causality, a message can be received only after it has been sent. Therefore, we can define the *happened-before* relation (denoted by →) on a set of events as follows (assuming that sending and receiving a message constitutes an event):

1. If A and B are events in the same process, and A was executed before B, then $A \rightarrow B$.

2. If A is the event of sending a message by one process and B is the event of receiving that message by another process, then $A \rightarrow B$.

3. If $A \rightarrow B$ and $B \rightarrow C$ then $A \rightarrow C$.

Since an event cannot happen before itself, the → relation is an irreflexive partial ordering.

If two events, A and B, are not related by the → relation (that is, A did not happen before B, and B did not happen before A), then we say that these two events were executed *concurrently*. In this case, neither event can causally affect the other. If, however, $A \rightarrow B$, then it is possible for event A to causally affect event B.

The definitions of concurrency and *happened-before* can best be illustrated by a space-time diagram, such as Figure 13.9. The horizontal direction represents space (that is, different processes), and the vertical direction represents time. The labeled vertical lines denote processes (or processors). The labeled dots denote events. A wavy line denotes a message sent from one process to another. Using this diagram, it is clear that events A and B are concurrent if and only if no path exists from either A to B or from B to A.

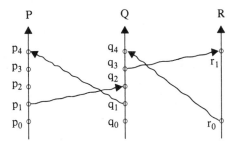

Figure 13.9   Relative time for three concurrent processes

For example, consider Figure 13.9. Some of the events related by the *happened-before* relation are:

$$p_1 \rightarrow q_2$$
$$r_0 \rightarrow q_4$$
$$q_3 \rightarrow r_1$$
$$p_1 \rightarrow q_4 \quad \text{(since } p_1 \rightarrow q_2 \text{ and } q_2 \rightarrow q_4\text{)}.$$

Some of the concurrent events in the system are:

$$q_0 \text{ and } p_2$$
$$r_0 \text{ and } q_3$$
$$r_0 \text{ and } p_3$$
$$q_3 \text{ and } p_3.$$

We cannot know which of two concurrent events, such as q_0 and p_2, happened first. However, since neither event can affect the other (there is no way for one to know if the other has occurred yet), it is not important which of them actually happens first. It is only important that any processes that care about the order of two concurrent events agree on some order.

13.7.2 Implementation

To be able to determine that an event A happened before an event B, we need either a common clock or a set of perfectly synchronized clocks. Since in a distributed system neither of these is available, we must define the *happened-before* relation without the use of physical clocks.

We associate with each system event a *time stamp*. We can then define the *global ordering* requirement: for every pair of events A and B, if $A - B$ then the time stamp of A is less than the time stamp of B. (Note that the converse need not be true.)

How do we enforce the global ordering requirement in a distributed environment? We define within *each* process p_i a *logical clock*, LC_i. The logical clock can be implemented as a simple counter which is incremented between any two successive events executed within a process. Since the logical clock has a monotonically increasing value, it assigns a unique number to every event and if an event A occurs before event B in process p_i, then $LC_i(A) < LC_i(B)$. The time stamp for an event is the value of the logical clock for that event. Clearly, this scheme ensures that for any two events in the same process, the global ordering requirement is met.

Unfortunately, this scheme does not ensure that the global ordering requirement is met across processes. To illustrate the problem, consider two processes p_1 and p_2 that communicate with each other. Suppose that p_1 sends a message to p_2 (event A) with $LC_1(A) = 200$, and p_2 receives the message (event B) with $LC_2(B) = 195$ (because the processor for p_2 is slower than the processor for p_1 and so its logical clock ticks slower). This situation violates our requirement, since $A \rightarrow B$, but the time stamp of A is greater than the time stamp of B.

To resolve this difficulty, we require a process to advance its logical clock when it receives a message whose time stamp is greater than the current value of its logical clock. In particular, if process p_i receives a message (event B) with time stamp t and $LC_i(B) < t$, then it should advance its clock so that $LC_i(B) = t+1$. Thus, in the example above, when p_2 receives the message from p_1, it will advance its logical clock so that $LC_2(B) = 201$.

Finally, to realize a total ordering, we need only to observe that with our time stamp ordering scheme, if the time stamps of two events A and B are the same, then they are concurrent. In this case, we may use process identity to break ties and create a total ordering.

13.8 Synchronization

To solve synchronization problems in a distributed system, we must provide a mechanism to allow us to implement *distributed semaphores*. To simplify our discussion, we restrict our attention here to the problem of implementing a binary semaphore initialized to 1. This is equivalent to solving the mutual exclusion problem. Since we have already shown that a semaphore can be implemented if mutual exclusion is provided in the context of a centralized system, we are only concerned here with a distributed environment in which n processes, each of which reside at a different processor, want to invoke mutual exclusion. To simplify our discussion, we assume that processes are uniquely numbered from 1 to n, and that there is a one-to-one mapping between processes and processors (that is, each process has its own processor).

13.8.1 Centralized Approach

In a centralized approach to providing mutual exclusion, one of the processes in the system is chosen to coordinate the entry to the critical section. Each process that wants to invoke mutual exclusion sends a *request* message to the coordinator. When the process receives a *reply* message from the coordinator, it can proceed to enter its critical section.

After exiting its critical section, the process sends a *release* message to the coordinator and proceeds with its execution.

On receiving a *request* message, the coordinator checks to see whether some other process is in its critical section. If no process is in its critical section, the coordinator immediately sends back a *reply* message. Otherwise, the request is queued. When the coordinator receives a *release* message, it removes one of the request messages from the queue (in accordance with some scheduling algorithm) and sends a *reply* message to the requesting process.

It should be clear that this algorithm ensures mutual exclusion. In addition, if the scheduling policy within the coordinator is fair (such as First-Come-First-Served scheduling), no starvation can occur. This scheme requires three messages per critical section entry: a request, a reply, and a release.

If the coordinator process fails, then a new process must take its place. In Section 13.10, below, we discuss the issue of how such a failure is detected, as well as various algorithms for electing a unique new coordinator. Once a new coordinator has been elected, it must poll all the processes in the system, to reconstruct its request queue. Once the queue has been constructed, the computation may resume.

13.8.2 Fully Distributed Approach

If we want to distribute the decision making across the entire system, then the solution is far more complicated. The first such solution was proposed by Lamport [1978a], who used his event-ordering scheme (Section 13.7) to totally order all the requests to critical sections, serving processes in a first-come-first-served order. Lamport's scheme requires $3 \times (n-1)$ messages per critical section entry. Subsequently, Ricart and Agrawala [1981] proposed a distributed algorithm (also based on Lamport's event-ordering scheme) which requires only $2 \times (n-1)$ messages. We present their algorithm.

When a process p wants to enter its critical section, it generates a new time stamp, TS, and sends the message *request(p,TS)* to all other processes in the system (including itself). On receiving a *request* message, a process may reply immediately (that is, send a *reply* message back to p), or it may defer sending a reply back (because it is already in its critical section, for example). A process that has received a *reply* message from all other processes in the system can enter its critical section. After exiting its critical section, the process sends *reply* messages to all of its deferred requests.

The decision whether process p replies immediately to a *request(q,TS)* message or defers it is based on three factors:

a. If process p is in its critical section, then it defers its reply to q.

b. If process p does *not* want to enter its critical section, then a *reply* is immediately sent out to q.

c. If process p wants to enter its critical section but has not yet entered it, then it compares its own request time stamp, say TS_p, with the time stamp TS_q of the incoming request made by process q. If TS_q is less than TS_p, then a *reply* is immediately sent out to q (q asked first). Otherwise, the reply is deferred.

Ricart and Agrawala [1981] have shown that this algorithm exhibits the following desirable behavior:

a. Mutual exclusion is obtained.

b. Freedom from deadlock is ensured.

c. Freedom from starvation is ensured, since entry to the critical section is scheduled according to the time stamp ordering. The time stamp ordering ensures that processes are served in a first-come-first-served order.

d. The number of messages required is $2 \times (n-1)$. This is the minimum number of required messages per critical section entry when processes act independently and concurrently.

To illustrate how the algorithm functions, consider a system consisting of process 1, process 2, and process 3. Suppose that process 1 and process 3 want to enter their critical sections. Process 1 then sends a *request* (process 1, time stamp 10) message to processes 2 and 3, while process 3 sends a *request* (process 3, time stamp 4) message to processes 1 and 2. The time stamps 4 and 10 were obtained from the logical clocks described in Section 13.7. When process 2 receives these *request* messages, it immediately replies. When process 1 receives the *request* from process 3 it replies immediately, since the time stamp (10) on its own request message is greater than the time stamp (4) for process 3. When process 3 receives the *request* from process 1, it defers its reply, since the time stamp (4) on its request message is less than the time stamp (10) for the message of process 1. On receiving replies from both process 1 and process 2, process 3 can enter its critical section. After exiting its critical section, process 3 sends a *reply* to process 1, which can then enter its critical section.

It should be noted that this scheme requires the participation of all of the processes in the system. This approach has two undesirable consequences:

1. The processes need to know the identity of all other processes in the system. When a new process joins the group of processes participating in the mutual exclusion algorithm, the following actions need to be taken:

    a. The process must receive the names of all the other processes in the group.

    b. The name of the new process must be distributed to all the other processes in the group.

    This task is not as trivial as it may seem, since some *request* and *reply* messages may be circulating in the system when the new process joins the group. We refer the interested reader to the paper by Ricart and Agrawala [1981] for more details.

2. If one of the processes fails, then the entire scheme collapses. This difficulty can be resolved by continuously monitoring the state of all the processes in the system. If one of them fails, then all other processes are notified, so that they will no longer send *request* messages to the failed process. When a process recovers, it must initiate the procedure that allows it to rejoin the group.

13.8.3 Token Passing Approach

Another method of providing mutual execution is to circulate a token among the processes in the system. A token is a special type of message that is passed around the system. Possession of the token entitles its holder to enter the critical section. Since there is only a single token in the system, only one process can be in its critical section at a time.

Ring Structured System

We assume that the processes in the system are *logically* organized in a ring structure (Figure 13.5). The physical communication network need not be a ring. As long as the processes are connected to each other, it is possible to implement a logical ring. To implement mutual exclusion, the token is passed around the ring. When a process receives the token it may enter its critical section, keeping the token. After the process exits its critical section, the token is passed around again. If the process receiving the token does not want to enter its critical section, it passes the token to its neighbor.

It should be clear that only one process can be in its critical section at a time, since there is only a single token. In addition, if the ring is unidirectional, freedom from starvation is ensured. The number of messages required to implement mutual exclusion may vary from one message per entry, in the case of high contention (that is, every process wants to enter its critical section), to an infinite number of messages, in the case of low contention (that is, no one wants to enter its critical section).

Two types of failure must be considered. First, if the token is lost, an election is called and the elected process generates a new token. Second, if a process fails, a new logical ring must be established. There are a number of different algorithms for election and for reconstructing a logical ring. In Section 13.12 below we present an election algorithm. We leave it as an exercise for the reader to develop an algorithm for reconstructing the ring.

Non-Ring Structured Systems

In contrast to the ring structured system, a process holding the token may send it to any of the processes in the system. In addition, the token need not be passed around if no process wishes to enter the critical section.

The algorithm presented below, due to Chandy [1982], ensures that each process requesting entry to its critical section will receive the token within a finite time of requesting entry. There are n processes in the system indexed from 1 to n. Associated with the token is a vector $T = (T_1, T_2, ..., T_n)$, where T_i indicates the number of times process p_i has entered its critical section.

When a process p_i wants to enter its critical section for the m_ith time it sends the message $request(p_i, m_i)$ to all the other processes in the system. It then waits until it receives the token. At that time it sets $T_i := m_i$ in the token vector T, and enters its critical section. After exiting the critical section, process p_i examines the incoming request queue. If the queue is empty it continues with its normal execution until it receives a request message from some other process. In either case, once the queue is not empty, process p_i removes the first request, say (p_j, m_j), from the queue (which is maintained in FIFO order). If $m_j > T_j$ then p_i sends the token to p_j. Otherwise it discards this request (it is an old request that has already been satisfied), removes the next request from the queue and it proceeds as above. This continues until the queue is either empty or the token is sent out to another process.

13.9 Deadlock Handling

The deadlock prevention, avoidance, and detection algorithms presented in Chapter 8 can also be used in a distributed system, provided that appropriate modifications are made. For example, the resource ordering deadlock prevention technique can be used by simply defining a *global* ordering among the system events. That is, all resources in the entire system are assigned unique numbers, and a process may request a resource (at any processor) with unique number i only if it is not holding a resource with a unique number less than or equal to i. Similarly, the banker's algorithm can be used in a distributed system by designating one of the processes in the system (the *banker*) as the process that maintains the information necessary to carry out the banker's algorithm. Every resource request must be channeled through the banker.

These two schemes can be used in dealing with the deadlock problem in a distributed environment. The first scheme is simple to implement and requires very little overhead. The second scheme can also be simply implemented, but it may require too much overhead. The banker may become a bottleneck, since the number of messages to and from the banker may be large. Thus the banker's scheme does not seem to be of practical use in a distributed system.

In this section we present two alternative schemes, which are the most commonly used today, for dealing with the deadlock problem in a distributed system. The first scheme is based on deadlock prevention, while the second one is based on deadlock detection. For simplicity, we consider only the case of a single instance of each resource type.

13.9.1 Time Stamp Ordering Approach

For deadlock prevention, we want to design the system to prevent at least one of the four necessary conditions from holding. The approach we will discuss prevents the circular wait condition by preempting resources if necessary. To control the preemption, we assign a unique priority number to each process. These numbers are used to decide whether a process p_i should wait for a process p_j. For example, we could let p_i wait for p_j if p_i has a higher priority than p_j; otherwise p_i is rolled back. This scheme prevents deadlocks because for every edge (p_i, p_j) in the wait-for graph, p_i has a higher priority than p_j. Thus a cycle cannot exist.

One difficulty with this scheme is the possibility of starvation. Some processes with very low priority may always be rolled back. To avoid this difficulty, Rosenkrantz et al. [1978] have proposed the use of time stamps as priorities. Each process in the system is assigned a unique time stamp when it is created. Two complementary deadlock prevention schemes using time stamps have been proposed.

- The **Wait-Die** scheme is based on a non-preemptive technique. When process p_i requests a resource currently held by p_j, p_i is allowed to wait only if it has a smaller time stamp than p_j (that is, p_i is older than p_j). Otherwise, p_i is rolled back (dies). For example, suppose that processes p_1, p_2, and p_3 have time stamps 5, 10, and 15, respectively. If p_1 requests a resource held by p_2, p_1 will wait. If p_3 requests a resource held by p_2, p_3 will be rolled back.

- The **Wound-Wait** scheme is based on a preemptive technique and is a counterpart to the *wait-die* system. When process p_i requests a resource currently held by p_j, then p_i is allowed to wait only if it has a larger time stamp than p_j (that is, p_i is younger than p_j). Otherwise, p_j is rolled back (p_j is *wounded* by p_i). Returning to our previous example, with processes p_1, p_2, and p_3, if p_1 requests a resource held by p_2, then the resource will be preempted from p_2 and p_2 will be rolled back. If p_3 requests a resource held by p_2, then p_3 will wait.

Both schemes can avoid starvation, provided that when a process is rolled back it is *not* assigned a new time stamp. Since time stamps always increase, a process which is rolled back will eventually have the smallest time stamp. Thus it will not be rolled back again. There are, however, significant differences in the way the two schemes operate.

- In the *wait-die* scheme, an older process must wait for a younger one to release its resource. Thus the older the process gets, the more it tends to wait. By contrast, in the *wound-wait* scheme, an older process never waits for a younger process.

- In the *wait-die* scheme, if a process p_i dies and is rolled back because it requested a resource held by process p_j, then p_i may reissue the same sequence of requests when it is restarted. If the resource is still held by p_j, then p_i will die again. Thus p_i may die several times before acquiring the needed resource. Contrast this series of events with what happens in the *wound-wait* scheme. Process p_i is wounded and rolled back because p_j requested a resource it holds. When p_i is restarted and requests the resource now being held by p_j, p_i waits. Thus there are fewer rollbacks in the *wound-wait* scheme.

The major problem with these two schemes is that some unnecessary rollbacks may occur.

13.9.2 Deadlock Detection

The deadlock prevention algorithm may preempt resources even if no deadlock has occurred. To prevent unnecessary preemptions, we can use a deadlock detection algorithm. We construct a wait-for graph describing the resource allocation state. Since we are assuming only a single resource of each type, a cycle in the wait-for graph represents a deadlock.

The main problem in a distributed system is deciding how to maintain the wait-for graph. We elaborate on this problem by describing several common techniques to deal with this issue. These schemes require that each site keep a *local* wait-for graph. The nodes of the graph correspond to all the processes (local as well as non-local) that are currently either holding or requesting any of the resources local to that site. For example, in Figure 13.10 we have a system consisting of two sites, each maintaining its local wait-for graph. Note that processes p_2 and p_3 appear in both graphs, indicating that the processes have requested resources at both sites.

These local wait-for graphs are constructed in the usual manner for local processes and resources. When a process p on site A needs a resource held by process q in site B, a request message is sent from p to q. The edge (p,q) is then inserted in the local wait-for graph of site B.

Clearly, if any local wait-for graph has a cycle, deadlock has occurred. On the other hand, the fact that there are no cycles in any of the local wait-for graphs does not mean that there are no deadlocks. To illustrate this problem, consider the system depicted in Figure 13.10. Each wait-for graph is acyclic; nevertheless, a deadlock exists in the system. To prove that a deadlock has not occurred, we must show that the *union* of all local graphs is acyclic. The graph (shown in Figure 13.11) obtained by taking the union of the two wait-for graphs of Figure 13.10

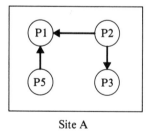

Site A

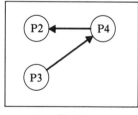

Site B

Figure 13.10   Local wait-for graphs

does indeed contain a cycle, implying that the system is in a deadlock state.

There are a number of different methods for organizing the wait-for graph in a distributed system. Several common schemes are described below.

Centralized Approach

In the centralized approach, a global wait-for graph is constructed as the union of all of the local wait-for graphs. It is maintained in a *single* process: the deadlock detection coordinator. Since there is communication delay in the system, we must distinguish between two types of wait-for graphs. The *real* graph describes the real but unknown state of the system at any instance in time, as would be seen by an omniscient observer. The *constructed* graph is an approximation generated by the controller during the execution of its algorithm. Obviously, the constructed graph must be generated in such a way that whenever the detection algorithm is invoked the reported results are correct in a sense that, if a deadlock exists it is reported properly, and if it reports a deadlock, then the system is indeed in a deadlock state. As we show below, it is not easy to construct such correct algorithms.

The wait-for graph may be constructed at different points in time:

1. Whenever a new edge is inserted or removed in one of the local wait-for graphs.

2. Periodically, when a number of changes have occurred in a wait-for graph.

3. Whenever the coordinator needs to invoke the cycle detection algorithm.

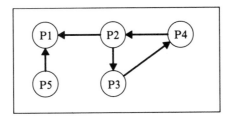

Figure 13.11   Global wait-for graph for Figure 13.10

To illustrate this, let us consider the first option. Whenever process A either inserts or removes an edge in its local graph, it must also send a message to the coordinator to notify it of this modification. On receiving such a message, the coordinator updates its global graph. Alternatively, process A can send a number of such changes in a single message periodically. Returning to our previous example, the coordinator process will maintain the wait-for graph as depicted in Figure 13.11. When site B inserts the edge (p_3, p_4) in its local wait-for graph, it also sends a message to the coordinator. Similarly, when site B deletes the edge (p_5, p_1), because p_1 has released a resource that was requested by p_5, an appropriate message is sent to the coordinator.

When the deadlock detection algorithm is invoked, the coordinator searches its global graph. If a cycle is found, a victim is selected to be rolled back. The coordinator must notify all the sites that a particular process has been selected as victim. The sites, in turn, roll back the victim process.

We note that in this scheme unnecessary rollbacks may result, as a result of two situations:

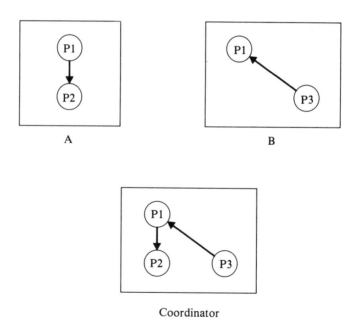

Figure 13.12   False cycles in the global wait-for graph

- *False cycles* may exist in the global wait-for graph. To illustrate this point, consider a snapshot of the system as depicted in Figure 13.12. Suppose that p_2 releases the resource it is holding in site A, resulting in the deletion of the edge (p_1, p_2) in A. Process p_2 then requests a resource held by p_3 at site B, resulting in the addition of the edge (p_2, p_3) in B. If the *insert* (p_2, p_3) message from B arrives before the *delete* (p_1, p_2) message from A, the coordinator may discover the false cycle $\{p_1, p_2, p_3\}$ after the *insert* (but before the *delete*). Deadlock recovery may be initiated, although no deadlock has occurred.

- Unnecessary rollbacks may also result when a *deadlock* has indeed occurred and a victim has been picked, while at the same time one of the processes was aborted for reasons unrelated to the deadlock (such as the process exceeding its allocated time). For example, suppose that site A in Figure 13.10 decides to abort p_2. At the same time, the coordinator has discovered a cycle and picked p_3 as a victim. Both p_2 and p_3 are now rolled back, although only p_2 needed to be rolled back.

We note that the same problems are inherited in solutions employing the other two options.

Let us now present a centralized deadlock detection algorithm, using option 3, which detects all deadlocks that actually occur, and does not detect false deadlocks. This algorithm is due to Stuart et al. [1984]. To avoid the report of false deadlocks, we require that requests from different sites be appended with unique identifiers (time stamps). When process p_i, at site A, requests a resource from p_j, at site B, a request message with time stamp n is sent. The edge (p_i, p_j, n) is inserted in the local wait-for of A. The edge (p_i, p_j, n) is inserted in the local wait-for graph of B only if p_j has received the request message and cannot immediately grant the requested resource. A request from p_i to p_j in the same site is handled in the usual manner; no time stamps are associated with the edge (p_i, p_j). The detection algorithm is then:

1. The controller sends an initiating message to each site in the system.

2. On receiving this message, a site sends its local wait-for graph to the coordinator. Note that each of these wait-for graphs contains all of the local information the site has about the state of the real graph. The graph reflects an instantaneous state of the site, but it is not synchronized with respect to any other site.

3. When the controller has received a reply from each site, it constructs a graph as follows:

   a. The constructed graph contains a vertex for every process in the system.

   b. The graph has an edge (p_i, p_j) if and only if (1) there is an edge (p_i, p_j) in one of the wait-for graphs or (2) an edge (p_i, p_j, n) (for some n) appears in more than one wait-for graph.

We assert that if there is a cycle in the constructed graph, then the system is in a deadlock state. If there is no cycle in the constructed graph, then the system was not in a deadlock state when the execution of the algorithm began.

Hierarchical Approach

The centralized deadlock detection algorithm requires all information to reside in one process. An alternative is to distribute the information among the various processes. The *hierarchical* deadlock detection algorithm is a distributed algorithm.

As in the case of the centralized approach, each site maintains its own local graph. In contrast to the centralized scheme, however, the global wait-for graph is distributed over a number of different *controllers*. These controllers are organized in a tree, where each leaf contains the local wait-for graph of a single site. Each non-leaf controller maintains a wait-for graph which contains relevant information from the graphs of the controllers in the subtree below it.

In particular, let A, B, and C be controllers such that C is the lowest common ancestor of A and B (C must be unique, since we are dealing with a tree). Suppose that node p_i appears in the local wait-for graph of controllers A and B. Then p_i must also appear in the local wait-for graph of:

1. Controller C.

2. Every controller in the path from C to A.

3. Every controller in the path from C to B.

In addition, if p_i and p_j appear in the wait-for graph of controller D and there exists a path from p_i to p_j in the wait-for graph of one of the children of D, then an edge (p_i, p_j) must be in the wait-for graph of D.

If a cycle exists in any of the wait-for graphs, then the system is deadlocked, and appropriate recovery steps must be taken.

To illustrate this algorithm, consider the system of Figure 13.10. A tree for this system is depicted in Figure 13.13. Since p_2 and p_3 appear in A and B, they also appear in C. Since there exists a path from p_2 to p_3 in A, the edge (p_2, p_3) is included in C. Similarly, since there exists a path from p_3 to p_2 in B, the edge (p_3, p_2) is included in C. Note that the wait-for graph in C contains a cycle, implying the presence of a deadlock.

We have not presented an algorithm for constructing and maintaining this hierarchy of controllers. This is left as an exercise to the reader.

Fully Distributed Approach

Menasce and Muntz [1979] proposed a distributed algorithm in which every site constructs a wait-for graph which represents a part of the total graph, depending on the dynamic behavior of the system. The idea is that if a deadlock exists, a cycle will appear in (at least) one of the partial graphs. This algorithm has two undesirable properties. First it could fail to detect some deadlocks. Second, it could discover false deadlocks. Gligor and Shattuck [1980] proposed a modification of the algorithm to fix the first problem. They also noted that the modified

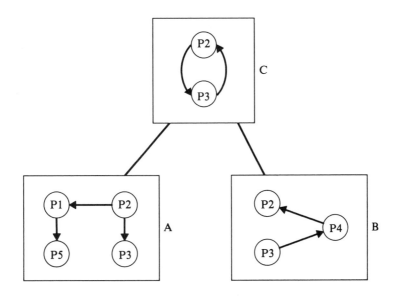

Figure 13.13   Hierarchical wait-for graph

algorithm is too expensive to be practical. Obermarck [1982] proposed another distributed method, again involving construction of partial graphs in every site. This algorithm also suffers from the problem of reporting false deadlocks.

13.10 Robustness

A distributed system may suffer from various types of hardware failure. The failure of a link, the failure of a processor, and the loss of a message are the most common failures. In order for the system to be robust, it must therefore *detect* any of these failures, *reconfigure* the system so that computation may continue, and *recover* when a processor or a link is repaired.

13.10.1 Failure Detection

In an environment with no shared memory, it is generally not possible to differentiate between link failure, processor failure, and message loss. We can usually detect that one of these failures has occurred, but we may not be able to identify what kind of failure it is. Once a failure has been detected, appropriate action must be taken, depending on the particular application.

To detect link and processor failure, a *hand shaking* procedure is used. Suppose that processors A and B have a direct physical link between them. At fixed intervals, both processors send each other an *I-am-up* message. If processor A does not receive this message within a predetermined time period it can assume either that processor B has failed, that the link between A and B has failed, or that the message from B has been lost. At this point processor A has two choices. It can wait for another time period to receive an *I-am-up* message from B, or it can send an *Are-you-up?* message to B.

If processor A does not receive an *I-am-up* message or a reply to its inquiry, the whole procedure can be repeated. The only thing that processor A can safely conclude is that some type of failure has occurred.

Processor A can try to differentiate between link failure and processor failure by sending an *Are-you-up?* message to B by another route (if one exists). If and when B receives this message, it immediately replies positively. This positive reply tells A that B is up, and that the failure is in the direct link between them. Since it is not known in advance how long it will take the message to travel from A to B and back, a *time-out* scheme must be used. At the time A sends the *Are-you-up?* message, it specifies a time interval during which it is willing to wait for the reply from B. If A receives the reply message within that time interval, then it can safely conclude that B is up. If, however, it does not receive the reply message within the time interval (that is, a time-out occurs), then A may only conclude that one or more of the following situations has occurred:

1. Processor B is down.

2. The direct link (if one exists) from A to B is down.

3. The alternative path from A to B is down.

4. The message has been lost.

Processor A cannot, however, decide which of the above has indeed occurred.

13.10.2 Reconfiguration

Suppose that processor A has discovered, through the mechanism described above, that a failure has occurred. It must then initiate a procedure that will allow the system to reconfigure and continue with its normal mode of operation.

- If a direct link from A to B has failed, this information must be broadcast to every processor in the system so that the various routing tables can be updated accordingly.

- If it is believed that a processor has failed (because it can no longer be reached), then every processor in the system must be so notified, so that they will no longer attempt to use the services of the failed processor. The failure of a processor which serves as a central coordinator for some activity (such as deadlock detection), requires the election of a new coordinator. Similarly, if the processor is part of a logical ring, then a new logical ring must be constructed. Note that if the processor has not failed (that is, it is up but cannot be reached), then we may have the undesirable situation where two processors serve as the coordinator. When the network is partitioned, the two coordinators (each for its own partition) may initiate conflicting actions. For example, if the coordinators are responsible for implementing mutual exclusion, we may have a situation where two processes may be executing simultaneously in their critical sections.

13.10.3 Recovery from Failure

When a failed link or processor is repaired, it must be gracefully and smoothly integrated into the system.

a. A link between A and B has failed. When it is repaired, both A and B must be notified. This notification can be accomplished by continuously repeating the hand shaking procedure, described in Section 13.10.1.

b. Processor B has failed. When it recovers, it must notify all other processors that it is up again. Processor B then may have to receive various information from the other processors to update its local tables, such as routing table information, a list of processors that are down, or undelivered messages and mail. Note that if the processor has not failed, but simply could not be reached, then this information is still required.

13.11 Reaching Agreement

In order for a system to be reliable we need a mechanism that allows a set of processes to agree on a common "value". There are several reasons why such an agreement may not take place. First, the communication medium may be faulty, resulting in lost or garbled messages. Second, the processes themselves may be faulty, resulting in unpredictable process behavior. The best we can hope for, in this case, is that processes fail in a clean way, stopping their execution without deviating from their normal execution pattern. In the worst case, processes may send garbled or incorrect messages to other processes or even collaborate with other failed processes in an attempt to destroy the integrity of the system.

This problem has been expressed as the *Byzantine Generals Problem* [Lamport et al. 1982]. Several divisions of the Byzantine army, each commanded by its own general, surround an enemy camp. The Byzantine generals must reach a common agreement on whether or not to attack the enemy at dawn. It is crucial that all generals agree since an attack by only some of the divisions would result in defeat. The various divisions are geographically dispersed and the generals can only communicate with each other with messengers who run from camp to camp. There are at least two major reasons why the generals may not be able to reach an agreement:

- Messengers may get caught by the enemy and thus be unable to deliver their messages. This corresponds to unreliable communication in a computer system and is discussed further in Section 13.11.1.

- Generals may be *traitors*, trying to prevent the *loyal* generals from reaching an agreement. This corresponds to faulty processes in a computer system and is discussed further in Section 13.11.2.

13.11.1 Unreliable Communications

Let us assume that if processes fail, they do so in a clean way, and that the communication medium is unreliable. Suppose that process p_i at site A, which has sent a message to process p_j at site B, needs to know whether p_j has received the message in order to decide how to proceed with its computation. For example, p_i may decide to compute a function S if p_j has received its message, or to compute a function F if p_j has not received the message (because of some hardware failure).

To detect failures, a *time-out* scheme similar to the one described in Section 13.10.1 may be used. When p_i sends a message out, it also specifies a time interval during which it is willing to wait for an acknowledgment message from p_j. When p_j receives the message, it immediately sends an acknowledgment to p_i. If p_i receives the acknowledgment message within the specified time interval, it can safely conclude that p_j has received its message. If, however, a time-out occurs, then p_i needs to retransmit its message and wait for an acknowledgment. This procedure continues until p_i either gets the acknowledgment message back, or is notified by the system that processor B is down. In the first case, it will compute S, while in the latter it will compute F. Note that if these are the only two viable alternatives, p_i must wait until it has been notified that one of the situations has occurred.

Suppose now that p_j also needs to know that p_i has received its acknowledgment message, in order to decide on how to proceed with its computation. For example, p_j may want to compute S only if it is assured that p_i got its acknowledgment. In other words, p_i and p_j will compute S if and only if both have agreed on it. It turns out that in the presence of failure it is not possible to accomplish this task. More precisely, it is not possible in a distributed environment for processes p_i and p_j to completely agree on their respective states.

Let us prove this claim. Suppose that there exists a minimal sequence of message transfers such that after the messages have been delivered, both processes agree to compute S. Let m' be the last message sent by p_i to p_j. Since p_i does not know if its message will arrive at p_j (since the message may be lost due to a failure), p_i will execute S regardless of the outcome of the message delivery. Thus m' could be removed from the sequence without affecting the decision procedure. Hence, the original sequence was not minimal, contradicting our assumption and showing that there is no sequence. The processes can never be sure that both will compute S.

13.11.2 Faulty Processes

Let us assume that the communication medium is reliable but that processes can fail in unpredicatable ways. Consider a system of n processes, of which no more that m are faulty. Suppose that each process p_i has some private value of V_i. We wish to devise an algorithm which allows each nonfaulty process p_i to construct a vector $X_i = (A_{i,1}, A_{i,2}, ..., A_{i,n})$ such that:

a. If p_j is a nonfaulty process that $A_{i,j} = V_j$.

b. If p_i and p_j are both nonfaulty processes then $X_i = X_j$.

There are a number of solutions to this problem, referred to in the literature as the *General Byzantine Problem*, all sharing the following properties.

1. A correct algorithm can be devised only if $n \geq 3 \times m + 1$.

2. The worst case delay for reaching agreement is proportionate to $m+1$ message passing delays.

3. The number of messages required for reaching agreement is very high. This is because no single process is trustworthy, so all processes must collect all information and make their own decisions.

Rather than presenting a general solution, which is quite complicated, we will present an algorithm for the simple case where $m = 1$, and $n = 4$. The general solution can be found in [Pease et al. 1980].

The algorithm requires two rounds of information exchange.

1. Each process sends its private value to the other four processes.

2. Each process sends the information it has obtained in the first round to all other processes.

A faulty process obviously may refuse to send messages. In this case a nonfaulty process can choose an arbitrary value and pretend that value was sent by that process.

Once these two rounds are completed a nonfaulty process p_i can construct its vector $X_i = (A_{i,1}, A_{i,2}, A_{i,3}, A_{i,4})$ as follows:

a. $A_{i,i} = V_i$.

b. For $j \neq i$, if at least two of the three values reported for process p_j (in the two rounds of exchange) agree, then the majority value is used to set $A_{i,j}$. Otherwise, a default value, say Nil, is used to set $A_{i,j}$.

13.12 Election Algorithms

As pointed out in Section 13.8.1, many distributed algorithms employ a coordinator process which performs functions needed by the other processes in the system. These functions include enforcing mutual exclusion, maintaining a global wait-for graph for deadlock detection, or controlling an input or output device in the system. If the coordinator process fails due to the failure of the processor at which it resides, the system can continue execution only by restarting a new copy of the coordinator on some other processor. The algorithms that determine where a new copy of the coordinator should be restarted are called *election* algorithms.

Election algorithms assume that a unique priority number is associated with each active process in the system. For ease of notation we shall assume that the priority number of process p_i is i. Also, to simplify our discussion, we assume a one-to-one correspondence between processes and processors, and thus refer to both as processes. The coordinator is always the process with the largest priority number. Hence, when a coordinator fails, the algorithm must elect that active process with the largest priority number. This number must be sent to each active process in the system. Additionally, the algorithm must provide a mechanism for a recovered process to identify the current coordinator.

In this section we present two interesting examples of election algorithms for two different configurations of distributed systems. The first algorithm is applicable to systems where every process can send a message to every other process in the system. The second algorithm is applicable to systems organized as a ring (logically or physically). Both algorithms require n^2 messages for an election, where n is the number of processes in the system.

13.12.1 The Bully Algorithm

Suppose that process p_i sends a request that is not answered by the coordinator within a time interval T. In this situation, it is assumed that the coordinator has failed, and p_i tries to elect itself as the new coordinator. This task is completed through the following algorithm due to Garcia-Molina [1982].

Process p_i sends an election message to every process with a higher priority number. Process p_i then waits for a time interval T for an answer from any one of these processes.

If no response is received within time T, it is assumed that all processes with numbers greater than i have failed, and p_i elects itself the new coordinator. Process p_i restarts a new copy of the coordinator and sends a message to inform all active processes with priority numbers less than i that p_i is the process at which the new coordinator resides.

However, if an answer is received, p_i begins a time interval T', waiting to receive a message informing it that a process with a higher priority number has been elected. (Some other process is electing itself coordinator, and should report the results within time T'.) If no message is sent within T', then the process with a higher number is assumed to have failed, and process p_i should restart the algorithm.

At any time during execution, p_i may receive one of the following two messages from process p_j:

a. p_j is the new coordinator ($j > i$). Process p_i, in turn, records this information.

b. p_j started an election ($j < i$). Process p_i sends a response to p_j and begins its own election algorithm, provided that p_i has not already initiated such an election.

The process that completes its algorithm has the highest number and is elected as the coordinator. It has sent its number to all active processes with smaller numbers. After a failed process recovers, it immediately begins execution of the same algorithm. If there are no active processes with higher numbers, the recovered process forces all processes with lower numbers to let it become the coordinator process, even if there is a currently active coordinator with a lower number. For this reason, it is termed the *bully* algorithm.

Let us demonstrate the operation of the algorithm with a simple example of a system consisting of processes p_1 through p_4. The operations are as follows:

1. All processes are active, with p_4 as the coordinator process.

2. p_1 and p_4 fail. p_2 determines p_4 has failed by sending a request which is not answered within time T. p_2 then begins its election algorithm by sending a request to p_3.

3. p_3 receives the request, responds to p_2, and begins its own algorithm by sending an election request to p_4.

4. p_2 receives p_3's response, and begins waiting for an interval T'.

5. p_4 does not respond within an interval T, so p_3 elects itself the new coordinator, and sends the number 3 to p_2 and p_1 (which p_1 does not receive, since it has failed).

6. Later, when p_1 recovers, it sends an election request to p_2, p_3, and p_4.

7. p_2 and p_3 respond to p_1 and begin their own election algorithms. p_3 will again be elected, using the same events as before.

8. Finally, p_4 recovers and notifies p_1, p_2, and p_3 that it is the current coordinator. (p_4 sends no election requests, since it is the process with the highest number in the system.)

13.12.2 A Ring Algorithm

This algorithm assumes that the links are unidirectional, and that processes send their messages to their right neighbors. The algorithm is due to Le Lann [1977]. The main data structure used by the algorithm is the *active list*, a list which contains the priority numbers of all active processes in the system when the algorithm ends; each process maintains its own active list. The algorithm works as follows:

1. If process p_i detects a coordinator failure, it creates a new active list which is initially empty. It then sends a message *elect(i)* to its right neighbor, and adds the number i to its active list.

2. If p_i receives a message *elect(j)* from the process on the left, it must respond in one of three ways:

a. If this is the first *elect* message it has seen or sent, p_i creates a new active list with the numbers i and j. It then sends the message *elect(i)*, followed by the message *elect(j)*.

b. If $i \neq j$ (that is, the message received does not contain p_i's number), then p_i adds j to its active list and forwards the message to its right neighbor.

c. If $i = j$ (that is, p_i receives the message *elect(i)*), then the active list for p_i now contains the numbers of all the active processes in the system. Process p_i can now determine the largest number in the active list to identify the new coordinator process.

This algorithm does not specify how a recovering process determines the number of the current coordinator process. One solution would be to require a recovering process to send an inquiry message. This message is forwarded around the ring to the current coordinator, which in turn sends a reply containing its number.

13.13 Summary

A distributed system is a collection of processors that do not share memory or a clock. Instead, each processor has its own local memory, and the processors communicate with each other through various communication lines, such as high-speed buses or telephone lines. The processors in a distributed system vary in size and function. They may include small microprocessors, work stations, minicomputers, and large general-purpose computer systems.

Principally, there are two types of distributed systems: computer networks and local area networks. The main difference between the two is in the way they are geographically distributed. Computer networks are composed of a number of autonomous processors that are distributed over a large geographical area (such as the United States), while local area networks are composed of processors that are distributed over small geographical areas, such as a single building or a number of adjacent buildings.

The processors in the system are connected through a communication network which can be configured in a number of different ways. The network may be fully or partially connected. It may be a tree, a star, a ring, or a multi-access bus. The communication network design must consider routing and connection strategies, and the problems of contention and security.

A distributed system provides the user with access to the various resources the system provides. Access to a shared resource can be provided by data migration, computation migration, or job migration. A distributed file system must consider two major issues: transparency (Does a user access all files in the same manner regardless of where they are in the network?) and locality (Where do files reside in the system?).

In a distributed system with no common memory and no common clock, it is sometimes impossible to determine the exact order in which two events occur. The happened-before relation is only a partial ordering of the events in distributed systems. Time stamps can be used to provide a consistent event ordering in a distributed system.

A centralized scheme can be used for implementing mutual exclusion and deadlock detection. Alternative distributed algorithms include the token-passing algorithm for synchronization of a ring structured network, and a hierarchical deadlock detection algorithm.

A distributed system may suffer from various types of hardware failure. In order for the system to be fault tolerant, it must detect failures and reconfigure the system. When the failure is repaired, the system must be reconfigured again. Two algorithms, the bully algorithm and a ring algorithm, can be used to elect a new coordinator in case of failures.

Exercises

13.1 What are the main differences between a computer network and a local area network?

13.2 Contrast the various network topologies in terms of reliability.

13.3 Why do most computer networks employ only a partially connected topology?

13.4 What are the advantages and disadvantages in making the computer network transparent to the user?

13.5 Compare and contrast a centralized file system with a decentralized one.

13.6 Is it always crucial to know that the message you have sent has arrived at its destination safely? If the answer is yes, explain why. If the answer is no, give appropriate examples.

13.7 Your company is building a computer network and you are asked to write an algorithm for achieving mutual exclusion. Which scheme would you use and why?

13.8 Present an algorithm for reconstructing a logical ring in case a process in the ring fails.

13.9 Your company is building a computer network and you are asked to develop a scheme for dealing with the deadlock problem.

    a. Would you use a deadlock detection scheme, or a deadlock prevention scheme?

    b. If you chose a deadlock prevention scheme, which one will you use and why?

    c. If you chose a deadlock detection scheme, which one would you use and why?

13.10 Write an algorithm for maintaining the hierarchical deadlock detection scheme presented in Section 13.9.2.

13.11 Why is deadlock detection much more expensive in a distributed environment than in a centralized one?

Bibliographic Notes

Kahn [1972], Pyke [1973], Enslow [1973], Doll [1974], and Crowther et al. [1975] have provided general overviews of computer networks. A thorough discussion of several of the earlier networks was provided by Peterson and Veit [1971]. Forsdick et al. [1978], Donnelley [1979], and Ward [1980] discussed operating systems for computer networks.

A large number of private and public computer networks have emerged in the past few years, including the Arpanet [McQuillan and Walden 1977], Tymenet [Kopf 1977], Datapac [McGibbon et al. 1978], Telenet [Newport and Kaul 1977], the Nordic Public Data Network [Larsson 1976], and Transpac [Danet et al. 1976].

Discussions concerning local area networks (LANs) have been written by Metcalfe and Boggs [1976] and Clark et al. [1978]. A special issue of *Computer Networks*, December 1979, included nine papers on LANs covering such subjects as hardware, software, simulation, and examples. A taxonomy and extensive list of LANs was presented by Thurber and Freeman [1980]. Farber and Larson [1972], Pierce [1972], Fraser [1975], Clark et al. [1978], Liu [1978], Needham [1979], and Wilkes and Wheeler [1979] discussed various types of ring structured LANs.

Feng [1981] surveyed the various network topologies. Boorstyn and Frank [1977], Gerla and Kleinrock [1977], and Schwartz [1977] discussed topology design problems.

Nutt [1977], Gula [1978], and Jones and Schwarz [1980] discussed multiprocessing. A survey on multiprocessor organization was written by Enslow [1977]. A discussion of multiprocessor hardware was given by Satyanarayanan [1980a, 1980b]. Kimbleton and Schneider [1975], and Forsdick et al. [1978] presented an overview of computer networks.

Discussions concerning distributed file systems are offered by Gien [1978] (the File Transfer Protocol scheme), Israel et al. [1978], and Sturgis et al. [1980] (general discussions concerning the design and use of distributed file systems), Swinehart et al. [1979] (the Woodstock file system), Birrell and Needham [1980] (a universal file server), Dion [1980] (the Cambridge file server), Fridrich and Older [1981] (the FELIX file server), Casey [1972], and Chu [1969] (file allocation in a distributed environment).

Rivest et al. [1978], Diffie and Hellman [1979], Lempel [1979], Simmons [1979], Davies [1980], and Denning [1982b] are concerned with the use of cryptography in computer systems.

The first general algorithm for implementing mutual exclusion in a distributed environment was due to Lamport [1978a]; this algorithm required $3 \times n$ messages per entry. A refinement of this algorithm by Ricart and Agrawala [1981] reduced the number of message to the lower bound of $2 \times n$ messages. The token-passing algorithm for ring structured systems was due to Le Lann [1977].

The issue of distributed synchronization was discussed by Reed and Kanodia [1979] (shared memory environment), Banino et al. [1979] (shared broadcast channel environment), Lamport [1978a, 1978b], and Schneider [1982] (totally disjoint processes).

The time-stamp distributed deadlock detection algorithm was due to Rosenkrantz et al. [1978]. The hierarchical scheme was due to Menasce and Muntz [1979]. A deadlock detection scheme in which the wait-for graph is distributed over the network was proposed by Menasce and Muntz [1979]. This algorithm was shown to be incorrect by Gligor and Shattuck [1980], who also proposed a modification to the algorithm. Obermarck [1982] has further modified this basic algorithm to get better performance.

The problem of deadlock prevention and avoidance in a packet switched data transport system has been discussed by Merlin and Schweitzer [1980a, 1980b] and Gelernter [1981]. Toueg and Ullman [1979] and Toueg [1980] discussed deadlock-free packet switching networks.

The Unix Operating System

Although operating system concepts can be considered in purely theoretical terms, it is often useful to see them in practice. This chapter presents an in-depth examination of the 4.2BSD operating system, a version of Unix, as an example of the various concepts presented in this book. By examining a complete, real system, we can see how the various concepts discussed in this book relate both to each other and to practice. We consider first a brief history of Unix and a presentation of its user and programmer interfaces. Then we present the internal data structures and algorithms used by the Unix kernel to support the user/programmer interface.

14.1 History

The first version of Unix was developed in 1969 by Ken Thompson of the Research Group at Bell Laboratories to use an otherwise idle PDP-7. He was soon joined by Dennis Ritchie. Thompson, Ritchie, and others in the Research Group produced the early versions of Unix.

Ritchie had previously worked on the Multics project, and Multics was a strong influence on the newer operating system. Even the name Unix is merely a pun on Multics. The basic organization of the file system, the idea of the command interpreter (the shell) as a user process, the use of a separate process for each command, the original line-editing characters (# to erase the last character and @ to erase the entire line), and numerous other features came directly from Multics. Ideas from various other operating systems, such as MIT's CTSS and the XDS-940 system, were also used.

Ritchie and Thompson worked quietly on Unix for many years. Their work on the first version allowed them to move it to a PDP-11/20, for a second version. A third version resulted from rewriting most of the operating system in the systems programming language C, instead of the previously used assembly language. C was developed at Bell Labs to support Unix. Unix was also moved to larger PDP-11 models, such as the 11/45 and 11/70. Multiprogramming and other enhancements were added when it was rewritten in C and moved to systems (like the 11/45) with hardware support for multiprogramming.

As Unix developed, it became widely used within Bell Labs and gradually spread to a few universities. The first version widely available outside Bell Labs was Version 6, in 1976. (The version number for early Unix systems corresponds to the edition number of the *Unix Programmer's Manual* that was current when the distribution was made; the code and the manuals were revised independently.)

In 1978, Version 7 was distributed. This Unix system ran on the PDP-11/70 and the Interdata 8/32, and is the ancestor of most modern Unix systems. In particular, it was soon ported to other PDP-11 models and to the VAX computer line. The version available on the VAX was known as 32V.

After the distribution of Version 7 in 1978, the Unix Support Group (USG) assumed administrative control and responsibility from the Research group for distributions of Unix within AT&T, the parent organization for Bell Labs. Unix was becoming a product, not simply a research tool. The Research group has continued with their own version of Unix to support their own internal computing, however. The system currently (1985) in development by the Research group at Bell Labs is Version 8, which is available only within Bell Labs.

USG mainly provided support for Unix within AT&T. The first external distribution from USG was System III, in 1982. System III incorporated features of Version 7, 32V, and also of several Unix systems developed by groups other than Research. Features of UNIX/RT, a real-time Unix system, as well as numerous portions of the Programmer's Work Bench (PWB) were included in System III.

USG released System V in 1983; it is largely derived from System III. The divestiture of the various Bell operating companies from AT&T has left AT&T in a position to aggressively market System V. USG has been restructured as the Unix System Development Laboratory (USDL), whose current distribution, released in 1984, is Unix System V Release 2 (V.2).

The small size, modularity, and clean design of early Unix systems led to Unix-based work at numerous other computer science organizations such as Rand, BBN, the University of Illinois, Harvard, Purdue, and even DEC. The most influential of the non-Bell Labs and non-AT&T Unix development groups, however, has been the University of California at Berkeley.

The first Berkeley VAX Unix work was the addition in 1978 of virtual memory, demand paging, and page replacement to 32V by Bill Joy and Ozalp Babaoglu to produce 3BSD. The large virtual memory space of 3BSD allowed the development of very large programs, such as Berkeley's own Franz Lisp. The memory management work convinced the Defense Advanced Research Projects Agency (DARPA) to fund Berkeley for the development of a standard Unix system for government use (4BSD).

The 4BSD work for DARPA was guided by a steering committee which included many notable people from the Unix and networking communities. One of the goals of this project was to provide support for the DARPA Internet networking protocols (TCP/IP). This support was provided in a general manner. It is possible in 4.2BSD to uniformly communicate among diverse network facilities, including local area networks (such as Ethernets and token rings) and long-haul computer networks (such as DARPA's Arpanet).

In addition, Berkeley adapted many features from contemporary operating systems to improve the design and implementation of Unix. Many of the terminal line editing functions of the TENEX operating system were provided by a new terminal driver. A new user interface (the C Shell), a new text editor (ex/vi), compilers for Pascal and Lisp, and many new systems programs were written at Berkeley. For 4.2BSD, certain efficiency improvements were motivated by comparison with the VMS operating system.

Unix software from Berkeley is released in so-called *Berkeley Software Distributions*. It is convenient to refer to the Berkeley VAX Unix systems following 3BSD as 4BSD, although there were actually several specific

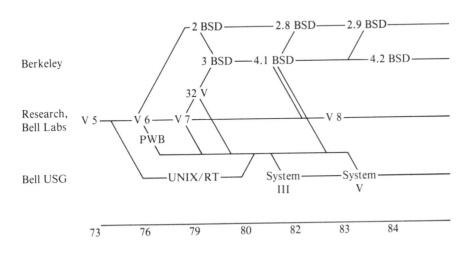

Figure 14.1   History of Unix versions

releases, most notably 4.1BSD and now 4.2BSD. The generic numbers 2BSD and 4BSD are used for the PDP-11 and VAX distributions of Berkeley Unix. 4.2BSD, first distributed in 1983, is the culmination of the original Berkeley DARPA Unix project, although further research proceeds at Berkeley. 2.9BSD is the equivalent version for PDP-11 systems.

Figure 14.1 summarizes the relationships between the various versions of Unix.

4BSD was the operating system of choice for VAXes from its initial release (1979) until the release of System III (1982). 4BSD is still the best choice for many research and networking installations. Many organizations would buy a 32V license and order 4BSD from Berkeley without even bothering to get a 32V tape.

The current set of Unix systems is not limited to Version 8, System V (Release 2), and 4.2BSD, however. As Unix has grown in popularity, it has been moved to many different computers and computer systems. A wide variety of Unix, and Unix-like, operating systems have been created. DEC supports its Unix (called Ultrix) for VAXes; Microsoft rewrote Unix for the Intel 8088 and called it Xenix; IBM has Unix on its PC and its mainframes. Unix is also available from Amdahl, Sun, NBI, MassComp, Hewlett-Packard, Gould, Data General, Perkin-Elmer, and a host of other vendors, including, of course, AT&T. Most of these systems are based on Version 7, System III, 4.2BSD, or System V.

We believe that Unix has become and will remain an important part of both operating system theory and practice. Unix is an excellent vehicle for academic study. For example, both the Tunis operating system [Holt 1983] and the Xinu operating system [Comer 1984] are based upon the concepts of Unix, but were developed explicitly for classroom study. Ritchie and Thompson were honored in 1983 by the ACM Turing award for their work on Unix.

The specific Unix version used in this chapter is the VAX version of 4.2BSD. This system is used because it implements many interesting operating system concepts, such as demand paging and networking. The VAX implementation is used because 4.2BSD was developed on the VAX and that machine still represents a convenient point of reference, despite the recent proliferation of implementations on other hardware (such as the Motorola 68000 or National 32032).

14.2 Design Principles

Unix was designed to be a time-sharing system. The standard user interface (the shell) is simple and may be replaced by another, if desired. The file system is a multi-level tree, which allows users to create their own subdirectories. All user data files are simply a sequence of bytes.

Disk files and I/O devices are treated as similarly as possible. Thus device dependencies and peculiarities are kept in the kernel as much as possible, and even in the kernel most of them are confined to the device drivers.

Unix supports multiple processes. A process can easily create new processes. CPU scheduling is a simple priority algorithm. Memory management is a variable region (MVT) algorithm with swapping. 4.2BSD uses demand paging as a mechanism to support memory management and cpu scheduling decisions.

Unix is an excellent example of an operating system for a personal computer. It was originated first by one programmer, Ken Thompson, and then another, Dennis Ritchie, as a system for their own convenience. As such, it is small enough to understand. Most of the algorithms were selected for *simplicity*, not speed or sophistication. Its clean design has resulted in many imitations and modifications.

Although the designers of Unix had a significant amount of knowledge about other operating systems, Unix had no elaborate design spelled out before its implementation. This flexibility appears to been one of the key factors in the development of the system. There were some design principles involved, however, even though they were not spelled out at the outset.

Unix was designed by programmers for programmers. Thus it has always been interactive, and facilities for program development have always been a high priority. Such facilities include the program *make* (which may be used to check to see which of a collection of source files for a program need to be compiled and then do so) and the *Source Code Control System (SCCS)* (which is used to keep successive versions of files available without having to store the entire contents of each step).

The operating system is mostly written in C, a systems programming language. C was developed to support Unix since neither Thompson nor Ritchie enjoyed programming in assembly language. The avoidance of assembly language was also necessary because of the uncertainty about the machine or machines on which Unix would be run. It has greatly simplified the problems of moving Unix from one hardware system to another.

From the beginning, Unix development systems have had all the Unix sources available on-line, and the developers have used the systems under development as their primary systems. This has greatly facilitated the discovery of deficiencies and their fixes as well as new possibilities and their implementations. It has also encouraged the plethora of Unix variants existing today, but the benefits have outweighed the disadvantages: if something is broken, it can be fixed at a local site, rather than having to wait for the next release of the system. Such fixes, as well as new facilities, may be incorporated into later distributions.

The size constraints of the PDP-11 (and earlier computers used for Unix) have forced a certain elegance. Where other systems have elaborate algorithms for dealing with pathological conditions, Unix just does a controlled crash (a *panic*), and instead tries to arrange to prevent rather than cure such conditions. Where other systems would use brute force or macro expansion, Unix mostly has had to develop more subtle, or at least simpler, approaches.

14.3 Programmer Interface

As with all computer systems, Unix consists of two separable parts: the kernel and the systems programs. One may roughly view the Unix operating system as being layered as in Figure 14.2. Everything below the system call interface and above the physical hardware is the kernel. The kernel provides the file system, cpu scheduling, memory management, and other operating system functions through system calls. Systems programs use the kernel-supported system calls to provide useful functions, such as compilation and file manipulation.

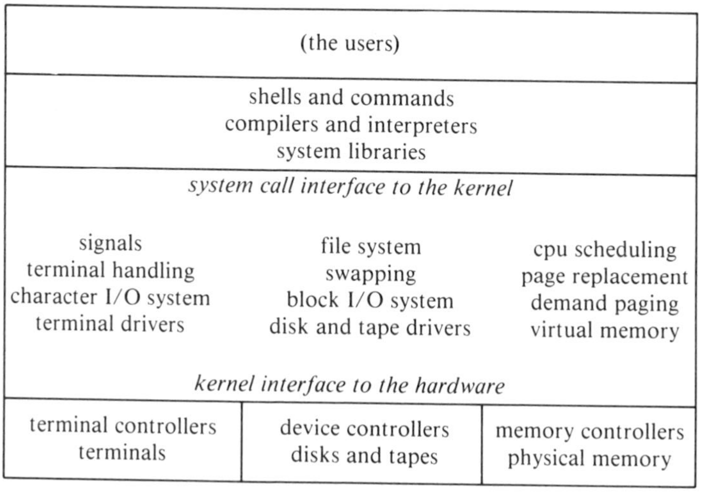

(the users)		
shells and commands compilers and interpreters system libraries		
system call interface to the kernel		
signals terminal handling character I/O system terminal drivers	file system swapping block I/O system disk and tape drivers	cpu scheduling page replacement demand paging virtual memory
kernel interface to the hardware		
terminal controllers terminals	device controllers disks and tapes	memory controllers physical memory

Figure 14.2   4.2BSD layer structure

System calls define the *programmer interface* to Unix; the set of systems programs commonly available defines the *user interface*. The programmer and user interface define the context that the kernel must support.

System calls in VAX 4.2BSD are made by a trap to location 40 of the VAX interrupt vectors. Parameters are passed to the kernel on the hardware stack; the kernel returns values in registers R0 and R1. Register R0 may also return an error code. The carry bit distinguishes a normal return from an error return.

This level of detail is seldom seen by the Unix programmer, however. Most systems programs are written in C, and the *Unix Programmer's Manual* presents all system calls as C functions. A system program written in C for 4.2BSD on the VAX can generally be moved to another 4.2BSD system and simply recompiled even though hardware details may be quite different. The details of system calls are known only to the compiler. This is a major reason for the portability of Unix programs.

System calls for Unix can be roughly grouped into three categories: file manipulation, process control, and information manipulation. In Chapter 2, we listed a fourth, device manipulation, but since devices in Unix are treated as (special) files, the same system calls support both files and devices.

14.3.1 File Manipulation

A *file* in Unix is a sequence of bytes. Different programs expect various levels of structure, but the kernel does not impose a structure on files. For instance, the convention for text files is lines of ASCII characters separated by a single newline character (which is the linefeed character in ASCII), but the kernel knows nothing of this convention.

Files are organized in tree-structured *directories*. Directories are themselves files that contain information on how to find other files. A *pathname* to a file is a text string that identifies a file by specifying a path through the directory structure to the file. Syntactically it consists of individual file name elements separated by the slash character. For example, in */usr/local/font* the first slash indicates the root of the directory tree, called the *root* directory. The next element, *usr*, is a subdirectory of the root, *local* is a subdirectory of *usr*, and *font* is a file or directory in the directory *local*. Whether *font* is an ordinary file or a directory cannot be determined from the pathname syntax.

Unix has both *absolute pathnames* and *relative pathnames*. Absolute pathnames start at the root of the file system and are distinguished by a slash at the beginning of the pathname; */usr/local/font* is an absolute pathname. Relative pathnames start at the *current directory*, which is an attribute of the process accessing the pathname. Thus, *local/font* indicates a file or directory named *font* in the directory *local* in the current directory, which might or might not be */usr*.

A file may be known by more than one name in one or more directories. Such multiple names are known as *links* and all links are treated equally by the operating system. 4.2BSD also supports *symbolic links*, which are files containing the absolute pathname of another file. The two kinds of links are also known as *hard links* and *soft links*. Soft (symbolic) links, unlike hard links, may point to directories and may cross file system boundaries.

The file name "." in a directory is a hard link to the directory itself. The file name ".." is a hard link to the parent directory. Thus, if the current directory is */user/jlp/programs*, then *../bin/wdf* refers to */user/jlp/bin/wdf*.

Hardware devices have names in the file system. These *device special files* or *special files* are known to the kernel as device interfaces, but are nonetheless accessed by the user by much the same system calls as other files.

Figure 14.3 shows a typical Unix file system. The root (/) normally contains a small number of directories as well as */vmunix*, the binary boot image of the operating system; */dev* contains the device special files, such as */dev/console*, */dev/lp0*, */dev/mt0*, and so on; */bin* contains the binaries of the essential Unix systems programs. Other binaries may be in */usr/bin* (for "applications" systems programs such as text formatters), */usr/ucb* (for systems programs written by Berkeley rather than AT&T), or */usr/local/bin* (for systems programs written by the local site). Library files, such as the C, Pascal, and Fortran library subroutines, are kept in */lib* (or */usr/lib* or */usr/local/lib*).

The files of users themselves are stored in a separate directory for each user, typically in */user*. Thus, the user directory for *carol* would normally be in */user/carol*. For a large system, these directories may be further grouped to ease administration, creating a file structure with */user/prof/avi* and */user/staff/carol*. Administrative files and programs, such as the password file, are kept in */etc*. Temporary files can be put in */tmp*, which is normally erased once a day, or */usr/tmp*.

Each of these directories may have considerably more structure. For example, the font description tables for the troff formatter for the Merganthaler 202 typesetter are kept in */usr/lib/troff/dev202*. All of the conventions concerning the location of specific files and directories have been defined by programmers and their programs; the operating system kernel depends only on the existence of */etc/init*, which is used to initialize terminal processes.

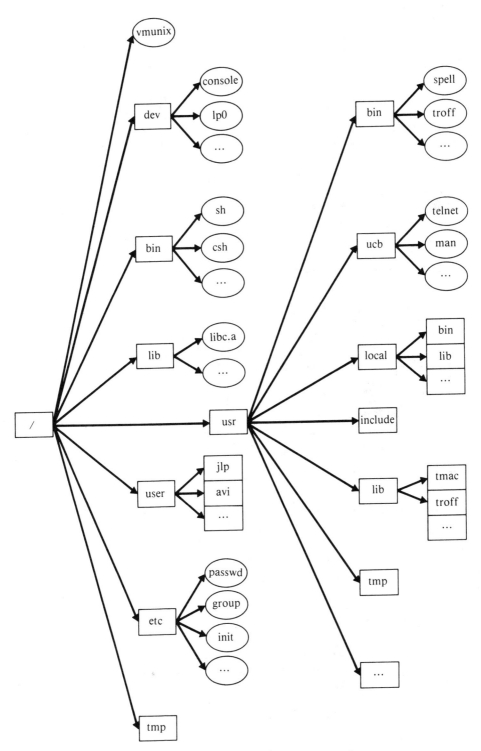

Figure 14.3 Typical Unix directory structure

System calls for basic file manipulation are *creat, open, read, write, close,* and *unlink.* The *creat* system call, given a pathname, creates an (empty) file. A file is opened by the *open* system call, which takes a pathname and a mode (such as read, write, or read/write) and returns a small integer, called a *file descriptor.* The descriptor is an index into a small table of open files for this process. Descriptors start at 0 and seldom get higher than 6 or 7 for typical programs, depending on the maximum number of simultaneously open files. A file descriptor may then be passed to a *read* or *write* system call (along with a buffer address and the number of bytes to transfer) to perform data transfers to or from the file. A file is closed by passing its file descriptor to the *close* system call.

Each *read* or *write* updates the current offset into the file, which is used to determine the position in the file for the next *read* or *write.* The *lseek* system call allows the position to be explicitly reset. There is an additional system call, *ioctl,* for manipulating device parameters.

Information about the file (such as its size, protection modes, owner, and so on) can be obtained by the *stat* system call. Three system calls allow some of this information to be changed: *rename* (change file name), *chmod* (change the protection modes), and *chown* (change the owner). The *link* system call makes a hard link for an existing file, creating a new name for an existing file. A link is removed by the *unlink* system call; if it is the last link, the file is deleted.

Directories are made by the *mkdir* system call and deleted by *rmdir.* The current directory is changed by *chdir.*

14.3.2 Process Control

A process is a program in execution. Processes are identified by their *process identifier,* which is an integer. A new process is produced by the *fork* system call, which creates two almost identical processes each with a *copy* of the original address space: the same program and the same variables with the same values. Both processes (the parent and the child) continue execution at the instruction after the *fork* with one difference: the return code for the *fork* is zero for the new (child) process while the (non-zero) process identifier of the child is returned to the parent.

Typically, the *execve* system call is used after a fork by one of the two processes to replace its virtual memory space with a new program. The *execve* system call loads a binary file into memory (destroying the memory image of the program containing the *execve* system call) and starts its execution.

A process may terminate by using the *exit* system call, and its parent process may wait for that event by using the *wait* system call. The *wait* system call provides the process id of a terminated child so that the parent can tell which of possibly several children terminated.

Together, *exit* and *wait* may be considered analogous to the abstract *join* primitive of Chapter 9, just as *fork* and *execve* together are analogous to the abstract *fork* primitive. From the viewpoint of the calling process, one may liken *fork* and *wait* to a subroutine call and return, while *execve* is more like a go-to.

The simplest form of communication between processes is by *pipes*, which may be created before the *fork* and whose endpoints are then set up between the *fork* and the *execve*. A pipe is essentially a queue of bytes between two processes. The pipe is accessed by a file descriptor, like an ordinary file. One process writes into the pipe and the other reads from the pipe. The size of the pipe (typically 4096 bytes) is fixed by the system. Reading from an empty pipe or writing into a full pipe causes the process to be blocked until the state of the pipe changes.

All user processes are descendants of one original process, called *init* (which has process identifier 1). Each terminal port available for interactive use has a *getty* process forked for it by *init*. Getty initializes terminal line parameters and waits for a user's *login name*, which it passes through an *execve* as an argument to a *login* process. *Login* collects the user's password, encrypts it, and compares it to an encrypted string taken from the file /etc/passwd. If the comparison is successful, the user is allowed to log in. *Login* executes a *shell*, or command interpreter, after setting the numeric *user identifier* of the process to that of the user logging in. (The shell and the user identifier are found in /etc/passwd by the user's login name.) This shell is what the user ordinarily communicates with for the rest of the login session, while the shell itself forks subprocesses for the commands the user tells it to execute.

The user identifier is used by the kernel to determine the user's permissions for certain system calls, especially those involving file accesses. There is also a *group identifier* which is used to provide similar privileges to a collection of users. In 4.2BSD a process may be in several groups simultaneously. The *login* process puts the shell in all the groups permitted to the user by the files /etc/passwd and /etc/group.

There are actually two user identifiers used by the kernel: the *effective user identifier* is the identifier used to determine file access permissions. If the file of a program being loaded by an *execve* has the *setuid* bit set in its inode, the effective user id of the process is set to the user identifier of the owner of the file, while the *real user identifier* is left as it was. This allows certain processes to have more than ordinary privileges while still being executable by ordinary users. The setuid idea is patented by Dennis Ritchie (U.S. Patent 4,135,240) and is one of the distinctive features of Unix. There is a similar *setgid* bit for groups.

14.3.3 Signals

Signals are a facility for handling exceptional conditions similar to software interrupts. There are 19 different signals, each corresponding to a certain condition. A signal may be generated by a keyboard interrupt, by an error in a process, such as a bad memory reference, or by a number of asynchronous events such as timers or job control signals from the shell. Almost any signal may also be generated by the *kill* system call.

The *interrupt* signal, SIGINT, is used to stop a command before it completes. It is usually produced by the ^C character (ASCII 3) or, in the more traditional configuration, the *delete* character (ASCII 127). In 4.2BSD the important keyboard characters are defined by a table for each terminal and can be easily redefined. The *quit* signal, SIGQUIT, is usually produced by the ^\ character (ASCII 28). The *quit* signal both stops the currently executing program and dumps its current memory image to a file named *core* in the current directory. The core file can be used by debuggers. SIGILL is produced by an illegal instruction and SIGSEGV by an attempt to address memory outside of the legal virtual memory space of a process.

Arrangements can be made for most signals to be ignored (to have no effect), or for a routine in the user process (a signal handler) to be called. There is one signal (the *kill* signal, number nine, SIGKILL) that cannot be ignored or caught by a signal handler. SIGKILL is used, for example, to kill a runaway process that is ignoring other signals such as SIGINT or SIGQUIT.

Signals can be lost: if another of the same kind is sent before a previous one has been accepted by the process to which it is directed, the first one will be overwritten and only the last one will be seen by the process.

14.3.4 Information Manipulation

System calls exist to set and return both an interval timer (*getitimer/setitimer*) and the current time in microseconds since 1 January 1970 (*gettimeofday/settimeofday*). In addition, processes can ask for their process identifier (*getpid*), their group identifier (*getgid*), the name of the machine on which they are executing (*gethostname*), and many other values.

14.3.5 Library Routines

The system call interface to Unix is supported and augmented by a large collection of library routines and header files. The header files provide the definition of complex data structures used in system calls. In addition, a large library of functions provides additional program support.

For example, the Unix I/O system calls provide for the reading and writing of blocks of bytes. Some applications may want to read and write only one byte at a time. While it would be possible to read and write one byte at a time, this would require a system call for each byte, a very high overhead. Instead a set of standard library routines (the standard I/O package accessed through the header file *stdio.h*) provides another interface, which reads and writes several thousand bytes at a time using local buffers and transfers between these buffers (in user memory) when I/O is desired. Formatted I/O is also supported by the standard I/O package.

Additional library support is provided for mathematical functions, network access, data conversion, and so on. The 4.2BSD kernel supports 153 system calls, while the C program library has 336 library functions. Although the library functions eventually result in system calls where necessary (for example, the *getchar* library routine will result in a *read* system call if the file buffer is empty), it is generally unnecessary for the programmer to distinguish between the basic set of kernel system calls and the additional functions provided by library functions.

14.4 User Interface

Both the programmer and the user of a Unix system deal mainly with the set of systems programs that have been written and are available for execution. These programs make the necessary system calls to support their function, but the system calls themselves are contained within the program and need not be obvious to the user.

The common systems programs can be grouped into several categories; most of them are file or directory oriented. For example, to manipulate directories: *mkdir* makes a new directory, *rmdir* removes a directory, *cd* changes the current directory to another, and *pwd* prints the absolute pathname of the current (working) directory.

The *ls* program lists the names of the files in the current directory. Any of 18 options can ask that properties of the files be displayed also. For example, the *-l* option asks for a long listing, showing the file name, owner, protection, date and time of creation, and size (in bytes). The *cp* program creates a new file that is a copy of an existing file. The *mv* program moves a file from one place to another in the directory tree. In most cases this simply requires a renaming of the file, but if need be, the file is copied to the new location and the old copy is deleted. A file is deleted by the *rm* program (which makes an *unlink* system call).

To display a file on the terminal, a user can run *cat*. The *cat* program takes a list of files and concatenates them, copying the result to the standard output, commonly the terminal. On a high-speed CRT, of course, the file may speed by too fast to be read. The *more* program displays the file one screen at a time, pausing until the user types a character to continue to the next screen. The *head* program displays just the first few lines of a file, while *tail* shows the last few lines.

These are the basic systems programs widely used in Unix. In addition, there are a number of editors (*ed, sed, emacs, vi, ...*), compilers (C, Pascal, Fortran, ...), and text formatters (*troff, tex, scribe, ...*). There are also programs for sorting (*sort*) and comparing files (*cmp, diff*), looking for patterns (*grep, awk*), sending mail to other users (*mail*), and many other activities.

14.4.1 Shells and Commands

Programs, both systems programs and user-written programs, are normally executed by a command interpreter. The command interpreter in Unix is a user process like any other. It is called a *shell*, as it surrounds the kernel of the operating system. Users can write their own shell, and there are in fact several shells in general use. The *Bourne shell*, written by Steve Bourne, is probably the most widely used, or at least the most widely available. The *C shell*, mostly the work of Bill Joy, is the most popular on BSD systems.

The common shells share much of their command language syntax. Unix is normally an interactive system. The shell indicates its readiness to accept another command by typing a prompt, and the user types a command on a single line. For instance, in the line

% ls -l

the per cent sign is the usual C shell prompt and the *ls -l* (typed by the user) is the (long) list directory command. Commands may take arguments, which the user types after the command name on the same line, separated by white space (spaces or tabs).

Although there are a few commands built into the shells (such as *cd*), a typical command is an executable binary object file. A list of several directories, the *search path*, is kept by the shell. For each command, each of the directories in the search path is searched for a file of the same name. If a file is found, it is loaded and executed. The search path can be set by the user. The directories /bin and /usr/bin are almost always in the search path, and a typical search path on a BSD system might be

(. /usr/local/bin /usr/ucb /bin /usr/bin)

The ls command's object file is /bin/ls and the shell itself is /bin/sh (the Bourne shell) or /bin/csh (the C shell).

Execution of a command is done by a *fork* system call followed by an *execve* of the object file. The shell usually then does a *wait* to suspend its own execution until the command completes (Figure 14.4). There is a simple syntax (an ampersand [&] at the end of the command line) to indicate that the shell should *not* wait. A command left running in this manner while the shell continues to interpret further commands is said to be a *background* command, or to be running in the background. Processes for which the shell *does* wait are said to run in the *foreground*.

The C shell in 4.2BSD systems provides a facility called *job control* (partially implemented in the kernel). Job control allows processes to be moved between the foreground and the background. They can be stopped and restarted on various conditions, such as a background job wanting input from the user's terminal. This allows most of the control of processes provided by windowing or layering interfaces, but requires no special hardware.

14.4.2 Standard I/O

Processes may open files as they like, but most processes expect three file descriptors (numbers 0, 1, and 2) to be open when they start. They are known as *standard input* (0), *standard output* (1), and *standard error* (2). These file descriptors are inherited across the *execve* (and possibly the

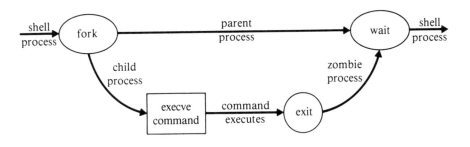

Figure 14.4   A shell forks a subprocess to execute a command

fork) that created the process. All three are frequently open to the user's terminal. Thus the program can read what the user types by reading standard input, and the program can send output to the user's screen by writing to standard output. The standard error file descriptor is also open for writing and is used for error output; standard output is used for ordinary output. Most programs can also accept a file (rather than a terminal) for standard input and standard output.

The common shells have a simple syntax for changing what files are open for the standard I/O streams of a process. Changing a standard file is called *I/O redirection*. The syntax for I/O redirection is shown in Figure 14.5. In this example, the *ls* command produces a listing of the names of files in the current directory, the *pr* command formats that list into pages suitable for a printer, and the *lpr* command spools the formatted output to a printer, such as */dev/lp0*.

14.4.3 Pipelines, Filters, and Shell Scripts

The three-step example of Figure 14.5 could have been done in the one command

% ls | pr | lpr

Each vertical bar tells the shell to arrange for the output of the preceding command to be passed as input to the following command. A pipe is used to carry the data from one process to the other. One process writes into one end of the pipe, and another process reads from the other end. In the example, the write end of one pipe would be set up by the shell to be the standard output of *ls* and the read end of the pipe would be the standard input of *pr*; there would be another pipe between *pr* and *lpr*.

A command like *pr* that passes its standard input to its standard output, performing some processing on it, is called a *filter*. Many Unix commands may be used as filters. Complicated functions may be pieced together as pipelines of common commands. Also, common functions, such as output formatting, need not be built into numerous commands,

```
% ls > filea              # direct output of ls to file filea
% pr < filea > fileb      # input from filea and output to fileb
% lpr < fileb             # input from fileb
```

Figure 14.5   Standard I/O redirection

since the output of almost any program may be piped through *pr* (or some other appropriate filter).

Both of the common Unix shells are also programming languages, with shell variables and the usual higher-level programming language control constructs (loops, conditionals). The execution of a command is analogous to a subroutine call. A file of shell commands, a *shell script*, may be executed like any other command, with the appropriate shell being invoked automatically to read it. *Shell programming* may thus be used to combine ordinary programs conveniently for quite sophisticated applications without the necessity of any programming in conventional languages.

This external user view is commonly thought of as the definition of Unix and yet it is the most easily changed definition. Writing a new shell with a quite different syntax and semantics would greatly change the user view while not changing the kernel or even the programmer interface. For example, work is proceeding at several sites to develop menu-driven and iconic interfaces for Unix. The heart of Unix is, of course, its kernel. The remaining sections of this chapter examine the kernel and its data structures and operation. We start with the file system.

14.5 File System

The Unix file system supports two main objects: files and directories. Directories are in fact just files with a special format, so the representation of a file is the basic Unix concept.

14.5.1 Blocks and Fragments

Most of the file system is taken up by *data blocks*, which contain whatever the users have put in their files. Let us consider how these data blocks are stored on the disk.

The hardware disk sector is usually 512 bytes. A block size larger than 512 bytes is desirable for speed. However, since Unix file systems usually contain a very large number of small files, much larger blocks would cause excessive internal fragmentation. This is why the earlier 4.1BSD file system was limited to a 1024-byte block.

The 4.2BSD solution is to use *two* block sizes: all the blocks of a file are of a large *block* size (such as 8192), except the last. The last block is an appropriate multiple of a smaller *fragment* size (for example 1024) to fill out the file. Thus an 18000-byte file would have two 8192-byte blocks and one 2048-byte fragment (which would not be completely filled).

The *block* and *fragment* sizes are set during file system creation according to the intended use of the file system: if many small files are expected, the fragment size should be small; if repeated transfers of large files are expected, the basic block size should be large. Implementation details force a maximum block/fragment ratio of 8/1, and a minimum block size of 4096, so typical choices are 4096/512 for the former case and 8192/1024 for the latter.

Suppose data is written to a file in transfer sizes of 1024 bytes while the block and fragment sizes of the file system are 4096 and 512 bytes. The file system will allocate a 1024-byte fragment to contain the data from the first transfer. The next transfer will cause a new 2048-byte fragment to be allocated. The data from the original fragment must be copied into this new fragment, followed by the second 1024-byte transfer. The allocation routines do attempt to find space on the disk immediately following the existing fragment so that no copying is necessary, but, if this is not possible, up to seven copies may be required before the fragment becomes a block. Provisions have been made for programs to discover the block size for a file so that transfers of that size may be made, in order to avoid fragment recopying.

14.5.2 Inodes

A file is represented by an *inode*. An inode is a record that stores most of the information about a specific file on the disk. The name *inode* (pronounced *EYE node*) is derived from "index node" and was originally spelled "i-node"; the hyphen fell out of use over the years. It is sometimes spelled *I node*.

The inode contains the user and group identifiers of the file, its times of last modification and access, a count of the number of hard links (directory entries) to the file, and the type of the file (plain file, directory, symbolic link, character device, block device, or socket). In addition, the inode contains 15 pointers to the disk blocks containing the data bytes of the file. The first 12 of these pointers point to *direct blocks*; that is, they directly contain addresses of blocks that contain data of the file. Thus, the data for small files (no more than 12 blocks) can be referenced immediately, since a copy of the inode is kept in main memory while a file is open. If the block size is 4096 bytes, then up to 48K bytes of data may be accessed directly from the inode.

The next three pointers in the inode point to *indirect blocks*. If the file is large enough to use indirect blocks, the indirect blocks are each of the major block size; the fragment size applies only to data blocks. The first indirect block pointer is the address of a *single indirect block*. The single indirect block is an index block, containing not data but the addresses of blocks which do contain data. Then there is a *double indirect block* pointer, the address of a block that contains the addresses of blocks which contain pointers to the actual data blocks. The last pointer would contain the address of a *triple indirect block*, however, there is no need for it. The minimum block size for a file system in 4.2BSD is 4096 bytes, so files with as many as 2^{32} bytes will only use double, not triple, indirection. That is, since each block pointer takes four bytes, we have 49,152 bytes accessible in direct blocks, 4,194,304 bytes accessible by a single indirection, and 4,294,967,296 bytes reachable through double indirection, for a total of 4,299,210,752 bytes, which is larger than 2^{32} bytes. The number 2^{32} is significant because the file offset in the file structure in main memory is kept in a 32-bit word. Files therefore cannot be larger than 2^{32} bytes. Four gigabytes is large enough for most purposes.

14.5.3 Directories

There is no distinction between plain files and directories at this level of implementation; directory contents are kept in data blocks and directories are represented by an inode in the same way as plain files. Only the inode type field distinguishes between plain files and directories. Plain files are not assumed to have a structure, however, while directories have a specific structure. In Version 7, file names were limited to 14 characters, so directories were a list of 16-byte entries: 2 bytes for an inumber and 14 bytes for a file name.

In 4.2BSD, file names are of variable length, up to 255 bytes, and so directory entries are also of variable length. Each entry contains first the length of the entry, then the file name and its inumber. This variable length entry makes the directory management and search routines more difficult, but greatly improves the ability of users to choose meaningful names for their files and directories, with no practical limit on the length of the name.

The first two names in every directory are "." and "..". New directory entries are added to the directory in the first space available, generally after the existing files. A linear search is used.

The user refers to a file by a pathname, while the file system uses the inode as its definition of a file. Thus the kernel has to map the user's pathname to an inode. The directories are used for this mapping.

First a starting directory is determined. If the first character of the pathname is "/", the starting directory is the root directory. If the pathname starts with any character other than a slash, the starting directory is the current directory of the current process. The starting directory is checked for existence, proper file type, and access permissions, and an error is returned if necessary. The inode of the starting directory is always available.

The next element of the pathname, up to the next "/", or the end of the pathname, is a file name. The starting directory is searched for this name, and an error returned if it is not found. If there is another element in the pathname, the current inode must refer to a directory, and an error is returned if it does not, or if access is denied. This directory is searched as was the previous one. This process continues until the end of the pathname is reached and the desired inode is returned.

Hard links are simply directory entries like any other. Symbolic links are handled for the most part by starting the search over with the pathname taken from the contents of the symbolic link. Infinite loops are prevented by counting the number of symbolic links encountered during a pathname search and returning an error when a limit (8) is exceeded.

Non-disk files (such as devices) do not have data blocks allocated on the disk. The kernel notices these file types (as indicated in the inode) and calls appropriate drivers to handle I/O for them.

Once the inode is found by, for instance, the *open* system call, a *file structure* is allocated to point to the inode. The file descriptor given to the user refers to this file structure.

14.5.4 Mapping a File Descriptor to an Inode

System calls that refer to open files indicate the file by passing a file descriptor as an argument. The file descriptor is used by the kernel to index a table of open files for the current process. Each entry of the table contains a pointer to a *file structure*. This file structure in turn points to the inode (Figure 14.6).

The *read* and *write* system calls do not take a position in the file as an argument. Rather the kernel keeps a *file offset*, which is updated by an appropriate amount after each *read* or *write* according to the amount of data actually transferred. The offset can be set directly by the *lseek* system call. If the file descriptor indexed an array of inode pointers instead of file pointers, this offset would have to be kept in the inode. Since more than one process may open the same file, and each such process needs its own offset for the file, keeping the offset in the inode is inappropriate. Thus the file structure is used to contain the offset.

File structures are inherited by the child process after a *fork*, so several processes may also have the *same* offset into a file.

The *inode structure* pointed to by the file structure is an in-core copy of the inode on the disk and is allocated out of a fixed-length table. The

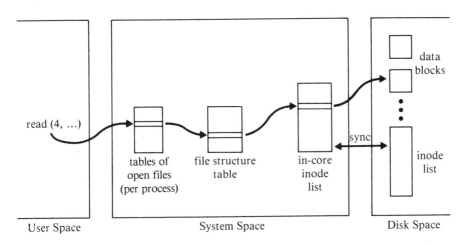

Figure 14.6   File system control blocks

in-core inode has a few extra fields, such as a reference count of how many file structures are pointing at it, and the file structure has a similar reference count for how many file descriptors refer to it.

14.5.5 Disk Structures

The file system that the user sees is supported by data on a mass storage device, usually a disk. The user ordinarily knows of only one file system, but this one logical file system may actually consist of several *physical* file systems, each on a different device. Since device characteristics differ, each separate hardware device defines its own physical file system. In fact, it is generally desirable to partition large physical devices, such as disks, into multiple *logical* devices. Each logical device defines a physical file system. Figure 14.7 illustrates how a directory structure is partitioned into file systems, which are mapped onto logical devices, which are partitions of physical devices.

Partitioning a physical device into multiple file systems has several benefits. Different file systems can support different uses. Although most partitions would be used by the file system, at least one will be necessary for a swap area for the virtual memory software. Reliability is improved, since software damage is generally limited to only one file system. Efficiency can be improved by varying the file system parameters (such as the block and fragment sizes) for each partition. Also, separate file systems prevent one program from using all available space for a large file, since files cannot be split across file systems.

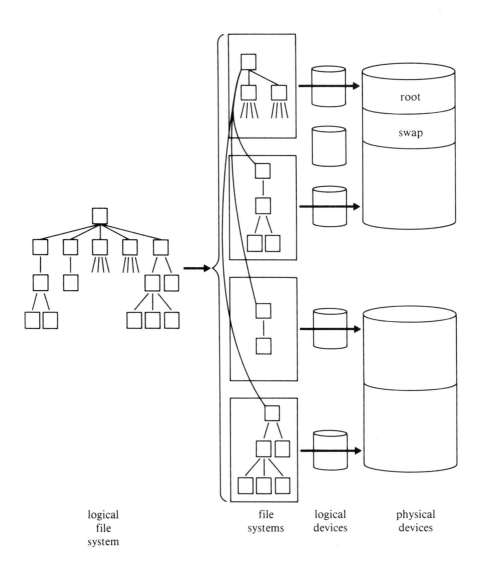

logical	file	logical	physical
file	systems	devices	devices
system			

Figure 14.7   Mapping a logical file system to physical devices

The actual number of file systems on a drive varies according to the size of the disk and the purpose of the computer system as a whole. One file system, the *root file system*, is always available. Others may be *mounted*, that is, integrated into the directory hierarchy of the root file system.

A bit in the inode structure indicates that the inode has a file system mounted on it. A reference to this file causes the *mount table* to be searched to find the device number of the mounted device. The device number is used to find the inode of the root directory of the mounted file system, and that inode is used. Conversely, if a pathname element is ".." and the directory being searched is the root directory of a file system that is mounted, the mount table must be searched to find the inode it is mounted on, and that inode is used.

Each file system is a separate system resource and represents a set of files. The first sector on the logical device is the *boot block*, containing a primary bootstrap program, which may be used to call a secondary bootstrap program residing in the next 7.5K bytes. The *super-block* contains static parameters of the file system. These include the total size of the file system, the block and fragment sizes of the data blocks, and assorted parameters that affect allocation policies.

14.5.6 Implementations

The user interface to the file system is simple and well defined. This has allowed the implementation of the file system itself to be changed without significant effect on the user. The file system was changed between Version 6 and Version 7, and again between Version 7 and 4BSD. For Version 7, the size of inodes doubled, the maximum file and file system sizes increased, and the details of free list handling and super-block information changed. At that time also, *seek* (with a 16-bit offset) became *lseek* (with a 32-bit offset) to allow for specifying offsets properly in the larger files then permitted, but few other changes were visible outside the kernel.

In 4.0BSD the size of blocks used in the file system was increased from 512 bytes to 1024 bytes. Although this produced increased internal fragmentation on the disk, it doubled throughput, due mainly to the greater amount of data accessed on each disk transfer. This idea was later adopted by System V, along with a number of other ideas, device drivers, and programs.

14.5.7 Layout and Allocation Policies

The kernel uses a *logical device number/inode number* pair to identify a file. The logical device number defines the file system involved. The inodes in the file system are numbered in sequence. In the Version 7 file system, all inodes are in an array immediately following a single super-block at the beginning of the logical device, with the data blocks following the inodes. The *inumber* is effectively just an index into this array.

With the Version 7 file system, a block of a file can be anywhere on the disk between the end of the inode array and the end of the file system. Free blocks are kept in a linked list in the super-block. Blocks are pushed onto the front of the free list, and removed from the front as needed for new files or to extend existing files. Thus, the blocks of a file may be arbitrarily far from both the inode and each other. Furthermore, the more a file system of this kind is used, the more disorganized the blocks in a file become. This process can only be reversed by reinitializing and restoring the entire file system, which is not a convenient thing to do.

Another difficulty is the reliability of the file system. For speed, the super-block of each mounted file system is kept in memory. This allows the kernel to quickly access a super-block, especially for using the free list. Every 30 seconds, the super-block is written to the disk, to keep the in-core and disk copies synchronized (the *sync* system call). However, it is not uncommon for system bugs or hardware failures to destroy the in-core super-block during a system crash. The free list is then lost, and must be constructed by a lengthy examination of all blocks in the file system.

The 4.2BSD file system implementation is radically different from that of Version 7. This reimplementation was done primarily for efficiency and robustness, and most such changes are invisible outside the kernel. There were some other changes introduced at the same time, such as symbolic links and long file names (up to 255 characters), that are visible at both the system call and the user levels. Most of the changes required for these features were not in the kernel, however, but in the programs that use them.

Space allocation is especially different. The major new concept in 4.2BSD is the *cylinder group*. The cylinder group was introduced to allow localization of the blocks in a file. Each cylinder group occupies one or more consecutive cylinders of the disk so that disk accesses within the cylinder group require minimal disk head movement. Every cylinder group has a super-block, a cylinder block, an array of inodes, and some data blocks (Figure 14.8).

The super-block is identical in each cylinder group, so that it may be recovered from any one of them in the event of disk corruption. The *cylinder block* contains dynamic parameters of the particular cylinder group. These include a bit map of free data blocks and fragments and a bit map of free inodes. Statistics on recent progress of the allocation strategies are also kept here.

The header information in a cylinder group (the super-block, the cylinder block, and the inodes) is not always at the beginning of the cylinder group. If it were, the header information for every cylinder

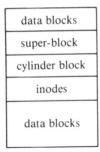

| data blocks |
| super-block |
| cylinder block |
| inodes |
| data blocks |

Figure 14.8   4.2BSD cylinder group

group might be on the same disk platter; a single disk head crash could wipe them all out. Therefore each cylinder group has its header information at a different offset from the beginning of the group.

It is common for the directory listing command *ls* to read all the inodes of every file in a directory, making it desirable for all such inodes to be close together. For this reason the inode for a file is usually allocated from the same cylinder group as the inode of its parent directory. Not everything can be localized, however, so an inode for a new directory is put in a *different* cylinder group from that of its parent directory. The cylinder group chosen for such a new directory inode is that with the greatest number of unused inodes.

To reduce disk head seeks involved in accessing the data blocks of a file, blocks are allocated from the same cylinder group as much as possible. Since a single file cannot be allowed to take up all the blocks in a cylinder group, a file exceeding a certain size (such as 32Kbytes) has further block allocation redirected to a different cylinder group, the new group being chosen from among those having more than average free space. If the file continues to grow, allocation is again redirected (at each megabyte) to yet another cylinder group. Thus all the blocks of a small file are likely to be in the same cylinder group, and the number of long seeks involved in accessing a large file is kept small.

There are two levels of disk block allocation routines. The global policy routines select a desired disk block according to the above considerations. The local policy routines use the specific information recorded in the cylinder blocks to choose a block near the one requested. If the requested block is not in use, it is returned. Otherwise, the block rotationally closest to it in the same cylinder or a block in a different cylinder but the same cylinder group is returned. If there are no more blocks in the cylinder group, a quadratic rehash is done among all the other cylinder groups to find a block, and if that fails an exhaustive search is done. If enough free space (typically 10 per cent), is left in the file system, blocks usually are found where desired, the quadratic rehash and exhaustive search are not used, and performance of the file system does not degrade with use.

The 4.2BSD file system is capable of using 30 per cent or more of the bandwidth of a typical disk, in contrast to about 3 per cent or less for the Version 7 file system.

14.6 Process Management

A major design problem for operating systems is the representation of processes. One major difference between Unix and many other systems is the ease of creating and manipulating multiple processes. These processes are represented in Unix by various control blocks. There are no system control blocks accessible in the virtual address space of a user process; control blocks associated with a process are stored in the kernel. The information in these control blocks is used by the kernel for process control and cpu scheduling.

14.6.1 Process Control Blocks

The most basic data structure associated with processes is the *process structure*. A process structure contains everything that is necessary to know about a process when it is swapped out, such as its unique process identifier, scheduling information (like the priority of the process), and pointers to other control blocks. There is an array of process structures, whose length is defined at system linking time. The process structures of ready processes are kept linked together by the scheduler in a doubly linked list (the ready queue), and there are pointers from each process structure to the process's parent, its youngest living child, and various other relatives of interest, such as a list of processes sharing the same program code (text).

The *virtual address space* of a user process is divided into text (program code), data, and stack segments. The data and stack segments are always in the same address space, but may grow separately, and usually in opposite directions: most frequently the stack grows down as the data grows up towards it. The text segment is sometimes (as on a PDP-11 with separate instruction and data space) in a different address space from the data and stack and is usually read-only.

Every process with sharable text (almost all, under 4.2BSD) has a pointer from its process structure to a *text structure*. The text structure records how many processes are using the text segment, a pointer into a list of their process structures, and where the page table for the text segment can be found on disk when it is swapped. The text structure itself is always resident in main memory: an array of such structures is allocated at system link time. The text, data, and stack segments for the processes may be swapped. When the segments are swapped in, they are paged.

The *page tables* record information on the mapping from the process's virtual memory to physical memory. The process structure contains pointers to the page table, for use when the process is resident in main memory, or the address of the process on the swap device, when it is swapped. There is no special separate page table for a shared text segment; every process sharing it has entries for its pages in the process's page table.

Information about the process that is needed only when the process is resident (that is, not swapped out) is kept in the *user structure* (or *u structure*) rather than the process structure. The *u* structure is mapped into kernel virtual data space. A copy of the VAX process control block is kept here for saving the process's general registers, stack pointer, program counter, and page table base registers when the process is not running. There is space to keep system call parameters and return values. All user and group identifiers associated with the process (not just the effective user identifier kept in the process structure) are kept here. Signals, timers, and quotas have data structures here. Of more obvious relevance to the ordinary user, the current directory and the table of open files is maintained in the user structure.

Every process has both a user and a system phase. Most ordinary work is done by the *user process*, but when a system call is made, it is the *system process* that performs the system call. The system and user phases of a process never execute simultaneously. The system process has a different stack than the user process. The *kernel stack* for the process immediately follows the user structure: the kernel stack and the user structure together compose the *system data segment* for the process.

Figure 14.9 illustrates how the process structure is used to find the various parts of a process.

The *fork* system call allocates a new process structure (with a new process identifier) for the child process and copies the user structure. There is ordinarily no need for a new text structure, as the processes share their text; the appropriate counters and lists are merely updated. A new page table is constructed, and new main memory is allocated for the data and stack segments of the child process. The copying of the the user structure preserves open file descriptors, user and group identifiers, signal handling, and most similar properties of a process.

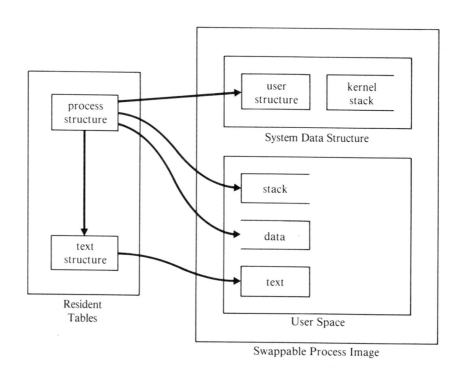

Figure 14.9 CPU scheduling components

The *vfork* system call does *not* copy the data and stack to the new process, rather the new process simply shares the page table of the old one. A new user structure and a new process structure are still created. A common use of this system call is by a shell to execute a command and wait for its completion. The parent process uses *vfork* to produce the child process. Since the child process wishes to immediately use an *execve* to completely change its virtual address space, there is no need for a complete copy of the parent process. Such data structures as are necessary for manipulating pipes may be kept in registers between the *vfork* and the *execve*. Files may be closed in one process without affecting the other process, since the kernel data structures involved depend on the user structure, which is not shared. The parent uses *wait* to suspend its execution until the child terminates, so that the parent will not change memory the child needs.

When the parent process is large, *vfork* can produce substantial savings in system cpu time. However, it is a fairly dangerous system call since any memory change occurs in both processes until the *execve* occurs. An alternative is to share all pages by duplicating the page table, but to mark the entries of both page tables as *copy-on-write*. The hardware protection bits are set to trap any attempt to write in these shared pages. If such a trap occurs, a new frame is allocated and the shared page is copied to the new frame. The page tables are adjusted to show that this page is no longer shared (and therefore need no longer be write-protected), and execution can resume. Hardware bugs with the VAX/750 prevented 4.2BSD from including a copy-on-write fork operation.

An *execve* system call creates no new process or user structure, rather the text and data of the process are replaced. Open files are preserved (although there is a way to specify that certain file descriptors are to be closed on an *execve*). Most signal handling properties are preserved, but arrangements to call a specific user routine on a signal are cancelled, for obvious reasons. The process identifier and most other properties of the process are unchanged.

14.6.2 CPU Scheduling

CPU scheduling in Unix is designed to benefit interactive processes. Processes are given small cpu time slices by a priority algorithm that reduces to round-robin for cpu-bound jobs.

Every process has a *scheduling priority* associated with it; larger numbers are lower priority. Processes doing disk I/O or other important tasks have negative priorities and cannot be killed by signals. Ordinary user processes have positive priorities and thus are all less likely to be run than any system process, although user processes may have precedence over one another: the *nice* command affects this.

The more cpu time a process accumulates, the lower (more positive) its priority becomes, and the reverse, so there is negative feedback in cpu scheduling and it is difficult for a single process to take all cpu time. Process aging is employed to prevent starvation.

Older Unix systems used a one second quantum for the round-robin scheduling: 4.2BSD reschedules processes every 1/10 second and recomputes priorities every second. The round-robin scheduling is accomplished by the *timeout* mechanism, which tells the clock interrupt driver to call a kernel subroutine after a specified interval; the subroutine to be called in this case causes the rescheduling and then resubmits a *timeout* to call itself again. The priority recomputation is also timed by a subroutine that resubmits a *timeout* for itself.

There is no preemption of one process by another in the kernel. A process may relinquish the cpu because it is waiting on I/O or because its time slice has expired. When a process chooses to relinquish the cpu, it goes to sleep on an *event*. The kernel primitive used for this is called *sleep* (not to be confused with the user-level library routine of the same name). It takes an argument, which is by convention the address of a kernel data structure related to an *event* the process wants to occur before it is awakened. When the event occurs, the system process that knows about it calls *wakeup* with the address corresponding to the event, and *all* processes that had done a *sleep* on the same address are put in the ready queue to be run.

For example, a process waiting for disk I/O to complete will *sleep* on the address of the buffer header corresponding to the data being transferred. When the interrupt routine for the disk driver notes the transfer is complete, it calls *wakeup* on the buffer header. The interrupt uses the kernel stack for whatever process happened to be running at the time, and the *wakeup* is done from that system process.

The process that actually does run is chosen by the scheduler. *Sleep* takes a second argument, which is the scheduling priority to be used for this purpose. This priority argument, if negative, also prevents the process from being prematurely awakened by some exceptional event, such as a *signal*.

When a signal is generated, it is queued until the system half of the affected process next runs. This usually happens soon, since the signal normally causes the process to be awakened if it has been waiting for some other condition.

There is no memory associated with events and the caller of the routine that does a *sleep* on an event must be prepared to deal with a premature return, including the possibility that the reason for waiting has vanished.

There are *race conditions* involved in the event mechanism. If a process decides (because of checking a flag in memory, for instance) to sleep on an event and the event occurs before the process can execute the primitive that does the actual sleep on the event, the process sleeping may then sleep forever. This is prevented by raising the hardware processor priority during the critical section so that no interrupts can occur, and thus only the process desiring the event can run until it is sleeping. Hardware processor priority is used in this manner to protect critical regions throughout the kernel and is the greatest obstacle to porting Unix to multiple processor machines.

Many processes such as text editors are I/O-bound and will usually be scheduled mainly on the basis of waiting for I/O. Experience suggests that the Unix scheduler performs best with I/O-bound jobs, as can be observed when there are several cpu-bound jobs like text formatters or language interpreters running.

What has been referred to here as cpu scheduling corresponds closely to the *short-term scheduling* of Chapter 4, although the negative feedback property of the priority scheme provides some long-term scheduling in that it largely determines the long-term *job mix*. *Medium-term scheduling* is done by the swapping mechanism described below.

14.7 Memory Management

Much of Unix's early development was done on a PDP-11. The PDP-11 has only eight segments in its virtual address space, and each of these are at most 8192 bytes. The larger machines like the PDP-11/70 allow separate instruction and address spaces, which effectively double the address space and number of segments, but this is still not much. In addition, the kernel was even more severely constrained due to dedicating one data segment to interrupt vectors, another to point at the per-process system data segment, and yet another for the UNIBUS registers. Further, on the smaller PDP-11s, total physical memory was limited to 256K bytes. The total memory resources were insufficient to justify or support complex memory management algorithms. Thus, Unix swapped the entire process memory image.

14.7.1 Swapping

Pre-3BSD Unix systems used swapping exclusively to handle memory contention among processes: if there is too much contention, processes are swapped out until enough memory is available. Also, a few large processes can force many small processes out of memory, and a process larger than non-kernel main memory cannot be run at all. The system data segment (the *u* structure and kernel stack) and the user data segment (text [if non-sharable], data, and stack) are kept in contiguous main memory for swap transfer efficiency, so external fragmentation of memory can be a serious problem.

Allocation of both main memory and swap space is done first-fit. When the size of a process's memory image increases (due to either stack expansion or data expansion), a new piece of memory big enough for the whole image is allocated. The memory image is copied, the old memory is freed, and the appropriate tables are updated. (An attempt is made in some systems to find memory contiguous to the end of the current piece to avoid some copying.) If no single piece of main memory is large enough, the process is swapped out in such a way that it will be swapped back in with the new size.

There is no need to swap a sharable text segment out, because it is read-only, and there is no need to read in a sharable text segment for a process when another instance is already in core. This is one of the main reasons for keeping track of sharable text segments: less swap traffic. The other reason is the reduced amount of main memory required for multiple processes using the same text segment.

Decisions on which processes to swap in or out are made by the the *scheduler process*, process 0 (also known as the *swapper* process). The *scheduler* wakes up at least once every four seconds to check for processes to be swapped in or out. A process is more likely to be swapped out if it is idle, has been in main memory a long time, or is large; if no easy candidates are found, other processes are picked by age. A process is more likely to be swapped in if it has been swapped out a long time, or is small. There are checks to prevent thrashing, basically by not letting a process be swapped out if it has not been in core for a certain amount of time.

If jobs do not need to be swapped out, the process table is searched for a process deserving to be brought in (determined by how small it is and how long it has been swapped). If there is not enough memory available, processes are swapped out until there is.

In 4.2BSD, swap space is allocated in pieces that are multiples of a power of two and a minimum size (for example, 32 pages), up to a maximum that is determined by the size of the swap space partition on the disk. If several logical disk partitions may be used for swapping, they should be the same size, for this reason. The several logical disk partitions should also be on separate disk arms to minimize disk seeks.

Many Unix systems still use the swapping scheme described above. All USG systems, including System V, do. All Berkeley Unix systems, on the other hand, including 4.2BSD, depend primarily on paging for memory contention management and only secondarily on swapping. A scheme very similar in outline to the traditional one is used to determine what processes get swapped in or out, but the details differ and the influence of swapping is less.

14.7.2 Paging

Berkeley introduced paging to Unix with 3BSD. 4.2BSD is a demand paged virtual memory system. External fragmentation of memory is eliminated by paging. (There is of course internal fragmentation, but this is negligible with a reasonably small page size.) Swapping can be kept to a minimum because more jobs can be kept in main memory since not all of any of them has to be resident.

Demand paging is done in a straightforward manner. When a process needs a page and the page is not there, a page fault to the kernel occurs, a frame of main memory is allocated, and the proper disk page is read into it.

There are a few optimizations. If the page needed is still in the page table for the process, but has been marked invalid by the page replacement process, it can be marked valid and used without any I/O transfer. Pages can similarly be retrieved from the list of free frames. When most processes are started, many of their pages are prepaged and put on the free list for recovery by this mechanism. Arrangements may also be made for a process to have no prepaging on startup, but this is seldom done, as it results in more page fault overhead, being closer to pure demand paging.

If the page has to be fetched from disk, it must be locked for the duration. Once the page is fetched and mapped properly, it must not be unlocked if raw physical I/O is being done on it.

The *page replacement* algorithm is more interesting. The VAX has no hardware memory page reference bit. This makes many memory management algorithms, such as page fault frequency, unusable. 4.2BSD uses a modified *Global Clock Least Recently Used* (LRU) algorithm. The map of all non-kernel main memory (the *core map* or *cmap*) is swept linearly and repeatedly by a software *clock hand*. When the clock hand reaches a given frame, if the frame is marked as in use by some software condition (for example, physical I/O is in progress using it), or the frame is already free, it is left untouched and the clock hand sweeps to the next frame. Otherwise, the corresponding text or process page table entry for this frame is located. If the entry is already invalid, the frame is added to the free list, otherwise the page table entry is made invalid but reclaimable (that is, if it does not get paged out by the next time it is wanted, it can just be made valid again). Of course if the page is dirty (the VAX *does* have a dirty bit) it must first be written to disk before being added to the free list.

There are checks to make sure the number of valid data pages for a process does not fall too low, and to keep the paging device from being flooded with requests. There is also a mechanism by which a process may limit the amount of main memory it uses.

The LRU clock hand is implemented in the *pagedaemon*, which is process 2 (remember the *scheduler* is process 0 and *init* is process 1). This process spends most of its time sleeping, but a check is done several times a second (scheduled by a *timeout*) to see if action is necessary, and if so, process 2 is awakened. Whenever the number of free frames falls below a threshold, *lotsfree*, the *pagedaemon* is awakened; thus if there is always a lot of free memory, the *pagedaemon* imposes no load on the system because it never runs.

The sweep of the clock hand each time the *pagedaemon* process is awakened (that is, the number of frames scanned, which is usually more than the number paged out), is determined both by the number of frames lacking to reach *lotsfree* and by the number of frames the *scheduler* has determined are needed for various reasons (the more frames needed, the longer the sweep). If the number of frames free rises to *lotsfree* before the expected sweep is completed, the hand stops and the *pagedaemon* process sleeps. The parameters that determine the range of the clock hand sweep are determined at system startup according to the amount of main memory so that *pagedaemon* should not use more than 10 per cent of all cpu time.

If the *scheduler* decides the paging system is overloaded, processes will be swapped out whole until the overload is relieved. This usually happens only if several conditions are met: high load average, free memory has fallen below a very low limit, *minfree*, and the average memory available over recent time is less than a desirable amount, *desfree*, where *lotsfree* > *desfree* > *minfree*. In other words, only a chronic shortage of memory with several processes trying to run will cause swapping, and even then free memory has to be *very* low at the moment. (An excessive paging rate or a need for memory by the kernel itself may also enter into the calculations in rare cases.) Processes may of course be swapped by the *scheduler* for other reasons (such as just not running for a long time).

The parameter *lotsfree* is usually 1/4 of the memory in the map the clock hand sweeps, and *desfree* and *minfree* are usually the same across different systems, but are limited to fractions of available memory.

Every process's text segment is by default a shared, read-only text segment. This is practical with paging, since there is no external fragmentation, and the swap space gained by sharing more than offsets the negligible amount of overhead involved, since the kernel virtual space is large.

CPU scheduling, swapping, and paging interact: the lower the priority of a process, the more likely its pages will be paged out and the more likely it will be swapped in its entirety.

The age preferences in choosing processes to swap guard against thrashing, but paging does so more effectively. Ideally, processes will not be swapped out unless they are idle, since each process will need only a small working set of pages in main memory at any one time, and the *pagedaemon* will reclaim unused pages for use by other processes, so most runnable processes will never be completely swapped out.

The amount of memory the process will need is some fraction of its total virtual size, up to 1/2 if it has been swapped a long time.

For I/O efficiency, the VAX 512-byte hardware pages are too small, so they are clustered in groups of two so that all paging I/O is actually done in 1024-byte chunks. In other words, the effective page size is not tied to the hardware page size of the machine, although it must be a multiple of the hardware page size.

14.8 I/O System

One of the purposes of an operating system is to hide the peculiarities of specific hardware devices from the user. For example, the file system presents a simple consistent storage facility (the file) independent of the underlying disk hardware. In Unix, the peculiarities of I/O devices are also hidden from the bulk of the kernel itself by the *I/O system*. The I/O system consists of a buffer caching system, general device driver code, and drivers for specific hardware devices. Only this last part, the device driver, knows the peculiarities of a specific device.

The major parts of the I/O system may be diagrammed as in Figure 14.10.

There are three main kinds of I/O in 4.2BSD: block devices, character devices, and the *socket* interface. The socket interface, together with its protocols and network interfaces, will be treated later in Section 14.9.1.

Block devices include disks and tapes. Their distinguishing characteristic is that they are directly addressable in a fixed block size, usually 512 bytes. A block device driver is required to isolate details of tracks, cylinders, and so on, from the rest of the kernel. Block devices are accessible directly through appropriate device special files (such as */dev/rp0*), but are more commonly accessed indirectly through the file system. In either case, transfers are buffered through the *block buffer cache*, which has a profound effect on efficiency.

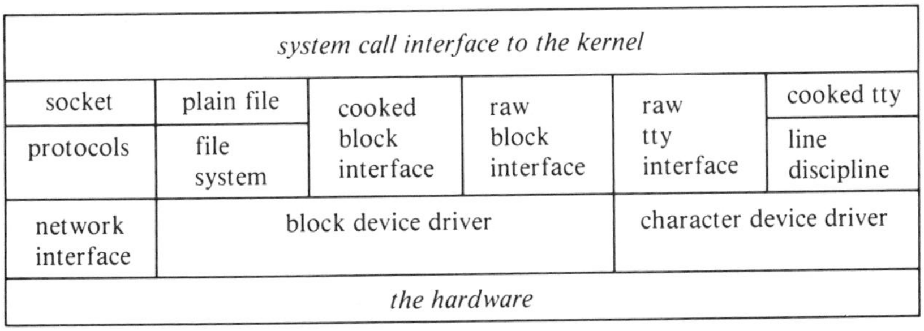

system call interface to the kernel					
socket	plain file	cooked	raw	raw	cooked tty
protocols	file system	block interface	block interface	tty interface	line discipline
network interface	block device driver			character device driver	
the hardware					

Figure 14.10   4.2BSD kernel I/O structure

Character devices include terminals and line printers, but also almost everything else (except network interfaces) that does not use the block buffer cache. For instance, */dev/mem* is an interface to physical main memory and */dev/null* is a bottomless sink for data and an endless source of end-of-file markers. Some devices, such as high-speed graphics interfaces may have their own buffers or may always do I/O directly into the user's data space; since they do not use the block buffer cache, they are classed as character devices.

Terminals and terminal-like devices use *C-lists*, which are buffers smaller than those of the block buffer cache.

"Block" devices and "character" devices are the two main device classes. Device drivers are accessed by one of two arrays of entry points. One array is for block devices; the other is for character devices. A device is distinguished by a class (block or character) and a *device number*. The device number consists of two parts. The *major device number* is used to index the array for character or block devices to find entries into the appropriate device driver. The *minor device number* is interpreted by the device driver as, for example, a logical disk partition or a terminal line.

A device driver is connected to the rest of the kernel only by the entry points recorded in the array for its class, and by its use of common buffering systems. This segregation is important for portability, and also for configuring systems.

14.8.1 Block Buffer Cache

The block devices use a block buffer cache. The buffer cache consists of a number of buffer headers, each of which points to a piece of physical memory as well as a device number and a block number on the device. The buffer headers are kept in several linked lists.

- Information that is never written out, such as super-blocks of file systems.

- Blocks in use (the cache) in least recently used order.

- Empty buffers with no memory or disk blocks associated with them.

The buffers in these lists are also hashed by device and block number for search efficiency.

When a block is wanted from a device (a read), the cache is searched. If the block is found, it is used and no I/O transfer is necessary. If it is not found, a buffer is chosen from the list of empty buffers, the device number and block number associated with it are updated, memory is found for it, and the new data is transferred into it from the device. If there are no empty buffers, the least recently used buffer is written to its device and the buffer is reused.

On a write, if the block in question is already in the buffer cache, the new data is put in the buffer (overwriting any previous data), the buffer header is marked to indicate the buffer has been modified, and no I/O is immediately necessary. The data will be written when the buffer is needed for other data. If the block is not found in the buffer cache, an empty buffer is chosen (as with a read) and a transfer is done to this buffer.

Writes are periodically forced for dirty buffer blocks in order to minimize potential file system inconsistencies after a crash.

The amount of data in a buffer in 4.2BSD is variable, up to a maximum over all file systems, usually 8K bytes. The minimum size is the paging cluster size, usually 1024 bytes. Buffers are page-cluster aligned and any page cluster may be mapped into only one buffer at a time, just as any disk block may be mapped into only one buffer at a time.

The amount of data in a buffer may grow as a user process writes more data following that already in the buffer. When this happens, a new buffer large enough to hold all the data is allocated and the original data is copied into it, followed by the new data. If a buffer shrinks, a buffer is taken off the empty queue, excess pages are put in it, and that buffer is released to be written to disk.

Some devices, such as magnetic tapes, require blocks to be written in a certain order, so facilities are provided to force synchronous writes of buffers to these devices. Blocks of directories are also written synchronously.

The size of the buffer cache can have a profound effect on the performance of a system, since if it is large enough the percentage of cache hits can be quite high and the number of actual I/O transfers low.

There are some interesting interactions between the buffer cache, the file system, and the disk drivers. When data is written to a disk file, it is buffered in the cache, and the disk driver sorts its output queue according to disk address. These two things allow the disk driver to minimize disk head seeks and to write data at times optimized for disk rotation. When data is read from a disk file, the block I/O system does some read-ahead; however, reads are much nearer to asynchronous than writes. Thus output to the disk through the file system is often faster than input for large transfers, counter to intuition.

14.8.2 Raw Device Interfaces

Almost every block device also has a character interface, and these are called *raw device interfaces*. Such an interface differs from the *block interface* in that the block buffer cache is bypassed.

Each disk driver maintains a queue of pending transfers. Each record in the queue specifies whether it is a read or a write, a main memory address for the transfer, a device address for the transfer (usually the 512 byte block number), and a transfer size (in bytes). It is simple to map the information from a block buffer to what is required for this queue.

It is almost as simple to map a piece of main memory corresponding to part of a user process's virtual address space in a similar manner. This is what a raw disk interface, for instance, does. Unbuffered transfers directly to or from a user's virtual address space are thus allowed. The size of the transfer is limited by the physical device, some of which require an even number of bytes. The software restricts the size of a single transfer to what will fit in a 16-bit word; this is an artifact of the system's PDP-11 history and of the PDP-11 derivation of many of the devices themselves.

The kernel accomplishes transfers for swapping and paging simply by putting the appropriate request on the queue for the appropriate device. No special swapping or paging device driver is needed.

The 4.2BSD file system implementation was actually written and largely tested as a user process that used a raw disk interface before the code was moved into the kernel.

14.8.3 C-Lists

Terminal drivers use a character buffering system. This involves small blocks of characters (usually 28 bytes) kept in linked lists. There are routines to enqueue and dequeue characters for such lists. Although all free character buffers are kept in a single free list, most device drivers that use them limit the number of characters that may be queued at one time for a terminal line.

A write system call to a terminal enqueues characters on a list for the device. An initial transfer is started, and interrupts cause dequeueing of characters and further transfers.

Input is similarly interrupt driven. Terminal drivers typically support *two* input queues, however, and conversion from the first (raw queue) to the other (canonical queue) is triggered by the interrupt routine putting an end of line character on the raw queue. The process doing a read on the device is then awakened and its system phase does the conversion, and the characters thus put on the canonical queue are then available to be returned to the user process by the read.

It is also possible to have the device driver bypass the canonical queue and return characters directly from the raw queue. This is known as "raw mode".

14.9 Interprocess Communication

Many tasks can be accomplished in isolated processes, but many others require interprocess communication. Isolated computing systems have long served for many applications, but networking is increasingly important. With the increasing use of personal workstations, resource sharing is becoming more common. Interprocess communication has not traditionally been one of Unix's strong points.

Most Unix systems have not permitted *shared memory* because the PDP-11 hardware did not encourage it. System V does support a shared memory facility, and one was planned for 4.2BSD but was not implemented due to time constraints. In any case, shared memory presents a problem in a networked environment, since network accesses can never be as fast as memory accesses on the local machine. While one could, of course, pretend that memory was shared between two separate machines by copying data across a network transparently, still the major benefit of shared memory (speed) would be lost.

14.9.1 Sockets

The *pipe* (discussed in Section 14.4.3) is the IPC mechanism most characteristic of Unix. A pipe permits a reliable uni-directional byte stream between two processes. It is traditionally implemented as an ordinary file, with a few exceptions. It has no name in the file system, being created instead by the *pipe* system call. Its size is fixed and when a process attempts to write to a full pipe, the process is suspended. Once all data previously written into the pipe has been read out, writing continues at the beginning of the file (pipes are not true circular buffers). One benefit of the small size (usually 4096 bytes) of pipes is that pipe data is seldom actually written to disk, usually being kept in memory by the normal block buffer cache.

In 4.2BSD, pipes are implemented as a special case of the *socket* mechanism. The 4.2BSD socket mechanism provides a general interface not only to facilities such as pipes, which are local to one machine, but also to networking facilities.

A *socket* is an endpoint of communication. A socket in use usually has an *address* bound to it. The nature of the address depends on the *communication domain* of the socket. A characteristic property of a domain is that processes communicating in the same domain use the same *address format*. A single socket can communicate in only one domain.

The two domains currently implemented in 4.2BSD are the Unix domain (AF_UNIX) and the Internet domain (AF_INET). The address format of the Unix domain is ordinary file system pathnames, such as */alpha/beta/gamma*. Processes communicating in the Internet domain use DARPA Internet communications protocols (such as TCP/IP) and Internet addresses, which consist of a 32-bit host number and a 32-bit port number.

There are several *socket types*, which represent classes of services. Each type may or may not be implemented in any communication domain. If a type is implemented in a given domain, it may be implemented by one or more protocols, which may be selected by the user.

- **Stream** sockets provide reliable, duplex, sequenced data streams. No data is lost or duplicated in delivery, and there are no record boundaries. This type is supported in the Internet domain by the TCP protocol. In the Unix domain, pipes are implemented as a pair of communicating stream sockets.

- **Sequenced packet** sockets would provide data streams like those of stream sockets, except that record boundaries would be provided. This type is currently unsupported, but corresponds to the Xerox XNS protocol.

- **Datagram** sockets transfer messages of variable size in either direction. There is no guarantee that such messages will arrive in the same order they were sent, or that they will be unduplicated, or that they will arrive at all, but the original message (record) size is preserved in any datagram that does arrive. This type is supported in the Internet domain by the UDP protocol.

- **Reliably delivered message** sockets would transfer messages that would be guaranteed to arrive, and would otherwise be like the messages transferred using datagram sockets. This type is currently unsupported.

- **Raw** sockets allow direct access by processes to the protocols that support the other socket types. The protocols accessible include not only the uppermost ones, but also lower level protocols. For example, in the Internet domain it is possible to reach TCP, IP beneath that, or an Ethernet protocol beneath that. This capability is useful for developing new protocols.

The socket facility has a set of system calls specific to it. The *socket* system call creates a socket. It takes as arguments specifications of the communication domain, the socket type, and the protocol to be used to support that type. The value returned is a small integer called a *socket descriptor*, which is in the same name space as file descriptors. The socket descriptor indexes the array of open "files" in the *u* structure in the kernel, and has a file structure allocated for it. The 4.2BSD file structure may point to a *socket* structure instead of an inode. In this case, certain socket information (such as a the socket's type, message count, and the data in its input and output queues) is kept directly in the socket structure.

For another process to address a socket, the socket must have a name. A name is bound to a socket by the *bind* system call, which takes the socket descriptor, a pointer to the name, and the length of the name as a byte string. The contents and length of the byte string depend on the address format. The *connect* system call is used to initiate a connection. The arguments are syntactically the same as for *bind*, and the socket descriptor represents the local socket while the address is that of the foreign socket to attempt to connect to.

Many processes that communicate using the socket IPC follow the *client/server model*. In this model, the *server* process provides a *service* to the *client* process. When the service is available, the server process listens on a well-known address, and the client process uses *connect*, as above, to reach it.

A server process uses *socket* to create a socket and *bind* to bind the well-known address of its service to it. Then it uses the *listen* system call to tell the kernel it is ready to accept connections from clients, and how many pending connections the kernel should queue until the server can service them. Finally, the server uses the *accept* system call to accept individual connections. Both *listen* and *accept* take as an argument the socket descriptor of the original socket. *Accept* returns a new socket descriptor corresponding to the new connection; the original socket descriptor is still open for further connections. The server usually uses *fork* to produce a new process after the *accept* to service the client while the original server process continues to listen for more connections.

There are also system calls for setting parameters of a connection and for returning the address of the foreign socket after an *accept*.

When a connection for a socket type such as a stream socket is established, the addresses of both endpoints are known and no further addressing information is needed to transfer data. The ordinary *read* and *write* system calls may then be used to transfer data.

The simplest way to terminate a connection and destroy the associated socket is to use the *close* system call on its socket descriptor.

One may also wish to terminate only one direction of communication of a duplex connection, and the *shutdown* system call may be used for this.

Some socket types, such as datagram sockets, do not support connections, and instead their sockets exchange datagrams that must be individually addressed. The system calls *sendto* and *recvfrom* are used for such connections. Both take as arguments a socket descriptor, a buffer pointer and the length of the buffer, and an address buffer pointer and length. The address buffer contains the address to send to for *sendto* and is filled in with the address of the datagram just received by *recvfrom*. The amount of data actually transferred is returned by both system calls.

The *select* system call may be used to multiplex data transfers on several file descriptors and/or socket descriptors. It may even be used to allow one server process to listen for client connections for many services and *fork* a process for each connection as it is made. This is done by doing *socket*, *bind*, and *listen* for each service, and then doing *select* on all the socket descriptors. When *select* indicates activity on a descriptor, the server does an *accept* on it and forks a process on the new descriptor returned by *accept*, leaving the parent process to do a *select* again.

14.9.2 Network Support

Almost all current Unix systems support the UUCP network facilities, which are mostly used over dial-up phone lines to support the UUCP mail network and the USENET news network. These are, however, at best rudimentary networking facilities, as they do not even support remote login, much less remote procedure call or distributed file systems. These facilities are also almost completely implemented as user processes, and are not part of the operating system proper.

4.2BSD supports the DARPA Internet protocols UDP, TCP, IP, and ICMP on a wide range of Ethernet, token ring, and Arpanet interfaces. The framework in the kernel to support this is intended to facilitate the implementation of further protocols, and all are accessible via the socket interface. The first version of the code involved was written by Rob Gurwitz of BBN as an add-on package for 4.1BSD.

The International Standards Organization's (ISO) Open System Interconnection (OSI) Reference Model for networking prescribes seven layers of network protocols and strict methods of communication between them. An implementation of a protocol may only communicate with a peer entity speaking the same protocol at the same layer, or with the protocol-protocol interface of a protocol in the layer immediately above or below in the same system.

The 4.2BSD networking implementation, and to a certain extent the *socket* facility, is more oriented towards the Arpanet Reference Model (ARM). The Arpanet in its original form served as proof-of-concept for many networking concepts such as packet switching and protocol layering. It serves today as a communications utility for researchers. Together with its sibling networks in the DARPA Internet, it is also a testbed for internet gateway research. The ARM predates the ISO model and the latter was in large part inspired by the Arpanet research.

While the ISO model is often interpreted as requiring a limit of one protocol communicating per layer, the ARM allows several protocols in the same layer. There are only three protocol layers in the ARM:

- **Process/Applications** subsumes the Application, Presentation, and Session layers of the ISO model. Such user-level programs as the File Transfer Protocol (FTP) and Telnet (remote login) exist at this level.

- **Host-Host** corresponds to ISO's Transport and the top part of its Network layers. Both the Transmission Control Protocol (TCP) and the Internet Protocol (IP) are in this layer, with TCP on top of IP. TCP corresponds to an ISO Transport protocol and IP performs the addressing functions of the ISO network layer.

- **Network interface** spans the lower part of the ISO network layer and all of the Data Link layer. The protocols involved here depend on the physical network type. The Arpanet uses the IMP-Host protocols, while an Ethernet uses Ethernet protocols.

- **Network hardware**. The ARM is primarily concerned with software, so there is no explicit network hardware layer; however, any actual network will have hardware corresponding to the ISO hardware layer.

The networking framework in 4.2BSD is more generalized than either the ISO model or the ARM, although it is most closely related to the latter. See Figure 14.11.

User processes communicate with network protocols (and thus with other processes on other machines) via the *socket* facility, which corresponds to the ISO Session layer, as it is responsible for setting up and controlling communications.

Sockets are supported by *protocols*; possibly by several, layered one on another. A protocol may provide services such as reliable delivery,

ISO Reference Model	ARPANET Reference Model	4.2BSD Layers	Example Layering
Application	Process/ Applications	User Programs and Libraries	telnet
Presentation			
Session		Sockets	SOCK-STREAM
Transport	Host– Host	Protocols	TCP
Network			IP
	Network Interface	Network Interfaces	Ethernet Driver
Data Link			
Hardware	Network Hardware	Network Hardware	Interlan Controller

Figure 14.11   Network reference models and layering

suppression of duplicate transmissions, flow control, or addressing, depending on the socket type being supported and the services required by any higher protocols.

A protocol may communicate with another protocol or with the network interface that is appropriate for the network hardware. There is little restriction in the general framework on what protocols may communicate with what other protocols, or on how many protocols may be layered on top of one another. The user process may, by means of the raw socket type, directly access any layer of protocol from the uppermost used to support one of the other socket types, such as streams, down to a raw network interface. This capability is used by routing processes and also for new protocol development.

There tends to be one *network interface* driver per network controller type. The network interface is responsible for handling characteristics specific to the local network being addressed in such a way that the protocols using the interface need not be concerned with them.

The functions of the network interface depend largely on the *network hardware*, which is whatever is necessary for the network it is connected to. Some networks may support reliable transmission at this level, but most do not. Some provide broadcast addressing, but many do not.

There are projects in progress at various organizations to implement protocols other than the DARPA Internet ones, including the protocols ISO has thus far adopted to fit the OSI model.

The socket facility and the networking framework use a common set of memory buffers, or *mbuf*s. These are intermediate in size between the large buffers used by the block I/O system and the C-lists used by character devices. An *mbuf* is 128 bytes long, 112 bytes of which may be used for data; the rest is used for pointers to link the *mbuf* into queues and to indicate how much of the data area is actually in use.

Data is ordinarily passed between layers (socket/protocol, protocol/protocol, or protocol/network interface) in *mbuf*s. This ability to pass the buffers containing the data eliminates some data copying, but there is still frequently a need to remove or add protocol headers. It is also convenient and efficient for many purposes to be able to hold data of the size of the memory management page. Thus it is possible for the data of an *mbuf* to reside not in the *mbuf* itself, but elsewhere in memory. There is an *mbuf* page table for this purpose, as well as a pool of pages dedicated for *mbuf* use.

14.10 Summary

Unix was developed at Bell Labs as a research project. As it has changed over the past 15 years, it has become an important and powerful operating system. Many versions of Unix exist. 4.2BSD was developed at Berkeley for the VAX, but has been ported to many other computer systems.

Unix provides a file system with tree-structured directories. Files are supported by the kernel as unstructured sequences of bytes. Direct access and sequential access are supported through system calls and library routines.

Files are stored as an array of fixed-size data blocks with perhaps a trailing fragment. The data blocks are found by pointers in the inode. Directory entries point to inodes. Disk space is allocated from cylinder groups to minimize head movement and improve performance.

Unix is a multiprogrammed system. Processes can easily create new processes with the *fork* system call. Processes can communicate with pipes, or more generally, sockets.

Processes are represented by two structures: the process structure and the user structure. CPU scheduling is a priority algorithm with dynamically computed priorities that reduces to round-robin in the extreme case.

4.2BSD memory management is swapping supported by paging. A pagedaemon process uses a modified second chance page replacement algorithm to try to keep enough free frames to support the executing processes.

Page and file I/O uses a block buffer cache to minimize the amount of actual I/O. Terminal devices use a separate character buffering system.

4.2BSD provides a large amount of network support. The socket concept provides the programming mechanism to access other processes, even across a network. Sockets are supported by various protocols.

Bibliographic Notes

The best general description of Unix is Ritchie and Thompson [1974]. Much of the history of Unix is given in Ritchie [1979]. The most influential ancestor of Unix is Multics, which is thoroughly examined in Organick [1972]. Differences between the two main modern strains of Unix, 4.2BSD and System V, are given in Chambers and Quarterman [1983].

Possibly the best book on general programming under Unix, especially on the use of the shell and facilities such as *yacc* and *sed*, is Kernighan and Pike [1984]. Two others of interest are Bourne [1983] and McGilton and Morgan [1983]. The best-supported language under Unix is C [Kernighan and Ritchie 1978]. C is also the system's implementation language.

The set of documentation that comes with Unix systems is called the *Unix Programmer's Manual* (UPM) and is traditionally organized in two volumes. *Volume 1* contains short entries for every command, system call, and subroutine package in the system and is also available on-line via the *man* command. *Volume 2 - Supplementary Documents* (usually divided into *Volume 2A* and *Volume 2B* for convenience of binding) contains assorted papers relevant to the system and manuals for those commands or packages too complex to describe in a page or two. Berkeley systems add *Volume 2C* to contain documents concerning Berkeley-specific features.

The Version 7 file system is described in Thompson [1978] and the 4.2BSD file system in McKusick et al. [1984]. The basic reference for processes is Thompson [1978]. The 4.2BSD memory management system is described in Babaoglu and Joy [1981]. The I/O system is described in Thompson [1978].

Two useful papers on communications under 4.2BSD are Leffler et al. [1983] and Leffler et al. [1978], both in UPM *Volume 2C*.

The ISO Reference Model is given in ISO [1981]. The Arpanet Reference Model is set forth and contrasted with the ISO Reference Model in Padlipsky [1982].

There are many useful papers in the two special issues of *The Bell System Technical Journal* on Unix [BSTJ 1978, BSTJ 1984]. Other papers of interest have appeared at various USENIX conferences and are available in the proceedings of those conferences.

15

Historical Perspective

In Chapter 1, we presented a short historical survey of the development of operating systems. That survey was brief and without much detail, since the fundamental concepts of operating systems (cpu scheduling, memory management, processes, and so on) had not yet been presented. By the time we finished with Chapter 13, however, the basic concepts were well understood. We were thus in a position to examine how our concepts have been applied in a real operating system, Unix.

In this chapter, we briefly discuss several other highly influential operating systems. Some of them (such as the XDS-940 or the THE system) were one-of-a-kind systems; others (such as OS/360) are widely used. The order of presentation has been chosen to highlight the similarities and differences of the systems, and is not strictly chronological or ordered by importance. The serious student of operating systems should be familiar with all of these systems.

The treatment of each system is still very brief, but each section contains references to further reading. The papers, written by the designers of the systems, are important both for their technical content, and, perhaps more importantly, for their style and flavor. This chapter is somewhat of a *Bibliographic Notes* for the entire book.

15.1 Atlas

The Atlas operating system [Kilburn et al. 1961, Howarth et al. 1961, Fotheringham 1961, Kilburn et al. 1962, Morris et al. 1962] was designed at the University of Manchester in England in the late 1950s and early 1960s. Many of its basic features, which were quite new and novel at the time, have become standard parts of modern operating systems. Device drivers were a major part of the system. In addition, system calls were added by a set of special instructions called extra codes.

Atlas was a batch operating system with spooling. Spooling allowed the system to schedule jobs according to the availability of peripheral devices, such as magnetic tape units, paper tape readers, paper tape punches, line printers, card readers, or card punches.

The most remarkable feature of Atlas, however, was its memory management. Core memory was quite new and very expensive at the time. Many computers, like the IBM 650, used a drum for primary memory. The Atlas system used a drum for its main memory, but had a small amount of core memory that was used as a cache for the drum. Demand paging was used to transfer information between core memory and the drum automatically.

The Atlas system used a Ferranti computer with 48-bit words. Addresses were 24 bits, but were encoded in decimal, which allowed only 1,000,000 words to be addressed. At that time, this was a very large address space. The physical memory for Atlas was a 98K word drum and 16K words of core. Memory was divided into 512-word pages, providing 32 frames in physical memory. An associative memory of 32 registers implemented the mapping from a virtual address to a physical address.

If a page fault occurred, a page replacement algorithm was invoked. One memory frame was always kept empty, so that a drum transfer could start immediately. The page replacement algorithm attempted to predict the future memory accessing behavior based on past behavior. A reference bit for each frame was set whenever the frame was accessed. The reference bits were read into memory every 1024 instructions. The last 32 values of the reference bit were used to define the time since the last reference (t_1) and the interval between the last two references (t_2). Pages were chosen for replacement in the following order:

1. Any page with $t_1 > t_2 + 1$. This page is no longer considered to be in use.

2. If $t_1 \le t_2$ for all pages, then replace that page with the largest $t_2 - t_1$.

The page replacement algorithm assumes programs access memory in loops. If the time between the last two references is t_2, then another reference is expected t_2 time units later. If a reference does not occur ($t_1 > t_2$), it is assumed that the page is no longer being used and it is replaced. If all pages are still in use, then the page that will not be needed for the longest time is replaced. The time to the next reference is expected to be $t_2 - t_1$.

15.2 XDS-940

The XDS-940 operating system [Lichtenberger and Pirtle 1965, Lampson et al. 1966] was designed at the University of California at Berkeley. Like the Atlas system, it used paging for memory management. Unlike the Atlas system, the XDS-940 was a time-shared system.

The paging was used only for relocation, not for demand paging. The virtual memory of any user process was only 16K words, while the physical memory was 64K words. Pages were 2K words each. The page table was kept in registers. Since physical memory was larger than virtual memory, several user processes could be in memory at the same time. The number of users could be increased by sharing pages when they contained read-only reentrant code. Processes were kept on a drum and swapped in and out of memory as necessary.

The XDS-940 system was constructed from a modified XDS-930. The modifications were typical of the changes made to a basic computer to allow an operating system to be properly written. A user/monitor mode was added. Certain instructions, such as I/O and Halt, were defined to be privileged. An attempt to execute a privileged instruction in user mode would trap to the operating system.

A system call instruction (SYSPOP) was added to the user mode instruction set. This instruction was used to create new resources, such as files, allowing the operating system to manage the physical resources. Files, for example, were allocated in 256-word blocks on the drum. A bit map was used to manage free drum blocks. Each file had an index block with pointers to the actual data blocks. Index blocks were chained together.

The XDS-940 system also provided system calls to allow processes to create, start, suspend, and destroy subprocesses. A user programmer could construct a system of processes. Separate processes could share memory for communication and synchronization. Process creation defines a tree structure, where a process is the root and its subprocesses are nodes below it in the tree. Each of the subprocesses could, in turn, create more subprocesses.

15.3 THE

The THE operating system [Dijkstra 1968a, Bron 1972, McKeag and Wilson 1976 (Chapter 3)] was designed at the Technische Hogeschool at Eindhoven in the Netherlands. It is a batch system running on a Dutch computer, the EL X8, with 32K of 27-bit words. The system was mainly noted for its clean design, particularly its layer structure, and the use of

a set of concurrent processes employing semaphores for
synchronization.

Unlike the XDS-940 system, however, the set of processes in the
THE system was static. The operating system itself was designed as a
set of cooperating processes. In addition, five user processes were
created, which served as the active agents to compile, execute, and print
user programs. When one job was finished, the process would return to
the input queue to select another job.

A priority cpu-scheduling algorithm was used. The priorities are
recomputed every two seconds and were inversely proportional to the
amount of cpu time used recently (in the last eight to ten seconds). This
scheme gave higher priority to I/O-bound processes and new processes.

Memory management was limited by the lack of hardware support.
However, since the system was quite limited and user programs could
only be written in Algol, a software paging scheme was used. The Algol
compiler automatically generated calls to system routines, which made
sure the requested information was in memory, swapping if necessary.
The backing store was a 512K word drum. A 512-word page was used,
with a LRU page replacement strategy.

Another major concern of the THE system was deadlock control.
The banker's algorithm was used to provide deadlock avoidance.

Closely related to the THE system is the Venus system [Liskov
1972a]. The Venus system was also a layer structure design, using
semaphores to synchronize processes. The lower levels of the design
were implemented in microcode, however, providing a much faster
system. The memory management was changed to a paged-segmented
memory. The system was also designed as a time-sharing system, rather
than batch.

15.4 RC 4000

The RC 4000 system, like the THE system, was notable primarily for its
design concepts. It was designed for the Danish RC 4000 computer by
Regenecentralen, particularly by Brinch Hansen [1970, 1973a (Chapter
8)]. The objective was not to design a batch system or a time-sharing
system or any other specific system. Rather, the goal was to create an
operating system nucleus, or kernel, upon which others could build a
complete operating system [Lauesen 1975]. Thus the system structure
was layered, and only the lower levels, the kernel, were provided.

The kernel supported a collection of concurrent processes. Processes
were supported by a round-robin cpu scheduler. Although processes
could share memory, the primary communication and synchronization

mechanism was the *message system* provided by the kernel. Processes can communicate with each other by exchanging fixed-size messages of eight words in length. All messages are stored in buffers from a common buffer pool. When a message buffer is no longer required it is returned to the common pool.

A *message queue* is associated with each process. It contains all the messages that have been sent to that process, but have not yet been received. Messages are removed from the queue in FIFO order. The system supports four primitive operations, which are executed atomically:

- **send-message** (**in** *receiver*, **in** *message*, **out** *buffer*).

- **wait-message** (**out** *sender*, **out** *message*, **out** *buffer*).

- **send-answer** (**out** *result*, **in** *message*, **in** *buffer*).

- **wait-answer** (**out** *result*, **out** *message*, **in** *buffer*).

The last two operations allow processes to exchange several messages at a time.

These primitives require that a process service its message queue in a FIFO order, and that it block itself while other processes are handling its messages. To remove these restrictions, two additional communication primitives are provided. They allow a process to wait for the arrival of the next message or answer and service its queue in any order:

- **wait-event** (**in** *previous-buffer*, **out** *next-buffer*, **out** *result*).

- **get-event** (**out** *buffer*).

I/O devices were also treated as processes. The device drivers were code that converted the device interrupts and registers into messages. Thus a process would write to a terminal by sending it a message. The device driver would receive the message and output the character to the terminal. An input character would interrupt the system and transfer to a device driver. The device driver would create a message from the input character and send it to a waiting process.

Brinch Hansen has continued his work on operating systems, and especially the principles of operating system design. The language Concurrent Pascal [Brinch Hansen 1975] was defined to allow the writing of operating systems in a higher-level language. Concurrent Pascal has been used to define the Solo operating system [Brinch Hansen 1977].

Solo is a single-user multiprogrammed operating system for the PDP-11/45. It consists of a collection of concurrent processes. The most important aspect of the Solo system is that the use of a higher-level language allowed the entire system to be programmed by two people in less than a year. The system is sufficiently compact to be studied as an example in a course on operating systems.

15.5 CTSS

The CTSS (Compatible Time-Sharing System) system [Corbato et al. 1962, Crisman et al. 1964] was designed at MIT as an experimental time-sharing system. It was implemented on an IBM 7090 and eventually supported up to 32 interactive users. The users were provided with a set of interactive commands, which allowed them to manipulate files and compile and run programs through a terminal.

The 7090 had a 32K memory, made up of 36-bit words. The monitor used 5K words, leaving 27K for the users. User memory images were swapped between memory and a fast drum. CPU scheduling employed a multi-level feedback queue algorithm. The time quantum for level i was 2^i time units. If a program did not finish its cpu burst in one time quantum, it was moved down to the next level of the queue, giving it twice as much time. The program at the highest level (with the shortest quantum) was run first. The initial level of a program was determined by its size, so that its time quantum was at least as long as its swap time.

CTSS was extremely successful, and continued to be used as late as 1972. Although it was quite limited, it succeeded in demonstrating that time-sharing was a convenient and practical mode of computing. One result of CTSS was increased development of time-sharing systems. Another result was the development of Multics.

15.6 Multics

Multics was designed at MIT [Corbato and Vyssotsky 1965, Daley and Dennis 1968, Organick 1972, Corbato et al. 1972] as a natural extension of CTSS. CTSS and other early time-sharing systems were so successful that there was an immediate desire to proceed quickly to bigger and better systems. As larger computers became available, the designers of CTSS set out to create a time-sharing *utility*. Computing service would be provided like electrical power. Large computer systems would be connected by telephone wires to terminals in offices and homes throughout a city. The operating system would be a time-shared system running continuously with a vast file system of shared programs and data.

Multics was designed by a team from MIT, GE (which later sold its computer department to Honeywell), and Bell Labs (which dropped out of the project in 1969). The basic GE 635 computer was modified to a new computer system called the GE 645, mainly by the addition of paged-segmentation memory hardware.

A virtual address was composed of an 18-bit segment number and a 16-bit word offset. The segments are then paged in 1K word pages. The second-chance page replacement algorithm was used.

The segmented virtual address space was merged into the file system; each segment was a file. Segments were addressed by the name of the file. The file system itself was a multi-level tree structure, allowing users to create their own subdirectory structures.

Like CTSS, Multics used a multi-level feedback queue for cpu scheduling. Protection was accomplished by an access list associated with each file and a set of protection rings for executing processes. The system, which was written almost entirely in PL/1 [Corbato 1969], was about 300,000 lines of code. It was extended to a multiprocessor system, allowing a cpu to be taken out of service for maintenance while the system continued running.

15.7 OS/360

The longest line of operating system development is undoubtedly for IBM computers. The early IBM computers, like the IBM 7090 and 7094, are prime examples of the development of common I/O subroutines, followed by a resident monitor, privileged instructions, memory protection, and simple batch processing. These systems were developed separately, often by each site independently. As a result, IBM was faced with many different computers, with different languages and different system software.

The IBM/360 was designed to alter this situation. The IBM/360 was designed as a family of computers spanning the complete range from small business machines to large scientific machines. Only one set of software would be needed for these systems, which all used the same operating system: OS/360 [Mealy et al. 1966]. This arrangement was supposed to reduce the maintenance problems for IBM and allow users to move programs and applications freely from one IBM system to another.

Unfortunately, OS/360 tried to be all things for all people. As a result, it did none of them especially well. The file system included a type field that defined the type of each file, and different file types were defined for fixed-length and variable-length records and for blocked and unblocked files. Contiguous allocation was used, so the user had to guess the size of each output file. The control card language Job Control Language (JCL) added parameters for every possible option, making it incomprehensible to the average user.

The memory management routines were hampered by the architecture. Although a base-register addressing mode was used, the program could access and modify the base register, so that absolute addresses were generated by the cpu. This arrangement prevented dynamic relocation; the program was bound to physical memory at load time. Two separate versions of the operating system were produced: OS/MFT used fixed regions and OS/MVT used variable regions.

The system was written in assembly language by thousands of programmers, resulting in millions of lines of code. The operating system itself required large amounts of memory for its code and tables. Operating system overhead often consumed half of the total cpu cycles. Over the years, new versions were released to add new features and fix errors. However, fixing one error often caused another in some remote part of the system, so that the number of known errors in the system was fairly constant.

Virtual memory was added to OS/360 with the change to the IBM 370 architecture. The underlying hardware provided a segmented-paged virtual memory. New versions of OS used this hardware in different ways. OS/VS1 created one large virtual address space, and ran OS/MFT in that virtual memory. Thus the operating system itself was paged, as well as user programs. OS/VS2 Release 1 ran OS/MVT in virtual memory. Finally, OS/VS2 Release 2, which is now called MVS, provided each user with their own virtual memory.

MVS is still basically a batch operating system. The CTSS system was run on an IBM 7094, but MIT decided that the address space of the 360, IBM's successor to the 7094, was too small for Multics, so they switched vendors. IBM then decided to create its own time-sharing system, TSS/360 [Comfort 1965, Lett and Konigsford 1968]. Like Multics, TSS/360 was supposed to be a large time-shared utility. The basic 360 architecture was modified in the model 67 to provide virtual memory. Several sites purchased the 360/67 in anticipation of TSS/360.

TSS/360 was delayed [Schwemm 1972], however, so other time-sharing systems were developed as temporary systems until TSS/360 was available. A time-sharing option (TSO) was added to OS/360. IBM's Cambridge Scientific Center developed CMS as a single-user system and CP/67 to provide a virtual machine to run it on [Meyer and Seawright 1970, Parmelee et al. 1972]. The University of Michigan developed the

Michigan Terminal System (MTS) [Alexander 1972]; Stanford developed Wylbur [Fajman 1973].

When TSS/360 was eventually delivered, it was a failure. It was too large and too slow. As a result, no site would switch from its temporary system to TSS/360. Today time-sharing on IBM systems is largely provided either by TSO under MVS or by CMS under CP/67 (renamed VM).

What went wrong with TSS/360 and Multics? Part of the problem was that these were really quite advanced systems and too large and too complex to be understood. Another problem was the assumption that computing power would be available from a large remote computer by time-sharing. It now appears that most computing will be done by small individual machines -- personal computers -- not by a large remote time-shared system trying to be all things to all users.

15.8 Other Systems

There are, of course, more operating systems, most of them with some interesting properties. The MCP operating system for the Burroughs computer family [McKeag and Wilson 1976] was the first to be written in a system programming language. It also supported segmentation and multiple cpus. The SCOPE operating system for the CDC 6600 [McKeag and Wilson 1976] was also a multi-cpu system. The coordination and synchronization of the multiple processes was surprisingly well designed. Tenex [Bobrow et al. 1972] was an early demand paging system for the PDP-10, which has had a great influence on subsequent time-sharing systems, such as TOPS-20 for the DEC-20. The VMS operating system for the VAX is based on the RSX operating system for the PDP-11. CP/M is the most common operating system for 8-bit microcomputer systems, while MS-DOS is the most common system for 16-bit microcomputers.

Bibliography

[Abate and Dubner 1969] J. Abate and H. Dubner, "Optimizing the Performance of a Drumlike Storage," *IEEE Transactions on Computers*, Volume C-18, Number 11, (November 1969), pages 992-996.

[Abell et al. 1970] V. A. Abell, S. Rosen, and R. E. Wagner, "Scheduling in a General Purpose Operating System," *Proceedings of the AFIPS Fall Joint Computer Conference*, (1970), pages 89-96.

[Agerwala and Flynn 1973] T. Agerwala and M. Flynn, "Comments on Capabilities, Limitations, and 'Correctness' of Petri Nets," *Proceedings of the ACM First Annual Symposium on Computer Architecture*, (1973), pages 81-86.

[Aho et al. 1971] A. V. Aho, P. J. Denning, and J. D. Ullman, "Principles of Optimal Page Replacement," *Journal of the ACM*, Volume 18, Number 1, (January 1971), pages 80-93.

[Alderson et al. 1972] A. Alderson, W. C. Lynch, and B. Randell, "Thrashing in a Multiprogrammed Paging System," *in* [Hoare and Perrott 1972], pages 152-167.

[Alexander 1972] M. T. Alexander, "Organization and Features of the Michigan Terminal System," *Proceedings of the AFIPS Spring Joint Computer Conference*, (1972), pages 585-591.

[Anderson 1972] J. Anderson, "Computer Security Technology Planning Study," Technical Report ESD-TR-73-51, Air Force Electrical Systems Division, (October 1972).

[Andrews 1981] G. R. Andrews, "Synchronizing Resources," *ACM Transactions on Programming Languages and Systems*, Volume 3, Number 4, (October 1981), pages 405-430.

[Apt et al. 1980] K. R. Apt, N. Francez, and W. P. DeRoever, "A Proof of Communicating Sequential Processes," *ACM Transactions on Programming Languages and Systems*, Volume 2, Number 3, (July 1980), pages 359-385.

[Arden and Boettner 1969] B. Arden and D. Boettner, "Measurement and Performance of a Multiprogramming System," *Proceedings of the Second ACM Symposium on Operating Systems Principles*, (October 1969), pages 130-146.

[Atwood 1976] J. W. Atwood, "Concurrency in Operating Systems," *Computer*, Volume 9, Number 10, (October 1976), pages 18-26.

[Babaoglu and Joy 1981] O. Babaoglu and W. N. Joy, "Converting a Swap-Based System to do Paging in an Architecture Lacking Page-Referenced Bits," *Proceedings of the Eighth Symposium on Operating Systems Principles*, (December 1981), pages 78-86.

[Baer and Sager 1972] J. L. Baer and G. R. Sager, "Measurement and Improvement of Program Behavior Under Paging Systems," *in* [Frieberger 1972], pages 241-264.

[Banino et al. 1979] J. S. Banino, C. Kaiser, and H. Zimmermann, "Synchronization for Distributed Systems using a Single Broadcast Channel," *Proceedings of the First International Conference on Distributed Computing Systems*, (October 1979), pages 330-338.

[Barron 1974] D. W. Barron, "Job Control Languages and Job Control Programs," *Computer Journal*, Volume 17, Number 3, (August 1974), pages 282-286.

[Bartlett 1978] J. F. Bartlett, "A 'Nonstop' Operating System," *Proceedings of the Eleventh Hawaii International Conference on System Science*, (January 1978), pages 103-117.

[Baskett 1971] F. Baskett, "The Dependence of Computer System Queues Upon Processing Time Distribution and Central Processor Scheduling," *Proceedings of the Third ACM Symposium on Operating Systems Principles*, (October 1971), pages 109-113.

[Batson et al. 1970] A. P. Batson, S. Ju, and D. Wood, "Measurements of Segment Size," *Communications of the ACM*, Volume 13, Number 3, (March 1970), pages 155-159.

[Bayer et al. 1978] R. Bayer, R. M. Graham, and G. Seegmuller (Editors), *Operating Systems -- An Advanced Course*, Lecture Notes in Computer Science, Volume 60, Springer-Verlag, Berlin, (1978).

[Bays 1977] C. Bays, "A Comparison of Next-Fit, First-Fit, and Best-Fit," *Communications of the ACM*, Volume 20, Number 3, (March 1977), pages 191-192.

[Belady 1966] L. A. Belady, "A Study of Replacement Algorithms for a Virtual-Storage Computer," *IBM Systems Journal*, Volume 5, Number 2, (1966), pages 78-101.

[Belady and Kuehner 1969] L. A. Belady and C. J. Kuehner, "Dynamic Space Sharing in Computer Systems," *Communications of the ACM*, Volume 12, Number 5, (May 1969), pages 282-288.

[Belady et al. 1969] L. A. Belady, R. A. Nelson, and G. S. Shedler, "An Anomaly in Space-Time Characteristics of Certain Programs Running in a Paging Machine," *Communications of the ACM*, Volume 12, Number 6, (June 1969), pages 349-353.

[Bell and Newell 1971] C. G. Bell and A. Newell, *Computer Structures: Readings and Examples*, McGraw-Hill, New York, (1971).

[Bensoussan et al. 1972] A. Bensoussan, C. T. Clingen, and R. C. Daley, "The Multics Virtual Memory: Concepts and Design," *Communications of the ACM*, Volume 15, Number 5, (May 1972), pages 308-318.

[Bernstein 1966] A. J. Bernstein, "Program Analysis for Parallel Processing," *IEEE Transactions on Electronic Computers*, Volume EC-15, Number 5, (October 1966), pages 757-762.

[Bernstein and Siegel 1975] A. J. Bernstein and P. Siegel, "A Computer Architecture for Level Structured Operating Systems," *IEEE Transactions on Computers*, Volume C-24, Number 8, (August 1975), pages 785-793.

[Birrell and Needham 1980] A. D. Birrell and R. M. Needham, "A Universal File Server," *IEEE Transactions on Software Engineering*, Volume SE-6, Number 5, (September 1980), pages 450-453.

[Bobrow et al. 1972] D. G. Bobrow, J. D. Burchfiel, D. L. Murphy, and R. S. Tomlinson, "TENEX, a Paged Time Sharing System for the PDP-10," *Communications of the ACM*, Volume 15, Number 3, (March 1972), pages 135-143.

[Boorstyn and Frank 1977] R. R. Boorstyn and H. Frank, "Large-Scale Network Topological Optimization," *IEEE Transactions on Communications*, Volume COM-25, Number 1, (January 1977), pages 29-47.

[Bourne 1978] S. R. Bourne, "The Unix Shell," *in* [BSTJ 1978], pages 1971-1990.

[Bourne 1983] S. R. Bourne, *The Unix System*, Addison-Wesley, Reading, Massachusetts, (1983).

[Branstad 1973] D. K. Branstad, "Privacy and Protection in Operating Systems," *Computer*, Volume 6, Number 1, (January 1973), pages 43-46.

[Bratman and Boldt 1959] H. Bratman and I. V. Boldt, "The SHARE 709 System: Supervisory Control," *Journal of the ACM*, Volume 6, Number 2, (April 1959), pages 152-155.

[Brawn and Gustavson 1968] B. Brawn and F. G. Gustavson, "Program Behavior in a Paging Environment," *Proceedings of the AFIPS Fall Joint Computer Conference*, (1968), pages 1019-1032.

[Brinch Hansen 1970] P. Brinch Hansen, "The Nucleus of a Multiprogramming System," *Communications of the ACM*, Volume 13, Number 4, (April 1970), pages 238-241 and 250.

[Brinch Hansen 1971] P. Brinch Hansen, "An Analysis of Response Ratio Scheduling," *Proceedings of the IFIP Congress 71*, (1971), pages 479-484.

[Brinch Hansen 1972a] P. Brinch Hansen, "A Comparison of Two Synchronizing Concepts," *Acta Informatica*, Volume 1, Fasc. 3, (1972), pages 190-199.

[Brinch Hansen 1972b] P. Brinch Hansen, "Structured Multiprogramming," *Communications of the ACM*, Volume 15, Number 7, (July 1972), pages 574-578.

[Brinch Hansen 1973a] P. Brinch Hansen, *Operating System Principles*, Prentice-Hall, Englewood Cliffs, New Jersey, (1973).

[Brinch Hansen 1973b] P. Brinch Hansen, "Concurrent Programming Concepts," *Computing Surveys*, Volume 5, Number 4, (December 1973), pages 223-245.

[Brinch Hansen 1975] P. Brinch Hansen, "The Programming Language Concurrent Pascal," *IEEE Transactions on Software Engineering*, Volume SE-1, Number 2, (June 1975), pages 199-207.

[Brinch Hansen 1977] P. Brinch Hansen, *The Architecture of Concurrent Programs*, Prentice-Hall, Englewood Cliffs, New Jersey, (1977).

[Brinch Hansen 1978] P. Brinch Hansen, "Distributed Processes: A Concurrent Programming Concept," *Communications of the ACM*, Volume 21, Number 11, (November 1978), pages 934-941.

[Bron 1972] C. Bron, "Allocation of Virtual Store in the THE Multiprogramming System," *in* [Hoare and Perrott 1972], pages 168-193.

[Brown 1970] G. D. Brown, *System/360 Job Control Language*, John Wiley and Sons, New York, (1970).

[Brown 1978] H. Brown, "Recent Developments in Command Languages," *Information Technology: Proceedings of the Third Jerusalem Conference on Information Technology*, North-Holland, Amsterdam, (1978), pages 453-460.

[Browne et al. 1972] J. C. Browne, J. Lan, and F. Baskett, "The Interaction of Multiprogramming Job Scheduling and CPU Scheduling," *Proceedings of the AFIPS Fall Joint Computer Conference*, (1972), pages 13-22.

[Brunt and Tuffs 1976] R. F. Brunt and D. E. Tuffs, "A User-Oriented Approach to Control Languages," *Software -- Practice and Experience*, Volume 6, Number 1, (January-March 1976), pages 93-108.

[BSTJ 1978] "Unix Time-Sharing System," *The Bell System Technical Journal*, Volume 57, Number 6, Part 2, (July-August 1978).

[BSTJ 1984] "The Unix System," *The Bell System Technical Journal*, Volume 63, Number 8, Part 2, (October 1984).

[Bull and Packham 1971] G. M. Bull and S. F. G. Packham, *Time Sharing Systems*, McGraw-Hill, London, (1971).

[Bunt 1976] R. B. Bunt, "Scheduling Techniques for Operating Systems," *Computer*, Volume 9, Number 10, (October 1976), pages 10-17.

[Burns 1978] J. E. Burns, "Mutual Exclusion with Linear Waiting Using Binary Shared Variables," *SIGACT News*, Volume 10, Number 2, (Summer 1978), pages 42-47.

[Burns and Lynch 1980] J. E. Burns and N. A. Lynch, "Mutual Exclusion Using Indivisible Reads and Writes," *Proceedings of the 18th Annual Allerton Conference on Communication, Control and Computing*, (1980), pages 833-842.

[Burns et al. 1982] J. E. Burns, P. Jackson, N. A. Lynch, M. J. Fischer, and G. L. Peterson, "Data Requirements for Implementation of N-Process Mutual Exclusion Using a Single Shared Variable," *Journal of the ACM*, Volume 29, Number 1, (January 1982), pages 183-205.

[Buxton and Randell 1970] J. N. Buxton and B. Randell (Editors), *Software Engineering Techniques*, NATO Science Committee, Brussels, (1970).

[Buzen 1971] J. P. Buzen, "Queuing Network Models of Multiprogramming," Ph.D. Thesis, Harvard University, (1971).

[Buzen 1973] J. P. Buzen, "Computational Algorithms for Closed Queuing Networks with Exponential Servers," *Communications of the ACM*, Volume 16, Number 9, (September 1973), pages 527-531.

[Calingaert 1982] P. Calingaert, *Operating System Elements: A User Perspective*, Prentice Hall, Englewood Cliffs, New Jersey, (1982).

[Casey 1972] R. G. Casey, "Allocation of Copies of Files in an Information Network," *Proceedings of the AFIPS Spring Joint Computer Conference*, (1972), pages 617-625.

[Cerf 1972] V. G. Cerf, "Multiprocessors, Semaphores, and a Graph Model of Computation," Ph.D. Thesis, University of California At Los Angeles, (1972).

[Chambers and Quarterman 1983] J. Chambers and J. Quarterman, "Unix System V and 4.1C BSD," *USENIX Association Conference Proceedings*, Toronto, (Summer 1983), page 267-291.

[Chandy 1982] K. M. Chandy, "A Mutual Exclusion Algorithm for Distributed Systems," Technical Report, University of Texas, (1982).

[Chapin 1969] N. Chapin, "Common File Organization Techniques Compared," *Proceedings of the AFIPS Fall Joint Computer Conference*, (1969), pages 413-422.

[Cheriton et al. 1979] D. R. Cheriton, M. A. Malcolm, L. S. Melen, and G. R. Sager, "Thoth, a Portable Real-Time Operating System," *Communications of the ACM*, Volume 22, Number 2, (February 1979), pages 105-115.

[Chu 1969] W. W. Chu, "Optimal File Allocation in a Multiple Computer System," *IEEE Transactions on Computers*, Volume C-18, Number 10, (October 1969), pages 885-889.

[Clark et al. 1978] D. D. Clark, K. T. Pogran, and D. P. Reed, "An Introduction to Local Area Networks," *Proceedings of the IEEE*, Volume 66, Number 11, (November 1978), pages 1497-1517.

[Coffman and Kleinrock 1968a] E. G. Coffman and L. Kleinrock, "Computer Scheduling Methods and Their Countermeasures," *Proceedings of the AFIPS Spring Joint Computer Conference*, (1968), pages 11-21.

[Coffman and Kleinrock 1968b] E. G. Coffman and L. Kleinrock, "Feedback Queuing Models for Time-Shared Systems," *Journal of the ACM*, Volume 15, Number 4, (October 1968), pages 549-576.

[Coffman and Varian 1968] E. G. Coffman and L. C. Varian, "Further Experimental Data on the Behavior of Programs in a Paging Environment," *Communications of the ACM*, Volume 11, Number 7, (July 1968), pages 471-474.

[Coffman 1969] E. G. Coffman, "Analysis of a Drum Input/Output Queue Under Scheduling Operation in a Paged Computer System," *Journal of the ACM*, Volume 16, Number 1, (January 1969), pages 73-90.

[Coffman et al. 1971] E. G. Coffman, M. J. Elphick, and A. Shoshani, "System Deadlocks," *Computing Surveys*, Volume 3, Number 2, (June 1971), pages 67-78; *reprinted in* [Freeman 1975], pages 153-167.

[Coffman and Ryan 1972] E. G. Coffman and T. A. Ryan, "A Study of Storage Partitioning using a Mathematical Model of Locality," *Communications of the ACM*, Volume 15, Number 3, (March 1972), pages 185-190.

[Coffman and Denning 1973] E. G. Coffman and P. J. Denning, *Operating Systems Theory*, Prentice-Hall, Englewood Cliffs, New Jersey, (1973).

[Cohen and Jefferson 1975] E. S. Cohen and D. Jefferson, "Protection in the Hydra Operating System," *Proceedings of the Fifth Symposium on Operating Systems Principles*, (November 1975), pages 141-160.

[Colin 1971] A. J. T. Colin, *Introduction to Operating Systems*, Macdonald, London, (1971).

[Comber 1969] E. V. Comber, "Management of Confidential Information," *Proceedings of the AFIPS Fall Joint Computer Conference*, (1969), pages 135-143.

[Comeau 1967] L. W. Comeau, "A Study of the Effect of User Program Optimization in a Paging System," *Proceedings of the First ACM Symposium on Operating Systems Principles*, (October 1967).

[Comer 1984] D. Comer, *Operating System Design: the Xinu Approach*, Prentice-Hall, Englewood Cliffs, New Jersey, (1984).

[Comfort 1965] W. T. Comfort, "A Computing System Design for User Service," *Proceedings of the AFIPS Fall Joint Computer Conference*, (1965), pages 619-628.

[Conway 1963] M. Conway, "A Multiprocessor System Design," *Proceedings of the AFIPS Fall Joint Computer Conference*, (1963), pages 139-146.

[Conway et al. 1967] R. W. Conway, W. L. Maxwell, and L. W. Miller, *Theory of Scheduling*, Addison-Wesley, Reading, Massachusetts, (1967).

[Conway et al. 1972] R. W. Conway, W. L. Maxwell, and H. L. Morgan, "On the Implementation of Security Measures in Information Systems," *Communications of the ACM*, Volume 15, Number 4, (April 1972), pages 211-220.

[Cook 1980] R. P. Cook, "*MOD: A Language for Distributed Programing," *IEEE Transactions on Software Engineering*, Volume SE-6, Number 6, (November 1980), pages 563-571.

[Corbato et al. 1962] F. J. Corbato, M. Merwin-Daggett, and R. C. Daley, "An Experimental Time-Sharing System," *Proceedings of the AFIPS Spring Joint Computer Conference*, (1962), pages 335-344.

[Corbato and Vyssotsky 1965] F. J. Corbato and V. A. Vyssotsky, "Introduction and Overview of the Multics System," *Proceedings of the AFIPS Fall Joint Computer Conference*, (1965), pages 185-196; *reprinted in* [Rosen 1967], pages 714-730.

[Corbato 1969] F. J. Corbato, "PL/1 As a Tool for System Programming," *Datamation*, Volume 15, Number 5, (May 1969), pages 68-76.

[Corbato et al. 1972] F. J. Corbato, J. H. Saltzer, and C. T. Clingen, "Multics -- The First Seven Years," *Proceedings of the AFIPS Spring Joint Computer Conference*, (1972), pages 571-583.

[Cosserat 1974] D. C. Cosserat, "A Data Model Based on the Capability Protection Mechanism," *Proceedings of the IRIA International Workshop on Protection in Operating Systems*, (1974), pages 35-54.

[Courtois et al. 1971] P. J. Courtois, F. Heymans, and D. L. Parnas, "Concurrent Control with 'Readers' and 'Writers'," *Communications of the ACM*, Volume 14, Number 10, (October 1971), pages 667-668.

[Cox 1975] G. W. Cox, "Portability and Adaptability in Operating System Design," Ph.D. Thesis, Purdue University, (1975).

[Crisman 1965] P. A. Crisman (Editor), *The Compatible Time-Sharing System: A Programmer's Guide*, Second Edition, MIT Press, Cambridge, Massachusetts, (1965).

[Crowther et al. 1975] W. R. Crowther, F. E. Heart, A. A. McKenzie, J. M. McQuillan, and D. C. Walden, "Issues in Packet Switching Network Design," *Proceedings of the AFIPS National Computer Conference*, (1975), pages 161-176.

[Cuttle and Robinson 1970] G. Cuttle and P. B. Robinson (Editors), *Executive Programs and Operating Systems*, Macdonald, London, (1970).

[Dahl et al. 1968] O. J. Dahl, B. Myhrhaug, and K. Nygaard, "The SIMULA 67 Common Base Language," Technical Report, Norwegian Computing Center, Oslo, Norway, (1968).

[Daley and Neumann 1965] R. C. Daley and P. G. Neumann, "A General Purpose File System for Secondary Storage," *Proceedings of the AFIPS Fall Joint Computer Conference*, (1965), pages 213-229.

[Daley and Dennis 1968] R. C. Daley and J. B. Dennis, "Virtual Memory, Processes, and Sharing in Multics," *Communications of the ACM*, Volume 11, Number 5, (May 1968), pages 306-312.

[Danet et al. 1976] A. Danet, R. Despres, A. Le Rest, G. Pichon, and S. Ritzenthaler, "The French Public Packet Switching Service: The Transpac Network," *Proceedings of the Third International Conference on Computer Communication*, (1976), pages 251-260.

[Davies 1980] D. W. Davies, "Protection," *Distributed Systems: An Advanced Course*, Springer-Verlag, Berlin, (1980).

[deBruijn 1967] N. G. deBruijn, "Additional Comments on a Problem in Concurrent Programming and Control," *Communications of the ACM*, Volume 10, Number 3, (March 1967), pages 137-138.

[DeMeis and Weizer 1969] W. M. DeMeis and N. Weizer, "Measurements and Analysis of a Demand Paging Time Sharing System," *Proceedings of the ACM National Conference*, (August 1969), pages 201-216.

[Denning 1967] P. J. Denning, "Effects of Scheduling on File Memory Operations," *Proceedings of the AFIPS Spring Joint Computer Conference*, (1967), pages 9-21.

[Denning 1968] P. J. Denning, "The Working Set Model for Program Behavior," *Communications of the ACM*, Volume 11, Number 5, (May 1968), pages 323-333.

[Denning 1970] P. J. Denning, "Virtual Memory," *Computing Surveys*, Volume 2, Number 3, (September 1970), pages 153-189.

[Denning 1971] P. J. Denning, "Third Generation Computer System," *Computing Surveys*, Volume 3, Number 4, (December 1971), pages 175-216.

[Denning and Schwartz 1972] P. J. Denning and S. C. Schwartz, "Properties of the Working Set Model," *Communications of the ACM*, Volume 15, Number 3, (March 1972), pages 191-198.

[Denning 1976] P. J. Denning, "Fault-Tolerant Operating Systems," *Computing Surveys*, Volume 8, Number 4, (December 1976), pages 359-389.

[Denning 1980a] P. J. Denning, "Working Sets Past and Present," *IEEE Transactions on Software Engineering*, Volume SE-6, Number 1, (January 1980), pages 64-84; *see also* [Lanciaux 1978], pages 115-148.

[Denning 1980b] P. J. Denning, "Another Look at Operating Systems," *Operating Systems Review*, Volume 14, Number 4, (October 1980), pages 78-82.

[Denning 1982a] P. J. Denning, "Are Operating Systems Obsolete?," *Communications of the ACM*, Volume 25, Number 4, (April 1982), pages 225-227.

[Denning 1982b] D. Denning, *Cryptography and Data Security*, Addison-Wesley, Reading, Massachusetts, (1982).

[Dennis 1965] J. B. Dennis, "Segmentation and the Design of Multiprogrammed Compute Systems," *Journal of the ACM*, Volume 12, Number 4, (October 1965), pages 589-602.

[Dennis and Van Horn 1966] J. B. Dennis and E. C. Van Horn, "Programming Semantics for Multiprogrammed Computations," *Communications of the ACM*, Volume 9, Number 3, (March 1966), pages 143-155.

[Dependahl and Presser 1976] R. H. Dependahl and L. Presser, "File Input/Output Control Logic," *Computer*, Volume 9, Number 10, (October 1976), pages 38-42.

[Devillers 1977] R. Devillers, "Game Interpretation of the Deadlock Avoidance Problem," *Communications of the ACM*, Volume 20, Number 10, (October 1977), pages 741-745.

[Diffie and Hellman 1979] W. Diffie and M. E. Hellman, "Privacy and Authentication," *Proceedings of the IEEE*, Volume 67, Number 3, (March 1979), pages 397-427.

[Dijkstra 1965a] E. W. Dijkstra, "Cooperating Sequential Processes," Technical Report EWD-123, Technological University, Eindhoven, The Netherlands, (1965); *reprinted in* [Genuys 1968], pages 43-112.

[Dijkstra 1965b] E. W. Dijkstra, "Solution of a Problem in Concurrent Programming Control," *Communications of the ACM*, Volume 8, Number 9, (September 1965), page 569.

[Dijkstra 1968a] E. W. Dijkstra, "Go To Statement Considered Harmful," *Communications of the ACM*, Volume 11, Number 3, (March 1968), pages 147-148.

[Dijkstra 1968b] E. W. Dijkstra, "The Structure of the THE Multiprogramming System," *Communications of the ACM*, Volume 11, Number 5, (May 1968), pages 341-346.

[Dijkstra 1971] E. W. Dijkstra, "Hierarchical Ordering of Sequential Processes," *Acta Informatica*, Volume 1, Fasc. 2, (1971), pages 115-138; *reprinted in* [Hoare and Perrott 1972], pages 72-93.

[Dijkstra 1975] E. W. Dijkstra, "Guarded Commands, Non-Determinacy and Formal Derivation of Programs," *Communications of the ACM*, Volume 18, Number 8, (August 1975), pages 453-457.

[Dion 1980] J. Dion, "The Cambridge File Server," *Operating Systems Review*, Volume 14, Number 4, (October 1980), pages 26-35.

[Dodd 1969] G. G. Dodd, "Elements of Data Management Systems," *Computing Surveys*, Volume 1, Number 2, (June 1969), pages 117-133; *reprinted in* [Freeman 1975], pages 314-334.

[Doherty 1970] W. J. Doherty, "Scheduling TSS/360 for Responsiveness," *Proceedings of the AFIPS Fall Joint Computer Conference*, (1970), pages 97-111.

[Doll 1974] D. R. Doll, "Telecommunications Turbulence and the Computer Network Evolution," *Computer*, Volume 7, Number 2, (February 1974), pages 13-22.

[Donnelley 1979] J. E. Donnelley, "Components of a Network Operating System," *Computer Networks*, Volume 3, Number 6, (December 1979), pages 389-399.

[Doran 1976] R. W. Doran, "Virtual Memory," *Computer*, Volume 9, Number 10, (October 1976), pages 27-37.

[Doran and Thomas 1980] R. W. Doran and L. K. Thomas, "Variants of the Software to Mutual Exclusion," *Information Processing Letters*, Volume 10, Numbers 4/5, (July 1980), pages 206-208.

[Eisenberg and McGuire 1972] M. A. Eisenberg and M. R. McGuire, "Further Comments on Dijkstra's Concurrent Programming Control

Problem," *Communications of the ACM*, Volume 15, Number 11, (November 1972), page 999.

[Ekanadham and Bernstein 1979] K. Ekanadham and A. J. Bernstein, "Conditional Capabilities," *IEEE Transactions on Software Engineering*, Volume SE-5, Number 5, (September 1979), pages 458-464.

[England 1974] D. M. England, "Capability Concept Mechanism and Structure in System 250," *Proceedings of the IRIA International Workshop on Protection in Operating Systems*, (August 1974), pages 63-82.

[Enslow 1973] P. H. Enslow, "Non-Technical Issues in Network Design Economic, Legal, Social, and Other Considerations," *Computer*, Volume 6, Number 8, (August 1973), pages 20-30.

[Enslow 1977] P. H. Enslow, "Multiprocessor Organization -- A Survey," *Computing Surveys*, Volume 9, Number 1, (March 1977), pages 103-129.

[Evans and Leclerc 1967] D. C. Evans and J. Y. Leclerc, "Address Mapping and the Control of Access in an Interactive Computer," *Proceedings of the AFIPS Spring Joint Computer Conference*, (1967), pages 23-32.

[Fabry 1971] R. S. Fabry, "Preliminary Description of a Supervisor for a Machine Oriented Around Capabilities," Quarterly Progress Report, University of Chicago, (March 1971).

[Fabry 1974] R. S. Fabry, "Capability-Based Addressing," *Communications of the ACM*, Volume 17, Number 7, (July 1974), pages 403-412.

[Fajman 1973] R. Fajman, "WYLBUR: An Interactive Text Editing and Remote Job Entry System," *Communications of the ACM*, Volume 16, Number 5, (May 1973), pages 314-322.

[Farber and Larson 1972] D. J. Farber and K. C. Larson, "The System Architecture of the Distributed Computer System -- The Communications System," *Symposium on Computer Networks*, (April 1972).

[Feldman 1979] J. A. Feldman, "High Level Programming for Distributed Computing," *Communications of the ACM*, Volume 22, Number 6, (June 1979), pages 353-368.

[Feng 1981] T. Feng, "A Survey of Interconnection Networks," *Computer*, Volume 14, Number 12, (December 1981), pages 12-27.

[Fine et al. 1966] G. H. Fine, C. W. Jackson, and P. V. McIsaac, "Dynamic Program Behavior Under Paging," *Proceedings of the ACM National Conference*, (August 1966), pages 223-228.

[Fontao 1971] R. O. Fontao, "A Concurrent Algorithm for Avoiding Deadlocks," *Proceedings of the Third ACM Symposium on Operating Systems Principles*, (October 1971), pages 72-79.

[Forsdick et al. 1978] H. C. Forsdick, R. E. Schantz, and R. H. Thomas, "Operating Systems for Computer Networks," *Computer*, Volume 11, Number 1, (January 1978), pages 48-57.

[Fotheringham 1961] J. Fotheringham, "Dynamic Storage Allocation in the Atlas Computer Including an Automatic Use of a Backing Store," *Communications of the ACM*, Volume 4, Number 10, (October 1961), pages 435-436.

[Frailey 1973] D. J. Frailey, "A Practical Approach to Managing Resources and Avoiding Deadlock," *Communications of the ACM*, Volume 16, Number 5, (May 1973), pages 323-329.

[Frank 1969] H. Frank, "Analysis and Optimization of Disk Storage Devices for Time-Sharing Systems," *Journal of the ACM*, Volume 16, Number 4, (October 1969), pages 602-620.

[Frank 1976] G. R. Frank, "Job Control in the MU5 Operating System," *Computer Journal*, Volume 19, Number 2, (May 1976), pages 139-143.

[Fraser 1969] A. G. Fraser, "Integrity of a Mass Storage Filing System," *Computer Journal*, Volume 12, Number 1, (February 1969), pages 1-5.

[Fraser 1972] A. G. Fraser, "The Integrity of a Disc Based File System," *in* [Hoare and Perrott 1972], pages 227-248.

[Fraser 1975] A. G. Fraser, "Loops for Data Communication," *Datamation*, Volume 21, Number 2, (February 1975), pages 51-56.

[Freeman 1975] P. Freeman (Editor), *Software Systems Principles*, Science Research Associates, Palo Alto, California, (1975).

[Freibergs 1968] I. F. Freibergs, "The Dynamic Behavior of Programs," *Proceedings of the AFIPS Fall Joint Computer Conference*, (1968), pages 1163-1167.

[Fridrich and Older 1981] M. Fridrich and W. Older, "The Felix File Server," *Proceedings of the Eighth Symposium on Operating Systems Principles*, (December 1981), pages 37-46.

[Frieberger 1972] W. Frieberger (Editor), *Statistical Computer Performance Evaluation*, Academic Press, New York, (1972).

[Fuller 1972] S. H. Fuller, "An Optimal Drum Scheduling Algorithm," *IEEE Transactions on Computers*, Volume C-21, Number 11, (November 1972), pages 1153-1165.

[Fuller 1974] S. H. Fuller, "Minimal-Total-Processing-Time Drum and Disk Scheduling Disciplines," *Communications of the ACM*, Volume 17, Number 7, (July 1974), pages 376-381.

[Garcia-Molina 1982] H. Garcia-Molina, "Election in a Distributed Computing System," *IEEE Transactions on Computers*, Volume C-31, Number 1, (January 1982), pages 48-59.

[Gelernter 1981] D. Gelernter, "A DAG Based Algorithm for Prevention of Store-and-Forward Deadlock in Packet Networks," *IEEE Transactions on Computers*, Volume C-30, Number 10, (October 1981), pages 709-715.

[Genuys 1968] F. Genuys (Editor), *Programming Languages*, Academic Press, London, (1968).

[Gerla and Kleinrock 1977] M. Gerla and L. Kleinrock, "On the Topological Design of Distributed Computer Networks," *IEEE Transactions on Communications*, Volume COM-25, Number 1, (January 1977), pages 48-60.

[Gien 1978] M. Gien, "A File Transfer Protocol FTP," *Computer Networks*, Volume 2, Numbers 4/5, (September-October 1978), pages 312-319.

[Gligor and Shattuck 1980] V. D. Gligor and S. H. Shattuck, "On Deadlock Detection in Distributed Systems," *IEEE Transactions on Software Engineering*, Volume SE-6, Number 5, (September 1980), pages 435-440.

[Gold 1978] E. M. Gold, "Deadlock Prediction: Easy and Difficult Cases," *SIAM Journal of Computing*, Volume 7, Number 3, (August 1978), pages 320-336.

[Gotlieb and MacEwen 1973] C. C. Gotlieb and G. H. MacEwen, "Performance of Movable-Head Disk Scheduling Disciplines," *Journal of the ACM*, Volume 20, Number 4, (October 1973), pages 604-623.

[Graham 1968] R. M. Graham, "Protection in an Information Processing Utility," *Communications of the ACM*, Volume 11, Number 5, (May 1968), pages 365-369.

[Graham et al. 1971] R. M. Graham, G. J. Clancy, and D. B. DeVancey, "A Software Design and Evaluation System," *Proceedings of the*

ACM-SIGOPS Workshop on System Performance Evaluation, (1971), pages 200-213.

[Graham and Denning 1972] G. S. Graham and P. J. Denning, "Protection -- Principles and Practice," *Proceedings of the AFIPS Spring Joint Computer Conference*, (1972), pages 417-429.

[Graham 1975] R. M. Graham, *Principles of Systems Programming*, John Wiley and Sons, New York, (1975).

[Gram and Hertweck 1975] C. Gram and F. R. Hertweck, "Command Languages: Design Considerations and Basic Concepts," *in* [Unger 1975], pages 43-67.

[Gula 1978] J. L. Gula, "Operating System Considerations for Multiprocessor Architecture," *Proceedings of the Seventh Texas Conference on Computing Systems*, (1978), pages 7-1 to 7-6.

[Gustavson 1968] F. G. Gustavson, "Program Behavior in a Paging Environment," *Proceedings of the AFIPS Fall Joint Computer Conference*, (1968), pages 1019-1032.

[Habermann 1969] A. N. Habermann, "Prevention of System Deadlocks," *Communications of the ACM*, Volume 12, Number 7, (July 1969), pages 373-377 and 385.

[Habermann 1972] A. N. Habermann, "Synchronization of Communicating Processes," *Communications of the ACM*, Volume 15, Number 3, (March 1972), pages 171-176.

[Habermann 1976] A. N. Habermann, *Introduction to Operating System Design*, Science Research Associates, Palo Alto, California, (1976).

[Habermann et al. 1976] A. N. Habermann, L. Flon, and L. Cooprider, "Modularization and Hierarchy in a Family of Operating Systems," *Communications of the ACM*, Volume 19, Number 5, (May 1976), pages 266-272.

[Hall et al. 1980] D. E. Hall, D. K. Scherrer, and J. S. Sventek, "A Virtual Operating System," *Communications of the ACM*, Volume 23, Number 9, (September 1980), pages 495-502.

[Harrison et al. 1976] M. A. Harrison, W. L. Ruzzo, and J. D. Ullman, "Protection in Operating Systems," *Communications of the ACM*, Volume 19, Number 8, (August 1976), pages 461-471.

[Hatfield and Gerald 1971] D. Hatfield and J. Gerald, "Program Restructuring for Virtual Memory," *IBM Systems Journal*, Volume 10, Number 3, (1971), pages 168-192.

[Hatfield 1972] D. Hatfield, "Experiments on Page Size, Program Access Patterns, and Virtual Memory Performance," *IBM Journal of Research and Development*, Volume 16, Number 1, (January 1972), pages 58-62.

[Havender 1968] J. W. Havender, "Avoiding Deadlock in Multitasking Systems," *IBM Systems Journal*, Volume 7, Number 2, (1968), pages 74-84.

[Henderson and Zalcstein 1980] P. Henderson and Y. Zalcstein, "Synchronization Problems Solvable By Generalized PV Systems," *Journal of the ACM*, Volume 27, Number 1, (January 1980), pages 60-71.

[Hoare 1972a] C. A. R. Hoare, "Operating Systems: Their Purpose, Objectives, Functions and Scope," *in* [Hoare and Perrott 1972], pages 11-19.

[Hoare 1972b] C. A. R. Hoare, "Towards a Theory of Parallel Programming," *in* [Hoare and Perrott 1972], pages 61-71.

[Hoare and McKeag 1972] C. A. R. Hoare and R. M. McKeag, "A Survey of Store Management Techniques," *in* [Hoare and Perrott 1972], pages 117-151.

[Hoare and Perrott 1972] C. A. R. Hoare and R. H. Perrott (Editors), *Operating Systems Techniques*, Academic Press, London, (1972).

[Hoare 1974] C. A. R. Hoare, "Monitors: An Operating System Structuring Concept," *Communications of the ACM*, Volume 17, Number 10, (October 1974), pages 549-557; Erratum in *Communications of the ACM*, Volume 18, Number 2, (February 1975), page 95.

[Hoare 1978] C. A. R. Hoare, "Communicating Sequential Processes," *Communications of the ACM*, Volume 21, Number 8, (August 1978), pages 666-677.

[Hoare 1981] C. A. R. Hoare, "A Calculus of Total Correctness for Communicating Processes," *Science of Computer Programming*, Volume 1, Numbers 1/2, (October 1981), pages 49-72.

[Hoffman 1977] L. J. Hoffman, *Modern Methods for Computer Security and Privacy*, Prentice-Hall, Englewood Cliffs, New Jersey, (1977).

[Hofri 1980] M. Hofri, "Disk Scheduling: FCFS vs. SSTF Revisited," *Communications of the ACM*, Volume 23, Number 11, (November 1980), pages 645-653; *see also* [Lanciaux 1978], pages 181-198.

[Holt 1971a] R. C. Holt, "Comments on Prevention of System Deadlocks," *Communications of the ACM*, Volume 14, Number 1, (January 1971), pages 36-38.

[Holt 1971b] R. C. Holt, "On Deadlock in Computer Systems," Ph.D. Thesis, Cornell University, (1971).

[Holt 1972] R. C. Holt, "Some Deadlock Properties of Computer Systems," *Computing Surveys*, Volume 4, Number 3, (September 1972), pages 179-196.

[Holt et al. 1978] R. C. Holt, G. S. Graham, E. D. Lazowska, and M. A. Scott, *Structured Concurrent Programming with Operating System Applications*, Addison-Wesley, Reading, Massachusetts, (1978).

[Holt 1983] R. C. Holt, *Concurrent Euclid, the Unix System, and Tunis*, Addison-Wesley, Reading, Massachusetts, (1983).

[Horning and Randell 1973] J. J. Horning and B. Randell, "Process Structuring," *Computing Surveys*, Volume 5, Number 1, (March 1973), pages 5-30.

[Howard 1973] J. H. Howard, "Mixed Solutions for the Deadlock Problem," *Communications of the ACM*, Volume 16, Number 7, (July 1973), pages 427-430.

[Howard 1976a] J. H. Howard, "Proving Monitors," *Communications of the ACM*, Volume 19, Number 5, (May 1976), pages 273-279.

[Howard 1976b] J. H. Howard, "Signaling in Monitors," *Proceedings of the Second International Conference on Software Engineering*, (October 1976), pages 47-52.

[Howarth et al. 1961] D. J. Howarth, R. B. Payne, and F. H. Sumner, "The Manchester University Atlas Operating System, Part II: User's Description," *Computer Journal*, Volume 4, Number 3, (October 1961), pages 226-229.

[Hsiao et al. 1979] D. K. Hsiao, D. S. Kerr, and S. E. Madnick, *Computer Security*, Academic Press, New York, (1979).

[Hyman 1966] H. Hyman, "Comments on a Problem in Concurrent Programming Control," *Communications of the ACM*, Volume 9, Number 1, (January 1966), page 45.

[Ichbiah et al. 1980] J. Ichbiah, et al., "Reference Manual for the Ada Programming Language," Technical Report, United States Department of Defense, (July 1980); *also* "The Programming Language Ada: Reference Manual," Lecture Notes in Computer Science, Volume 106, Springer-Verlag, Berlin, (1981).

[Iliffe and Jodeit 1962] J. K. Iliffe and J. G. Jodeit, "A Dynamic Storage Allocation System," *Computer Journal*, Volume 5, Number 3, (October 1962), pages 200-209.

[Isloor and Marsland 1980] S. S. Isloor and T. A. Marsland, "The Deadlock Problem: An Overview," *Computer*, Volume 13, Number 9, (September 1980), pages 58-78.

[ISO 1981] "ISO Open Systems Interconnection - Basic Reference Model," ISO/TC 97/SC 16 N 719, *International Organization for Standardization*, (August 1981).

[Israel et al. 1978] J. Israel, J. G. Mitchell, and H. E. Sturgis, "Separating Data From Function in a Distributed File System," *in* [Lanciaux 1978], pages 17-27.

[Jones 1973] A. K. Jones, "Protection in Programmed Systems," Ph.D. Thesis, Carnegie-Mellon University, (1973).

[Jones and Liskov 1976] A. K. Jones and B. H. Liskov, "A Language Extension Mechanism for Controlling Access to Shared Data," *Proceedings of the Second International Conference on Software Engineering*, (1976), pages 62-68.

[Jones 1978] A. K. Jones, "Protection Mechanisms and the Enforcement of Security Policies," *in* [Bayer et al. 1978], pages 228-251.

[Jones and Liskov 1978] A. K. Jones and B. H. Liskov, "A Language Extension for Expressing Constraints on Data Access," *Communications of the ACM*, Volume 21, Number 5, (May 1978), pages 358-367.

[Jones and Schwarz 1980] A. K. Jones and P. Schwarz, "Experience Using Multiprocessor Systems -- A Status Report," *Computing Surveys*, Volume 12, Number 2, (June 1980), pages 121-165.

[Kahn 1972] R. Kahn, "Resource-Sharing Computer Communications Networks," *Proceedings of the IEEE*, Volume 60, Number 11, (November 1972), pages 1397-1407.

[Kahn et al. 1981] K. C. Kahn, W. M. Corwin, T. D. Dennis, H. D'Hooge, D. E. Hubka, L. A. Hutchins, J. T. Montague, F. J. Pollack, and M. R. Gifkins, "iMAX: A Multiprocessor Operating System for an Object-Based Computer," *Proceedings of the Eighth Symposium on Operating Systems Principles*, (December 1981), pages 127-136.

[Kameda 1980] T. Kameda, "Testing Deadlock-Freedom of Computer Systems," *Journal of the ACM*, Volume 27, Number 2, (April 1980), pages 270-280.

[Katzan 1973] H. Katzan, *Operating Systems: A Pragmatic Approach*, Van Nostrand-Reinhold, New York, (1973).

[Katzman 1978] J. A. Katzman, "A Fault-Tolerant Computer System," *Proceedings of the Eleventh Hawaii International Conference on System Science*, (1978), pages 85-102.

[Keller 1972] R. Keller, "Vector Replacement Systems: A Formalism for Modeling Asynchronous Systems," Technical Report, Princeton University, (December 1972).

[Kernighan and Ritchie 1978] B. W. Kernighan and D. M. Ritchie, *The C Programming Language*, Prentice-Hall, Englewood Cliffs, New Jersey, (1978).

[Kernighan and Pike 1984] B. W. Kernighan and R. Pike, *The Unix Programming Environment*, Prentice-Hall, Englewood Cliffs, New Jersey, (1984).

[Kessels 1977] J. L. W. Kessels, "An Alternative to Event Queues for Synchronization in Monitors," *Communications of the ACM*, Volume 20, Number 7, (July 1977), pages 500-503.

[Kieburtz and Silberschatz 1978] R. B. Kieburtz and A. Silberschatz, "Capability Managers," *IEEE Transactions on Software Engineering*, Volume SE-4, Number 6, (November 1978), pages 467-477.

[Kieburtz and Silberschatz 1983] R. B. Kieburtz and A. Silberschatz, "Access Right Expressions," *ACM Transactions on Programming Languages and Systems*, Volume 5, Number 1, (January 1983), pages 78-96.

[Kilburn et al. 1961] T. Kilburn, D. J. Howarth, R. B. Payne, and F. H. Sumner, "The Manchester University Atlas Operating System Part I: Internal Organization," *Computer Journal*, Volume 4, Number 3, (October 1961), pages 222-225.

[Kilburn et al. 1962] T. Kilburn, D. B. G. Edwards, M. J. Lanigan, and F. H. Sumner, "One-Level Storage System," *IEEE Transactions on Electronic Computers*, Volume EC-11, Number 2, (April 1962), pages 223-235; *reprinted in* [Bell and Newell 1971], pages 276-290.

[Kimbleton and Schneider 1975] S. R. Kimbleton and G. M. Schneider, "Computer Communication Networks: Approaches, Objectives, and Performance Considerations," *Computing Surveys*, Volume 7, Number 3, (September 1975), pages 129-173.

[Kleinrock 1970] L. Kleinrock, "A Continuum of Time-Sharing Scheduling Algorithms," *Proceedings of the AFIPS Spring Joint Computer Conference*, (1970), pages 453-458.

[Kleinrock 1975] L. Kleinrock, *Queueing Systems, Volume II: Computer Applications*, Wiley-Interscience, New York, (1975).

[Knight 1968] D. C. Knight, "An Algorithm for Scheduling Storage on a Non-Paged Computer," *Computer Journal*, Volume 11, Number 1, (February 1968), pages 17-21.

[Knuth 1966] D. E. Knuth, "Additional Comments on a Problem in Concurrent Programming Control," *Communications of the ACM*, Volume 9, Number 5, (May 1966), pages 321-322.

[Knuth 1973] D. E. Knuth, *The Art of Computer Programming, Volume 1: Fundamental Algorithms, Second Edition*, Addison-Wesley, Reading, Massachusetts, (1973).

[Kopf 1977] J. Kopf, "TYMNET as a Multiplexed Packet Network," *Proceedings of the AFIPS National Computer Conference*, (1977), pages 609-613.

[Kosaraju 1973] S. Kosaraju, "Limitations of Dijkstra's Semaphore Primitives and Petri Nets," *Operating Systems Review*, Volume 7, Number 4, (October 1973), pages 122-126.

[Kuck and Lawrie 1970] D. J. Kuck and D. H. Lawrie, "The Use and Performance of Memory Hierarchies: A Survey," *Software Engineering, Volume 1*, Academic Press, New York, (1970), pages 45-78.

[Kurzban et al. 1975] S. A. Kurzban, T. S. Heines, and A. P. Sayers, *Operating System Principles*, Petrocelli/Charter, New York, (1975).

[Lamport 1974] L. Lamport, "A New Solution of Dijkstra's Concurrent Programming Problem," *Communications of the ACM*, Volume 17, Number 8, (August 1974), pages 453-455.

[Lamport 1977] L. Lamport, "Proving the Correctness of Multiprocess Programs," *IEEE Transactions on Software Engineering*, Volume SE-3, Number 2, (March 1977), pages 125-133.

[Lamport 1978a] L. Lamport, "Time, Clocks, and the Ordering of Events in a Distributed System," *Communications of the ACM*, Volume 21, Number 7, (July 1978), pages 558-565.

[Lamport 1978b] L. Lamport, "The Implementation of Reliable Distributed Multiprocess Systems," *Computer Networks*, Volume 2, Number 2, (April 1978), pages 95-114.

[Lamport et al. 1982] L. Lamport, R. Shostak, and M. Pease, "The Byzantine Generals Problem," *ACM Transactions on Programming Languages and Systems*, Volume 4, Number 3, (July 1982), pages 382-401.

[Lampson et al. 1966] B. W. Lampson, W. W. Lichtenberger, and M. W. Pirtle, "A User Machine in a Time-Sharing System," *Proceedings of the IEEE*, Volume 54, Number 12, (December 1966), pages 1766-1774.

[Lampson 1968] B. W. Lampson, "A Scheduling Philosophy for Multiprocessing Systems," *Communications of the ACM*, Volume 11, Number 5, (May 1968), pages 347-360.

[Lampson 1969] B. W. Lampson, "Dynamic Protection Structures," *Proceedings of the AFIPS Fall Joint Computer Conference*, (1969), pages 27-38.

[Lampson 1971] B. W. Lampson, "Protection," *Proceedings of the Fifth Annual Princeton Conference on Information Science Systems*, (1971), pages 437-443; *reprinted in Operating Systems Review*, Volume 8, Number 1, (January 1974), pages 18-24.

[Lampson 1973] B. W. Lampson, "A Note on the Confinement Problem," *Communications of the ACM*, Volume 16, Number 10, (October 1973), pages 613-615.

[Lampson and Sturgis 1976] B. W. Lampson and H. E. Sturgis, "Reflections on an Operating System Design," *Communications of the ACM*, Volume 19, Number 5, (May 1976), pages 251-265.

[Lampson and Redell 1980] B. W. Lampson and D. D. Redell, "Experience with Processes and Monitors in Mesa," *Communications of the ACM*, Volume 23, Number 2, (February 1980), pages 105-117.

[Lanciaux 1978] D. Lanciaux (Editor), *Operating Systems: Theory and Practice*, North-Holland, Amsterdam, (1978).

[Lang 1969] C. A. Lang, "SAL -- Systems Assembly Languages," *Proceedings of the AFIPS Spring Joint Computer Conference*, (1969), pages 543-555.

[Lang 1970] C. A. Lang, "Languages for Writing Systems Programs," *in* [Buxton and Randell 1970], pages 101-106.

[Larsson 1976] T. Larsson, "A Public Data Network in the Nordic Countries," *Proceedings of the Third International Conference on Computer Communication*, (August 1976), pages 246-250.

[Lauesen 1975] S. Lauesen, "A Large Semaphore Based Operating System," *Communications of the ACM*, Volume 18, Number 7, (July 1975), pages 377-389.

[Leffler et al. 1978] S. J. Leffler, R. S. Fabry, and W. N. Joy, "A 4.2BSD Interprocess Communication Primer," *Unix Programmer's Manual*, Volume 2C, University of California at Berkeley, (1978).

[Leffler et al. 1983] S. J. Leffler, W. N. Joy, R. S. Fabry, "4.2BSD Networking Implementation Notes, Revised July, 1983" *Unix Programmer's Manual*, Volume 2C, University of California at Berkeley, (1983).

[Lefkovitz 1969] D. Lefkovitz, *File Structures for On-Line Systems*, Spartan Books, New York, (1969).

[Le Lann 1977] G. Le Lann, "Distributed Systems -- Toward a Formal Approach," *Proceedings of the IFIP Congress 77*, (1977), pages 155-160.

[Lempel 1979] A. Lempel, "Cryptology in Transition," *Computing Surveys*, Volume 11, Number 4, (December 1979), pages 286-303.

[Lett and Konigsford 1968] A. L. Lett and W. L. Konigsford, "TSS/360: A Time-Shared Operating System," *Proceedings of the AFIPS Fall Joint Computer Conference*, (1968), pages 15-28.

[Levin et al. 1975] R. Levin, E. S. Cohen, W. M. Corwin, F. J. Pollack, and W. A. Wulf, "Policy/Mechanism Separation in Hydra," *Proceedings of the Fifth Symposium on Operating Systems Principles*, (November 1975), pages 132-140.

[Levin and Gries 1981] G. M. Levin and D. Gries, "A Proof Technique for Communicating Sequential Processes," *Acta Informatica*, Volume 15, Fasc. 3, (1981), pages 281-302.

[Levy 1978] J. V. Levy, "A Multiple Computer System for Reliable Transaction Processing," *ACM SIGSMALL Newsletter*, Volume 4, Number 5, (October 1978), pages 5-22.

[Levy 1984] H. M. Levy, *Capability-Based Computer Systems*, Digital Press, Bedford, Massachusetts, (1974).

[Lichtenberger and Pirtle 1965] W. W. Lichtenberger and M. W. Pirtle, "A Facility for Experimentation in Man-Machine Interaction," *Proceedings of the AFIPS Fall Joint Computer Conference*, (1965), pages 589-598.

[Licklider and Clark 1962] J. C. R. Licklider and W. E. Clark, "On-Line Man-Computer Communication," *Proceedings of the AFIPS Spring Joint Computer Conference*, (1962), pages 113-128.

[Linde 1975] R. R. Linde, "Operating System Penetration," *Proceedings of the AFIPS National Computer Conference*, (1975), pages 361-368.

[Linden 1976] T. A. Linden, "Operating System Structures to Support Security and Reliable Software," *Computing Surveys*, Volume 8, Number 4, (December 1976), pages 409-445.

[Lions 1977] J. Lions, *A Commentary on the Unix Operating System*, Department of Computer Science, The University of New South Wales, (June 1977).

[Lipner 1975] S. Lipner, "A Comment on the Confinement Problem," *Operating System Review*, Volume 9, Number 5, (November 1975), pages 192-196.

[Liptay 1968] J. S. Liptay, "Structural Aspects of the System/360 Model 85: II The Cache," *IBM Systems Journal*, Volume 7, Number 1, (1968), pages 15-21.

[Lipton 1974] R. Lipton, "On Synchronization Primitive Systems," Ph.D. Thesis, Carnegie-Mellon University, (1974).

[Liskov 1972a] B. H. Liskov, "The Design of the Venus Operating System," *Communications of the ACM*, Volume 15, Number 3, (March 1972), pages 144-149.

[Liskov 1972b] B. H. Liskov, "A Design Methodology for Reliable Software Systems," *Proceedings of the AFIPS Fall Joint Computer Conference*, (1972), pages 191-200.

[Liskov and Zilles 1974] B. H. Liskov and S. N. Zilles, "Programming with Abstract Data Types," *Proceedings ACM SIGPLAN Conference on Very High Level Languages*, (April 1974), pages 50-59.

[Liskov and Zilles 1975] B. H. Liskov and S. N. Zilles, "Specification Techniques for Data Abstractions," *IEEE Transactions on Software Engineering*, Volume SE-1, Number 1, (March 1975), pages 7-19.

[Lister and Maynard 1976] A. M. Lister and K. J. Maynard, "An Implementation of Monitors," *Software -- Practice and Experience*, Volume 6, Number 3, (July 1976), pages 377-386.

[Lister 1979] A. M. Lister, *Fundamentals of Operating Systems*, Macmillan, London, (1979).

[Little 1961] J. D. C. Little, "A Proof of the Queuing Formula L=λW," *Operations Research*, Volume 9, Number 3, (May 1961), pages 383-387.

[Liu 1978] M. T. Liu, "Distributed Loop Computer Networks," *in* [Yovits 1978], pages 163-221.

[Lomet 1980] D. Lomet, "Subsystems of Processes with Deadlock Avoidance," *IEEE Transactions on Software Engineering*, Volume SE-6, Number 3, (May 1980), pages 297-303.

[Lorin 1972] H. Lorin, *Parallelism in Hardware and Software -- Real and Apparent Concurrency*, Prentice-Hall, Englewood Cliffs, New Jersey, (1972).

[Lucas 1971] H. C. Lucas, "Performance Evaluation and Monitoring," *Computing Surveys*, Volume 3, Number 3, (September 1971), pages 79-91.

[Lynch 1967] W. C. Lynch, "Description of a High Capacity Fast Turnaround University Computing Center," *Proceedings of the ACM National Conference*, (August 1967), pages 273-288.

[Lynch 1972a] W. C. Lynch, "An Operating System Design for the Computer Utility Environment," *in* [Hoare and Perrott 1972], pages 341-350.

[Lynch 1972b] W. C. Lynch, "Do Disk Arms Move?," *Performance Evaluation Review, ACM Sigmetrics Newsletter*, Volume 1, (December 1972), pages 3-16.

[Lynch 1972c] W. C. Lynch, "Operating System Performance," *Communications of the ACM*, Volume 15, Number 7, (July 1972), pages 579-586.

[Madnick and Alsop 1969] S. E. Madnick and J. W. Alsop, "A Modular Approach to File System Design," *Proceedings of the AFIPS Spring Joint Computer Conference*, (1969), pages 1-14.

[Madnick and Donovan 1974] S. E. Madnick and J. J. Donovan, *Operating Systems*, McGraw-Hill, New York, (1974).

[Mattson et al. 1970] R. L. Mattson, J. Gecsei, D. R. Slutz, and I. L. Traiger, "Evaluation Techniques for Storage Hierarchies," *IBM Systems Journal*, Volume 9, Number 2, (1970), pages 78-117.

[McGibbon et al. 1978] C. I. McGibbon, H. Gibbs, and S. C. K. Young, "DATAPAC -- Initial Experiences with a Commercial Packet Network," *Proceedings of the Fourth International Conference on Computer Communication*, (September 1978), pages 103-108.

[McGilton and Morgan 1983] H. McGilton and R. Morgan, *Introducing the Unix System*, McGraw-Hill, New York, (1983).

[McGraw and Andrews 1979] J. R. McGraw and G. R. Andrews, "Access Control in Parallel Programs," *IEEE Transactions on Software Engineering*, Volume SE-5, Number 1, (January 1979), pages 1-9.

[McKeag and Wilson 1976] R. M. McKeag and R. Wilson, *Studies in Operating Systems*, Academic Press, London, (1976).

[McKellar and Coffman 1969] A. McKellar and E. G. Coffman, "The Organization of Matrices and Matrix Operations in a Paged Multiprogramming Environment," *Communications of the ACM*, Volume 12, Number 3, (March 1969), pages 153-165.

[McKinney 1969] J. M. McKinney, "A Survey of Analytical Time-Sharing Models," *Computing Surveys*, Volume 1, Number 2, (June 1969), pages 105-116.

[McKusick et al. 1984] M. K. McKusick, W. N. Joy, S. J. Leffler, and R. S. Fabry, "A Fast File System for Unix," *ACM Transactions on Computer Systems*, Volume 2, Number 3, (August 1984), pages 181-197.

[McQuillan and Walden 1977] J. M. McQuillan and D. C. Walden, "The ARPA Network Design Decisions," *Computer Networks*, Volume 1, Number 5, (August 1977), pages 243-289.

[Mealy et al. 1966] G. H. Mealy, B. I. Witt, and W. A. Clark, "The Functional Structure of OS/360," *IBM Systems Journal*, Volume 5, Number 1, (1966), pages 3-51.

[Menasce and Muntz 1979] D. Menasce and R. R. Muntz, "Locking and Deadlock Detection in Distributed Data Bases," *IEEE Transactions on Software Engineering*, Volume SE-5, Number 3, (May 1979), pages 195-202.

[Merlin and Schweitzer 1980a] P. M. Merlin and P. J. Schweitzer, "Deadlock Avoidance in Store-and-Forward Networks -- I: Store and Forward Deadlock," *IEEE Transactions on Communications*, Volume COM-28, Number 3, (March 1980), pages 345-354.

[Merlin and Schweitzer 1980b] P. M. Merlin and P. J. Schweitzer, "Deadlock Avoidance in Store-and-Forward Networks -- II: Other Deadlock Types," *IEEE Transactions on Communications*, Volume COM-28, Number 3, (March 1980), pages 355-360.

[Metcalfe and Boggs 1976] R. M. Metcalfe and D. R. Boggs, "Ethernet: Distributed Packet Switching for Local Computer Networks," *Com-*

munications of the ACM, Volume 19, Number 7, (July 1976), pages 395-404.

[Meyer and Seawright 1970] R. A. Meyer and L. H. Seawright, "A Virtual Machine Time-Sharing System," *IBM Systems Journal*, Volume 9, Number 3, (1970), pages 199-218.

[Miller 1978] R. Miller, "Unix -- A Portable Operating System," *Proceedings of the Australian Universities Computer Science Seminar*, (February 1978), pages 23-25.

[Minoura 1982] T. Minoura, "Deadlock Avoidance Revisited," *Journal of the ACM*, Volume 29, Number 4, (October 1982), pages 1023-1048.

[Misra and Chandy 1981] J. Misra and K. M. Chandy, "Proofs of Networks of Processes," *IEEE Transactions on Software Engineering*, Volume SE-7, Number 4, (July 1981), pages 417-426.

[Morenoff and McLean 1967] E. Morenoff and J. B. McLean, "Inter-Program Communications, Program String Structures and Buffer Files," *Proceedings of the AFIPS Spring Joint Computer Conference*, (1967), pages 175-183.

[Morris et al. 1967] D. Morris, F. H. Sumner, and M. T. Wyld, "An Appraisal of the Atlas Supervisor," *Proceedings of the ACM National Conference*, (August 1967), pages 67-75.

[Morris 1973] J. H. Morris, "Protection in Programming Languages," *Communications of the ACM*, Volume 16, Number 1, (January 1973), pages 15-21.

[Morris and Thompson 1979] R. Morris and K. Thompson, "Password Security: A Case History," *Communications of the ACM*, Volume 22, Number 11, (November 1979), pages 594-597.

[Muntz 1975] R. R. Muntz, "Scheduling and Resource Allocation in Computer Systems," *in* [Freeman 1975], pages 269-304.

[Needham and Walker 1974] R. M. Needham and R. D. H. Walker, "Protection and Process Management in the CAP Computer," *Proceedings of the IRIA International Workshop on Protection in Operating Systems*, (1974), pages 155-160.

[Needham and Walker 1977] R. M. Needham and R. D. H. Walker, "The Cambridge CAP Computer and its Protection System," *Proceedings of the Sixth Symposium on Operating Systems Principles*, (November 1977), pages 1-10.

[Needham 1979] R. M. Needham, "System Aspects of the Cambridge Ring," *Proceedings of the Seventh Symposium on Operating Systems Principles*, (December 1979), pages 82-85.

[Nelson and Gordon 1978] D. C. Nelson and R. C. Gordon, "Computer Cells -- A Network Architecture for Data Flow Computing," *Proceedings of the IEEE COMPCON Conference*, (1978), pages 296-301.

[Neuhold 1978] E. J. Neuhold (Editor), *Formal Description of Programming Concepts*, North-Holland, Amsterdam, (1978).

[Neumann et al. 1975] P. G. Neumann, L. Robinson, K. N. Levitt, R. S. Boyer, and A. R. Saxena, "A Provably Secure Operating System," Technical Report, Stanford Research Institute, (June 1975).

[Newcomer et al. 1976] J. M. Newcomer, E. S. Cohen, W. M. Corwin, D. Jefferson, T. Lane, R. Levin, F. J. Pollack, and W. A. Wulf, "Hydra: Basic Kernel Reference Manual," Computer Science Department, Carnegie-Mellon University, (November 1976).

[Newport and Kaul 1977] C. B. Newport and P. Kaul, "Communications Processors for TELENET's Third Generation Packet Switching Network," *Proceedings of the IEEE Electronics and Aerospace Systems Convention*, (September 1977), pages 8-2A to 8-2L.

[Nutt 1977] G. J. Nutt, "A Parallel Processor Operating System Comparison," *IEEE Transactions on Software Engineering*, Volume SE-3, Number 6, (November 1977), pages 467-475.

[Obermarck 1982] R. Obermarck, "Distributed Deadlock Detection Algorithm," *ACM Transactions on Database Systems*, Volume 7, Number 2, (June 1982), pages 187-208.

[Operdeck and Chu 1974] H. Operdeck and W. W. Chu, "Performance of the Page Fault Frequency Algorithm in a Multiprogramming Environment," *Proceedings of the IFIP Congress 74*, (1974), pages 235-241.

[Oppenheimer and Weizer 1968] G. Oppenheimer and N. Weizer, "Resource Management for a Medium-Scale Time-Sharing Operating System," *Communications of the ACM*, Volume 11, Number 5, (May 1968), pages 313-322.

[Organick 1972] E. I. Organick, *The Multics System: An Examination of its Structure*, MIT Press, Cambridge, Massachusetts, (1972).

[Organick 1973] E. I. Organick, *Computer System Organization: The B5700/B6700 Series*, Academic Press, New York, (1973).

[Owicki and Gries 1976a] S. S. Owicki and D. Gries, "Verifying Properties of Parallel Programs: An Axiomatic Approach," *Communications of the ACM*, Volume 19, Number 5, (May 1976), pages 279-285.

[Owicki and Gries 1976b] S. S. Owicki and D. Gries, "An Axiomatic Proof Technique for Parallel Programs," *Acta Informatica*, Volume 6, Fasc. 4, (1976), pages 319-340.

[Owicki 1978] S. S. Owicki, "Verifying Concurrent Programs with Shared Data Classes," *in* [Neuhold 1978], pages 279-299.

[Padlipsky 1982] M.A. Padlipsky, "A Perspective on the Arpanet Reference Model," RFC 871, Network Information Center, SRI International, Menlo Park, California, (September 1982).

[Parmelee et al. 1972] R. P. Parmelee, T. I. Peterson, C. C. Tillman, and D. Hatfield, "Virtual Storage and Virtual Machine Concepts," *IBM Systems Journal*, Volume 11, Number 2, (1972), pages 99-130.

[Parnas and Darringer 1967] D. L. Parnas and J. A. Darringer, "SODAS and a Methodology for System Design," *Proceedings of the AFIPS Fall Joint Computer Conference*, (1967), pages 449-474.

[Parnas 1971] D. L. Parnas, "Information Distribution Aspects of Design Methodology," *Proceedings of the IFIP Congress 71*, (1971), pages 339-344.

[Parnas 1972a] D. L. Parnas, "A Technique for Software Module Specification with Examples," *Communications of the ACM*, Volume 15, Number 5, (May 1972), pages 330-336.

[Parnas 1972b] D. L. Parnas, "Some Conclusions from an Experiment in Software Engineering Techniques," *Proceedings of the AFIPS Fall Joint Computer Conference*, (1972), pages 325-329.

[Parnas 1972c] D. L. Parnas, "On the Criteria to be Used in Decomposing Systems into Modules," *Communications of the ACM*, Volume 15, Number 12, (December 1972), pages 1053-1058.

[Parnas and Habermann 1972] D. L. Parnas and A. N. Habermann, "Comment on Deadlock Prevention Method," *Communications of the ACM*, Volume 15, Number 9, (September 1972), pages 840-841.

[Parnas 1975a] D. L. Parnas, "On a Solution to the Cigarette Smokers' Problem without Conditional Statements," *Communications of the ACM*, Volume 18, Number 3, (March 1975), pages 181-183.

[Parnas 1975b] D. L. Parnas, "The Influence of Software Structure on Reliability," *Proceedings of the International Conference on Reliable Software*, (April 1975), pages 358-362.

[Patil 1971] S. Patil, "Limitations and Capabilities of Dijkstra's Semaphore Primitives for Coordination Among Processes," Technical Report, Massachusetts Institute of Technology, (February 1971).

[Pease et al. 1980] M. Pease, R. Shostak, and L. Lamport, "Reaching Agreement in the Presence of Faults," *Journal of the ACM*, Volume 27, Number 2, (April 1980), pages 228-234.

[Perros 1980] H. G. Perros, "A Regression Model for Predicting the Response Time of a Disc I/O System," *Computer Journal*, Volume 23, Number 1, (February 1980), pages 34-36.

[Peterson and Veit 1971] J. J. Peterson and S. A. Veit, "Survey of Computer Networks," Technical Report, Mitre Corporation, (September 1971).

[Peterson 1981] G. L. Peterson, "Myths About the Mutual Exclusion Problem," *Information Processing Letters*, Volume 12, Number 3, (June 1981), pages 115-116.

[Pierce 1972] J. R. Pierce, "Network for Block Switching of Data," *The Bell System Technical Journal*, Volume 51, Number 6, (July-August 1972), pages 1133-1145.

[Popek 1974] G. J. Popek, "Protection Structures," *Computer*, Volume 7, Number 6, (June 1974), pages 22-23.

[Popek et al. 1979] G. J. Popek, M. Kampe, C. S. Kline, A. Stoughton, M. Urban, and E. Walton, "UCLA Secure Unix," *Proceedings of the AFIPS National Computer Conference*, (1979), pages 355-364.

[Presser 1975] L. Presser, "Multiprogramming Coordination," *Computing Surveys*, Volume 7, Number 1, (March 1975), pages 21-44.

[Prieve and Fabry 1976] B. G. Prieve and R. S. Fabry, "VMIN -- An Optimal Variable-Space Page Replacement Algorithm," *Communications of the ACM*, Volume 19, Number 5, (May 1976), pages 295-297.

[Pyke 1973] T. Pyke, "Computer Networking Technology -- A State of the Art Review," *Computer*, Volume 6, Number 8, (August 1973), pages 12-19.

[Randell and Kuehner 1968] B. Randell and C. J. Kuehner, "Dynamic Storage Allocation Systems," *Communications of the ACM*, Volume 11, Number 5, (May 1968), pages 197-304.

[Randell 1969] B. Randell, "A Note on Storage Fragmentation and Program Segmentation," *Communications of the ACM*, Volume 12, Number 7, (July 1969), pages 365-372.

[Randell 1975] B. Randell, "System Structure for Software Fault Tolerance," *IEEE Transactions on Software Engineering*, Volume SE-1, Number 2, (June 1975), pages 220-232.

[Randell et al. 1978] B. Randell, P. A. Lee, and P. C. Treleaven, "Reliability Issues in Computing System Design," *Computing Surveys*, Volume 10, Number 2, (June 1978), pages 123-165.

[Rashid and Robertson 1981] R. Rashid and G. Robertson, "Accent: A Communication Oriented Network Operating System Kernel," *Proceedings of the Eighth Symposium on Operating Systems Principles*, (December 1981), pages 64-75.

[Redell 1974] D. D. Redell, "Naming and Protection in Extendible Operating Systems," Ph.D. Thesis, University of California At Berkeley, (1974).

[Redell and Fabry 1974] D. D. Redell and R. S. Fabry, "Selective Revocation of Capabilities," *Proceedings of the IRIA International Workshop on Protection in Operating Systems*, (1974), pages 197-210.

[Reed and Kanodia 1979] D. P. Reed and R. K. Kanodia, "Synchronization with Eventcounts and Sequences," *Communications of the ACM*, Volume 22, Number 2, (February 1979), pages 115-123.

[Ricart and Agrawala 1981] G. Ricart and A. K. Agrawala, "An Optimal Algorithm for Mutual Exclusion in Computer Networks," *Communications of the ACM*, Volume 24, Number 1, (January 1981), pages 9-17.

[Richards 1969] M. Richards, "BCPL: A Tool for Compiler Writing and System Programming," *Proceedings of the AFIPS Spring Joint Computer Conference*, (1969), pages 557-566.

[Ritchie 1979] D. M. Ritchie, "The Evolution of the Unix Time-Sharing System," *Language Design and Programming Methodology*, Lecture Notes in Computer Science, Volume 79, Springer-Verlag, Berlin, (1979), pages 25-35.

[Ritchie and Thompson 1974] D. M. Ritchie and K. Thompson, "The Unix Time-Sharing System," *Communications of the ACM*, Volume 17, Number 7, (July 1974), pages 365-375; *see also* [BSTJ 1978], pages 1905-1929.

[Rivest et al. 1978] R. L. Rivest, A. Shamir, and L. Adleman, "On Digital Signatures and Public Key Cryptosystems," *Communications of the ACM*, Volume 21, Number 2, (February 1978), pages 120-126.

[Robinson et al. 1975] L. Robinson, K. N. Levitt, P. G. Neumann, and A. R. Saxena, "On Attaining Reliable Software for a Secure Operating System," *Proceedings of the International Conference on Reliable Software*, (April 1975), pages 267-284.

[Rosen 1967] S. Rosen (Editor), *Programming Systems and Languages*, McGraw-Hill, New York, (1967).

[Rosen 1969] S. Rosen, "Electronic Computers: A Historical Survey," *Computing Surveys*, Volume 1, Number 1, (March 1969), pages 7-36.

[Rosenkrantz et al. 1978] D. J. Rosenkrantz, R. E. Stearns, and P. M. Lewis II, "System Level Concurrency Control for Distributed Database Systems," *ACM Transactions on Database Systems*, Volume 3, Number 2, (June 1978), pages 178-198.

[Rosin 1969] R. F. Rosin, "Supervisory and Monitor Systems," *Computing Surveys*, Volume 1, Number 1, (March 1969), pages 37-54.

[Rushby 1981] J. M. Rushby, "Design and Verification of Secure Systems," *Proceedings of the Eighth Symposium on Operating Systems Principles*, (December 1981), pages 12-21.

[Saltzer 1974] J. H. Saltzer, "Protection and the Control of Information Sharing in Multics," *Communications of the ACM*, Volume 17, Number 7, (July 1974), pages 388-402.

[Saltzer and Schroeder 1975] J. H. Saltzer and M. D. Schroeder, "The Protection of Information in Computer Systems," *Proceedings of the IEEE*, Volume 63, Number 9, (September 1975), pages 1278-1308.

[Sammet 1971] J. E. Sammet, "Brief Survey of Languages Used in Systems Implementation," *ACM SIGPLAN Notices*, Volume 6, Number 9, (September 1971), pages 2-19.

[Satyanarayanan 1980a] M. Satyanarayanan, *Multiprocessors: A Comparative Study*, Prentice-Hall, Englewood Cliffs, New Jersey, (1980).

[Satyanarayanan 1980b] M. Satyanarayanan, "Commercial Multiprocessing Systems," *Computer*, Volume 13, Number 5, (May 1980), pages 75-96.

[Saxena and Bredt 1975] A. R. Saxena and T. H. Bredt, "A Structured Specification of a Hierarchical Operating System," *Proceedings of the*

International Conference on Reliable Software, (April 1975), pages 310-318.

[Sayers 1971] A. P. Sayers (Editor), *Operating Systems Survey*, Auerbach, Princeton, New Jersey, (1971).

[Sayre 1969] D. Sayre, "Is Automatic 'Folding' of Programs Efficient Enough to Replace Manual?," *Communications of the ACM*, Volume 12, Number 12, (December 1969), pages 656-660.

[Schmid 1976] H. A. Schmid, "On the Efficient Implementation of Conditional Critical Regions and the Construction of Monitors," *Acta Informatica*, Volume 6, Fasc. 3, (1976), pages 227-279.

[Schneider 1982] F. B. Schneider, "Synchronization in Distributed Programs," *ACM Transactions on Programming Languages and Systems*, Volume 4, Number 2, (April 1982), pages 125-148.

[Schrage 1967] L. E. Schrage, "The Queue M/G/1 with Feedback to Lower Priority Queues," *Management Science*, Volume 13, Number 7, (March 1967), pages 466-474.

[Schroeder and Saltzer 1972] M. D. Schroeder and J. H. Saltzer, "A Hardware Architecture for Implementing Protection Rings," *Communications of the ACM*, Volume 15, Number 3, (March 1972), pages 157-170.

[Schwartz et al. 1964] J. I. Schwartz, E. G. Coffman, and C. Weissman, "A General Purpose Time-Sharing System," *Proceedings of the AFIPS Spring Joint Computer Conference*, (1964), pages 397-411.

[Schwartz and Weissman 1967] J. I. Schwartz and C. Weissman, "The SDC Time-Sharing System Revisited," *Proceedings of the ACM National Conference*, (August 1967), pages 263-271.

[Schwartz 1977] M. Schwartz, *Computer-Communication Network Design and Analysis*, Prentice-Hall, Englewood Cliffs, New Jersey, (1977).

[Schwemm 1972] R. E. Schwemm, "Experience Gained in the Development and Use of TSS," *Proceedings of the AFIPS Spring Joint Computer Conference*, (1972), pages 559-569.

[Seawright and MacKinnon 1979] L. H. Seawright and R. A. MacKinnon, "VM/370 -- A Study of Multiplicity and Usefulness," *IBM Systems Journal*, Volume 18, Number 1, (1979), pages 4-17.

[Sevick 1972] K. C. Sevick, "Project SUE as a Learning Experience," *Proceedings of the AFIPS Fall Joint Computer Conference*, (1972), pages 571-578.

[Shaw 1974] A. C. Shaw, *The Logical Design of Operating Systems,* Prentice-Hall, Englewood Cliffs, New Jersey, (1974).

[Shore 1975] J. E. Shore, "On the External Storage Fragmentation Produced by First-Fit and Best-Fit Allocation Strategies," *Communications of the ACM,* Volume 18, Number 8, (August 1975), pages 433-440.

[Shoshani and Coffman 1970] A. Shoshani and E. G. Coffman, "Prevention, Detection and Recovery from System Deadlocks," *Proceedings of the Fourth Annual Princeton Conference on Information Sciences and Systems,* (March 1970).

[Silberschatz et al. 1977] A. Silberschatz, R. B. Kieburtz, and A. J. Bernstein, "Extending Concurrent Pascal to Allow Dynamic Resource Management," *IEEE Transactions on Software Engineering,* Volume SE-3, Number 3, (May 1977), pages 210-217.

[Simmons 1979] G. J. Simmons, "Symmetric and Asymmetric Encryption," *Computing Surveys,* Volume 11, Number 4, (December 1979), pages 304-330.

[Stone and Fuller 1973] H. S. Stone and S. H. Fuller, "On the Near Optimality of the Shortest-Latency-Time-First Drum Scheduling Discipline," *Communications of the ACM,* Volume 16, Number 6, (June 1973), pages 352-353.

[Stone 1980] H. S. Stone, "The Coming Revolution in Operating Systems Courses," *Operating Systems Review,* Volume 14, Number 4, (October 1980), pages 72-77.

[Strachey 1959] C. Strachey, "Time Sharing in Large Fast Computers," *Proceedings of the International Conference on Information Processing,* UNESCO, Paris, (June 1959), pages 336-341.

[Stuart et al. 1984] D. Stuart, G. Buckley, and A. Silberschatz, "A Centralized Deadlock Detection Algorithm," Technical Report, University of Texas, (1984).

[Sturgis et al. 1980] H. E. Sturgis, J. G. Mitchell, and J. Israel, "Issues in the Design and Use of a Distributed File System," *Operating Systems Review,* Volume 14, Number 3, (July 1980), pages 55-69.

[Svobodova 1976] L. Svobodova, *Computer Performance Measurement and Evaluation,* Elsevier North-Holland, New York, (1976).

[Swinehart et al. 1979] D. Swinehart, G. McDaniel, and D. R. Boggs, "WFS: A Simple Shared File System for a Distributed Environment,"

Proceedings of the Seventh Symposium on Operating Systems Principles, (December 1979), pages 9-17.

[Teorey 1972] T. J. Teorey, "Properties of Disk Scheduling Policies in Multiprogrammed Computer Systems," *Proceedings of the AFIPS Fall Joint Computer Conference,* (1972), pages 1-11.

[Teorey and Pinkerton 1972] T. J. Teorey and T. B. Pinkerton, "A Comparative Analysis of Disk Scheduling Policies," *Communications of the ACM,* Volume 15, Number 3, (March 1972), pages 177-184.

[Thompson 1978] K. Thompson, "Unix Implementation," *in* [BSTJ 1978], pages 1931-1946.

[Thornton 1970] J. E. Thornton, *Design of a Computer: The Control Data 6600,* Scott, Foresman and Company, (1970).

[Thurber and Freeman 1980] K. J. Thurber and H. A. Freeman, "Updated Bibliography on Local Computer Networks," *Computer Architecture News,* Volume 8, (April 1980), pages 20-28.

[Toueg and Ullman 1979] S. Toueg and J. D. Ullman, "Deadlock-Free Packet Switching Networks," *Proceedings of the ACM Symposium on Theory of Computing,* (May 1979), pages 89-98.

[Toueg 1980] S. Toueg, "Deadlock- and Livelock-Free Packet Switching Networks," *Proceedings of the ACM Symposium on Theory of Computing,* (April 1980), pages 94-99.

[Tsichritzis and Bernstein 1974] D. C. Tsichritzis and P. A. Bernstein, *Operating Systems,* Academic Press, New York, (1974).

[Unger 1972] C. Unger (Editor), *Command Languages,* North-Holland, Amsterdam, (1972).

[Vantilborgh and Van Lamsweerde 1972] H. Vantilborgh and A. Van Lamsweerde, "On an Extension of Dijkstra's Semaphore Primitives," *Information Processing Letters,* Volume 1, (1972), pages 181-186.

[Vareha et al. 1969] A. L. Vareha, R. M. Rutledge, and M. M. Gold, "Strategies for Structuring Two-Level Memories in a Paging Environment," *Proceedings of the Second ACM Symposium on Operating Systems Principles,* (October 1969), pages 54-59.

[Varney 1971] R. C. Varney, "Process Selection in a Hierarchical Operating System," *Proceedings of the Third ACM Symposium on Operating Systems Principles,* (October 1971), pages 106-108.

[Ward 1980] A. A. Ward, "TRIX: A Network-Oriented Operating System," *Proceedings of the IEEE COMPCON Conference*, (1980), pages 344-349.

[Warwick 1970] M. Warwick, "Introduction to Operating System Concepts," *in* [Cuttle and Robinson 1970], Chapter 1.

[Watson 1970] R. W. Watson, *Timesharing System Design Concepts*, McGraw-Hill, New York, (1970).

[Weingarten 1966] A. Weingarten, "The Eschenbach Drum Scheme," *Communications of the ACM*, Volume 9, Number 7, (July 1966), pages 509-512.

[Weissman 1969] C. Weissman, "Security Controls in the ADEPT-50 Time-Sharing System," *Proceedings of the AFIPS Fall Joint Computer Conference*, (1969), pages 119-134.

[Weizer 1981] N. Weizer, "A History of Operating Systems," *Datamation*, Volume 27, Number 1, (January 1981), pages 118-126.

[Welsh and Bustard 1979] J. Welsh and D. W. Bustard, "Pascal-Plus -- Another Language for Modular Multiprogramming," *Software -- Practice and Experience*, Volume 9, Number 11, (November 1979), pages 947-957.

[Wilhelm 1976] N. C. Wilhelm, "An Anomaly in Disk Scheduling: A Comparison of FCFS and SSTF Seek Scheduling using an Empirical Model for Disk Accesses," *Communications of the ACM*, Volume 19, Number 1, (January 1976), pages 13-17.

[Wilkes 1975] M. V. Wilkes, *Time-Sharing Computer Systems, Third Edition*, Macdonald, London, (1975).

[Wilkes and Wheeler 1979] M. V. Wilkes and D. J. Wheeler, "The Cambridge Digital Communication Ring," *Proceedings Local Area Computer Network Symposium*, (May 1979).

[Williams 1972] R. K. Williams, "System 250 -- Basic Concepts," *Proceedings of the I. E. R. E. Conference on Computers -- System and Technology*, (1972), pages 157-168.

[Winograd et al. 1971] J. Winograd, S. J. Morganstein, and R. Herman, "Simulation Studies of a Virtual Memory, Time-Shared, Demand Paging Operating System," *Proceedings of the Third ACM Symposium on Operating Systems Principles*, (October 1971), pages 149-155.

[Wirth 1968] N. Wirth, "PL360 -- A Programming Language for the 360 Computers," *Journal of the ACM*, Volume 15, Number 1, (January 1968), pages 37-74.

[Wirth 1971] N. Wirth, "The Programming Language Pascal," *Acta Informatica*, Volume 1, Fasc. 1, (1971), pages 35-63.

[Wirth 1977] N. Wirth, "Modula: A Programming Language for Modular Multiprogramming," *Software -- Practice and Experience*, Volume 7, Number 1, (January-February 1977), pages 3-35.

[Wolman 1965] E. Wolman, "A Fixed Optimum Cell-Size for Records of Various Lengths," *Journal of the ACM*, Volume 12, Number 1, (January 1965), pages 53-70.

[Wulf 1969] W. A. Wulf, "Performance Monitors for Multiprogramming Systems," *Proceedings of the Second ACM Symposium on Operating Systems Principles*, (October 1969), pages 175-181.

[Wulf et al. 1971] W. A. Wulf, D. B. Russell, and A. N. Habermann, "BLISS: A Language for Systems Programming," *Communications of the ACM*, Volume 14, Number 12, (December 1971), pages 780-790.

[Wulf et al. 1974] W. A. Wulf, E. S. Cohen, W. M. Corwin, A. K. Jones, R. Levin, C. Pierson, and F. J. Pollack, "Hydra: The Kernel of a Multiprocessor Operating System," *Communications of the ACM*, Volume 17, Number 6, (June 1974), pages 337-345.

[Wulf 1975] W. A. Wulf, "Reliable Hardware/Software Architecture," *IEEE Transactions on Software Engineering*, Volume SE-1, Number 2, (June 1975), pages 233-240.

[Wulf et al. 1981] W. A. Wulf, R. Levin, and S. P. Harbison, *Hydra/C.mmp: An Experimental Computer System*, McGraw-Hill, New York, (1981).

[Yovits 1978] M. C. Yovits (Editor), *Advances in Computers*, Academic Press, New York, (1978).

[Zurcher and Randell 1968] F. W. Zurcher and B. Randell, "Iterative Multi-Level Modeling -- A Methodology for Computer System Design," *Proceedings of the IFIP Congress 68*, (1968), pages 867-871.

Index